KT-133-880

Legal
Aspects of
Nursing

Fifth edition

Bridgit Dimond MA LLB D.S.A. A.H.S.M.
Barrister-at-Law
Emeritus Professor University of Glamorgan

PEARSON
Education

Harlow, England • London • New York • Boston • San Francisco • Toronto
Sydney • Tokyo • Singapore • Hong Kong • Seoul • Taipei • New Delhi
Cape Town • Madrid • Mexico City • Amsterdam • Munich • Paris • Milan

Pearson Education Limited
Edinburgh Gate
Harlow
Essex CM20 2JE
England

and Associated Companies throughout the world

Visit us on the World Wide Web at:
www.pearsoned.co.uk

First published 1990
Fifth edition published 2008

© Prentice Hall Europe 1990, 1995
© Pearson Education Limited 2002, 2005, 2008

The right of Bridgit Dimond to be identified as author of this work has
been asserted by her in accordance with the Copyright, Designs and
Patents Act 1988.

All rights reserved. No part of this publication may be reproduced, stored in
a retrieval system, or transmitted in any form or by any means, electronic,
mechanical, photocopying, recording or otherwise, without either the prior
written permission of the publisher or a licence permitting restricted copying
in the United Kingdom issued by the Copyright Licensing Agency Ltd, Saffron
House, 6-10 Kirby Street, London EC1N 8TS.

Crown Copyright material is reproduced with the permission of the Controller
of HMSO and the Queen's Printer for Scotland. Law Commission Reports are
reproduced under the terms of the Click-Use Licence.

ISBN: 978-1-4058-5875-5

British Library Cataloguing-in-Publication Data
A catalogue record for this book is available from the British Library

Library of Congress Cataloging-in-Publication Data
Dimond, Bridgit.
  Legal aspects of nursing / Bridgit Dimond.-- 5th ed.
    p. ; cm.
  Includes bibliographical references and index.
  ISBN-13: 978-1-4058-5875-5
  1. Nursing--Law and legislation--Great Britain.
  [DNLM: 1. Legislation, Nursing--Great Britain. WY 33 FA1 D582L 2008]
  I. Title.
  KD2968.N8D56 2008
  344.4104'14--dc22

                         2008009455

10 9 8 7 6 5 4 3 2 1
12 11 10 09 08

Typeset in 9/12pt Interstate Light by 35
Printed by Ashford Colour Press Ltd., Gosport

The publisher's policy is to use paper manufactured from sustainable forests.

WITHDRAWN

MKH LIBRARY

C20408571

€1.50

Legal Aspects of Nursing

MKH LIBRARY SERVICES   FINE

Visit the *Legal Aspects of Nursing*, fifth edition **mylawchamber** site at **www.mylawchamber.co.uk/dimond** to access valuable learning material.

For students

Do you want to give yourself a head start come exam time?

Companion Website support

- Use the multiple choice questions, online glossary and practice exam questions to test yourself on each topic throughout the course
- Use the live weblinks to help you read more widely around the subject, and really impress your lecturers

For more information please contact your local Pearson Education sales representative or visit **www.mylawchamber.co.uk/dimond**

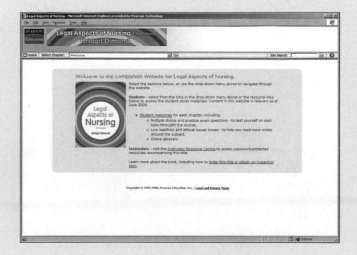

PEARSON EDUCATION

NURSING&HEALTH

FIRST FOR HEALTH

We work with leading authors to develop the strongest
educational materials in nursing and healthcare, bringing
cutting-edge thinking and best learning practice to
a global market.

Under a range of well-known imprints, including
Pearson Education, we craft high quality print and
electronic publications which help readers to understand
and apply their content, whether studying or at work.

To find out more about the complete range of our
publishing please visit us on the World Wide Web at:
www.pearsoned.co.uk

To Clare and Bec

Brief contents

Part III General areas   585

Contents

Part III General areas

Visit the *Legal Aspects of Nursing*, fifth edition **mylawchamber** site at **www.mylawchamber.co.uk/dimond** to access valuable learning material.

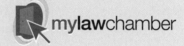

For students

Do you want to give yourself a head start come exam time?

Companion Website support
- Use the multiple choice questions, online glossary and practice exam questions to test yourself on each topic throughout the course
- Use the live weblinks to help you read more widely around the subject, and really impress your lecturers

For more information please contact your local Pearson Education sales representative or visit **www.mylawchamber.co.uk/dimond**

Guided tour

How can I get the most from my study?

This chapter discusses sections at the start of each chapter provide you with an instant point of reference that highlights what you can expect to learn within each chapter. You can use these as a checklist of key concepts during the course of your reading.

Will difficult concepts in law be presented in a manageable way?

Diagrams and **flowcharts** are used throughout to highlight complex legal processes.

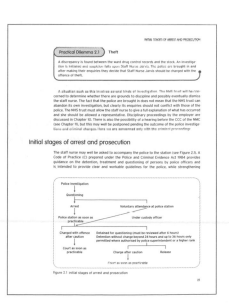

Summary information boxes pick out key points, examples and list the essential information and legal principles of a given topic. These can be found at regular intervals throughout chapters.

How can I contextualise all the theory I'll be learning?

Use the **practical dilemmas** located throughout the text to test that you understand the topics you are reading in relation to possible real life situations.

How will I know which are the most relevant cases and statutes to be aware of?

Key case boxes explicitly highlight the key facts and related legal principle of the essential cases you need to know.

Key statute boxes identify some of the most important statutory provisions and articles to learn for your studies.

How can I check I've understood what I've read?

Reflection questions at the end of each chapter can be used to test that you have followed and understood the key issues raised within the chapter.

How can I develop my understanding from the chapter?

Further exercises at the end of each chapter provide practical tasks that will help you apply what you have learnt and extend your knowledge.

Visit the *Legal Aspects of Nursing*, fifth edition **mylawchamber**
site at **www.mylawchamber.co.uk/dimond** to access:

Companion Website support
- Use the multiple choice questions, online glossary and practice exam questions to test yourself on each topic throughout the course. The site includes weblinks to help you read more widely around the subject.

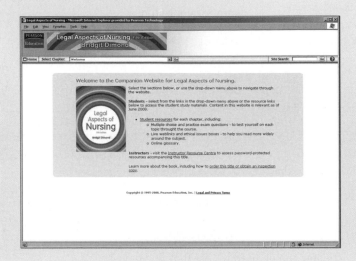

Table of cases

Table of statutes

Abbreviations

The health services are awash with abbreviations and jargon. It would, however, be immeasurably tedious and unrealistic to ignore these and always use the full words. Some of the most commonly used abbreviations are therefore set out here. Where there is any possibility of confusion, words are spelt out in full.

ABI	Association of British Insurers
ABPI	Association of the British Pharmaceutical Industry
ACAS	Advisory, Conciliation and Arbitration Service
ACGT	Advisory Committee on Genetic Testing
ADR	Adverse Drug Reaction
A&E	accident and emergency department
AGMR	Advisory Group on Medical Research
AID	artificial insemination by donor
AIDS	acquired immune deficiency syndrome
AIH	artificial insemination by husband
AIP	artificial insemination by partner
AMHP	Approved Mental Health Professional
ARC	AIDS-related complex
ASW	approved social worker
BID	brought in dead
BMA	British Medical Association
BMJ	*British Medical Journal*
BNF	*British National Formulary*
BP	blood pressure
BPAS	British Pregnancy Advisory Service
CAB	Citizens' Advice Bureau
CAM	complementary and alternative medicines
CCC	Conduct and Competence Committee
CCETSW	Central Council for Education and Training in Social Work
CCIAG	Critical Care Information Advisory Group
CDRP	crime and disorder reduction partnerships
CE	Conformité Européenne (marking following EC directive 93/68/EEC)
CESDI	Confidential Enquiry into Stillbirths and Deaths in Infancy
CESU	clinical effectiveness support unit
CFA	Conditional Fee Agreement
CGWTs	Care Group Workforce Teams
CHAI	Commission for Health Audit and Inspection (known as the Healthcare Commission)
CHC	community health council

CHI	Commission for Health Improvement (now CHAI)
CHRE	Council for Healthcare Regulatory Excellence (formerly CRHCP)
CICA	Criminal Injuries Compensation Authority
CNR	cell nuclear replacement
CNST	Clinical Negligence Scheme for Trusts
COREC	Central Office for Research Ethics Committees (replaced 2007 by NRES)
COSHH	Control of Substances Hazardous to Health (Regulations)
CPD	Continuing Professional Development
CPN	community psychiatric nurse
CPPIH	Commission for Patient and Public Involvement in Health
CPR	cardio pulmonary resuscitation
CPS	Crown Prosecution Service
CRHCP	Council for the Regulation of Health Care Professionals (now *see* CHRE)
CSAG	Clinical Standards Advisory Group
CSCI	Commission for Social Care Inspection
CSIP	Care Services Improvement Partnership
CSSD	central sterile supply department
D and C	dilation and curettage
DBERR	Department for Business, Enterprise and Regulatory Reform
DCSF	Department for Children, Schools and Families (formerly DfES)
DH	Department of Health
DHA	district health authority
DHSS	Department of Health and Social Security (divided in 1989 into DH, Department of Health, and DSS, Department of Social Security)
DNAR	do not attempt resuscitation
DNR	do not resuscitate
DPA	Data Protection Act 1998
DSS	Department of Social Security
EC	European Community
ECHR	European Court of Human Rights
ECL	emergency care leads
ECP	Extended Care Practitioner
ECT	Electro Convulsive Therapy
EEA	European Economic Area
EHR	Electronic Health Record
EL	executive letter (guidance from DH)
ELS	Existing Liabilities Scheme
EPR	Electronic Patient Record
ERG	External Reference Group
ET	embryo transfer
EWC	expected week of confinement
GDC	General Dental Council
GIFT	gamete intrafallopian transfer
GMC	General Medical Council
GP	general practitioner
GSL	General Sales List
GTAC	Gene Therapy Advisory Committee
GUM	genito-urinary medicine
GWC	General Whitley Council

HAI	hospital acquired infection
HASC(CHS)A	Health and Social Care (Community Health and Standards) Act 2003
HASWA	Health and Safety at Work Act
HCSS	healthcare support staff
HFEA	Human Fertilisation and Embryology Authority
HGAC	Human Genetics Advisory Commission
HGC	Human Genetics Commission
HIV	human immunodeficiency virus
HPA	Health Protection Agency
HPC	Health Professional Council
HSC	Health and Safety Commission
HSC	Health Service Commissioner
HSC	Health Service Circular
HSE	Health and Safety Executive
HTA	Human Tissue Authority
IAG	Independent Advisory Group
ICAS	Independent Complaints Advocacy Services
ICRS	Integrated Care Records Service
IC(T)U	intensive care (treatment) unit
IM and T	information management and technology
IMCA	Independent Mental Capacity Advocate
IMHA	Independent Mental Health Advocate
IV	intravenous(ly)
IVF	*in vitro* fertilisation
LA	local authority
LBC	liquid-based cytology
LHB	local health board (equivalent of PCT in Wales)
LINKS	Local Involvement Networks
LOLER	Lifting Operations and Lifting Equipment Regulations
LPA	Lasting Power of Attorney
LREC	local research ethical committee
LSA	Local Supervising Authority
LSP	local service provider
MA	Maternity Allowance
MCA	Medicines Control Agency (*see* MHRA)
MDA	Medical Devices Agency (*see* MHRA)
MDU	Medical Defence Union
MHAC	Mental Health Act Commission
MHRA	Medicines and Healthcare products Regulatory Agency (since 1 April 2003)
MPP	maternity period pay
MREC	Multi-Centre Research Ethics Committee
MRSA	methicillin-resistant *Staphylococcus aureus*
NAI	non-accidental injury
NAO	National Audit Office
NASP	national application service provider
NCAA	National Clinical Assessment Authority
NCAS	National Clinical Assessment Service
NCSC	National Care Standards Commission
NFR	not for resuscitation

NHS	National Health Service
NHSBT	NHS Blood and Transplant
NHSFT	NHS Foundation Trust
NHSLA	National Health Service Litigation Authority
NHSU	National Health Service University
NICE	National Institute for Health and Clinical Excellence
NIHR	National Institute for Health Research
NMC	Nursing and Midwifery Council
NMW	national minimum wage
NPFiT	National Programme for Information Technology
NPRB	National Pay Review Body
NPSA	National Patient Safety Agency
NRES	National Research Ethics Service (replaced COREC in 2007)
NRT	Nicotine Replacement Therapy
NSF	National Service Framework
ODP	operating department practitioner
OFV	opportunities for volunteering scheme
OOS	Occupational Overuse Syndrome
OTC	over the counter
PALS	patient advice and liaison service
PBC	prudential borrowing code
PCC	professional conduct committee
PCG	primary care group
PCMH	Plea and Case Management Hearing
PCT	primary care trust
PGD	pre-implantation genetic diagnosis
PGD	Patient Group Directions
PIAG	patient information advisory group
POM	prescription-only medicine
POVA	protection of vulnerable adults
PPE	personal protective equipment
PPIFs	patient and public involvement forums
PREP	post-registration education and practice
PRN	*pro re nata* (as required, whenever necessary)
PUWER	Provision and Use of Work Equipment Regulations
PVS	persistent vegetative state
QA	Quality Assurance
QC	Queen's Counsel
QW	qualifying week
RATE	Regulatory Authority for Tissue and Embryos
RCM	Royal College of Midwifery
RCN	Royal College of Nursing
RCP	Royal College of Psychiatrists
REC	research ethics committee
RIDDOR	Reporting of Injuries, Diseases and Dangerous Occurrences Regulations
RMN	Registered Mental Nurse
RMO	responsible medical officer
RSI	repetitive strain injury
SAP	single assessment process

SCIE	Social Care Institute for Excellence
SCPHN	specialist community public health nurse
SEN	state enrolled nurse
SLA	service level agreement
SMP	statutory maternity pay
SRSC	safety representative and safety committee
SSI	Social Services Inspectorate
SSP	statutory sick pay
TB	tuberculosis
T+P	temperature and pulse
TUR & ER 93	Trade Union Reform and Employee Rights Act 1993
UKCC	United Kingdom Central Council for Nursing, Midwifery and Health Visiting
UKECA	United Kingdom Ethics Committee Authority
ULTRA	Unrelated Live Transplant Regulatory Authority
VD	venereal disease
WDC	Workforce Development Confederation

Foreword to first edition

The author, Bridgit Dimond, is well known to nurses working in Wales. She has assisted many of us in developing an increased awareness of the need for expert legal advice and knowledge of the law to inform our practice in the interests of our patients, our colleagues and ourselves.

The text of the book illustrates very graphically that she has skilfully drawn her material from frequent contact with nurses, midwives and health visitors working in a variety of settings. The topics are relevant to the work of the practitioner, the educator and the manager and presented in a form that encourages the reader to delve further into the subject. Although this book is seen by the author primarily as a work of reference, the very fact that many of the issues identified are at the centre of the profound changes taking place in the pattern and organisation of services, and within the nursing profession itself, ensures that it will have wider interest and will assist nurses considerably with understanding their responsibilities in a period of significant development.

Bridgit Dimond has, through this publication, yet again provided valuable assistance for improving the practice of nursing – by encouraging nurses to acquire a deeper understanding of the relevant legal aspects of the work of nursing.

Miss M. Bull
Chief Nursing Officer
Welsh Office

Foreword to third edition

With the first edition of *Legal Aspects of Nursing*, Bridgit Dimond quite rightly acquired an enviable reputation for having written the foremost text in the field. Her book established a new standard of comprehensiveness and clarity. Accessible to the non-lawyer yet unyielding in its attention to the detail of the law, it provided nurses and others with a superb reference and guide to professional practice.

While many of the principles that inform effective professional practice are enduring, the health and legal landscape have changed significantly in recent years. There can be few areas of modern life that are more dynamic than healthcare and the law

In the third edition Bridgit Dimond has maintained the high standards established in the first but she has updated and extended the text to take account of new laws, cases and developments in professional regulation and practice. As before, she very ably draws out the implications for nurses, exposing the important issues and identifying the key points that need to underpin accountable practice.

Patients and client protection should be paramount in professional thinking, but *Legal Aspects of Nursing* does not espouse the defensive practice sometimes associated with a preoccupation with the law. Rather, it encourages a positive approach to nursing based on a firm understanding of the legal implications and potential ramifications for professional practice.

The challenge of making the law both relevant and accessible to nurses should not be underestimated. Bridgit Dimond has achieved it again with this third edition of *Legal Aspects of Nursing*.

Sarah Mullally
Chief Nursing Officer
Department of Health

Preface to first edition

I make no apologies for producing a book on law for nurses. It is apparent to me that nurses are increasingly aware of the need for up-to-date legal knowledge, that they realise that they practise their profession within the constraints and limitations of the law and very occasionally with the powers of the law and that they are increasingly held responsible. The approach adopted here is, however, a practical one. I attempt to start with the problems and move outwards to the legal significance of the events described. The result is very different from the traditional textbook approach. My aim is not to teach the nurse the academic niceties of contract law or of the law of negligence but, rather, to take some everyday situations in which the nurse finds herself and examine the legal consequences of the situations so that she comes to an understanding of the legal principles that arise. In this way her legal understanding will develop and she will then be able to apply those principles to similar situations.

I am aware of the dangers of this approach. Any situation is, of course, very complex; there are considerable dangers of oversimplification. However, I am not of the persuasion that because a little knowledge is a dangerous thing law must be kept for the lawyers. It is essential that nurses understand the legal implications of their work so that they can protect both themselves and their patients. With a basic understanding of the law they should know when they need to seek expert legal advice and also know what elementary precautions they should be taking to protect themselves. Where possible, actual wording of acts of Parliament has been placed in figures, so that it would not break the flow of the text, and so that the nurse can see the actual wording. It is anticipated that the book would be used as a source book to dip into rather than be read from cover to cover. The appendices thus include much reference information and the index has been designed with this purpose in mind. I have not flinched from including some of the technical legal terms and have given the case references so that the nurse who wishes to pursue the subject in more detail can follow the cases.

Many of the problems discussed here are ones cited to me by hundreds of nurses in seminars I have conducted throughout the country and this explains the apparent concentration on issues relating to negligence litigation. This is a field that nurses are considerably anxious about and constantly ask questions on problems relating to the extended role, responsibility for others and aspects relating to resourcing.

A note of caution: there are many situations that arise where there are no clear legal guidelines; the dilemmas arising are of an ethical rather than a legal dimension. The law is both narrower and wider than the field of ethics. There are some problems where ethical issues arise and where the law as yet provides no specific guidelines other than the basic legal principles, for example many issues arising from the developments in reproductive technology have still not been covered by legislation although, following the Warnock Report, this situation is about to be changed. In other respects, the law is wider than ethical issues: for example the need to register a birth, marriage or death raises no ethical issues other than that of obeying the law. Some of these ethical issues will be covered although, clearly, it is only where there is a breach of the law that specific guidance can be given. This is not to say that ethical issues are not important. It is simply that there is no space for their discussion here. However, reference is made in the extended reading list to books that deal solely with these issues.

Some of the discussion relates to nursing procedure and practice that does not have legal status. However, it is considered essential to include this in a work of this kind.

A word about terminology. I have used the term 'nurse' to cover all categories of nursing staff from auxiliary to nursing officer. When it is significant that the nurse has a particular rank, then I have used the appropriate grade. I have also tended to refer to the nurse as she; this is not meant to be sexist: it simply covers the vast majority of nursing staff and is less clumsy than any contrived alternative such as 'he/she'. To illustrate practical situations two different terms have been applied: **situation** to describe an imaginary series of events that could well occur but, in fact, the names are fictitious and not intended to refer to any actual persons living or dead; **case** to cover actual cases that were heard before the courts. Not all of these refer to nursing staff; indeed the actual number of cases in which nurses have personally been defendant or accused are comparatively rare. Many of the cases involve medical staff or are not directly concerned with the health professions. However, principles that do arise are significant for nursing practice and on that account have been included. Because law even more than healthcare is a jargon-dominated profession, a glossary has been included to explain those legal terms that could cause difficulties.

The aim is to provide some practical guidance to nursing staff on the many problems that they might encounter. Part I of the book deals with those general problems facing all nursing staff, covering principles of professional negligence and the rights of the patient and also those areas where the nurse herself is a victim of an accident or assault etc. Part II deals with those specialist areas that are more likely to be encountered by nurses working in different fields but they may also be of general interest. Finally, certain areas that seem to require attention in their own right such as property matters, handling complaints, drugs and AIDS are considered separately, in Part III. Appendices provide additional useful information to which the nurse may wish to refer. I have endeavoured to state the law for England and Wales at 31 August 1989.

I am grateful for the support and encouragement of so many in the preparation of this book. I am considerably indebted to Tessa Shellens and Dr Sue Revel who painstakingly read through the draft and offered much advice and guidance and to Mrs Brenda Hall, my indexer, for her patience, tenacity and thoroughness. I also thank Ann Cross for her detective work. In addition, I am grateful to the following who read individual sections: Dawn O'Brien, Val Taylor, Margaret Winter, Anne Ryall-Davies, Sylvia Parker, Sue Bowers, Yvonne Peters, Gillian Davies, Helen Gray, Keith Weeks, Heather Anderson, Duncan Bloy, Helen Power, Jean Jones and Jean Whyte. The responsibility for the accuracy and contents of the book, however, remains mine. I also acknowledge the support and encouragement of my publishers, particularly Cathy Peck and Mike Cash.

Finally, I am conscious of the great debt I owe to my family whose delight in my work is encouragement in itself. I thank you all.

Preface to fifth edition

Once again one struggles to keep up with the many significant changes which have taken place since 2004 when the fourth edition of this book was published. The most momentous must be the Mental Capacity Act 2005 which has implications for almost all registered healthcare practitioners in whichever specialty they work. Its coming into force in October 2007 should facilitate the work of those who are in situations where decisions have to be made on behalf of those who lack the mental capacity to make their own decisions. Other significant areas of change in the law include the Human Tissue Act 2004, the NHS Redress Act 2006, the Corporate Manslaughter and Corporate Homicide Act 2007, the Health Act 2006 and many other statutory developments.

Significant changes have also taken place within the NHS with new initiatives, quangos, and reorganisations under way. Regulation and inspection have been tightened with the Healthcare Commission making major recommendations on deficiencies within healthcare, particularly in relation to the control of hospital acquired infection and another overhaul of the inspection machinery for the public and private health and social services being planned.

This fifth edition, like its predecessors, seeks to use practical examples to illustrate the impact of the law in specific situations with the aim of ensuring that the student and registered practitioner understand how the law operates within the changing context of their work. It is hoped that this book will continue to be a resource not only for those undertaking their pre-registration training but also for those who already have a basic understanding of the many areas of law which affect their practice.

Acknowledgements

I wish to convey my thanks to the Stationery Office for being able to print sections of the statutes and the statutory instruments, and to the various law reports for the quotations from the cases. In the preparation of this fifth edition, I am grateful once again to so many people – not least the hundreds of nurses who have raised legal concerns at the seminars and conferences I have spoken at – that it is invidious to mention just a few by name. My special thanks are due to Bette who prepared the index and tables and provided constant encouragement and support, as did my daughters Clare and Bec to whom this book is dedicated.

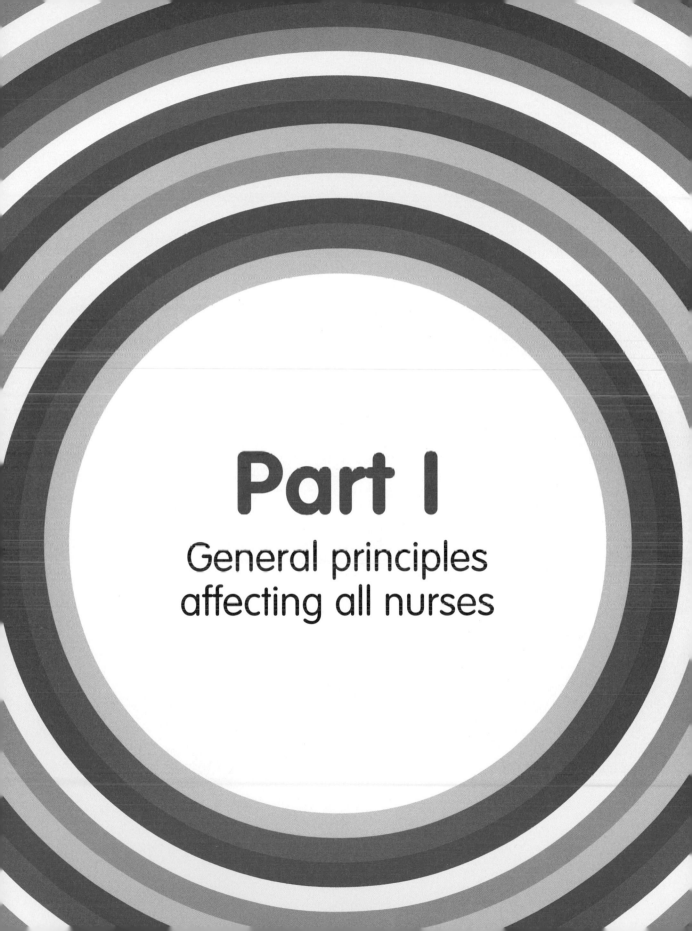

Part I
General principles affecting all nurses

Chapter 1
Introduction:
four arenas of accountability, the legal system and human rights

This chapter discusses

+ Accountability
+ Criminal liability
+ Professional liability
+ Civil liability
+ Accountability to employer
+ Relationship between the four arenas of accountability
+ Sources of law
+ Differences between civil and criminal law
+ Civil actions
+ Legal personnel and legal complaints
+ Legal language
+ Legal aid and conditional fees
+ Human Rights Act 1998
+ Freedom of Information Act 2000

Introduction

This book is about the accountability of the nurse, which means that it is concerned with how far the nurse can be held in law to account for her actions. No distinction is drawn in this context between responsibility and accountability. Responsibility is seen as being liable to be called to account, answerable for, accountable for. Space does not permit discussion of the moral or ethical dimensions. There may be circumstances in which a nurse could be held morally responsible but there is no legal liability. For example, if a nurse fails to volunteer her services at the scene of a road accident the law at present recognises no legal duty to volunteer help and thus any legal action brought against the nurse would fail. The Nursing and Midwifery Council (NMC) may, however, consider that she was guilty of professional misconduct and states in its Code of professional conduct: standards for performance, conduct and ethics[1] (replacing the Code of Professional Conduct) that there is professional duty upon the registered practitioner at all times. Paragraph 8.5 states:

> *In an emergency, in or outside the work setting, you have a professional duty to provide care. The care provided would be judged against what could reasonably be expected from someone with your knowledge, skills and abilities when placed in those particular circumstances.*

Many would hold that there is a moral duty to use her skills to help a fellow human being. Obviously, the law and ethics overlap, but each is both wider and narrower than the other. The further reading section promotes further consideration of the moral dilemmas in healthcare. The topics to be covered in this chapter are shown above.

Accountability

In this book we are concerned with the legal aspects of the accountability of the nurse. Many problems arise, however. Can a nurse, who does not have control over the resources, be held liable for harm suffered by a patient? Can a nurse be held responsible if she is ignorant, through lack of training, of certain procedures, and as a result the patient is harmed? Issues such as these are of significant concern to the nurse.

In order to be responsible it is necessary to have knowledge and this includes legal knowledge. Ignorance of the law is no defence and the nurse should be aware of the limits that the law imposes on her and also of the power it gives her. The increase in litigation over past years and the possibility of the nurse being personally involved in court proceedings is also a major anxiety for nurses.

Four main arenas of accountability in law are identified and discussed in detail. It might be considered that the most important has been omitted, i.e. accountability to oneself. This, however, is the moral dimension. There are no legal means of enforcing this form of accountability, although many would recognise it as being at the heart of the best of professional competence and skill.

Figure 1.1 illustrates the many areas of law that concern the nurse and most of these topics are considered in Part I. Some of the more specialist areas, e.g. the Abortion Act, are considered in Part II of the book, which deals with different specialties. In this introductory chapter, the four fields of accountability that the nurse faces will be considered.

When a patient suffers harm or there is loss of or damage to property, the nurse may be called to account in four different courts and tribunals. Not all actions will be heard in all four but we shall give an example incident to illustrate the different procedures that could involve all four. Figure 1.2 illustrates the four arenas of accountability: accountability in the civil and criminal courts, in disciplinary proceedings and before the committees of the NMC.

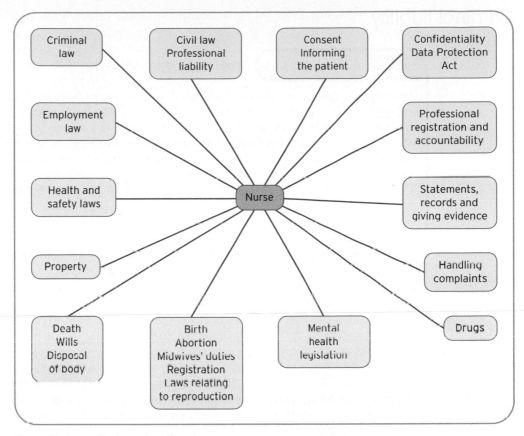

Figure 1.1 Areas that concern the nurse

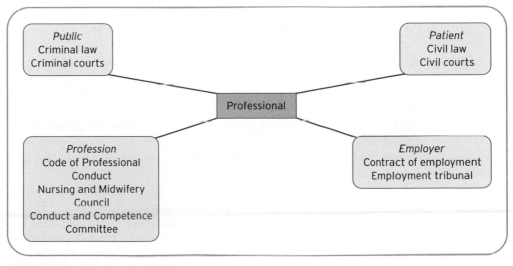

Figure 1.2 Arenas of accountability

Criminal liability

> ### Practical Dilemma 1.1   The wrong drug
>
> Staff Nurse Greaves was under considerable pressure on the children's ward. A spate of very seriously ill patients being admitted and a few absences from flu put great strains on the ward. A junior doctor wrote up a 4-year-old child with suspected meningitis for a high dose of antibiotics and told the staff nurse that he was prescribing a higher dose than was usual because of the severity of the child's condition. Normally, Staff Nurse Greaves would have checked the dose in the *British National Formulary* (*BNF*), but since they were so busy she took the doctor's word for it and gave the child the dose indicated on the sheet. Not long afterwards, the child showed signs of kidney failure and, despite efforts to save him, he died. Subsequently, the post mortem investigations revealed that the child had been given a thousandfold overdose of the antibiotic.

Death in circumstances such as those described in Practical Dilemma 1.1 would have to be reported to the coroner, who would immediately take control of the whole case, would probably order a post mortem, which the relatives would have no right to refuse, and may hold an inquest to establish the cause of death. Details of the coroner's powers and the progress of an inquest and the changes following the Shipman Inquiry[2] are discussed in Chapter 29. The staff nurse is likely to be asked to provide a statement and may well be called to give evidence at the inquest. The Chief Officer of Police or the Director of Public Prosecutions can request the coroner to adjourn the inquest on the grounds that a person may be charged with an offence committed in circumstances connected with the death of the deceased. The coroner also has the power to adjourn the hearing.

In a case like this, it is highly likely that, after investigation by the police, a decision might be taken to prosecute the nurse and the doctor for a criminal offence in connection with the child's death. Offences are classified as indictable or summary. An indictable offence is one that is heard before a judge and jury in the Crown Court, such as murder, manslaughter, rape and very serious offences. A summary offence is one heard by the magistrates in a magistrates' court, such as driving without due care and attention and some parking offences. Many offences can be tried in either a magistrates' court or the Crown Court. (For further discussion on this, see Chapter 2.)

Figure 1.3 shows the system of our criminal courts. Even where a case is to be heard in the Crown Court because it concerns an offence that can be tried only on indictment, the magistrates will still hear the case as examining justices to decide if the case is to be committed for trial.

In a situation like the one just described, it is quite likely that the inquest would be adjourned and that criminal proceedings would then take place against the staff. The prosecution has the burden of establishing to the satisfaction of the jury that the accused is guilty beyond reasonable doubt of the offence.

Once the jury has found the accused guilty, the judge has considerable discretion over sentencing. Only where the accused has been found guilty of murder is the judge compelled to sentence him to life imprisonment. The judge sets a minimum period to be served (tariff period), the parole board determine how much longer he must serve to protect the public and after release the convicted person remains on licence for the rest of his life. Proposals made to abolish the mandatory life sentence following a murder conviction were made by the

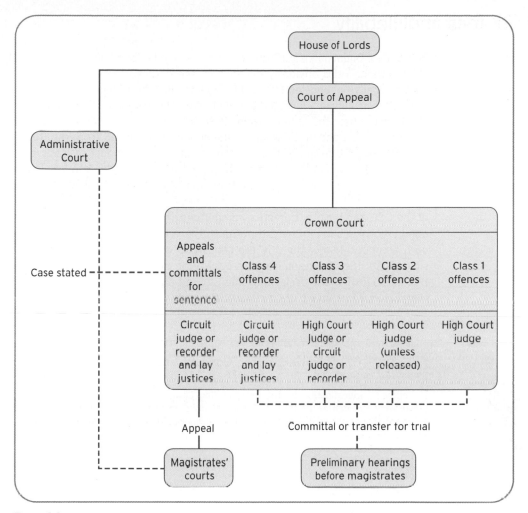

Figure 1.3 System of criminal courts

House of Lords Select Committee in 1988. In 2006 the Law Commission published a consultation paper on a new Homicide Act which set out a list of provisional proposals reforming the law on homicide[3] (see Chapter 2). In other, non-murder, cases, the judge has a discretion that ranges from an absolute discharge to imprisonment. There is a right of both the prosecution and the defendant to appeal against sentencing.

Criminal charges in relation to the care of the patient are rare, but when they do arise they attract considerable publicity. The trial of Dr Arthur in connection with the death of a severely handicapped Down's syndrome baby, the committal proceedings of Dr Hamilton on a charge under the Infant Life Preservation Act, the conviction of Dr Nigel Cox (for causing the death of a woman suffering from rheumatoid arthritis by prescribing and administering potassium chloride) and the case of Dr Shipman, who was convicted of the murder of 15 women, have raised serious issues in relation to the position of the doctor and the criminal law. (The nature of criminal proceedings is considered at greater length in Chapter 2 and laws relating to death in Chapter 29.)

Professional liability

In Practical Dilemma 1.1, Staff Nurse Greaves could be found guilty of causing the death of the child, although this obviously depends on the detailed facts of the case. The result would automatically be reported to the Nursing and Midwifery Council (NMC), and it is highly likely that, after preliminary investigation had taken place, a Conduct and Competence Committee (CCC) would hear the case to decide if Staff Nurse Greaves is unfit to practise by reason of her misconduct and, if so, whether she should be removed from the Register. Information goes to the NMC from a variety of sources about the conduct of a nurse and in a case like this the police would also report it to the registration body. Non-criminal misconduct may also be reported. The nurse could argue that the special circumstances of the case do not warrant her being removed from the Register. (The full details of the powers and procedures of the CCC and the other practice committees are discussed in Chapter 11.) In contrast to the criminal prosecution in the Crown Court, there is no jury here and the members who make up the constitution of the CCC are concerned with protecting the public from an irresponsible nurse; their intention is not to punish the nurse. The powers of the CCC are set out in Box 1.1. Following any decision by the CCC, an appeal on a point of law can be made to the High Court which can instigate a judicial review.

Box 1.1   **Powers of the Conduct and Competence Committee**

Following investigation by the Investigating Committee and referral to the Conduct and Competence Committee of the NMC, the Conduct and Competence Committee after a finding of unfitness to practise by the nurse can take one of the following courses:

(i) no action
(ii) refer respondent to the Health Committee or to screeners
(iii) postpone decision or issue interim order
(iv) strike off the Register
(v) issue a caution or condition order
(vi) suspend from registration.

Civil liability

The death of the child gives the child's personal representative the right to sue in the civil courts (see Figure 1.4) for the negligence that led to the child's death. The action could be brought against the nurse and the doctor personally, or against the NHS trust, which could be sued either for its direct responsibility for the death of the child or its vicarious (indirect) liability for the negligence of its staff while acting in the course of employment. If the NHS trust is found vicariously liable, then it has a right under the contract of employment to seek an indemnity from the negligent employee, although this right is rarely exercised. (The vicarious liability of the employer is considered in Chapter 4.) The claimant, i.e. the person who is bringing a civil action for negligence, must show fault on the part of the person or organisation he is suing. Box 1.2 shows the elements that must be established by the claimant and the

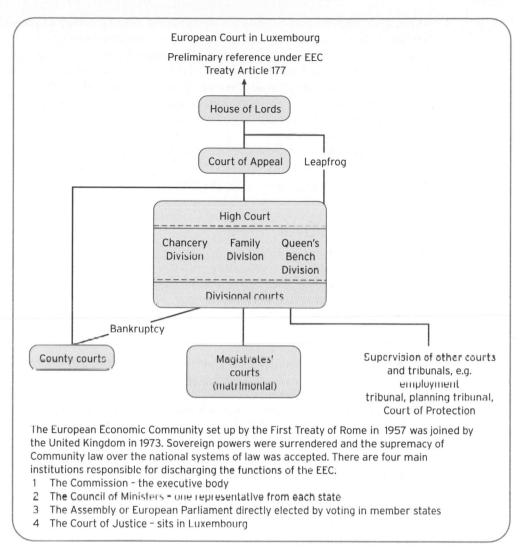

The European Economic Community set up by the First Treaty of Rome in 1957 was joined by the United Kingdom in 1973. Sovereign powers were surrendered and the supremacy of Community law over the national systems of law was accepted. There are four main institutions responsible for discharging the functions of the EEC.

1　The Commission – the executive body
2　The Council of Ministers – one representative from each state
3　The Assembly or European Parliament directly elected by voting in member states
4　The Court of Justice – sits in Luxembourg

Figure 1.4 The civil courts

Box 1.2　Elements in an action for negligence

1　A duty of care is owed by the defendant to the claimant.
2　There is a breach in the standard of the duty of care owed.
3　This breach has caused reasonably foreseeable harm.
4　Harm.

Importance of these elements in a claim for compensation for negligence is considered in Chapter 3.

Because of rising costs and awards of compensation, and owing to the injustice to claimants should they fail to obtain compensation, many associations are now urging the adoption of a system of no-fault liability. The DH has introduced a new NHS redress scheme,[4] which, when implemented, will operate alongside the existing system of claiming compensation for clinical negligence through the civil courts. (See Chapter 6.)

In the situation that Staff Nurse Greaves faces here, it is particularly unlikely that the NHS trust would defend an action for vicarious liability for her negligence if she had already been found guilty of a criminal offence. They would be more likely to offer a sum in compensation for the death of the child, the only likely dispute being over the appropriate sum of compensation. (The problems of quantifying harm and putting a monetary figure on loss suffered are discussed in Chapter 6.)

In the civil courts, the claimant has to establish liability of the defendant on a balance of probabilities. This is an easier task than that facing the prosecution in the criminal courts, where proof is required beyond reasonable doubt.

Accountability to employer

Finally, the staff nurse has to account to her employer. There is an implied term (i.e. a term that may never even be discussed or written down but which is assumed by the courts to exist unless there is evidence to the contrary) in every contract of employment that the employee will obey the reasonable instructions of the employer and will use all care and skill in carrying out her duties. (See Chapter 10 on implied terms in the contract of employment.) In a case such as this where it is evident that the employee has been grossly negligent, then that employee is in breach of contract and the employer can take appropriate disciplinary action. This might mean a warning - oral or written - demotion, suspension or even dismissal. (Disciplinary powers of the employer are considered in Chapter 10.)

In the case discussed here, the employer might initially suspend the staff nurse on full pay pending an inquiry and then, after all reasonable enquiries have been made and she has had an opportunity to respond, dismiss her. If she has the requisite length of continuous service, the staff nurse would be able to apply to an employment tribunal for a hearing of unfair dismissal. At this hearing the tribunal is concerned with the following issues:

1 What was the reason for the dismissal and was it one recognised by statute (i.e. Act of Parliament)?

2 Did the employer act reasonably in treating that reason as justification for dismissal?

(This is considered in more detail in Chapter 10.)

Relationship between the four arenas of accountability

In a situation such as the one described here, if the staff nurse has been grossly negligent, then consistent results for all four hearings are likely: she will be found guilty in the criminal courts; liable in the civil court; removed from the Register by the NMC; and dismissed by the employer. However, this is not necessarily so and cases are on record where the employer dismisses the nurse, but the NMC keeps her on the Register, or where the employer does not dismiss the nurse, but she is removed from the Register (in which case, of course, the nurse would lose her registered post). In addition, a criminal charge may fail where a civil charge succeeds. The reason for the lack of consistency is that the four forums are concerned with different aspects of the situation and have different standards of proof.

Sources of law

A brief word is appropriate on what is meant by the term 'law' and what its origin is. The law derives from two main sources:

1 *Acts of Parliament and Statutory Instruments that are enacted under the powers given by the former*: These are known as statutory sources, include the legislation of the European Community and take precedence over all other laws. Laws of the European Community automatically become part of the law of the United Kingdom (see Figure 1.4). The Council and the Commission have law-making powers and this can be in the form of Regulations or Directives. The Human Rights Act 1998 is in a special position (see pages 14–18).

2 *The common law (also known as case law or judge-made law)*: This is made up of the decisions by judges in individual cases that are often, but not always, interpretations of statute law. The judge, in deciding a particular case, is bound by a previous decision on the law made by judges in an earlier case if it is relevant to the facts before him and if that decision was made by a higher court than the one in which he is sitting. There is a recognised order of precedence so that, for example, a decision by the House of Lords is binding on all other courts except itself, but would be subject to relevant precedents of the European Court of Justice. The decisions are recorded by officially recognised reporters, so that in a case similar to a previous one the earlier decision can be put before the court. If the facts and the situation are comparable and the decision was made by a court whose decisions are binding, then the earlier precedent will be followed. If there are grounds for distinguishing the case then a different decision may follow.

Of vital importance to the system of precedence is a reliable procedure for recording the facts and decisions on any court case. Each court has a recognised system of reporting and the case is quoted by a reference that should enable the full report of the case to be found easily. An example is given in the Glossary (see 'Citation').

Similarly, Acts of Parliament and Statutory Instruments have chapter numbers for each year or a serial number.

There are recognised rules for interpreting Acts of Parliament and in relation to the following of precedents. Ultimately, however, if the law is unsatisfactory and fails to provide justice, the courts look to the Houses of Parliament to remedy the situation by new legislation. There is a right of appeal on matters of law to courts of higher jurisdiction. An appeal can be taken to the Court of Appeal and from there to the House of Lords, if permission is granted. Until the House of Lords has pronounced on a particular point of law, there may be considerable uncertainty as to what the law in a given situation is. A considerable number of medical law cases have been referred to the House of Lords in recent years.

Department of Health (DH) circulars, Department of Social Security (DSS) circulars and NMC codes of practice are not legally binding, but they are recommended practice. Breach of these codes may be evidence of failure to follow the approved practice, but cannot in itself result in successful civil or criminal action. This does not apply to the Midwives' Rules, which do have statutory force.

Differences between civil and criminal law

What is the difference between the civil law and the criminal law? The only safe answer is that a breach of the criminal law can be followed by prosecution in the criminal courts, whereas liability in civil law is actionable in the civil courts and may or may not be a crime. There is no necessary moral difference between the two. Prior to the Suicide Act of 1961 (which decriminalised an attempt to commit suicide), suicide and attempted suicide were crimes and as such the latter was subject to criminal proceedings. To many people, however, suicide may still be regarded as morally wrong irrespective of its non-criminal status and it is still a criminal offence to assist someone in a suicide attempt. Some acts may be both criminal and civil wrongs: thus to drive without due care and attention and cause harm can be followed by both criminal and civil proceedings.

How does one know if an act is a civil wrong? One way would be to consider previous cases to find out if there is a precedent. The ultimate way would be to establish in the House of Lords whether a particular action gives rise to civil liability. There is, for example, an increasing acceptance by the courts that information given in specific circumstances can give rise to an action for breach of confidence. Liability in civil law is thus a growth area.

Civil actions

A civil action for negligence will be the main one considered here in relation to the liability of the nurse or NHS trust, but there are other civil actions which will be considered briefly. The various forms of civil action are shown in Box 1.3. All these, except actions for breach of contract, are known as torts, i.e. civil wrongs.

Box 1.3 — **Some forms of civil action**

1 Torts
    Negligence
    Trespass to property
            to land
            and to the person
    False imprisonment
    Wrongful interference
    Breach of a statutory duty
    Nuisance
    Defamation
    Malicious prosecution
    Deliberate interference with interests in trade or business
2 Breach of contract

The action for breach of a statutory duty arises when an Act of Parliament or Statutory Regulations place duties on organisations or individuals. In certain circumstances where an individual suffers harm as a result of the breach of these statutory duties, an action for compensation may ensue in the civil courts. For example, many of the provisions of the Factories Acts give rise to such actions. In contrast, a breach of the general duties under the Health and Safety at Work Act does not give rise to such an action, although breach of the regulations made under the Health and Safety at Work Act may do so. This is considered in Chapter 12.

Defamation is another tort that is considered in Chapter 9. An action for nuisance is not considered and is unlikely to concern the nurse at work. An action for breach of contract will be briefly considered in Chapter 10 in connection with the nurse's contract of employment. An action for trespass to the person exists where a person alleges that they have been touched without their consent, and this is considered further in Chapter 7.

Legal personnel and legal complaints

At present we have a divided legal profession: solicitors and barristers (counsel). There are about 90,000 solicitors and about 10,000 barristers. The former are the main link with the client. Thus in Practical Dilemma 1.1, if the parents of the child decided to take civil action against the NHS trust, they would consult a solicitor, who would give them advice and possibly prepare an application for financial aid. If the case were to proceed, he would probably instruct counsel (i.e. a barrister) to prepare the pleadings (see Chapter 6) and represent the client in court. Under Part III of the Access to Justice Act 1999, major reforms were made to the law on lawyers' rights of audience before the courts and rights to conduct litigation and as a result all lawyers have full rights of audience before any court, subject only to meeting reasonable training requirements. The Act replaced the Lord Chancellor's Advisory Committee on Legal Education and Conduct with a new Legal Services Consultative Panel. The Act also made changes relating to complaints against lawyers. It gave additional powers to the Law Society and the Legal Services Ombudsman to strengthen the system for handling complaints against lawyers and created a Legal Services Complaints Commissioner to set targets for the handling of complaints by the professional bodies. The House of Lords has decided that professional work in court is no longer immune from actions for negligence.[5]

These reforms may in the long term lead to a single legal profession. At present the initial training for both solicitors and barristers is the same (a law degree or Part 1 of the Common Professional Examination). Would-be solicitors then undertake practical training with a firm of solicitors, and then take the Law Society's Part 2 examination, called the Legal Practice Course, while would-be barristers study for the Bar to which they are 'called'. They must join one of the Inns of Court and must dine there on a specified number of occasions. The barrister must then undertake pupillage, where they are attached to a practising barrister. Barristers usually work together in chambers managed by a clerk who negotiates and collects the fees from solicitors. Fees are at present negotiated in advance and include a brief fee for accepting a case and a refresher fee, which is a daily fee for each day that the case is in court. Senior barristers and solicitor-advocates are eligible to 'take silk', i.e. they become Queen's Counsel (QC) appointed by the Lord Chancellor. A new independent selection procedure has now been introduced and candidates are appointed by the Lord Chancellor on the recommendation of an independent panel. The term lawyer includes both solicitor and barrister.

Legal language

Lawyers, like any profession, have their own language, which can create barriers. In April 1999, new procedures for civil litigation were introduced together with a simplification of language to assist communication: thus the term plaintiff (used to describe a person bringing a civil action) was replaced by the word claimant; a writ (the document issued by the court which begins the civil case) is replaced by claim form. A glossary is provided to assist the reader with any specialist terms. It is the aim of this book to break down the barriers between the law and the nurse and to facilitate communication.

Legal aid and conditional fees

Major changes have been made to the legal aid system under the Access to Justice Act 1999.

Part I of the Act provided for two new schemes, replacing the existing legal aid scheme, to secure the provision of publicly funded legal services for people who need them. It established a *Legal Services Commission* to run the two schemes; and enabled the Lord Chancellor to give the Commission orders, directions and guidance about how it should exercise its functions. It required the Commission to establish, maintain and develop a *Community Legal Service*. The Community Legal Service fund has replaced the legal aid fund in civil and family cases. The Commission is also responsible for a *Criminal Defence Service*, which replaced the legal aid scheme in criminal cases. The new scheme is intended to ensure that people suspected or accused of a crime are properly represented, while securing better value for money than is possible under the legal aid scheme. The Legal Services Commission is empowered to secure these services through contracts with lawyers in private practice or by providing them through salaried defenders (employed directly by the Commission or by non-profit-making organisations established for the purpose). Under the Criminal Defence Services Act 2006 the Legal Services Commission is given the power to grant rights of representation instead of the court and a test of financial eligibility for the grant of such funding and contributions towards it is introduced.

Part II of the Access to Justice Act 1999 made changes to facilitate the private funding of litigation. Over recent years a scheme known as 'no win, no fee' or conditional fee system has been introduced. By this system, potential litigants can agree with lawyers terms on which they will be represented. Insurance cover is taken out to meet the expenses of witnesses and other costs arising in case the action is lost. The 1999 Act amended the law on conditional fee agreements between lawyers and their clients; in particular it allows the additional fees payable to a solicitor in a successful case in a no win, no fee agreement to be recovered from the other side. (See Chapter 6 for further consideration of this.)

Human Rights Act 1998

The United Kingdom was a signatory of the European Convention for the Protection of Human Rights and Fundamental Freedoms in 1950. However, anyone who sought to bring an action for breach of their human rights, as set out in the Convention, was unable to take the case to the courts in this country but had to go to the European Court of Human Rights in Strasbourg. (NB: This is *not* the court of the European Community, the European Court of Justice, which meets in Luxembourg.) It was estimated that to take a case to Strasbourg cost over £30,000 and took over five years. The Human Rights Act 1998 came into force on 2 October 2000. (It came into force in Scotland on devolution.) It has three main effects: first, it is unlawful for a public authority (or organisation exercising functions of a public nature) to breach the rights set out in the Convention; second, from 2 October 2000 an allegation of a breach of the rights can be brought in the courts of this country; and third, judges can make a declaration that legislation that is raised in a case before them is incompatible with the articles of the Convention and the legislation will then be referred back to Parliament for reconsideration. The Act is not retrospective, but any person concerned about an infringement before 2 October 2000 could take a case to Strasbourg, depending on time limits.

Action can be brought against a public authority or organisation exercising functions of a public nature for breach of the Convention articles in the courts of this country. An example of a declaration of the court of law incompatible with the articles of Human Rights is a declaration of the House of Lords,[6] which held that present marriage laws in the country that prevented a transsexual marrying following his gender change (because the law did not recognise the change of gender) were incompatible with Human Rights articles; a Gender Recognition Act 2004 was passed and implemented, which enables applicants who meet specified criteria to apply for a replacement birth certificate and are allowed to marry in their adopted sex.

Appendix A sets out Schedule 1 to the Human Rights Act 1998. The alarmist prophecies of a huge increase in litigation were not realised, although there has been an increase in the number of cases alleging breach of the articles, often alongside another course of action. Some of the more significant articles will be considered below, but articles are also considered in relevant chapters. It is recommended that healthcare staff should undertake a proactive exercise in identifying possible breaches of the Act and be proactive in taking any necessary remedial action. Further information is available from the Ministry of Justice website,[7] which took over the responsibilities on Human Rights from the Department for Constitutional Affairs (DCA) in 2007 and will in due course reprint the guidance on the Human Rights Act published by the DCA.[8] In June 2007 the House of Lords[9] decided, in a majority decision, that private care homes under contract with local authorities for the provision of places were not exercising functions of a public nature for the purposes of the Human Rights Act. This has led to an understandable reaction from many charities concerned with the care of vulnerable adults that overriding legislation be passed. A private member's Bill was introduced into the House of Commons by Andrew Dismore MP to change the definition.

Right to life

> **Statute** | **Article 2(1)**
>
> Everyone's right to life shall be protected by law. No one shall be deprived of his life intentionally save in the execution of a sentence of a court following his conviction for a crime for which this penalty is provided by law. (The sixth Protocol Article 1 states that 'The death penalty shall be abolished. No one shall be condemned to such penalty or executed.')

Claims have been made that this right to life could be used as the basis for legal action when resources are refused or when decisions are made for a person not to be resuscitated or treatment is withdrawn or withheld. For example, in a case where parents challenged a not for resuscitation (NFR) decision for their severely disabled baby,[10] the court held that the full palliative care recommended by the doctors, allowing the baby to die with dignity, was not a breach of either Article 2 or Article 3 (see below) of the European Convention for the Protection of Human Rights and Fundamental Freedoms. The President of the Family Division, Dame Elizabeth Butler-Sloss, held that the withdrawal of life-sustaining medical treatment was not contrary to Article 2 of the Human Rights Convention and the right to life, where the patient was in a persistent vegetative state. The ruling was made on 25 October 2000 in cases involving Mrs M, 49 years, who suffered brain damage during an operation abroad in 1997 and was diagnosed as being in a persistent vegetative state (PVS) in October 1998 and Mrs H, 36, who fell ill in America as a result of pancreatitis at Christmas 1999.[11]

Diane Pretty failed in her attempt to see the Suicide Act 1961 (which makes it an offence for her husband to aid and abet her suicide) as incompatible with her right to a dignified death and therefore a breach of Articles 2, 3, 8 and 14.[12] She took her case to the European Court of Human Rights but failed.[13] Article 2 has also been relied upon by those who claim that there has been a miscarriage of justice in relation to a death in custody or near death. Thus in one case[14] the claimant, who was assessed as a real suicide risk in prison, attempted to hang himself and was left severely brain damaged. A prison investigation took place but the report was not published. The Secretary of State proposed a private inquiry by the Prisons and Probation Ombudsman but the claimant sought judicial review of this proposal arguing that Article 2 rights implied an obligation on the State to carry out an effective investigation into the circumstances relating to a death. The judge upheld the claim, setting out the characteristics of an effective investigation. The Secretary of State appealed and the Court of Appeal held that any investigation should be held in public but the claimant's representatives would not be entitled to cross-examine witnesses. In a subsequent case a young man attempted suicide in Feltham Young Offenders Institution and was left brain-damaged. The Court of Appeal held that in such a situation Article 2 rights required that there was a clear obligation on the Secretary of State to ensure that there was an effective inquiry into the near death.[15] A breach of Article 2 was successfully claimed when a witness for the prosecution who was known to be subject to intimidation did not receive police protection and was murdered before the trial took place.[16] Article 2 rights were also considered by the House of Lords when considering a coroner's refusal to resume an inquest[17] (see Chapter 29).

Right not to be subjected to inhuman or degrading treatment

> ### Statute   Article 3
>
> Article 3 of the Convention states that:
>
> *No one shall be subjected to torture or to inhuman or degrading treatment or punishment.*

It could be argued that patients who spend six hours on a stretcher in a corridor outside the A&E department while a bed is being sought are being subjected to both degrading and inhuman treatment. The physical conditions in some hospitals or nursing or residential care homes may be seen to be an infringement of this right. Other examples could probably be given where patients are not treated with dignity or humanity. In the field of manual handling, there have been suggestions that to require a person to use a hoist is contrary to their human rights. However, it is thought that such an argument will not succeed, since if the alternative to a hoist is manual handling by another person, then that might be contrary to the rights of the other. This issue was considered in a manual handling case involving East Sussex County Council (see Chapter 12). The High Court has held that requiring an asylum seeker to sleep rough was inhuman and degrading treatment under Article 3. It was insufficient for the Home Office to provide a list of charities for the homeless.[18] In a case where a woman died after being imprisoned, her children won a case in the European Court of Human Rights that the conditions of her imprisonment prior to her death were inhuman and degrading and therefore a breach of Article 3. There were serious lapses of procedures to monitor her condition, especially her weight loss (from 50 kg to 40 kg) and her vomiting and to arrange for earlier hospital admission.[19]

Right to liberty and security

> **Statute**   **Article 5**
>
> Article 5 of the Convention states:
>
> *Everyone has the right to liberty and security of person. No one shall be deprived of his liberty save in accordance with a procedure prescribed by law.*

The use of common law powers (i.e. powers recognised by the courts as in the *Re F*[20] case) to detain mentally incapacitated adults in psychiatric hospitals was regarded as a breach of this article, since, although the article envisages the lawful detention of persons of unsound mind, a decision of the House of Lords did not lay down a procedure. This issue was raised in the Bournewood case[21] where the European Court of Human Rights ruled against the UK. The case is discussed in Chapters 7 and 20. Amendments to the Mental Capacity Act 2005 to fill the gap revealed by the Bournewood case have been made by the Mental Health Act 2007 and are considered in Chapter 20.

Right to a fair trial

> **Statute**   **Article 6**
>
> Article 6 of the Convention states:
>
> *In the determination of his civil rights and obligations or of any criminal charge against him, everyone is entitled to a fair and public hearing within a reasonable time by an independent and impartial tribunal established by law.*

This will apply to disciplinary hearings as well as courts and tribunals. Hearings must be independent and impartial. In criminal prosecutions, the accused is presumed innocent until proved guilty. A GP's claim that his suspension from his practice was a breach of Article 6 was not upheld since the suspension was an interim measure during which his pay was maintained. There was, however, a breach of the right to protection of property under Article 1 of the First Protocol to the Convention.[22]

Right to respect for private and family life, home and correspondence

> **Statute**   **Article 8**
>
> Under Article 8 of the Convention:
>
> *Everyone has the right to respect for his private and family life, his home and his correspondence.*

It was argued by a father[23] whose wife wished to obtain an abortion that for it to be undertaken against the wishes of the father was contrary to Article 8. This is considered in Chapter 15. Failures to recognise confidential information or support the privacy of patients may lead to court action against hospitals and other organisations. In a case heard by the European Court of Human Rights, it was held that the fact that the rights in law of an unmarried father differed from those of a married father were not a breach of Article 8 since there was an objective and reasonable justification for the difference in treatment.[24] The High Court held that restrictions on child visits to patients in high-security hospitals who had committed murder, manslaughter or certain sexual offences, unless the child was one of a permitted category, were lawful and not in breach of Article 8 of the European Convention on Human Rights.[25] The onus of establishing family life lay on an applicant. The High Court also held that a prisoner serving a life sentence for murder did not have a right to his wife to be artificially inseminated with his sperm. The right to found a family did not mean that an individual was guaranteed to the right at all times to conceive children.[26]

Other significant articles include Article 9, freedom of thought, conscience and religion; Article 10, freedom of expression; and Article 14, prohibition of discrimination. As cases come before the courts, case law will develop on the interpretation to be given to the various articles and the extent to which the NHS is recognising the rights of its staff and its patients.

Freedom of Information Act 2000

This Act, which gives a right of access to information held by public authorities, was brought into force by 2005. An Information Commissioner has been appointed to monitor both the FOI Act and the Data Protection Act 1998 and codes of practice and guidance have been issued. There are many exceptions to the right of access including personal information, information provided in confidence and legal professional privilege. Both Acts are considered in Chapter 8. Information on both the Data Protection Act and the Freedom of Information Act is available from the Information Commissioner's Office website.[27]

Reflection questions

1 What is the difference between law that derives from a statute and the common law?
2 What is the difference between a solicitor and a barrister?
3 Look at the glossary and identify those words with which you are not familiar.

Further exercises

1 Consider any situation you know of where a patient (almost) suffered harm as a result of a careless act by a professional and analyse the potential consequences as far as the civil and criminal courts, the CCC and the employment tribunal are concerned. Refer to Chapters 2, 3, 10 and 11 for more details.
2 Try to arrange a visit to one of the four forums described here or a coroner's court (see Chapter 29) and draw up a plan for the procedure that you witness.
3 With colleagues, choose any Article in the Convention on Human Rights (see Appendix A) that is relevant to your work and decide on the extent to which there are any infringements of that right. What action could you take?

References

[1] Nursing and Midwifery Council, Code of professional conduct: standards for performance, conduct and ethics, NMC, 2004

[2] Shipman Inquiry Third Report: Death and Cremation Certification, 14 July 2003; www.the-shipman-inquiry.org.uk/reports.asp

[3] Law Commission, A new Homicide Act for England and Wales, Consultation paper 177, 2006

[4] Department of Health, Making Amends: a consultation paper setting out proposals for reforming the approach to clinical negligence in the NHS, CMO, June 2003

[5] *Arthur JS Hall and Co.* (a firm) v. *Simons* [2000] 3 WLR 543 HL

[6] *Bellinger* v. *Bellinger* [2003] UKHL 21; [2003] 2 WLR 1174

[7] http://www.justice.gov.uk/hract; www.humanrights.gov.uk/whatsnew.htm

[8] Department for Constitutional Affairs, Study Guide on Human Rights Act 1998, 2nd edition, October 2002; now available from the Department of Justice: www.justice.gov.uk www.dca.gov

[9] *YL* v. *Birmingham City Council* [2007] UKHL 22; *The Times*, 21 June 2007

[10] *National Health Service Trust A* v. *D and Others* [2000] Lloyd's Rep Med 411

[11] *NHS Trust A* v. *M; NHS Trust B* v. *H* [2001] 1 All ER 801

[12] *R (on the application of Pretty)* v. *DPP* [2001] UKHL 61, [2001] 3 WLR 1598

[13] *Pretty* v. *UK* ECHR Current Law 380 June 2002 2346/02; [2002] 35 EHRR 1; [2002] 2 FLR 45

[14] *R (on the application of D)* v. *Secretary of State for the Home Department (Inquest intervening)* [2006] EWCA Civ 143, [2006] 3 All ER 946

[15] *R (on the application of JL)* v. *Secretary of State for the Home Department* [2007] EWCA Civ 767

[16] *Van Colle and another* v. *Chief Constable of Hertfordshire Police* [2006] EWHC 360 QBD, [2006] 3 All ER 963

[17] *R (on the application of Hurst)* v. *London Northern District Coroner* [2007] UKHL 13, [2007] 2 All ER 1025

[18] *R (Limbuela)* v. *Secretary of State for the Home Department, The Times Law Report,* 9 February 2004

[19] *McGlinchey and Others* v. *The United Kingdom* [2003] Lloyd's Rep Med 265

[20] *In re F (Mental Patient: Sterilisation)* [1990] 2 AC 1, [1989] 2 WLR 1025, [1989] 2 All ER 545

[21] *R* v. *Bournewood Community and Mental Health NHS Trust ex p L* [1998] 3 All ER 289; *HL* v. *United Kingdom* [2004] ECHR 471 Application No 45508/99, 5 October 2004; *Times Law Report,* 19 October 2004

[22] *R (on the application of Malik)* v. *Waltham Forest Primary Care Trust* (Secretary of State for Health, interested party) [2006] EWHC 487 admin, [2006] 3 All ER 71

[23] *Paton* v. *UK* (1980) 3 EHRR 408

[24] *B* v. *UK* [2000] 1 FLR 1 ECtHR

[25] *R* v. *Secretary of State for Health ex parte Lally, The Times,* 26 October 2000; [2001] 1 FLR 406

[26] *R* v. *Secretary of State for the Home Department ex p Mellor* [2000] 2 FLR 951

[27] www.ico.gov.uk

Chapter 2
Actions in the criminal courts and defences to criminal charges

Introduction

In this chapter, we consider the course followed if criminal proceedings are brought against a nurse and the ways in which she could defend herself. It must be emphasised that the burden is on the prosecution to establish the guilt of the accused beyond reasonable doubt. The accused still has a right of silence at all stages of the prosecution, but failure by the accused to answer questions or mention something she relies on later in court or failure to give evidence may allow adverse inferences to be drawn during the trial.

> **Practical Dilemma 2.1**   **Theft**
>
> A discrepancy is found between the ward drug control records and the stock. An investigation is initiated and suspicion falls upon Staff Nurse Jarvis. The police are brought in and after making their enquiries they decide that Staff Nurse Jarvis should be charged with the offence of theft.

A situation such as this involves several kinds of investigation. The NHS trust will be concerned to determine whether there are grounds to discipline and possibly eventually dismiss the staff nurse. The fact that the police are brought in does not mean that the NHS trust can abandon its own investigation, but clearly its enquiries should not conflict with those of the police. The NHS trust must allow the staff nurse to give a full explanation of what has occurred and she should be allowed a representative. Disciplinary proceedings by the employer are discussed in Chapter 10. There is also the possibility of a hearing before the CCC of the NMC (see Chapter 11), but this may well be postponed pending the outcome of the police investigations and criminal charges. Here we are concerned only with the criminal proceedings.

Initial stages of arrest and prosecution

The staff nurse may well be asked to accompany the police to the station (see Figure 2.1). A Code of Practice (C) prepared under the Police and Criminal Evidence Act 1984 provides guidance on the detention, treatment and questioning of persons by police officers and is intended to provide clear and workable guidelines for the police, while strengthening

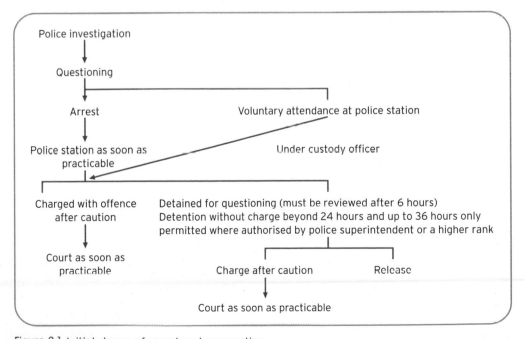

Figure 2.1 Initial stages of arrest and prosecution

safeguards for the public at the same time. The Codes of Practice were revised in 2003 and again in 2004[1] and cover: Code of Practice A: exercise of police officers of their statutory powers of stop and search; B: searches of premises and seizure of property; C: detention, treatment and questioning of persons by police officers (C includes annexes on A: intimate and strip search; B: delay in notifying arrest or allowing access to legal advice; C: restriction on drawing adverse inference from silence and the terms of the caution; D: written statements under caution; E: provisions for mentally ill and mentally vulnerable people; F: agreements between countries on notification of those arrested and detained; G: fitness to be interviewed; and H: detained persons: observation list); D: identification of persons by police officers; and E: tape-recording interviews with suspects. The Code of Practice must be readily available at all police stations. The Code applies both to those who have been arrested and those who have voluntarily attended the police station. One of the most important safeguards is the right of the detained person to have access to free legal advice at the police station before and during any interview.

The staff nurse may have been arrested before she is taken to the police station or she may be arrested there. In either case, she should be given a caution as soon as there are grounds to suspect her of the offence and before she is questioned about it for the purpose of obtaining evidence that may be given to a court in a prosecution. The caution should be given in the following terms: 'You do not have to say anything but it may harm your defence if you do not mention when questioned something which you later rely on in court. Anything you do say may be given in evidence.'

Minor deviations may be a breach of the Code, but do not necessarily affect the fairness of the trial and make the evidence inadmissible under S. 78 of the Police and Criminal Evidence Act. The documentation that the police must retain is shown in Box 2.1. The Code sets out rules for the police in the interview. The usual procedure now is for the interview to be tape-recorded and the guidelines and Code of Practice for tape-recording should be followed.

Box 2.1 **Documentation kept by the police**

Custody records should be kept for each person who is brought to a police station under arrest or who is arrested at the police station after attending there voluntarily. He is entitled on request to be supplied with a copy when he leaves the police station.

The information must be recorded as soon as practicable and should include the following:

1 Grounds for a person's detention.

2 Detained person's property.

3 Request made for a person to be informed and action taken; any letters or messages sent, calls made or visits received and any refusal on the part of a person to have information about himself or his whereabouts given to an outside enquirer.

4 Any request for legal advice and the action taken on it.

5 Replacement clothing and meals offered.

6 Medical examination by a police surgeon, or request for one and the arrangements made; any medication the detained person is on.

7 An interview record should record:
   + the times at which the detained person is not in the custody of the custody officer and why, and the reason for any refusal to deliver him out of that custody
   + any intoxicating liquor supplied to a detained person
   + any decision to delay a break in an interview
   + a written record of the interview (unless tape-recorded) signed by the detained person as correct.

> **Box 2.1 continued**
>
> **8** Any action taken to call an interpreter and any agreement to be interviewed in the absence of an interpreter.
>
> **9** Grounds for and the extent of any delay in conducting a review.
>
> **10** Anything a detained person says when charged, any questions put after the charge and answers given relating to the offence shall be contemporaneously recorded in full on the forms provided and the record signed by the detained person.
>
> **11** Details of any intimate or strip search: which parts were searched, by whom, who was present, reasons and the result.
>
> **12** Grounds for any action in delaying the notification of an arrest or allowing access to legal advice.

When the officer considers that there is sufficient evidence to prosecute a detained person, he should bring her before the custody officer without delay, who will then be responsible for considering whether or not she should be charged. A further caution must then be given. In addition, a written notice should be given showing the particulars of the offence with which she is charged and including the name of the officer in the case (except where in terrorist cases or where naming the officer would cause reasonable fear of danger), their police station and a reference number for the case. Questions relating to an offence may not be put to a person after she has been charged with that offence or after she has been informed that she may be prosecuted for it, unless they are necessary to prevent or minimise harm or loss to some other person or to the public, to clear up an ambiguity in a previous answer or statement or where it is in the interests of justice that she should have an opportunity to comment on some fresh information. Before these additional questions are put, the accused must be given another caution. Annexe D to the Code of Practice gives rules on written statements given under caution.

The Criminal Justice Act 2003 has introduced the power of a constable, investigating officer or person authorised by a relevant prosecutor to give a conditional caution provided five requirements are satisfied: evidence the offender has committed the offence; there is sufficient evidence to charge the person and a conditional caution should be given; the offender admits the offence; the effect of the conditional caution is explained; and the offender signs a document setting out specified details. The Secretary of State must prepare a Code of Practice in relation to conditional cautions covering specified topics (CJA 2003 SS. 22–5).

Role of the Crown Prosecution Service

Since the introduction of the Crown Prosecution Service, the responsibility for the conduct of most criminal proceedings is on the Crown Prosecution Service, the head of which is the Director of Public Prosecution, who acts under the Attorney General. They have the responsibility of instituting criminal proceedings and appearing for the prosecution.

Magistrates' courts

If the staff nurse is charged with the offence of theft, she would probably be given police bail and told to appear at a magistrates' court. Almost all criminal cases begin in a magistrates' court and 98 per cent are dealt with completely there. The remaining cases go before the

Crown Courts before judge and jury or are dismissed by the magistrates at the committal proceedings.

Indictable-only offences can be heard only before a judge and jury in the Crown Court, summary offences can be heard only by magistrates, but many offences are triable either way. Box 2.2 shows the classification of the offences and Box 2.3 shows the course of a hearing.

Box 2.2   Classification of offences

1. Offences triable only on indictment (i.e. by judge and jury): murder; genocide; infanticide; causing death by reckless driving; robbery; treason; wounding with intent and many others.
2. Offences triable only summarily (i.e. by magistrates): drunk and disorderly; careless driving; assault on police; and other offences set down by statute, such as the Road Traffic Act 1972 and Schedule 1 of the Criminal Law Act 1977.
3. Offences triable either way (by judge and jury or by magistrates) – case can be heard by magistrates in summary trial or on indictment in the Crown Court. New powers for magistrates in respect of offences triable either way are given in Schedule 3 of the Criminal Justice Act 2003. Offences include: theft; handling, obtaining property or pecuniary advantage by deception; assault occasioning actual bodily harm.

Box 2.3   Course of a hearing in a magistrates' court

The magistrates' courts hear:

(a) offences that are triable only as summary offences, e.g. careless driving
(b) offences that are triable either way.

Hearing

1. Plea:
   - a plea of guilty must be unequivocal
   - a plea of guilty may be made by post, but only to summary non-imprisonable offences.
2. Summary trial where the defendant pleads not guilty:
   - A Prosecution:
     1. Opening speech by prosecution lawyer.
     2. Examination in chief of prosecution witnesses.
     3. Cross-examination by defence.
     4. Re-examination by prosecution lawyer.
   - B Submission by defence of no case to answer (if appropriate). Prosecution have the right to reply and magistrates determine the question.
   - C Defence case:
     1. Defendant can remain silent or give evidence. (The court may in certain circumstances draw adverse inferences from silence.)
     2. Defence witnesses are called.
     3. Defence lawyer addresses the magistrates.
   - D The finding: the magistrates determine the guilt or innocence and determine the sentence if a guilty verdict and if they feel their powers are adequate.

When the staff nurse is brought before the magistrates on a charge of theft she will be asked to indicate a plea. If she indicates a plea of guilty to the summary offence, she will be sentenced by the magistrates. If she pleads not guilty, she will be tried by the magistrates.

If she is charged with an offence that is triable either way (i.e. as a summary offence before the magistrates or on indictment by a judge and jury) and she indicates a plea of guilty, then the magistrates will decide whether she should be sentenced by them; if they consider their powers are inadequate, they may then commit her to the Crown Court for sentencing. If she indicates that she intends to plead not guilty or declines to indicate a plea, the magistrate will then decide whether the trial should be before them or whether the defendant should be committed to the Crown Court for trial. If the magistrates decide the case is suitable for trial before them, the defendant will be asked to consent to that procedure. The defendant has the right at that stage to elect trial by judge and jury at the Crown Court. New procedures under the Criminal Justice Act 2003 enable the magistrates to give an indication, if the accused were to plead guilty, of whether a custodial sentence would be imposed.

The Criminal Justice Act 2003 limits the choice of the accused to opt for trial by jury, thus reducing the number of cases that would be heard in the Crown Court.

Committal proceedings

If, by the same token, Staff Nurse Jarvis elects to have the case heard in the Crown Court, she would in the past have faced committal proceedings before the magistrates where they act as examining justices and decide if there is sufficient evidence for the case to be committed to the Crown Court. There used to be two forms of committal proceedings: old style where there is a mini hearing of the prosecution evidence which the defence can challenge, and the new style committal proceedings where the defendant agrees that there is a case to answer. With the implementation of Schedule 3 of the Criminal Justice Act 2003 committal proceedings are abolished and once the magistrates decide that an 'either way' offence should be tried in the Crown Court, it will be sent there directly and a date for the Plea and Case Management Hearing agreed. Indictable-only cases are transferred to the Crown Court immediately (i.e. at first appearance before the magistrates), and sometimes before witness statements are taken. At this preliminary hearing a timetable will be set for the service of the prosecution evidence, service of defence statements and a date for the Plea and Case Management Hearing (PCMH).

Crown Court proceedings

Let us assume that Staff Nurse Jarvis's case is committed to the Crown Court for trial, since it is an offence which is triable either way. (If she had been charged with an indictable-only offence, the case would have been transferred to the Crown Court.) The procedure followed is shown in Box 2.4. Changes have been made regarding the right to challenge the jury (see Box 2.5). Once the jury have been sworn in, the hearing follows the same path as that in a magistrates' court, but only counsel or solicitor-advocate can represent the accused before the court and a barrister may therefore have been briefed by Staff Nurse Jarvis's solicitor.

Box 2.4 Procedure in the Crown Court

1 Attendance of the defendant (in person or by video link if the defendant has been remanded in custody).

2 The indictment (the document embodying the charge(s) brought by the Crown against the defendant) is read by the clerk to the accused and he is asked whether he pleads guilty or not guilty. This is known as the arraignment.
 The accused can:
 (a) plead guilty – if accepted, court proceeds to sentencing
 (b) plead not guilty – see point 4, below
 (c) stand silent – if mute of malice (this is determined by the jury) a plea of not guilty entered – if mute by visitation of God, court will decide if accused is fit to plead (see insanity, below)
 (d) object on legal grounds – e.g. indictment is invalid and should be quashed; the accused has already been tried for the same offence (i.e. a plea of *autrefois*, acquit or convict).

3 Directions for smooth running of the trial: identification of all the issues.

4 Empanelling of the jury: if the defendant has pleaded not guilty to any count on the indictment, a jury must be empanelled. The jury is not usually present during the arraignment so that they are kept in ignorance if the accused has pleaded guilty to some offences and not guilty to others, unless the guilty pleas are admissible in the trial.
 The jurors are called in after the arraignment and the names of 12 are called out. They can be challenged by defence or prosecution for cause (see Box 2.5). They are then sworn in and the clerk reads the indictment to them, tells them the defendant has pleaded not guilty and that their charge is to say, having heard the evidence, whether he be 'guilty' or 'not guilty'.

5 The hearing
 A Prosecution:
  1 Opening speech by the prosecution.
  2 Prosecution evidence:
   Examination in chief: prosecution witnesses questioned by the prosecution.
  3 Cross-examination – to discredit witnesses, leading questions can be used and earlier inconsistent statements by the witness can be put to him.
  4 Re-examination – to offset the effects of cross-examination. It cannot be used to produce new evidence which should have been brought out in the examination in chief.
  5 Written statements of witnesses whose evidence the defence does not wish to dispute will be read out.
  6 Challenges to admissibility of evidence: the defence can (in the absence of the jury) challenge the admissibility of evidence. The judge will rule on the admissibility and if he upholds the defence objections to the evidence, all reference to the evidence must be omitted.
 B Defence:
  1 Defence submission: after the conclusion of the prosecution evidence, the defence can ask the trial judge to direct the jury as a matter of law that they should acquit the defendant:
   (a) either because the prosecution has failed to produce any evidence to establish some essential ingredient of the offence
   (b) or because the evidence produced is so weak or so discredited by cross-examination that no reasonable jury could convict. If the defence submission is upheld, an acquittal is directed.
   If this submission fails then the defence case is put.
  2 Case for the defence: an opening speech can be made where the defendant and other witnesses are being called to give evidence as to facts (not where only the defendant is called or the other witnesses are only as to character).
   Procedure as above.
   Examination in chief.
   Cross-examination.
   Re-examination.
 C Closing speeches: by prosecution and defence counsel.
 D Summing up by judge.
 E Verdict of jury.
 F Sentencing following finding of guilt.

> ### Box 2.5　Challenging the jury
>
> *Prosecution*: Can ask for any would-be juror to 'stand by' until they have gone right through the panel. Can challenge for cause (e.g. ineligibility, disqualification, presumed or actual bias).
>
> *Defence*: Has lost right to three peremptory challenges (i.e. challenging without having to give any reasons).
>
> Can challenge for cause (e.g. ineligibility, disqualification, presumed or actual bias). (There have been changes to the rules on ineligibility to sit as a juror and now judges, barristers, police officers, prison officers and others who were formerly ineligible to sit can be summoned.)
>
> The effect of challenging for cause is that if either side can show that a juror is personally concerned in the facts of the particular case or closely connected with a party to the proceedings or with a prospective witness he can be removed. A challenge for cause should not succeed if the only ground for bias is so insubstantial as to be unlikely to affect the jurors' approach to the case. The challenging party says 'challenge' immediately before the juror takes the oath. He then has the burden of satisfying the judge on a balance of probabilities that his objection is well founded and produce *prima facie* evidence of this.

The charges on the indictment must be put to Staff Nurse Jarvis at the Plea and Case Management Hearing. If she pleads not guilty, directions will be given to ensure the smooth running of the trial and a trial date will be fixed. The trial will then proceed as set out in Box 2.4. There will be an opening address by the prosecution counsel, setting out the elements that the prosecution have to prove and the standard of proof. This has no evidential value, but can be an important scene setting for the jury. The prosecution then calls its witnesses who are examined in chief, which means that the witness cannot be asked leading questions. The witness can be cross-examined by the defence and here leading questions, designed to show the irrelevance of this evidence or in some other way discredit it, can be asked (see Chapter 9 on evidence in court). After the cross-examination has finished, the party calling that witness can re-examine the witness on points arising from the cross-examination. The judge can call a halt to the case on completion of the prosecution evidence if he is not satisfied that there is sufficient evidence to go before the jury, in which case the jury is asked to bring in a not-guilty verdict. For example, in a Crown Court hearing in Cardiff when two surgeons from Prince Philip Hospital Llanelli were charged with manslaughter following the removal of the wrong kidney, the pathologist giving evidence for the prosecution could not confirm that death was caused by the removal of the wrong kidney and thus the judge instructed the jury to bring forward a not-guilty verdict, since the causal link between an alleged act of gross negligence and the death had not been established by the prosecution. An NMC report[2] on 29 October 2003 stated that two nurses were convicted of manslaughter when an elderly patient died from septicaemia resulting from pressure sores while a resident in a nursing home, of which the nurses were managers. Their defence that it was the system, rather than themselves, that was to blame was rejected.

If the case proceeds, the defence calls its witnesses. At present, although the accused does not have to give evidence, the judge may in certain circumstances allow adverse inferences to be drawn by the jury.

After all the evidence has been given, the defence and prosecution conclude their cases in final speeches. The judge then sums up the case for the jury. He has the task of explaining to the jury all the relevant directions of law: the elements of the crime that the prosecution must prove the accused committed, the nature of the burden of proof that is on the prosecution; and he analyses the evidence which both sides have put before the jury.

The jurors then retire to decide their verdict and elect a foreman after they have retired. Initially, the jury is asked to return a unanimous verdict. If it is clear that they can never reach a unanimous verdict, then they can return to court and can be given instructions on returning a majority verdict which must be at least 10 to 2. The minimum period of jury discussion before a majority verdict is possible is 2 hours and 10 minutes but in practice it may be a much longer time.

If the jury decide that the staff nurse is guilty, evidence of previous convictions (until this moment usually kept secret from the jury, but under the Criminal Justice Act 2003 evidence of bad character is admissible in certain circumstances) and her present social and economic circumstances will be given before sentencing. Sentencing will usually be adjourned for a pre-sentence report from a probation officer. Box 2.6 sets out the powers of sentencing.

Box 2.6 Sentencing in the Crown Court

Absolute/conditional discharge.

Bindover.

Fine (and compensation).

Community service.

Suspended sentence.

Prison sentence.

Hospital order, Section 37 Mental Health Act 1983.

Hospital order and restriction order, Sections 37 and 41 Mental Health Act 1983.

The staff nurse has the right to appeal against the finding of guilt on the grounds that the conviction is unsafe. She also has the right to appeal against the sentence imposed. The prosecution can appeal against sentencing by way of a reference by the Attorney General and it has the right to appeal on a point of law.

Elements of a crime

In order to establish guilt, the prosecution must be able to show that each element of the crime charged is proved so that the jury is sure. Each crime thus has its ingredients that make up that particular offence. Examples are given of the elements of some crimes in Box 2.7.

Box 2.7 Examples of the definition of certain crimes

1 Assault (common law offence):
    actus reus: an act that causes the victim to fear the immediate application of force against him
    mens rea: an intention to cause the victim to apprehend the immediate application of force or recklessness as to whether the victim might apprehend immediate force.
2 Battery (common law offence):
    actus reus: an act that results in the application of force to the person of another
    mens rea: an intention to apply force or recklessness as to whether force might be applied.

> **Box 2.7 continued**
>
> **3** Wounding or causing really serious harm, Section 18 Offences Against the Person Act 1861:
> *actus reus*: wound or cause any really serious harm to any person
> *mens rea*: unlawfully with intent to do really serious harm or an intent to resist or prevent lawful apprehension or detaining of any person.
>
> **4** Wounding or inflicting really serious harm, Section 20 Offences Against the Person Act 1861:
> *actus reus*: to wound or inflict any really serious harm on any other person, either with or without any weapon or instrument
> *mens rea*: unlawfully and maliciously (intentional or recklessly and without lawful justification).
>
> **5** Theft, Section 1(1) Theft Act 1968:
> *actus reus*: appropriate property that belongs to another
> *mens rea*: dishonest with the intention of permanently depriving the true owner of that property.

Mental and physical elements

There is a further breakdown of the elements that have to be established to prove that a crime has taken place, i.e. between the *actus reus* and the *mens rea*. The *mens rea*, or mental element, includes all those elements that relate to the mind of the accused. The *actus reus* is everything else. There are some crimes where there is no requirement to show a mental element. For example, the sale of medicine by a person who was not qualified and while unsupervised by a pharmacist and which was contrary to Section 52 of the Medicines Act 1968 was held to be an absolute offence.[3] The law has now been changed to require a mental element to be proved.

If there were no requirement for the prosecution to establish a mental element in the crime of theft, Staff Nurse Jarvis could be successfully prosecuted for theft in circumstances where someone had accidentally dropped a bottle of tablets in the staff nurse's open bag and she had therefore taken them home inadvertently. In order to secure a conviction, whether the prosecution takes place in the magistrates' court or in the Crown Court, all the elements, mental and physical, must be shown to have existed at the time it was alleged that the crime was committed.

Several cases where health professionals have been convicted of criminal offences are now discussed.

Case of Dr Nigel Cox[4]

Dr Nigel Cox, a rheumatologist in Winchester, was convicted of attempted murder of a patient to whom he had administered potassium chloride, after repeated doses of heroin failed to control her pain. (The prosecution conceded that the patient might have died anyway even if Cox had not administered the drugs so he was only charged with attempted murder.) He was given a prison sentence of one year suspended for 12 months. The patient was 70 years old, terminally ill with rheumatoid arthritis, with gastric ulcer and gangrene and in considerable pain. Her relatives were concerned at her condition. Dr Cox was also brought before his employers, the Wessex Regional Health Authority, to face disciplinary proceedings, but retained his post. He was also brought before professional conduct proceedings of the General Medical Council, which admonished him but noted that he acted in good faith and allowed him to stay on the Register. The Cox case contrasts with that of Dr Bodkin Adams,[5] who was charged with the murder of an elderly patient in Eastbourne. The judge directed the jury that a doctor was not guilty of murder if he prescribed medication for pain relief appropriate to a person's needs, even if, incidentally, the medication shortened that person's life.

Case of Dr Adomako

Gross professional negligence can constitute both a criminal offence of manslaughter and also grounds for an action for compensation in the tort of negligence, as the case of Dr Adomako shows (see Case 2.1). Dr Adomako was an anaesthetist who failed to realise during an operation that a tube had become disconnected, as a result of which the patient died. He was prosecuted in the criminal courts and convicted of manslaughter.

Case 2.1   *R v. Adomako* (1995)

Manslaughter by an anaesthetist[6]

At approximately 11.05 a.m. a disconnection occurred at the endotracheal tube connection. The supply of oxygen to the patient ceased and led to a cardiac arrest at 11.14 a.m. During this period, the defendant failed to notice or remedy the disconnection. He first became aware that something was amiss when an alarm sounded on the Dinamap machine, which monitors the patient's blood pressure. From the evidence it appeared that some four and a half minutes had elapsed between the disconnection and the sounding of the alarm. When the alarm sounded, the defendant responded in various ways by checking the equipment and administering atropine to raise the patient's pulse. But at no stage before the cardiac arrest did he check the integrity of the endotracheal tube connection. The disconnection was not discovered until after resuscitation measures had been commenced.

He accepted at his criminal trial that he had been negligent. The issue was whether his conduct was criminal i.e. whether there was gross negligence. He was convicted of involuntary manslaughter, but appealed against conviction. He lost his appeal in the Court of Appeal and then appealed to the House of Lords.

The House of Lords clarified the legal situation.[7]

The stages that the House of Lords suggested should be followed are set out in Box 2.8.

Box 2.8   House of Lords ruling in Adomako case

1 The ordinary principles of the law of negligence should be applied to ascertain whether or not the defendant had been in breach of a duty of care towards the victim who had died.

2 If such a breach of duty was established, the next question was whether that breach caused the death of the victim.

3 If so, the jury had to go on to consider whether that breach of duty should be characterised as gross negligence and therefore as a crime. That would depend on the seriousness of the breach of duty committed by the defendant in all the circumstances in which the defendant was placed when it occurred.

Box 2.8 continued

4 The jury would have to consider whether the extent to which the defendant's conduct departed from the proper standard of care incumbent on him, involving as it must have done a risk of death to the patient, was such that it should be judged criminal.

The judge was required to give the jury a direction on the meaning of gross negligence as had been given in the present case by the Court of Appeal.

The jury might properly find gross negligence on proof of:

(a) indifference to an obvious risk of injury to health or of

(b) actual foresight of the risk coupled either
  (i) with a determination nevertheless to run it or
  (ii) with an intention to avoid it but involving such a high degree of negligence in the attempted avoidance as the jury considered justified conviction or

(c) of inattention or failure to advert to a serious risk going beyond mere inadvertence in respect of an obvious and important matter which the defendant's duty demanded he should address.

[Lettering and numbering are the author's.]

The House of Lords held that the Court of Appeal had applied the correct test and the appeal was dismissed.

There would also be vicarious liability on his employers in the civil courts for his negligence in causing the death of the patient.

The Corporate Manslaughter and Corporate Homicide Act 2007

The Law Commission[8] recommended that the law should be changed to enable it to be made easier for corporations and statutory bodies to be prosecuted for manslaughter. The government accepted the recommendations and the Corporate Manslaughter and Corporate Homicide Act was enacted in 2007. The Act abolishes the common law offence of corporate manslaughter by gross negligence and replaces it with statutory offences which can be committed by a specified organisation if its activities are managed or organised in a way which (a) causes a person's death, and (b) amounts to a gross breach of a relevant duty of care owed by the organisation to the deceased. An organisation is guilty of an offence under this section only if the way in which its activities are managed or organised by its senior management is a substantial element in the breach of the duty of care. The organisations specified include 'corporations' and also the Department of Health. The duty of care is defined widely and includes duties to a detained patient, but excludes any duty of care owed by a public authority in respect of a decision as to matters of public policy (including in particular the allocation of public resources or the weighing of competing public interests). Duty of care also excludes emergency responses carried out by an NHS body or ambulance service (see Chapter 12 on the link with health and safety legislation).

Alarmist fears that the Act would lead to the end of corporate team-building activities when it came into force on 6 April 2008 were rejected by the Chief Executive of the Royal Society for the Prevention of Accidents in a letter to *The Times* on 6 December 2007. He pointed out that the Act is there to strengthen the sanctions against negligent employers who, by ignoring good safety practice and necessary regulation, kill their staff and members of the public. It is not designed to undermine a spirit of enterprise, nor to inhibit a creative, fun atmosphere that can be so valuable in welding work colleagues into a team.[9]

Case of Dr Shipman

On 31 January 2000 Dr Shipman, a general practitioner, was found guilty of the murder of 15 patients and was suspected of having killed many more. The atrocious offences raised serious concerns about the inadequacy of professional regulation and control. An inquiry set up by the Secretary of State has published six reports.[10] The first considered how many patients Shipman killed, the means employed and the period over which the killings took place. The second report examined the conduct of the police investigation. The third report considered the present system for death and cremation certification and for the investigation of deaths by coroners and is considered in Chapter 29. The fourth Shipman report, which was published in July 2004,[11] considered the regulation of controlled drugs in the community and is considered in Chapter 28. The fifth report of this inquiry was published in December 2004.[12] It considered the handling of complaints against GPs, the raising of concerns about GPs, the procedures of the General Medical Council and the revalidation of doctors and makes significant recommendations for the more effective regulation of GPs. The sixth and final Shipman report considered how many patients Shipman killed during his career as a junior doctor at Pontefract General Infirmary and in his time at Hyde.[13]

Case of Beverley Allitt

Following the deaths and injuries to children caused by the nurse Beverley Allitt, an independent inquiry was set up. Its recommendations are considered in Chapter 5.

Case of Kevin Cobb

Kevin Cobb was found guilty of the manslaughter of a nurse and also convicted of drugging three female patients and raping two of them.[14]

Administration of drug by epidural instead of intravenous injection

In 2003 a junior doctor in Nottingham pleaded guilty to the manslaughter of a patient suffering from leukaemia. Instead of administering the anti-drug intravenously, he administered it epidurally and the patient died. The doctor was given a prison sentence. The National Patient Safety Agency has aimed at preventing the recurrence of such mistakes (see Chapters 12 and 28).

Defences

The main defences to a criminal act are shown in Box 2.9. They are all given here for completeness, but not all of them are relevant to Staff Nurse Jarvis's case.

> ### Box 2.9 — Main defences to a criminal offence
>
> 1 Absence of any of the elements making up the offence: *actus reus* or *mens rea*.
> 2 Infancy:
>   below 10 years no crime.
> 3 Insanity:
>   **(a)** unfit to plead and stand trial;
>   **(b)** not guilty by reason of insanity at the time of the crime.
> 4 Diminished responsibility and provocation (which reduce murder to manslaughter).
> 5 Mistake. (Sometimes this is a statutory defence but usually only where the defendant has taken all reasonable steps. Normally the statute places the burden of proof on the defendant on a balance of probabilities.)
> 6 Necessity (now known as 'duress of circumstances').
> 7 Duress.
> 8 Superior orders.
> 9 Self-defence.

Absence of any of the elements making up the offence

It will be apparent from what has been said thus far that if the accused can show that any of the required elements, either *actus reus* or *mens rea*, as defined in the Act of Parliament or the common law definition of the crime, are missing, then there should be an acquittal. Even though it is usually for the prosecution to show they exist rather than for the defence to prove their absence, it would clearly be an advantage for the defence to show their absence. Thus, for example, in the offence of theft, one of the elements is that the property that has been taken belonged to another. If the defence can show that the property did not belong to anyone but had, in fact, been abandoned, then that would be a successful defence.

Infancy

Children under 10 years are exempt from criminal responsibility and cannot be found guilty of a crime. The infant is known as *doli incapax*.

Minors over 10 years are presumed to be responsible for their actions but there are considerable procedural differences from the way in which an adult is proceeded against. The UK was criticised by the European Court of Human Rights for its handling of child criminals following the conviction of two boys for the killing of Jamie Bulger.[15] The Court held that Article 6 had been breached by the way the trial had been conducted. However, the court did not find that there was a breach of Article 3 (inhuman or degrading treatment).

Insanity

Insanity can be pleaded before or when the trial takes place so that the accused is held unable by reason of insanity to stand trial. Alternatively, it can be pleaded as a defence to the crime on the basis that at the time the crime was committed the accused was insane. The definition of insanity as a defence is based on the M'Naghten Rules, which were laid down in 1843. The basic propositions are:

> *[E]very man is presumed to be sane and to possess a sufficient degree of reason to be responsible for his crimes, until the contrary be proved.*
>
> *[To] establish a defence on ground of insanity, it must be clearly proved that at the time of the committing of the act, the party accused was labouring under such a defect of reason, from disease of mind, as not to know the nature and quality of the act he was doing, or if he did know it, that he did not know he was doing what was wrong.*

Since 1843 there have been many interpretations and refinements of this definition, but the substance has survived.

Diminished responsibility and provocation

These statutory defences are provided by the Homicide Act 1957, apply only to murder and have the effect of enabling the accused charged with murder to be found guilty of manslaughter on grounds of diminished responsibility or provocation. The Law Commission published a consultation paper in 2006 which set out proposals for a new Homicide Act.[16] It put forward the proposal that the structure of a reformed law of homicide should comprise three general offences plus specific offences: 1st degree murder would have a mandatory life sentence; 2nd degree murder would have a discretionary life sentence; manslaughter would have a fixed term of years maximum imprisonment; and specific offences such as assisting suicide and infanticide should have a fixed term of years maximum imprisonment.

Mistake

A defendant can argue self-defence if he honestly but mistakenly believed he was under attack. This can be an effective defence where it prevents the accused from being able to form the required mental element (i.e. *mens rea*) to be guilty of the offence charged. For example, a defendant to a charge of theft could argue that he honestly but mistakenly believed that he had permission to take the goods, i.e. mistake negatives dishonesty. Mistake of law is not sufficient, for knowledge that an act is a crime is not usually a necessary ingredient of the *mens rea*.

Necessity

There is no recognised principle that necessity is a valid defence to any crime.

Duress

This will be a valid defence where it can be established that the force or compulsion was such that the accused had no choice. There must be an immediate threat of death or serious harm. It is unlikely to be accepted as a defence to a charge of murder, but has been invoked in other lesser crimes.

Superior orders

It is not a defence for the accused to argue that the crime was committed in obedience to the orders of a superior. However, it might be possible for a defendant to show that as a result of the orders she lacked the required mental element for the crime and that she was acting reasonably in all the circumstances. The issue of obeying orders as a defence in the civil courts is considered in Chapter 4.

Self-defence

Reasonable force can be used to defend oneself or another person against an attack. However, greater force than is reasonable would result in the possibility of the defender being liable to prosecution for assault or, in the event of the assailant dying, murder or manslaughter. This is considered further in Chapter 12.

Criminal injuries compensation

A scheme to compensate those who have suffered personal injuries as the result of criminal action has been in existence since 1964. A new scheme for compensation following injuries or death as a result of a crime was established on 1 April 1996 under the Criminal Injuries Compensation Act 1995, based on a statutory scale of awards known as the 'tariff'. Details of the current scheme,[17] which has been in operation since April 2001, are available from the Criminal Injuries Compensation Authority (CICA) headquarters in Glasgow.[18] Claims are processed by the CICA and claims officers and adjudicators on a panel determine whether a claim can be met. Evidence is obtained from applicants, the police, medical bodies and others such as witnesses to the incident. The CICA determines whether payments are to be made to victims of criminal acts. Those eligible (and these include the victims of crime as well as the dependants of homicide victims) must have reported the crime to the police as soon as possible. The application should be made within two years of the incident, but exceptions can be made to both these requirements. Payments are made against a tariff system up to a maximum of £500,000 (see Paragraph 24 of the scheme) and include the following items:

medical expenses

mental health expenses

lost wages for disabled victims (but not for the first 28 full weeks of lost earnings or earning capacity)

lost support for dependants of homicide victims

funerals

travel

rehabilitation for disabled victims

pain and suffering

bereavement

loss of parental services.

Procedure for claiming

The procedure is for an application form (available from the CICA, local victim support schemes, Crown Court witness service, local police stations or local citizens' advice bureaux) to be completed and sent to the CICA. Claims officers at the CICA initially consider the claim to determine whether it comes within the scheme's eligibility criteria. The claim will either be rejected or an offer will be made to the claimant. Once the CICA is notified that the offer has been accepted, the compensation will be paid. In certain circumstances an interim award may be made with the final award awaiting further details, for example of the victim's prognosis. Claimants may be asked to attend a centre for medical examination. A claimant has the right to contest the result of the review by appealing to the Criminal Injuries Compensation Appeals Panel. The appellant has 90 days from the date of the notification of the decision within which to appeal to the Panel, which is independent of the CICA itself. There is no appeal against the decision of the Panel. The CICA can itself reopen a case after its final decision has been made if the medical condition has deteriorated to such extent that it would be unjust to keep to the original award (Paragraphs 56 and 57 of the scheme).

The National Audit Office in December 2007 reported that victims of violent crimes waited almost 17 months before being paid compensation. The CICA took an average of 151 days to resolve a case even though there had been a 23 per cent fall in the number of applications over the past 7 years.[19]

Information relating to the CICA can be obtained from its website[20] and should be available to all NHS staff, who should ensure that, if they are injured at work, they can check on their eligibility to receive compensation.

Tariff

There is a scale of payments covering 25 levels with level 1, the minimum claim payable, set at £1,000 and level 25 set at £250,000, which relates to the kind of injury sustained. Level 25 includes quadriplegia/tetraplegia (paralysis of all four limbs); level 1 covers multiple minor injuries or disabling but temporary mental anxiety lasting more than 6 weeks, medically verified. Where compensateable injuries come under several different levels, then the highest level award is paid out for the highest rated injury, then 30 per cent of the tariff for the next serious injury and 15 per cent of the tariff for the next serious injury. If a person qualifies for lost earnings and/or special expenses, additional compensation of up to £250,000 is payable. The maximum compensation payable is £500,000.

Withholding of compensation

The scheme permits compensation to be refused if the claimant has a criminal record or whose conduct led to their being injured. In addition, people who fail to cooperate in bringing an offender to justice may be refused compensation. The CICA has discretion to withhold or reduce an award on these grounds. Paragraph 13 of the 2001 scheme sets out the grounds for the withholding or reduction of an award.

The fact that the aggressor is a mentally disturbed patient against whom a prosecution may not succeed on the grounds of insanity will be left out of the account in deciding whether compensation should be paid.

Order that the convicted defendant make a compensation payment to the victim

Judges and magistrates also have the power to order a defendant to make a payment to the victim of the offence of which they have been convicted. Before making the order, the judge has to take into account the defendant's ability to pay the amount ordered.

Conclusions

Most of the Criminal Justice Act 2003 has now been implemented and significant changes to the procedure in the criminal courts have taken place. New powers to combat terrorism have strengthened the police, but raised issues in relation to the respect for human rights. The creation of the new offence of corporate manslaughter may place a heavy burden on senior managers and board members of primary care and NHS trusts. The effect of these changes on the role of the registered nurse practitioner remains to be seen.

Reflection questions

In the case of Staff Nurse Jarvis, trace the course that would be followed if:

(a) she were tried in a magistrates' court

(b) she were tried in the Crown Court

(c) she pleaded guilty in the magistrates' court

(d) she pleaded guilty in the Crown Court.

Further exercises

1 What do you consider are the advantages and disadvantages of trial before magistrates compared with a jury trial for an offence that is triable either way?

2 What evidence do you consider the prosecution would require in a case similar to that of Staff Nurse Jarvis and what evidence would the defence seek?

3 Visit your local magistrates' court and Crown Court and analyse the difference between the two in terms of formality, procedure and justice to the accused.

References

[1] Home Office Police and Criminal Evidence Act 1984 S. 60(1)(a) and S. 60(1) Codes of Practice, The Stationery Office, revised editions, London, 2003 and 2004, www.homeoffice.gov.uk/crimpol/poice/system/pacecodes.html

[2] www.nmc-uk.org/nmc/main/news/nurses_guilty_of_manslaughter

[3] *Pharmaceutical Society of Great Britain* v. *Logan* (1982) Crim LR 443

[4] *R* v. *Cox* (1992) 12 BMLR 38

[5] *R* v. *Bodkin Adams* [1957] Crim LR 365

[6] *R* v. *Adomako* [1995] 1 AC 171; [1994] 3 All ER 79

[7] Ibid.

[8] Law Commission Report No. 237, Legislating the Criminal Code: involuntary manslaughter, The Stationery Office, London, 1996

[9] Deadly Team-Building, *The Times*, 6 December 2007. http://www.timesonline.co.uk/tol/comment/letters/articles3006690.ece (last accessed 25 January 2008)

[10] Shipman Inquiry First Report: Death Disguised, 19 July 2002; www.the-shipman-inquiry.org.uk/reports.asp; Shipman Inquiry Second Report: The Police Investigation of March

1998, 14 July 2003; www.the-shipman-inquiry.org.uk/reports.asp; Shipman Inquiry Third Report: Death and Cremation Certification, 14 July 2003; www.the-shipman-inquiry.org.uk/reports.asp

[11] Shipman Inquiry Fourth Report: The Regulation of Controlled Drugs in the Community published 15 July 2004, Cm 6249, The Stationery Office; www.the-shipman-inquiry.org.uk/reports.asp

[12] The Shipman Inquiry Fifth Report: Safeguarding Patients: Lessons from the Past – Proposals for the Future. Command Paper CM 6394, December 2004, The Stationery Office; www.the-shipman-inquiry.org.uk/reports.asp

[13] The Shipman Inquiry Sixth Report: Shipman: The Final Report, January 2005, The Stationery Office; www.the-shipman-inquiry.org.uk/reports.asp

[14] Robert Munro, Victim's mother's chaperone call, *Nursing Times*, 25 May 2000, 96(21), p. 8

[15] *T* v. *United Kingdom*; *V* v. *United Kingdom* [2000] 2 All ER 1024 ECtHR

[16] Law Commission, A new Homicide Act for England and Wales, Consultation paper 177, 2006

[17] Criminal Injuries Compensation Scheme 2001, Issue No. 1 (4/01), Home Office, 1 April 2001

[18] Criminal Injuries Compensation Authority, Tay House, 300 Bath Street, Glasgow G2 4JR; Tel 014 133 12726; Fax 014 133 12287/014 133 33148

[19] National Audit Office, *Compensating victims of violent crime*, NAO, London, 2007.

[20] www.cica.gov.uk

Chapter 3
Liability in a civil court case for negligence

This chapter discusses

+ Duty of care
+ Standard of care
+ Causation
+ Harm

Introduction

Litigation to obtain compensation in the civil courts is one of the growth areas of recent years. The National Audit Office has estimated that almost £4 billion is required to meet actual and potential claims from events that have occurred. In claims of up to £50,000 more than half the cost is paid to lawyers. There is therefore clear evidence of an increase in litigation and the number of civil claims.[1] A similar figure was assessed as being required in 2007. There is a lack of clear evidence about the extent of clinical negligence. The National Patient Safety Agency was criticised by the Public Accounts Committee in 2006 because it was unable to give the number of patients who had been injured as a result of medical errors.

If harm has occurred to a patient, then the patient or his/her representatives can seek compensation. However, not all harm is compensateable. Accidents to patients are infinite: they include incidents where the patient falls out of bed, pressure sores develop, the wrong dose of medicine is given, it is given at the wrong time or at the wrong site by the wrong method or the expiry date is passed, the wrong limb is amputated, the treatment is given to the wrong patient, the patient dies as the result of a mistake. Some of these are the result of negligence and the victims may receive compensation. Not all accidents, however, will result in the payment of compensation to the patient or relatives.

This chapter looks at the circumstances that must exist for compensation to be payable and the type of harm for which compensation will be paid. The personal liability of the nurse and the liability of her employer are considered in Chapter 4. The calculation of compensation is considered in Chapter 6.

The elements that must be established by the claimant in a case of negligence before the civil courts are set out in Box 1.2. In this section we are concerned with four basic questions:

1   What is meant by the term 'duty of care'; when does the nurse owe a duty of care; and to whom is it owed?

2   What is the appropriate standard of care and what criteria determine whether the nurse is in breach of that duty?

3   What is meant by 'reasonably foreseeably caused' and why and how must the claimant prove this in an action for negligence?

4   What type of harm do the courts recognise as capable of being compensated?

This chapter will answer these questions by providing examples where patients have been harmed. The next chapter will consider some specific problems of liability in relation to inexperienced staff, team responsibility, limits on resources and also the liability of the NHS trust. The topics covered in this chapter are shown above.

Duty of care

Difficulties can arise as to whether a duty of care exists, especially outside the immediate employment situation. A duty of care is not owed universally and the claimant bringing the action has to show that a duty of care was owed to him or her personally.

The legal test of whether a duty of care exists was laid down in the case of *Donoghue* v. *Stevenson*.[2] In this case, manufacturers were held to owe a duty of care to the ultimate consumer. The facts of this case were that a person who was bought a bottle of ginger beer discovered the decomposed remains of a snail when half the beer had been drunk and sued the manufacturer, arguing that the manufacturer owed a duty of care to the consumer. In the case, Lord Atkin stated that:

> *You must take reasonable care to avoid acts or omissions which you can reasonably foresee would be likely to injure your neighbour. Who then in law is my neighbour? The answer seems to be persons who are so closely and directly affected by my act that I ought reasonably to have them in contemplation as being so affected when I am directing my mind to the acts or omissions which are called in question.*

In other words, a duty of care can be said to exist if one can see that one's actions are reasonably likely to cause harm to another person.

In recent years, there have been several cases on whether a duty of care is owed to an individual by different public services: the ambulance service, social services, the police and the fire service. In a recent case, the Court of Appeal held that although the ambulance service owed no duty to the public at large to respond to a telephone call for help, once a 999 call had been accepted, it was arguable that the ambulance service did have an obligation to provide the service for a named individual at a specified address. Subsequently the Court of Appeal dismissed an appeal by the London Ambulance Authority that it should pay the victim £362,377. The facts of the case are shown in Case 3.1.

Case 3.1   *Kent v. Griffiths and Others* **(2000)**

Ambulance slow to arrive[3]

A doctor called an ambulance for a woman who was asthmatic at 4.27 p.m. on 16 February 1991. The standards recommended were that the ambulance should come within 14 minutes. The husband phoned again at 4.39 p.m. and was told they would be there within 7 to 8 minutes. The doctor phoned at 4.55 p.m. and was told it would be a couple of minutes. The ambulance arrived at 5.05 p.m., 38 minutes after the first call. (A record prepared by a member of the crew indicated that it had arrived after 22 minutes.) During the journey, the claimant was given oxygen, but on the way suffered a respiratory arrest with tragic consequences, including serious memory impairment, change of personality and miscarriage. The judge found that the record of the ambulance's arrival had been falsified. The Court of Appeal refused to strike out the case as disclosing no reasonable cause of action for negligence, but held that the case should continue to trial.

The Court of Appeal held that a duty of care could be owed by the ambulance service which was comparable to hospital services rather than to the police or fire services.

In the second appeal, the Court of Appeal held that the acceptance of the call in the present case established the duty of care. It was delay that caused the further injuries. If wrong information had not been given about the arrival of the ambulance, other means of transport could have been used.

Educational psychologist

In the case of *Phelps* v. *Hillingdon London Borough Council*,[4] the Court of Appeal held that an educational psychologist, employed by a local education authority to give advice to it in respect of children in its schools suffering from learning difficulties, did not owe a duty of care to such a child, unless he or she had assumed responsibility for that child. The House of Lords, however, allowed the appeal.[5] It held that a local education authority is liable for the negligent actions of a teacher or educational psychologist and can be sued for a failure to provide an education commensurate with a child's needs. The House of Lords gave a judgment on four cases: the Phelps case against London Borough of Hillingdon; Marcus Jarvis against Hampshire County Council (failing to diagnose dyslexia); G against Bromley (failure to provide him with computer technology and suitable training to help him deal with a muscular problem); and Rhiannon Anderton against Clwyd County Council (she sought pre-action disclosure of educational records: to succeed she had to show that she was suffering from personal injury).

The House of Lords emphasised that liability for negligence by a council would require exceptional circumstances. It held that a failure to improve a condition from which a child suffered could count as personal injury. It rejected the argument that providing psychological advice was part of a multidisciplinary approach that, in the past, has justified immunity from negligence in care claims.

Placing of foster child

In the case of *W and Others* v. *Essex County Council and Another*,[6] the local authority (LA) placed a foster child with a couple, having given an assurance that he was not a known sex abuser. In fact, the LA knew that the boy had been cautioned three years previously for indecent assault on his sister. The boy subsequently sexually abused three of the claimants' children. The foster parents' claim for psychiatric shock failed in the High Court and the Court of Appeal on the grounds that the court held that no duty of care was owed to them at common law. The children succeeded since they were not subject to any statutory duty by the LA, but were living at home with their parents and express assurances had been given that a sexual abuser would not be placed in that home.

The House of Lords[7] allowed the parents' appeal on the grounds that the parents should not be barred from pursuing their claim: the parents could be seen as victims of the situation, the psychiatric injury they suffered could be seen as within the range of psychiatric injury recognised by law and it could be argued that the local authority owed a duty of care to the parents. They should therefore be allowed to pursue their claim.

In a similar case, the House of Lords[8] allowed the claim by a boy who had been in local authority care all his life to pursue an action against the local authority for psychiatric damage he had suffered as a result of the authority's breach of statutory duty and negligence in failing to place him for adoption or place him in suitable foster homes. Where there has been clinical negligence by a hospital, a legal action arises, not because of the statutory duty on the NHS to provide a service, but because of what it has done in accepting a patient for treatment.[9]

See Chapter 13 for child protection cases, where the courts have held that a duty of care is not owed to parents where a child has been removed as a result of abuse being wrongly suspected.

Does a nurse have a duty to volunteer help?

Practical Dilemma 3.1   Volunteering help

A nurse on her way to work passes a road accident. She sees that a man is still trapped in a vehicle. Does she have an obligation to stop and render first aid? If she does stop and help and something goes wrong, would she be liable?

Unless there is a pre-existing relationship between the parties (for example, if the nurse has caused the accident or if she is employed to assist people in such circumstances), she has no duty in law to stop and render first aid. So if, for example, someone saw her drive past and, knowing that she was a nurse, believed that she could have saved the victim, she was consequently sued, the action would fail. Her failure to help is not actionable. There is in law no duty to volunteer help. There must be a pre-existing duty. However, once the nurse undertakes the duty of care, she is then bound to follow the standard of care that would be expected of a reasonable person. So, for example, imagine that she moves the victim and causes spinal injury. If it can be shown that she should have anticipated the dangers of moving a person when a spinal injury was possible, and if there were no immediate danger in leaving the man where he was, then she could be sued for any further injuries she had caused him.

While there is no legal duty, the NMC has made it clear in its Code of Professional Conduct[10] that there is professional duty upon the registered practitioner at all times. Paragraph 8.5 states:

In an emergency, in or outside the work setting, you have a professional duty to provide care. The care provided would be judged against what could reasonably be expected from someone with your knowledge, skills and abilities when placed in those particular circumstances.

The nurse who failed to volunteer help could therefore not be held legally liable in the civil courts for failing to act; she could, however, face professional conduct proceedings (see Chapter 11). Where the nurse has volunteered help in such a situation, it is unlikely that her employer would accept any responsibility for her actions (i.e. would not be vicariously liable, see page 67) and therefore the nurse would have to rely on personal insurance cover in the event of any action being brought against her. This cover, known as cover for Samaritan actions, is provided by some professional associations.

Practical Dilemma 3.2 | **A fall in the night**

Mary Smith is in the post-operative ward following a gall bladder operation. She becomes very disturbed during the night and Staff Nurse Janice Parker hears a crash and rushes to the ward. She finds Mrs Smith on the floor

---

How is the civil liability of the staff nurse determined? The questions to be answered are:

1 Does Staff Nurse Parker owe a duty of care to Mrs Smith?
2 Is she in breach of the duty of care?
3 Has her breach of care led to reasonably foreseeable harm?
4 Has the patient suffered compensateable harm?

To win compensation in a civil case, Mary Smith would have to show that the staff nurse failed to follow the approved accepted practice without good reason in carrying out her duty of care towards her and that, as a reasonably foreseeable result, she suffered harm.

Does a duty of care arise?

A nurse, by virtue of the nurse/patient relationship, does owe a duty of care to her patients. Whether a duty of care exists will be decided by established legal principles. There is no doubt that, in these circumstances, the nurse does owe a duty of care to the patient.

Once it is decided that a duty of care is owed, the next question is: has there been a breach of this duty? Before this can be answered, the nature of the standard of care owed must be established.

Standard of care

Approved practice

> ### Case 3.2   *Whitehouse v. Jordan* (1981)
>
> **Birth traumas**[11]
>
> Stuart Whitehouse was born on 7 January 1970 with severe brain damage. His mother alleged that the brain damage was caused because the doctor pulled too hard and too long with forceps, as a consequence of which the baby was severely disabled. The doctor denied the allegations.

The House of Lords stated that whether an error of judgement was negligence or not depended on the facts of the situation. The test to be applied to determine if there was negligence was the Bolam Test (from an earlier case in 1957).[12] In applying this test in this case, the House of Lords decided that Mr Jordan had not been negligent. The Bolam Test is as follows:

> *When you get a situation that involves the use of some special skill or competence, then the test as to whether there has been negligence or not is . . . the standard of the ordinary skilled man exercising and professing to have that special skill. If a surgeon failed to measure up to that in any respect ('clinical judgement' or otherwise), he had been negligent and should be so adjudged.*

In the last sentence, 'any other professional' can be substituted for 'surgeon'. Thus the negligence of a nurse is to be determined by the standard of the ordinary skilled nurse.

Let us turn again to Practical Dilemma 3.2, of the patient falling out of bed, and see how the court would decide whether or not Staff Nurse Janice Parker was in breach of care in relation to the patient Mary Smith.

What would the ordinary skilled nurse be expected to do in those circumstances? Was it reasonably foreseeable that this patient was likely to be restless? If so, what additional precautions should have been taken? Was she in the right location and was she adequately supervised? Had the patient called earlier for help or a bedpan and did that request go unheard or unmet? In the actual court hearing, expert evidence would be given as to what would have been expected of a nurse in that context and the judge would decide what should be regarded as acceptable practice in that context.

Deviation from approved practice

It does not follow that simply to fail to follow the accepted practice is, in itself, evidence of negligence since there may well be very strong reasons why the usual properly accepted practice was not followed in a particular case. The following case illustrates this point.

Case 3.3   *Maynard v. West Midlands (1984)*

Biopsy[13]

A consultant physician and a consultant surgeon, while recognising that the most likely diagnosis of the patient's illness was tuberculosis (TB), took the view that Hodgkin's disease, carcinoma and sarcoidosis were also possibilities. Because Hodgkin's disease is fatal unless remedial steps are taken in its early stages, they decided that, rather than wait several weeks for the result of a sputum test, the operation of mediastinoscopy should be performed to provide a biopsy. This involved some risk of damage to the left laryngeal recurrent nerve, even if correctly performed. The operation was carried out properly, but that damage did in fact occur. The biopsy proved negative and it was subsequently confirmed that the patient did have TB and not Hodgkin's disease. The patient brought an action against the health authority, claiming that the decision to perform the biopsy rather than wait for the result of the TB test had been negligent.

At the trial, a distinguished body of medical opinion was called approving of the action of the consultants in carrying out the operation, but the judge said that he preferred the evidence of an expert witness called for the claimant, who had stated that the case had almost certainly been one of TB from the outset and should have been so diagnosed and that it had been wrong and dangerous to undertake the operation. The trial judge gave judgment for the claimant. The defendants succeeded before the Court of Appeal and the claimant therefore appealed to the House of Lords. The House of Lords held that in the medical profession there was room for differences of opinion and practice and that a court's preference for one body of opinion over another was no basis for a conclusion of negligence. Where it was alleged that a fully considered decision by two consultants in their own special field had been negligent, it was not sufficient to establish negligence for the claimant to show that there was a body of competent professional opinion that considered that the decision had been wrong if there was also a body of equally competent professional opinion that supported the decision as having been reasonable in the circumstances. The claimant therefore lost the appeal and the case.

While this decision might seem very hard for the patient, it is only fair to the professional staff where a decision has been made carefully and with great consideration and is supported by substantial professional opinion, even if not everyone would have followed the same practice. In applying this to nursing staff, it can be said that in most circumstances the nurse will be expected to follow the standards of practice laid down by her profession or the local policy of her employer, but there may be very exceptional circumstances where it is justifiable not to follow the accepted practice. In a more recent case, the Court of Appeal has suggested that where there was more than one acceptable standard, competence should be gauged by the lowest of them.[14] The Bolam Test applied where there was a conscious choice of available courses made by a trained professional. It was inappropriate where the alleged neglect lay in an oversight.

The wording of the Congenital Disabilities (Civil Liability) Act 1976 (which allows right of action in cases of prenatal infliction of harm) puts the point very clearly. (This Act is considered in detail in Chapter 14.)

Statute	**Congenital Disabilities (Civil Liability) Act 1976 Section 1(5)**

The defendant is not answerable to the child, for anything he did or omitted to do when responsible in a professional capacity for treating or advising the parent, if he took reasonable care having due regard to then received professional opinion applicable to the particular class of case; but that does not mean that he is answerable only because he departed from received opinion.

The courts rely on expert evidence to decide on what is a reasonable standard of care and the House of Lords in the Bolitho case emphasised that such expert opinion must flow logically and reasonably from the specific circumstances:

> *The use of the adjectives 'responsible, reasonable and respectable' (in the Bolam case) all showed that the court had to be satisfied that the exponents of the body of opinion relied upon could demonstrate that such opinion had a logical basis.*[15]

Following the changes to the civil procedure as a result of the Woolf Reforms, parties to a civil action are required, if possible, to agree on experts who are to give evidence of the required standards and the extent to which what actually happened measured up to that standard.

The application of the Bolam Test was considered in the work of the laboratory screeners who read the slides for cervical cytology.[16] The High Court and Court of Appeal held that the Bolam Test did not apply where no professional judgement was required by the employee. The evidence of expert witnesses that the Standards of the Cervical Screening Programme, which required an absolute confidence test, had not been complied with was accepted by the judge. The full facts of the case are given in Chapter 23.

Policies, protocol, procedures, guidelines and their effect

The questions arise: When must I follow a procedure and when should I not follow it? Is there any difference in law between a policy, a procedure and a guideline and their effect? In the main, guidance issued by an employer, by a professional association or by the registration body should as far as is reasonable be followed. However, there may be specific circumstances that make the following of a particular procedure inappropriate and therefore any reasonable practitioner would modify compliance with the procedure accordingly. Clearly, advice from others would be required to ascertain whether rigid compliance with the procedure would be justified. The courts require a reasonable standard to be followed; a standard that would be supported by competent professional opinion and practice. Where the practitioner decides that circumstances justify a modification of the usual procedure, it is essential that she record exactly why the usual practice was not followed.

Procedures, policies, protocols and guidelines do not have a recognised hierarchy in courts of law. The same principles would apply to them all. In general, they should be followed, if it would be reasonable to do so. If a policy, etc. is issued by an NHS trust that is not acceptable in the light of professional practice, it should be challenged as soon as possible and a revised policy that does accord with reasonable standards of care issued. Reference should be made to the work by Brian Hurwitz where this issue is considered in detail.[17] The significance of protocols has become more important as the work of the National Institute for Health and Clinical Excellence (NICE) has expanded (see Chapter 5). In its NHS Plan, the government has stated its intention that NICE's work in undertaking appraisals and setting guidelines will increase by 50 per cent. Eventually, NICE guidelines are likely to be incorporated into the Bolam Test of reasonable practice, but it will be open for a health professional to argue that the guidelines were not appropriate in the particular circumstances of the patient she was caring for. In the case of *Early* v. *Newham HA*,[18] the judge accepted that guidelines drafted locally by consultants on intubation could be seen as satisfying the Bolam Test. In a case in 2005[19] where a ventouse delivery was attempted at 9 cm of dilation and led to spastic tetraplegia and cerebral palsy in the baby, the court held that the clinician had failed to follow both the guidelines of the Royal College of Obstetricians and Gynaecologists and also the hospital's own guidelines and held the defendant NHS trust liable. The Bolam Test was applied in a case where a patient alleged that had her general practitioner referred her for orthopaedic surgery the same day as she was seen by him, she would not have suffered from the severe side effects of the loss of function of her bowels and bladder. She failed since it was established that her GP's views were in accordance with the practice accepted as proper and there was no evidence that had there been a same-day referral, she would have had an operation immediately.[20] John Tingle and Charles Foster have edited a useful book showing the interlink between law, policy and practice on clinical guidelines.[21] (See also Chapter 24 on the scope of professional practice and clinical guidelines.)

The situation is thus as follows:

1 There is no breach of the standard of care if the professional has acted in accordance with the practice accepted as proper by a responsible body of professionals skilled in that particular art and this was appropriate in the circumstances of the case.

2 There is no breach of the standard of care if there is no acceptable body of opinion covering that situation, but what the professional did was considered reasonable in all the circumstances.

3 There is no breach of the standard of care if the professional did not follow the accepted practice, but his actions were reasonable in all the circumstances and would be supported by competent professional opinion.

Reasonable foreseeability

Other criteria are considered in determining if the professional has been negligent. One of the basic principles of the law of negligence is that precautions can be taken only against reasonably known risks.

> ### Case 3.4   *Roe* v. *Ministry of Health* (1954)
>
> **Ampoules in phenol**[22]
>
> A local anaesthetic was given by injection in a hospital. The ampoule, which was stored in phenol to sterilise it, contained invisible cracks caused by some mishandling in the hospital, through which the phenol seeped into the ampoule. The injection caused paralysis.

The patient sued the anaesthetist and nurses and their employer. The patient, however, lost the case. The possibility of seepage through invisible cracks was not known at that time and precautions against an unforeseeable possibility are not required of the defendant. However, successful defence may, of course, mean that the next claimant has a greater chance of winning since such risks are now known. The standard of care thus increases.

The judge, Lord Denning, said in this case:

It is so easy to be wise after the event and to condemn as negligence that which was only a misadventure. We ought always to be on our guard against it, especially in cases against hospitals and doctors. Medical science has conferred great benefits on mankind, but these benefits are attended by considerable risks. Every surgical operation is attended by risks. We cannot take the benefits without taking the risks. Every advance in technique is also attended by risks. Doctors like the rest of us have to learn by experience; and experience often teaches in a hard way. Something goes wrong and shows up a weakness, and then it is put right . . . We must not look at the 1947 accident with 1954 spectacles.

Exactly the same could be said of practice today and of nurses as well as doctors. There may be many occasions when one looks back and says, 'I would do things differently if I were to do it again', but that does not mean the professional has been negligent.

Keeping up to date

When one looks at the many professional journals that exist, the question must arise as to what extent the professional can be expected to master all this knowledge. How up to date is one expected to be?

> ### Case 3.5   *Crawford v. Charing Cross Hospital* (1953)
>
> **A recent article**[23]
>
> A patient developed brachial palsy during a blood transfusion. An article had appeared in the *Lancet* six months previously describing this hazard.

The patient lost the case on the grounds that, provided the professional staff were following the accepted approved practice at that time, it could not be said that they were negligent in failing to apply or be aware of recent knowledge.

Articles in magazines and journals can be of very different status. Some are pure research articles, the lessons from which have not yet been absorbed into current accepted practice; others are controversial and their conclusions may never become part of recognised procedure. Other instructions, however, would have immediate effect. Thus, if a directive from the Medicines and Healthcare Products Regulatory Agency warned against prescribing a particular drug to a patient, to ignore that instruction might well be evidence of negligence. Nursing staff who had received comparable instructions from their profession or senior nurse management would be expected to be aware of these orders and to comply. The instructions would become part of the accepted practice.

Balancing the risks

As the earlier quotation from Lord Denning points out, there are hazards in modern medicine and much of professional discretion is concerned with balancing the risks of taking action A compared with action B or compared with taking no action at all.

> ## Practical Dilemma 3.3   Meningitis
>
> A patient is admitted with a provisional diagnosis of meningitis. She was immediately barrier nursed in a single room, even though that meant moving a very sick patient on to a four-bed ward. The patient who was moved died in the night. There was criticism from relatives that the patient should not have been moved and also a suggestion that the death was accelerated. Was the nurse at fault if, the next day, it is discovered that the suspected meningitis patient was only suffering from a non-fatal virus?

Provided the nurse used her professional judgement in making the decision to give the single room to that particular patient, with the knowledge available to her at that time, then there should be no finding of negligence. In fact, if meningitis had been confirmed, then the nurse may well have been negligent in not taking precautions to prevent any danger of staff or patients being infected. She has to use her judgement in determining the degree of risk to both patients.

Causation

The third element in the claimant's case against the NHS trust or the nurse is to establish that there is a causal link between the breach of the duty of care by the nurse and the harm suffered by the claimant. It is possible for the nurse to fail in her duty of care to the patient and for the patient to suffer harm, yet for the nurse or her employer not to be liable in civil law. This is because one of the essential elements that the claimant must establish in an action for negligence is that there is a causal link between the failure of the defendant to follow the approved practice and the harm suffered by the patient. The possibility that this harm could occur must be reasonably foreseeable and must also take place.

Factual causation

> ## Case 3.6   *Barnett* v. *Chelsea HMC* (1968)
>
> **Causation**[24]
>
> A patient attended the casualty department after drinking tea that, unknown to him, had been contaminated with arsenic and that caused prolonged vomiting. The doctor did not examine him, but sent a message that he should see his own doctor. He died a few hours later.

The widow failed in her action because it was established that the patient would have died even if properly examined and treated. In this case, the pathological evidence on the progress of arsenic poisoning and the projected timetable of events had the patient been examined and admitted was of vital importance.

In such circumstances, although a civil action fails there are likely to be professional and disciplinary proceedings by the professional body and the employer.

Barnett's case (Case 3.6) was an example of a lack of factual connection between the breach of duty of care and the harm suffered by the patient.

Another example of a case that has been before the House of Lords is the following.

Case 3.7   *Wilsher v. Essex AHA* (1988)

Blindness, but how caused?[25]

In the Wilsher case (considered on page 62, Case 4.3) the House of Lords decided that the case should be reheard by a new High Court judge on the issue of whether it was the defendant's negligence that had caused the harm to the child. In this case, it was agreed that there were several different factors that could have caused the child to become blind and the negligence by the defendant was only one of these. The trial judge had failed to make a relevant finding of fact and could not presume that it was the defendant's negligence that had caused the harm.

Following the House of Lords' ruling, the parties came to a settlement and compensation was paid to the parents for the child.

Case 3.8   *Kay v. Ayrshire and Arran Health Board* (1987)

The cause of deafness[26]

A child suffering from meningitis was given 300,000 units of penicillin instead of 10,000 units. The mistake was discovered and remedial action taken. The health authority admitted liability and made an offer to the parents for the additional pain and suffering that the negligence caused the boy. However, the parents argued that the overdose had caused the boy to become deaf and they rejected the board's offer, claiming instead many thousands of pounds more because they held the health authority liable for the deafness.

The House of Lords decided that the parents had not made out the factual causation between the overdose and the deafness and thus that the boy was not entitled to the larger amount. It is a well-known fact that meningitis itself can cause deafness.

Reasonably foreseeable consequence

In a civil case for negligence, the claimant also has to establish that the harm that occurred was a reasonably foreseeable consequence of breach of duty by the defendant.

Practical Dilemma 3.4   Reasonable foreseeability

In breach of her duty of care, a nurse failed to dispose properly of contaminated dressings, which were left on a stainless steel trolley in the treatment area. By chance, two boys broke into the room looking for syringes and needles. When they heard footsteps approaching, they grabbed as much as they could from the trolley and ran off, taking a dressing with them. Subsequently, an outbreak of disease attributable to the dressing occurred in the neighbourhood. Was the nurse responsible in law for this?

The nurse was certainly at fault in not disposing correctly of the dressings. However, it could be argued that the subsequent events were not reasonably foreseeable and, in any event, the chain of causation between the nurse's action and the outbreak of the disease was broken by the action of the boys. This is sometimes known as a *novus actus interveniens* (i.e. a new act intervening).

Taking one's claimant as one finds him

There is one important exception to the rule that the harm resulting from the breach of duty is reasonably foreseeable, known as the thin skull rule or 'you take your claimant as you find him'.

Practical Dilemma 3.5   The thin skull rule

A nurse puts some drops in the wrong eye. They were meant to dilate the pupil in the other eye. They would not normally have caused any harm, but because of an existing defect in that eye the patient became blind.

The nurse in this case is clearly negligent. However, in the majority of patients her error would have caused no, or very little, harm. In this case, however, even though she could not have predicted the outcome, she would be liable for the harm that has occurred on the basis of the doctrine 'you take your claimant as you find him'.

Case 3.9   *Smith v. Leech Brain* (1961)

The thin skull rule[27]

An accident occurred at work when a labourer was splashed with a piece of molten metal and his lower lip was burnt. The burn was treated and the labourer thought nothing more about it. However, the place where the burn had been began to ulcerate and get larger. He consulted his general practitioner who sent him to hospital where cancer was diagnosed. Treatment by radium needles enabled the lip to heal and destroyed the primary growth. Subsequently, however, secondary growths were observed. He had six operations and died of cancer just over three years after the accident. His widow claimed compensation from the employers.

They admitted liability for the original accident, but denied that they were responsible for the man's death. Lord Parker in the Queen's Bench Division held that the test was not whether the defendants could reasonably have foreseen that a burn would cause cancer and that Mr Smith would die. The test was whether these defendants could reasonably foresee the type of injury that he suffered, namely the burn. The amount of damage that he suffers as a result of that burn depends on the characteristics and constitution of the victim. The widow therefore won her case.

In a case involving harm to a child who was playing about on a boat,[28] the House of Lords held that ingenuity of children in finding unexpected ways of doing mischief to themselves and others should not be underestimated. Reasonable foreseeability was not a fixed point on the scale of probability and the child won his case against the local authority as occupiers. (The case is discussed on page 289 in Case 12.2.)

Loss of a chance

Case 3.10   *Hotson v. Berkshire AHA (1987)*

A lost chance[29]

A 13-year-old boy fell out of a tree and suffered a slipped femoral epiphysis. He attended the A&E department, but the doctor failed to carry out an X-ray of the hip. The boy suffered considerable pain and returned to hospital five days later, when the fracture was diagnosed. He developed avascular necrosis of the femoral head which medical evidence suggested occurred in 75 per cent of patients. Expert evidence for the claimant was that as a result of the delay in diagnosis he lost a 25 per cent chance of avoiding this complication. The judge awarded the boy £150 damages for the pain suffered by him for the five days, which he would have been spared by prompt diagnosis and treatment. In addition, the boy was awarded 25 per cent of the damages that would have been awarded had the entire injury been attributable to negligence (i.e. 25 per cent of £45,000), for the loss of the chance of recovery.

The House of Lords allowed the health authority's appeal, holding that the claimant had not established that the defendant's negligence had caused the avascular necrosis. The question of causation was to be determined on the balance of probabilities with the onus on the claimant.

The loss of a chance argument by a claimant is particularly difficult in cases where there has been failure to diagnose a condition such as a malignancy. In such a case the patient may have died even had the correct diagnosis been made, but would attempt to argue that had the correct diagnosis been made, then he would have been in that category which would have obtained remission following the appropriate treatment. In order to obtain compensation when there has been negligence in diagnosis, the claimant may have to rely on the specific consequences of delayed diagnosis such as further protracted treatment, additional pain and suffering, or other harm, rather than being able to claim that he or she would have been cured.

The House of Lords in a majority judgment[30] reaffirmed the use of the balance of probabilities test of causation in a 'lost chance' case and dismissed the claimant's appeal. The claimant alleged that negligent misdiagnosis of his tumour had caused a nine-month delay in the start of treatment. The trial judge held that this delay had reduced the claimant's chance of a cure from 42 per cent to 25 per cent.

Harm

Not all forms of harm are compensateable by the civil courts. Grief itself is not a ground for a claim, although there is now a statutory right for compensation for bereavement where the death has resulted from negligence. This is considered in Chapter 6 where the basis for the amount of compensation is discussed. The court recognises that harm that involves personal injury or death or loss or damage of property should be compensated if the other elements of negligence can be proved. However, the harm must be a reasonably foreseeable consequence of the breach of duty: it must not be too remote. This is a particularly difficult question when economic loss has occurred and the courts have limited the liability of the defendants to reasonably foreseeable economic loss. Similar difficulties arise over determining the liability for causing nervous shock or post-traumatic stress as it is now termed.

Post-traumatic stress

> ### Case 3.11   *McLoughlin v. O'Brian* (1982)
>
> **Post-traumatic stress syndrome (nervous shock)**[31]
>
> Mr Thomas McLoughlin and his three children George (aged 17), Kathleen (aged 7) and Gillian (aged 3) were in a motorcar driven by George when it was in collision with a lorry. George was not at fault. Mrs McLoughlin, who was not in the vehicle, was told by a friend who was in the car behind (with Michael, another McLoughlin child, aged 11, who was a passenger) that George had probably died and that he was uncertain of the condition of the husband or the other children. She was driven to the hospital and saw Michael who told her that Gillian was dead. She was taken down the corridor and through a window she saw Kathleen, crying with her face cut and begrimed with dirt and oil. She could hear George shouting and screaming. She was taken to her husband who was sitting with his head in his hands. His shirt was hanging off him and he was covered in mud and oil. He saw his wife and started sobbing. She was then taken to see George. The whole of the left face and left side were covered. He appeared to recognise her and then lapsed into unconsciousness. Finally, she was taken to see Kathleen who by now had been cleaned up. The child was too upset to speak and simply clung to her mother. As a result of this experience Mrs McLoughlin suffered from severe shock, organic depression and a change of personality. She was normally a person of reasonable fortitude.

Obviously, in a case like this, damages would be payable to the husband and the children for the harm that they had suffered, but in addition to that, compensation was claimed by Mrs McLoughlin for nervous shock. The defendants argued that she was too remote from the defendants' negligence: she was not herself a direct victim of the accident, neither was she a bystander witnessing what happened. The House of Lords decided that she was entitled to receive compensation since she was so closely related to those injured and the nervous shock that she suffered was close in both space and time.

Lord Wilberforce said:

It is necessary to consider three elements inherent in any claim: The class of persons whose claims should be recognised; the proximity of such persons to the accident; and the means by which the shock is caused. As regards the class of persons the possible range is between the closest possible of family ties, of parent and child or husband and wife, and the ordinary bystander. Existing law recognises the claims of the first; it denies that of the second, either on the basis that such persons must be assumed to be possessed of fortitude sufficient to enable them to endure the calamities of modern life or that defendants cannot be expected to compensate the world at large.

Any persons wishing to claim compensation for nervous shock (now referred to as post-traumatic stress syndrome) would have to show that they were actually suffering from a mental illness and not just grief and that they were sufficiently closely related to the objects of the defendant's negligence and also in time and space.

The law has been further clarified by the House of Lords in the case of *Alcock* v. *Chief Constable South Yorkshire Police*.[32] In this case, people who were present at or who watched the disaster at Hillsborough where 95 people died (as a result of overcrowding in the stadium, allegedly due to negligence by the police) brought a claim in respect of post-traumatic stress syndrome. The House of Lords held that in order to establish a claim in respect of psychiatric illness resulting from shock it was necessary to show not only that such injury was reasonably foreseeable, but also that the relationship between the claimant and the defendant was sufficiently proximate. Proximity could include not only blood ties, but also ties of love and affection. The closeness would have to be proved in each individual case. The claimant would also have to show propinquity in time and space to the accident or its immediate aftermath. It was held that those claimants who viewed the disaster on television could not be said to be equivalent to being within sight and hearing of the event or its immediate aftermath.

In *White and Others* v. *Chief Constable of the South Yorkshire Police and Others*,[33] police officers sued for post-traumatic stress syndrome following the same disaster. The House of Lords decided that merely being an employee of the person/organisation responsible for the negligence did not automatically create sufficient proximity for the claimant to succeed in obtaining compensation for post-traumatic stress syndrome. The employee had to satisfy the usual rules of establishing proximity. To obtain compensation for psychiatric illness, a rescuer would have to show that he had objectively exposed himself to danger or reasonably believed that he was doing so. Rescuers were not entitled to claim compensation when they were not within the range of foreseeable physical injury and their psychiatric injury was caused by witnessing or participating in the aftermath of accidents that caused death or injury to others. The police therefore failed in their claim.

Both the McLoughlin and Alcock cases were referred to in a case in 1998,[34] where a mother failed in her case to obtain compensation for psychiatric illness following the abduction and death of her daughter by a mentally ill outpatient. The Court of Appeal held that the judge was correct to find that there was no proximity between the mother, the daughter and the Tees Health Authority. It was also relevant to consider how the offences could have been avoided even if sufficient proximity were established, having regard to the difficulty in identifying and protecting potential victims and to the limited effectiveness of the health authority's powers under the Mental Health Act 1983.[35]

The High Court[36] applied these House of Lords' cases in a situation where a fire officer sued his son, claiming damages for psychiatric harm suffered as a result of attending the scene of an accident in which the son had suffered head injuries. The accident occurred as a result of the son driving a car negligently after drinking. The court held that a victim of self-inflicted injuries owed no duty of care to a secondary party who, after witnessing the event from which the injuries resulted or its aftermath, suffered psychiatric injury. In addition, in the circumstances of the case, to allow one family member to sue another would potentially result in an objectionable form of intra-family litigation.

An event may, in practice, cover a period of time as the following case shows.

Case 3.12   *N. Glamorgan NHS Trust* v. *Walters* (2003)

Delayed transfer[37]

A 10-month-old boy was admitted to hospital suspected of suffering from hepatitis. The doctors failed to diagnose that this was acute and accepted that had it been properly diagnosed and treated by means of a liver transplant, he may have lived. During the night he suffered

> **Case 3.12 continued**
>
> a fit and the mother was told by the nurse that it was unlikely that he had suffered any brain damage. In fact, there had been a major epileptic seizure that led to a coma and irreparable brain damage. A scan was carried out and the mother was told incorrectly that it showed no brain damage. He was transferred to a London hospital where he was placed on a life support machine. A further scan showed that he had suffered severe brain damage and the parents agreed that it was in the boy's best interests for the life support to be turned off. He died in his mother's arms. She was subsequently told that had he been transferred earlier he would have had a far better chance of survival.

It was agreed that the mother was suffering from a pathological grief reaction, which was a result of witnessing, experiencing and participating in the events described. The judge found that the mother was a secondary victim and her psychiatric injury was caused by sight and sound of a horrifying event that had covered a period of time. The defendants appealed to the Court of Appeal on the grounds that the 36-hour period could not be regarded in law as one horrifying event, but the claimant's appreciation was not sudden. The Court of Appeal held that the 36-hour period could be viewed as a single horrifying event and the judge was correct to find that the claimant's appreciation of the events was sudden as opposed to an accumulation of gradual assaults on her mind.

A similar decision is seen in another Court of Appeal case[38] where the claimant suffered post-traumatic stress syndrome after her daughter was killed in a road accident when a car mounted the pavement. The claimant rushed to the scene of the accident, which was cordoned off, and she was prevented from crossing the tape. She was told that her daughter was dead and she screamed hysterically and collapsed to the ground. Subsequently at the mortuary, while the worst of the injuries on the girl's lower part were covered by a blanket, the mother saw that the daughter's face and head were disfigured. She cradled the daughter saying she was cold. She lost her case on the grounds that the judge could not accept that what happened in the mortuary could be said to be part of the aftermath. The shock from which she suffered was a result of what she had been told by the police. The Court of Appeal allowed the claimant's appeal holding that the immediate aftermath extended from the moment of the accident until the moment that the claimant left the mortuary. The judge had artificially separated out the mortuary visit from what was an uninterrupted sequence of events.

This topic of post-traumatic stress syndrome relates to the nurse in two ways. First, she may herself be the victim of post-traumatic stress arising from another person's negligence, in which case she needs to know whether she is likely to obtain compensation. Second, in her own work she should be aware of the dangers of causing stress shock in others and the possibility of claims for compensation arising out of this.

Conclusions

Claims in respect of clinical negligence are increasing in the NHS and the nurse needs to be aware of the basic legal provisions which apply in order that she can protect both the patient and herself. An NHS redress scheme is being introduced as an alternative to civil litigation through the courts and this is considered in Chapter 6.

> ### Reflection questions
>
> **1** Consider the duty of care possibly owed by the nurse of an NHS trust and discuss whether and on what grounds you think a duty would be owed in the following circumstances:
>
> **(a)** an informal patient who wanders away from the hospital and damages cars in the vicinity of the hospital
>
> **(b)** a detained patient who does likewise
>
> **(c)** a patient in the A&E department who, after an attempted suicide, insists on taking his own discharge and is shortly afterwards found dead on a railway line
>
> **(d)** a doctor in a cinema who gives a person having a cardiac arrest the wrong treatment
>
> **(e)** a community nurse who is caring for a neighbour, not on her list, and who accidentally leaves the door open. The neighbour is mugged and the house burgled.
>
> **2** If there has been a negligent act but no harm has occurred to the patient, what remedies are available (if any) for the patient to obtain compensation?
>
> **3** How would you determine the standard of care that should be adopted in carrying out the following procedures:
>
> **(a)** lifting
>
> **(b)** administering medication
>
> **(c)** informing patients of their rights
>
> **(d)** advising relatives on the procedures to be followed in dealing with death?

Further exercises

1 Why do you consider that causation is an important element in an action for negligence? Would it be fairer to the claimant if causation did not need to be proved?

2 A new scheme for compensation for clinical negligence has been established by the Department of Health (see Chapter 6 on the NHS redress scheme). Contrast the new scheme with the elements of a negligence action set out in this chapter and consider the extent to which a claimant would benefit from the NHS redress scheme.

References

[1] National Audit Office, Handling Clinical Negligence Claims in England, Report of the Comptroller and Auditor General, House of Commons Session 2000-2001, 3 May 2001

[2] *Donoghue* v. *Stevenson* [1932] AC 562

[3] *Kent* v. *Griffiths and Others*, The Times Law Report, 23 December 1998; The Times Law Report, 10 February 2000; [2000] 2 All ER 474

[4] *Phelps* v. *Hillingdon London Borough Council* [1998] 1 All ER 421

[5] *Phelps* v. *Hillingdon London Borough Council; Anderton* v. *Clwyd CC; Jarvis* v. *Hampshire CC; Re G (A Minor)* [2000] 4 All ER 504

[6] *W and Others* v. *Essex County Council and Another* [1998] 3 All ER 111

[7] *W and Others* v. *Essex County Council and Another* [2000] 2 All ER 237 HL, [2000] 2 WLR 601, [2000] 1 FLR 657

[8] *Barrett* v. *Enfield LBC* [1999] 2 FLR 426

[9] *Gorringe* v. *Calderdale MBC* [2004] UKHL 15, [2004] 1 WLR 1057

[10] Nursing and Midwifery Council, Code of Professional Conduct: standards for performance, conduct and ethics, NMC, 2004

11 *Whitehouse v. Jordan* [1981] 1 All ER 267

12 *Bolam v. Friern Barnet HMC* [1957] 2 All ER 118

13 *Maynard v. West Midlands RHA* [1984] 1 WLR 634

14 *Michael Hyde and Associates Ltd v. JD Williams and Co. Ltd*, The Times Law Report, 4 August 2000

15 *Bolitho v. City and Hackney Health Authority* [1997] 3 WLR 115

16 *Penney, Palmer and Cannon v. East Kent Health Authority* [2000] Lloyd's Rep Med p. 41 CA

17 Brian Hurwitz, *Clinical Guidelines and the Law*, Radcliffe Medical Press, Abingdon, 1998

18 *Early v. Newham HA* [1994] 5 Med LR 214

19 *Fotedar v. St George's Healthcare NHS Trust* [2005] EWHC 1327 QBD

20 *Zarb v. Odetoyinbo* [2006] EWHC 2880

21 John Tingle and Charles Foster, *Clinical Guidelines: Law, Policy and Practice*, Cavendish Publishing, London, 2002

22 *Roe v. Minister of Health* (1954) 2 QB 66

23 *Crawford v. Charing Cross Hospital, The Times*, 8 December 1953

24 *Barnett v. Chelsea HMC* [1968] 1 All ER 1068

25 *Wilsher v. Essex Area Health Authority* [1986] 3 All ER 801 CA, [1988] 1 All ER 871 HL

26 *Kay v. Ayrshire and Arran Health Board* [1987] 2 All ER 417

27 *Smith v. Leech Brain & Co. Ltd* [1961] 3 All ER 1159 QBD

28 *Jolley v. Sutton London Borough Council*, The Times Law Report, 24 May 2000; [2000] 1 WLR 1082

29 *Hotson v. East Berks HA* [1987] AC 750

30 *Gregg v. Scott* [2005] UKHL 2

31 *McLoughlin v. O'Brian* [1982] 2 All ER 298

32 *Alcock v. Chief Constable of the South Yorkshire Police* (1992) 2 AC 310 HL

33 *White and Others v. Chief Constable of the South Yorkshire Police and Others* [1999] 1 All ER 1

34 *Palmer v. Tees Health Authority and Another*, The Times Law Report, 1 June 1998; [1998] Lloyd's Rep Med 447 QBD

35 *Palmer v. Tees HA* (2000) 2 LGLR 69 CA

36 *Greatorex v. Greatorex and Another* (Pope, Pr 20 Defendant) [2000] 4 All ER 769

37 *North Glamorgan NHS Trust v. Walters*, Lloyd's Rep Med 2 [2003] 49 CA

38 *Giulietta Galli-Atkinson v. Sudhaker Seghal*, Lloyd's Rep Med 6 [2003] 285

Chapter 4

Specific problem areas in civil liability:
personal liability of the nurse, vicarious liability of the employer and managerial issues

Introduction

In this chapter, we explore some of the particular difficulties that can arise in determining the liability of a professional in some specific situations, beginning with liability for negligence in communicating. In addition, we consider the problems that can arise from inadequate resources;

the nurse as a manager; and the liability of the employer. (The scope of professional practice and the role of clinical nurse specialist and consultant nurse are considered in Chapter 24.)

Negligence in communication

It is possible to be negligent in failing to communicate with the appropriate person at the correct time and in the proper way.

> **Case 4.1** **_Coles_ v. _Reading HMC_ (1963)**
>
> **Crushed fingers**[1]
>
> Mr Coles suffered a crush injury to his finger. He went to the cottage hospital where the nurse cleaned the wound of dust and dirt and told him to go to a proper hospital where he would have an anti-tetanus injection. But neither she nor anyone else impressed on him the purpose and importance of the visit and so he did not go. He later saw his general practitioner who believed that he had had the injection and so he did not give him one. He subsequently died of tetanus.

In this case, there was negligence by all those professional staff (including the nurse) who had failed to communicate adequately with other professionals and with the patient. Failure to communicate, if it falls short of the required professional standard, can be regarded as negligence and is actionable if it causes reasonably foreseeable harm to the patient.

Failure to communicate rarely causes such devastating harm as in this tetanus case, but there are other well-known examples where it is vital that the patient receives certain information and it cannot be assumed that the patient is aware of the dangers. For example, in head injury cases there may be no detectable sign of head injury when the patient is seen in the A&E department. However, it is essential that the patient be warned to return if certain symptoms appear. Comparable instructions must be given after plastering and in many other situations. In such circumstances, it is advisable for a strict procedure to be implemented to ensure that the correct information is given both by word of mouth and in writing. If there is likely to be any dispute as to whether the information was given and/or where there are considerable dangers if the patient is not informed, it is possible to ask the patient to acknowledge in writing his receipt of that information. This procedure has the added advantage of making the patient aware of the importance of the information or instructions.

Negligence in instructing others is considered in further detail in Chapter 18, which deals with the law and the nurse educator. Liability for a negligent misstatement was found when a local authority recommended a registered childminder to a mother despite an earlier case of non-accidental injury by the minder.[2]

Inexperience

Does a newly qualified nurse have to follow the same standard of care as an experienced nurse?

In practical terms, it is, of course, impossible to expect the same standard of care from the junior nurse as from the experienced senior nurse. However, in law that is what the patient is entitled to expect. You cannot say in defence to a patient, 'The reason that you were given the wrong drug is that nurse X administered it and she has only just qualified.' The patient is entitled to receive the accepted standard of care whoever provides it. It is, however, essential that staff work within their field of competence and that work requiring greater experience is performed by those with the appropriate skills or that those lacking in experience have adequate supervision to ensure the task is safely undertaken. This point is discussed in the Wilsher case (considered on pages 62-3).

Case 4.2 *Nettleship v. Weston* (1971)

A learner driver[3]

Mr Nettleship was teaching Mrs Weston to drive in her husband's car. On the third lesson, he was helping her by moving the gear lever, applying the handbrake and occasionally helping with the steering. In the course of the lesson, they made a slow left-hand turn after stopping at a halt sign. However, Mrs Weston did not straighten up the wheel and panicked. Mr Nettleship got hold of the handbrake with one hand and tried to get hold of the steering wheel with the other. The car hit a lamp standard. Mr Nettleship broke his kneecap. He claimed compensation and succeeded before the Court of Appeal.

The crucial question in the case was: Since Mrs Weston was not a qualified driver, was the standard of care that she owed to the instructor lower than would otherwise have been the case? The court decided not. They preferred to have one standard of driving, not a variable standard depending on the characteristics of the individual driver. 'The certainties of a general standard are preferable to the vagaries of a fluctuating standard' (Lord Justice Megaw).

This might seem irrelevant to the standard of the nurse but Lord Justice Megaw, in discussing the issue, used the example of the young surgeon:

> *Suppose that to the knowledge of the patient, a young surgeon, whom the patient has chosen to operate on him, has only just qualified. If the operation goes wrong because of the surgeon's inexperience, is there a defence on the basis that the standard of care and skill was lower than the standard of a competent and experienced surgeon? In cases such as the present it is preferable that there should be a reasonably certain and reasonably ascertainable standard of care, even if on occasion that may appear to work hardly against an inexperienced driver.*

Mr Nettleship obtained his compensation, subject to a reduction for contributory negligence.

Practical Dilemma 4.1 No experience

Ruth Evans is recently qualified and is a staff nurse at Roger Park Hospital. She is asked to work initially on the orthopaedic ward until a vacancy occurs on the children's ward, which is her chosen specialty. The orthopaedic consultant suggests that Fred Timms, who has recently been taken off traction, could start some mobility exercises. Ruth, following this advice, approaches Fred's bed with a nursing auxiliary and with a pair of crutches. She suggests that Fred should manoeuvre himself to the side of the bed and gently put his sound leg on the floor. Then, when he feels steady enough, he should take the crutches and start to walk. Fred shifts to the side of the bed, puts his sound leg on the floor, but as he stands up holding on to the crutches, they slide away from him and he falls heavily to the ground. Subsequently, X-rays reveal a further fracture of the injured leg and a fresh fracture in the other leg. Where does Ruth stand as far as liability is concerned? Is the fact that she has only just commenced on the orthopaedic ward and has never specialised in it a good defence for her personally against any potential court action that Fred might bring?

It is quite likely that if this case were investigated it would be established that there was a recognised procedure for mobilisation of orthopaedic patients, which would most likely involve the physiotherapist, and that Ruth had failed to follow this and probably was not even aware of its existence. This would be no defence against Fred. If he can establish the four elements of negligence – (a) a duty of care was owed to him, (b) Ruth was in breach of that duty by failing to follow the accepted approved practice and that (c) as a reasonably foreseeable consequence, he has (d) been caused harm – then he would succeed in his action. Ruth would be held to be negligent. Fred is, however, more likely to sue the NHS trust as Ruth's employer on the grounds that it is vicariously liable for her negligence (see page 67, below) and is also directly liable for failing to ensure a system of supervision of inexperienced staff. Other staff may also be held negligent. For example, who should have ensured that Ruth had the requisite training, that she was made aware of ward procedures and that she had adequate support? Someone else should have ensured that she was aware of the role of the physiotherapist.

In practice, of course, the experience of individual staff varies greatly and even where staff have had the same experience and training, their level of skill and manual dexterity may also vary greatly. However, the patient should be assured that the recognised approved standard of care will be given. Occasionally, a patient may require a higher standard.

For example, Mr Links may have held himself up as a specialist in a complex ear operation that is not often performed because of its particular hazards and difficulties. A general practitioner might refer a patient to Mr Links because of his particular skill. If Mr Links then fails to perform the operation carefully and the patient suffers harm, it is no defence for Mr Links to claim that he knows he did not perform it correctly, but no other ear surgeon could have done it. He has held himself up as having that particular skill. Of course, it would have to be shown that he had failed to perform the operation with the required level of care and skill. The fact that things go wrong does not in itself mean that there has been negligence.

Team liability and apportionment of responsibility

Team liability

If harm is caused by another member of the team, is the nurse responsible?

Work in the health service is, above all, team oriented. Very few tasks are performed entirely on one's own. In the community, particular tasks are often allocated not purely on a professional basis, but on a key worker basis, which enables one person to take responsibility for a wide range of tasks.

Practical Dilemma 4.2   **The team**

Jane is a third-year student who, together with other members of staff on the ward, is caring for orthopaedic patients. The nursing process is in operation. One day Jane is asked to work in the plaster unit where it is her task to bind the plaster bandage around the patients' limbs. One of the patients, a young boy called Sam, has a broken wrist and Jane is told to strap it up. She bandages the wrist and then calls the sister to look at it. The sister glances at it, but does not touch it and the boy's mother is asked to bring him back in three weeks' time. No instructions are given about checking the tightness of the bandage or moving the hand. Three weeks later the boy returns with his mother and it is noticed that the bandage has been put on too tightly and it appears that permanent damage has been done to the boy's hand. What is Jane's responsibility?

Jane is, of course, the person who actually bandaged his wrist. Whether the trust is vicariously responsible for her actions will depend on any memorandum of agreement between her college of nurse training and the NHS trust offering clinical placements. Jane's personal liability will depend on such questions as: Had Jane been trained to plaster? Was such a task entirely within her competence? Should she have refused to undertake an activity for which she was not competent? Was her level of expertise such that the sister should have checked her work? If, for example, it should have been quite clear that Jane was too inexperienced to undertake the task without supervision, the fact that she asked the sister to check over the work might be sufficient to relieve her of personal responsibility. The failure to communicate to the parent the need to check on the plaster is also a breach of duty and liability will depend on who had the responsibility of ensuring that this was done. As has been noted in the first section of this chapter, failure to communicate can itself be grounds for an allegation of negligence.

The team may be a group of nurses working together – it might be a multidisciplinary group. In the following case, the team was made up of doctors and nurses working under one consultant.

Case 4.3   *Wilsher* v. *Essex AHA* (1986)

No team liability[4]

A premature baby was placed in a special care baby unit staffed by a medical team consisting of two consultants, a senior registrar, several junior doctors and trained nurses. A junior doctor, while monitoring the oxygen intake, inadvertently put the catheter in a vein rather than in an artery. He asked the senior registrar to check what he had done. The registrar failed to see the mistake and several hours later made exactly the same mistake himself. As a result, the catheter failed to monitor the oxygen correctly and it was alleged that the child suffered from an incurable condition of the retina resulting in near blindness.

At the trial, the judge awarded £116,199 to the child. The health authority appealed to the Court of Appeal on the grounds that (1) there had been no breach of duty of care owed to the child because the standard of care required of doctors in the unit was only that reasonably required of doctors having the same formal qualifications and practical experience as the doctors in the unit; and (2) the child had failed to show that the health authority's actions had caused or contributed to his condition since excess oxygen was merely one of several different factors, any one of which could have caused or contributed to the eye condition from which the child suffered. (This last point is known as *causation* and is discussed in Chapter 3.)

On the point of the standard of care, the Court of Appeal held that there was no concept of team negligence, in the sense that each individual team member was required to observe standards demanded of the unit as a whole, because it could not be right, for example, to expose a student nurse to an action for negligence for her failure to possess the experience of a consultant. The standard of care required was that of the ordinary skilled person exercising and professing to have that special skill, but that standard was to be determined in the context of the particular posts in the unit rather than according to the general rank or status of the people filling the posts, since the duty ought to be tailored to the acts which the doctor had elected to perform rather than to the doctor himself. It followed that inexperience was no defence to an action for negligence. One judge, however, stated that an inexperienced doctor who was called on to exercise a specialist skill and who made a mistake nevertheless satisfied the necessary standard of care if he had sought the advice and help of his superior when necessary. The court in this case applied the same standard as the court in the Whitehouse and Jordan case (see page 44), i.e. the Bolam Test. The judges held that the junior doctor had not been negligent and had upheld the relevant standard of care by consulting his superior. His superior had, however, been negligent in failing to notice that the catheter had been mistakenly inserted in a vein rather than an artery and, accordingly, the health authority was vicariously liable for the registrar's negligence.

An additional finding was that there was no reason why, in certain circumstances, a health authority could not be directly liable to a claimant if it failed to provide sufficient or properly qualified and competent medical staff for the unit (see page 73 on direct liability). The House of Lords subsequently ordered a new trial on the issue of causation and the parties then settled the case (see Chapter 3).

Apportioning responsibility

Although there is no concept of team negligence in law, each person is individually responsible for his/her negligence; it does not follow that there are no occasions of multiple liability, i.e. in a given situation several different professionals might be individually responsible for their own individual negligence. An example of this is given in Chapter 28 on the prescribing of medicines.[5] Under the Civil Liability (Contribution) Act 1978, if there are several defendants, a successful claimant can recover damages from any one of the defendants. That defendant may then sue the other defendants to recover a sum that represents their responsibility for the harm which has occurred.

Taking instructions: refusal to obey

General principles

When we look at the scope of professional practice (see Chapter 24), we will consider the possibility that the nurse might have to refuse to undertake a task where, for example, she was not trained to perform it or where she had insufficient time to undertake it safely. In this section, we look at the wider field of obeying orders.

> ### Practical Dilemma 4.3   Orders are orders
>
> A registrar decides that Margaret Brown should be prescribed a new drug that has only just been released on to the market and writes her up for it. The staff nurse on that ward is not familiar with the drug and says that she would like to check it with the pharmacist before she administers it. The doctor is furious with this insolence and says that if he has written it up then she should administer it without questioning his competence. The nurse says that she needs some understanding of the drug before she gives it to the patient. The doctor insists she gives it. Where does the nurse stand?

This is a simplified version of situations that often confront the nurse. This particular example raises the issue of what the nurse's responsibility is in relation to the administration of drugs, but examples could be given from other fields such as obeying the order 'not for resuscitation', not passing certain information on to a patient, etc.

It is impossible to give an answer that would apply to every situation. In an emergency, for example, certain risks have to be taken which would not be appropriate in non-urgent circumstances. In Practical Dilemma 4.3, the nurse would be quite correct in obtaining further information about the drug in question. When she administers a drug she must be sure that she is administering the right drug, at the right time, in the right place, at the right dosage, in the right way, to the right patient. She should not administer a drug of which she has no knowledge without taking all reasonable steps to ascertain that it is appropriate for that particular patient. If in this situation she were to go ahead and administer the drug on the orders of the doctor and the patient were to die or suffer harm as a result, she could be held to be negligent in any civil action (for which her employers would be held vicariously liable) since she failed to follow the reasonable standards of care expected of a nurse. She could also face professional disciplinary proceedings before the CCC of the NMC and disciplinary proceedings before her own line manager because she failed to use all care and skill in carrying out her contract of employment. If the patient died, the nurse might have to appear in the coroner's court and there might also be criminal proceedings brought against both her and the doctor. (See the NMC Code of Professional Conduct: standards for conduct, performance and ethics[6] Paragraph 1.4, 'You have a duty of care to your patients and clients, who are entitled to receive safe and competent care.')

In all these courts and hearings, saying, 'I was only carrying out orders' will not be sufficient defence on its own. In the civil courts, the professional proceedings and the employer's disciplinary proceedings, the nurse would have to show that what she did was reasonable having regard to the approved accepted practice to be expected from any qualified nurse. In the criminal courts, she would have to show that her acts did not constitute the ingredients of the particular charge and/or that she lacked the required mental state. (See Chapter 2.)

Obeying orders in an emergency

In certain circumstances, time does not permit the usual practice to be followed, but the risks taken must be balanced against the risk of the patient dying.

Practical Dilemma 4.4   Emergency

A patient has been brought into the A&E department with severe bleeding. A blood sample is taken for cross-matching and he is immediately put on an intravenous infusion of plasma. The doctor places the cannula in the patient's arm for the intravenous infusion and asks the nurse to set up a saline solution for administration straightaway. Staff Nurse Bryant takes the bag that the doctor is holding out to her and attaches it to the IV line. She does not check the bag. The patient's condition worsens and he eventually dies. It is then discovered that the doctor inadvertently gave the nurse a bag containing a substance other than saline. What is the nurse's liability?

It is clear that a quick check of the label on the bag would not have delayed the patient's treatment and could have been done by the nurse without any difficulty. It is most likely that she would be found personally negligent in these circumstances (although her employer would have to pay compensation because of its vicarious liability for her negligence) and any defence of 'but that was the bag the doctor gave me' would be unlikely to succeed. There could be other circumstances where emergency life-saving measures are required and the nurse would be unable to make the same checks. Very rarely, however, would the defence of 'obeying orders' succeed, since as a professionally qualified person the nurse would be expected to act responsibly and carefully and to ensure that her own personal actions are safe.

Nurses sometimes complain that the misgivings they express to doctors are ignored. What do they do then? Obviously, it depends on the circumstances. Where her misgivings concern treatment that could be harmful to the patient and if one doctor ignored her concern, then the nurse should express her misgivings to her own line manager and, if necessary, the advice of a more senior doctor should be sought. Much depends on the approach made by the nurse and the nature of the relationship and understanding that exists between the nurse and the doctor. Undoubtedly, encouragement of a team approach to patient care could prevent many unnecessary confrontations of this kind. It should, of course, be stressed that a nurse should not disobey the instructions of a doctor lightly; she should have compelling reasons from the patient's point of view. She should ensure that she keeps detailed records indicating the reasons for her actions and that her nurse manager is brought in at the earliest opportunity. If it should happen that the nurse's attitude was unreasonable then she would, of course, face disciplinary action and, if the patient has been harmed as a result of the nurse's action, civil proceedings and professional misconduct proceedings. (See the discussion of whistleblowing later in this chapter.)

In a case heard by the Court of Appeal in 1942,[7] Lord Goddard said:

> If a doctor in a moment of carelessness, perhaps by the use of a wrong symbol in a prescription, ordered a dose which to an experienced ward sister was obviously incorrect and dangerous, I think it might well be held to be negligence if she administered it without obtaining confirmation from the doctor or higher authority. In the stress of an operation, however, I should suppose that the first thing required of a nurse would be an unhesitating obedience to the orders of the surgeon.

Since 1942, as the recognition of the nurse's personal professional accountability has strengthened, the number of occasions on which a nurse would be expected to obey orders without question has clearly diminished.

Nurse as manager

Delegation and supervision

As the scope of professional practice develops (see Chapter 24), more and more work that is currently undertaken by registered staff will have to be delegated to healthcare support workers under the supervision of registered practitioners. Delegation may take place to other trained staff, learners and nursing assistants and also volunteers. On some occasions, these volunteers may be very unwilling helpers as, for example, where youth training schemes include an attachment to a hospital. If such persons are assigned to work on a ward or department and the nurse manager is responsible for them, then she would have to ensure that their training and the tasks delegated to them are appropriate and that adequate supervision is provided. The NMC has published updated guidance on delegation to non-registered staff.[8]

As a manager, the nurse would be responsible for ensuring that the resources were effectively used and were sufficient for treating patients according to the approved standard of care. If harm is caused by inadequate resources and it is established that she failed to take the appropriate measures to prevent unreasonable risks arising, then she may well be liable (see below and page 76).

Pressure on the manager

Practical Dilemma 4.5   Manager's nightmare

Nursing Officer Janice Clarke is on duty and is informed by the staff in the surgical ward that, although they are on intake and have three empty beds, owing to illness and the failure to fill vacancies they are so far below their establishment that the situation is dangerous and the present staff cannot cope with any more patients.

Obviously, the nursing officer would ensure that the facts are correct and that the nurses on that ward are using their time appropriately and not undertaking tasks that could safely be left, in order to give priority to the work that is most important. Having assured herself that the situation is critical, she would then look internally at other wards and decide whether staff could be transferred. She might also have to consider bringing in bank or agency nurses. If necessary, she would consider the situation on a district basis, which might mean that she would have to discuss the possibility of another hospital taking over the intake at the present. Ultimately, she might have to bring in other districts or at least refer the problems to a more senior manager. The decision might be made that waiting list admissions are cancelled for the time being. Clearly, at all stages in this decision the evidence of the individual ward staff on the dangers and hazards is vital for informed decisions to be made. Like the ward sister or staff nurse, the nursing officer herself should keep records of the reasons behind the actions she has taken since this information may well be relevant to a court or CCC hearing. (Whistleblowing is considered below.)

Covering several wards

Another difficulty that can arise in this context is where a ward sister is in charge of her own ward and also holds the drug cupboard keys for another ward because there is no trained nurse on that ward. In such a situation, the ward sister would have the same responsibilities for both wards. Her tasks of delegation and supervision become extremely difficult and if something goes wrong on one ward in her absence, she may well be liable if that task required her personal supervision. If such problems were likely, then she would obviously have to ensure that this was made known to the senior nurse management and ultimately the NHS trust whose duty it is to take reasonable steps to provide the appropriate facilities.

Practical Dilemma 4.6   On holiday

Marion is ward sister of an acute surgical ward of 30 patients. When she is on holiday, a patient is given a pre-medication prior to the form of consent for his operation being signed. The mistake is discovered and because it was felt that there was no doubt that the patient wanted to have the operation he was still asked to sign the form. He was then taken to theatre. Subsequently, he disputed the extent of his operation, as he had understood that the operation was only exploratory, but he received radical surgery including the provision of a colostomy. He argued that had he known that this was a possibility he would not have agreed to have the operation and he could not remember signing any form of consent. The circumstances of his signature then were discovered. Since the ward sister was on holiday at the time, is there any possibility of her being liable?

It would be cheering for ward sisters and managers if the question could be answered with a definite 'no'. However, this is not possible. A manager has a continuing responsibility to ensure that procedures and policies are designed and implemented to prevent any likelihood of harm to the patient. A vital question to be answered would be: Had a procedure been established to ensure that the nursing staff checked that the consent form had been signed before administration of pre-medication? It would be the ward sister's responsibility to ensure that those procedures that come under the responsibility of the nursing staff are carried out competently and diligently, even when she is not there. In this example, the doctor would be liable for failing to obtain consent. In addition, as far as the immediate responsibility is concerned, the manager in charge of the ward at the time would also share liability for the events, but if, for example, it were established that there was no clear system for ensuring a correct procedure in relation to the checking of consent forms prior to the pre-medication being given, then the ward sister who should have implemented and supervised such a procedure would share some responsibility for the events. It is likely, too, that evidence of similar events in the past would be used to show the deficiencies in overall ward management in this particular context. In these circumstances, the ward sister's liability is not vicarious (see next section), i.e. it does not concern taking responsibility for the fault of others. It is directly her own personal liability for failing in her management role. If, of course, it can be shown that a sound practice had been implemented and was not followed on that occasion owing to the negligence of the staff on duty at that time, then there is less likelihood that the ward sister would be held liable.

Her failings in her responsibilities as manager could result in her having to give evidence in the civil courts, if her employer were to be sued for its vicarious liability for her negligence and, in addition, it could result in her facing a hearing for professional misconduct before the CCC of the NMC. The definition of unfitness to practise by reason of conduct unworthy of a nurse, which may justify removal from the Register, is sufficiently wide to cover mismanagement by a nurse. It is thus an increasing feature of the CCC hearings that as well as hearing a case against an individual nurse who has been at fault in the care of patients, that nurse's manager or managers may also appear before the CCC to answer the charge of misconduct in failing to take responsibility for the situation and having shown a failure in management. Similar principles would apply if, for example, a nurse were known to be on drugs or under the influence of drink at work. If this were known or should have reasonably been known to the managers (they cannot simply turn a blind eye and pretend to be ignorant) and they failed to take appropriate action, then they may well face a hearing for unfitness to practise.

The Royal College of Nursing has provided guidance on the principles of good management practice[9] covering the topics of: vision and strategy; leadership; managing people; managing financial resources; management of care; and quality and risk management. Its aim is to provide a template for managers to develop their own performance standards. It emphasises the importance of regular updating. (The implications of clinical governance are considered in Chapter 5.)

Vicarious liability of employer

Vicarious liability

The NHS trust or employer has two forms of liability in negligence: one is known as direct liability, i.e. the trust itself is at fault; the other is known as vicarious liability or indirect liability, i.e. the trust is responsible for the faults of others, mainly its employees. In this first section, we look at the vicarious liability of the employer, which could be a health authority, an NHS trust, a primary care trust, a private hospital, a company or even a general practitioner who employs his own staff.

> ### Practical Dilemma 4.7   Assault on behalf of the employer
>
> Kate was a staff nurse in casualty where, at weekends, there tended to be a problem with drunks. The hospital was close to the town centre and to several pubs and not infrequently people needing some assistance were accompanied by friends who were incoherent and abusive. One evening Kate was very busy and therefore extremely annoyed to find some very obstreperous men accompanying another man who had a cut head. She asked them to leave him and wait outside. They refused to go. She said she would have to summon the police if they did not leave quietly. One particularly aggressive visitor moved towards the treatment trolley and Kate, fearing that he would knock it over, raised her arm to prevent him. He was taken by surprise at her actions and fell heavily to the ground, catching his head on the side of the trolley. Kate has subsequently learnt that he intends to sue her and her employer.

In a personal action against her for assault, Kate would have to prove that she took reasonable action in self-defence or in protecting her employer's property or in evicting on behalf of the occupier a trespasser who refused to go. In such cases, it is more likely that the claimant would sue the NHS trust responsible for the wrongs of its employees. The claimant does not have to choose whether to sue the employer or the employee. He can sue both. The obvious advantage of suing the employer is that funds will be available to pay him should he win the case. To win against the employer, he has to establish the following:

1 Kate was negligent or was liable for a civil wrong (see below).

2 Kate was an employee (see below).

3 Kate was acting in the course of her employment (see below).

There is no problem with the second element in this case. Kate was an employee, but there may be cases where this is not so clear, for example, if Kate were an agency nurse it might not always be obvious whether Kate is considered to be an employee of the authority to which she is sent or whether she continues to be an employee of the agency.

In practice, the first element could cause some considerable difficulty. Much would depend on the circumstances of the assault: whether she had lost her temper, the level of provocation she was subjected to, etc. Let us assume, for the purpose of this discussion, that it was established as a matter of fact that Kate had acted unlawfully and that personal action against her would therefore succeed.

In the course of employment

In the employer's interests

The third element now needs to be considered. Was the nurse acting in the course of her employment when she assaulted the visitor? The test used to answer this question is as follows: What was she employed to do and when she carried out that act was she acting for the benefit of her employer? In this case, she was clearly not employed as a bouncer, but she was trying to prevent a trolley from being upset by an obstreperous visitor (or even trespasser). This could certainly be seen as being in the interests of the employer's business. Even if there were a clear policy that nursing staff should not attempt to deal with aggressive visitors on their own, this should not necessarily prevent the act from being in the course of employment. The performance of a prohibited act does not on its own mean that the employee has ceased to be acting in the course of employment. All the facts have to be considered. If it can be shown that all three elements were present, the NHS trust could be held vicariously liable for the harm caused by the nurse.

There have been difficulties in establishing whether an act is in the course of employment, and Box 4.1 sets out the criteria which have been used by the courts to decide if an act is in the course of employment.

Box 4.1

The term may cover:

1 Acts authorised by employer.
2 Acts not authorised by employer, but
   (a) performed for the purpose of the employer's business
   (b) prohibited acts, but the prohibition does not take the conduct outside the sphere of employment[10]
   (c) acts incidental to the employment, undertaken for the employee's benefit while the employee is working on the employer's business (e.g. smoking on duty)[11]
   (d) acts for the protection of the employer's property and business[12]
   (e) dishonest or fraudulent acts of the employee, if the employer is under a duty to the person suffering the loss[13]

Outside the job description

Practical Dilemma 4.8   Helping others

Ann Barrett was a staff nurse on a medical ward and was concerned that the kitchen had not sent up the diets. She telephoned for them and was told that she would have to wait since there were no porters available. Rather than wait, she decided to fetch them herself. She went to the kitchen, passing the notice saying: 'No admission, kitchen staff only.' She went across to the diet bay and as she did so she knocked into a cook who was removing a pan of gravy from the stove. The gravy splashed over the cook and also over Ann. What remedies do the cook and Ann have in this situation and is the employer vicariously liable for Ann's negligence?

The cook could, of course, sue Ann personally. Ann owed a duty of care to the cook and, by her carelessness, she caused reasonably foreseeable harm to the cook. However, is the employer vicariously liable for Ann's actions? There is no doubt that she is an employee. There is also no doubt that she was negligent in knocking into the cook. However, is the third element satisfied, i.e. was she acting in the course of employment when she went to the kitchens and when she knocked into the cook? She was employed as a nurse, not as a kitchen porter, but she was acting in the care of the patients (her employer's business) when she went to the kitchens. Even if there were a clear prohibition on non-kitchen staff entering the kitchens, this would not in itself remove the act from the course of employment. The crucial point would be whether she was acting on the employer's business when she entered the kitchen and the answer to that in this case is yes. It would be very different if she entered the kitchen to have a chat on non-hospital business with a friend of hers who worked there.

It is not, of course, uncommon for staff in the health service to step outside the strict confines of their job descriptions. If the employer is aware of this and turns a blind eye to it, then it could be said that he condones it and accepts that the employee's duties have been expanded to include the additional tasks. In such cases, if the employee acts negligently while carrying out these duties, it could be argued that he or she is acting within the course of his or her employment. In addition, particularly during times of industrial action, employers specifically authorise staff to cover for the strikers or those working to rule. In such cases, the employees are acting in the course of their employment: they have the express authorisation of the employer.

Activities incidental to the work

> **Practical Dilemma 4.9**   **Smoking on duty**
>
> There was a clear and enforced policy at Roger Park Hospital that there was no smoking except in authorised areas. One of the nurses ignored these instructions and regularly smoked with the patients in the ward area. On one such occasion, she accidentally dropped the cigarette and burned a patient's foot. He threatened to sue the NHS trust. Was the nurse acting in the course of employment?

The answer is probably yes, based on the following case.

> **Case 4.4**   ***Century Insurance Co. Ltd v. Northern Ireland Road Transport Board* (1942)**
>
> **Lighting up**[14]
>
> A tanker driver ignored his instructions not to light matches when loading or unloading his vehicle and, as a result, the tanker, a vehicle belonging to the garage and several nearby houses were destroyed.

In this case, the court held that even though the act of lighting a cigarette is for the employee's own comfort and even though it is prohibited, the act could not be separated from the circumstances of his employment. The driver was held to be negligent in the course of performing his authorised work and the employers (and therefore their insurers) were liable.

In our example of the smoking nurse, it is highly likely that she will face disciplinary proceedings and possibly even dismissal, yet she may still be held to be acting in the course of employment and therefore the employer is liable.

In Case 4.5 the House of Lords held that school owners were vicariously liable for acts of sexual abuse committed by the school warden against pupils – the abusive acts were sufficiently connected with his work as to be in the course of employment.

> ### Case 4.5   *Lister* v. *Hesley Hall* (2001)
>
> **Sexual abuse by warden**[15]
>
> The board of governors were sued by the victims of abuse by the warden at Hesley Hall, a children's home, because of its vicarious liability for his actions. The Home denied liability on the grounds that the abuse was not committed in the course of his employment. The House of Lords held that it was vicariously liable for the acts of the warden in abusing the claimants: the Home had undertaken the care of the children and entrusted the performance of that duty to the warden and there was therefore sufficiently close connection between his employment and the acts committed by him.
>
> The House of Lords stated that the approach which was best when determining whether a wrongful act was to be deemed to be done by the employee in the course of his employment was to concentrate on the relative closeness of the connection between the nature of the employment and the particular wrongdoing. The defendant undertook to care for the claimants through the services of a warden, so there was a very close connection between the torts of the warden and the defendant. The torts were also committed at a time and place when the warden was busy caring for the claimants. The warden was carrying out his duties though in an unauthorised and improper mode

What if a nurse is off duty?

There can be no easy answer. It depends entirely on what she is doing and in what way she has been negligent. In a recent case, the Court of Appeal allowed an appeal with costs against the decision of the PCC who found that a nurse was guilty of misconduct when she refused to answer a heart patient's call for help because she was having her tea break. The decision was based on the fact that it had not been established that the nurse knew it was an emergency. However, this case was before the Professional Conduct Committee and different principles might apply in a civil case.

In one case, for example, some employees in their employer's van left the authorised route and went to a café to have a snack. On the way back, they had an accident and the court held that they were not acting in the course of employment.[16] It might have been different had they deviated from their route to collect goods for the employer.

Non-employees

It will be recalled that, in order to establish vicarious liability, it must be established that the negligent person is an employee of the defendant. Box 4.2 shows some of the criteria used by the courts to decide if an individual is an employee. Case 4.6 illustrates this principle.

> ### Box 4.2
>
> 1. The employee agrees that in consideration of a wage or other remuneration he will provide his own work and skill in performance of some service for the employer.
> 2. He agrees, expressly or impliedly, that in the performance of that service he will be subject to the other's control in a sufficient degree to make that other the employer.
> 3. The other provisions of the contract are consistent with its being a contract of service. 'Control in itself is not always conclusive', *Ready-Mixed Concrete (South-East) Ltd* v. *Ministry of Pensions and National Insurance* [1968] 1 All ER 433.

> ### Case 4.6   *Watkins v. Birmingham City Council* (1975)
>
> **Classroom chaos**[17]
>
> A deputy headmistress was injured when she fell over a tricycle that had been negligently placed near a classroom door by a 10-year-old boy in the course of carrying out his assigned task of distributing milk in the classrooms. There was a strict rule that tricycles were not to be removed from their safe position in the middle of the assembly hall.

The Court of Appeal held that the boy was not an employee of the authority, that he was doing those duties as part of his education and that the authority was therefore not vicariously liable.

In a recent case,[18] the Court of Appeal held that it was necessary for a contract of employment to contain an obligation on the part of the employee to provide services personally. A contract that allowed services to be provided by another person was a contract for services and not a contract of service.

Liability for negligence of volunteers

What about volunteers? Do the same principles apply? Is the NHS trust liable for the negligent acts of the volunteer? If we follow the basic principles of vicarious liability, it could be argued that since the volunteer is not an employee, then the NHS trust should not be liable. However, the philosophy that underlies the concept of vicarious liability is one of public policy, i.e. the person or organisation that has set in motion a particular activity that has caused harm should bear the loss rather than an innocent victim. In addition, one of the essential elements in the principle of vicarious liability is that the master is in control of the servant's activity. Unfortunately, there is no decided case on whether the NHS trust would be liable to a third person for the negligence of a volunteer. Much would, of course, depend on the circumstances of the volunteer's negligence. It may be that the NHS trust or its staff are themselves at fault in failing to provide adequate training or supervision, or have delegated an entirely inappropriate task to the volunteer. Circular HSG (92)15 advised providers to define clearly the scope or limits of volunteers' activities and accept liability for the results of such activities. The Department of Health has published guidance on volunteering in health and social care including an opportunities for volunteering scheme (OFV) with grants available for small local voluntary organisations.[19]

Liability for independent contractors

> ### Practical Dilemma 4.10   Agency liability
>
> Mary Downs is employed by a nursing agency and is often sent to work in NHS hospitals that call on the agency for additional staff to cover any crises. While she is assisting on the ITU, she fails to notice that one of the monitoring machines has ceased to function and she then discovers that the patient has died. The relatives wish to bring a complaint or even take the NHS trust or the agency to court.

In a case like this, there may well be direct responsibility of the NHS trust for failing to provide a machine that had an effective alarm system or had been satisfactorily maintained. If there is also negligence on the part of the agency nurse, does it make any difference that she is not an employee of the NHS trust, but is employed by the agency? Could the NHS trust still be liable for her negligence? The answer would depend to a considerable extent on the agreement between the NHS trust and the agency on the terms of employment of their staff. In the unlikely event that this has not been predetermined, the control test would be applied. The general or permanent employer has to shift the presumption of responsibility for the negligence of the employee on to the hirer. He can do this by showing that the control of the employee has passed to the hirer. In a health service context, this should be relatively easy since an agency staff nurse sent to help out at an NHS hospital would automatically become part of the ward/department, would be under the control of the ward sister or departmental head and would be subject to their supervision. In most cases, unless there is a clear agreement to the contrary, the NHS trust would probably be vicariously liable for the negligence of the agency staff.

Direct liability of employer

The Secretary of State has a statutory duty (i.e. one laid down by Act of Parliament) under the NHS Act 1977 (now re-enacted in the National Health Service Act 2006) to provide medical services throughout England and Wales and to direct the appropriate health service bodies to exercise these functions on his behalf. It has been argued that if any employee or independent contractor or agency person is negligent, then there is a breach of duty under the Act and the NHS trust is primarily liable, without having to establish all the elements of vicarious liability. This was the opinion of Lord Denning in the case now described.

Case 4.7   *Cassidy v. Ministry of Health* (1939)

A hand operation[20]

The patient lost the use of his left hand and had severe pain and suffering as a result of negligent treatment following an operation on his hand. The evidence showed a *prima facie* case of negligence on the part of the persons in whose care the plaintiff was, although it was not clear whether this was to be imputed to Dr Fahrni, the full-time assistant medical officer, to the house surgeon or to one of the nurses.

The Court of Appeal held that the hospital authority was liable. Lord Denning said:

Whenever (hospital authorities) accept a patient for treatment, they must use reasonable care and skill to cure him of his ailment. The hospital authorities cannot, of course, do it by themselves. They have no ears to listen through the stethoscope, and no hands to hold the knife. They must do it by the staff which they employ, and, if their staff are negligent in giving the treatment, they are just as liable for that negligence as is anyone else who employs others to do his duties for him . . . I decline to enter into the question whether any of the surgeons were employed only under a contract for services, as distinct from a contract of service. The evidence is meagre enough in all conscience on that point, but the liability of the hospital authorities should not, and does not, depend on nice considerations of that sort. The plaintiff knew nothing of the terms on which they employed their staff. All he knew was that he was treated in the hospital by people whom the hospital authorities appointed, and the hospital authorities must be answerable for the way in which he was treated.

This suggests that the NHS trust cannot delegate its duty by providing competent trained staff. It will always be primarily responsible for any negligence to the patients whether the negligent person is an employee, a volunteer, an independent contractor or an agency employee.

A case on this point is that of *Wilsher* v. *Essex Area Health Authority*,[21] discussed earlier. In this case, it was held that there was no reason why, in certain circumstances, a health authority could not be directly liable to a plaintiff (claimant) if it failed to provide sufficient or properly qualified and competent medical staff for the unit. In a case where the Ministry of Defence ceased to arrange direct care for British forces in Germany, their families entered into an arrangement whereby an English NHS trust procured services in Germany and a baby was brain-damaged. The High Court held that there was no negligence by the NHS trust and there was no appeal against that finding. The Court of Appeal held that the Ministry of Defence was not liable.[22] It considered that there was no non-delegatable duty which made the Ministry liable for acts of negligence by the provider. The extent of the direct liability of an NHS trust for services provided by a private provider, or provider overseas remains to be established.

It must be pointed out, however, that even where it is possible to hold the NHS trust directly liable for the harm caused to the patient under the principle set out by Lord Denning, those individuals who were negligent could still face an action for their personal liability. In addition, if the NHS trust pays out compensation as a result of its negligence, it would be possible for it to seek an indemnity from the negligent person. At present, this indemnity is rarely sought.

Indemnity from the employee at fault

This indemnity arises as a result of an implied term in the contract of employment, that the employee will indemnify the employer as a result of any losses caused by a breach of contract by the employee. In these circumstances, this would be a breach of the term 'to use all reasonable care and skill'.

| Case 4.8 | *Lister* v. *Romford Ice and Cold Storage Co. Ltd* (1957) |

Family trouble[23]

Lister was employed as a lorry driver who worked with his father. He negligently ran down his father while backing the lorry in a yard. The father recovered damages from the employers on the grounds of their vicarious liability for the negligence of their employee. The employers' insurers then brought an action against the son for damages for breach of an implied term in his contract of employment that he would exercise reasonable care and skill in his driving. The son in his defence claimed that he was entitled to the benefit of any insurance that his employer either had or should have taken out. Therefore, they could not claim an indemnity from him.

The House of Lords held by a majority decision that they could claim an indemnity from the employee and they refused to imply a term in the contract of employment that the employer would not seek to claim an indemnity from the negligent employee.

Case 4.9   *Jones v. Manchester Corporation* (1952)

Anaesthetic[24]

The widow of a patient who died as a result of negligent hospital treatment sued for damages. The hospital board claimed an indemnity from Dr Wilkes, an inexperienced physician, who had administered the fatal anaesthetic under the instructions of Dr Sejrup, a house surgeon.

The Court of Appeal rejected this claim for an indemnity partly because the hospital itself was at fault.

Claims brought against the NHS organisations are handled by the NHS Litigation Authority (NHSLA). Trusts have joined in a clinical negligence scheme (CNST) whereby resources are pooled and claims over a certain amount are met from the pool. (This is discussed further in Chapter 6.)

The NMC published a consultation paper[25] in June 2002 on whether a clause should be included in the Code of Professional Conduct requiring registered practitioners to take out public indemnity cover. The background to the paper was that independent midwives who were no longer able to secure cheap indemnity cover through the Royal College of Midwives were not taking out any cover, because of its costs (often over £8000 annually). Following the consultation, the NMC decided[26] that the best approach was not to enforce indemnity insurance but to offer a recommendation to independent practitioners that they should maintain adequate professional indemnity insurance in respect of their practice.

A new clause 9 was therefore included in the amended Code of Professional Conduct:

9 Indemnity insurance

9.1 The NMC recommends that a registered nurse, midwife or specialist community public health nurse, in advising, treating and caring for patients/clients, has professional indemnity insurance. This is in the interests of clients, patients and registrants in the event of claims of professional negligence.

9.2 Some employers accept vicarious liability for the negligent acts and/or omissions of their employees. Such cover does not normally extend to activities undertaken outside the registrant's employment. Independent practice would not normally be covered by vicarious liability, while agency work may not. It is the individual registrant's responsibility to establish their insurance status and take appropriate action.

9.3 In situations where employers do not accept vicarious liability, the NMC recommends that registrants obtain adequate professional indemnity insurance. If unable to secure professional indemnity insurance, a registrant will need to demonstrate that all their clients/patients are fully informed of this fact and the implications this might have in the event of a claim for professional negligence.[27]

For employees who are covered by the employer's vicarious liability, the need for personal public indemnity cover will only become necessary if they work outside the course of employment and therefore the employer does not accept vicarious liability, for example if they undertake Good Samaritan acts. Professional associations often provide cover for such actions by their members. Clearly all those who undertake private practice will require personal public indemnity cover for their private work. There are plans that from 2009 registered health professionals will be required to take out professional indemnity cover.

Pressure from inadequate resources

Unfortunately, harm to the patient can occur due to shortage of staff, inadequate equipment and unsafe premises. This section deals with the liability of those concerned. The NMC Code of Professional Conduct[28] Paragraph 8.3 sets out clearly the practitioner's duty in relation to the environment of care:

> *Where you cannot remedy circumstances in the environment of care that could jeopardise standards of practice, you must report them to a senior person with sufficient authority to manage them and also, in the case of midwifery, to the supervisor of midwives. This must be supported by a written record.*

General principles

> **Practical Dilemma 4.11**   **Resources**
>
> Pauline Cross is working on a busy geriatric ward with only two staff. The patients are severely confused and can do little for themselves. As she is transferring a patient from a wheelchair into bed, the patient falls to the floor and breaks her hip bone. Is Pauline likely to be held responsible in law for the patient's injuries?

It could be argued that this incident took place because there was inadequate staffing. However, there are many factors to be considered. Were they so short-staffed that even when priorities were set it would have been impossible for another member of the staff to help Pauline? Had the staff been trained in manual handling and was a risk assessment carried out? Was such an incident reasonably foreseeable such that additional precautions should have been taken or was it an inevitable accident? If the conclusion is that the accident was avoidable and another nurse should have been assigned to assist Pauline, then this will not automatically relieve Pauline of responsibility, especially if she were in charge of the ward. The question arises whether it would not have been possible to have transferred the patient to bed later when more help would have been available. Alternatively, could the tasks that were occupying the other nurses have been given a lower priority?

Even if all the questions could be answered negatively, i.e. they were so short-staffed that they could not take the necessary foreseeable precautions to ensure the patient was put to bed safely, Pauline may still be responsible. If she was in charge of the ward, had she warned her senior nurse management of the staffing difficulties and suggested remedial action such as discharging patients to other wards or home or suggesting the use of agency nurses if nurses could not be transferred from other wards? Failure to take such action where her management role requires it would mean that Pauline would have to share some measure of responsibility for the occurrence (see the section on the nurse as manager on page 65).

Employer's responsibility

If a patient is harmed because of an accident that would not have occurred had reasonable resources been available, then the patient would have a valid action to recover compensation in the civil courts. It is no defence to say to a patient, 'We are sorry we amputated the wrong leg, but Wednesday is our busiest day and we had a lot of staff off with influenza.' A patient is entitled to the approved standard of care. Even in an emergency situation, staff would be expected to take additional precautions to prevent further harm arising on the basis of a clear order of priorities. In such circumstances, the patient would be able to sue the NHS trust for its vicarious liability for the negligence of the staff. However, it is probable, too, that an action of direct liability also might succeed against the trust because harm was caused to the patient as a result of inadequate resources. If there has been a failure to provide a reasonable standard according to the Bolam Test, it does not matter what the cause was: staffing shortages, lack of equipment, or inexperience, there will either be direct liability of the organisation or vicarious liability for the negligence of its staff.[29] The claimant must, of course, be able to show that there is a causal link between the failure to maintain the reasonable standard of care and the harm which has occurred.[30]

Case 4.10   *McCormack v. Redpath Brown* (1961)

Inadequate resources (1)[31]

A casualty officer, through pressure of work, made only a brief examination and treated a major head injury on the assumption that it was a minor one.

Both he and the health authority were held liable. The judge held that pressure of work was no defence to the patient's claim.

Case 4.11   *Deacon v. McVicar and Another* (1984)

Inadequate resources (2)[32]

Several allegations were made by a patient that she was not treated with proper professional care and skill during the delivery of her first child. A Shirodkar suture had been fitted at an earlier stage because of an incompetent cervix. It was important that the suture should be removed promptly once labour had commenced, otherwise there was a danger that the cervix could be damaged. The patient claimed that the staff had failed to act speedily and as a consequence her cervix was damaged. The defendants claimed that the ward was very busy that night and the patient received appropriate care.

At the defendants' request, the judge directed that the notes of the other patients should be made available to show what was going on in the labour ward that evening. He did so with reluctance because he did not wish a breach of the duty of confidentiality owed to the patients and the defendants had not pleaded any special emergency that prevented speedier attention to the patient. These patients were referred to by code names. Their notes were exhaustively examined in the course of the evidence. 'In summary they showed that the doctors were busy and that the patient bringing the action was not the only patient who presented problems. But they did not show there was anything to prevent the doctors performing a vaginal examination or removing the suture sooner than they did.'

One of the criticisms was that the doctors had failed to give the patient sufficient priority. The doctor in his defence said that on a busy labour ward the doctors do not sit down and work out a list of priorities. The judge, however, had to decide if the patient had been kept waiting too long. He said: 'I appreciate that one must not be too critical of what goes on in a busy ward but it is difficult to understand why the patient did not have a vaginal examination until two hours after admission. Other ladies were admitted at about the same time as she was and whose cases were of no greater urgency had their examinations far sooner.'

Commenting on the statement of one of the experts for the defence who had said, 'I think the time scale is within the pattern of what occurs in a busy ward', the judge said:

> That may well be, but it does not resolve the question whether this particular patient was given proper care . . . I do not pinpoint any particular moment when a particular doctor did something wrong. It was rather a case where there was a lack of sufficient sense of urgency on all sides. In these circumstances I hold that the second defendants (Leicester Health Authority) did not treat the patient with proper professional care and skill.

The patient was awarded £1,500.

Several important points emerge from this case:

1 The assessment of priorities can be carried out negligently or not at all and can itself form the basis of a claim for compensation.
2 To ascertain the workload and other demands, it is possible with the approval of the judge for the records of other patients to be made available. It is essential that comprehensive records are always kept.

Coping under pressure

One question often asked by nursing staff in relation to shortage of resources is, 'What happens if we are dangerously short of staff and yet we cope? What is the situation then?' This is a frequent situation. Yet if no person suffers harm as a result of the inadequate levels, then there can be no action for negligence, since harm must be established. However, it would be part of the duties of the nurse, both in her professional duties and as a manager, to ensure that senior levels are notified of any dangers or hazards so that harm does not eventually occur. An inadequate number of trained staff in proportion to the demands of patients could lead to inexperienced people administering drugs, using specialised equipment or assisting doctors in complex treatments and patients could therefore suffer overdoses or other forms of harm. In extreme situations, where it is impossible to obtain sufficient numbers of staff to run a service safely or to run a service with the correct skill mix, then the provision of that service may have to be transferred to other providers.

Legal requirements on staffing

Another question that is raised is: 'What are the legal staffing levels or of what legal significance is a particular staffing ratio that has been recommended by different researchers?' Minimum staffing levels or ratios are unlikely to be laid down by Act of Parliament or by the courts. Under the principles relating to liability in negligence, sufficient resources must be provided to ensure that the patients being cared for are provided with the approved accepted standard of care (i.e. the Bolam Test; see page 44). All circumstances must be taken into account in determining whether this has been provided in respect of a given patient who has suffered harm. Obviously, evidence could be given of the extent to which the staffing levels had fallen below the levels considered by experts in the field to be the minimum consistent with good practice, but this is evidence, not law.

Failures by management

What does the nurse do if she has drawn the attention of management to a situation that she considers dangerous and nothing is done about it? Whatever the situation, whether it is concerned with inadequate resources or incompetent staff, the nurse should not give up if she feels her concern about a dangerous situation is being ignored. She has a duty to ensure that the patients are cared for appropriately. She should therefore put her concerns in writing with evidence of hazards that have occurred. Her report would need to be a detailed account that is meaningful to management of the levels of staffing and the needs of the patients. If nothing is done, she should then be prepared to refer the matter to a higher level of management. Eventually, if she is still concerned that the dangers are being ignored, she should take the matter to her NHS trust or the NMC and utilise the procedure set up under the Public Interest Disclosure Act 1998. This is preferable to bringing the local or national press into a field that should be sorted out internally.

Public Interest Disclosure Act 1998 and whistleblowing

Nurses are required under the Code of Professional Conduct (see Paragraph 8.3, quoted above) to bring hazards and dangers to the attention of management. Practitioners whose fitness to practise is doubted must also be reported to the NMC.[33] Many nurses have feared victimisation (see report on Rodney Ledward, Chapter 5, page 107). To allay such fears and prevent victimisation, the NHS Management Executive issued Guidelines for Staff on Relations with the Public and the Media (1993). This emphasised that under no circumstances are employees who express their views about health service issues in accordance with this guidance to be penalised in any way for doing so (Paragraph 6). Each NHS employer has a duty to establish a procedure for employees to raise concerns. Statutory provision was made in the Public Interest Disclosure Act 1998 to ensure that a procedure is set up to ensure that staff who raise justifiable concerns are protected from victimisation. Justifiable concerns are shown in Box 4.3. (Guidance has been issued by the Department of Health (HSC (99)198 followed by a policy pack[34] and by the RCN.[35]) The charity Public Concern at Work provides a helpline and information service for the promotion and protection of responsible whistleblowing.[36] A claim by an employee of the North Glamorgan NHS trust that he had been unfairly dismissed because he had made allegations of fraud against other employees was allowed to proceed on the grounds that in a fact-sensitive situation such as a whistleblowing claim a full hearing was necessary to resolve the dispute.[37]

The protected disclosures in Box 4.3 are extensive and would cover most of the situations in which a registered practitioner would have a professional duty to inform an appropriate person or authority under the Code of Professional Conduct.

> **Box 4.3** **Protected disclosures under the Public Interest Disclosure Act 1998**
>
> 1 That a criminal offence has been, is being or is likely to be committed.
> 2 That a person has failed, is failing or is likely to fail to comply with any legal obligation to which he is subject.
> 3 That a miscarriage of justice has occurred, is occurring or is likely to occur.
> 4 That the health or safety of any individual has been, is being or is likely to be endangered.
> 5 That the environment has been, is being or is likely to be damaged.
> 6 That information tending to show any matter falling within any of the above paragraphs has been, is being or is likely to be deliberately concealed.

Under the Act, the disclosure is only protected if certain conditions are satisfied. The employee must have made the disclosure in good faith to his employer; or where the employee reasonably believes that a person other than the employer is to blame, then the disclosure can be made to that other person. Disclosure is also protected if it is made in the course of obtaining legal advice; or if the employer is a body any of whose members are appointed by a minister of the Crown, then the disclosure can be made to a minister of the Crown. This would cover disclosures by employees working within the NHS. Disclosures to prescribed persons are protected if made in good faith to a person prescribed by the Secretary of State and the worker reasonably believes that the relevant failure is within the concern of that person and the information is substantially true. (More persons and organisations (including the General Social Care Council, the Health and Safety Executive, local authorities responsible for enforcing health and safety legislation and the Information Commissioner) were added to the list of prescribed persons by amending regulations in 2003.[38]) Other disclosures are protected if the conditions set out in Box 4.4 are satisfied.

> **Box 4.4** **Conditions for other protected disclosures**
>
> 1 The employee makes the disclosure in good faith.
> 2 He reasonably believes that the information disclosed, and any allegations contained in it, are substantially true.
> 3 He does not make the disclosure for personal gain.
> 4 Any of the conditions in subsection 2 is met (see below).
> 5 In all the circumstances of the case, it is reasonable for him to make the disclosure.

The subsection 2 conditions referred to in Box 4.4 include the reasonable belief that the employee would be subjected to detriment by his employer if he makes the disclosure. Factors determining the reasonableness of the disclosure include the identity of the person to whom it is made; the seriousness of the failure; whether it is continuing or likely to occur in future; whether the disclosure is made in breach of a duty of confidentiality; previous disclosures to the employer or to another person prescribed by the Secretary of State; and compliance with any procedure specified for making disclosures.

Disclosures relating to exceptionally serious failures

Special provisions apply to a disclosure of an exceptionally serious failure. Such a disclosure is protected if the employee makes the disclosure in good faith, reasonably believing the allegations to be true, not making the disclosure for personal gain and in all the circumstances it is reasonable to make the disclosure and to that particular person.

Gagging of an employee

The Act states that any provision in an agreement is void in so far as it purports to preclude an employee from making a protected disclosure. Thus, if a trust attempts to introduce a term into a contract of employment that prevents an employee making a disclosure that comes under the protection of the Act, that term is void.

Before the Public Interest Disclosure Act, a student nurse reported a Rampton Hospital nurse for ill treating and assaulting patients.[39] The abuser was subsequently convicted in the criminal courts and struck off the UKCC Register. The student nurse, however, suffered considerable abuse after blowing the whistle. Such victimisation should now lead to compensation for the whistleblower. In one of the first cases to be reported after the coming into force of the Act, an accountant who was dismissed after blowing the whistle on his managing director's expense claims was awarded compensation of £293,441 by an employment tribunal. The tribunal held that he was victimised for raising genuine concerns.[40] A report by the charity Public Concern at Work in April 2003 claimed that 1,200 claims had been made in the first three years after the Public Interest Disclosure Act came into force and more than £10 million is being awarded in compensation to whistleblowers every year. The following case is reported by the charity Public Concern at Work.

Case 4.12   *Kay v. Northumberland Healthcare NHS Trust (2001)*

A protected disclosure bid[41]

Kay managed a ward for the elderly. Kay internally raised concerns about bed shortage but was told there were no resources. The problem worsened and some elderly patients were moved to a gynaecological ward. Kay wrote a satirical open letter to the Prime Minister for his local paper. With the trust's agreement, Kay was photographed for the local press. When the letter was published, the trust gave a final written warning for totally unprofessional and unacceptable conduct. Kay won his case as the disclosure was protected because (a) disclosure under 43G of the 1998 Act was balanced with Article 10 and freedom of expression in the European Convention on Human Rights, (b) Kay did not know of the trust's whistleblowing policy, (c) there was no reasonable expectation of action following earlier concerns, and (d) it was a serious public concern.

Kennedy Report

The Kennedy Report[42] following the inquiry into children's heart surgery at Bristol Royal Infirmary recommended that there should be openness and honesty in the NHS and a partnership between patients and professionals. It covered the topics shown in Box 4.5.

> **Box 4.5**   **Subjects covered by recommendations of the Bristol Inquiry**
>
> 1 Respect and honesty.
> 2 A health service which is well led.
> 3 Competent healthcare professionals.
> 4 The safety of care.
> 5 Care of an appropriate standard.
> 6 Public involvement through empowerment.
> 7 Care of children.
> 8 Healthcare services and the treatment for children with congenital health disease.

The Bristol Inquiry recognised the principles set out in Box 4.6.

> **Box 4.6**   **Principles recognised by the Bristol Inquiry**
>
> + The patient must be at the centre of everything that the NHS does.
> + The commitment and dedication of staff in the NHS must be valued and acknowledged; those caring for patients must themselves be supported and cared for.
> + There must be openness and transparency in everything the NHS does.
> + The impact of the way in which services are organised on the quality of care that patients receive must be recognised: the quality of care depends on systems and on facilities, as well as on individual healthcare professionals.
> + All those involved in healthcare . . . must recognise and acknowledge the contribution of the others in the service of patients.
> + The safety of patients must be the foundation of the NHS's commitment to the quality of its services.
> + Sentinel events, that is, errors, other adverse events and near misses, that occur during the care of patients, must be seen as opportunities to learn, not just as reasons to blame.
> + There must be clear and understood systems of responsibility and accountability: a culture of blame is no substitute for such systems.
> + The quality of healthcare must be guided by agreed standards, compliance with which is regularly monitored.
> + The role of central government in relation to the NHS should be:
>   - to act as its HQ in terms of management
>   - to create independent mechanisms for regulating the quality of healthcare and the competence of healthcare professionals.
> + The various independent bodies must themselves be coordinated so as to avoid the fragmentation of responsibility that arose in the past.

In considering the topic of 'respect and honesty', the Report recommended that:

Patients in their journey through the healthcare system are entitled to be treated with respect and honesty and to be involved, wherever possible, in decisions about their care.

To achieve this aim the Report makes recommendations on achieving a partnership between healthcare professionals and the patient, whereby the patient and the professional meet as equals with different expertise. Patients must be kept informed about their treatment and care. Communications must be improved, including the use of tape-recording facilities to enable patients, should they so wish, to make a tape-recording of a discussion with a healthcare professional when a diagnosis, course of treatment or prognosis is being discussed. Support services should be provided for patients including counselling and a professional bereavement service. Voluntary organisations that provide care and support for patients should, where they meet the appropriate standards, receive state funding to contribute their services. Consent to treatment should be seen as a process and not simply the signing of a form. Feedback from patients should be encouraged. There should be a duty of candour, to tell a patient if adverse events have occurred, and patients should receive an acknowledgement, an explanation and an apology. Complaints should be dealt with swiftly and thoroughly, keeping the patient informed, and the present system of compensation should be reviewed.

The Department of Health announced its response to the Report in 2002 and both the full response and an executive summary are available from the Department of Health website.[43] Many of these recommendations are being implemented across the NHS and the consultation paper on a new system of compensation, which includes a duty of candour, is considered in Chapter 6. The discussion in this section only covers a small part of the significant recommendations made in the Bristol Report and it is recommended that practitioners should obtain a copy from the website[44] and discuss the implementation of the recommendations with colleagues.

Conclusions

This chapter has covered a wide range of topics relating to the role of the nurse in communicating, delegating, managing and dealing with inadequate resources. It has also considered the direct and vicarious liability of the employer. Nurses and employers, however, work within the wider scope of the NHS and it is the structure and management of the NHS to which we now turn.

Reflection questions

1 There can be liability for failure to communicate. Apply this principle to your particular post and consider how and to what extent communication with the patient could be improved.

2 Consider any work you undertake as a member of a team and assess the extent to which it is clear where the boundaries of individual responsibility lie.

3 There are times when it is essential that a nurse obeys the orders of a doctor without question and others when it is imperative that she check that the instructions are appropriate. What distinguishing features would decide whether an order falls in the first category or in the second?

4 What is the difference between direct and vicarious liability?

5 In what way do you think that the liability of the NHS trust for the safety of the volunteer differs from its liability for the safety of staff (see, in addition, Chapter 12)?

6 An employee can be liable for the negligent actions of another person if the employee should not have delegated a task to him or, having correctly delegated it, has failed to provide the appropriate level of supervision. Apply this principle to the role of the nurse manager in relation to junior registered staff, learners, volunteers and untrained assistants.

Further exercises

1 Obtain a copy of your NHS trust's policy on the use of volunteers and study in particular those parts that relate to liability for the negligence of volunteers.

2 Obtain a copy of your employer's policy on whistleblowing and familiarise yourself with its contents. Do you understand how the procedure would work in practice?

3 Obtain a copy of the Bristol Inquiry Report and consider the extent to which your department could implement any of its recommendations that are not yet in place.

References

1 *Coles* v. *Reading HMC* (1963) 107 SJ 115
2 *Harrison* v. *Surrey County Council and Others*, The Times Law Report, 27 January 1994
3 *Nettleship* v. *Weston* [1971] 3 All ER 581
4 *Wilsher* v. *Essex Area Health Authority* [1986] 3 All ER 801 CA; [1988] 1 All ER 871 HL
5 *Dwyer* v. *Roderick*, 20 June 1984 QBD
6 Nursing and Midwifery Council, Code of Professional Conduct: standards for conduct, performance and ethics, NMC, 2004
7 *Gold* v. *Essex County Council* [1942] 2 All ER 237
8 Nursing and Midwifery Council, New advice for delegation to non-regulated healthcare staff, NMC, 2007
9 Royal College of Nursing, Guidance on Good Management Practice, Order No. 001001, RCN, March 1999
10 *Rose* v. *Plenty* [1976] 1 All ER 97
11 *Century Insurance Co. Ltd* v. *Northern Ireland Road Transport Board* [1942] 1 All ER 491
12 *Poland* v. *Parr and Sons* CA [1926] All ER 177
13 *Lloyd* v. *Grace Smith & Co.* [1912] AC 716; *Morris* v. *C.W. Martin & Sons Ltd* [1965] 2 All ER 725
14 *Century Insurance Co. Ltd* v. *Northern Ireland Road Transport Board* [1942] 1 All ER 491
15 *Lister & Others* v. *Hesley Hall Ltd* [2001] UKHL 22; [2002] 1 AC 215; The Times Law Report, 10 May 2001; [2001] 2 WLR 1311
16 *Hilton* v. *Thomas Burton (Rhodes) Ltd* [1961] 1 WLR 705
17 *Watkins* v. *Birmingham City Council*, The Times, 1 August 1975
18 *Express and Echo Publications Ltd* v. *Tanton*, The Times, 7 April 1999
19 Department of Health, Opportunities for Volunteering Scheme: general notes of guidance, DH, 2004; www.dh.gov.uk/volunteering
20 *Cassidy* v. *Ministry of Health* [1939] 2 KB 14
21 *Wilsher* v. *Essex Area Health Authority* [1986] 3 All ER 801 CA
22 *A.* v. *Ministry of Defence* [2004] EWCA 641
23 *Lister* v. *Romford Ice and Cold Storage Co. Ltd* [1957] 1 All ER 125 HL
24 *Jones* v. *Manchester Corporation* [1952] 2 All ER 125 CA
25 www.nmc-uk.org/cms/content/consultation/indemnity
26 www.nmc-uk.org/nmc/main/consultation/indemnity_insurance
27 Nursing and Midwifery Council, Code of Professional Conduct: standards for conduct, performance and ethics, NMC, 2004
28 Ibid.
29 *Ball* v. *Wirral Health Authority* [2003] WLR 117
30 *Aisha Qureshi* v. *Royal Brompton and Harefield NHS Trust* [2006] EWHC 298 QB

31 *McCormack* v. *Redpath Brown, The Times*, 24 March 1961

32 *Deacon* v. *McVicar and Another*, 7 January 1984, QBD

33 UKCC, Reporting Unfitness to Practise – Information for Employers and Managers, UKCC, August 1996

34 Department of Health, Whistleblowing, in the NHS policy pack, July 2003

35 Royal College of Nursing, Blowing the Whistle, Order No. 001 510, RCN, May 2001

36 www.pcaw.co.uk/policy_pub/

37 *Ezsias* v. *North Glamorgan NHS Trust* [2007] EWCA Civ 330

38 Public Interest Disclosure (Prescribed Persons) (Amendment) Order SI 2003 No. 1993

39 News item, *Nursing Times*, 8 June 2000, 96(23), p. 4

40 Jenny Booth, Man who shopped boss wins £290,000, *The Times*, 11 July 2000

41 *Kay* v. *Northumberland Healthcare NHS Trust* 2001, available on the Public Concern at Work website: www.pcaw.co.uk/policy_pub

42 Bristol Royal Infirmary Inquiry (Kennedy Report), Learning from Bristol: the report of the public inquiry into children's heart surgery at the Bristol Royal Infirmary 1984–1995 (chaired by Professor Ian Kennedy), Command Paper Cm 5207, July 2001; http://www.bristol-inquiry.org.uk/

43 Department of Health's Response to the Report of the Public Inquiry into children's heart surgery at the Bristol Royal Infirmary 1984–1995, DH, January 2002, Cm 5363; www.dh.gov.uk/bristolinquiryresponse/bristolresponseexecsum.htm

44 http://www.bristol-inquiry.org.uk/

Chapter 5
Statutory functions and management of the NHS

Introduction

This chapter considers the statutory background to the NHS and the functions of the Secretary of State. It also looks at changes in the NHS following the Health Act 1999, the NHS Reform and Health Care Professions Act 2002 and the Health and Social Care (Community Health and Standards) Act 2003, including the duty of quality, the Healthcare Commission and the National Institute for Health and Clinical Excellence. (Many of the earlier legislative provisions have been consolidated in the National Health Service Act 2006.) Issues of resource management and the Public Interest Disclosure Act 1998 are considered in relation to whistle-blowing in Chapter 4. The role of NHS Professionals is considered in Chapter 10, page 251.

National Health Service

The National Health Service (NHS) was set up on 5 July 1948 as a result of the National Health Service Act 1946. It was based on the principle that services should be provided free at the point of delivery unless there was clear statutory authorisation for any charges. Charges for prescriptions were the first to be introduced. The duty to provide services was placed on the Secretary of State who delegated these functions to regional hospital boards, hospital management committees and other statutory organisations. Family practitioner services were administered by the executive councils, later superseded by the family practitioner committees. A major reorganisation of healthcare provision took place in 1973 and the statutory duties were re-enacted in the National Health Service Act 1977. Health Service legislation has since been consolidated in the National Health Service Act 2006 with the NHS Consequential Amendments Act 2006 and separate legislation for Wales. The duties placed on the Secretary of State are shown in the following Statute.

Statute | **Duties of the Secretary of State under the National Health Service Act 2006**

Secretary of State's duty as to health service

Section 1(1) The Secretary of State must continue the promotion in England of a comprehensive health service designed to secure improvement:

    a. In the physical and mental health of the people in England; and
    b. In the prevention, diagnosis and treatment of illness.

1(2) The Secretary of State must for that purpose provide or secure the provision of services in accordance with this Act.

1(3) The services so provided shall be free of charge except in so far as the making and recovery of charges is expressly provided for by or under any enactment, whenever passed.

Secretary of State's general power as to services

2(1) The Secretary of State may:

    a. provide such services as he considers appropriate for the purpose of discharging any duty imposed on him by this Act; and

---

Statute continued

b. do any other thing which is calculated to facilitate, or is conducive or incidental to, the discharge of such a duty.

2(2) Subsection (1) does not affect:

a. the Secretary of State's powers apart from this section,

b. Chapter 1 of Part 7 [of this Act] (pharmaceutical services).

Services generally

3(1) The Secretary of State must provide throughout England, to such extent as he considers necessary to meet all reasonable requirements –

a. Hospital accommodation;

b. Other accommodation for the purpose of any service provided under this Act;

c. Medical, dental, nursing and ambulance services;

d. Such other facilities for the care of pregnant women, women who are breast feeding and young children as he considers are appropriate as part of the health service;

e. Such other services or facilities for the prevention of illness, the care of persons suffering from illness and the after-care of persons who have suffered from illness as he considers are appropriate as part of the health service;

f. Such other services as are required for the diagnosis and treatment of illness.

3(2) For the purposes of the duty in subsection (1) services provided under

a. section 83(2) (primary medical services), section 99(2) (primary dental services) or section 115(4) (primary ophthalmic services) or

b. a general medical services contract, a general dental services contract or a general ophthalmic services contract

must be regarded as provided by the Secretary of State.

3(3) This section does not affect Chapter 1 of Part 7 (pharmaceutical services)

Other services which the Secretary of State has a duty to provide are set out in Schedule 1 of the NHS Act 2006 and include the medical inspection of pupils, contraceptive services, provision of vehicles for disabled persons, microbiological services and research activities.

Part 4 of the 2006 NHS Act covers primary medical services; Part 5 the provision of dental services; Part 6 ophthalmic services and Part 7 pharmaceutical services.

Enforcement of statutory duties

There have been several cases where patients who have waited a considerable time for operations or for other treatments have brought legal action to enforce the provision for them of health services. By and large, the courts have taken the view that it is not for the court to become involved in issues relating to resource allocation, unless there are clear failures in public duty. (See Case 5.1.) However, a recent decision of the High Court held that the NHS should pay for a patient to have treatment abroad, if the patient had waited a significantly long time for NHS treatment.[1]

Where a patient is kept waiting for treatment, there is an interesting distinction in the following three situations.

1 Where the treatment has commenced, it must be carried out according to the accepted approved standard. If a negligent act occurs that causes harm to the patient, then this is actionable by the patient.

2 Where treatment has not commenced and the patient has to wait on a waiting list, then even though the patient's condition might deteriorate this is not actionable provided the health service body has carried out its provision of health services rationally. It may, of course, be the subject of a complaint since the provider has failed to comply with the standards set by the Department of Health, but these standards do not have any legal effect unless they are already incorporated in an Act of Parliament or a decided case or unless they infringe the European Convention on Human Rights.

3 As a result of the recent case, where it is held that the patient has waited an unreasonable length of time for treatment, the NHS may be obliged to pay for treatment provided abroad.

Case 5.1   R v. Secretary of State for Health (1979)

Inadequate resources[2]

Orthopaedic patients at a hospital in Birmingham, who had waited for treatment for periods longer than was medically advisable, brought an action against the Secretary of State, the regional health authority and the area health authority. They were seeking a declaration that the defendants were in breach of their duty under Section 1 of the National Health Service Act 1977 to continue to promote a comprehensive health service designed to secure improvement in health and the prevention of illness and under Section 3 to provide accommodation, facilities and services for those purposes.

The judge held that it was not the function of the court to direct Parliament as to what funds to make available to the health service and how to allocate them. The Secretary of State's duty under Section 3 to provide services 'to such extent as he considers necessary', gave him discretion as to the disposition of financial resources. The court could interfere only if the Secretary of State acted so as to frustrate the policy of the Act or as no reasonable minister could have acted. No such breach had been shown in the present case. The court could not grant mandamus (see glossary) or a declaration against area or regional authorities since specific remedies against them were available by Section 85 and Part V of the 1977 Act. Nor, if a breach were proved, did the Act admit of relief by way of damages. The application was therefore dismissed.

The reasoning behind the above ruling was confirmed in the following case.

Case 5.2   In re Walker Application (1987)

Postponed operation[3]

Mrs Walker's baby son required a heart operation and was on the waiting list. A date was fixed for the operation to be performed but was postponed by the Birmingham Health Authority. She applied to the court for a judicial review of the decision of the health authority. The High Court judge refused her application. She appealed to the Court of Appeal which upheld the earlier decision.

The health authority had accepted that the regional district health authorities could be subject to judicial review where there was reason to believe that they might be in breach of their public duties. There would always be individuals who believed that treatment was not provided quickly enough, but the financial resources were finite and always would be. The court held that it was not for the court to substitute its own judgment for that of those responsible for the allocation of resources. It would interfere only if there had been a failure to allocate funds in a way that was unreasonable or where there had been breaches of public duties. Mrs Walker's application was refused.

Case 5.3   *R* v. *Cambridge HA* (1995)

Bone marrow transplant postponed operation[4]

A 10-year-old girl was suffering from acute myeloid leukaemia and required a further session of chemotherapy and a second bone marrow transplant to survive. It was estimated that the chance of success was between 10 per cent and 20 per cent. Costs of the drug and transplant were estimated as £15,000 and £60,000 respectively. The health authority refused to resource this and the father challenged its decision. The High Court upheld his application for judicial review. The health authority appealed to the Court of Appeal and the case was heard that same day. The Court of Appeal held that the four criticisms made by the trial judge of the health authority's decision were not acceptable. The court should confine itself to the lawfulness of the decision. It held that it was not in the best interests of the child to undergo further treatment and that resources had to be taken into account.

While the general principle that the courts will not intervene in resourcing issues of the NHS appears to continue to be accepted by the courts, there have been several cases where health authorities have been held liable for failure to provide services and in one case it was ruled that in certain circumstances the NHS should pay for treatment overseas.

In one case,[5] the health authority decided that it would not enable Beta Interferon to be prescribed for patients in its catchment area, since it was not yet proved to be clinically effective for the treatment of multiple sclerosis. A sufferer from multiple sclerosis challenged this refusal of the health authority and succeeded on the grounds that the health authority had failed to follow the guidance issued by the Department of Health.[6] A declaration was granted that the policy adopted by the health authority was unlawful and an order of mandamus was made requiring the defendants to formulate and implement a policy that took full and proper account of national policy as stated in the circular. In a later case the Court of Appeal held that the policy of a primary care trust on the availability of Herceptin for breast cancer was irrational since there were no clinical or personal considerations which led to one patient being preferred over another. It asked the PCT to formulate a lawful policy upon which to base decisions in particular cases, including that of Mrs Rogers, in the future.[7] On 18 July 2007 the High Court ruled that, whilst the primary care trust policy on Avastin was entirely rational and sensible, the PCT had made a flawed and irrational decision when it refused to fund the drug Avastin for cancer treatment for a specific patient, Ms Otley.[8] As a consequence the PCT agreed to fund five cycles of treatment for her, the treatment being reviewed after those treatments and a CT scan. The guidance issued by NICE on drugs for Alzheimer's were challenged in a case in 2007[9] (see below).

Another case concerned three transsexuals who wished to undergo gender reassignment.[10] The Health Authority refused to fund such treatment on the grounds that it had been assigned a low priority in its lists of procedures considered to be clinically ineffective in terms of health gain. Under this policy, gender reassignment surgery was listed among others as a procedure for which no treatment, apart from that provided by the authority's general psychiatric and psychology services, would be commissioned, save in the event of overriding clinical need or exceptional circumstances. The transsexuals sought judicial review of the health authority's refusal and the judge granted an order quashing the authority's decision and the policy on which it was based. The health authority then took the case to the Court of Appeal, but lost its appeal. The Court of Appeal held that:

1 While the precise allocation and weighting of priorities is a matter for the judgement of the authority and not for the court, it is vital for an authority:
   (a) to accurately assess the nature and seriousness of each type of illness
   (b) to determine the effectiveness of various forms of treatment for it and
   (c) to give proper effect to that assessment and that determination in the formulation and individual application of its policy.

2 The authority's policy was flawed in two respects:
   (a) it did not treat transsexualism as an illness, but as an attitude of mind which did not warrant medical treatment
   (b) the ostensible provision that it made for exceptions in individual cases and its manner of considering them amounted to the operation of a 'blanket policy' against funding treatment for the condition because it did not believe in such treatment.

3 The authority were not genuinely applying the policy to the individual exceptions.

4 Article 3 and Article 8 of the European Convention on Human Rights (see Chapter 1) did not give a right to free healthcare and did not apply to this situation, where the challenge is to a health authority's allocation of finite funds. Neither were the patients victims of discrimination on the grounds of sex.

In another case[11] a woman was waiting for a hip replacement operation and went abroad for treatment after being told that she would have to wait a year for the operation on the NHS. She asked her local hospital in Bedford to pay for the trip under the E112 certificate scheme, but Bedford Primary Care Trust refused on the grounds that the wait was within the government's waiting times guidelines. She brought an action for judicial review of the PCT's refusal, claiming that its decision was unlawful and infringed her rights under Articles 3 and 8 of the European Convention on Human Rights.

The judge held, based on Article 49 of the EC Treaty[12] (which prohibited restrictions on freedom to provide services within the Community), that prior authorisation for treatment by an NHS patient in another member state of the European Union at the expense of the NHS could be refused on the ground of lack of medical necessity only if the same or equally effective treatment could be obtained without undue delay at an NHS establishment. He also held that in assessing what amounted to undue delay, regard had to be had to all the circumstances of the specific case, including the patient's medical condition and, where appropriate, the degree of pain and the nature and extent of the patient's disability. Consideration of NHS waiting times and waiting lists were relevant, when having regard to all the circumstances. On the facts of the case, however, the claimant did not recover the money, since the local hospital had offered her an earlier operation. The Court of Appeal referred the case to the European Court of Justice (EJC) for a preliminary ruling on the application of Article 49 and Article 22 of Regulation 1408/71. The EJC held that under Article 22(1) the organisation was required to establish that the waiting list did not exceed an acceptable period; Article 49 did not preclude reimbursement of the cost of hospital treatment to be provided in another member state. A refusal to grant prior authorisation could not be based purely on the existence of waiting lists; the claimant was entitled to be reimbursed the cost of the healthcare received under Article 22(1)(c) and the cost of ancillary costs under Article 49.[13] A draft Directive of the European Union was published on 19 December 2007 which stated that if the appropriate care for the patient's condition cannot be provided in their own country without undue delay, then they will be authorised to go abroad, and any additional costs of treatment will be covered by public funds. The government has stated its intention to oppose the directive.[14]

It is inevitable that there will always be a gap between the demands that are made for healthcare and the resources to meet those demands. Decisions will therefore have to be made on priorities and who is refused treatment. New developments in technology, such as the identification of the human genome and the treatment possibilities for identified genetic diseases, are just one example of increasing pressures. The Human Rights Act 1998 has seldom been successfully relied upon in disputes over access to services.

Distinction between statutory duties and guidance from the Department of Health

In fulfilling its statutory duties, the government issues circulars providing guidance to NHS organisations on how they should function. These are available from the DH website.[15]

While in general the advice in these circulars is not the law as such, there is a clear responsibility on organisations to follow the recommendations. The failure by a health authority to follow DH guidelines on the prescribing of Beta Interferon led to a successful action being brought by a patient suffering from multiple sclerosis[16] (see above). In a contrasting case,[17] a court held that government circular 1998/158, which limited the powers of GPs to prescribe Viagra, was unlawful in that by preventing the issue of a prescription, where the GP considered it to be justified, the clinical judgement of the GP was usurped. As a consequence regulations were then issued by the Secretary of State which placed restrictions on the prescription of Viagra on the grounds of cost to the NHS. Pfizer's challenge to the legality of these regulations on the basis of an EC Directive (89/105) failed.

Strategic health authorities

Strategic health authorities are established by the Secretary of State under the provisions of the NHS Reform and Health Care Professions Act 2002 and were created by the amalgamation of several smaller health authorities. They are responsible for contracting for the provision of health services in a given area and ensuring that the health needs within their catchment area are met (Sections 13-17 and Schedule 2 of the NHS Act 2006). In accordance with the NHS Plan they must set up with the Department of Health an Annual Delivery Agreement which sets targets for them to achieve. Their main functions are to develop plans for improving health services in their area, ensure that local health services are of a high quality and are performing well, increase the capacity of the local health services to provide more services and take steps to ensure that national priorities are integrated into local health service plans.

Each Strategic Health Authority is required to make arrangements to ensure that it receives advice from persons with professional expertise relating to the physical or mental health of individuals to enable it to exercise its functions effectively (Section 17 of NHS Act

2006). Members of the strategic health authority are required to comply with a Code of Accountability and a Code of Conduct, drawn up by the Department of Health.

NHS trusts

NHS trusts were established following the NHS and Community Care Act 1990. This Act saw the introduction of the internal market in the NHS. NHS trusts were established that provided services under a non-legally enforceable contract or agreement with the health authorities. In addition, group fundholding practices of general practitioners were established which were allocated the funds to purchase services for the patients on their lists from the providers. Competition was expected to take place between providers of health services to obtain the agreements for the purchase of their services. However, this organisation was radically changed following the White Paper on the NHS and the Health Act 1999 (see below). Legislation relating to NHS trusts has now been consolidated in the NHS Act 2006 Sections 25 to 27 and under Schedules 4 and 5. The NHS trust duty is to provide goods and services for the purposes of the health service and each trust is required to exercise its functions effectively, efficiently and economically (Section 26 NHS Act 2006).

Foundation trusts

After considerable controversy, the Health and Social Care (Community Health and Standards) Act was passed in 2003 and foundation hospital trusts were set up in April 2004. The statutory provisions have now been consolidated in the National Health Service Act 2006 Sections 30–65 and Schedules 7, 8, 9 and 10. The Act defines an NHS foundation trust as 'a public benefit corporation which is authorised to provide goods and services for the purposes of the health service in England'. A body corporate known as the Independent Regulator of NHS Foundation Trusts (called Monitor)[18] is set up under Section 31 of the 2006 Act with additional provisions relating to membership, tenure of office, general and specific powers, finance and reports set out in Schedule 8. Monitor has a duty to exercise its functions in a manner consistent with the performance by the Secretary of State of the duties under Sections 1, 3 and 258 of the NHS Act 2006 (duty as to health service and services generally and as to university clinical teaching and research). NHS trusts can apply to Monitor for authorisation to become an NHS foundation trust. The application must describe the goods and services it intends to provide together with a copy of the proposed constitution of the trust. Monitor must maintain a register of NHS foundation trusts together with, for each, a copy of its constitution, latest annual report and accounts and any notice relating to its being a failing NHS foundation trust. Once an NHS foundation trust is established, it ceases to be regarded as the servant or agent of the Crown or as enjoying any status, immunity or privilege of the Crown.

The main differences between an NHS foundation trust and an NHS trust are as follows:

An NHS foundation trust is an independent public benefit corporation, not under the direct control of the Secretary of State.

An NHS foundation trust comes under the control of an independent regulator which gives an authorisation for the establishment of the NHS foundation trust and must secure that the principle purpose of the trust is the provision of goods and services for the purposes of the health service in England (these include education and training, accommodation and other facilities and carrying out research). An authorisation can restrict the provision of private healthcare by the NHS foundation trust.

Ownership and accountability for the NHS foundation trust is in the hands of the local community rather than the Secretary of State.

NHS foundation trusts are able to raise capital (within overall limits and according to a prudential borrowing code (PBC) – Section 41) and retain any operating surplus. (The PBC is to be drawn up by the regulator and placed before Parliament.[19])

NHS foundation trusts are expected to comply with national standards and targets, but are not subject to directions from the Secretary of State or performance management by strategic health authorities and the Department of Health. (They are, however, subject to inspections and inquiries carried out by the Healthcare Commission (CHAI), which must report to the regulator.)

Individuals with an interest in the development and well-being of an NHS foundation trust can register as members. These members become responsible as owners of the trust.

Each NHS foundation trust has a board of governors, which ensures that the local community is directly involved in the governance of the trust. Regulations make provision for the conduct of elections for membership of the board of governors.

Primary care trust patient forums for any PCT area served by an NHS foundation trust will have the right to inspect the NHS foundation trust's services, commission independent advocacy in relation to services provided by the NHS foundation trust, promote the involvement of members of the public in consultations, decisions and policy development by the NHS foundation trust and advise the trust on encouraging public involvement and monitor its success in achieving public involvement. (Patient forums are to be abolished following publication of the DH report *A Stronger Local Voice* in 2006; see Chapter 27.)

An NHS foundation trust may do anything which appears to it to be necessary or expedient for the purpose of or in connection with its functions (S. 47(1)) including the acquiring and disposing of property, entering into contracts, accepting gifts of property and employing staff (S. 47(2)).

The authorisation must require an NHS foundation trust to disclose such information as the Secretary of State specifies to the regulator and may require an NHS foundation trust to allow the regulator to enter and inspect premises owned or controlled by the trust.

Sections 56 and 57 provide for the mergers of NHS foundation trusts with NHS foundation trusts and/or NHS trusts.

Bill Moyes was appointed in December 2003 as chair of the Independent Regulator of NHS Foundation Trusts, i.e. Monitor. He has the responsibility of authorising, monitoring and regulating NHS foundation trusts and works with a board of up to five members, including the chair and a deputy chair. The Healthcare Commission carried out a review of NHS foundation trusts in 2005.[20] It found that in their first year of operation NHS foundation trusts were making progress in developing new services and improving accountability to their local population, but it had not found at that stage any significant difference in quality of care and access to services between the foundation and other acute NHS trusts. The report made significant recommendations including a clearer policy framework, issues relating to competition and future flexibility, commissioning and regulation. It is available on the Healthcare Commission website.

Failing NHS foundation trusts

If Monitor is satisfied that an NHS foundation trust is contravening or failing to comply with the terms of its authorisation then it may serve a notice on the trust that the board of governors is required to do a specified thing, or that all of the directors or the members of the board of governors are removed and replaced with interim directors or members or suspended (S. 52). The directors can be required to take steps to obtain a moratorium or propose a voluntary arrangement under insolvency legislation. Ultimately, Monitor can make an order (after following a specified procedure) providing for the dissolution of the trust and the transfer of its property or liabilities to another NHS foundation trust, a PCT, an NHS trust or the Secretary of State.

Community and primary care services

The NHS and Community Care Act 1990 changed the basis of community care, implementing the recommendations of the Griffiths Report.[21] Instead of places in nursing homes and residential care homes being funded on a means-tested basis by social security, funds were given to the local authority social services departments to become the purchasers of places, on a means-tested basis, for those residents in its catchment area who required nursing or residential care (see Chapter 23 for community provisions).

Abolition of the internal market

The White Paper on the NHS[22] envisaged major initiatives in the management of the NHS, which were brought into force following the passing of the Health Act 1999. These developments included a statutory duty of quality set out in Section 18 of the Health Act 1999, which is the statutory basis for the concept of clinical governance and has since been replaced by Section 45 of the Health and Social Care (Community Health and Standards) Act 2003; the establishment of the Commission for Health Improvement with considerable powers of inspection and audit; the setting up of the National Institute for Clinical Excellence (subsequently renamed National Institute for Health and Clinical Excellence) and the development of National Service Frameworks for specific specialties.

White Paper on the new NHS

The main features of the White Paper on the NHS are shown in Box 5.1.

Box 5.1 — Main features of the White Paper

1 Abolition of the internal market and GP fundholding.
2 Establishment of primary care groups leading to primary care trusts.
3 Establishment of the National Institute for Health and Clinical Excellence.
4 Establishment of the Commission for Health Improvement.
5 Setting up of National Service Frameworks.
6 Introduction of NHS Direct.
7 Introduction of clinical governance.

Changes in the organisation of primary care services

Family practitioner services were once organised by the health authorities (replacing the family health service authorities in this function). Following the White Paper on the NHS[23] and the Health Act 1999 this function has now passed to primary care groups, which eventually obtained primary care trust status. The PCTs hold contracts with general practitioners, pharmacists and dentists to provide services in their areas. The practitioners have in the past not usually become employees of the health authority, but provided services as independent contractors following terms and conditions of service that are nationally agreed. Under these terms of service, general practitioners were required to provide 24-hour care for the patients on their list. While some partnerships still provide personal cover for their patients, in practice there have been recent changes in the provision of out-of-hours services, including the formation of GP cooperatives and the use of deputising services. In October 2000, a review of out-of-hours care was published,[24] which proposed a flexible, national model of integrated out-of-hours provision with defined quality standards, ensuring that patient access should be based on a single telephone call and all professionals providing the service should work together. The RCN has identified the knowledge and skills that nurses need to make primary care groups a success.[25]

The early legislation permitted considerable flexibility in the way in which primary care trusts were organised and managed. Their functions and powers are set out in Chapter 5 of the NHS Plan[26] and are shown in Box 5.2. Care trusts, which provide health and social services, have been set up under the Health Act 1999 and Health and Social Care Act 2001 (see below).

Box 5.2   Functions of primary care trusts

1 To exercise functions in accordance with any directions or agreement with the strategic health authority or other NHS body.

2 To make provision for primary medical services, primary dental services, and provide premises for such services and pharmaceutical and ophthalmic services.

3 To prepare a plan which sets out a strategy for improving the health of the people for whom it is responsible and the provision of healthcare to such people and keep such plan under review.

4 To promote the health of the local population.

5 To commission health services for their populations.

6 To monitor performance.

7 To develop primary care by joint working across practices.

8 To better integrate primary care and community health services and work more closely with social services on both planning and delivery.

Primary care trusts

All primary care groups have now become primary care trusts, i.e. freestanding organisations. Such trusts may include community health services from existing trusts. (In Wales the PCTs equivalent are local health boards.) All or part of an existing community NHS trust could combine with a primary care trust in order to better integrate services and management support. The White Paper specifically stated that these new trusts would not be expected to take responsibility for specialised mental health or learning disability services. It considered that: 'On mental health, where health and social care boundaries are not fixed and where joint work is particularly important, and where an integrated range of services from community to hospital care is required, specialist mental health NHS trusts are likely to be the best mechanism for co-ordinating service delivery.'

The powers recognised in Schedule 1 Part III of the Health Act 1999 (as re-enacted in the NHS Act 2006 Sections 18–24 and Schedule 3) are shown in Box 5.3.

Box 5.3   **Powers of the primary care trust**

'A Primary Care Trust may do anything which appears to it to be necessary or expedient for the purpose of or in connection with the exercise of its functions.
   In particular it may:

1   acquire and dispose of property

2   enter into contracts and

3   accept gifts of property (including property to be held on trust . . .).'

Specific powers and duties are also outlined in Schedule I Part III Paragraphs 14, 15 and 16 of the Health Act 1999 (re-enacted in the NHS Act 2006 Schedule 3 Part 3). These include the power to conduct, commission or assist the conduct of research, together with making officers available or providing facilities for research. It is a specific requirement of the PCT that, as soon as practicable after the end of each financial year, every PCT shall prepare a report of the trust's activities during that year and shall send a copy of the report to each strategic health authority within whose area the trust's area falls and to the Secretary of State.

New contractual arrangements from April 2004

From April 2004 significant changes have taken place in the role of the primary care trust and its relationship with general practitioners. An allocation on a cash-limited basis is now given to each primary care trust by the Department of Health for the provision of primary care (replacing the old GMS non-cash-limited arrangements). PCTs are required to commission six directed enhanced services and other enhanced services and can choose from four different sources: general medical services (GMS), primary medical services (PMS), alternative providers (such as voluntary sector, commercial providers, NHS trusts or other PCTs) or direct PCT provision. The previous medical, supplement and services lists were replaced by the new single primary medical services performers' list. General practitioners who have provided general medical services in the past have a new contract which began in April 2004 and is with the PCT. Contractors had to decide whether to form and contract as an NHS health service body or have a private law contract. Under the new contract to provide GMS, GPs are required to provide essential services, have the expectation and right to provide additional services and the right to provide certain of the directed enhanced services.[27] Contractors are subject to statutory requirements relating to quality, including a new duty of clinical governance. There are significant implications for nurses if more GPs opt to be directly employed by the PCT and cease to be self-employed practitioners. Practice nurses in particular are less likely to be the employee of a GP practice and become instead employees of the PCT.

Employment issues

Part V of Schedule 1 of the Health Act 1999 (now re-enacted in the NHS Act 2006 Schedule 3 Part 5) sets rules on the transfer of staff and empowers the Secretary of State to order transfer to a primary care trust of any employees of a health authority, an NHS trust or a primary care trust. The contract of employment of an employee is not terminated by the transfer. An employee is enabled to object to the transfer. It is important for employees to obtain advice about their transfer to a primary care trust, especially where they are likely to suffer a detriment as a result of the transfer. However, for the vast majority of employees, while in theory they could argue that they do not want to be transferred, in practice, if they fail to agree, they would be without a job.

Care trusts

The NHS Plan[28] envisaged that care trusts would be established to commission and provide social services as well as community healthcare (see Chapter 23). Further provisions to regulate care trusts are contained in the Health and Social Care Act 2001 Part 3. Care trusts enable social services as well as health services to be provided by the same trust. Section 45 enables an organisation to be designated as a care trust (following an application by a local partnership of primary care trust and LA), where:

> a primary care trust or an NHS trust is, or is to be, a party to any existing or proposed LA delegation arrangements
>
> the relevant authority is of the opinion that designation of the trust as a care trust would be likely to promote the effective exercise by the trust of prescribed health-related functions of a local authority (in accordance with the arrangements) in conjunction with prescribed NHS functions of the trust.

Under Section 45(9) the designation of a body as a care trust shall not affect any of the functions, rights or liabilities of that body in its capacity as a primary care trust or NHS trust as the case may be. Regulations for applications and consultations on care trusts were enacted in 2001.[29]

Partnership arrangements

Section 31 of the Health Act 1999 enables partnership arrangements to be set up[30] to improve services for users, through pooled funds and the delegation of functions (lead commissioning and integrated provision). Guidance sets out details on who can make use of these arrangements and the conditions necessary.[31] Partnership arrangements can be directed under Section 46 of the Health and Social Care Act 2001 when it is considered that an NHS body or a local authority is failing in the exercise of its functions. (Children's trusts are considered in Chapter 13.)

Clinical governance

One of the most significant changes envisaged by the government in its White Paper was the concept of clinical governance. It is defined as:

A framework through which NHS organisations are accountable for continuously improving the quality of their services.[32]

The idea of clinical governance is basically simple. In the past, the trust board and its chief executive have been responsible for the financial probity of the organisation; there has been no statutory responsibility of the trust for the overall quality of the organisation. Under the concept of clinical governance, the board and its chief executive are responsible for the quality of clinical services provided by the organisation. In theory, this could mean that a board is removed or a chief executive dismissed if a baby suffers brain damage at birth as a result of negligence or a mother dies in childbirth.

The concept of clinical governance was based on the statutory duty of quality under Section 18 of the Health Act 1999 which has now been replaced by Section 45 of the Health and Social Care (Community Health and Standards) Act 2003.

Duty of quality

Section 45 of the Health and Social Care (Community Health and Standards) Act 2003 is shown in the Statute below.

Statute | **Section 45 of the Health and Social Care (Community Health and Standards) Act 2003**

It is the duty of each NHS body to put and keep in place arrangements for the purpose of monitoring and improving the quality of healthcare provided by and for that body.

Healthcare means the services provided to individuals for or in connection with the prevention, diagnosis or treatment of illness and the promotion and protection of public health.

The duty falls primarily on the chief executive of each strategic health authority, NHS trust and PCT to implement. In practice, each chief executive designates officers to be responsible for quality or clinical governance in specified areas of clinical practice. Government guidance was published in March 1999.[33] This follows from the original consultation document, 'A First Class Service: quality in the new NHS'.[34] The aim to develop quality within the NHS is to be secured in three ways:

1 setting clear national quality standards

2 ensuring local delivery of high-quality clinical services

3 effective systems for monitoring the quality of services.

The Clinical Effectiveness Support Unit (CESU) is a sister organisation to the NHS Clinical Governance Support Team in Wales.

Guidance for nurses on clinical governance has been provided by the RCN.[35] It defines clinical governance as 'an umbrella term for everything that helps to maintain and improve high standards of patient care' and in a series of case studies, shows the implications for nurses. Appendix 2 of the 2003 resource pack provides a list of clinical governance resources with websites and relevant publications.

Standard setting

Following the White Paper, there has been greater emphasis on standard setting in the light of research findings on clinical effectiveness and excellence. Standard setting and monitoring will become an even more significant part of the practitioner's professional responsibilities. (Standards in relation to the law are discussed in Chapter 3 on the law of negligence.)

Under Section 46 of the Health and Social Care (Community Health and Standards) Act 2003 the Secretary of State has the power to prepare and publish statements of standards in relation to the provision of healthcare by and for English NHS bodies and cross-border SHAs and must keep these standards under review, consulting such persons as he considers appropriate before publishing a statement. These standards are to be taken into account by every English NHS body and cross-border SHA in discharging its duty under Section 45 of the Act, which is set out on page 99. CHAI will have regard to the adherence to these standards in its inspections, inquiries and investigations (see below).

Commission for Health Audit and Inspection (CHAI) (Healthcare Commission)

The predecessor to the Commission for Health Audit and Inspection was the Commission for Health Improvement (CHI). (CHI's forerunner, the Clinical Standards Advisory Group (CSAG), had been set up under the NHS and Community Care Act 1990 as a statutory body to advise UK health ministers on standards of clinical care. It was abolished on 1 November 1999 under the Health Act 1999, its duties being taken over by the Commission for Health Improvement.) The Commission for Health Audit and Inspection (CHAI), known as the Healthcare Commission, replaced CHI on 1 April 2004. The chairman was Sir Ian Kennedy. Its functions, constitution and powers are set out in the Health and Social Care (Community Health and Standards) Act 2003 supplemented by regulations set out in Statutory Instruments. Its functions are listed in Box 5.4.

Box 5.4   **Functions of the Healthcare Commission**

General duties:

1 Encouraging improvement in the provision of healthcare by and for NHS bodies and being concerned in particular with:
   a. the availability of, and access to, healthcare
   b. the quality and effectiveness of healthcare
   c. the economy and efficiency of the provision of healthcare
   d. the availability and quality of information provided to the public about healthcare
   e. the need to safeguard and promote the rights and welfare of children
   f. the effectiveness of measures taken for the purpose of paragraph e, by the body in question and any person who provides, or is to provide, healthcare for that body.

8 Publishing data relating to the provision of healthcare by and for NHS bodies.

9 Conducting annual reviews of the provision of healthcare by and for each English NHS body and each cross-border SHA and award a performance rating to each such body, using criteria which it has devised and published and has been approved by the Secretary of State. It can conduct inspections for the purpose of these reviews.

> ### Box 5.4 continued
>
> **10** Other reviews and investigations into the provision of healthcare or particular kinds of healthcare and publication of a report.
>
> **11** Where a review or investigation has been conducted by CHAI it must make a report to the Secretary of State if it is of the view that there are significant failings in the provision of healthcare or the running of the NHS body or cross-border SHA or any body providing healthcare for an English NHS body or cross-border SHA. This report may include recommendations on special measures to remedy the failings.
>
> **12** Keep the Secretary of State or Welsh Assembly informed about the provision of healthcare by and for any NHS body.
>
> **13** Review the quality of data obtained by others in relation to the provision of healthcare by and for NHS bodies, including the methods used in the collection and analysis of such data and the validity of conclusions drawn from such data.
>
> **14** Promote the effective coordination of reviews or assessments carried out by public bodies or other persons in relation to the provision of healthcare by or for English NHS bodies and cross-border SHAs.

Other functions set out in the Health and Social Care (Community Health and Standards) Act 2003 include:

Promoting or undertaking comparative or other studies designed to enable it to make recommendations for improving economy, efficiency and effectiveness in the exercise of any of the functions of an English NHS body either at its own initiative or at the request of the body concerned.

The Secretary of State has the power to enact regulations requiring CHAI to undertake other functions.

The Secretary of State has power under the 2003 Act to make regulations on the procedure to be followed in making representations to CHAI before the award of a performance rating; on the procedure to be followed in making representations to CHAI before the publication of a report following a review or investigation. CHAI must report its findings on NHS foundation trusts to the independent regulator responsible for the regulation of foundation trusts (see below).

The functions originally performed by the National Care Standards Commission (NCSC) in respect of the registration and standards of independent hospitals, independent clinics and independent medical agencies have been transferred to CHAI under Section 102 of the Health and Social Care (Community Health and Standards) Act 2003. Other functions of the NCSC relating to children's homes, care homes, residential family centres, domiciliary care agencies, nurses agencies, fostering agencies, voluntary adoption agencies and adoption support agencies have been transferred to the Commission for Social Care Inspection (CSCI). Similar general functions have been given to CHAI in relation to informing the Secretary of State about the provision of independent health services and the availability and quality of the services and the general duty of encouraging improvement in the quality of independent health services provided in England. CHAI and CSCI also have a significant role to play in the handling of complaints about health and social services and this role is discussed in Chapter 27.

Under Schedule 6 to the Health and Social Care (Community Health and Standards) Act 2003, the Healthcare Commission's (CHAI's) status is described as not being 'regarded as the servant or agent of the Crown or as enjoying any status, immunity or privilege of the Crown'.

Its general powers and duties state that it 'may do anything which appears to it to be necessary or expedient for the purpose of, or in connection with the exercise of its functions'. That includes, in particular, cooperating with other public authorities in the UK, acquiring and disposing of land and other property, entering into contracts and providing training. It has a duty to carry out its functions effectively, efficiently and economically.

Prior to the establishment of CHAI, its chairman designate published a consultation document on a vision of how CHAI would operate.[36] The intention is that the vision should be rewritten in the light of the feedback from the consultation. Further information on its role, publications and inspections can be obtained from its website.[37]

Proposals are being discussed for the establishment of a single regulatory body in 2009 which will result from the merger of the Healthcare Commission, the Commission for Social Care Inspection and the Mental Health Act Commission.

Audit Commission

The Audit Commission is a non-departmental public body sponsored by the Office of the Deputy Prime Minister with the Department of Health and the National Assembly for Wales. It is responsible for ensuring that public money is used economically, efficiently and effectively. Its reports are available from its website.[38] The Audit Commission covers local government, housing, health, criminal justice and community safety, working in audit, inspection, collecting information to measure performance, assessing local authorities and carrying out national studies. It has 18 commissioners and a chairman and employs 2,500 people led by a chief executive. Its income is the fees charged for its work and government grants. It audits NHS trusts, PCTs and strategic health authorities to review the quality of their financial systems and it also works with foundation trusts. From 2004 the Healthcare Commission took over responsibility for inspecting and assessing health services and in ensuring value for money nationally. The Commission for Social Care Inspection (CSCI) took over the responsibility for regulating social care. The Audit Commission in Wales merged with the Welsh part of the National Audit Office to create a new, independent, unified audit and inspection organisation in April 2005. A Concordat was agreed between the bodies that regulate, audit, inspect or review elements of health and healthcare in England. It sets out that bodies which undertake audit and inspection should continuously monitor their practices in line with the Concordat and publish an annual review of progress with implementing it. There is a comparable Concordat in Wales.

National Institute for Health and Clinical Excellence (NICE)

The National Institute for Clinical Excellence (NICE) (subsequently renamed National Institute for Health and Clinical Excellence) was established on 1 April 1999 to promote clinical excellence and cost-effectiveness.[39] It is an independent organisation for providing national guidance on treatments and care for those using the NHS in England and Wales. It can be accessed on its website.[40] The original intention was that it would bring to an end postcode prescribing, where there were significant regional and local differences in the treatments, particularly medicines, that were available within the NHS. It produces guidance in three areas of health: public health (guidance on the promotion of good health and the prevention of ill health for those working in the NHS, local authorities and the wider public and voluntary sector); health technologies (guidance on the use of new and existing medicines, treatment and procedures within the NHS); and clinical practice (guidance on the appropriate treatment and care of people with specific diseases and conditions within the NHS). Further information can be obtained from its publication *About NICE guidance: what does it mean for me?* which is available on its website. Recent recommendations to help the NHS reduce ineffective practice include guidance on asthma inhaler devices, atopic dermatitis, caesarean section, chronic obstructive pulmonary disease, eating disorders, fertility, long-acting reversible contraception, multiple sclerosis, post-traumatic stress disorder, preoperative tests and footcare in Type 2 diabetes.

Guidance issued by NICE on restricting the use of specified drugs to treat Alzheimer's Disease to patients with moderate-severe levels of the disease was challenged in a court case in 2007.[41] Eisai Ltd sought judicial review of the processes followed by NICE in its assessment of the drugs. The judge found that NICE did appropriately take into account the benefits which the drugs brought to carers, it did reflect the costs of long-term care in its calculations, it did not breach principles of procedural fairness by providing a read-only version of the economic model, it was not irrational in concluding that there was no cumulative benefit to patients after six months' treatment with the drugs and its assessment and consideration of a 2000 Alzheimer's Disease study was not irrational. However, the judge did rule that NICE was in breach of its duties under the Disability Discrimination Act and the Race Relations Act by not offering specific advice regarding people with learning disabilities and people who lacked English as a first language in its technology appraisal guidance. As a consequence of the case, NICE was asked to revise its guidance within 28 days and the revised guidance can be seen on its website.[42]

Implementation and the effects of national guidelines

A memorandum of understanding on appraisal of health interventions was published by the Department of Health in August 1999. This set out the ground rules under which NICE would carry out the appraisal of individual health interventions.[43] In discussing the legal status of guidance, the memorandum states that:

> *All guidance must be fully reasoned and written in terms which makes clear that it is guidance. Guidance for clinicians does not override their professional responsibility to make the appropriate decision in the circumstances of the individual patient, in consultation with the patient or guardian/carer and in the light of locally agreed policies. Similarly, guidance to NHS trusts and commissioners must make clear that it does not take away their discretion under administrative law to take account of individual circumstances.*

In practice, in the determination of reasonable professional practice (the Bolam Test;[44] see Chapter 3), the fact that a specific treatment has been endorsed as clinically effective by NICE will carry weight in deciding what is reasonable practice and a clinician may have to show what the individual circumstances were that justified a different treatment for a particular patient. Patients who claim that they have suffered as a result of a failure to provide a reasonable standard of care could use evidence of clinical effectiveness and research-based practice to illustrate failings in the care provided to them. It could be argued, therefore, that failure to follow the recommendations of NICE will be *prima facie* evidence of a failure to follow a reasonable standard of care according to the Bolam Test.

In addition, since the aim of NICE recommendations is to end the postcode lottery, strategic health authorities and PCTs that decide they do not have the funds to make available medicines and treatments that NICE has recommended as clinically effective within their catchment area may find that their decisions are subject to judicial review.

NICE has been concerned at ensuring implementation of its guidance. A cancer charity pointed to the wide variations in the prescribing of the drug Herceptin, used for breast cancer.[45] In December 2003 the chief executive of NICE stated that in future NICE would concentrate on the implementation of its guidelines and that it was discussing with the Healthcare Commission sanctions being taken against those hospitals that fail to follow guidelines for prescribing drugs and for best clinical practice. NICE has set up an implementation programme to help support implementation of NICE guidance. Its implementation team works alongside the guidance developers, the communications team and the field-based teams to ensure intelligent dissemination to the appropriate target audience, work to encourage a supportive environment, provide tools to support putting NICE guidance into practice and generally encourage implementation. Further information is available on the NICE website.

National Service Frameworks (NSFs)

The White Paper on the NHS[46] set out a package of measures to raise standards within the NHS and these were further elaborated in the NHS Plan.[47] Included in this programme of action was the introduction of National Service Frameworks (NSFs). The circular[48] explaining their function stated:

NSFs will set national standards and define service models for a defined service or care group; put in place strategies to support implementation; and establish performance measures against which progress within an agreed timescale will be measured. The Commission for Health Improvement (CHI) (now the Healthcare Commission) will assure progress through a programme of systematic service reviews.

NSFs cover the following areas: cancer; children; coronary heart disease; diabetes; long-term health conditions; mental health; older people; paediatric intensive care; renal services and chronic obstructive pulmonary disease. Each NSF is developed with the assistance of an external reference group (ERG) which brings together health professionals, service users and carers, health service managers, partner agencies and other advocates. ERGs adopt an inclusive process to engage the full range of views. The Department of Health supports the ERGs and manages the overall process. In addition, the Department of Health makes a general invitation to professionals and the public to send in their views and their examples of good practice to the Department of Health website.[49] Guidance is issued by the Department of Health in the form of health service circulars (HSCs) on the implementation of NSFs. For example, HSC 2001/026 sets out the standards defined in the NSF for diabetes.[50] Twelve standards are laid down from prevention of Type 2 diabetes to the detection and management of long-term complications. Standard 9 relates to diabetes and pregnancy. Failure by an NHS organisation to comply with the NSF could lead to a complaint by a patient but the patient could not sue for breach of a statutory duty since the NSF does not in itself create statutory duties. However, it would be possible for the Secretary of State, in setting standards under Section 46 of the Health and Social Care (Community Health and Standards) Act 2003, to create a statutory duty binding on NHS bodies to comply with NSFs. One of the statutory duties of the Healthcare Commission is to monitor and review the implementation of standards set out in the NSFs and by NICE. Its reports on the NSFs can be found on its website.[51] The first NSF which it reviewed was on coronary heart disease.

The work of NICE contributes to the development of National Service Frameworks. For example, NICE has undertaken investigations into Type 1 diabetes to develop clinical guidelines and these will contribute to the implementation of the Diabetes National Service Framework.

NHS Direct and walk-in clinics

The pilot scheme whereby patients could phone direct to a 24-hour helpline and get immediate advice from a registered nurse was followed by the implementation of NHS Direct across the country. The service provides both clinical advice to support self-care and appropriate self-referral to NHS services as well as access to more general advice and information. An improved NHS Direct Online website including a new interactive enquiry service was launched in November 2001.[52] In April 2003 it was announced[53] that the success of NHS Direct has led to plans for considerable expansion over the next three years and a strategy document was published.[54] Its call capacity was to be doubled to 16 million calls annually with an 80 per cent increase in funding. The intention was to enable NHS to:

provide a single access point to the NHS out-of-hours services

handle all low-priority 999 ambulance calls

establish a new national NHS Direct digital TV service

become a distinct national organisation, independent of the Department of Health with funding devolved from Whitehall direct to PCTs.

In a press release in November 2000,[55] the Department of Health stated that the helpline has received over 3.5 million calls and takes an average of 60,000 calls a week, expected to rise to 100,000 by the end of the year. It is the largest telephone-based healthcare provider in the world. It provides a nurse-led telephone advice line; a website;[56] an NHS Direct Healthcare Guide which is available in Safeways (now Morrisons) and in high-street pharmacies; and NHS Direct information kiosks. Guidance for nurses has been provided by the RCN on nurse telephone consultation services.[57] It states on the topic of professional and legal issues that: 'There is no reason why a properly trained and experienced nurse providing telephone consultation should be at any greater risk of being held liable for negligence than nurses operating in other clinical settings.' As in any other clinical setting, it is essential that a nurse works within her competence. In November 2003 the 20-millionth caller to NHS Direct was noted. In a press release, the Department of Health stated that the Secretary of State hailed NHS Direct as one of the most popular health service reforms of the past few years.[58] The Commission for Health Improvement reported that 90 per cent of respondents who had used NHS Direct in England were either completely satisfied or satisfied to some extent with the way their call was dealt with.[59]

A press announcement[60] publicised the setting up of more direct access clinics run by nurses, to which any person can go for assistance and advice on healthcare. The clinics aim, in the words of the press release:

[To] offer quick access to a range of NHS services including free consultations, minor treatments, health information and advice on self-treatment. They are based in convenient locations that allow the public easy access and have opening hours tailored to suit modern lifestyles, including early mornings, late evenings, and weekends. The centres will have close links with local GPs ensuring continuity of care for their patients.

The advantages to the public are clearly apparent: fast service, no wait, close to work, easy access, immediate advice and speedy prescriptions. Many of the clinics are planned to be linked with GP surgeries through information technology. However, perhaps one of the advantages for some people is the anonymity that such clinics may provide: pregnancy testing, and other immediate tests without any receptionist recognising the patient. A practical guide to establishing an NHS Walk-in Centre was published by the DH in June 2007.[61] It covers premises, staffing and training.

Nurses and expanded role practice in NHS Direct and walk-in clinics

NHS Direct and the walk-in clinics depend heavily on nursing staff who are the main group employed in these areas. Nurses have to be sure that they work within the scope of their professional competence. This is considered in Chapter 24. In February 2000, nurses who work in walk-in centres were added to the list of the nurses who were able to have limited prescribing powers.[62] (See Chapter 28.)

Patient safety

In June 2000,[63] the government published a press release on the setting up of a national system for the NHS to learn from experience. This led to the establishment of the National Patient Safety Agency and a national reporting system of all adverse incidents. The NPSA is considered in Chapter 12. The need for a national system of the reporting of untoward incidents is apparent from some of the reports and evidence of professional misconduct described below. The Health Act 2006 Section 14 enables the Secretary of State to issue a code of practice relating to healthcare-associated infections which must be taken account of by the Healthcare Commission in conducting a review.

Beverly Allitt

Beverly Allitt, a state enrolled nurse, was convicted of murdering four children, of attempting to murder three others and of causing grievous bodily harm to six more. She was sentenced to life imprisonment on every count. An independent inquiry,[64] chaired by Sir Cecil Clothier, made significant and substantial recommendations on the selection procedures for nurses, including the prohibition of employment of those with a personality disorder, and that there should be formal health screening; that post mortem reports should be sent by the coroner to doctors involved in the patient's care; that there should be a review of paediatric pathology services; that there should be a review of sickness information being referred to occupational health and of the criteria for management referrals to occupational health; that there should be untoward incident reports if there is a failure of an alarm on monitoring equipment; and that reports of serious untoward incidents should be made in writing to district and regional health authorities. The Department of Health drew the attention of NHS managers to the report's recommendations.[65] The report accepted that no measures can afford complete protection against a determined miscreant and emphasised that:

> Our principal recommendation is that the Grantham disaster should serve to heighten awareness in all those caring for children of the possibility of malevolent intervention as a cause of unexplained clinical events.

A High Court judge ruled on 6 December 2007 that Beverly Allitt must serve a minimum of 30 years in custody and will therefore be over 60 years old before she is eligible for release.

Shipman Inquiry

It was apparent from the prosecution of a general practitioner, Dr Shipman, for the murder of 15 patients, that the principal recommendation of the Allitt Inquiry applies as much to the care of adults as to children. An inquiry was set up after his conviction and several reports have been published: the first[66] identified the patients for whose deaths he was probably responsible (possibly over 200), the second[67] reviewed a police investigation into early police enquiries and the third[68] made fundamental recommendations on the reform of the present system of death certification and the office and function of the coroner. (This third report is discussed in Chapter 29.) The fourth Shipman report, which was published in July 2004,[69] considered the regulation of controlled drugs in the community and is considered in Chapter 28. The fifth report of this inquiry was published in December 2004[70] and was concerned with the complaints against and the regulation of doctors. The sixth, and final, Shipman report considered how many patients Shipman killed during his career as a junior doctor at Pontefract General Infirmary and in his time at Hyde.[71] Shipman committed suicide in Wakefield prison on 13 January 2004.

Dr Ledward

Dr Ledward was a gynaecologist working in south-east England who was struck off by the GMC after being found guilty of negligence in 13 operations. An inquiry into the conduct of Rodney Ledward[72] found that there had been a climate of fear and intimidation preventing nurses and junior doctors from telling tales in case they lost their jobs. The inquiry recommended that: each trust should develop a list of untoward non-clinical events that should trigger an incident report; each Royal College should identify a minimum list of untoward clinical events that should trigger the completion of an incident report; the person completing the form should generally identify themselves to encourage a culture of openness in the NHS; the earlier that concerns about a doctor's practice are noted, the sooner they can be rectified. Further, clinical governance should apply to the private sector as well as the NHS. It was subsequently reported[73] that 59 women are suing the Kent and Medway Health Authority and East Kent Hospitals NHS Trust for damages. They allege that they were raped or sexually assaulted by Rodney Ledward when they were in his care in the early 1980s. He died in 2000.

Reports of other inquiries which can be downloaded from the Department of Health website include the inquiry into Clifford Ayling (a GP from Kent who was convicted of indecently assaulting women patients); Richard Neale (a gynaecologist who was struck off the GMC register for poor standards in a number of cases) and the Kerr/Haslam Inquiry (two psychiatrists in Yorkshire about whom several patients raised concerns).

Corporate manslaughter and corporate homicide

In 2007 the Corporate Manslaughter and Corporate Homicide Act was passed which abolishes the common law offence of corporate manslaughter as a result of gross negligence and replaces it by new statutory offences. The Act is considered in Chapter 2 and its link with health and safety offences in Chapter 12. As a consequence of this legislation an NHS organisation may be prosecuted as a result of its senior management being in substantial breach of a duty of care owed to the deceased. Emergency activities are excluded from the offence as are decisions made by a public authority on matters of public policy (including in particular the allocation of public resources or the weighing of competing public interests).

The extent of prosecutions in the NHS under this Act and the impact, if any, upon the management of NHS organisations remain to be seen.

National Health Service Plan

In July 2000 the NHS Plan[74] was published. It described itself as: 'A Plan for investment in the NHS with sustained increases in funding. This is a Plan for reform with far-reaching changes across the NHS.'

The executive summary stated that the investment in the NHS 'has to be accompanied by reform'. The reforms envisaged are set out in Box 5.5. In addition to these reforms, specific targets and dates are set in the NHS Plan. These include:

By 2004 all patients should be able to have a GP appointment within 48 hours.

By the end of 2005, the maximum wait for an outpatient appointment will be three months and for inpatients, six months.

Specific targets were also set for cancer care, heart disease, mental illness services and services for the elderly. (The implications of the NHS Plan for the care of the elderly are considered in Chapter 19 and for community and primary care in Chapter 23.)

Box 5.5 **Major reforms of the NHS Plan**

Principles of subsidiarity.

National standards.

Regular inspections by CHI.

NICE will ensure cost-effective drugs are not dependent on where one lives.

A Modernisation Agency will be set up.

£500 million performance fund.

Linking of NHS and social services with new agreements to pool resources: new care trusts to commission health and social care in a single organisation.

New contracts for GPs and hospital doctors to reflect quality and productivity; limitation on newly qualified consultants to do private work.

Expansion of roles for nurses and other health professionals.

Individual learning accounts for support staff worth £150 million.

Increase in number of nurse consultants to 1,000.

Leadership centre to be set up for developing managerial and clinical leaders.

Patients to have more powers and influence in the NHS:
(a) will receive copies of letters about care
(b) will have better information to choose GP
(c) patient advocates and advisers in each hospital
(d) proper redress when operations are cancelled
(e) patients' surveys and forums to help services become more patient centred.

Concordat with private providers of healthcare to enable NHS to make better use of facilities in private hospitals.

In order to ensure implementation of the NHS Plan, the government set up an *NHS Modernisation Agency*. Its first task was allocated in August 2000 when it was required to visit the seven hospitals with the longest waiting times. The action teams of the NHS Modernisation Agency would then decide how the additional money to be made available under the NHS Plan would be spent at these hospitals in order to bring down the waiting lists within six months. An *NHS Modernisation Board* was established to advise the Secretary of State on, and help oversee, implementation of the NHS Plan. A member of the Modernisation Board serves on the taskforces which have been set up to drive forward implementation of the NHS Plan. The NHS Modernisation Board is chaired by the Secretary of State and includes the Department of Health's permanent secretary, the NHS Chief Executive and representatives from leading healthcare organisations, people who work in the NHS and patient and citizen representatives. Its role is to ensure that those involved in the implementation of the NHS Plan are making real and speedy progress. It also oversees the progress of the Department of Health, the Modernisation Agency, the taskforces, the NHS and the social care community. It publishes an annual report.[75] The next stage of the NHS Modernisation Agency, announced by the DH in February 2007, is designed to place stronger emphasis on local implementation with a devolution of skills and resources to support this.

Within the modernisation agenda were plans for a major reform of the NHS pay scheme for staff (except doctors, dentists and senior managers). This is considered in Chapter 10. Under the NHS Plan, an NHS University has been established (subsequently absorbed into the NHS Institute for Innovation and Improvement), which is considered in Chapter 11.

A White Paper was published in 2005, 'Our Health, Our Care', which sets out how health and social care services are to change in the future. It was based on two consultations: Independence, Well-being and Choice and a listening exercise. The aim of future changes is to make services more flexible and responsible to communities and those who work in the service, to provide a service which is tailored to the specific health and social care needs of individuals, give users more control over the treatment they receive, and work with health and social care professionals and services to get the most appropriate treatment or care for their needs.

Patient representation and involvement

Another of the aims of the NHS Plan was to increase the representation of the patient in strategic planning and decision making within the NHS. As a consequence new organisations were established following the Health and Social Care Act 2001 and NHS Reform and Health Care Professions Act 2002: the Commission for Patient and Public Involvement in Health (CPPIH), independent complaints and advice services (ICAS), patient advice and liaison services (PALS) and patients' forums are considered in Chapter 27. In December 2003[76] the Department of Health published a command paper, 'Building on the Best', which outlined the results of the national consultation on extending patient choice and the steps towards enabling every patient to have a choice of when, where and how they are treated. The choices will cover pharmacists having the power to provide repeat prescriptions for up to a year and the range of medicines that are available over the counter without prescription will be expanded. Minor ailment schemes will be introduced to allow patients who are exempt from prescription charges to get over-the-counter treatments direct from the pharmacist. Primary care services will be expanded to include nurse-led clinics and polyclinics, the provision of more diagnostic tests and X-rays. Also of significance for the NHS in terms of patient involvement are the recommendations of the Report of the Bristol Inquiry[77] which are considered in Chapter 4.

Conclusions

This chapter has considered the statutory duties placed on the Secretary of State and the new organisations that have been introduced in recent years to ensure that there are accountability and high standards of care provided in the NHS. In February 2004 the Department of Health announced a national pricelist for operations with the aim that by 2008 hospitals and trusts would be paid according to a national tariff for every operation, treatment or procedure.[78] A week later it was announced that the hospital star ratings scheme would be abolished in 2006.[79] Such changes and reversals of policy are perhaps one of the frustrating elements for staff in the NHS. It could be argued that there have been too many reorganisations and initiatives within the NHS in recent times and health professionals now need a time of stability. A major reorganisation of the bodies for inspection of health and social care is to take place in 2009 when the Healthcare Commission, the Commission for Social Care and Inspection and the Mental Health Act Commission are to be integrated into a single powerful regulatory body.

At the time of writing, the new Secretary of State, Alan Johnson, has announced a review of the NHS to be chaired by Lord Darzi, a surgeon and junior minister within the Department of Health. The review has four main tasks:

+ To put clinical decisions at the centre of the NHS.

+ To improve patient care, particularly for those with long-term and life-threatening conditions.

+ To make care more accessible and convenient.

+ To establish a vision for the next decade based less on central direction and more on patient control.

It remains to be seen if this third review in recent years leads to higher morale of NHS staff and greater public appreciation of the NHS.

Reflection questions

1 Assess the likely contribution of NICE, CHAI and the statutory duty of quality to the standards of care within your own sphere of professional practice.

2 Discuss the national scheme for the reporting of adverse healthcare incidents. How does it operate within your particular field of work?

Further exercises

1 Ascertain if there have been any prosecutions for corporate manslaughter or corporate homicide in the NHS and identify the implications of this new offence for your own organisation.

2 Analyse the NHS Plan and consider specifically the effects that it could have in the area in which you work. To what extent do you consider that it affects your own working practices?

References

[1] *R (Watts) v. Bedford Primary Care Trust and Another*, The Times Law Report, 3 October 2003; [2004] EWCA Civ 166; (C372/04) [2006] ECJ

[2] *R v. Secretary of State for Social Services ex parte Hincks and Others*, Solicitors' Journal, 29 June 1979, 436

[3] *R v. Central Birmingham HA ex p Walker* (1987) 3 BMLR 32

[4] *R v. Cambridge Health Authority ex parte B (A Minor)* (1995) 23 BMLR 1 CA; [1995] 2 All ER 129

[5] *R v. North Derbyshire Health Authority* [1997] 8 Med LR 327

[6] NHS Executive Letter, EL (95)97

[7] *R (on the application of Rogers) v. Swindon NHS Primary Care Trust and Another* [2006] EWCA Civ 392

[8] *R (on the application of Otley) v. Barking and Dagenham NHS Primary Care Trust* [2007] EWHC 1927

[9] *Eisai Ltd v. National Institute for Health and Clinical Excellence (Alzheimer's Society and Shire Pharmaceuticals Ltd Interested parties)* [2007] EWHC 1941

[10] *North West Lancashire Health Authority v. A, D and G* [1999] Lloyd's Rep Med; (1999) 2 CCL Rep 419; [2000] 1 WLR 977

[11] *R (Watts) v. Bedford Primary Care Trust and Another*, The Times Law Report, 3 October 2003; [2003] EWHC 2228; [2004] EWCA Civ 166, (C372/04) [2006] ECJ

[12] (Previously Article 59) EC Treaty (OJ 1992 C224/6)

[13] *R (Watts) v. Bedford Primary Care Trust and Another* (C372/04) [2006] ECJ

[14] David Charter, Patients to beat NHS queues in EU plan for open health market, *The Times*, 18 December 2007

[15] www.dh.gov.uk/

[16] *R v. North Derbyshire Health Authority* [1997] 8 Med LR 327

[17] *R v. Secretary of State for Health ex p Pfizer Ltd* [1999] 3 CMLR 875; Lloyd's Rep Med 289

[18] www.dh.gov.uk/nhsfoundationtrusts/independentregulator.htm

[19] www.dh.gov.uk/nhsfoundationtrusts/finance.htm

[20] Healthcare Commission, The Healthcare Commission's review of NHS Foundation Trusts, July 2005

[21] Sir Roy Griffiths, Community Care: agenda for action, HMSO, 1988; followed by Command Paper 849, Caring for People: community care in the next decade and beyond, HMSO, November 1989

[22] White Paper on the NHS, The New NHS – modern, dependable, The Stationery Office, London, 1997

[23] Ibid.

[24] Department of Health, Raising Standards for Patients: new partnerships in out-of-hours care, DH, October 2000

[25] Royal College of Nursing, The New Primary Care Groups, Order No. 000924, RCN, October 1998

[26] Department of Health, The NHS Plan: a plan for investment, a plan for reform, Cm 4818-1, The Stationery Office, London, July 2000

[27] Department of Health, Delivering Investment in General Practice: implementing the new GMS contract, DH, December 2003

[28] Department of Health, The NHS Plan: a plan for investment, a plan for reform, Cm 4818-1, The Stationery Office, London, July 2000

[29] Care Trusts (Applications and Consultation) Regulations 2001, SI 2001 No. 3788

30 Health Act 1999 Partnership Arrangements SI 2000 No. 617

31 HSC 2000/010; LAC (2000)9 Implementation of the Health Act 1999 Partnership Arrangements

32 Department of Health, A First Class Service: quality in the new NHS, DH, 1998

33 HSC 1999/065 Clinical Governance: quality in the new NHS, NHS Executive, 1999

34 HSC 1998/113 A First Class Service: quality in the new NHS, NHS Executive, 1998

35 Royal College of Nursing, Clinical Governance: how nurses can get involved, Order No. 001171, RCN, March 2000; Royal College of Nursing, Clinical Governance: an RCN resource guide, Order No. 002036, RCN, June 2003

36 CHAI, Vision for CHAI, 2003

37 www.healthcarecommission.org.uk/

38 www.audit-commission.gov.uk/aboutus/index.asp

39 National Institute for Clinical Excellence (Establishment and Constitution) Regulations SI 1999 No. 220; amendments SI 2002 Nos 1759 and 1760

40 www.nice.org.uk

41 *Eisai Ltd* v. *National Institute for Health and Clinical Excellence (Alzheimer's Society and Shire Pharmaceuticals Ltd Interested parties)* [2007] EWHC 1941

42 http://guidance.nice.org.uk/TA111

43 Department of Health, Memorandum of Understanding on Appraisal of Health Interventions, DH, August 1999

44 *Bolam* v. *Friern Barnet Hospital Management Committee* [1957] 1 WLR 582

45 CancerBACUP, Herceptin NICE Implementation Audit: key findings, 2003; www.cancerbacup.org.uk

46 Department of Health, The New NHS – modern, dependable, HMSO, London, 1997

47 Department of Health, The NHS Plan: a plan for investment, a plan for reform, Cm 4818-1, The Stationery Office London, July 2000

48 Health Service Circular HSC 1998/074, National Service Frameworks

49 www.dh.gov.uk

50 Department of Health HSC 2001/026, Diabetes National Service Framework: standards

51 www.healthcarecommission.org.uk/

52 Department of Health press release 2001/0573, Personalised health information at the touch of a button, 29 November 2001

53 Department of Health press release 2003/0165, NHS Direct to more than double in size, 15 April 2003

54 Department of Health, Developing NHS Direct, DH, April 2003

55 Department of Health press release 2000/0679, 20 November 2000

56 http://www.nhsdirect.nhs.uk

57 Royal College of Nursing, Nurse Telephone Consultation Services: information and good practice, Order No. 000995, RCN, no date

58 Department of Health press release 2003/0432, November 2003

59 Commission for Health Improvement, What CHI has found in NHS Direct, CHI, 2003; www.chi.nhs.uk

60 Department of Health press release, Frank Dobson announces more NHS walk-in clinics, 30 September 1999; HSC 1999/116, NHS primary care walk-in centres

61 Department of Health, Establishing an NHS Walk-in Centre, June 2007

62 The National Health Service (Pharmaceutical Services) Amendment Regulations 2000, SI 2000 No. 121

63 Department of Health press release 2000/349, National system for NHS to learn from experience, 13 June 2000

[64] Clothier Report, The Allitt Inquiry: an independent inquiry relating to deaths and injuries on the children's ward at Grantham and Kesteven General Hospital during the period February to April 1991, HMSO, London, 1994

[65] DGM (95) 71 The Allitt Inquiry

[66] Shipman Inquiry First Report: Death Disguised, 19 July 2002; www.the-shipman-inquiry. org.uk/reports.asp

[67] Shipman Inquiry Second Report: The Police Investigation of March 1998, 14 July 2003; www.the-shipman-inquiry.org.uk/reports.asp

[68] Shipman Inquiry Third Report: Death and Cremation Certification, 14 July 2003; www. the-shipman-inquiry.org.uk/reports.asp

[69] Shipman Inquiry Fourth Report: The Regulation of Controlled Drugs in the Community published 15 July 2004 Cm 6249, The Stationery Office; www.the-shipman-inquiry.org.uk/ reports.asp

[70] The Shipman Inquiry Fifth Report: Safeguarding Patients: Lessons from the Past – Proposals for the Future. Command Paper CM 6394, December 2004, The Stationery Office; www.the-shipman-inquiry.org.uk/reports.asp

[71] The Shipman Inquiry Sixth Report: Shipman: The Final Report, January 2005, The Stationery Office; www.the-shipman-inquiry.org.uk/reports.asp

[72] Jean Ritchie, Inquiry into Quality and Practice within the NHS arising from the Actions of Rodney Ledward, DH, 2000

[73] News item, *The Times*, 4 November 2003

[74] Department of Health. The NHS Plan: a plan for investment, a plan for reform, Cm 4818 1, The Stationery Office, London, July 2000

[75] Department of Health, The NHS Modernisation Board's Annual Report 2003; www. dh.gov.uk/modernisationboardreport/index.htm

[76] Department of Health press release 2003/0504, 9 December 2003

[77] Bristol Royal Infirmary Inquiry (Kennedy Report), Learning from Bristol: the report of the public inquiry into children's heart surgery at the Bristol Royal Infirmary 1984–1995, Command Paper Cm 5207; www.bristol-inquiry.org.uk

[78] Department of Health press release 2004/0042, NHS reference costs and national tariff published today, 2004

[79] Oliver Wright, Hospital star ratings to be scrapped, *The Times*, 9 February 2004

Chapter 6
Progress of a civil claim: defences and compensation

> ### This chapter discusses

> + Civil proceedings
> + Compensation in civil proceedings for negligence
> + Defences to a civil action
> + Clinical Negligence Scheme for Trusts (CNST) and the NHS Litigation Authority (NHSLA)
> + NHS Redress Act 2006

Introduction

This chapter considers the likely course that any civil case against a nurse and/or NHS trust might follow, the ways in which compensation in the civil courts is assessed and the defences that may be available. It takes into account the major reforms in civil procedure which came into effect in April 1999, following the Report on Access to Justice by Lord Woolf[1] and the more recent changes including the NHS Redress Act 2006.

Civil proceedings

Two issues

In any civil case there are two separate issues:

1 Is the defendant liable?
2 How much compensation is payable?

It is sometimes possible that one of these issues has been agreed, e.g. the defendant accepts liability, but disagrees with the amount of compensation claimed by the victim, or that the amount of compensation that would be payable is agreed, but the defendant refuses to accept liability for that sum. Sometimes both issues are disputed. Evidence will therefore be required on both issues. The elements to establish liability and the kinds of harm for which compensation is payable are discussed in Chapter 3.

A nurse is first likely to be asked by management to provide a statement on the events. Care should be taken in the completion of this and guidelines are given in Chapter 9. If the victim has sought advice and has decided to commence an action, the next stages are set out below. These are stages in the High Court. Claims can be brought in the small claims court for up to £5,000 (£1,000 for personal injury cases). The County Court, which deals with claims up to £50,000, is speedier and less formal than the High Court, but the stages are similar (see Chapter 1 for civil courts).

Mediation

One of the results of the Woolf reforms in civil justice is that the parties are encouraged to resolve the dispute before going to court using mediation or other forms of resolution such as alternative dispute resolution. Often such processes can be linked with the complaints procedure (see Chapter 27) to avoid litigation. In mediation, an independent mediator attempts to assist the parties to reach an agreement to resolve the dispute. Unlike arbitration, the parties are under no compulsion to accept any ruling by the independent person.

Case management

The overriding principle enshrined in the new Civil Procedure Rules[2] (see Box 6.1) is that all cases should be dealt with justly. The court must seek to give effect to this overriding principle when it exercises any powers under the rules and when it interprets any rule. The parties also have a duty to help the court to further this overriding objective. The court in furthering this principle of dealing with cases justly must actively manage the cases. Active management includes:

1 Encouraging the parties to cooperate with each other in the conduct of the proceedings.
2 Identifying the issues at an early stage.
3 Deciding promptly which issues need full investigation and trial and accordingly disposing summarily of the others.
4 Deciding the order in which the issues are to be resolved.
5 Encouraging the parties to use an alternative dispute resolution procedure if the court considers that appropriate and facilitating the use of such procedure.

6 Helping the parties to settle the whole or part of the case.

7 Fixing timetables or otherwise controlling the progress of the case.

8 Considering whether the likely benefits of taking a particular step justify the cost of taking it.

9 Dealing with as many aspects of the case as it can on the same occasion.

10 Dealing with the case without the parties needing to attend court.

11 Making use of technology.

12 Giving directions to ensure that the trial of a case proceeds quickly and efficiently.

Box 6.1

The Civil Procedure Rules are a new procedural code with the overriding objective of enabling the court to deal with cases justly. They are available online.[3]

Dealing with a case justly includes, so far as is practicable:

1 Ensuring that the parties are on an equal footing.

2 Saving expense.

3 Dealing with the case in ways which are proportionate:
  (a) to the amount of money involved;
  (b) to the importance of the case;
  (c) to the complexity of the issues; and
  (d) to the financial position of each party.

4 Ensuring that it is dealt with expeditiously and fairly.

5 Allotting to it an appropriate share of the court's resources, while taking into account the need to allot resources to other cases.

A prime mechanism for judicially-led case management is the introduction of three tracks:

1 small claims track

2 fast track

3 multi-track.

The court allocates each case to one of these three tracks on the basis of information provided by the claimant on the statement of case. If it does not have enough information to allocate the claim then it will make an order requiring one or more parties to provide further information within 14 days.

Small claims track (CPR Part 27)

This provides a procedure for straightforward claims that do not exceed £5,000, without the need for substantial pre-hearing preparation and the formalities of a traditional trial and where costs are kept low.

Fast track (CPR Part 28)

Factors deciding whether a case is allocated to the fast track include: the limits likely to be placed on disclosure; the extent to which expert evidence may be necessary; and whether the trial will last longer than a day. Case management directions will be given at the allocation stage or at the listing stage.

Multi-track (CPR Part 29)

Other cases may be allocated to be dealt with on a multi-track basis and dealt with at a civil trial centre.

Pre-action protocol

Lord Woolf found that one of the major sources of increased costs and delay in clinical negligence litigation is at the pre-litigation stage and he therefore recommended the development and introduction of a pre-action protocol. A draft protocol was drawn up in 1997 by the Clinical Disputes Forum and was formally launched on 23 July 1998.[4] The protocol sets a standard of good practice with emphasis on better handling of potential disputes and more effective and efficient management of information and investigation. It also sets out the steps to be followed where litigation is in prospect.

Summary judgment or other early termination

Part of the court's duty of active case management is the summary disposal of issues that do not need full investigation and trial. The court can strike out a statement of case or give a summary judgment where either claimant or defendant has no reasonable prospect of success.

Disclosure and inspection of documents

A party discloses a document by stating that the document exists or has existed. Rules relating to the disclosure and inspection of documents are to be found in Part 31 of the Civil Procedure Rules. There are rules relating to standard disclosure that list the documents that are to be disclosed. These include:

1 the documents on which the party relies
2 the documents that adversely affect his own case or another party's case or support another party's case
3 the documents that he is required to disclose by a relevant practice direction.

A party is required to make a reasonable search for any relevant documents. Some documents are obtainable before a case begins under the Supreme Court Act 1981, Section 33. The nurse may well not be aware of this activity unless she is being personally sued or unless good communication ensures that she is kept in the picture. In *Harris* v. *Newcastle HA* [1989] 2 All ER 273, the court allowed pre-trial disclosure of records relating to events 26 years before, even though the health authority intended to plead that the case was out of time. The emphasis now is on full disclosure by each party to ensure that the case can be dealt with as promptly as possible.

Claim form is issued

This marks the beginning of the case. There are important time limits (discussed below) within which the claim form (originally known as a writ) is issued. The claim form indicates that action is now being commenced. It is preceded by what is known as a letter before action, i.e. a warning by the claimant (usually the claimant's solicitor) that if there is no acceptance of the claim, then the legal action will commence. The claim form usually names the NHS trust as the defendant, but it is possible for an individual employee to be named as a party and more than one defendant can be named.

Service of claim form (CPR Part 6)

This must be sent to the defendant within four months of its issue. (In the past there was a requirement for personal service, i.e. the claim form had to be handed to the defendant personally. Now, however, the claim form is sent to a known address.) The defendant must then respond by filing a defence or an admission or filing an acknowledgement of service. If the defendant fails to respond, the claimant may be able to obtain judgment in default.

The drafting of the documents or statements of case (these were once known as pleadings) is arranged by the respective parties' solicitors, who often instruct counsel (i.e. barristers). A litigant may, however, represent himself personally. Strict time limits are laid down for the service and response to the documents. Under the Woolf reforms, the documents exchanged between the parties should be simpler and be verified by the parties. If there are uncertainties, the court can require the parties to clarify any matter in dispute.

Pre-trial review

Eventually, there will be an assessment of the situation by the parties, together with a registrar or judge, account taken of the number of witnesses to attend, exchange of any experts' medical reports and, finally, the case will be set down for hearing.

Payment into court

Rules about offers to settle and payments into court are set out in Parts 36 and 37 of the Civil Procedure Rules. In some cases where there is dispute over the amount of compensation, but liability is accepted, the defendant will probably be advised to pay a sum in settlement of the case into court. If the claimant accepts this payment in, then the defendant will be liable for the claimant's costs up to that point. The court will be notified that there has been a settlement of the case. A payment in may also be made where the defendant does not accept liability, but he is not confident of winning the case and rather than risk losing and having to pay the costs of both sides he offers a sum in full and final settlement.

If the claimant decides that the payment in is not acceptable, the case will continue. In these circumstances, the judge is not told that there has been a payment in. He will not therefore be influenced by that in determining the case and deciding what compensation to award. If he awards less than the payment in or if he decides there is no liability by the defendant, then the claimant will have to pay both the defendant's costs from the time of the payment in as well as his own, since, of course, had the claimant accepted that sum deemed reasonable in comparison with the judge's award, there would have been no time-consuming and costly court hearing. These costs may well exceed the amount of the award. The judge has a discretion over whether to award the defendant the costs in these circumstances. An example of a refusal to accept a reasonable offer and becoming liable for the costs of a defendant is a case brought by a tourism student who sued his college for not warning him of leeches on a barefoot walk through a jungle. He was awarded £4,795 but could have to pay the college's court costs because he refused an offer of £10,000 (*The Times*, 29 November 2007).

The hearing

Claimant's case

Examination in chief

This is when questions are put to the witness by the party that has called him to give evidence.

The claimant has the burden of establishing to the satisfaction of the judge, on a balance of probabilities, that there has been negligence or some other alleged civil wrong. The claimant will therefore be asked to give evidence first.

His witnesses will be sworn in, in turn, and will then give evidence under examination of the claimant's legal representative. This has, in the past, usually been a barrister (counsel), instructed by the solicitor; but increasingly solicitors are taking on an advocacy role. Sometimes the claimant appears personally. This initial questioning is known as examination in chief. The witness cannot be asked leading questions when being examined in chief. Counsel will have before him the proof of the witness statements to the solicitor and will take him through this to bring his evidence to the court.

Expert evidence

Expert evidence from witnesses may be required on the nature of the standard of care that should have been provided or on the amount of compensation payable. The new Civil Procedure Rules have led to major changes in the giving of expert evidence and these are discussed in Chapter 9.

Cross-examination

Counsel for the defence is then able to question the witness, i.e. cross-examine. Here the task is to discredit the evidence by showing that it is irrelevant, unreliable or for some other reason is of no weight against the defendant. Alternatively, the witness can be used to support the case of the other side. Leading questions are allowed when the witness is under cross-examination. The judge will, however, intervene to protect the witness from harassment. (See Chapter 9 on giving evidence in court.) At this stage, the judge may wish to question the witness to clarify points on which he is not certain.

Re-examination

Finally, the side calling that witness has the chance of repairing any damage that the cross-examination has inflicted, but the re-examination is confined to points that have arisen during cross-examination or under questioning by the judge. All the claimant's witnesses give evidence in this way.

When the case for the claimant has ended, the judge has the opportunity of ending the case at this point and of finding against the claimant on the grounds that he has not established a *prima facie* case and therefore the defence is not required to give evidence. He cannot, of course, decide at this point against the defendant because the defence has not as yet given evidence.

Defendant's case

If the case proceeds, the defence must put forward its witnesses who are examined in chief, cross-examined and then re-examined as previously described. If it is alleged that the nurse has been negligent, she will be called as a witness for the defence. Several years may have elapsed since the events and her recall may be limited or even nil. She is able to refresh her memory by referring to contemporaneous records and therefore she should refer to the case notes. In this situation, she will appreciate the value of detailed, accurate, clear information on those events. Counsel who examines her in chief will have a copy of statements she has previously given. She should ensure that she had help in making this statement and prior to the court hearing she should be instructed on the procedure to be followed and some of the pitfalls she may encounter. Most of those who have appeared in court describe the event as particularly harrowing and preparation is essential. (Giving evidence in court is discussed further in Chapter 9.)

Judge's summing up

After summaries by counsel, the judge then has the task of making his or her judgment. This may be reserved, i.e. the parties are notified that they will be informed of the outcome, or it might be given immediately. The judge will determine both liability and damages (whichever are in dispute). The party having to pay costs will usually depend on the outcome, i.e. the loser pays the costs of both sides. There is no jury in a civil case (except in defamation cases).

Res ipsa loquitur

In certain cases, inferences can be made from the facts about the existence of negligence.[5] If the claimant can establish that it is a *res ipsa loquitur* situation ('the matter speaks for itself'), then the defendant can be asked to show how the incident occurred without negligence on his part. The claimant would have to show the following factors to raise a presumption of *res ipsa loquitur*:

1 What has occurred would not normally occur if reasonable care were taken.
2 The events were under the control or management of the defendant.
3 The defendant has not offered any reasonable explanation for what occurred.

The most obvious example is leaving a swab inside a patient or amputating the wrong limb. The doctrine was applied when a patient went into hospital with two stiff fingers and was discharged with four stiff fingers: he was entitled to receive an explanation from the hospital as to how this could have happened without negligence on its part.[6] This procedure gives the claimant a technical advantage that is very necessary when he is ignorant of the actual events that caused harm. If the defendant fails to give a reasonable explanation of the events, the court can draw the inference that there was negligence. In a case brought against Tesco by a woman who slipped on some yoghurt that had been spilt on the floor, the doctrine was applied and Tesco found liable.[7] In medical negligence cases the effect of *res ipsa loquitur* is to enable the claimant to force the defendant to respond at peril of having a finding of negligence made against him.[8]

Compensation in civil proceedings for negligence

Nurses sometimes meet patients who are hesitant to undertake all the necessary physiotherapy and other rehabilitative work lest the compensation will be reduced because they are seen to have made a full recovery. However, the powers of the court to make provisional awards or award interim amounts of compensation should make it easier for a claimant to focus on rehabilitation. There is also a duty on a claimant to mitigate or reduce their loss. In medical cases the test will be whether in all the circumstances and the medical advice given the claimant acted reasonably (for example, in refusing surgery).[9] The chance of a recommended remedial operation failing to rectify the claimant's condition has to be taken into account in determining compensation payable.

Practical Dilemma 6.1 | **Leslie's leg**

Leslie was travelling on his motorbike when a car started to overtake him. Unfortunately, a lorry was coming in the opposite direction and the vehicle pulled in to the side, knocking Leslie off. Leslie was admitted to the orthopaedic ward from A&E. He suffered a serious compound fracture. The prognosis was that he was unlikely to make a complete recovery and could anticipate further problems with the leg, a slight limp and a vulnerability to arthritis later on. He had been advised not to expect to return to his existing job (a PE instructor) for at least nine months. How will his likely compensation be calculated?

Special damages

Leslie will first be entitled to receive special damages. These are amounts to cover specific losses that have already been suffered and where the amount can therefore be accurately stated. For example, the loss and damage to his motorbike, damage to his clothing, loss of wages up to the present day. Interest is allowed on the items.

General damages

The headings under which such damages are calculated are shown in Box 6.2.

Box 6.2

1 Special damages: expenses and losses to the date of judgment.
2 General damages:
  (a) *non-pecuniary loss*:
    pain and suffering
    loss of amenity
  (b) *pecuniary loss*:
    loss of earnings
    loss of earning capacity
    cost of future care and expenses
    interest.

Non-pecuniary loss (i.e. non-financial loss)

1 *Pain and suffering*: this is to cover the pain from the injury itself, as well as from any consequential medical treatment and worry about the effects of the injury on the patient's lifestyle. It could also include damages for the mental suffering resulting from the fact that

the person's life has been shortened. (Administration of Justice Act 1982, Section 1(1)(a) introduced this form of compensation since there is no longer any compensation for the actual shortening of life itself. This used to be known as 'loss of expectation of life' and was abolished by this Act.)

2 *Loss of amenity*: Leslie will be able to recover additional compensation if it is established that his activities will be restricted because of the injuries to his leg. Clearly, if his leg had to be amputated, then he would recover an additional sum for that loss.

These non-pecuniary losses are notoriously difficult to calculate. How can money ever be an adequate compensation for blindness or loss of the ability to have children or to enjoy normal activities? The answer is that it cannot. However, since there is no other form of compensation, the non-pecuniary loss has to be converted into pecuniary form. Judges follow precedents in calculating the awards. They examine decisions in preceding cases, taking into account any relevant differences between the present case and the earlier cases and allowing for inflation. A judge's award is subject to appeal.

Pecuniary loss

1 *Loss of earnings*: Leslie's loss of future earnings would be calculated by determining his net annual loss multiplied by a figure to cover the number of years the disability will last. The figure takes into account the fact that the compensation will be paid out all at once rather than each week or month over the next few years. (Structured payments are now being introduced.)

2 *Loss of earning capacity*: because of his injury Leslie may never be able to work as a PE instructor again. Alternatively, he may retain his job initially, but with the risk that if he loses it he might never get similar paid work again because of his disability. He is entitled to be compensated for this risk.

3 *Expenses*: Leslie would also be entitled to recover reasonable expenses in getting to and from hospital, medical and similar expenses (e.g. physiotherapy) and, in some circumstances, domestic help.

4 *Interest*: interest is payable on the pecuniary loss already suffered and on the non-pecuniary loss.

5 *Deductions*: deductions are made in respect of the value of certain social security benefits, which are paid to the compensation recovery unit.

Interim payments can be made by the court under the Rules of the Supreme Court. The claimant can apply for an interim payment at any time after the claim form has been served on the defendant. Thus, where the defendant has admitted liability, but disputes the amount of damages payable, the court could make an order for an interim payment to be made. Because of the uncertainty of prognosis, there is the power for an order of provisional damages for personal injuries to be made if there is a chance that at some time in the future the injured person will, as a result of the act or omission, develop some serious disease or suffer some serious deterioration in his physical or mental condition (Supreme Court Act 1981, Section 32A and Rules of Supreme Court 0.37, pp. 7-10). Provisional damages in relation to exposure to asbestos were awarded in one case.[10] Where large settlements are to be paid, parties often agree a structured settlement whereby an annuity is purchased with part of the lump sum, thus providing an income to the claimant for life.

In December 2003 £5.75 million in agreed damages was awarded to Matthew King, then aged eight, who had been starved of oxygen at birth and suffered from cerebral palsy. South

---

Case 6.1   *Webster v. Hammersmith Hospital NHS Trust* (2002)

Brain damage at birth[11]

The girl, aged seven at the date of hearing, suffered brain injury at birth. Liability was admitted by the defendants. The birth injury resulted in dyskinetic choreo-athetoid cerebral palsy producing severe physical disability in all four limbs, but leaving her awareness and intelligence intact. She was likely to live to the age of 65 years. She could not walk unaided and would always be dependent on a wheelchair, with the assistance of one (and in many circumstances, two) carers for any venture taking her out of her home. She had good sight and hearing but her speech was dysarthric and difficult to understand. She was a gifted child with high verbal ability. She was very determined in her attitude to life. She would be likely to have had a university education and to have pursued some form of professional career. General damages of £180,000 were awarded within a total award of £4,186,221 made up as follows:

Past losses: Travel (£394); incidental (£2,195); aids (£3,144); past care (£45,000); property (£70,000); interest (£120,733)

Future loss: Loss of earnings £407,000; aids (£416.257); care up to age 19 (£546,601); care 19+ (£1,946,185); IT equipment (£75,000); physio (£37,000); property (£400,000); investment (£18,780); pain, suffering and loss of amenity (£180,000); interest (£5,500)

Total: £4,186,221

Kent Hospitals NHS Trust admitted liability for his injuries, but the valuation of his claim had been deferred so that his needs could be assessed.[12] In January 2004 Oliver Davies, then eight years old, received £3.4 million damages for oxygen starvation at birth which led to acute cerebral palsy. Oxford Radcliffe Hospitals NHS Trust admitted liability. There had been an inexcusable delay in arranging an emergency delivery.[13]

Where there has been a failure to diagnose a terminal condition such as cancer, damages can be awarded for the loss of a chance of successful treatment being given, but it may be difficult for the claimant to establish, on a balance of probabilities, that it was more probable than not that the outcome would have been materially different had the diagnosis been made earlier.[14] (See Chapter 3.)

An example of the assessment of compensation is shown in Box 6.3.[15]

Calculating amount of compensation

The House of Lords ruled that in awarding compensation, victims should not be expected to speculate on the stock market and therefore lower levels of return based on index-linked government securities can be used as the basis of calculation. The effect of this ruling will be to increase the capital amount awarded to victims. In the case itself, James Thomas, a cerebral palsy victim as a result of negligence at birth, was awarded £1,285,000 by the High Court judge, but this was reduced by the Court of Appeal by £300,000 on the basis that the capital could be invested in the higher-return (but more risky) equities. The House of Lords restored the original amount.[16] Subsequently the Lord Chancellor issued a statement[17] which recognised that the use of index-linked government stock as the basis for calculation was appropriate, even though the Court of Protection invested client funds partly in equities.

Courts were able to adopt a different rate if there were exceptional circumstances under Section 1(2) of the Damages Act 1996.

Box 6.3	**Example of an assessment of compensation:** *Inman* v. *Cambridge Health Authority*, **January 1998**

Spastic quadriplegic cerebral palsy sustained at birth

The claimant was aged nine when the settlement was approved. As a result of a late delivery, he was severely acidotic at birth and had suffered bilateral cerebral cortical damage resulting in quadriplegic cerebral palsy. The defendants admitted negligence by the midwife in failing to summon an obstetrician, but they denied causation. Damages were eventually agreed as follows:

	£
General damages	125,000
Interest	12,500
Past care	58,500
Accommodation	50,000
Other past expenses	139,000
Future care	600,000
Claimant's loss of earnings	115,000
Accommodation (future)	40,000
Other future expenses	225,000
Education	50,000
Total	**1,300,000**

A structured settlement was eventually agreed after some dispute and approved by the judge. A sum of £689,000 was returned to the defendants to provide £20,000 per year to the claimant to the age of 19 and thereafter £35,000.

The Law Commission recommended changes to the present system relating to the quantifying of damages for personal injury[18] in 1996 and suggested, among other recommendations, that the NHS should be able to recover the costs arising from the treatment of road traffic and other accident victims. It is estimated that this might bring in £120 million to the NHS. A later report by the Law Commission[19] in 1999 recommended that compensation for non-pecuniary loss (e.g. pain, suffering and loss of amenity) should be increased and this could be implemented through the courts' decisions on damages. The Court of Appeal gave judgment in March 2000[20] and decided that a modest increase was required to bring some awards up to a figure that was fair, reasonable and just. It recommended that damages for claims above £10,000 should be raised by a maximum of about 35 per cent with increases tapering downwards. The Court of Appeal acknowledged that the life expectancy for many seriously injured claimants has increased and they can now survive for many years. There is likely to be a significant impact on the NHS as a result of this judgment, although not perhaps as much as if the Law Commission recommendations had been supported in full. The continuity of future periodic payments as a result of the possible failure of the NHS Foundation was questioned in one case. The judge held that the continuity was reasonably secured because arrangements had been agreed whereby the NHS Litigation Authority was the source of the payments and was therefore legally responsible for the payments.[21]

The new statutory scheme for compensation following clinical negligence may have considerable effect on the levels of compensation paid out. (See NHS redress scheme on page 133.)

The principles of determining the compensation payable when a child is born following a failed sterilisation or a failure to advise a woman that the foetus is suffering from disabilities (and therefore the possibility of a termination not being discussed) are considered in Chapter 15.

Defences to a civil action

A considerable number of claims that are brought against NHS trusts and health authorities are dropped before they reach a final outcome and many of those that survive to the end are unsuccessful. They may fail because on investigation there are no grounds for negligence or some of the other defences succeed. This section looks at the defences open to a nurse or her employer in civil actions for negligence.

Denial of facts

It often happens that, when things go wrong, it is one person's word against another. The patient might complain that the nurse has been negligent, but the nurse might be able to show that the events were not as the patient describes. Many court cases are simply disputes over facts. Where only two people are involved, with no other witnesses and no other circumstantial evidence, if such a case comes before the courts, the judge will have to decide, on the basis of the evidence in court and the way the parties stand up to cross-examination, which account of the events is acceptable. Records of what took place can be of considerable significance in determining the outcome of the hearing.

In civil cases, the burden is on the claimant to establish, on a balance of probabilities, that the defendant has been negligent.

A missing element

Even where the facts are not disputed, it might still be possible for an action for negligence to be defended on the grounds that one of the essential elements is missing. From Chapter 3 it will be recalled that to succeed in a negligence case it is necessary for the claimant to establish that a duty of care was owed by the defendant, that the defendant was in breach of this duty and that this breach caused reasonably foreseeable harm to the claimant. If one of these elements has not been established on a balance of probabilities, then the defendant will win the case.

Contributory negligence

Practical Dilemma 6.2   Walking aids

Fred, who has recently had an operation for a fractured leg, has been receiving help from the physiotherapist in walking with crutches. Fred asks a nursing auxiliary, who has only just come on to the ward, for help in going to the toilet. She is not aware that Fred has been told not to try to walk yet unless he is accompanied by a qualified person. She assists him out of bed and on to the crutches. As she does so, the crutches slip from under Fred and he falls to the ground, sustaining another fracture.

In this situation, the nursing auxiliary or the ward management are clearly at fault in allowing Fred out of bed in these circumstances. However, Fred is also at fault. He should have followed instructions. Fred's responsibility for the harm that has occurred depends to a large extent on his level of understanding, how clear the instructions were to him and how reasonable it was to expect him to have waited for experienced help in using the crutches. If he were to sue the NHS trust and its staff, they may well defend themselves on the grounds that he was partly at fault in not taking care of himself. This defence is known as a defence of contributory negligence. The defendant is saying to the claimant: 'You failed to take care of yourself and that has led to or increased the harm that you have suffered.' If the judge is satisfied that the defendant has succeeded in this defence, he is able to reduce the compensation by the extent to which he considers the claimant's fault has contributed to the harm. The wording of Section 1 of the Law Reform (Contributory Negligence) Act 1945 is shown in the following Statute:

Statute   **Law Reform (Contributory Negligence) Act 1945 Section 1**

Section 1(1) Where any person suffers damage as the result partly of his own fault and partly of any other person or persons a claim in respect of that damage shall not be defeated by reason of the fault of the person suffering the damage, but the damages recoverable in respect thereof shall be reduced to such an extent as the court thinks just and equitable having regard to the claimant's share in responsibility for the damage.

Case 6.2   *Froom v. Butcher* (1975)

No seat belt[22]

Mr Froom was driving his car carefully at a speed of 30–35 mph with his wife sitting beside him and his daughter in the back seat. The front seats were fitted with seatbelts, but neither Mr nor Mrs Froom was wearing one. Unfortunately, Mr Froom's car was struck head on by a car travelling at speed in the opposite direction and on the wrong side of the road as it had pulled out to overtake a line of traffic.

The trial judge decided that failure to wear a seatbelt was not contributory negligence. The defendant appealed to the Court of Appeal and won his appeal. Lord Denning emphasised that where the damage to the claimant would not have been reduced by failure to wear the seatbelt, then there should be no reduction of compensation, but where, as here, the injuries would have been reduced by wearing a seatbelt, there should be a reduction of compensation. In Mr Froom's case, the injuries to the head and chest would have been prevented by wearing a seatbelt. His finger would have been broken anyway and therefore there was no reduction on that account. The overall deduction of compensation for Mr Froom's contributory negligence was held to be 20 per cent. (This case was heard before the wearing of front seatbelts was compulsory.)

Reductions of compensation on grounds of contributory negligence can vary from 95 per cent to 5 per cent. When it is larger, then there is held to be no liability on the part of the defendant; when it is smaller it is considered to be too insignificant to count. To succeed, the defendant has to establish that the claimant failed to take reasonable care of himself and that this failure contributed to the harm he suffered, or increased it.

Contributory negligence and children

Lord Denning has said:

> *A very young child cannot be guilty of contributory negligence. An older child may be; but it depends on the circumstances. A judge should only find a child guilty of contributory negligence if he or she is of such an age as reasonably to be expected to take precautions for his or her own safety: and then he or she is only to be found guilty if blame should be attached to him or her.*

In the same case, Lord Justice Salmon said:

> *The question as to whether the plaintiff can be said to have been guilty of contributory negligence depends on whether any ordinary child of 13½ years could be expected to have done any more than this child did. I say 'any ordinary child'. I do not mean a paragon of prudence; nor do I mean a scatter-brain child; but the ordinary girl of 13½ [the age of the child in that case].*[23]

Willing assumption of risk (*volenti non fit injuria*)

Sometimes, where there is a known risk, the possibility of this taking place is accepted and the defendant is not liable. The most obvious example is dangerous sports where both players and spectators are at some risk. If that risk occurs, it is assumed that there will be no court action, but that the risk has been willingly accepted. For example, in a rugby match it is possible that a player may be seriously injured, even though no rules have been broken and there is no criminal act. This is a risk of the game and is accepted by the players. If, of course, the rules have been broken and thus resulted in injuries, then the injured player may well have an action for assault.

In the health service context, the agreement by the patient that treatment can proceed counts not only as consent to what would otherwise constitute a trespass to the person, but it is also an acceptance of the possibility that those hazards that are an inextricable risk of that particular treatment could occur. Consent, however, does not imply consent to the risk that the professional will be negligent (see Chapter 7 on consent).

Practical Dilemma 6.3   **Blood donor**

Rachel had been giving blood for many years. She was summoned on one occasion to the session. As the needle was inserted and the cannula put in place, she felt an appalling pain. She shrieked and the needle was quickly withdrawn and a new painless site was found. After the session, Rachel found that it was very difficult to move her hand, arm and fingers. She was examined by a doctor who sent her for tests and eventually she was told that a very rare damage to the nerve had occurred. However, she was assured that with physiotherapy she would soon recover full function. Unfortunately, this did not prove to be true. She was eventually forced to take early retirement on the grounds of ill health and did not recover full arm or hand movement. She sought advice about suing the doctor and was given an expert's report that such a rare event could occur without any negligence on the part of the doctor, so that there was no point in suing either the doctor or the blood transfusion authority. However, Rachel argued that if she had known of the risk she would not have agreed to give blood unless she had been given an assurance that in the event of the risk taking place she would have received compensation.

As the law stands at present, unless Rachel can show negligence by the professional staff or the employer, she would be unable to recover compensation in court. We do not have a system of no-fault liability. As a volunteer, she can be assumed to have accepted the possibility of those risks occurring, although she may well be able to show that there was a breach of the duty owed to her as a volunteer if certain risks were not pointed out to her. The Pearson Report on compensation for personal injuries recommended that there should be an acceptance of no-fault liability for volunteers in medical research. These recommendations have not yet been implemented in law (although pharmaceutical companies offer compensation on a no-fault liability basis to those who take part in drug trials (see Chapter 28)) and it could be argued that if the recommendations ever are implemented they should be extended to cover such situations as donation of blood. In such situations, many NHS trusts would make an *ex gratia* payment, i.e. a payment without any acceptance or implication of liability on its part.

To establish a defence of willing assumption of risk, the defendant has to show that the claimant knew of the risk, willingly consented to run it and waived any right to sue for compensation. If it is successfully pleaded, it operates as a total defence.

Sometimes employers have tried to rely on this defence when sued by an employee for injuries at work. For example, it has been said that back injuries are an occupational hazard for nurses; all psychiatric nurses accept the risk of physical violence; CSSD assistants are likely to suffer from 'sharp' injuries as an occupational hazard. However, it is quite clear that where there is a failure of the employer in his duty to care for the employee's safety, then the defence of willing assumption of risk will not prevail. (See Chapter 12 on health and safety law.)

Exemption from liability

NHS trust premises are a blaze of exemption notices: 'no responsibility is taken for cars parked in this area'; 'the "X" NHS trust accepts no liability for patients' property'. How effective are these notices if the NHS trust or its employees are negligent? Can a patient be persuaded to sign a form saying that he will not hold the 'X' NHS trust liable in any respect? Sometimes an NHS trust responds to a complaint by asking for a declaration that if the complaint is to be pursued and an investigation conducted, then the NHS trust requires an assurance that there will be no civil action. Can such a declaration be held against the person who signed? The answer to these questions is to a considerable extent given by reference to the Unfair Contract Terms Act 1977. This Act prevents anyone in the course of any business activity (and this covers professional, local and public authority activity) from exempting himself from negligence if that negligence gives rise to personal injury or death. Any agreement, notice or clause to that effect is void (see the Statute on pages 129–30).

Practical Dilemma 6.4　　No liability

A surgeon said: 'I am prepared to carry out upon you a very risky operation and I want you to sign that you will exempt me from all blame if anything goes wrong.' The patient, in his desire to have the operation, signed the form, but, unfortunately, the surgeon made a very careless error that no competent surgeon would have made, leaving the patient severely disabled.

Is the patient bound by that form? The answer is no. The Unfair Contract Terms Act prevents the surgeon relying on that form as a defence against the patient. He cannot exclude or restrict his liability for death or personal injury resulting from his negligence. The same principles do not apply to loss of or damage to property. Under the Unfair Contract Terms Act 1977, an exemption for damage to or loss of property is valid if it is reasonable (see the Statute below). (For further discussion on this, see Chapter 25.)

Limitation of time

Most civil court actions must be brought within a certain length of time. The time limit for actions concerning personal injury and death is three years from the cause of action arising or the date of the knowledge of the cause of action arising. The issue of the claim form marks the beginning of the court action and it is the time that elapses from the cause arising to the day the claim form is issued that is critical.

Knowledge of the harm

If a patient did not realise that he was suffering from the effects of someone's negligence in that time, then the time limit does not apply till he has that knowledge. It used to be law that if the claimant was out of time for whatever reason then he was barred from proceeding with the case. The injustice of this rule is very easy to see from cases involving such long-term diseases as pneumoconiosis, asbestosis and similar conditions. The law was therefore amended so that the period did not start to run until the claimant had knowledge of the facts shown in the Statute on page 130.

The potential claimant cannot, however, simply turn a blind eye to knowledge that any reasonable person would acquire from the facts around him. If, however, he had no knowledge of the facts, then he is not barred from proceeding.

Statute   **Sections from the Unfair Contract Terms Act 1977**

1 Scope of Part I

1 For the purposes of this part of this Act, 'negligence' means the breach:
   (a) of any obligation, arising from the express or implied terms of a contract, to take reasonable care or exercise skill in the performance of the contract
   (b) of any common law duty to take reasonable care or exercise reasonable skill (but not stricter duty)
   (c) of the common duty of care imposed by the Occupiers' Liability Act 1957 or the Occupiers' Liability Act (Northern Ireland) 1957.

2 This part of this Act is subject to Part III; and in relation to contracts, the operation of Sections 2 to 4 and 7 is subject to the exceptions made by Schedule 1.

3 In the case of both contract and tort, Sections 2 to 7 apply (except where the contrary is stated in Section 6(4)) only to business liability, that is liability for breach of obligations or duties arising:
   (a) from things done or to be done by a person in the course of a business (whether his own business or another's), or
   (b) from the occupation of premises used for business purposes of the occupier; and references to liability are to be read accordingly.

Statute continued

4 In relation to any breach of duty or obligation, it is immaterial for any purpose of this part of this Act whether the breach was inadvertent or intentional, or whether liability for it arises directly or vicariously.

2 Negligence liability

1 A person cannot by reference to any contract term or to a notice given to persons generally or to particular persons exclude or restrict his liability for death or personal injury resulting from negligence.

2 In the case of other loss or damage, a person cannot so exclude or restrict his liability for negligence except insofar as the term or notice satisfies the requirement of reasonableness.

3 Where a contract term or notice purports to exclude or restrict liability for negligence a person's agreement to or awareness of it is not of itself to be taken as indicating his voluntary acceptance of any risk.

11 The 'reasonableness' test

3 In relation to a notice (not being a notice having contractual effect), the requirement of reasonableness under this Act is that it should be fair and reasonable to allow reliance on it, having regard to all the circumstances obtaining when the liability arose or (but for the notice) would have arisen.

4 Where by reference to a contract term or notice a person seeks to restrict liability to a specified sum of money, and the question arises (under this or any other Act) whether the term or notice satisfies the requirement of reasonableness, regard shall be had in particular (but without prejudice to subsection (2) above in the case of contract terms) to:

   (a) the resources which he could expect to be available to him for the purpose of meeting the liability should it arise and
   (b) how far it was open to him to cover himself by insurance.

5 It is for those claiming that a contract term or notice satisfies the requirements of reasonableness to show that it does.

14 Interpretation of Part I

In this part of this Act: 'business' includes a profession and the activities of any government department or local or public authority.

Statute | **Limitation Act 1980 S. 14: Definition of knowledge**

(a) that the injury in question was significant

(b) that the injury was attributable in whole or in part to the act or omission which is alleged to constitute negligence

(c) the identity of the defendant, and

(d) the identity of any other defendant.

The term 'significant' is further defined as where 'the person whose date of knowledge is in question would reasonably have considered it sufficiently serious to justify instituting proceeding against a defendant who did not dispute liability'.

> ## Practical Dilemma 6.5   Delay
>
> Claire French was admitted for an appendectomy. The operation was performed success-fully and she was discharged. From time to time, however, she complained of violent stomach pain for which she took very strong pain killers. Some six years after the first operation, she was admitted to hospital in intense agony and no pain killer could relieve it. The consultant was reluctant to operate since he could not identify any possible cause for which surgery was the solution. However, a laparoscopy was performed and it was then discovered that a swab had been left behind in the previous operation. The consultant was completely open with Claire about his findings and assured her that from now on she should not get any pain. She felt that she should be compensated for the fact that she had already suffered much pain and had had to endure the risks, pain and suffering of a second operation. Is she entitled to compensation?

As a result of the changes to the Limitation Act 1980, she would not be barred on the grounds of exceeding the time limit, which would run from the time she was informed of the cause of her suffering. The House of Lords has eased the time limit of those suing for rape or sexual assault[24].

Judge's discretion to extend time limit

In addition, the judge has the discretion to allow a case to proceed that would otherwise be outside the time limit where it would be just to the claimant to permit him to continue. A judge refused to extend the time limit in the following case.

> ## Case 6.3   *Fenech v. E. London and City Health Authority (2000)*
>
> **No extension of time**[25]
>
> On 5 July 1960 the claimant gave birth to her first child. Afterwards, the doctor suturing her episiotomy informed her that the needle that he had been using had broken. In fact, a two-inch piece of the needle had been left inside the wound. The claimant experienced pain in the area of the episiotomy, but was too embarrassed to discuss her symptoms with her general practitioner. She gave birth to five more children. In 1983, she came under the care of a female gynaecologist and underwent a number of negative investigations and operations over a period of 11 years. The fragment of the needle was identified on a hip X-ray when she was being reviewed by orthopaedic surgeons in 1991, but it was not until a repeat X-ray in 1994 that she was informed of the needle's presence. She issued proceedings in January 1997 and the issue of limitation was tried as a preliminary point. At the County Court, her claim was held to be statute barred: although she had not attained actual knowledge until 1994, she had had constructive knowledge 'long before 1994'. She appealed to the Court of Appeal on the grounds that the judge had erred in refusing to take into account her embarrassment when considering when she ought reasonably to have sought medical advice and the defendant could not prove that such earlier advice would have led to an earlier detection of the needle fragment.

The Court of Appeal dismissed the appeal on the grounds that she should have sought medical advice earlier, she failed to give the gynaecologist sufficient information about her symptoms and while the 1991 X-ray had revealed the fragment of the needle, its significance and relationship to her gynaecological problems were not realised by the orthopaedic specialists who were reviewing her for a hip replacement.

In contrast, in the case of *Amanda Godfrey* v. *Gloucester Royal Infirmary NHS Trust*,[26] in which the claimant argued that while she had been told following an ultra scan that her baby (who was born in 1995) had severe abnormalities, she did not have sufficient information to make a decision about a termination until she read the medical report in 2001, the judge did not accept this argument but was still prepared to exercise his discretion under Section 33 of the Limitation Act 1980 and held that it was equitable to allow the case to proceed.

Extension of the time limit on other grounds

Where minors under 18 years of age have suffered personal injury, there is no time barrier to bringing an action until they reach the age of 18 years, at which time the time limit comes into operation. (See Chapter 13 on children.) The same principle applies to those of unsound mind whose disorder prevents them from bringing an action within the appropriate time limits. The time limits do not commence until the disorder ceases, which in most cases will be at death.

Legal aid and conditional fees

One of the recent changes in civil justice is the withdrawal of legal aid in personal injury claims. The introduction of conditional fee systems into civil litigation, sometimes referred to as 'no win, no fee', enables an agreement to be drawn up between solicitor and client, whereby the former would act on behalf of the latter in civil proceedings and only claim a fee if the outcome is satisfactory to the client. Regulations[27] that came into force in June 2003 enable clients to enter into simpler, more transparent conditional fee agreements (CFAs) with the solicitors and enable solicitors to guarantee to clients that they will get all the damages awarded. In some cases, especially those involving clinical negligence, it may be necessary for the client to purchase insurance cover for possible witnesses and other costs.

Clinical Negligence Scheme for Trusts (CNST) and the NHS Litigation Authority (NHSLA)

The CNST was established in 1996[28] to administer a scheme where trusts and other NHS bodies take part in a voluntary scheme whereby compensation is met from a pooling system. The payment into the pool depends on an assessment of the risk presented by that particular trust and amounts over a specified minimum will be met from the pool. The CNST visits organisations that belong or wish to belong to the scheme in order to assess their risk: they examine, in particular, the standard of risk assessment and management in the organisation; and the standards of record keeping. In the light of their assessment, premiums payable into the scheme are assessed. Over 95 per cent of NHS trusts are members of CNST. Liabilities prior to April 1995 are covered by the Existing Liabilities Scheme (ELS), which is centrally funded.

The NHS Litigation Authority (NHSLA) is a special health authority, i.e. a statutory body set up in 1995 to oversee the CNST in the handling of claims. The NHSLA uses an approved list of solicitors to handle litigation. In one case discussed earlier,[29] when the parties disputed the details for the setting up of a structured settlement, the claimant gave notice that they would ask the judge to summon the NHSLA's chief executive to explain why the defendants were attempting to charge the claimant for setting up the structured settlement. The defendants then reached agreement with the claimant. The NHSLA is subject to an annual performance review.

NHS redress scheme

The costs of compensation resulting from clinical negligence in the NHS has been constantly growing. The National Audit Office reported in May 2001 that almost £4 billion would be required to meet the costs of known and anticipated claims in the NHS.[30] A high proportion of that sum goes to lawyers. The National Audit Office made far-reaching recommendations in relation to the number of claims, the costs of settling them and the time taken, suggesting action to be taken by the Litigation Authority and the Legal Services Commission to bring cases to a conclusion. It recommended that the DH, the Lord Chancellor's Department and the Legal Services Commission should investigate alternative ways of satisfactorily resolving the small and medium-sized claims. In the light of the National Audit Office Report, the Department of Health announced in July 2001[31] that it was setting up a committee under the chairmanship of the Chief Medical Officer of Health to consider a new scheme for compensation for clinical negligence. A consultation paper was published in July 2001.[32] This was followed, on 30 June 2003, by a further consultation document *Making Amends*.[33] *Making Amends* provided a comprehensive account of the background to the present situation. It looked at the present system of medical negligence litigation and its costs. It analysed public attitudes and concerns and the earlier reviews of the negligence system by the Pearson Commission,[34] the Woolf Report on Access to Justice[35] and the National Audit Office Report in 2001.[36] It considered recent action taken to reform civil court procedures, claims handling by the NHS Litigation Authority and the use of alternative dispute resolution. It analysed systems of no-fault liability in Denmark, Finland, France, New Zealand, Norway and Sweden and discussed no-fault liability as an option along with continued reform of the present tort process, a tariff-based national tribunal or a composite option drawing on all three. The scheme eventually recommended in *Making Amends* was a composite package of reform drawing on the best elements of these three options. It included suggestions for the care and compensation for severely neurologically impaired babies; for the NHS redress scheme to be part of the system for handling complaints; for the retention of right to pursue litigation through the courts and changes to the existing scheme for civil proceedings; and for a duty of candour to be placed on healthcare professionals and managers to inform patients where they become aware of a possible negligent action or omission.

NHS Redress Act 2006

The NHS Redress Act which was eventually agreed was a very much less radical scheme than that proposed in the consultation paper *Making Amends*. It gives power to the Secretary of State to establish a scheme for the purpose of enabling redress to be provided without recourse to civil proceedings. Regulations are to be drawn up giving the details. The scheme can cover services provided by the Secretary of State, a primary care trust or a designated strategic health authority or an organisation or person providing services under an arrangement with these bodies. Excluded from the redress scheme are primary dental services, primary medical services, general ophthalmic services and pharmaceutical services. A scheme does not apply in relation to a liability that is or has been the subject of civil proceedings (S. 2(2)). Ordinarily the scheme will provide for the following redress:

(a) an offer of compensation in satisfaction of any right to bring civil proceedings

(b) giving an explanation

(c) giving an apology

(d) giving a report on the action which has been or will be taken to prevent similar cases arising.

The scheme may make provision for compensation to take the form of entry into a contract to provide care or treatment or of financial compensation or both. It can also detail the circumstances in which different forms of compensation may be offered. The scheme can set the upper limit on the amount of financial compensation to be offered and if it does not do so, it must specify an upper limit on the amount of financial compensation that may be included in such an offer in respect of pain and suffering. The scheme may not specify any other limit on what may be included in such an offer by way of financial compensation. The scheme can detail the following provisions relating to the commencement of proceedings:

(a) who may commence proceedings

(b) how proceedings are commenced

(c) time limits for commencing

(d) circumstances precluding proceedings being commenced

(e) proceedings being commenced in specified circumstances

(f) notification of the commencement of proceedings in specified circumstances.

The scheme may also make provision for proceedings under the scheme including details of the investigation of cases, decisions about the application of the scheme, the time limits within which an offer can be accepted, certain settlements in specified cases to be subject to approval by the court and the termination of proceedings under the scheme.

The scheme must make provision for the findings of an investigation of a case to be recorded in a report and make provision for a copy of the report to be provided on request to the individual seeking redress. However, no copy of an investigation report need be provided before an offer is made under the scheme or proceedings are terminated or in other specified circumstances. A settlement agreement must include a waiver of the right to bring civil proceedings in respect of the liability to which the settlement relates and the scheme must also provide for the termination of proceedings under the scheme if the liability to which the proceedings related becomes the subject of civil proceedings. The scheme must also provide for the suspension of the limitation period under the Limitation Act 1980.

The provision of legal advice (from a specified list of persons) without charge to individuals seeking redress may be specified under the scheme. The scheme may also include the provision of other services including the services of medical experts who must be instructed jointly by the scheme authority and the individual seeking redress. The Secretary of State also has a duty to arrange, to such extent as he considers necessary to meet all reasonable requirements, for the provision of assistance (by way of representation or otherwise) to those seeking redress (S. 9(1)). Payments may be made to any person under these arrangements, who should be independent of any person to whose conduct the case related or who is involved in dealing with the case. The Secretary of State can make provision about the membership of the scheme and the functions of members. Section 10 sets out the members' responsibilities, including the duty to publish an annual report. The Secretary of State may also make provision for the scheme authority, i.e. the special health authority, to have specified functions. The scheme must include provision requiring the scheme authority and the members of the scheme, in carrying out their functions under the scheme, to have regard in particular to the desirability of redress being provided without recourse to civil proceedings (S. 12). Section 13 specifies a general duty of cooperation between the scheme authority and the Commission for Healthcare Audit and Inspection, and between the scheme authority and the National Patient Safety Agency. Regulations may determine provisions about complaints on the handling and consideration of complaints relating to the scheme (S. 14) and the remit of the Health Service Comissioner is extended to include complaints about the exercise of functions under a scheme established under the NHS Redress Act 2006.

Conclusions

The need for urgent reform of the current system for obtaining compensation for clinical negligence has been clear. There was concern from Parliament: the Public Accounts Committee investigated the handling of clinical negligence cases[37] and the Health Service Committee of the House of Commons recommended a review of the possibility of no-fault compensation being introduced.[38] The NHS redress scheme does not contain the radical proposals set out in *Making Amends* and it remains to be seen whether the scheme will have the effect of reducing the extent of civil litigation in relation to the NHS and the cost of compensation.

Reflection questions

1 Look at the aspects of case management as set out on pages 115-17 and consider the extent to which this should ensure that cases are dealt with faster and more justly to the parties.

2 What is meant by *res ipsa loquitur*? In what situations in healthcare do you think it could apply?

3 What is the difference between pecuniary loss and non-pecuniary loss as a result of a civil wrong? How is compensation for the latter calculated?

4 What is meant by contributory negligence? What are the principles on which the judge works in deciding the level of deduction of compensation? (See the Statute on page 126.)

5 Are there any tasks that you perform that are likely to cause harm to you? Do you consider the principle of *volenti non fit injuria* applies to any of them and, if so, why?

Further exercises

1 Examine the notices in your hospital that disclaim any responsibility for loss or damage. Consider any ways in which they might not be completely effective in the light of the Unfair Contract Terms Act 1977.

2 What action do you consider could be taken to reduce the level and therefore the cost of litigation within the NHS?

3 Obtain a copy of your local NHS redress scheme and contrast its workings with legal action through civil proceedings.

References

[1] Lord Woolf, Access to Justice. Full details of the Civil Procedure Rules are available on the website at http://www.open.gov.uk/lcd/civil/procrules_fin/crules.htm

[2] Ian Grainger and Michael Fealy, *Introduction to the New Civil Procedure Rules*, Cavendish Publications Ltd, London, 1999

[3] www.justice.gov.uk/civil/procrules_fin/contents/parts/

[4] NHS Executive, Handling Clinical Negligence Claims, HSC 1998/183

[5] *Roe* v. *Minister of Health* [1954] 2 QB 66

[6] *Cassidy* v. *Ministry of Health* [1951] 2 KB 343

[7] *Ward* v. *Tesco Stores Ltd* [1976] 1 WLR 810 HL

[8] *Ratcliffe* v. *Plymouth and Torbay HA* [1998] PIQR P170

[9] *Selvanayagam* v. *University of West Indies* [1983] 1 All ER 824

[10] *Hurditch* v. *Sheffield HA* [1989] 2 All ER 869

[11] *Webster (A Child)* v. *Hammersmith Hospital NHS Trust*, February 2002 (taken from *Quantum of Damages*, Vol. 3, Kemp and Kemp, Sweet & Maxwell, 2008 edn, pp. 51507-8 and 51565-75)

[12] News item, £5.75m for palsy boy, *The Times*, 20 December 2003

[13] News item, Hospital payout, *The Times*, 20 January 2004

[14] *Gregg* v. *Scott* [2003] Lloyd's Rep Med 3 105

[15] *Inman* v. *Cambridge Health Authority*, January 1998 (taken from *Quantum of Damages*, Vol. 2, Kemp and Kemp, Sweet & Maxwell, 1998 edn)

[16] *Wells* v. *Wells* [1999] 1 AC 345

[17] Lord Chancellor Statement, 27 July 2001; Kemp and Kemp, *The Quantum of Damages*, Vol. 2, 36090/2, 2007 edn

[18] Law Commission, Damages for Personal Injury: medical, nursing and other expenses, The Stationery Office, London, 1996

[19] Law Commission Report No. 257, Personal Injury Compensation for Non-pecuniary Loss, 19 April 1999

[20] *Heil* v. *Rankin*, *The Times*, 24 March 2000; [2000] 2 WLR 1173

[21] *YM (A child)* v. *Gloucestershire Hospitals NHS Foundation Trust; Kanu* v. *King's College Hospital NHS Trust* [2006] EWHC 820; [2006] PIQR P27

[22] *Froom* v. *Butcher* [1975] 3 All ER 520

[23] *Gough* v. *Thorne* [1966] 3 All ER 398 CA

[24] *A v Hoare* (and other cases) [2008] UKHL 6

[25] *Alice Maud Fenech* v. *East London and City Health Authority* [2000] Lloyd's Rep Med p. 35 CA

[26] *Amanda Godfrey* v. *Gloucester Royal Infirmary NHS Trust* [2003] Lloyd's Rep Med 8 398

[27] Conditional Fee Agreements (Miscellaneous Amendments) Regulations 2003

[28] National Health Service (Clinical Negligence Scheme) Regulations XI 1996 No. 251; amendment regulations SI 2002 No. 1073

[29] *Inman* v. *Cambridge Health Authority*, January 1998 (taken from *Quantum of Damages*, Vol. 2, Kemp and Kemp, Sweet & Maxwell, 1998 edn)

[30] National Audit Office, Handling Clinical Negligence Claims in England, Report of the Comptroller and Auditor General, HC 403 Session 2000-2001, 3 May 2001

[31] Department of Health press release 2001/0313, New clinical compensation scheme for the NHS, 20 July 2001

[32] Ibid.

[33] Department of Health, *Making Amends*: a consultation paper setting out proposals for reforming the approach to clinical negligence in the NHS, CMO, June 2003

[34] Pearson Report, Royal Commission on Civil Liability and Compensation for Personal Injury, Cmnd 7054, HMSO, London, 1978

[35] Lord Woolf, Final Report: Access to Justice, HMSO, London, July 1996

[36] National Audit Office, Handling Clinical Negligence Claims in England, Report of the Comptroller and Auditor General, HC 403 Session 2000-2001, 3 May 2001

[37] Committee of Public Accounts HC 619-1 (1998-99) Hansard

[38] Health Select Committee HC 549 (1998-99) Hansard, October 1999

Chapter 7
Consent to treatment and informing the patient

Introduction

This chapter covers the principles relating to consent to treatment and giving information to the patient.

Basic principles

Any adult, mentally competent person has the right in law to consent to any touching of his person. If he is touched without consent or other lawful justification, then the person has the right of action in the civil courts of suing for trespass to the person – battery where the person is actually touched, assault where he fears that he will be touched. The fact that consent has been given will normally prevent a successful action for trespass. However, it may not prevent an action for negligence arising on the ground that there was a breach of the duty of care to inform the patient. This chapter explores both these aspects of consent and looks at the information that must be legally given to the patient and other questions that arise on informing the patient. Reference should be made to Chapter 13 on consent in relation to children and young persons – those under 18 years; to Chapter 20 on consent in relation to the mentally disordered; to Chapter 19 on consent in relation to the elderly; and to Chapter 17 in relation to consent to operations. The situation relating to AIDS and HIV is considered in Chapter 26.

Requirements of a valid consent

To be valid, consent must be given voluntarily by a mentally competent person without any duress or fraud. In the case of *Freeman* v. *Home Office*,[1] a prisoner challenged the legality of his being injected with drugs for his personality disorder on the basis that he had not given his consent and that being given medicine by a doctor in a custodial situation precluded consent being voluntarily given. The Court of Appeal refused to accept this proposition and agreed with the High Court judge that: 'Where, in a prison setting, a doctor has the power to influence a prisoner's situation and prospects, a court must be alive to the risk that what may appear, on the face of it, to be real consent is not in fact so.' There is a presumption that the patient is mentally competent, now enshrined in statutory form in Section 1(2) of the Mental Capacity Act 2005. However, this can be rebutted on a balance of probabilities (S. 2(4) of the Mental Capacity Act 2005) if there is evidence to the contrary. The criteria to be used in assessing competence are set by Ss. 2 and 3 of the Mental Capacity Act 2005 and shown on pages 146–147.

How should consent be given?

Figure 7.1 illustrates the different forms of giving consent. As far as the law is concerned, there is no specific requirement that consent for treatment should be given in any particular way. They are all equally valid. However, they vary considerably in their value as evidence in proving that consent was given. Consent in writing is by far the best form of evidence and is therefore the preferred method of obtaining the consent of the patient when any procedure involving some risk is contemplated. The Department of Health updated its guidance on consent to examination and treatment in 2001 and produced two publications: a reference guide to the principles on consent to examination and treatment[2] and a good practice in consent implementation guide.[3] These replace the guidance issued in 1990 and 1992 (HG (90)20 as amended by HSG (92)32 DH). The intention of the Department of Health is that the reference guide should be regularly updated. The forms recommended for use by the Department of Health in the implementation guide are considered below. The guidance is to be amended following the implementation of the Mental Capacity Act 2005.

Consent, it should be noted, is not a defence to an offence of causing actual bodily harm under the Offences Against the Person Act 1861.[4]

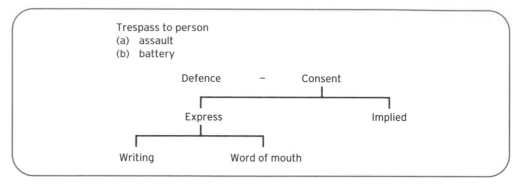

Figure 7.1 Various forms of consent to a trespass to the person

Consent in writing

The forms of consent to examination and treatment that are contained in the Department of Health implementation guidance[5] require the health professional providing the treatment (and this can include a nurse practitioner or midwife) to discuss with the patient the benefits of the treatment and also any serious or frequently occurring risks associated with it and also identify any additional procedures which may be necessary including the possibility of a blood transfusion or other specified procedure. Form 1 can be used for adults and young persons over 16 years and Form 3 for procedures where consciousness is not impaired. Form 2 can be used for parental consent on behalf of children (see Chapter 13) and Form 4 which is for use where the patient is mentally incapacitated is to be revised in the light of the Mental Capacity Act 2005 (see Chapter 20).

Consent is not simply a signature on a form: it is the result of a process of communication between patient and professional that may result in the patient signing a form, which is evidence that the patient agrees to the proposed treatment. Significant recommendations are made in the Kennedy Report[6] following the inquiry into the Bristol paediatric heart surgery on greater openness and honesty between health professionals and the patient. The recommendations on consent include those shown in Box 7.1 (numbers refer to recommendations in the Report).

Box 7.1   **Recommendations on consent in Kennedy Report**

1 In a patient-centred healthcare service patients must be involved, wherever possible, in decisions about their treatment and care.

5 Information should be tailored to the needs, circumstances and wishes of the individual.

23 We note and endorse the recent statement on consent produced by the DH reference guide to consent for examination and treatment (DH 2001). It should inform the practice of all health-care professionals in the NHS and be introduced into practice in all trusts.

24 The process of informing the patient, and obtaining consent to a course of treatment, should be regarded as a process and not a one-off event consisting of obtaining a patient's signature on a form.

25 The process of consent should apply not only to surgical procedures but also to all clinical procedures and examinations that involve any form of touching. This must not mean more forms: it means more communication.

26 As part of the process of obtaining consent, except when they have indicated otherwise, patients should be given sufficient information about what is to take place, the risks, uncertainties, and possible negative consequences of the proposed treatment, about any alternatives and about the likely outcome, to enable them to make a choice about how to proceed.

If a nurse were to become aware that the patient who has put his signature to a consent form has very little idea of what he has given consent to, then she should ensure that the health professional concerned gives more information to the patient about what is proposed. Where does the nurse stand if she is aware that the patient has signed a form without realising what is involved?

> ### Practical Dilemma 7.1   Ignorance is bliss
>
> Susan Smith had signed the form to consent to an operation for the investigation of a lump in her breast. She was very distressed to be undergoing surgery and ever since she had come into hospital had been able to understand and take in very little of what was said to her. The doctor had explained that a biopsy would be carried out and if that were positive further surgery would be undertaken. It was apparent to Staff Nurse Rachel Bryant that Susan had very little awareness that a radical mastectomy could be performed.

Where does Staff Nurse Bryant stand in relation to the proposed operation? The staff nurse has a legal duty to the patient and if she knows that the patient did not understand what she signed or failed to take in the information given by the doctor, she should arrange for the doctor to return and give the patient more information. From the court's point of view, the fact that the patient has signed the form and expressly agreed to a named procedure or course of treatment and that she understands that 'any procedure in addition to those described on this form will only be carried out if it is necessary to save my life or to prevent serious harm to my health' would be very strong evidence to defend any action for trespass to the person.

There is a possibility, however, of a successful action in negligence if the patient has not been given relevant information (see below). There is a clear duty on any health practitioner to take reasonable care that a patient receives the appropriate information before any consent form is signed and treatment proceeds. The nurse should, as far as possible, take appropriate steps to inform the relevant health practitioner if she discovers that this duty has not been carried out.

Consent by word of mouth

Many of the less risky treatments are carried out without any formal signature of the patient. Consent by word of mouth is valid, but it may be far more difficult to establish in court, since

> ### Case 7.1   *Davis v. Barking, Havering and Brentwood HA (1993)*
>
> **Consent to anaesthesia[7]**
>
> The claimant signed a consent form giving consent to a general anaesthetic. She was subsequently given a caudal block and, unfortunately, suffered some harm as a result. She claimed that she had not given consent to this block, which therefore amounted to a trespass to her person, i.e. battery. The High Court judge held that separate consent was not required for each part of the treatment.

it might be one person's word against another. Many of the day-to-day treatments and tests are, however, carried out on this basis.

The Department of Health recommends that consent in writing be obtained for any significant procedure such as a surgical operation or when the patient participates in a research project or a video recording (even if only minor procedures are involved).[8]

Implied consent

It is sometimes said that the fact that a patient comes into hospital means that he or she is giving his consent to anything that the consultant deems appropriate. That, however, is not supported in law. There are many choices of available treatment and when care is provided there must be evidence that the patient has agreed to that particular course. Similarly, it is said that when an unconscious patient is treated in the A&E department, he implies consent to being treated. This, however, is likewise not so. An unconscious patient implies nothing. The professionals care for him in the absence of consent as part of their duty to care for the patient out of necessity in an emergency[9] and could defend any subsequent action for trespass to the person on that basis. They would now be acting under the statutory duty provided by the Mental Capacity Act 2005 to act in the best interests of a mentally incapacitated person.

Implied consent is better reserved for situations where non-verbal communication by the patient makes it clear that he is giving consent. Nurses are familiar with the signs: the patient rolls up his sleeve for an injection; the patient opens his mouth as the nurse waves the thermometer in the air. Such actions indicate to the nurse that the patient agrees to the treatment/care proceeding. No words are spoken, there is no signature, but it is clear that the patient is in agreement. In an Australian case of 1891, a passenger on a ship who held out his hand to be vaccinated lost his action for battery.[10]

The weakness of implied consent is, however, that it is not always clear that the patient is agreeing to what the nurse intends to do. Thus the patient who rolls up his sleeve for blood pressure to be taken would get a nasty shock when the nurse gave him an injection, yet that is how the nurse has interpreted his non-verbal actions. To avoid such misunderstandings, it is preferable if the nurse tells the patient what she wishes to do and obtains a spoken consent from the patient. (The problems in giving day-to-day care to the confused elderly are considered in Chapter 19.)

Once a mentally competent patient has given a valid consent to treatment, then they cannot succeed in an action for trespass to the person,[11] but if it is claimed insufficient information on the risks of the treatment was given to them they would have to bring an action in negligence alleging a breach of the duty of care in failing to provide sufficient information (see page 154).

Right to refuse treatment

It is a basic principle of law in this country that an adult, mentally competent person has the right to refuse treatment and take his own discharge contrary to medical advice. The Court of Appeal has emphasised that provided the patient has the necessary mental capacity, which is assessed in relation to the decision to be made, then he or she can refuse to give consent for a good reason, a bad reason or no reason at all. This was the principle set out in the case of *Re MB* shown in Case 7.2.

> ### Case 7.2   *Re MB* (1997)
>
> **Consent to a Caesarean section**[12]
>
> A pregnant woman suffered from needle phobia as a result of which she was unable to agree to have an injection that would precede a Caesarean section. The High Court judge held that her needle phobia rendered her mentally incapacitated to take the decision not to have a Caesarean operation. The Court of Appeal confirmed that decision, but emphasised that had she been competent, she could have refused the operation. The Court of Appeal in *Re MB* laid down the steps and rules that should be followed when a health professional is faced with a patient who appears to be mentally incompetent. (This advice is set out in Box 14.4 on page 362.)

The ruling in *Re MB* was followed by the Court of Appeal in a case brought against St George's Hospital,[13] which is considered in Chapter 14.

Mental capacity of the patient

The fact that mentally capacitated adult patients can refuse life-saving treatment can be upsetting for staff, as the following case shows.

> ### Case 7.3   *Re C (An Adult: Refusal of Medical Treatment)* (1994)
>
> **The patient's autonomy**[14]
>
> The patient was a 68-year-old man who suffered from paranoid schizophrenia and was detained at Broadmoor Hospital. He developed gangrene in one foot and doctors believed an amputation to be a life-saving necessity. He refused to give consent and sought an injunction restraining the hospital from carrying out an amputation without his express written consent. He succeeded on the grounds that the evidence failed to establish that he lacked sufficient understanding of the nature, purpose and effects of the proposed treatment. Instead, the evidence showed that:
>
> 1   he had understood and retained the relevant treatment information
> 2   believed it, and
> 3   had arrived at a clear choice.

The sole issue in this case was whether the patient had the mental capacity to give a valid refusal. It should be noted that the presence of a mental disorder does not automatically mean that a person is incapable of making a valid decision in relation to treatment. *Re C* should be contrasted with a case[15] where a patient refused a blood transfusion which was required because she self-harmed. She described her blood as being evil and it was held that this was evidence of mental disorder which made her incapable of using and weighing the relevant information.

In *Re MB*[16] the Court of Appeal laid down a test for the competence of the patient which was applied in the case of Miss B, where a woman who had been paralysed refused to be placed on a ventilator and when that refusal was ignored applied to the court for the ventilator to be switched off. The facts are shown in the following case.

> ### Case 7.4   *Ms B (2002)*
>
> **Refusal to be ventilated**[17]
>
> Miss B suffered a ruptured blood vessel in her neck which damaged her spinal cord. As a consequence she was paralysed from the neck down and was on a ventilator. She was of sound mind and knew that there was no cure for her condition. She asked for the ventilator to be switched off. Her doctors wished her to try out some special rehabilitation to improve the standard of her care and felt that an intensive care ward was not a suitable location for such a decision to be made. They were reluctant to perform such an action as switching off the ventilator without the court's approval. Miss B applied to court for a declaration to be made that the ventilator could be switched off.

The main issue in the case was the mental competence of Miss B. If she were held to be mentally competent, she could refuse to have life-saving treatment for a good reason, a bad reason or no reason at all. She was interviewed by two psychiatrists who gave evidence to the court that she was mentally competent. The judge therefore held that she was entitled to refuse to be ventilated. The judge, Dame Elizabeth Butler-Sloss, President of the Family Division, held that Miss B possessed the requisite mental capacity to make decisions regarding her treatment and thus the administration of artificial respiration by the trust against her wishes amounted to an unlawful trespass. Dame Elizabeth Butler-Sloss restated the principles which had been laid down by the Court of Appeal in the case of St George's Healthcare Trust:

+ There was a presumption that a patient had the mental capacity to make decisions whether to consent to or refuse medical or surgical treatment offered.

+ If mental capacity was not an issue and the patient, having been given the relevant information and offered the available option, chose to refuse that treatment, that decision had to be respected by the doctors, considerations of what the best interests of the patient would involve were irrelevant.

+ Concern or doubts about the patient's mental capacity should be resolved as soon as possible by the doctors within the hospital or other normal medical procedures.

+ Meanwhile, the patient must be cared for in accordance with the judgement of the doctors as to the patient's best interests.

+ It was most important that those considering the issue should not confuse the question of mental capacity with the nature of the decision made by the patient, however grave the consequences. Since the view of the patient might reflect a difference in values rather than an absence of competence the assessment of capacity should be approached with that in mind and doctors should not allow an emotional reaction to or strong disagreement with the patient's decision to cloud their judgement in answering the primary question of capacity.

+ Where disagreement still existed about competence, it was of the utmost importance that the patient be fully informed, involved and engaged in the process, which could involve obtaining independent outside help, of resolving the disagreement since the patient's involvement could be crucial to a good outcome.

+ If the hospital were faced with a dilemma that doctors did not know how to resolve, this must be recognised and further steps taken as a matter of priority. Those in charge must not allow a situation of deadlock or drift to occur.

✚ If there was no disagreement about competence, but the doctors were for any reason unable to carry out the patient's wishes, it was their duty to find other doctors who would do so.

✚ If all appropriate steps to seek independent assistance from medical experts outside the hospital had failed the hospital should not hesitate to make an application to the High Court or seek the advice of the Official Solicitor.

✚ The treating clinicians and the hospital should always have in mind that a seriously physically disabled patient who was mentally competent had the same right to personal autonomy and to make decisions as any other person with mental capacity.

It was reported on 29 April 2002 that Miss B had died peacefully in her sleep after the ventilator had been switched off.

The patient therefore has a right to refuse treatment, but it must be clear that he has the requisite mental capacity. The case of *Re C* (Case 7.3) clearly brings out the clash between the patient's autonomy and the professional duty of care. Clearly, it would be essential for those in charge of the patient to take all reasonable precautions to ensure that the patient has appropriate counselling and all the necessary information and help in facing the future, but if this fails, it is the competent patient's right to refuse. Similarly, an adult Jehovah's Witness is able to refuse a blood transfusion. It was reported that a young mother who was a Jehovah's Witness died on 25 October 2007 after giving birth to twins because she refused a life-saving blood transfusion.[18] Different principles apply in relation to children and these are discussed in Chapter 13.

The Court of Appeal in the case of *Re T* (see Case 7.5) emphasised the importance of ensuring that, when a patient refuses treatment, the patient has the mental capacity to make a valid decision and has not been subjected to the undue influences of another.

Case 7.5   *Re T* (1992)

Refusal of blood transfusion[19]

A young pregnant woman was injured in a car accident and told the staff nurse that she did not want a blood transfusion. Her mother was a Jehovah's Witness. At the time, it was unlikely to be necessary. However, subsequently she went into labour and a Caesarean was necessary. She told medical staff that she would not want a transfusion and had signed a form to that effect. She was not told that it might be necessary to save her life. After the operation, she required blood as a life-saving measure and her father and co-habitee applied to court. The judge authorised the administration of blood on the ground that the evidence showed that she was not in a fit condition to make a valid decision.

(See also the case of *In Re S*,[20] discussed on page 361. For a case on refusal of treatment by a 16-year-old, see *In Re W* on page 331, Case 13.1.)

The common law principles relating to the presumption of capacity in the person over 16 years and the definition of capacity and best interests have now been placed on a statutory basis by the Mental Capacity Act 2005 (see pages 146–147 and 150–151).

Taking one's own discharge

It follows from what has been said so far that the adult, mentally competent patient is able to take his own discharge. However, this principle may, in practice, cause concern for staff.

> **Practical Dilemma 7.2**　　Self-discharge
>
> Don Pritchard was admitted from the A&E department with a suspected head injury. Before X-rays had been taken, he insisted on leaving the hospital, contrary to medical advice. The nursing staff knew that he was still very confused and it seemed likely that his aggression was a result of a brain injury.

This is a difficult situation because it could be argued here that, as a result of the brain injury, the patient was not mentally competent and therefore his decision to discharge himself was an irrational one. If the patient is mentally incapacitated and there is clear danger to the patient's life if he is allowed to leave, it could be argued that these are circumstances in which the staff would be justified in acting in an emergency to save the patient's life. If this does not apply, then the patient has the right to go. An assessment should be carried out of his mental competence. If he is deemed mentally competent, he cannot be compelled to stay, unless he presents a danger to other people. If possible, he should be persuaded to sign a form that he took his own discharge contrary to medical advice. However, it is not always possible to get this signature and therefore it is necessary to ensure that another member of staff can act as a witness to what occurred. In either case, it is essential that full records be made of the circumstances leading to the patient's discharge and the efforts made to persuade him to stay. If harm eventually befalls the patient as a result of his taking his own discharge contrary to medical advice, if there is evidence that the staff did all they could to persuade him to stay and if there was clear evidence that the patient was mentally competent, there is unlikely to be a successful action for negligence against the staff.

Definition of mental capacity under the Mental Capacity Act 2005

The definition of mental capacity under Sections 2 and 3 of the Mental Capacity Act is shown in the following Statute:

> **Statute**　　Sections 2 and 3 of the Mental Capacity Act 2005
>
> **Section 2 People who lack capacity**
>
> (1) For the purposes of this Act, a person lacks capacity in relation to a matter if at the material time he is unable to make a decision for himself in relation to the matter because of an impairment of, or a disturbance in the functioning of, the mind or brain.
>
> (2) It does not matter whether the impairment or disturbance is permanent or temporary.

Statute continued

(3) A lack of capacity cannot be established merely by reference to:

    (a) a person's age or appearance, or

    (b) a condition of his, or an aspect of his behaviour, which might lead others to make unjustified assumptions about his capacity.

(4) In proceedings under this Act or any other enactment, any question whether a person lacks capacity within the meaning of this Act must be decided on the balance of probabilities.

(5) No power which a person ('D') may exercise under this Act:

    (a) in relation to a person who lacks capacity, or

    (b) where D reasonably thinks that a person lacks capacity,

    is exercisable in relation to a person under 16.

(6) Subsection (5) is subject to section 18(3).

Section 3 Inability to make decisions

(1) For the purposes of section 2, a person is unable to make a decision for himself if he is unable:

    (a) to understand the information relevant to the decision,

    (b) to retain that information,

    (c) to use or weigh that information as part of the process of making the decision, or

    (d) to communicate his decision (whether by talking, using sign language or any other means).

(2) A person is not to be regarded as unable to understand the information relevant to a decision if he is able to understand an explanation of it given to him in a way that is appropriate to his circumstances (using simple language, visual aids or any other means).

(3) The fact that a person is able to retain the information relevant to a decision for a short period only does not prevent him from being regarded as able to make the decision.

(4) The information relevant to a decision includes information about the reasonably foreseeable consequences of:

    (a) deciding one way or another, or

    (b) failing to make the decision.

From this Statute it will be noted that there are two stages for the definition of mental capacity. The first is: is the person suffering from an impairment of, or a disturbance in, the functioning of the mind or brain? The second is: is the effect of the impairment or disturbance an inability to make a decision?

Hunger strikes

In an old case,[21] a suffragette went on hunger strike and was force-fed in prison. She lost her claim for trespass to the person. The court held that the prison doctor was justified in feeding her on the grounds that it was the duty of the officials to preserve the health and lives of prisoners. However, in a more recent case,[22] a prisoner went on hunger strike and the application was made to court to decide whether it was lawful for his doctors and nurses to abstain from force-feeding him. The judge held that there were four grounds for intervening against the prisoner's right of self-determination:

1 the interest that the state holds in preserving life
2 the interest of the state in preventing suicide
3 maintaining the integrity of the medical profession
4 the protection of the rights of innocent third parties.

He concluded that these did not overrule the right of self-determination of a mentally competent person and the prisoner could be permitted to starve himself to death, provided that he has the legal capacity.

In a more recent case,[23] the Moors murderer Ian Brady, who was in Ashworth Special Hospital, applied to court to be allowed to starve himself to death. The court held that he did not have the mental competence to make that decision. The decision to commence force-feeding was in all respects lawful, rational and fair. Brady was incapacitated by his mental illness. The failed attempts by the Ashworth Special Hospital Authority to discover who had leaked information about Brady to a journalist are considered in Chapter 8.

Amputation of healthy limbs

Media attention has been given to the condition of body dysmorphic disorder, where the patient wishes to have his healthy limbs removed. A surgeon in Falkirk and District Royal Infirmary, in a private operation, removed one lower limb from each of two patients who suffered from this disorder.[24] The hospital has subsequently banned such operations. In the absence of any doctor prepared to amputate, patients are known to have shot their limbs off or committed suicide. The General Medical Council has offered ethical guidance and the Medical Defence Union has emphasised that the utmost caution should be taken by doctors considering such an operation. They must be certain that the operation is right and that the patient has had full counselling as to the consequences. Everything must be carefully documented.[25] The House of Lords has held that consent is not a defence to an offence of grievous bodily harm.[26]

Defences to an action for trespass to the person

Consent is the main form of defence to an action for trespass to the person. However, it is not the only one and Box 7.2 shows the main defences.

Box 7.2 Defences to an action for trespass to the person

1 Consent.
2 Acting under a statutory power, e.g. Mental Capacity Act (see below), Mental Health Act 1983. (See Chapter 20.)
3 Making a lawful arrest.
4 Parental powers. (See Chapter 13.)

Patients lacking mental capacity

This issue is considered below under the defence of statutory powers and also in Chapter 20 in relation to mentally disordered persons. Where a patient lacks the capacity to give consent then treatment without consent may be given under statutory powers. Detention and compulsory treatment for mental disorder may be justified under the Mental Health Act 1983 (which is considered in Chapter 20). Alternatively, care and treatment can be given under the Mental Capacity Act 2005. Powers under this Act could be used not only if temporary restraint is justified in the interests of the patient but also if it is necessary to detain patients in hospitals or care homes when the use of the Mental Health Act powers is not required. This loss of liberty is possible under the Bournewood safeguards, which are explained below and considered in detail in Chapter 20. In this chapter we look at the provisions of the Mental Capacity Act 2005 and the care and treatment of those adults who are incapable of giving the requisite consent.

Unconscious patients

It was mentioned earlier that the doctors and nurses in their duty of care for the patient may take life-saving action. This was originally on the basis of their common law powers (recognised in the *Re F* case)[27] to act out of necessity in the best interests of a mentally incapacitated adult, but is now on the basis of the statutory powers in the Mental Capacity Act 2005. The Act requires actions to be taken in the best interests of a person who lacks mental capacity and this requires ascertaining from relatives and friends information about the personal beliefs and views and feelings of the patient. Where serious medical treatment decisions are to be made on behalf of a person who lacks mental capacity, then in the absence of a relative or informal carer person who can be consulted on the person's best interests, an independent mental capacity advocate must be appointed to report on the patient's best interest (see below). This topic of lack of mental capacity is also considered in relation to the care of the elderly in Chapter 19. The legal situation relating to a patient in a persistent vegetative state is considered in Chapter 16.

Case 7.6   *Malette v. Shulman* **(1991)**

Do not give me blood[28]

In a Canadian case, an unconscious patient was given a life-saving blood transfusion in spite of the fact that she was carrying a card refusing such treatment. She was awarded C$20,000. The doctor had ignored her written request not to give her blood and this constituted a trespass to her person.

In this case, the card setting out the wishes of the patient acted as a living will or advance directive. (These are now placed on a statutory footing under the Mental Capacity Act 2005 and are discussed in Chapter 16.)

Mental Capacity Act 2005

Where a practitioner takes measures to save the life of an unconscious patient, that is not a situation of implied consent, but a situation of necessity which is now covered by the Mental Capacity Act 2005. In such circumstances, the Mental Capacity Act 2005 recognises the duty of a professional to take action in the best interests of the patient following the accepted standard of care of the reasonable professional. The House of Lords had established the principle of acting out of necessity in the case of *Re F*,[29] which concerned the sterilisation of a woman who suffered from severe learning disabilities and was incapable of giving consent. However, the principle of acting out of necessity where an adult was incapable of giving consent also applied to day-to-day care. In the case of a girl of 18 with an intellectual age of between 5 and 8, the Court of Appeal held that the court had the power under its inherent jurisdiction and in the best interests of that person to hear the issues involving her future and to grant the necessary declarations.[30] The House of Lords (in the Bournewood[31] case) also held that the common law powers can be used to detain a mentally incapable adult if that is in the person's best interests but this was overruled by the European Court of Human Rights[32] (see page 154).

Recommendations were made by Law Commission No. 231[33] for a statutory duty to replace this common law power, with specific requirements depending on the seriousness of the treatment to be undertaken. Following further consultation by the Lord Chancellor,[34] the government published its proposals for decision making on behalf of mentally incapacitated adults[35] and this was followed by a draft Bill.[36] The Bill was subject to scrutiny by a Joint Committee of Parliament[37] and revised in the light of its recommendations. The Mental Capacity Act 2005 came into force partly on 1 April 2007 and on 1 October 2007. The Act will be considered under the following headings:

Principles

Definition of mental capacity

Best interests

Code of Practice

Independent mental capacity advocate

Lasting powers of attorney

Court of Protection, deputies and the Office of Public Guardian

The Bournewood safeguards

(In Chapter 16 will be found a discussion of the statutory provisions for advance decisions; the MCA 2005 protections provided in relation to research on those lacking capacity can be found in Chapter 18.)

Principles of the Mental Capacity Act 2005

The basic principles set out in Section 1 of the Act are shown below:

Statute	**Principles set down in Section 1 of the Mental Capacity Act 2005**

(1) The following principles apply for the purposes of this Act.

(2) A person must be assumed to have capacity unless it is established that he lacks capacity.

(3) A person is not to be treated as unable to make a decision unless all practicable steps to help him to do so have been taken without success.

Statute continued

Statute continued

(4) A person is not to be treated as unable to make a decision merely because he makes an unwise decision.

(5) An act done, or decision made, under this Act for or on behalf of a person who lacks capacity must be done, or made, in his best interests.

(6) Before the act is done, or the decision is made, regard must be had to whether the purpose for which it is needed can be as effectively achieved in a way that is less restrictive of the person's rights and freedom of action.

Definition of mental capacity

Sections 2 and 3 provide a statutory definition of mental capacity (see pages 146–7). The definition is decision-specific, i.e. a person may have the capacity to make a decision on one matter but not on another. For example, a person with learning disabilities may be able to decide on the food to eat and clothes to wear, but not whether to have an operation for an appendectomy.

Best interests

The Mental Capacity Act sets out the steps which must be taken in determining what are the best interests of the patient. They are shown in the Statute below:

Statute   **Best interests**

Section 4 of the Mental Capacity Act

(1) In determining for the purposes of this Act what is in a person's best interests, the person making the determination must not make it merely on the basis of:
   (a) the person's age or appearance, or
   (b) a condition of his, or an aspect of his behaviour, which might lead others to make unjustified assumptions about what might be in his best interests.

(2) The person making the determination must consider all the relevant circumstances and, in particular, take the following steps.

(3) He must consider:
   (a) whether it is likely that the person will at some time have capacity in relation to the matter in question, and
   (b) if it appears likely that he will, when that is likely to be.

(4) He must, so far as reasonably practicable, permit and encourage the person to participate, or to improve his ability to participate, as fully as possible in any act done for him and any decision affecting him.

(5) Where the determination relates to life-sustaining treatment he must not, in considering whether the treatment is in the best interests of the person concerned, be motivated by a desire to bring about his death.

Statute continued

(6) He must consider, so far as is reasonably ascertainable:

  (a) the person's past and present wishes and feelings (and, in particular, any relevant written statement made by him when he had capacity),

  (b) the beliefs and values that would be likely to influence his decision if he had capacity, and

  (c) the other factors that he would be likely to consider if he were able to do so.

(7) He must take into account, if it is practicable and appropriate to consult them, the views of:

  (a) anyone named by the person as someone to be consulted on the matter in question or on matters of that kind,

  (b) anyone engaged in caring for the person or interested in his welfare,

  (c) any donee of a lasting power of attorney granted by the person, and

  (d) any deputy appointed for the person by the court,

  as to what would be in the person's best interests and, in particular, as to the matters mentioned in subsection (6).

(8) The duties imposed by subsections (1) to (7) also apply in relation to the exercise of any powers which:

  (a) are exercisable under a lasting power of attorney, or

  (b) are exercisable by a person under this Act where he reasonably believes that another person lacks capacity.

(9) In the case of an act done, or a decision made, by a person other than the court, there is sufficient compliance with this section if (having complied with the requirements of subsections (1) to (7)) he reasonably believes that what he does or decides is in the best interests of the person concerned.

(10) 'Life-sustaining treatment' means treatment which in the view of a person providing health care for the person concerned is necessary to sustain life.

(11) 'Relevant circumstances' are those:

  (a) of which the person making the determination is aware, and

  (b) which it would be reasonable to regard as relevant.

The implication of the statutory steps which must be taken in determining what are a person's best interests is a modified best interest. For example if a person, who was once a firm believer in the sin of any surgical intervention, lost the mental capacity to make his decisions, then his earlier views on non-surgical intervention would be taken into account in determining what was in his best interests.

Code of Practice

The Department for Constitutional Affairs (now absorbed in the Ministry of Justice) prepared guidance on the Mental Capacity Act in the form of a Code of Practice. There is a statutory duty for those professionals involved in the care of those lacking mental capacity to have regard to the Code of Practice (S. 42(4)). It can be accessed via the Internet.[38] Whilst not statutorily bound by the Code of Practice, informal carers and others caring for those lacking the requisite mental capacity should find it of assistance both in determining whether a person lacks capacity and also in deciding what are the person's best interests.

Independent mental capacity advocate

Where serious medical treatment is proposed or accommodation arrangements are being made then, in the absence of an informal carer, relative or friend who can be consulted on behalf of a person lacking the capacity to make his or her own decisions, an independent mental capacity advocate must be appointed to report on the best interests of the patient. A report is given of one of the first situations where an independent mental capacity advocate was appointed where a patient had lost consciousness and had no meaningful brain activity and no next of kin had been traced.[39] The IMCA reported on the patient's best interests and the treating clinicians decided that antibiotics would not be administered for an infection and the patient passed away.

Lasting powers of attorney

The MCA enables a person, when competent, to set up a lasting power of attorney (LPA) by which the donee of the power can make decisions on his behalf. Unlike the earlier enduring power of attorney, which could only relate to the delegation of decisions relating to property and affairs, the lasting power of attorney can be set up for both property and affairs and also for decisions relating to personal welfare. There are different LPA forms for property and finance and for personal welfare. From 1 October 2007 enduring powers of attorney can no longer be set up, but those which are already in existence can continue to be used. There is one major difference between the two kinds of delegation. Although the donee under an LPA relating to property and affairs can exercise those powers while the donor still has the mental capacity to make his own decisions (for example, the donor might appoint an attorney to sell his house for him whilst he is abroad), the donee under an LPA relating to personal welfare decisions can only make decisions for the donor if the donor lacks the requisite capacity. Practical Dilemma 7.3 illustrates the effect of the appointment of an LPA for a patient in hospital.

Practical Dilemma 7.3   **Lasting power of attorney**

Meryl, the ward sister of a medical ward, was informed that a patient, Agnes, recently admitted with a severe chest infection and who appeared unable to make her own decisions, had set up an LPA giving the power to make personal welfare decisions to her daughter, Nicky. Meryl was concerned about whether Nicky could refuse antibiotics and resuscitation on Agnes's behalf if it were to be a life-saving necessity.

Nicky should be asked to show Meryl the LPA which Agnes has drawn up so that the specific instructions were made known to the ward team. Life-sustaining treatment, which was in her best interests, could only be refused on Agnes's behalf if she had specifically included that in the LPA, which had been appropriately drawn up, witnessed and registered. The LPA would only come into effect if Agnes lacked the capacity to make her own decisions.

Court of Protection, deputies and the Office of Public Guardian

Another significant innovation of the MCA 2005 was the establishment of a new Court of Protection with the jurisdiction to make decisions relating to personal welfare as well as property and finance. (The predecessor Court of Protection could only cover issues relating to property and affairs.) The Court can either make one-off decisions (with or without a court hearing) or appoint deputies with powers to make specific decisions on behalf of those lacking the requisite mental capacity who were over 16 years. Property decisions could be made on behalf of those under 16 years, if the mental capacity was likely to extend after they became 16 years. For example, if a young boy was badly brain-damaged in a road accident at 12 years old and received compensation from the driver responsible, decisions relating to the property and finances could be made by the Court of Protection while he was still under 16 years, because he was unlikely to recover his mental capacity. It might decide to appoint a deputy to make decisions relating to his finances. The MCA also set up an Office of Public Guardian. This keeps registers of deputies and LPAs and keeps a watching brief of their functioning. Complaints about the donee under an LPA who appeared not to be acting in the best interests of the donor could be made to the Office of Public Guardian which might decide to appoint a Visitor (General or Specific) to investigate the situation.

The Bournewood safeguards

The European Court of Human Rights ruled that there was a breach of Article 5.4 of the European Convention on Human Rights where a person with learning disabilities, and incapable of consenting to the admission, was detained in a hospital without being placed under the Mental Health Act 1983.[40] The facts of the case are given in Chapter 20. As a consequence of the case the UK government had to ensure that legislation was introduced to safeguard those who were incapable of giving consent to admission to hospitals and care homes but needed to be kept there for their safety, in a situation where the powers of detention under the Mental Health Act 1983 were inappropriate. Following extensive consultation the Department of Health decided in favour of amending the Mental Capacity Act 2005 to safeguard the rights of those kept in hospitals and care homes and ensure that there was no violation of Article 5. (See Chapter 20 for further details of the Bournewood safeguards.)

Mental Health Act 1983

Justification for acting without the consent of a patient may also be provided by the Mental Health Act 1983 (as amended by the Mental Health Act 2007) and this is considered in Chapter 20.

Giving information to a patient prior to consent being obtained

As has been mentioned, there are two main actions in relation to consent:

1 an action for trespass to the person

2 an action in negligence for a breach of the duty of care to inform the patient.

We now turn to the action for negligence. The courts have made it clear that if a competent patient has given a willing consent for a procedure, then an action for trespass to the person cannot proceed. If the patient alleges that he was not given significant information about possible side effects, then the action will be one of negligence. This raises the question of how much information must be given to the patient. The leading case on this question is the following.

| Case 7.7 | *Sidaway v. Bethlem Royal Hospital Governors* (1985) |

Failing to inform[41]

Amy Sidaway suffered from persistent pain in her neck and shoulder and was advised by a surgeon to have an operation on her spinal column to relieve the pain. The surgeon warned her of the possibility of disturbing a nerve root and the possible consequences of doing so, but did not mention the possibility of damage to the spinal cord, even though he would be operating within 3 millimetres of it. The risk of damage to the spinal cord was very small (less than 1 per cent), but if the risk materialised, the resulting injury could range from mild to very severe. Amy consented to the operation, which was performed with due care and skill. However, in the course of the operation, she suffered an injury to her spinal cord that resulted in her being severely disabled. She sued the surgeon and the hospital governors, alleging that the surgeon had been in breach of a duty owed to her to warn her of all possible risks inherent in the operation, with the result that she had not been in a position to give an informed consent to the operation. Amy lost the case before the trial judge and her appeal to the Court of Appeal. She then appealed to the House of Lords.

The House of Lords held that her appeal should fail. Three of the judges held that the test of liability in respect of a doctor's duty to warn his patient of risks inherent in treatment recommended by him was the same as the test applicable to diagnosis of treatment, i.e. the doctor was required to act in accordance with a practice accepted as proper by a responsible body of medical opinion. (This is known as the 'Bolam Test' and is discussed on page 11.) Since the surgeon's non-disclosure of risk of damage to the plaintiff's spinal cord accorded with a practice accepted as proper by a responsible body of neuro-surgical opinion, the defendants were not liable to the plaintiff.

The other two judges (Lord Scarman and Lord Templeman) were also of the opinion that Amy's appeal must fail since she had not proved on the evidence that the surgeon (who had died since the operation) had been in breach of duty by failing to warn her of the risks. Lord Scarman, whilst finding against her, alone of all the judges held that a patient had a right to give informed consent and he followed an American case,[42] where the 'prudent patient' test was applied to decide on the information a patient should be given prior to any consent, i.e. 'What would a reasonable prudent patient think significant if in the situation of this patient?' Lord Scarman concluded that:

> *English law must recognise a duty of the doctor to warn his patient of risk inherent in the treatment which he is proposing, and especially so if the treatment be surgery. The critical limitation is that the duty is confined to material risk. The test of materiality is whether in the circumstances of the particular case the court is satisfied that a reasonable person in the patient's position would be likely to attach significance to the risk. Even if the risk be material, the doctor will not be liable if on a reasonable assessment of his patient's condition he takes the view that a warning would be detrimental to his patient's health.*

Comment on the Sidaway case

While the case was concerned with treatment by a doctor, the same principles would apply to treatment by any other professional. Although the judges turned down Amy's appeal, their reasons for doing so were extremely varied. The majority applied the Bolam Test of the accepted approved professional practice.

Even Lord Scarman, who used the 'prudent patient' test, still agreed that there may well be exceptions where the doctor is entitled to use 'therapeutic privilege' in deciding what to tell or what not to tell the patient prior to any procedure. This exception means that in the end the professional must follow the accepted approved practice insofar as it is applicable to the particular needs of that specific patient.

The Sidaway case was cited and followed in the case of *Blyth* v. *Bloomsbury Health Authority*.

Case 7.8 — *Blyth* v. *Bloomsbury HA*

Depo-provera[43]

In this case, a patient had been given an injection of depo-provera and claimed that she had suffered harm as a result of it and that knowledge that was possessed by hospital researchers about some of the side effects of the drug was not made known to her at the time that she was prescribed it. The Court of Appeal applied the Bolam Test and the Sidaway case to the facts and decided that there was no negligence by the doctors who cared for her in the information they gave to her. They emphasised that the extent of the duty to give information is to be judged in the light of the state of medical knowledge at the time and one must avoid the danger of being wise after the event. In addition, they refused to interpret the Sidaway judgments as implying that where the patient asked specific rather than just general questions this meant that the doctor is under an obligation to tell the patient all he knows about the subject. 'The amount of information to be given must depend on all the circumstances, and as a general proposition it is governed by what is called the Bolam Test' (Lord Justice Neill).

Another important point is that in subsequent cases (see below), the courts have held that the professional's duty is not divisible. Diagnosis, treatment, carrying out that treatment and informing the patient are all part of the doctor's duty of care and cannot be separated into different boxes. Informing the patient of risks is as much a part of the clinical judgement of the doctor as all his other tasks.

The general proposition therefore is that a person giving information to the patient must follow the reasonable standard of approved practice, i.e. the Bolam Test. However, in one recent case, a judge held that what was purported to be the approved practice was not acceptable.

Case 7.9 — *Smith* v. *Tunbridge Wells HA* (1994)

Failure to warn[44]

Evidence given by experts to the court suggested that a body of experienced competent surgeons would not have warned the patient of a risk of impotence from the operation. The judge disagreed with this and held that the failure to warn of the risk of impotence was neither reasonable nor responsible and the surgeon was therefore in breach of his duty to warn the patient.

In the following case, the court had to decide if the doctors had followed the reasonable standard of care when they gave advice that the baby should not be induced.

Case 7.10   *Pearce v. United Bristol Healthcare NHS Trust* (1998)

Clinical opinion[45]

Mrs Pearce was expecting her sixth child. The expected date of delivery was 13 November 1991, but it had still not arrived on 27 November. She begged the consultant to give her an induced labour or a Caesarean section. He suggested that she should have a normal birth and let nature take its course. He pointed out that it would be very risky to induce the birth and she would take longer to recover from a Caesarean. He did not tell her that there was an increased risk of a stillbirth as a result of the delay in delivery between 13 and 27 November. She accepted his advice. The baby died *in utero* some time between 2 and 3 December.

The trial judge dismissed the claim. The Court of Appeal dismissed the appeal. It applied the reasoning in the Sidaway case and held that this was a case 'where it would not be proper for the courts to interfere with the clinical opinion of the expert medical man responsible for treating Mrs Pearce'. More recently the House of Lords has had to decide if the patient has to prove that he would not have had the treatment had he known of the serious risks of harm.

Case 7.11   *Chester v. Afshar* (2002)

Warning the patient of risks[46]

The patient suffered from severe back pain and gave consent to an operation for the removal of three intra-vertebral discs. The neurosurgeon failed to give a warning to her about the slight risk of post-operative paralysis which the patient suffered following the operation. The trial judge held that the doctor was not negligent in his conduct of the operation, but was negligent in failing to warn her of the slight risk of paralysis which she suffered. He also held that, had she been aware of the risk, she would have sought advice on alternatives to surgery and the operation would not have taken place when it did, if at all. He therefore held that there was a sufficient causal link between the defendant's failure to warn and the damage sustained by the claimant and that link was not broken by the possibility that the claimant might have consented to surgery in the future. He gave judgment for damages to be assessed. The defendant appealed to the Court of Appeal which dismissed the appeal. The defendant then appealed to the House of Lords which by a majority verdict dismissed his appeal.[47]

The House of Lords held that the claimant had shown that had she been notified of the risk, which in fact occurred, she would have had to think further about undergoing the surgery and therefore she had established a causal link between the breach and the injury she had sustained and the defendant was liable in damages. Lord Hope's reasoning is shown in Box 7.3.

Box 7.3 | *Chester* v. *Afshar* (Lord Hope)

I start with the proposition that the law which imposed the duty to warn on the doctor has at its heart the right of the patient to make an informed choice as to whether, and if so when and by whom, to be operated on. Patients may have, and are entitled to have, different views about these matters. All sorts of factors may be at work here – the patient's hopes and fears and personal circumstances, the nature of the condition that has to be treated and, above all, the patient's own views about whether the risk is worth running for the benefits that may come if the operation is to be carried out. For some the choice may be easy – simply to agree to or to decline the operation. But for many the choice will be a difficult one, requiring time to think, to take advice and to weigh up the alternatives. The duty is owed as much to the patient who, if warned, would find the decision difficult as to the patient who would find it simple and could give a clear answer to the doctor one way or the other immediately.

To leave the patient who would find the decision difficult without a remedy, as the normal approach to causation would indicate, would render the duty useless in the cases where it may be needed most. This would discriminate against those who cannot honestly say they would have declined the operation once and for all if they had been warned. I would find that result unacceptable. The function of the law is to enable rights to be vindicated and to provide remedies when duties have been breached. Unless this is done the duty is a hollow one, stripped of all practical force and devoid of all content. It will have lost its ability to protect the patient and thus to fulfil the only purpose which brought it into existence. On policy grounds therefore I would hold that the test of causation is satisfied in this case. The injury was intimately involved with the duty to warn. The duty was owed by the doctor who performed the surgery that Miss Chester consented to. It was the product of the very risk that she should have been warned about when she gave her consent. So I would hold that it can be regarded as having been caused, in the legal sense, by the breach of that duty.

The outcome of *Chester* v. *Ashfar*, therefore, was that the appeal by the surgeon failed and the patient won the case.

In the following case, the claimant also succeeded in his allegation that he had been given inadequate information.

Case 7.12 | *Chinchen* v. *University Hospital of Wales Healthcare NHS Trust* (2001)

Insufficient information[48]

In April 1996, C underwent surgery for a revision decompression of his spine. A consultant orthopaedic surgeon carried out the procedure. Four days later, C suffered loss of spinal fluid from the operation wound and was readmitted to hospital. In May a posterior exploration of C's lower lumbar spine was carried out. The dura was inspected and there was no obvious leak. A muscle patch was applied to the dura and C was later discharged and sent home. C suffered constant and debilitating pain and an inability to return to work after the procedures and claimed that he was not given proper advice before the decompression procedure. Had he received proper advice, he would not have consented to that procedure. The judge found in favour of C. The reasons for the judge's decision were:

The judge preferred C's recollections of the pre-operative discussion. Both C and his wife's version were the same, they were convincing witnesses and they had the benefit of consulting solicitors no later than a year after the operation and so events were fresh in their minds. The surgeon's evidence had changed and he had been in a difficult position, as

Case 7.12 continued

he had not had to try to recall the events until four years after the operation. On the evidence, C had not been advised of alternative procedures, neither had he been warned of the possible risks consequent on undergoing revision surgery. The surgeon had conveyed assurances that it would be fine and C had not been told that the surgery was urgent. The advice given did not satisfy the minimal standards of professional competence. There should have been a clear warning of the higher incidence of problems arising from revision surgery and other options should have been discussed. The surgeon admitted that he had not explained to C that any course of action was available other than surgery. In the instant circumstances, had C received the appropriate advice he would not have agreed to undergo the operation. The judge found that there was a causal and temporal connection between the surgery and the symptoms, which were different and worse very soon after the surgery. The two operations had occurred within a short period on a site previously operated on and had caused damage resulting in C's operation. The symptoms were much worse than they would have been without the surgery.

The case shows the importance of which side can prove what was actually said before the patient agreed to undergo the operation.

Non-therapeutic procedures

It was suggested in a case in 1987 (see Case 7.13) that the principles set out in the Sidaway case did not apply where non-therapeutic care was being provided but this was not accepted by the Court of Appeal.

Case 7.13   Gold v. Haringey Health Authority (1987)

Risk of sterilisation failing[49]

The claimant had two children and when she became pregnant agreed with her husband that they would have no further children after that pregnancy. She was seen by a consultant who suggested sterilisation following the birth of the child, but made no mention of the possibility of her husband having a vasectomy. Neither did he give her any warning of the risk of the sterilisation failing. The sterilisation operation was performed the day after the birth, but she subsequently became pregnant with her fourth child. She brought an action against the health authority alleging that there was negligence in failing to warn her of the risk of the operation failing and that the statement to her that the operation was irreversible amounted to a negligent misrepresentation.

The trial judge held that there was a distinction in the information that should be given in a non-therapeutic context compared with a decision on therapeutic treatment and that a sterilisation operation was non-therapeutic. He awarded her damages of £19,000. On appeal, the Court of Appeal held that the principles set out in the Sidaway case should apply in both contexts and it did not accept the validity of a distinction between therapeutic and non-therapeutic:

The [Bolam] principle does not depend on the context in which any act is performed or any advice given. It depends on a man professing skill or competence in a field beyond that possessed by the man on the Clapham omnibus. If the giving of contraceptive advice required no special skill, then I could see an argument that the Bolam Test should not apply. But that was not, and could not have been suggested. The fact (if it be a fact) that giving contraceptive advice involves a different sort of skill and competence from carrying out a surgical operation does not mean that the Bolam Test ceases to be applicable. It is clear from Lord Diplock's speech in Sidaway that a doctor's duty of care in relation to diagnosis, treatment and advice, whether the doctor be a specialist or general practitioner, is not to be dissected into its component parts. To dissect a doctor's advice into that given in a therapeutic context and that given in a contraceptive context would be to go against the whole thrust of [the decision in Sidaway].

The judge should have accepted the body of responsible medical opinion on the standard that should have been followed in giving her information.

Giving information to the terminally ill patient

In research reported by the Marie Curie Palliative Care Institute in Liverpool and the Royal College of Physicians[50] it was found that only 45 per cent of patients know that they are in 'the dying phase', compared with 80 per cent of their carers. If a patient is terminally ill, should the nurse tell the patient contrary to medical advice? What is the position if the relatives do not wish the patient to be told?

Practical Dilemma 7.4   Silence or lies?

Paul George has been operated on for 'ulcers'. Unknown to him, the surgeons actually found an inoperable tumour with wide spreading of the malignancy throughout the body. It is estimated that death is likely to occur in a few months. The consultant, who is normally in favour of a very open approach to patients, believes that Paul, who is 54, would not be able to cope with this news yet and he discusses this with Paul's wife, who agrees. The nursing staff are advised accordingly.

This kind of situation is in substance not unfamiliar to nursing staff and is repeated in different guises on many occasions. Unfortunately, however, it is the nursing staff who are most frequently with the patients and who are most likely to be asked: 'I don't have cancer, do I nurse?' or 'When am I likely to get out of here?' or 'Is it worth my while booking for this holiday next year?' and other direct or indirect questions designed to obtain a little more information for the patient as to where he stands. The questions that then arise in the nurse's mind are: Where does the patient stand in law? Does the patient have a legal enforceable right to obtain this information? What is the nurse's position in regard to the patient, the doctor and the relative?

Patient's rights

As has been seen in the discussion thus far, there is a duty on professional staff when advising certain forms of treatment to ensure that the patient is notified of any significant risks of substantial side effects. However, this duty on the professional is qualified by the power to withhold information in the rare cases where it is deemed to be in the patient's interest not to know. This is known as therapeutic privilege. Informing the patient that he is terminally ill may well come under this heading. Thus, if, in the opinion of the doctor, it would be harmful to tell a patient such disturbing news, then the doctor can withhold such information on the grounds that he is acting in the patient's best interest. A doctor may not withhold information about risks because he believes the patient would refuse consent if he were aware of them. There must be other reasons to justify withholding this information. There is no clear right in law for the patient to insist on being told and even where the patient is exercising his right under the Data Protection Act 1998, there is the power to withhold such data from him if serious harm would be caused to the patient's mental or physical health or condition (see Chapter 8).

The consultant or general practitioner has clinical responsibility for the patient. If in the doctor's opinion the patient would be harmed by any disclosure and he has exercised his judgement on this in accordance with the approved professional practice, then that decision must be accepted and implemented by the rest of the team of professionals. The nurses might disagree with the decision and, of course, they may well have the opportunity of persuading the doctor to change his mind, based on their own personal knowledge of the patient, his needs and his own understanding. Ultimately, however, they would be obliged to defer to the clinical decision of the doctor. Any nurse who flagrantly went against the doctor's view on this might well face disciplinary proceedings. What is clear at the present is that in the absence of any absolute statutory provision for accessing information, patients do not have a clear right to obtain this information. It may be that future cases based on the Articles of the European Convention of Human Rights may hold that keeping significant information from patients is a breach of Article 3 or Article 8 (see Appendix A).

The court has yet to deal directly with the question as to whether the patient has a right to be told and whether the doctor has a duty to tell when the patient is in a terminal condition. It is quite likely that if this is put before the courts, the court will apply the Bolam Test and leave it to the approved professional practice in relation to that particular patient.

Even if the patient is ultimately held to have such a right it does not follow that the nurse can ignore the instructions of the doctor. (This issue is considered in Chapter 4.)

Relatives' rights

It is not uncommon for relatives, on hearing of a particularly upsetting diagnosis, to ask for the patient not to be informed of that 'because he could not cope with that yet'. Often, perhaps, it is not the patient's inability to deal with the information, but the relatives' inability to cope with the patient's knowledge of it. The conspiracy of silence thus begins. As far as the law is concerned, unless the patient is mentally incompetent, this should not arise. The patient is entitled to have information about him kept confidential (see Chapter 8). It is a breach of this duty to the patient when the relative is told first. It is always open to the patient to say to the doctor, 'I would rather that my wife was not told about my diagnosis yet.' That is his right. Yet, when terminal illness or chronic sickness are concerned, the rules of confidentiality are broken and the relative is informed first. Obviously, there are exceptions to this duty of confidentiality when the patient is too ill to be told and decisions have to be made that therefore involve the relative. However, that should be the exception.

Let us return to the situation of Paul George (Practical Dilemma 7.4). If the nurse has received clear instructions that Paul should not be told that he is terminally ill, the nurse should not act contrary to these instructions. Neither, however, should she lie to Paul. If Paul makes it clear that he is seeking more information, the nurse should arrange for Paul to speak with the doctor concerned and express to the doctor her own views of Paul's needs. Ultimately, the wife has no right to insist that information is withheld from Paul. Obviously, because of her knowledge of Paul, she should be involved in any discussions on the correct approach.

Notifying the patient of negligence by a colleague

If a colleague has been negligent or even acts criminally, should the nurse inform the patient? This is not a hypothetical question as the cases of Beverly Allitt and Dr Shipman (see Chapters 2 and 5) show and it sometimes happens that a nurse is aware that a mistake has been made and that neither patient nor relatives have been made aware of this, although they may realise that all has not gone according to plan. What is the nurse to do in these circumstances? Does she have a duty to inform the patient?

The nurse's duty to the patient is to ensure that the patient receives all the appropriate care and treatment. If a mistake has been made, for example a colleague administers eye drops to the wrong eye, it is essential for the nurse to ensure that this is made known so that the patient can be given any necessary antidote. She should also ensure that steps are taken to prevent such an error occurring again and should therefore check that a report has been made to senior nurse management. Hopefully, if a nurse is at fault, she herself will have reported it, as part of her duties under the Code of Professional Conduct. Good practice should ensure that a full disclosure is given to the patient and it would be the consultant's responsibility to see that this was done and to reassure the patient about any future effects. The NMC has made it clear that where a practitioner has honestly admitted an error, she should be treated differently from a practitioner who has attempted to cover up a mistake.[51]

The nurse should take every action that she reasonably can to ensure that the patient is fully informed. Reference must also be made to the Code of Professional Conduct and the practitioner's duty to ensure that any untoward occurrences are brought to the attention of the appropriate officer. NHS trusts and health authorities are required to establish procedures to implement the Public Interest Disclosure Act 1998, known as the whistleblower's charter. Guidance is given in HSC 1999/198 by the Department of Health on the implementation of this Act. Its aim is to protect any employee who brings a protected disclosure (e.g. a criminal offence, health and safety danger, failure to fulfil legal duty) to the attention of the appropriate person in the organisation from any victimisation. (This legislation is further discussed in Chapter 4.) The Kennedy Report on Bristol paediatric heart surgery[52] recommended that there should be openness and honesty with patients. The National Patient Safety Agency's effectiveness depends on health professionals being prepared to admit when hazards exist or where accidents have occurred. In addition, a consultation paper on a new NHS redress scheme for compensation for clinical negligence (*Making Amends*) suggested that there should be a statutory duty of candour on health professionals (see Chapter 6). Such a statutory duty was not enacted in the NHS Redress Act 2006, but the recommendations of the Kennedy Report were in favour of openness between professionals and patients. The NHS Redress Act is considered in Chapter 6.

Conclusions

It is clear that there has been a move away from a paternalistic approach to consent to treatment towards an increasing emphasis on the rights of the patient to give consent and to receive the necessary information about the significant risks of substantial harm. It is likely that this trend will continue and health professionals will be increasingly required to ensure that they satisfy reasonable standards of practice in providing the patient with information about proposed treatments and investigations. Documentation of what information has been given is essential. The Mental Capacity Act 2005 has replaced the common law provisions in relation to decision making on behalf of those who lack the mental capacity to make their own decisions and its implications will be seen over the next few years.[53]

Reflection questions

1 What is meant by implied consent to treatment? Consider examples of implied consent from your own practice.
2 Consider the implications of the Mental Capacity Act for your particular specialty.
3 What is the difference between the 'Bolam Test' and the 'prudent patient' test so far as consent to treatment is concerned?

Further exercises

1 Obtain a copy of Form 1 of the Department of Health's recommended consent forms. How appropriate do you think it is to cover the wide range of treatments for which it is used? Could it be adapted to cover specific treatments that you provide?
2 Refer to the specialist subject areas in Part II of this book and consider the principles that apply to consent by children under 16, consent by young persons of 16 and 17, consent by the mentally disordered and by the unconscious patient.
3 Consider the first Schedule to the Human Rights Act 1998 (see Appendix A) and consider any other rights in relation to healthcare that you consider should be included.

References

1 *Freeman* v. *Home Offce* [1984] 1 All ER 1036
2 Department of Health, Reference Guide to Consent for Examination or Treatment, DH, 2001; www.dh.gov.uk/consent
3 Department of Health, Good Practice in Consent Implementation Guide, DH, November 2001
4 *R* v. *Brown and Others*, House of Lords, The Times Law Report, 12 March 1993
5 Department of Health, Good Practice in Consent Implementation Guide, DH, November 2001
6 Bristol Royal Infirmary Inquiry (Kennedy Report), Learning from Bristol: the report of the public inquiry into children's heart surgery at the Bristol Royal Infirmary 1984-1995, Command paper Cm 5207, The Stationery Office, London, 2001
7 *Davis* v. *Barking, Havering and Brentwood HA* [1993] 4 Med LR 85
8 Department of Health, Reference Guide to Consent for Examination or Treatment, DH, 2001 (Paragraph 12); www.dh.gov.uk/consent
9 *F* v. *West Berkshire Health Authority* [1989] 2 All ER 545; [1990] 2 AC 1
10 *O'Brien* v. *Cunard Steamship Co.* (1891) 28 NE 266
11 *Chatterton* v. *Gerson* [1981] 1 All ER 257
12 *Re MB (An adult: medical treatment)* [1997] 2 FLR 426

[13] *St George's Healthcare NHS Trust* v. *S* [1998] 3 All ER 673

[14] *Re C (An adult: refusal of medical treatment)* [1994] 1 All ER 819; (1993) 15 BMLR 77

[15] *NHS Trust* v. *Ms T* [2004] EWHC 1279

[16] *Re MB (An adult: medical treatment)* [1997] 2 FLR 426

[17] *Re B (Consent to treatment: capacity)*, The Times Law Report, 26 March 2002; [2002] 2 All ER 449

[18] Jehovah's Witness mother dies after refusing blood transfusion after giving birth to twins, *The Daily Mail*, 5 November 2007. http://www.dailymail.co.uk/pages/live/articles/news/news.html?in_article_id=491791&in_page_id=1770 (last accessed 25 January 2008)

[19] *In re T (An adult: refusal of medical treatment)* [1992] 4 All ER 649

[20] *In re S (An adult: refusal of medical treatment)* [1992] 4 All ER 671

[21] *Leigh* v. *Gladstone* (1909) 26 TLR 139

[22] *Secretary of State for the Home Department* v. *Robb* [1995] 1 All ER 677

[23] *R* v. *Collins, ex p Brady* (2001) 58 BMLR 173; [2000] Lloyd's Med Rep 355

[24] Gillian Harris, Surgeon happy he removed healthy limbs, *The Times*, 1 February 2000

[25] For further discussion of this topic, see B. Dimond, *Legal Aspects of Consent*, Quay Publications, Dinton, 2003

[26] *R* v. *Brown and Others*, The Times Law Report, 12 March 1993 HL

[27] *F* v. *West Berkshire Health Authority* [1989] 2 All ER 545

[28] *Malette* v. *Shulman* [1991] 2 Med LR 162

[29] *F* v. *West Berkshire Health Authority* [1989] 2 All ER 545

[30] *In re F (An adult: court's jurisdiction)*, The Times Law Report, 25 July 2000; [2000] 2 FLR 512

[31] *R* v. *Bournewood Community and Mental Health NHS Trust ex parte L* [1999] AC 458

[32] *HL* v. *United Kingdom* [2004] ECHR 720 Application No. 45508/99 5 October 2004; Times Law Report 19 October 2004

[33] Law Commission, Mental Incapacity, HMSO, London, 1995

[34] Lord Chancellor, Who Decides? Lord Chancellor's Office, The Stationery Office, London, 1997

[35] Lord Chancellor, Making Decisions, Lord Chancellor's Office, The Stationery Office, London, 1999

[36] Department of Health, Reference Guide to Consent for Examination or Treatment, DH, 2001; www.dh.gov.uk/consent

[37] House of Lords and House of Commons, Joint Committee on the Draft Mental Incapacity Bill Session 2002–3, HL paper 189-1; HC 1083-1

[38] www.justice.gov.uk/menincap/legis

[39] Robert Tobin, Pioneering use of Independent Mental Capacity Advocate, *Clinical Risk*, Vol. 13 No. 5, September 2007, p. 199

[40] *HL* v. *United Kingdom* [2004] ECHR 471 Application No 45508/99 5 October 2004; Times Law Report 19 October 2004

[41] *Sidaway* v. *Bethlem Royal Hospital Governors and Others* [1985] 1 All ER 643

[42] *Canterbury* v. *Spence* [1972] 464 F 2d 772

[43] *Blyth* v. *Bloomsbury Health Authority*, The Times, 11 February 1987; [1993] 4 Med LR 151

[44] *Smith* v. *Tunbridge Wells Health Authority* [1994] 5 Med LR 334

[45] *Pearce* v. *United Bristol Healthcare NHS Trust* (1998) 48 BMLR 118 CA

[46] *Chester* v. *Afshar*, The Times Law Report, 13 June 2002; [2002] 3 All ER 552 CA

[47] *Chester* v. *Afshar*, The Times Law Report, 19 October 2004 HL; [2004] UKHL 41; [2004] 3 WLR 927

[48] *Chinchen* v. *University Hospital of Wales Healthcare NHS Trust*, 8 November 2001 (*Current Law*, 340, April 2002)

[49] *Gold* v. *Haringey Health Authority* [1987] 2 All ER 888

[50] Rosemary Bennett, Patients 'not told they are dying', *The Times*, 5 December 2007. http://www.timesonline.co.uk/tol/news/uk/article3001103.ece (last accessed 25 January 2008)

[51] Nursing and Midwifery Council, *Guidelines on the Administration of Medicines*, 2002 (reprint of UKCC publication October 2000)

[52] Bristol Royal Infirmary Inquiry (Kennedy Report), Learning from Bristol: the report of the public inquiry into children's heart surgery at the Bristol Royal Infirmary 1984–1995, Command paper Cm 5207, The Stationery Office, London, 2001

[53] B Dimond, *Legal Aspects of Mental Capacity*, Blackwell Publishing, Oxford, 2008

Chapter 8
Data protection: confidentiality and access

This chapter discusses

+ Data Protection Act 1998
+ Data protection principles
+ First data protection principle
+ Duty of confidentiality
+ Caldicott Guardians
+ Freedom of Information Act 2000
+ Access to personal health records
+ Access to Medical Reports Act 1988

Data Protection Act 1998

The European Directive on Data Protection[1] was implemented in this country by the Data Protection Act 1998 (DPA). Member states were required to comply with its provisions by 24 October 1998, although the UK did not meet this target. Under the legislation, members have to establish a set of principles with which users of personal information must comply. The legislation also gives individuals the right to gain access to information held about them and provides for a supervisory authority to oversee and enforce the law. NHS guidance on the Act was provided by a circular in March 2000.[2] The NHS Information Authority was abolished in April 2005 and its work undertaken by NHS Connecting for Health and the Health and Social Care Information Centre. Information is available on NHS Connecting for Health website.[3] (The Information Security Management: Code of Practice prepared by the DH is considered in Chapter 9.) An explanation of the Data Protection Act 1998 is also available from the Data Protection Commissioner, now known as the Information Commissioner.[4] Good practice notes on the Data Protection Act 1998 are available from the Information Commissioner's website.[5]

The Data Protection Act 1998, unlike its 1984 predecessor, applies to manual records if they form part of a relevant filing system as well as to computerised records and provides tighter provisions on the processing of sensitive personal data. New rules for the transfer of personal data outside the European Community are set out.

Information Commissioner

The person responsible for the enforcement and overseeing of Data Protection legislation was known as the Data Protection Commissioner (the Registrar under the 1984 Act), but since that individual is now also responsible for the implementation of the Freedom of Information Act 2000, he/she is now known as the Information Commissioner, with both Acts coming within his or her jurisdiction, together with the Environmental Information Regulations and the Privacy and Electronic Communications Regulations. Good practice notes, codes of practice and technical guidance notes on all this legislation are available on the Information Commissioner's website.[6] The Information Commissioner's Office has legal powers to ensure that organisations comply with the legal requirements and details of cases where these powers of enforcement have been used are available on the ICO website. An application for judicial review by the Secretary of State of an information tribunal decision which had quashed a ministerial certificate claiming exemption from providing subject access on grounds of national security failed. The High Court held that the Information Commissioner had the power to check whether an exemption was properly claimed.[7]

Terminology

+ 'Personal data' are data that relate to a living person, who can be identified from those data or from those data together with other information in the possession of the data controller.

+ 'Sensitive personal data' are personal data consisting of information as specified in Section 2 of the 1998 Act. Section 2 includes racial or ethnic origins, political opinions and the physical or mental health or condition or sexual life of the data subject.

+ 'Data subject' is the individual who is the subject of the personal data.

+ 'Data controller' means a person who, either alone or with others, determines the purposes for which and the manner in which any personal data are, or are to be, processed.

+ 'Processing' includes obtaining, recording or holding information or carrying out any operation including retrieval or consultation or use of the information, and disclosure (definition abbreviated by author).

Human rights

The Data Protection Act 1998 must be read in conjunction with the Human Rights Act 1998 (see Chapter 1), since Article 8 recognises an individual's right to private and family life (see Appendix A of this book). The Freedom of Information Act 2000 gives a right to access to information held by public authorities, but this is subject to many exceptions including personal information where the Data Protection Act 1998 applies (S. 40 Freedom of Information Act 2000). The courts have issued injunctions to grant people lifetime anonymity. Thus, where two young boys had been convicted of killing James Bulger, a toddler, there was a fear for their safety (and therefore their Article 2 rights were at stake) if their new identities were disclosed, and an injunction was ordered forbidding disclosure of their identities;[8] a woman who had been convicted of manslaughter for killing two young children when she was 11 years old succeeded in obtaining an injunction to protect the privacy of herself and her daughter. There was no real fear of danger to her life (and therefore Article 2 rights), but her right to private and family life under Article 8 was threatened.[9]

Data protection principles

The Data Protection Act sets out eight principles that apply to the keeping of computerised data (see the Statute, below). These principles are designed to ensure that personal data shall be accurate, relevant, held only for specific defined purposes for which the user has been registered, not kept for longer than is necessary and not disclosed to unauthorised persons. In addition, a right of subject access is given (see below), i.e. the individual should be able, on payment of a small fee, to see what is contained about him and have a right to rectify that if it is not correct. The Commissioner has the power to enforce the duties under the Act and offenders can be prosecuted. The individual data subject has the right to apply to the courts for compensation for damage and any associated distress caused by a breach of these principles by the data user. (The provisions in relation to access to health records are considered below.) An orthopaedic surgeon lost his appeal against the refusal of the High Court to hold that removal of his name from the register of members of the Medical Defence Union breached principle one of the Data Protection Act 1998 in that his personal data was not processed fairly.[10]

Statute | **Principles of the Data Protection Act 1998 Schedule 1**

1 Personal data shall be processed fairly and lawfully and, in particular, shall not be processed unless:
  (a) at least one of the conditions in Schedule 2 is met, and
  (b) in the case of sensitive personal data, at least one of the conditions in Schedule 3 is also met.

> **Statute continued**
>
> **2** Personal data shall be obtained only for one or more specified and lawful purposes and shall not be further processed in any manner incompatible with that purpose or those purposes.
>
> **3** Personal data shall be adequate, relevant and not excessive in relation to the purpose or purposes for which they are processed.
>
> **4** Personal data shall be accurate and, where necessary, kept up to date.
>
> **5** Personal data processed for any purpose or purposes shall not be kept for longer than is necessary for that purpose(s).
>
> **6** Personal data shall be processed in accordance with the rights of data subjects under this Act.
>
> **7** Appropriate technical and organisational measures shall be taken against unauthorised or unlawful processing of personal data and against accidental loss or destruction of, or damage to, personal data.
>
> **8** Personal data shall not be transferred to a country or territory outside the European Economic Area unless that country or territory ensures an adequate level of protection for the rights and freedoms of data subjects in relation to the processing of personal data.

First data protection principle

This principle, which requires that personal data shall be processed fairly and lawfully, prevents the processing unless at least one of the conditions in Schedule 2 is met and, in the case of sensitive personal data, at least one of the conditions in Schedule 3 is also met. Schedules 2 and 3 are set out in the Department of Health guidance.[11] Schedule 2 includes the consent of the patient, contractual purposes and compliance with legal obligations necessary to protect the vital interests of the data subject or necessary for the administration of justice or for the legitimate purposes of the data controller. Schedule 3 includes the explicit consent of the patient, rights and obligations in connection with employment, where the processing is necessary to protect the vital interests of the data subject or another person, where the consent cannot be given by or on behalf of the data subject or where the data controller cannot reasonably be expected to obtain the consent. (Schedules 2 and 3 can be seen in Appendix C of this book.) The Privacy and Electronic Communications (EC Directive) Regulations 2003 controls the sending of unsolicited direct marketing by phone, fax, email and text messages and further information can be found on the ICO website. Guidance provided by the DH, GMC and the ICO on the use of IT equipment and access to patient data is considered in Chapter 9.

Information tribunals

The information tribunal hears appeals by data controllers against notices (usually enforcement notices) issued by the Information Commissioner under the Data Protection Act 1998 and also appeals against enforcement notices or information notices issued by the Commissioner under the Freedom of Information Act 2000 (see below). There is a separate national security appeals panel of the tribunal to hear appeals against exemptions from the Data Protection Act on grounds of national security.[12]

Duty of confidentiality

The patient is entitled to confidentiality of the information about him. There is therefore a duty on every professional and indeed every employee to ensure confidentiality of information. The duty arises:

1 from the duty of care in negligence discussed in Chapter 1

2 from the implied duties under the contract of employment (see Chapter 10)

3 from the duty to keep information that has been passed on in confidence, confidential, even when there is no pre-existing relationship or legally enforceable contract between the parties (a duty based on equity and only recently recognised by the courts and discussed in the case of *Stephens* v. *Avery and Others*).[13] In the case of Naomi Campbell, the House of Lords in a majority decision held that even though she had brought into the public domain the fact that she was being treated for drug addition, certain information could still be kept confidential, including the time, form and place of the drug therapy, and she was therefore entitled to damages against the Mirror Group Newspapers for that breach of confidence.[14] In this respect her right to privacy succeeded against the right to freedom of expression

4 from requirements by professional registration bodies as part of the professional conduct, such as the Nursing and Midwifery Council

5 from statutory duties such as the Data Protection Act 1998 and Article 8 of the European Convention of Human Rights (Schedule 1 of the Human Rights Act 1998; see Appendix A of this book).

Under the duties implied in the contract of employment, the employee has a responsibility to the employer to keep information acquired from work confidential. For the nurse, too, that duty is also spelled out by the Code of Professional Conduct: standards for conduct, performance and ethics[15] (see Box 8.1). (See Box 8.2 on page 172 for exceptions to the duty of confidentiality and Box 8.3 on page 180 for exceptions recognised by the NMC.)

Box 8.1 — **Paragraphs 5.1 and 5.2 of the Code of Professional Conduct of the NMC**

5.1 You must treat information about patients and clients as confidential and use it only for the purposes for which it was given. As it is impractical to obtain consent every time you need to share information with others, you should ensure that patients and clients understand that some information may be made available to other members of the team involved in the delivery of care. You must guard against breaches of confidentiality by protecting information from improper disclosure at all times.

5.2 You should seek patients' and clients' wishes regarding the sharing of information with their family and others. When a patient or client is considered incapable of giving permission, you should consult relevant colleagues.

While this code is not enforceable in a court of law, it reflects what the law upholds and is used by the NMC and its committees as a guideline in determining whether the nurse is guilty of professional misconduct and therefore whether her fitness to practise is impaired.

Difficulties arise not in understanding the duty of confidentiality, but in knowing when the exceptions arise and in what circumstances breaking the duty is permissible. Paragraph 5.3 of the Code of Professional Conduct of the NMC[16] sets out the circumstances in which disclosure is permissible. In a case brought by Ashworth Hospital against Mirror Group

Newspapers, the judge made an order requiring the newspaper group to disclose to the hospital the identity of the source of their information about a convicted murderer who was a patient at Ashworth. The Court of Appeal upheld this judgment, holding that the protection of patient information was of vital concern to the NHS.[17] Mirror Group Newspapers disclosed that the clinical notes had been received from a freelance investigative journalist, Mr Ackroyd. He then refused to identify his sources within the hospital. The hospital then sought an order requiring him to disclose the source of the notes. Mr Ackroyd stated that although he had been paid £1,250 from the *Mirror*, his sources at the hospital had not received any payment and were not motivated by financial gain, but to reveal publicly the way in which Ian Brady had been treated.

The Court of Appeal held that the protection of journalistic sources was one of the basic conditions of press freedom and the hospital had to establish an overriding public interest amounting to a pressing social need to which the need to keep press sources confidential should give way. The current case was different from the original MGN case, since as a journalist he was entitled to present different evidential material from a different perspective. The passage of time since the original case meant that there was no cloud of suspicion that was still blighting activity at the hospital and there had been no breach of confidentiality.[18] On 27 July 2007 the House of Lords refused leave to appeal against the Court of Appeal decision. Robin Ackroyd was thus not forced to disclose the source of his information.

The High Court has also recognised that in exceptional circumstances the court has the jurisdiction to extend the protection of confidentiality of information even to the extent of imposing restrictions on the press where a failure to do so would probably lead to serious physical injury or the death of the person seeking that confidentiality. Thus it granted an injunction to prohibit the publication of the details of the boys who killed James Bulger.[19]

The DH has issued an NHS Confidentiality Code of Practice. This supersedes the earlier advice on the protection and use of patient information issued in 1996.[20] The NHS Code of Practice covers the following areas:

+ confidentiality: definition, disclosing and using confidential patient information; patient consent to disclosing, obligations on individuals working in the NHS
+ providing a confidential service
+ using and disclosing confidential patient information
+ Annex A: detailed requirements in providing a confidential service
+ Annex B: confidentiality decisions
+ Annex C: index of confidential decisions in practice: health purposes, medical purposes other than healthcare, non-medical purposes.

A wider confidentiality communications strategy is at present being developed by the Department of Health and the NHS Information Authority and information is available on the NHS Information Authority website.[21]

Regulations on the disclosure of patient information

Powers are given to the Secretary of State under Sections 60 and 61 of the Health and Social Care Act 2001 (re-enacted in Sections 251 and 252 of the NHS Act 2006) to make regulations on the disclosure of patient information. This is subject to the scrutiny of the Patient Information Advisory Group (PIAG)[22] of the draft regulations and whether they are justified. (The terms of reference, membership and minutes of the PIAG are available from its website.)[23] Regulations have been drawn up following scrutiny by the PIAG relating to cancer registers and communicable diseases.[24] As a consequence disclosure to cancer registers and other specified registers of patient information were legitimated. The use of Department of Health powers should be consistent with human rights. The PIAG has supported the processing of the following databases without patient consent:

NHS-Wide Clearing Service

Hospital Episode Statistics

National Health Authority Information System

Patient Episode Database for Wales.

In 2003 the Department of Health issued a consultation paper on proposals to revise the regulations made under Section 60 of the 2001 Act so that provision for a number of essential NHS activities could be made, including the commissioning of healthcare services, call-up and recall of patients for cancer screening, monitoring performance and production of statistics on healthcare services and outcomes. Details of the applications approved by the PIAG can be found on its website.[25] Other studies are approved under by the Advisory Group for Medical Research (AGMR) on behalf of the PIAG and its register of approved schemes can be found on its website.[26] The PIAG has published a booklet for patients on its role in safeguarding confidential information[27] and another for health professionals and researchers.[28] It is envisaged that in time the NHS Connecting for Health programme will enable procedures to be developed to obtain consent from patients or for more effective and efficient means of anonymising health records for use by researchers. PIAG has published a procedure for responding to concerns and complaints about the use of patient-identifiable information which it will handle in conjunction with the Healthcare Commission.

Section 68 of the Health and Social Care (Community and Standards) Act 2003 gives powers to CHAI to access individual patient records. This raised concerns expressed by the NMC, GMC and Consumers' Association that insufficient weight was given to patient confidentiality and it was contrary to DH guidance. As a consequence CHAI (in its shadow form) agreed to develop a robust code of practice to protect patients' rights to confidentiality and a consultation exercise was held on a draft code of practice relating to access to personal patient information.[29] The Healthcare Commission published a draft charter in October 2007.

Exceptions to the duty of confidentiality

See Box 8.2.

Box 8.2   **Exceptions to the duty of confidentiality**

1 Consent of a patient.
2 Interests of patient.
3 Court orders:
      subpoena
      civil procedure rules.
4 Statutory duty to disclose:
      Road Traffic Act 1988 (as amended)
      Prevention of Terrorism (Temporary Provisions) Act 1988
      Public Health Acts
      Misuse of Drugs Acts.
5 Public interest.
6 Police.
7 Data Protection Act 1998 provisions.

Consent of the patient

The duty is owed to the patient and it is therefore in the patient's power to authorise disclosures to be made. Thus announcements to the press, notification of relatives and spouses and provision of information to a solicitor or to an insurance company are all legitimate disclosures with the consent of the patient. If the patient is unconscious and an adult, the consent of the relatives is often used to justify disclosure on behalf of the patient, but there may well be little justification for this in law, unless the patient has appointed that relative as his agent and given him that authority.

Practical Dilemma 8.1   Spouse's confidence

Annabel was involved in a serious road accident and admitted to hospital. While on the orthopaedic ward, a telephone request came in asking for information on her progress. The nurse taking the call asked who the caller was. The answer was 'her husband'. The nurse then gave the caller full details of Annabel's progress. She then told Annabel that her husband had phoned, asking for information about her; the nurse was surprised at Annabel's fury. It appeared that she had recently separated from him, she had not notified him of where she was now living and did not want any communication with him because of his violence.

The difficulties of the nurse's position in a situation like this are easily understood. In 99 out of 100 cases, Annabel would be delighted to receive a message of concern and interest. However, it is the 100th case that causes concern and procedures have to be established to prevent any unauthorised information being disclosed. Annabel is entitled to withhold information of her condition from her relatives and friends. In some cases, even an acknowledgement that a patient is on a particular ward, e.g. psychiatric or gynaecology (abortion), might be an unwarranted disclosure. In Practical Dilemma 8.1, the nurse was at fault in not checking with Annabel first and it is now standard practice not to disclose information over the phone unless checks on the caller have been made and the patient is agreeable to the information being given.

There can often be a problem in caring for elderly patients where the patient has made a special request to the nurses that the relatives should not be told about his/her condition. However, it can give rise to additional problems for staff. 'Where do I stand if I do not contact the relatives regarding the condition of the elderly patient because the elderly patient has asked me not to do so?' is a not infrequent question. Applying the principles discussed here, the patient does have the right to refuse to allow this information to be passed on. However, if the relatives are to care for the patient eventually, there may well be information that they need to know for the patient's own safety and thus disclosure is justified in the interests of the patient (see below).

Disclosure refused by the patient

In the following case the patient refused to permit disclosure of her records to her employer.

The Court of Appeal upheld the appeal and granted the 'unless' order. It stated that the court could not order a claimant to waive her right of confidentiality, but could stay proceedings until the claimant waived the right of confidentiality. Information requested from a claimant in a case of this kind should be confined to that which was relevant to the issues

173

Case 8.1   *Nicholson v. Halton General Hospital NHS Trust* (1999)

Waiver of patient's right to confidentiality[30]

The claimant issued proceedings against her employer alleging that she had sustained radial tunnel syndrome in her right wrist as a result of his negligence in requiring her to perform repetitive movements at work. She had undergone a remedial operation and the employer wished to have details of the reasons for the operation and the nature of the condition. She refused to give permission for the employer's legal and medical advisers to discuss the operation with her consultant. The employer sought an 'unless' order from the court, that unless she provided the necessary consent, the proceedings would be stayed. Her consultant also stated that he would not become involved unless instructed by the court. The judge refused the 'unless' order.

between the parties and a claimant could not restrict the information requested to a written rather than an oral form.

Disclosure to the press

Exactly the same principles apply when the press are asking for information about a patient. If the patient consents, the information can be given. If the patient refuses, then no information should be given and this includes a condition check, where the press phone up to find out the latest condition of the patient. Where the patient is unconscious, confidentiality should be respected.

Disclosure in the interests of the patient

Disclosure between professionals caring for the patient is justified on the basis that if information obtained by the doctor and relevant to the care of the patient is not passed on to the appropriate professional, then the patient might suffer. An obvious example is the patient's history of allergy to certain medication: if the pharmacist and the nurse were not told of a known allergy or allowed to see the records, they would be unable to ensure that the patient was given appropriate medication. Traditionally, nurses have not usually had difficulties over access to the patient's records. Other professional groups have encountered difficulties: occupational therapists, physiotherapists, social workers and other groups have sometimes been refused access to the patient's records on the grounds that it is unnecessary and also a breach of confidentiality. This is a difficult problem. On the one hand, the wider the range of people who have access to the medical records of the patient, the more difficult it is to maintain the duty of confidentiality. On the other hand, there are many situations where a professional caring for the patient, in ignorance of certain facts known to the doctor, could do the patient considerable harm.

The problem becomes even more complex when we consider the question of how much confidential information should be given to a volunteer who is taking the patient out. For example, if the volunteer is taking a patient with learning disabilities out for the day, it might be vital in the interests of the safety of the patient to advise the volunteer that the patient is epileptic and to ensure that the volunteer would know how to cope should the patient have a fit. Contrariwise, the fact that the patient had an abortion five years ago would be irrelevant and thus would be a disclosure that would not be justified in the interests of the patient.

In conclusion, it could be said that disclosure of confidential information to others is justified if it is necessary in the interests of the health and/or safety of the patient or the professional. Those to whom this information is disclosed would themselves be subject to the same duty of confidentiality. AIDS has raised many significant problems in this field and these are discussed further in Chapter 26.

Court orders

Subpoena

This is an order made by the court, which must be obeyed under threat of punishment for contempt of court.

The court has the power to subpoena any relevant evidence or witnesses in a case in the interests of justice. The court can also place conditions on an order for disclosure as in the case of *A Health Authority* v. *X*.[31] In this case, the health authority received information about a child protection case from the local authority from which it considered that there had been possible medical malpractice. The health authority sought an order for production of certain case papers, which the judge allowed and ordered the respondent doctor to produce the medical records. The judge placed certain conditions on the order to ensure the confidentiality of the documents and to prevent disclosure to third parties without the permission of the court. The health authority appealed against these conditions, but the Court of Appeal held the judge had been correct to exercise his discretion to impose conditions on the orders for disclosure.

There are only two exceptions to the power of the court to order disclosure and these are known as being privileged from disclosure.

Privilege on grounds of public interest (sometimes known as public interest immunity) An example of public interest protected from an order for disclosure is national security. It would usually be claimed by a minister of the Crown when a certificate is signed to the effect that disclosure of a particular document or information would be contrary to the public interest. Following the Scott Inquiry into the Matrix Churchill case, it was recommended that privilege on the grounds of the public interest should not be claimed when prosecution of a criminal offence was being brought. The House of Lords laid down guidelines for claiming privilege on grounds of public interest in a recent case.[32] It stated that withholding information (as an exception to the golden rule of disclosure) may be justified but it always had to be the minimum necessary to protect the public interest in question and could never imperil the overall fairness of the trial.

Legal professional privilege This second exception to the power of the court to order disclosure covers communications between client and legal adviser where litigation is envisaged or is taking place. In the interests of total disclosure between client and lawyer, and in the advancement of justice, these communications are free from an order of discovery or disclosure. Difficulties have arisen over the disclosure of statements taken from witnesses to an accident that might be used later in any court proceedings. Are such statements protected from disclosure on the grounds of legal professional privilege?

In the case of *Waugh* v. *British Railway Board*,[33] it was held that where a document comes into being after an accident and where there are two purposes for its use (e.g. management purposes to ensure that the accident does not happen again and legal purposes to defend any potential action), then if the dominant purpose is for management purposes, the document is not privileged from disclosure under the rules of professional legal privilege. This ruling by the House of Lords was upheld in the following case.

Case 8.2 *Lee v. SW Thames RHA (1985)*

Disclosure[34]

Marlon Lee, a young boy, was severely scalded and was initially treated in a hospital run by one health authority, then subsequently transferred to a burns hospital run by another district authority. Shortly afterwards, he developed breathing problems and was transferred to the first hospital by the ambulance that came under the South West Thames Regional Health Authority. He suffered brain damage, which was considered to be due to lack of oxygen. The mother asked for disclosure of the ambulance report produced by the regional health authority for the first hospital, but was refused it. Her application to the court for disclosure failed on the basis that the report was prepared in contemplation of litigation and to assist the legal advisers and disclosure could not be ordered even though it had been initiated as a result of the request by the first hospital authority, not by the authority responsible for the ambulance service.

This case shows the disadvantages faced by potential litigants since the health authority or NHS trust is, of course, both custodian of the records and a potential defendant and can use its first function to enable it to have immediate access to all the relevant records. (If the report can be defined as part of the personal health records of the patient, then access may be obtained under the data protection subject access provisions (see below) unless the exceptions apply.)

The test to decide whether communication between a solicitor and his client was privileged from disclosure was to consider whether it was made confidentially for the purposes of legal advice, constructing such purposes broadly.[35] A person could agree to a partial waiver of the right to legal professional privilege without having to lose the right entirely.[36] Section 42 of the Freedom of Information Act recognises the exception of legal professional privilege and an Awareness Guidance note is available from the Information Commissioner's website.[37]

Apart from these exceptions, the judge has the power to order the production of any evidence relevant to the case. There is no recognition of the privilege of confidential medical information, neither do the courts recognise the secrecy of the confessional. In the case of *Deacon* v. *McVicar*[38] (see Case 4.11, page 77), the judge ordered the production of the records of other maternity patients.

Health visitors are more likely than any other group of nurses to be summoned by subpoena to appear in court. They had adopted a procedure whereby they would normally require service of a subpoena before giving evidence in court. In this way, they were able to make it clear to their clients that they had no option but to attend court and were obliged to disclose confidential information. The Children Act 1989 has led to health visitors giving evidence in the interest of the child without waiting for a subpoena.

Disclosure in personal injury cases

Disclosure can be made of relevant records under the Supreme Court Act 1981, Sections 33 and 34: Section 33 enables disclosure to be made between parties to a case before litigation commences; Section 34 enables an order for disclosure to be made against a third party. In addition, as a result of pressure from the Health Service Commissioner and also from judges in several cases where there has been evidence of unnecessary delay in the production of medical records, NHS trusts nowadays rarely wait to be issued with an order for disclosure, but are more likely to produce the relevant documents when the solicitor requests them. Access by the claimant can be sought under the statutory provisions of the data protection legislation (see below). In addition, the Woolf reforms in civil justice have led to earlier disclosure of relevant information as part of the pre-action protocol (see Chapter 6).

Disclosure before trial

In addition to the rules under the Supreme Court Act 1981, the rules of the High Court enable an order for relevant information to be made once the claim form has been issued and the case commenced. This order for the production of documents is part of the exchange of information that takes place between the parties before the hearing takes place in the court. The aim is to ensure that the parties understand the main points in dispute and are not surprised when the oral hearing takes place. The days in court should thus be kept to a minimum and should take place only when there really is an outstanding issue between the parties. Changes to the civil law procedure have taken place following Lord Woolf's report on access to justice. The emphasis is on openness between the partners and early disclosure between them of all relevant information, including the reports of experts. Under the new system of case management by the courts introduced under the new Civil Procedure Rules, directions have been given to facilitate the exchange of information and the progress of the case (see Chapter 6).

In exceptional circumstances, the court could order disclosure to a person who was neither a party to the case nor a lawyer. Thus, in the case over the alleged harm caused by the drug Opren, the Court of Appeal allowed disclosure to the medical and scientific journalist and writer who was assisting the many claimants in their case against Eli Lilly.[39]

Disclosure to the patient and the right of subject access

The Data Protection Act 1998 gives the right of subject access to health records, subject to several exceptions. This is considered on pages 188–90.

Statutory duty to disclose

Whatever the views of the patient, there are certain circumstances in which disclosure of otherwise confidential information must be made by law. The following are the main provisions:

1 *Road Traffic Act 1988 Section 170 as amended by the Traffic Act 1991*: this requires any person to give information to the police relating to a road traffic accident involving personal injuries. A doctor was prosecuted under its predecessor for failing to disclose the relevant information and was fined £5.[40] His claim that he should not be required to give information that would be a breach of the patient's confidence was not accepted either by the trial judge or by the divisional court (see also Chapter 21). In a case in 1999,[41] it was held that there was a statutory duty to report a road accident, even when the driver was not actually driving at the time.

2 *Prevention of Terrorism (Temporary Provisions) Act 1988, Section 11 (Continuous Order SI 1993/747)*: this makes it an offence for any person having information, which he believes may be of material assistance in preventing terrorism or apprehending terrorists, to fail without reasonable cause to give that information to the police. This therefore places a burden on staff, for example in A&E departments, to disclose the existence of wounds that may have resulted from terrorist acts.

3 *Public Health (Control of Disease) Act 1984*: requires a medical practitioner attending a patient who appears to be suffering from a notifiable disease to notify the medical officer of the district of the name and whereabouts of the patient and the disease. Notifiable diseases include cholera, plague, smallpox and typhus. (See Chapter 26.)

4 *Abortion Act 1967*: requires doctors to inform the Chief Medical Officer of the DH of detailed information relating to the termination of pregnancy. (See Chapter 15.)

The Misuse of Drugs (Supply to Addicts) Regulations 1997 have abolished the requirement for a doctor to notify the Home Office of any patient who appears to be drug dependent, but a doctor is expected to notify the local drug misuse database. (See Chapter 28.)

Public interest

Unfortunately, many of the difficulties relating to the exceptions to the duty of confidentiality come under the broad heading of 'public interest' where there is little guidance from the courts.

Practical Dilemma 8.2   An epileptic lorry driver

Bill, a long-distance lorry driver, is diagnosed as having epilepsy, which is not yet under control through medication. The doctor has advised him to notify his employers and cease driving until the epilepsy is under control. Bill does not wish to do this since he has just been interviewed for the job of coach driver on the continent and he has been hoping for this chance for years. April, a nurse in the neurology ward, recognises Bill as her neighbour and is horrified when she hears from Bill's wife that Bill has been given the job of driving a coachload of schoolchildren to France. She knows several children who will be on that trip.

Many would argue that in these circumstances a breach of the duty of confidentiality owed to Bill is justified on grounds of the public interest. Obviously, there are advantages in Bill's being persuaded of the dangers of driving on the trip, but if he fails to disclose this and continues with his plans, then many would justify the doctor making the disclosure. If the doctor is adamant that he will not breach that confidence, does the nurse have any right to do so? The General Medical Council states specifically that it would defend any practitioner who disclosed confidential information in such circumstances. However, it is for each specific practitioner to decide personally if the particular circumstances justify disclosure in the public interest. There is no statutory definition of the public interest. Failure to notify the Vehicle Licensing Authority that a particular driver was not medically fit to drive could even be seen as a breach of a duty of care towards those persons who may be harmed as a result of that person driving. The success of such a hypothetical case would depend on establishing the following:

1 The doctor (or the nurse or other professional) owed a duty of care to the person who was eventually injured.

2 There was a breach of this duty in that the relevant information was not passed to the appropriate authority.

3 The personal injuries or death were a reasonably foreseeable result of that failure and were caused by that failure.

Until such a case is heard, or a law is enacted, a firm decision cannot be made, but some guidance is provided by the Tarasoff case heard in America and considered below. In addition, it should be pointed out that any person who drives a vehicle contrary to medical advice would himself be committing a criminal offence.

Case 8.3 **Tarasoff case (USA 1976)**

Confidentiality and psychotherapy[42]

A psychologist in California was told by a patient that he intended to kill a girl. The psychologist informed the campus police, who detained the man, but soon after released him. They did not inform the girl's parents of the danger to her. The patient subsequently killed the girl. The parents sued the university for breach of its duty of care to the girl in failing to warn them. They succeeded in a majority verdict. The court held that the therapist owes a legal duty of care not only to his patient, but also to his patient's would be victim. This duty of care is subject to scrutiny by judge and jury.

A dissenting judge, Judge Clark, was concerned that the very practice of psychiatry vitally depended on the reputation in the community that the psychiatrist would not tell. He considered that assurance of confidentiality was important to ensure patients were not deterred from seeking treatment; to ensure that they made a full disclosure to the doctor and to ensure that the patient maintains his trust in his doctor, which is vital for successful treatment. The NMC recognises that the public interest may be a justification for disclosing confidential information as Paragraph 5.3 shows (see Box 8.3 below).

The Court of Appeal has given guidance on the public duty of confidence.

Case 8.4 *W v. Egdell* **(1989)**

Disclosure in the public interest[43]

W, a psychiatric patient, brought an action against an independent psychiatrist, the health authority, the mental health review tribunal and the Secretary of State for breach of confidentiality. The psychiatrist had sent a copy of his report on W's mental condition to the hospital on grounds of public interest on the basis of W's particular circumstances. The High Court judge held that no distinction should be drawn between a psychiatrist who was independent and one employed by the health authority. The report did not come under the heading of legal professional privilege (see page 175). The judge relied on the General Medical Council's Advice on Standards of Professional Conduct and Medical Ethics and refused an injunction against the use or disclosure of the report and dismissed his claims for damage.

The Court of Appeal dismissed W's appeal and held that the balance came down in favour of the public interest in the disclosure of the report and against the public interest in the duty of confidentiality owed to the patient. Unlike the trial judge, the Court of Appeal considered the General Medical Council's rules as inappropriately relied on by the judge, since Dr Egdell did not have clinical responsibility for W. The Court of Appeal quoted Article 8(2) of the European Convention on Human Rights which permits intervention by a public authority in the duty of professional secrecy in the interests of public safety and the prevention of crime. (See Appendix A.)

The same considerations justified Dr Egdell's actions.

Box 8.3 — **Paragraphs 5.3 and 5.4 of the Code of Professional Conduct of the NMC**

5.3 If you are required to disclose information outside the team that will have personal consequences for patients or clients, you must obtain their consent. If the patient or client withholds consent, or if consent cannot be obtained for whatever reason, disclosures may be made only where:
- they can be justified in the public interest (usually where disclosure is essential to protect the patient or client or someone else from the risk of significant harm)
- they are required by law or by order of a court.

5.4 Where there is an issue of child protection, you must act at all times in accordance with national and local policies.

Practical Dilemma 8.3 — **Occupational health**

Brenda works as a nurse in the occupational health department and is horrified to discover that a paediatric nurse, Karen, has an unusual bacterial infection which makes it very dangerous for her to work in the unit, particularly with the premature babies. However, she knows that Karen has exhausted all her sick pay allowance from the authority and would be dependent on DSS benefits. She is bringing up two children on her own and would have great difficulty managing without her NHS pay. Karen herself is not ill: she appears to be a carrier rather than a sufferer of this particular germ and is anxious to continue to work and does not want her nursing officer to be notified.

An occupational health department is sometimes caught in the clash between its duty to keep information acquired from its clients/patients confidential and the interest of the employer in being aware of that information, especially where there is danger to the health or safety of other employees as a result of the person's medical condition. (The cases of *X* v. *Y*[44] and *H (A Healthcare Worker)* v. *Associated Newspapers Ltd*[45] and disclosure in relation to HIV/AIDS are considered separately in Chapter 26.) Exactly the same principles apply as in the situation described above, with the additional dimension of the employer's duty to other employees in the workplace. There is a clear duty owed by the employer to his employees under an implied term in the contract of employment (see Chapter 10), whereas the duty owed in the law of negligence in the situation of the epileptic lorry driver described in Practical Dilemma 8.2 is not at all clear.

In Brenda's case, there is clear justification for advising Karen that the information cannot be withheld. The dangers to the patients and to other staff are such that she cannot continue to work until she is free of the germ. Karen may have the right to claim the statutory right of payment on the grounds of medical suspension (see Chapter 10). This breach of confidentiality can be justified by reference to a preceding agreement, namely the contract of employment and the implied terms in it (see Chapter 10). Some authorities may well have an express term in their contract of employment authorising the occupational health department to notify the employer of any condition that would be dangerous to patients or other employees. Guidance is given by the Royal College of Nursing on confidentiality and the occupational health nurses.[46]

The Clothier Report following the conviction of Beverley Allitt[47] made recommendations for occupational health departments. It recommended that they should be involved in the selection of prospective employees and should monitor ongoing health problems of employees, alerting the employers when there were any serious risks to others. (See Chapter 12 for a consideration of a National Patient Safety Agency and Chapter 4 for whistleblowing.) The recommendations of the Clothier Report were reinforced by the report of an inquiry chaired by Richard Bullock following the case of Amanda Jenkinson, a Nottinghamshire nurse who was imprisoned for harming a patient. Similar recommendations were made to occupational health departments on risks from employees.

Disclosure to a registration body

In some cases, disclosure to a state registration body may be justified in the public interest, as the following case shows.

Case 8.5   *RE L (2000)*

Disclosure to a registration body in the public interest[48]

In care proceedings about a pre-school child, expert psychiatric evidence concluded that the mother was suffering from a severe personality disorder. The mother was a paediatric nurse and the three doctors involved in the case were agreed that there would be concern for any child in the mother's care. The court went on to consider whether the matter should be reported to the UKCC for the protection of any children who might be put at risk by contact with the mother in her professional capacity. The court decided that the court's judgment, the expert medical reports, and the minutes of the experts' two meetings should be given to the UKCC. The court had to decide on the balance of the rights of the mother and the child against the public interest in demanding protection from nurses who were, or who were potentially, unfit to practise.

Disclosures to the police

There are very few occasions on which the citizen is obliged as a duty by Act of Parliament to provide the police with information. The main statutes requiring disclosure are cited above. Many quandaries arise outside those areas and concern the powers of the police to require a professional to disclose confidential information during police investigations. Another difficulty is the position where, by chance, particularly through work in the community, the professional obtains evidence that a crime has been committed or is being committed: for example, stolen goods are seen in a client's home; there is evidence of drug abuse; there is evidence that a child is being physically or mentally ill-treated or sexually abused; there is evidence that a patient has had an illegal abortion; there has been an attempt to conceal the birth of a stillborn child; a wife has suffered a severe battering by the husband.

The police powers are contained in the Police and Criminal Evidence Act 1984. Medical records and human tissue or tissue fluid that has been taken for the purposes of diagnosis or medical treatment and which a person holds in confidence are subject to special procedures (see below).

> ### Statute — Sections 9, 12 and 14 from the Police and Criminal Evidence Act 1984
>
> *Section 9.* A constable may obtain access to excluded material or special procedure material by making an application under Schedule 1 Section 11. Excluded material means:
>
> **(a)** personal records which a person has acquired or created in course of any trade, business, profession . . . and which he holds in confidence
>
> **(b)** human tissue or tissue fluid which has been taken for the purposes of diagnosis or medical treatment and which a person holds in confidence
>
> **(c)** . . .
>
> *Section 12.* Personal records means documentary or records concerning an individual (whether living or dead) who can be identified from them and relating:
>
> **(a)** to his physical or mental health
>
> **(b)** to spiritual counselling or assistance given or to be given to him.
>
> *Section 14.* Special procedure material means material other than items subject to legal privilege and excluded material in the possession of a person who:
>
> **(a)** acquired or created it in course of any trade, business, profession or other occupation
>
> **(b)** and holds it subject to an express or implied undertaking to hold it in confidence.
>
> A circuit judge can make an order that the person who appears to be in possession of the specified material should produce it to a constable for him to take it away or give a constable access to it, not later than the end of the period of seven days from the date of the order. The judge must be satisfied that specific access conditions are fulfilled before making the order.

Disclosure where a criminal offence is believed to have taken place

> ### Practical Dilemma 8.4 — Rape?
>
> The police arrive at the A&E department one night enquiring about the possibility of a young man in his twenties having been admitted with severe lacerations to his face and neck. About two hours earlier, a girl of 15 had been found in a serious condition having suffered an attack. She had tried to defend herself by hitting the assailant in the face with a mirror. There was blood on the mirror and she believed she had cut him severely. The police arrive in the department and ask the duty nurse if they can go through the admissions during the last two hours.

The information required by the police is related to the medical records and thus comes under the special procedure. The police can make an application to a circuit judge for an order for the production of special procedure material. He will do so only if he is satisfied that certain conditions are present. However, these are the ultimate powers. It is unlikely that the police would be obliged to go to this length against an NHS trust. If it is known that the police can ultimately seek an order for disclosure, then the NHS trust policy is likely to be one of cooperation with them. In a case such as the rape case above, the nurse would be advised to call the medical officer in charge of the A&E department who would identify any patients who come within a fairly detailed description of the likely assailant. Giving the police the admission book would be beyond this duty.

In a case in 1993,[49] an order for disclosure to the police of the social security records giving dates of admission and discharge to the hospital was held not to come within the provisions of Schedule 1 of the Police and Criminal Evidence Act 1984.

Department of Health advice

The Department of Health in its NHS Confidentiality Code of Practice[50] (see page 171) considers disclosure to the police and states:

> *In the absence of a requirement to disclose there must be either explicit patient consent or a robust public interest justification. What is or isn't in the public interest is ultimately decided by the courts.*

> *Where disclosure is justified it should be limited to the minimum necessary to meet the need and patients should be informed of the disclosure unless it would defeat the purpose of the investigation, allow a potential criminal to escape or put staff or others at risk.*

The Department of Health quotes the definition of serious crime used by the GMC, i.e. 'a crime that puts someone at risk of death or serious harm and would usually be crimes against the person, such as abuse of children'.[51]

Practical Dilemma 8.5   Let me know!

The police are investigating a burglary in which the householder came back early and surprised the burglar, who fell from a first-floor window, but still managed to escape. The police have enquired at the various A&E departments in the vicinity. At one hospital, they heard of an admission following a road accident where a man said he fell from a motorcycle when it crashed against a tree. There were no witnesses. They believe that the injuries are comparable to those the burglar might have sustained. Since the patient is not yet fit for interrogation as he has just come from the operating theatre, the police ask the ward sister:

1 to let them know when he can be questioned, and
2 not to let him go until the police arrive.

What is the ward sister's position? Must she obey this order?

Notifying the police of the patient's fitness for questioning   There is no clear legal right for the police to insist that this is done. For example, if the ward sister decides that her duty is to the patient, not to the police, and thus fails to notify the police, could she then be prosecuted for obstructing the police in the execution of their duty? The answer is probably not, unless it can be shown that they had express legal powers to demand the information from her. In practice, of course, staff often rely on the help of the police when they have aggressive visitors, or even aggressive patients, and are therefore prepared to reciprocate. What we are concerned with here is the legal duty on the ward sister to provide this information and it is unlikely that this power exists.

Keeping the patient until the police arrive   The citizen does have wide powers of arrest, although they are, of course, more limited than police powers. The sister would have no statutory power of keeping the patient (which would, in fact, be arresting him) until the arrival of the police unless either she knows that an arrestable offence has been committed and the patient is guilty of this or she has reasonable grounds for suspecting that he is guilty. In the circumstances described above, it would not appear likely that the ward sister has those grounds since, as far as she knows, the patient could well have fallen from his motorcycle. She would therefore be on very weak ground if she refused to allow him to take his own discharge other than on the basis that she was acting out of her duty of care to save his life. In this situation, the police would have to provide a policeman to wait until such time as the patient could be questioned or taken to the police station under arrest.

Reporting crime to the police

Practical Dilemma 8.6   **Discovery in the community**

Jane, a health visitor, goes to enquire at a house where there is a young child of 18 months, since she has not seen her in the clinic and the child is due for several vaccinations and tests. While in the house, she notices the following: small burn marks on the child who looks very undernourished; four brand new video recorders in the corner of the room; and a pipe from the gas supply which bypasses the meter. One might question her imagination over the last item, but if this is in fact what she spotted, does she have any duty in respect of them?

1 *Non-accidental injury*: Jane's duty is to the child, so there can be no doubt that if she has reasonable grounds for suspecting that there is any abuse, then she must take the appropriate action to safeguard the child. There is a clear procedure for action if such a situation exists and Jane would have the responsibility to set it in motion. Even if Jane were a district nurse and visiting the mother rather than the child, she would still have a duty to ensure that the appropriate care was taken. (See Chapter 13 for child protection procedures.)

2 *Suspected stolen goods*: there is no duty on Jane to act as police informer in such circumstances. If, of course, the goods were subsequently found to be stolen and Jane were summoned to court as a witness, she would have to give evidence of what she had seen. What, however, if the goods were NHS trust property? Does she have a duty to inform her employer that goods are being stolen? The answer depends on whether a term can be implied into the contract of employment that any employee must inform the employer of any thefts from the workplace. There is no case that has decided the point, but it would appear to make business sense of the contract of employment if such a duty could be seen to be implied. (See Chapter 10 on implying terms into a contract of employment.)

3 *Gas*: it could be argued that the system for bypassing the meter is simply another case of stolen goods and theft. However, there are additional problems here, since there is a considerable public danger risking fire or an explosion. It could therefore be argued that Jane did have a public duty to notify the police, since her client and others could be in considerable danger.

Disclosure by the police to employers and the NMC

Where a registered practitioner is charged or convicted of an offence, the police would ensure that both the employers and the NMC or other registration body are informed.

> ## Case 8.6   *Woolgar v. Chief Constable of Sussex Police (1999)*
>
> **Disclosure to the UKCC**[52]
>
> Junia Woolgar, a registered nurse and matron of a nursing home, was arrested and interviewed by the police following the death of a patient in her care. The police concluded the investigation without bringing any charges and they referred the matter to the UKCC, which asked for further information. It was the practice of the police to seek the consent of those who had given statements. Ms W refused to give consent and sought an injunction to restrain the police from disclosing to the UKCC the contents of an interview they had taped. She appealed against the High Court judge's refusal to grant the injunction. The Court of Appeal held that the police were entitled to release the information to a regulatory body, if they were reasonably persuaded that it was relevant to an inquiry being conducted by the regulatory body. She lost her appeal.

Disclosure to parents

Information can be given to parents about their child's health if it is in the best interests of the child, and if a competent child has consented to the information being given. A mentally competent young person under 16 years has the right to request the withholding of information from the parents. This principle, established in the Gillick case, was upheld in the Axon case. In the Axon case[53] a mother of teenage daughters applied for judicial review of DH guidelines on advice and treatment of young people under 16 years on contraception, sexual and reproductive health which was based on the Gillick judgment. She claimed that she should have been told that her daughter had given consent to an abortion. The High Court dismissed her application, upholding the guidance laid down by Lord Fraser in the Gillick case. (See Chapter 13.)

Disclosure of information relating to a mentally incapacitated adult

In a case in 2002[54] the Court of Appeal recognised the duty of confidentiality owed to the mentally incapacitated adult, but in the circumstances, and taking account of the limited information required by his mother, allowed disclosure of information to her. She had applied in her capacity as nearest relative under the Mental Health Act 1983 for access to his medical records. Disclosure of information about those adults lacking mental capacity (who are outside the provisions of the 1983 Act) would now come under the Mental Capacity Act 2005 and the jurisdiction of the Court of Protection.

Disclosure under the Data Protection Act 1998

The disclosure of personal information should now be checked against the provisions of the Data Protection Act 1998. All personal health records, whether computerised or manually held, come within the definition of sensitive personal data and therefore at least one of the conditions in Schedule 2 and at least one of the conditions in Schedule 3 must be met. (Schedules 2 and 3 of the Data Protection Act 1998 can be seen in Appendix C of this book.)

Disclosure on an anonymous basis

The laws of confidentiality usually apply to the disclosure of information when the identity of the patient is made known. However, the Department of Health challenged a data-collecting company that was using information provided by GPs and pharmacists about prescribing habits.[55] The company believed the information would be useful to drug companies and would provide useful data for those interested in monitoring prescribing patterns. Even though the information would be anonymous, the Department of Health challenged the use of this information as a breach of the guidelines put forward by the Department of Health[56] in 1996. It succeeded before the High Court but the Court of Appeal[57] reversed this decision. It held that GPs and pharmacists providing prescription information that did not identify the patient was not a breach of confidence. Anonymous data did not involve a risk to the patient's privacy, even if, with effort, the patient could be identified. The DH withdrew its petition to appeal to the House of Lords because it intended to enact legislation.

In another case, a health authority sought to obtain disclosure of patient records in order to consider the compliance of a medical practice with the terms of service of the practitioners. Two patients had not given consent to the disclosure and therefore the GPs involved, not wishing to risk a breach of confidence by disclosing the information, applied to the court for a ruling as to whether they were entitled to make the disclosure. The court considered earlier cases heard by the European Court of Human Rights on medical data and Article 8[58] and ordered the disclosure of the records but on condition that the confidentiality of the personal information should be maintained and the patients' anonymity preserved as far as possible. The court also ordered that the data could not be disclosed more widely than was necessary to deal with the problem.[59]

Caldicott Guardians

Concern about the need to improve the way in which the NHS managed patient confidentiality led to the appointment of a committee chaired by Dame Fiona Caldicott. It reported in December 1997 and included in its recommendations the need to raise awareness of confidentiality requirements, and specifically recommended the establishment of a network of Caldicott Guardians of patient information throughout the NHS. Subsequently, a steering group was set up to oversee the implementation of the report's recommendations. A circular issued in 1999[60] gives advice on the appointment of the Guardians, the programme of work for the first year for improving the way each organisation handles confidential patient information and identifies the resources, training and other support for the Guardians.

Guardians

Each health authority, special health authority, NHS trust and primary care group was required to appoint a Caldicott Guardian by no later than 31 March 1999. Ideally, the Guardian would be at board level, be a senior health professional and have responsibility for promoting clinical governance within the organisation. The name and address of the Guardian was to be notified to the NHS Executive.[61] A manual for Caldicott Guardians was published in November 2006 and can be downloaded from the DH website.

Freedom of Information Act 2000

The Act gives a general right of access to information held by public authorities, but this right is subject to significant exceptions. The main exemptions from the duty are set out in Part 2 of the Act. Some of the exemptions are subject to a public interest test and these are shown in Box 8.4. Others are absolute exemptions and these are shown in Box 8.5. In addition to these exemptions, under Section 14 a request that is vexatious or that the public authority has already complied with does not have to be complied with. For the exemptions listed in Box 8.4, a public interest test applies. This means that a public authority must consider whether the public interest in withholding the exempt information outweighs the public interest in releasing it. The majority of exemptions fall into this category. For those exemptions listed in Box 8.5, there is no requirement for the public authority to consider the public interest.

Box 8.4 **Exempt information where the public interest test applies**

Information intended for future publication

National security

Defence

International relations

Relations within the UK

The economy

Investigations and proceedings conducted by public authorities

Law enforcement

Audit functions

Formulation of government policy

Prejudice to effective conduct of public affairs

Communication with Her Majesty, etc. and honours

Health and safety

Environmental information

Personal information

Legal professional privilege

Commercial interests

Box 8.5 **Absolute exemptions from the Act**

Information accessible to the applicant by other means

Information supplied by or relating to bodies dealing with security matters

Court records

Parliamentary privilege

Prejudice to effective conduct of public affairs

Personal information where the applicant is the subject of the information

Information provided in confidence

Prohibitions on disclosure where a disclosure is prohibited by an enactment or would constitute contempt of court

---

Data protection and freedom of information legislation

From Box 8.5 it will be noted that personal information where the applicant is the subject of the information is absolutely exempt from the Freedom of Information Act. Section 40 states that:

> *[A]ny information to which a request for information relates is exempt information if it constitutes personal data of which the applicant is the data subject.*

If a data subject wants access to personal information, then the route for that application is the Data Protection Act 1998 and in general the Freedom of Information Act 2000 tries to prevent an overlap between the two Acts.

Codes of practice

Codes of practice giving practical guidance to public authorities on the discharge of their duties under the Act have been issued by the Lord Chancellor as required under Section 45 of the Act[62] (referred to as the Section 45 Code of Practice). In December 2003 a model action plan for preparation for the implementation of the Freedom of Information Act 2000 was published.[63] While this model action plan is not compulsory, it was intended as a tool to disseminate ideas and best practice and to assist public authorities in creating a structured path towards full implementation of the Act in 2005.

Freedom of Information Act Awareness Guidance leaflets are available from the Information Commissioner's website.[64]

Conclusion on confidentiality

The NHS Confidentiality Code of Practice is of considerable guidance to healthcare staff in deciding whether the disclosure of confidential information is justified. However, the fact that many of the underpinning laws are based on common law, rather than statute, does make for difficulties. For example, whether a disclosure is justified as being in the public interest is determined by case law. The individual nurse practitioner still has to use her professional judgement in determining whether disclosure is justified and she is personally and professionally accountable for her decision. The Data Protection Act 1998 has tightened up access to and disclosure of personal information, putting more pressure on the decisions of the individual practitioner. Nurses should ensure that they make use of the existence of the Caldicott Guardian in their organisations to advise on issues relating to confidentiality and to assist in protecting the interests of the patient. If necessary, the protection of the Public Interest Disclosure Act 1998 could be sought if concerns on confidentiality need to be made known at a senior level within the organisation (see Chapter 4 and whistleblowing). The Human Rights Act, in enabling persons to bring actions against public authorities that have failed to uphold a person's right to respect for private and family life, as set out in Article 8, is likely to lead to more litigation where patients claim that confidentiality has not been respected.

Access to personal health records

The Data Protection Act 1998 gives a statutory right for data subjects to access personal information held on them (subject to exceptions discussed below). The Act applies to both computer records and records held in manual form. The 1998 Act replaces the Access to Health Records Act 1990 which gave access to manual records kept after 1 November 1991. The 1990 Act has been repealed except in respect of records of deceased patients. The definition of 'health record' would include nursing records, physiotherapy records, pathology laboratory records and all other records relating to the patient's health.

The Act enables data subjects:

1 to be informed whether personal data are processed

2 to be given a description of the data held, the purposes for which they are processed and to whom the data may be disclosed

3 to be given a copy of the information constituting the data

4 to be given information on the source of the data.

The data subject also has a right of rectification if the data recorded appear to be inaccurate. He/she can apply to the court for an order or to the Data Protection Commissioner (now the Information Commissioner) for an enforcement notice. The data controller would be required to rectify the data, block them or erase or destroy them. Alternatively, the court or commissioner could require that the record should be supplemented by a statement of the true facts.

Procedure for access

A request for access to personal health records must be made in writing to the holder of these records or the data controller, most likely the NHS trust or general practitioner or possibly the health authority, together with the required fee. The data controller should verify that the applicant is either the data subject or his authorised proxy acting on behalf of the data subject. A response must be given within 40 days of the full information being given, together with the fee, or the applicant informed that there are grounds for withholding the information. (Recent guidance, changed as a result of a Parliamentary debate,[65] from the Department of Health has suggested that NHS organisations should endeavour to comply with subject access requests within 21 days.[66])

The information can be withheld only on the grounds listed below. Failure to provide the fee or the necessary information required by the data controller would justify non-access. It may be that Informal access would be permitted outside the legislation. If the Data Protection Act principles are applied, the data subject would pay the required fee and within 40 days he should be given the required information.

Withholding information

The right of access to health records under the Data Protection Act 1998, like its predecessor, is not absolute and restrictions have been made by statutory instrument. The Data Protection (Subject Access Modifications) (Health) Order[67] modifies the right of access to health records in certain circumstances:

1 Where the access 'would be likely to cause serious harm to the physical or mental health or condition of the data subject or any other person (which may include a health professional)'. A data controller who is not a health professional shall not withhold information on these grounds unless he has first consulted the person who appears to be the appropriate health professional on whether this exception applies. The obligation to consult does not apply where the data subject has already seen or knows about the information that is the subject of the request.

2 Where the request for access is made by another person on behalf of the data subject, such as a parent for a child, access can be refused if the data subject had provided the information in the expectation that it would not be disclosed.

3 If giving access would reveal the identity of another person, unless that person has given consent to the disclosure or it is reasonable to comply with the access request without that consent. This does not apply if the third party is a health professional who has been involved in the care of the patient, unless serious harm to that health professional's physical or mental health or condition is likely to be caused by giving access (i.e. it comes within the first exception).

Certain information can be withheld if it is supplied in a report or other evidence given to the court by a local authority, health or social services board, health and social services trust, probation officer or other person in the course of any proceedings to which various statutes apply, including the Family Proceedings Courts, if, under the rules, the information may be withheld.

Correction of records

If a patient uses his right of access under the Data Protection Act to the health records and discovers that they are inaccurate, he can ask for them to be rectified. He also has the right to seek compensation for any harm that he has suffered as a result of the inaccuracy. Some say that the modifications to the right of access have taken much of the power out of the data access provisions. In addition, the data need not necessarily be supplied as a printout. The data user may choose to write or type the information to be supplied with any accompanying explanation.

Records of deceased persons

The only surviving provisions of the Access to Health Records Act 1990 are those relating to the records of deceased persons. Under Section 3(1)(f) of the Access to Health Records Act 1990 where a person has died, the patient's personal representative and any person who may have a claim arising out of the patient's death may apply for access to the deceased patients' health records. Where such an application is made, access shall not be given if the record includes a note, made at the patient's request, that he did not wish access to be given on such an application. Nor will access be given by the record holder to any part of the record, if he is of the opinion that it would disclose information which was not relevant to any claim which may arise out of the patient's death.

A life insurance company may seek information in order to decide whether to make a payment under a life assurance policy and require doctors to give information about the cause of death. Doctors could release information in accordance with the Access to Health Records Act 1990.

Access at common law

The Court of Appeal held In the case of Martin[68] there is no absolute right to access personal health records.

Access to Medical Reports Act 1988

This Act came into force on 1 January 1989. It gives an individual a right of access to any medical report relating to him that has been supplied by a medical practitioner for employment purposes or insurance purposes. Before any such medical report can be supplied, the individual must be notified that it is being requested and the individual must give his consent to that request. The medical practitioner must not supply the report unless he has the consent of the individual. He is also required to give the individual the opportunity of access to it and to be allowed to correct any errors. These provisions apply unless 21 days have elapsed since the practitioner notified him of his intention to provide a report. The medical report must be retained by the medical practitioner for at least six months from the date on which it was supplied.

There is an exemption from individual access where the medical practitioner is of the opinion that disclosure would be likely to cause serious harm to the physical or mental health of the individual or would indicate the intentions of the practitioner in respect of the individual or where the identity of another person would be made known.

Conclusions

The protection of patient confidentiality and the rights of access to information on health records continues to be a legal battleground. There are fears that the developing computerised system for patient records will provide inadequate protection for patient confidentiality. The Information Commissioner in his dual role as enforcement officer for both Data Protection and Freedom of Information legislation has a major role to play in ensuring that patient confidentiality is respected, but legitimate claims to access information held by public authorities is granted. Regular updating can be obtained via the Information Commissioner's website.[69] Serious losses of data by the Child Support Agency, the Driving Standards Agency, the Ministry of Works and Pensions and the Ministry of Defence in 2007 and 2008 have raised further concerns about the security of NHS information and strengthened the opposition of many doctors to the NHS electronic patient record systems. Proposed new powers for the Information Commissioner include criminal penalties for the most serious breaches of the data protection laws.

Reflection questions

1 Prepare guidelines for a new employee on the duty of confidentiality.

2 Do you consider that there is a breach of confidentiality if a nurse returns home and tells her husband that they are treating a patient with AIDS on the ward? She does not mention the patient's name.

3 Consider the exception to the duty of confidentiality entitled 'public interest' and consider examples from your own experience that may come under that heading. What justifications could you give for and against disclosure?

4 Do you consider that the patient should have an absolute right of access in law to health records? Justify your answer.

5 Hospitals are often seen as the most difficult institutions in which to keep personal matters secret. What action do you think could be taken to enforce the duty of confidentiality in practice?

Further exercises

1 Identify who the Caldicott Guardian is in your organisation and establish the role that he or she plays in maintaining standards of confidentiality.

2 Obtain information on the function of the Patient Information Advisory Group set up under Section 61 of the Health and Social Care Act 2001.[70]

References

1 European Directive on Data Protection adopted by the Council of the European Union in October 1995

2 NHS Executive, Data Protection Act 1998, HSC 2000/009 and supporting information: DH and NHS Executive, Data Protection Act 1998: Protection and Use of Patient Information; http://www.dh.gov.uk/dpa98/

3 www.connectingforhealth.nhs.uk/

4 http://www.ico.gov.uk/for_organisations/data_protection_guide

5 www.ico.gov.uk

6 Ibid.

7 *R (on the application of the Secretary of State for the Home Department) Information Tribunal (Information Commissioner, interested party)* [2006] EWHC 2958 Admin; [2007] 2 All ER 703

8 *Venables* v. *News Group Newspapers Ltd* [2001] Fam 430

9 *X (A woman formerly known as Mary Bell)* v. *SO* [2003] EWHC 1101; [2003] 2 FCR 686

10 *Johnson* v. *Medical Defence Union* [2007] EWCA 262

11 NHS Executive, Data Protection Act 1998, HSC 2000/009 and supporting information: DH and NHS Executive, Data Protection Act 1998: Protection and Use of Patient Information; http://www.dh.gov.uk/dpa98/

12 www.dca.gov.uk/foi/infcom.htm

13 *Stephens* v. *Avery and Others* [1988] 2 All ER 477

14 *Campbell* v. *MGN Ltd* [2004] UKHL 22; [2004] 2 AC 457 HL

15 Nursing and Midwifery Council, Code of Professional Conduct: standards for conduct, performance and ethics, NMC, 2004

16 Nursing and Midwifery Council, Code of Professional Conduct, London, NMC, 2002

17 *Ashworth Hospital Authority* v. *MGN Ltd* [2001] 1 All ER 991

18 *Mersey Care NHS Trust* v. *Ackroyd* [2007] EWCA 101

19 *Venables and Another* v. *News Group Newspapers Ltd and Others* [2001] 1 All ER FD

20 Department of Health, NHS Confidentiality Code of Practice, DH, 2003, available on www.dh.gov.uk/ipu/confiden/protect/ (superseding HSG (96) 18 LASSL (96)5)

21 www.nhsla.nhs.uk/confidentiality/pages/default.asp

22 Patient Information Advisory Group (Establishment) Regulations SI 2001 No. 2836 (amended by SI 2007 No. 2009)

23 www.dh.gov.uk/ipu/confiden/protect/

24 Statutory Instrument 2002 No. 1438

25 www.advisorybodies.doh.gov.uk/piag/register.htm

26 www.statistics.gov.uk/about/services/medicalresearch/apply/consent/agmr.asp

27 Patient Information Advisory Group, Your Health Records; available at www.connectingforhealth.nhs.uk/publications

28 Patient Information Advisory Group, Information about Patients; available at www.connectingforhealth.nhs.uk/publications

29 *NMC News*, 29 October 2003; www.nmc-uk.org/nmc/main/news/CHAI_toprotect_patient_data

30 *Nicholson v. Halton General Hospital NHS Trust, Current Law*, 46, November 1999

31 *A Health Authority v. X, The Independent*, 17 January; [2002] 2 All ER 780 CA

32 *R v. H; R v. C*, The Times Law Report, 6 February 2004

33 *Waugh v. British Railway Board* [1980] AC 521

34 *Lee v. South West Thames Regional Health Authority* [1985] 2 All ER 385

35 *Balabel and Another v. Air India, The Times*, 19 March 1988

36 *Fulham Leisure Holdings Ltd v. Nicholson Graham and Jones (a firm)* [2006] EWHC 158 Ch; [2006] 2 All ER 599

37 Information Commissioner, Freedom of Information Act Awareness Guidance No. 4, 2004, updated 2006

38 *Deacon v. McVicar and Another*, 7 January 1984 QBD

39 *Davies v. Eli Lilly and Co.* [1987] 1 All ER 801

40 *Hunter v. Mann* [1974] 1 QB 767

41 *Cawthorne v. Director of Public Prosecutions, The Times*, 31 August 1999

42 *Tarasoff v. Regents of the University of California* 17 Cal 3d 425 (1976) (USA)

43 *W v. Egdell* [1989] 1 All ER 1089 HC; [1990] 1 All ER 835 CA

44 *X v. Y and Another* [1988] 2 All ER 648

45 *H (A Healthcare Worker) v. Associated Newspapers Ltd; H (A Healthcare Worker) v. N (A Health Authority)* [2002] Civ 195; [2002] Lloyd's Rep Med 210 CA

46 Royal College of Nursing, Confidentiality – RCN, guide for occupational health nurses, RCN, no date

47 Clothier Report, The Allitt Inquiry: an independent inquiry relating to deaths and injuries on the children's ward at Grantham and Kesteven General Hospital during the period February to April 1991, HMSO, London, 1994

48 *Re L (Care Proceedings: disclosure to third parties)* [2000] 1 FLR 913

49 *R v. Cardiff Crown Court ex parte Kellam, The Times*, 3 May 1993

50 Department of Health, NHS Confidentiality Code of Practice, DH, 2003, available on www.dh.gov.uk/ipu/confiden/protect/ (superseding HSG (96)18 LASSL (96)5)

51 GMC guidance, Confidentiality: protecting and providing information, GMC, London, 2004

52 *Woolgar v. Chief Constable of Sussex Police and Another* [1999] 3 All ER 604 CA

53 *R (On the application of Axon) v. Secretary of State* [2006] EWHC 37 admin; [2006] 2 WLR 1130

54 *R (on the application of S) v. Plymouth City Council* [2002] EWCA Civ 388

55 *R v. Department of Health ex p Source Informatics Ltd* [1999] Lloyd's Rep Med 264; [1999] 4 All ER 185

56 Department of Health HSG (1996) 18, Protection and Use of Patient Information, DH circular, March 1996 (superseded by Department of Health, NHS Confidentiality Code of Practice, DH, 2003, available on www.dh.gov.uk/ipu/confiden/protect/)

57 *R v. Department of Health ex p Source Informatics Ltd* [2000] TLR 17, [2000] 1 All ER 786 CA

58 *Z v. Finland* (1998) 25 EHRR 371 and *MS v. Sweden* [1999] 28 EHRR 91

59 *A Health Authority v. X* [2001] 2 FLR 673 Fam Div, [2002] EWCA Civ 2014 CA

60 NHS Executive, HSC 1999/012, Caldicott Guardians, 31 January 1999

61 Raj Kaur, NHS Executive, 3E58 Quarry House, Leeds LS2 7UE; Fax 0113 254 6114

62 Lord Chancellor, Code of Practice on the Discharge of Public Authorities' Functions under Part 1 of the Freedom of Information Act 2000; Lord Chancellor, Code of Practice on the Management of Records (Section 46 Code of Practice); www.dataprotection.gov.uk

[63] www.dca.gov.uk/foi/map/modactplan.htm

[64] www.ico.gov.uk

[65] www.parliament.uk/hansard/hansard.cfm

[66] Department of Health, Guidance for Access to Health Records Requests under the Data Protection Act 1998, DH, June 2003

[67] Data Protection (Subject Access Modifications) (Health) Order Statutory Instrument 2000 No. 413

[68] *R* v. *Mid Glamorgan Family Health Services Authority, ex p. Martin* [1995] 1 All ER 356

[69] www.ico.gov.uk

[70] www.dh.gov.uk/ipu/confiden/act/index; 0113 254 6019 to contact the Secretariat of the Patient Information Advisory Group (PIAG)

Chapter 9
Record keeping, statements and evidence in court

This chapter discusses

+ Record keeping
+ Statements
+ Evidence in court
+ Defamation
+ Providing references

Record keeping

General principles

Record keeping is part of the professional duty of care owed by the nurse to the patient. As the NMC says in its 'Guidelines for Records and Record Keeping' (NMC, 2002):[1]

> *[Record keeping] is a tool of professional practice and one which should help the care process. It is not separate from this process and it is not an optional extra to be fitted in if circumstances allow.*

Failure, therefore, to maintain reasonable standards of record keeping could be evidence of professional misconduct and subject to professional conduct proceedings. The NMC has set out guidelines for good practice to assist the practitioner in fulfilling this professional duty.

NMC: 'Guidelines for Records and Record Keeping'

This document was first issued in 1998 and has been subsequently reprinted by the NMC. It is an invaluable guide to all practitioners. It provides guidelines for recording patient information and sets out the principles underpinning records and record keeping. Guidance is also provided in the former NHS training directorate booklets and by the NHS Executive.[2] The Audit Commission made recommendations to improve the standard of record keeping in hospitals in 1995.[3] It reviewed the situation in 1999 and concluded that, although progress had been made, there was still scope for further improvements.[4] Guidance is also available from the Clinical Negligence Scheme for Trusts, which monitors standards of record keeping and risk management by NHS organisations as part of its work in setting levels for membership of the NHS pool for sharing liability for compensation claims (see Chapter 6). The standards set by the CNST include in their criteria principles relating to documentation. For example, criterion 8 for the governance standard relates to clinical records management. Level 3 for this requires the organisation to demonstrate that there are processes in place to monitor the overall effectiveness of the approved documentation which describes the process for managing the risks associated with clinical records in all media. These standards, updated in April 2007, can be seen on the CNST website. Under the standard for learning from experience the organisation is required to have approved documentation which describes the process for investigating all incidents, complaints and claims.

Common errors noted in record keeping

These are listed in Box 9.1 and are the most common errors noted by a group of health visitors in record keeping.

> **Box 9.1**   Common errors in record keeping
>
> Times omitted.
> Illegible handwriting.
> Lack of entry in the record when an abortive call has been made.
> Abbreviations were ambiguous.
> Record of phone call (e.g. to social services) that omitted the name of the recipient (e.g. social worker).

> ### Box 9.1 continued
>
> Use of Tippex and covering up of errors.
>
> No signature.
>
> Absence of information about the child.
>
> Inaccuracies, especially of the date.
>
> Omission of date of medical check-up and hearing test and records for immunisation.
>
> Delay in completing the record; sometimes more than 24 hours elapsed before the records were completed.
>
> Record completed by someone who did not make visit.
>
> Inaccuracies of name, date of birth and address.
>
> Unprofessional terminology, e.g. 'dull as a doorstep'.
>
> Meaningless phrases, e.g. 'lovely child'.
>
> Opinion mixed up with facts.
>
> Reliance on information from neighbours without identifying the source.
>
> Subjective not objective comments, e.g. 'normal development'.

Clarity

Records should be meaningful, clear accounts of the patient's care. 'Had a good day', which is one of the most unhelpful statements, should not feature in the records. Why did she have a good day? Had her appetite returned? Had she spent most of the time sleeping? Alternatively, had she spent most of the day awake? Had she been of minimal trouble to the nursing staff? Had she in contrast been lively and interacted with the nursing staff? All these situations, many of them incompatible, are within the meaning of those words.

Comprehensiveness

Some nurses might see this paperwork as a distraction from the real task of nursing, i.e. caring for the patient. However, records are an integral part of nursing care. Failure to record an important item, e.g. administration of a drug, may mislead other professionals, such as those on a later nursing shift, and the patient could consequently be given an overdose. Accurate, comprehensive information relating to the care and the condition of the patient is a vital part of the professional role of the nurse. In addition, the information could be used for many other purposes of which the nurse may not be aware at the time.

Use of abbreviations

The NMC makes it clear in its 'Guidelines for Records and Record Keeping' that abbreviations should not be used. However, this advice is probably not very realistic in view of the number of everyday abbreviations that are used automatically and reasonably safely, such as BP (blood pressure), T (temperature) and so on. If these words were to be written out in full every time, they would add considerably to the time taken to complete records. There are dangers in the use of abbreviations:

1 PID: **p**elvic **i**nflammatory **d**isease or **p**rolapsed **i**ntervertebral **d**isc?

2 pt: **p**atient, **p**hysiotherapist or **p**art **t**ime?

3 CP: **c**erebral **p**alsy or **c**hartered **p**hysiotherapist?

4 MS: **m**ultiple **s**clerosis or **m**itral **s**tenosis?

5 NFR: **n**ot **f**or **r**esuscitation or **n**europhysiological **f**acilitation of **r**espiration?

6 NAD: **n**othing **a**bnormal **d**iscovered or **n**ot **a d**rop!

What is essential is that there should be an agreed list set up by each directorate or trust and it should be a disciplinary matter for anyone to use an abbreviation that is on that list but for another meaning or to use an abbreviation that is not on that list. The approved list should be reviewed at regular intervals. A list of the approved abbreviations could be attached to the front of the patient's records. Eventually there may be a recognised list of nationally agreed abbreviations, but this may be some time away. All that has been said about abbreviations also applies to the use of symbols and signs and other hieroglyphics. Their use can certainly assist record keeping, especially in spinal care, but there must be a clearly approved list available for both patients and health professionals to access.

Who should sign or write the records?

Any individual, and this would include unregistered staff or learners who have first-hand knowledge of any events regarding the care of the patient, should write up the relevant record and initial or sign it. Countersigning might be required by trained staff in certain circumstances and the procedure for this would be laid down locally. Any member of staff, registered or not, could be summoned to court to give evidence of what took place.

What about errors and mistakes?

If it is necessary to change what has been written, it is good practice for a line to be put through the incorrect statement and the correct statement made underneath rather than heavily scoring out the incorrect sentence or using correction fluid. Tippex and other such deletions should not be used on records. It should always be clear what was originally written and any corrections should be signed and dated. If the records are used in evidence, it should be clear what was originally written and why it was changed. It must be emphasised that these records are not proof of the truth of what they contain, but the writer of the records could be summoned to court to give direct evidence as to their accuracy and reliability.

Audit

Maintaining high standards in record keeping requires constant vigilance. Regular audit is necessary to identify errors and ensure that standards are met. The NMC Guidelines state (page 9):

> *Audit is one component of the risk management process, the aim of which is the promotion of quality . . .*

> *Audit can play a vital part in ensuring the quality of care that is delivered and this applies equally to the process of record keeping. By auditing your records, you can assess the standard of the record and identify areas for improvement and staff development. Audit tools should therefore be devised at a local level to monitor the standards of the records produced and to form a basis both for discussion and measurement.*

The Clinical Negligence Scheme for Trusts (see above) carries out regular monitoring of the standards of record keeping for those participants in the scheme. Their recommendations should assist in establishing and maintaining high standards. In addition, practitioners can learn from colleagues who have had to face questioning on their records before court or similar hearings.

Use in court

What constitutes a legal document?

There is sometimes confusion over what is a legal document. For example, are the nursing care plans legal documents? The answer is that any document requested by the court becomes a legal document. The court could subpoena the disclosure of Kardex or the nursing process documents, medical records, X-rays, pathology laboratory reports, social workers' records, any document in fact that may be relevant to the case. If they are missing, the writer of the records could be cross-examined as to the circumstances of their disappearance.

While the main purpose of record keeping is the care of the patient, considerable reliance will be placed on the records in any court hearing. Any weaknesses in record keeping will hamper the professional when it comes to giving evidence in court and will render her vulnerable in cross-examination, especially when there has been a considerable delay between the events recorded and the court hearing.

On some occasions, records may be looked at in a matter unconnected with the treatment of that particular patient. For example, in the case of *Deacon* v. *McVicar*[5] (see Case 4.11, page 77), there was a dispute as to the priority that a particular patient should have been given and the judge ordered the records of the other patients on the ward at the time to be disclosed in order to assess whether or not they would have been making demands on medical and nursing time at a particular point in time.

The preceding chapter considers the rules relating to the disclosure of medical records in cases of personal injury litigation, and the powers of the court to order the discovery of any relevant documents with only privileged records being exempt from disclosure. Health records are not proof of the truth of the facts stated in them, but the maker of the record must be called to give evidence as to the truth of what is contained in them. There are exceptions under civil evidence legislation that permit the records to be used in evidence without the presence of the maker (where, for example, the maker is dead or overseas), but due warning of the intent to use the records in evidence must be given to the other side.

Maintaining high standards of record keeping

The pressures of work and the lack of adequate time for record keeping make it extremely difficult to ensure that standards of record keeping are kept high. Constant vigilance is required. Clinical governance requires each NHS organisation to have a clear system of setting and maintaining high standards of record keeping on a multidisciplinary basis.

Computerised records

The White Paper on the NHS[6] envisaged a vast investment in information technology within the NHS that would ultimately link GP surgeries and hospitals to an NHS-wide information network. The government published an information strategy[7] on 24 September 1998 with a commitment to invest at least £1 billion over the lifetime of the strategy. By June 2000, £139 million from the Modernisation Fund had been provided for information technology investment in 2000/01. Investment is also being made in IT access by patients to the NHS. In October 2000 the terms of service for GPs were changed to enable their records to be kept on computers with no requirement for a manual back-up. GPs, however, have a choice. Electronic patient records will increasingly become the norm. Good practice guidelines have been drawn up by the Joint Computing Group of the General Practitioners' Committee and the Royal College of General Practitioners.[8] These guidelines will also be of use to other areas within healthcare as they cover such topics as: the purposes of patient records, the legal issues, hardware, electronic record requirements, maintaining security, confidentiality, training and regulatory requirements. On 4 February 2001 the Department of Health issued a press release saying that by March 2005 every person in the country would have their own electronic health record (EHR).[9] The electronic health record is defined by the Department of Health as holding summarised key data about patients, such as name, address, NHS number, registered GP and contact details, previous treatments, ongoing conditions, current medication, allergies and the date of any next appointments. It is intended that it will be securely protected, created with patient consent, with individual changes made only by authorised staff. The timetable for the electronic health record envisaged that 5 million people would have their own lifelong EHR by 2003, rising to around 25 million by 2004 and then everyone by March 2005. In addition, an electronic patient record (EPR) would be created at a later date which would provide full information about the patient's health admissions and consultation. In 2003, £2.3 million was invested in the National Programme for Information Technology (NPfiT) for the following three years. The NPfiT has four strands: an electronic integrated care records service (ICRS); electronic booking system; electronic transmission of prescriptions; and an underpinning IT infrastructure. The ICRS will create a basic health record, called 'the spine', for every patient and this will contain the essential information about the patient, who will eventually be able to access this record. Two committees have been set up to advise on the strategy and implementation: the National Clinical Advisory Board, which represents healthcare professionals, and the Public Advisory Board, which represents patients. The NPfiT carried out a qualitative and quantitative survey on the public view on electronic health records in October 2003, with the findings available on the website of Connecting for Health.[10] The details of the progress being made across the NHS can be obtained from the Department of Health website. In December 2003 the Department of Health announced that by 2010 each NHS patient would have an individual electronic NHS care record. This will detail key treatments and care within either the health service or social care. A contract to set up the infrastructure to support the electronic record system was awarded to BT in December 2003. The NHS care records service will connect 30,000 GPs and 270 acute, community and mental health NHS trusts in a single, secure national system.[11]

There are two parts to the NHS care records service:

1 Services that are common to all users nationally will be the responsibility of the national application service provider (NASP).

2 Services delivered at a more local level will be the responsibility of five local service providers (LSPs). Together, they will ensure the integration of existing local systems and implement the new systems, if necessary.

The NASP and the LSPs will make IT work across the NHS to support the creation of the NHS care records service.

The Department of Health pledged guarantees in May 2005 relating to patients' control over access to their health records.[12] The Care Record Guarantee, drawn up by the Care Record Development Board, included the commitments that access to records by NHS staff will be strictly limited to those having a need to know to provide effective treatment to a patient; patients will be able to block off parts of their record to stop it being shared with anyone in the NHS, except in an emergency, and individuals will be able to stop their information being seen by anyone outside the organisation which created it.

The Information Governance Toolkit can be downloaded from the website of NHS Connecting for Health.[13]

While computerisation will resolve some of the problems arising from manually held records, e.g. illegible spelling, the principles of good record keeping in terms of the content, clarity and accuracy of the information put on to the computer will still apply. Data protection requirements on security and access to the data are enforced through the criminal law (see Chapter 8).

Statements

Figure 9.1 illustrates some of the many occasions on which staff may be required to produce a statement. The statements produced on different occasions have very different purposes and effects. For example, where a statement is taken by the police, it can be used as formal evidence in criminal proceedings and the person who made the statement can be questioned on it. Where it has been made under caution, it can be used in evidence against an accused. In civil proceedings, the statement is not regarded as formal evidence, although the civil court now has the power to order disclosure of witnesses' statements.

The purpose of this section is to explore the principles of statement making and highlight some of the dangers.

Does one have to make a statement?

The one occasion on which one can refuse to make a statement is if it criminally implicates one. No one can be forced to answer a question if the effect of the answer is to incriminate her. There is a right to remain silent when questioned by the police about an alleged offence and also if a defendant in a criminal court, but failure to reply or remaining silent can result in an adverse conclusion being drawn about this failure in an address to the jury.

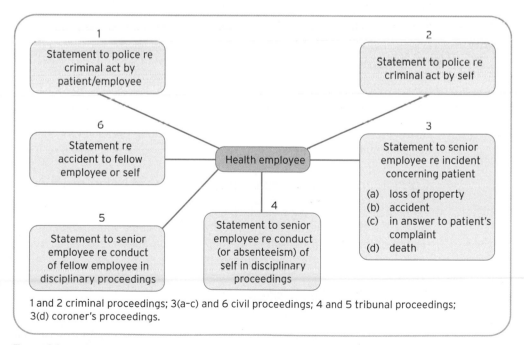

Figure 9.1 Occasions when a statement might be requested

There are considerable advantages in setting out exactly what took place as a record, although help and guidance are clearly essential. In general, a statement is required, not for self-defence, but as evidence of the events to which one was a witness. There have been examples where hospital staff have refused to participate in an inquiry set up by the health authority. For example, in the Shewin case, where a patient went into hospital for a gall bladder operation and suffered irreversible brain damage, the doctors initially refused to take part in the health authority inquiry. They eventually did so and were exonerated.[14]

In general, it could be argued that provided a member of staff is given appropriate guidance in making a statement, then the statement should be a valuable reminder at a later date of the details of what took place. It would seem to be reasonable to imply a term into the contract of employement that an National Health Service employee, in the course of his or her employment, would cooperate with the police and the coroner's court and would give a statement and information relevant to civil claims. It could also be argued that the employee should have assistance from senior managers or from the employer's solicitors in preparing a statement.

What is the status of a statement as evidence in court?

In criminal proceedings

Where the statement forms part of a police investigation and a caution has been given as to its effect, it could be used in evidence against the person who gave it, especially where the account they are now giving is entirely different from the statement.

Where the statement has been given by a person who is a witness to the events, then the statement, if it was made contemporaneously with the events described, can be used as an aid to memory. It must be emphasised that the statement is not in itself proof of the truth of the events therein described. Any number of lies or exaggerations can be recorded in a statement. However, except for certain exceptions, the person who made the statement would be expected to give evidence in court and could be cross-examined on the statement, from which the court could deduce the weight to be attached to the statement. Documentary evidence is permissible under the Criminal Justice Act 1988 SS. 23-28.

In civil proceedings

The statement can be used by its maker to refresh her memory. The court now has access to the statement; it can order disclosure of the witness statements. Written documents can be entered as evidence under the provisions of the Civil Evidence Act 1968. Further details relating to statements and documents can be found in the Civil Procedure Rules, which are available online.[15] (See below.)

Can the court always insist on the statement being produced?

In Chapter 8, the occasions on which documents are regarded as privileged were discussed. Where the statement, document, letter etc. have come into existence as a result of and for the purposes of proposed or existing litigation, they are covered by professional legal privilege and the courts cannot enforce disclosure.

Should one make a statement?

A distinction must again be made between the criminal and the civil courts. Where the police are investigating a crime and seeking information from witnesses, then it could be an offence to refuse to cooperate with them. There is, however, no duty to incriminate oneself.

In potential civil cases, there is no duty to make a statement, except possibly under the contract of employment (see above).

However, if one considers the time it takes for a case to come to court – in the civil courts sometimes as long as five or six years – it is highly unlikely that anyone would have a detailed recollection of the facts when they finally come under cross-examination or are giving evidence in chief. A detailed comprehensive statement of the events, drawn up at the time of the incident or events, is essential to refresh one's memory. In addition, a detailed, sensibly prepared statement may eliminate the chance of a nurse being called as a witness and thus save a needless attendance in court.

What points should be followed in making a statement?

Purpose

Before a statement is made, it is always advisable for its maker to have an idea of the purposes for which it is being made. Is it going to the coroner's office? Is it for internal information only? Is it to be used in a criminal prosecution? The purpose will affect the detail, style and content of the statement. The maker should therefore find out from the person who has asked for the statement who will read it and to what varied purposes it will be put. If there is any danger that the maker would incriminate herself, she should ask for legal advice before making the statement. It is not necessary to wait for a request before writing a statement about a certain occurrence. In some situations, it may be wise for a witness or participant to write down a brief account of the events immediately.

Guidance

Even in circumstances where there is no question of self-incrimination, it is always advisable to seek advice in making the statement. An objective reader can see gaps, ambiguities and confusion in a statement and give much valuable assistance.

Who should provide the guidance?

Normally, a senior nurse manager or the solicitor to the employer should provide this assistance. There will be occasions, however, where advice from a union officer is sought. In disciplinary proceedings, this depends on how far the proceedings have been taken. It would, for example, be contrary to the guidelines for good practice for management to refuse to allow an employee to receive the advice of the union representative prior to any formal disciplinary action being taken (see Chapter 10).

The essential elements in a statement are shown in Box 9.2.

Box 9.2   **Essential elements of a statement**

1. date and time of incident
2. full name of maker, position, grade and location
3. full name of any person involved, e.g. patient, visitor, other staff
4. date and time the statement was made
5. a full and detailed description of the events that occurred
6. signature
7. any supporting statement or document attached.

Principles to be followed

See Box 9.3.

| Box 9.3 | **Principles to be followed in preparing a statement** |

1 Accuracy
2 Factual
3 Avoid hearsay
4 Conciseness
5 Relevance
6 Clarity
7 Legibility
8 Overall impact
9 Keep copy.

Accuracy

It is essential that the statement should set out clearly the facts that took place. There should be no exaggeration or minimisation. The statement should be read through carefully to ensure that there are no inconsistencies, mistakes or other faults. There should be access to the relevant records so that the statement maker does not rely on memory in preparing the statement. If the record keeping has been of a high standard, this will facilitate the writing of the statement.

Keeping to the facts

The maker should, if at all possible, avoid value judgements and should keep to the facts. For example, a health visitor might have formed the opinion that one of her clients was lazy. If this is relevant to the statement, it is of far more value if she were to write down a description of the facts that led her to that opinion than to make value judgements. Thus 'there were 12 dirty milk bottles on the living room floor and piles of papers on every seat etc.' is more useful than expressing an opinion that may or may not be acceptable and is not on its own very meaningful. The facts on which those opinions are based are more useful. There are occasions where it is necessary to express opinions, especially where they led one to act in a particular way. Even here, however, it is still necessary to record the facts that led to those opinions. For example: 'Because I felt she was a danger to herself I put the cot sides up.' This statement needs to be amplified in order to expand on what has caused the nurse to believe that the patient was a danger to herself. For example, had she fallen out of bed? Had she tried to leave the ward? Was she in a confused state and, if so, how did she show it?

Where it is possible to check facts before making the statement, this should be done. For example, a statement that a patient had a high temperature should be checked against the patient's record; similarly, a description that the patient had been written up for a particular form of medication should be checked against the drug card. Sometimes it is helpful to draw a sketch of the ward layout or where the patient was found or where there is a need to identify the exact location, but only if the plan is a help rather than a further source of confusion.

Avoidance of hearsay

Hearsay is the recording or repetition of what someone else has seen or heard. If possible, it is best to avoid this as the person making the statement is only repeating what someone else has said and cannot give first-hand evidence of what was heard or seen. Imagine a situation where a nurse hears a fall in the night and runs in to the ward to find a patient on the floor. It is better for her statement to cover what she herself saw and heard rather than to repeat what another employee heard and saw. This other person should be asked to provide a statement of what she witnessed at first hand. Where the only witness to the events may have been another patient, it may be possible to obtain a statement from that patient, but that does depend on his physical and mental condition.

Conciseness

The statement must not ramble. It must be to the point in a logical sequence. Padding, waffle, meaningless generalisations should all be avoided. However, essential detail should not be sacrificed on the altar of brevity. The amount of detail required will, of course, depend on the facts described.

Relevance

It is a useful exercise to question oneself on the events to establish what detail a stranger to the situation would require. This questioning would have to take place in the context of the purpose for which the statement is required. In some circumstances, it may be important to describe the colour, material and style of the patient's clothes – in other circumstances, this may be entirely irrelevant. If there is any doubt as to what is relevant or not, one should err on the side of inclusion. What is in can always be omitted on the grounds of relevance at a later stage; what is left out is left out for good, because such details would soon be forgotten if not recorded.

Clarity

It is essential that the maker should read through the statement to ensure that it is clear and meaningful. If there are any doubts as to what is meant, it should be rewritten until one is sure that it is an exact clear record of what happened. Substitutes for any misleading or ambiguous words or phrases should be found. The use of clichés should be avoided. Abbreviations should be used only after the full terms are set out in full, with the abbreviation set out in brackets after the words. They should not be used for any other meaning. The level of technical language used should relate to the likely readership. In some circumstances, it will be necessary to explain technical procedures in full. In others, there will be no need. Emphasis should be on simplicity rather than complexity. The writer should make sure that he or she understands.

Legibility

If the statement is handwritten, it should be legible. If it is typed at a later date, then the typed copy must be checked for errors.

Overall impact

The statement should be read through and its overall impact assessed. Does it give sufficient detail? Is it clear exactly what happened? Is it accurate? Is there any further information that should be included? Is it internally consistent? Have any facts been checked?

Any necessary changes should be made and the maker should not sign the statement unless he or she is entirely satisfied with it. The maker must be satisfied with every aspect of the statement. The maker must not allow herself to be browbeaten into including information that is not within her knowledge or that she knows is not entirely accurate. Personal accountability must be accepted for the statement. Putting a signature to a statement implies that the maker is satisfied that it is accurate in every detail and she takes personal responsibility for it. A copy should always be kept. The confidentiality of the statement should be protected in accordance with the principles considered in Chapter 8.

Practical Dilemma 9.1   Scope of professional practice

The facts: The Roger Park NHS Trust had agreed with various nursing professional organisations that registered general nurses employed by the trust would be able to carry out, as part of their expanded scope of professional practice, certain clinical tasks formerly considered to be the sole responsibility of the medical staff. One of these tasks was the setting up of intravenous transfusions. Margery Broome, who had been employed by the NHS trust for three years as a staff nurse on a surgical ward was off sick when the appropriate course was held (on which she had been selected to go). She thus missed the intense tuition for this skill. No alternative course was suggested to her.

One weekend in December, when Margery was on duty and in charge of the ward, the consultant surgeon, Mr Browne, was on intake and the ward was under heavy pressure. The difficulties were aggravated by the fact that Mr Browne had had a long list on Saturday in an effort to reduce the waiting list (increased as a result of recent industrial action) and to prevent any further build-up before Christmas. Extra beds had been put up in the centre of the ward and the nursing team were particularly harassed because their numbers were reduced by a flu epidemic.

Mr Browne's registrar decided that Peter Price, a young man who had been operated on earlier in the week, should receive antibiotics by intravenous transfusion. He recommended that it should be set up immediately. He did not ask Margery if she was eligible to undertake the procedure; neither did she attempt to tell him that she had not yet been on the training course.

Margery collected the IV set and the intravenous antibiotics from the treatment room. She inserted a cannula into a vein in the arm and then set up a saline drip to which she added the antibiotics. While she was finishing this, another staff nurse came to ask if another extra bed could be put up for another emergency admission patient. As Margery Broome indicated where she wished the bed to be placed, she heard a call from another patient and saw that Peter Price had collapsed. She immediately requested that a doctor be called and initiated resuscitative measures. Despite emergency action being taken, Peter Price died. Peter's widow brought an action under the Fatal Accidents Acts and the Law Reform (Miscellaneous Provisions) Act 1934 against Margery Broome, Mr Browne, the registrar and the NHS trust, alleging that their negligence caused the death of her husband. Damages were agreed as being over £100,000. Liability is denied.

Margery Broome's statement follows. (How many errors can you spot based on the principles already discussed?)

Practical Dilemma 9.1 continued

Death of Peter Price

I certainly remember the day it happened. The morning began with a row with Mr Browne's registrar, Danladi Singh – I'm not racially prejudiced, but I knew from the moment he started that he would be difficult. He never understood the nursing difficulties. He was always admitting patients, never minding how the nursing staff would cope and since Mr Browne's illness, Singh had made all the decisions. Well, that morning we were on intake, Mr Browne was doing an additional list and Singh wanted me to ask medical records to send a telegram to ask the patient to come in the afternoon. Sister was off. I was in charge and I really blew my top. I told him of the difficulties we were in with the flu outbreak and the union dispute. I told him it wasn't fair on the patient – to call her in on a Saturday afternoon. He said it did not matter if it was Christmas Day or Saturday. That's partly the trouble with these foreigners. They don't make any attempt to understand the patients and their ways. Anyway, Singh agreed that he would not call her. I'm sure that it was because of this he then asked me to set up the IV. I knew I had missed the course, but I had seen it done many times by Sister and the doctors. Singh was too bad tempered to stay and help me, so I started to set it up on my own. I knew that we would soon be having patients back from theatre, so I wanted to get started.

Peter Price was making very good progress. He had had carcinoma of the stomach and I don't think they left much stomach after the operation. Singh always regarded Peter as an aggressive patient, but I never had much trouble with him. I did not have any difficulty getting the cannula in and I was not aware that he had any allergies to any antibiotics. I still do not know why he collapsed. Just as I was setting the rate of the IV, Janet Pritchard called me about an extra bed that Singh wanted for another emergency patient. I was really incensed. We were too overworked to have extra beds. A patient called out and I saw that Peter Price had collapsed. Pritchard and I rushed to him. I took out the cannula and Pritchard went to get Singh. It seemed as though he had a cardiac arrest or a fit of some sort. He was very blue and I started to do mouth-to-mouth resuscitation. Singh then came and took over. I am sure that the IV had nothing to do with his death.

There can seldom be a statement as bad as this, not only for the irrelevancies that it contains, but also the lack of essential information. The time and date of the events, as well as the time and date of the statement being made, are all missing. The staff on the ward who are potential witnesses should also be named with their appropriate grade. Far more information is required as to what exactly she did with the IV when her attention was diverted as well as more information about patient numbers and more specific information about the pressures: 'too overworked' is meaningless. Specific facts relating to the work pressure should be given along with any information relating to formal or informal complaints to senior nursing staff or medical staff about the pressures. In addition, it is clear that the whole style of the statement is wrong and unprofessional.

Evidence in court

Reference should be made to Chapters 2 and 6 for procedures followed in criminal and civil courts respectively.

Fears of giving evidence in court

There are few health professionals who relish the possibility of being required to give evidence in court. Preparation and guidance in facing the ordeal are essential, whether it is a criminal court, coroner's court, civil court, conduct and competence committee hearing or employment tribunal. Of equal importance, however, are comprehensive, clear and accurate records. Box 9.4 sets out some of the fears expressed by health visitors (probably the most likely of the nursing profession to face a court appearance).

Box 9.4 | **Fears over a court appearance**

Fear of the unknown.

Hearing the client call one a liar.

Publicity.

Waiting and the build-up in tension that can arise.

Remembering the detail of what took place.

Fear of being made to look a fool.

Being unable to express oneself concisely.

Contradicting oneself.

Omissions in one's statement on which one could be cross-examined.

Being made to feel guilty.

Downright rudeness and offensiveness of the others in court, especially the barristers.

Tension and nerves.

Being turned into the betrayer of the client.

Waste of time.

Being cross-examined by the client when he is not represented but is conducting his case personally.

Failure to understand the legal jargon, procedure and gestures.

Manipulation under cross-examination and being forced to change one's evidence.

Preparation for a court appearance

Experience in giving evidence in court will undoubtedly clear some of the anxieties illustrated in Box 9.4. Many can be solved by a private visit to a court hearing (they are all open to the public except for the few cases, such as children's and matrimonial proceedings, which are heard in private), and going on one's own or in a group without any personal involvement gives a sense of the procedure and language used and provides a chance of familiarising oneself with the process.

Witnesses are of two kinds: a witness of fact and an expert witness. The witness of fact is required to describe what she saw and did and give direct evidence of the facts in dispute. Her opinion is not usually required. An expert witness, by way of contrast, provides evidence of opinion of professional practice and approved standards of care or of causation or the appropriate level of compensation. The expert will be chosen because of her personal standing within a particular specialty.

If a nurse were asked to attend court as a witness of fact, a solicitor would normally assist in explaining the procedure and in preparing the nurse for giving evidence. Considerable expertise can often be built up within a department and the lessons learnt passed from one to another.

Confidence in the records that have been kept and the statements made should ensure that nerves are kept under control. The nurse should know the contents of the original records and where the entries appear so that there is no fumbling through the original records in the course of giving evidence.

Advice on court procedure and giving evidence in court is available from the county courts or High Court and also from the Internet at the Ministry of Justice website.[16] For example, leaflet Ex 341-w3 is entitled 'I have been asked to be a witness - What do I do?' It explains the different court proceedings, the role of a witness of fact and explains that, if the person does not wish to be a witness, a party to the case can secure a witness summons. Failure to respond to a witness summons can lead to the person being in contempt of court and a fine of up to £1,000. A witness could apply to have the summons withdrawn.

The Civil Procedure Rules Part 35, which can also be accessed via the Internet,[17] set down detailed rules relating to the role of the expert witness and the contents of the expert's report. The advice available from the website emphasises that:

> *You have a duty to the court to help the court with all matters within your expertise. Your duty to the court overrides any obligations you have to the party instructing you or paying for your reports.*

Practical issues such as 'What do I call the judge?' often worry potential witnesses:

+ a High Court judge is called 'My Lord' or 'My Lady'
+ a circuit judge is called 'Your Honour'
+ a district judge is called 'Sir' or 'Madam'.

Advice is also provided by the Royal College of Nursing for nurses asked to give evidence as expert witnesses.[18] The guidance includes in an appendix a copy of the Civil Procedure Rules 1999 on experts and assessors. Expert evidence has come into focus recently following the discrediting of evidence given in the trial of mothers accused of causing the deaths of their babies. Dr Meadows, a paediatrician, gave evidence for the prosecution in the trial of C for the murder of her two sons and she was convicted. Her second appeal to the Court of Appeal against the conviction succeeded on the grounds that the verdicts were unsafe because of material non-disclosure by the Crown's pathologist. A complaint was made to the GMC about the evidence of Dr Meadows, which the Court of Appeal had indicated was also probably unsafe. The GMC concluded that he was guilty of serious professional misconduct and ordered his name to be struck off the register. Meadows appealed against this striking off to the High Court, which found for him on the grounds that an expert witness should be immune from subsequent legal proceedings. The GMC appealed to the Court of Appeal, which held that immunity from suit did not apply to disciplinary, regulatory or fitness to practise proceedings. However, Meadows's mistake had not amounted to serious professional misconduct. He had not intended to mislead the trial court and he had honestly believed in the validity of his evidence when he gave it.[19]

Cross-examination

As far as the cross-examination is concerned, it should be remembered that following a few guidelines should limit the damage to one's evidence in chief.

Go prepared to the court hearing with the relevant records and documentation; read through the contemporaneous notes beforehand; go through the evidence with a senior nurse manager.

In court, be honest; do not exaggerate; do not be drawn into saying something that is not true; do not rush the answers; take time to think.

Be aware of the 'Catch-22' type question:

Q. You are a nurse?

A. Yes.

Q. You are therefore observant?

How do you answer this? If you say, 'Yes', the next questions could be:

Q. How fast was the car going?

A. Er . . . I'm not sure.

Q. But I thought you said you were observant?

If you say, 'No', the next question could be:

Q. Then your observations in this case are entirely useless?

A. Er.

If you answer the original question, 'Sometimes, it depends on what I am observing', it is likely to lead to a question or comment such as, 'Then we cannot rely on your evidence in this case'.

Such tactics are unlikely to have any effect on the judge's view, but they can sometimes influence the jury's thinking. (It must be remembered, however, that there is usually no jury in the civil court and the nurse's involvement in a jury trial in the Crown Court is likely to be rare.) What is more likely, however, is that the tactics used unnerve the person being cross-examined and cause difficulties for the future. The witness feels discredited. One way of avoiding the Catch-22 question is to expand on the answer so that one is answering fully and accurately.

Q. You are therefore observant?

A. My training has taught me to observe a patient's condition.

It is important under such pressure to avoid becoming angry or upset.

It is likewise important to avoid commenting on the relevance of the question. 'Do I have to answer that question, my Lord?' is fine on a TV drama, but unnecessarily dramatic in court. In most circumstances, one can rely on one's own lawyer or the judge to protect one from unnecessary harassment.

It must be remembered that in cross-examination there are two purposes. One is to discredit the witness's potentially hostile evidence against a client by showing the witness to be unreliable, dishonest, exaggerated, given to imagination, inconsistent (either internally, i.e. within her own evidence, or externally, i.e. in contrast to what another witness has said or what other evidence shows), unclear, confused, suffering from amnesia or (and this may be the most effective) irrelevant.

The other purpose of cross-examination is to build up the strength of the side undertaking the cross-examination. Thus, the witness being cross-examined can be used to bolster the good character and reputation of the defendant. 'What were his good qualities?' 'Was she a good mother?' 'Did you see her show any kindness to the child?' 'Did you like her?' is another Catch-22 question since once again to answer negatively implies that the witness being cross-examined is prejudiced; to answer affirmatively shows that the client has likeable qualities.

It is important in this context for the professionals to remember that in cases where they are giving evidence as witnesses as a result of their professional work, they are not on a particular side. They are called to give evidence of facts that they themselves witnessed. Their reputation does not hang on getting a particular outcome in a negligence case or in a non-accidental injury case. Where the client is personally cross-examining the professional, there should be no sense of betrayal since the professional would have been subpoenaed to attend court and is not there voluntarily.

Defamation

One concern of anyone asked to provide a statement or give evidence is that he or she could face an action for defamation. The main principles of such an action will be discussed very briefly here.

Defamation is either libel or slander. Libel is usually in writing or, at least, in a permanent form. Thus, broadcasting or a record would be considered to be libel. Slander is the spoken word. The main difference is that to succeed in an action for slander it is necessary to show that harm has occurred as a result of the slander, whereas in an action for libel it is not necessary to establish harm. There are four main exceptions to having to show harm resulting from a slander: imputation of a criminal offence; imputation that the individual suffers from a contagious or infectious disease; accusation of unchastity in a woman; imputations in respect of profession, business or office.

To be defamatory, the statement must tend to injure the reputation of the person to whom it refers, i.e. it tends to lower him in the estimation of right-thinking members of society generally. The statement must be untrue. Truth is a complete defence to an action for defamation. In addition, it must be 'published', i.e. spoken or made to an individual other than the claimant. Thus if, when we were alone together, I accused you incorrectly of having AIDS, this would not be defamatory since there is no publication. Contrariwise, if I said this to someone else about you, it could be actionable.

There are certain occasions that are said to be privileged, i.e. even though the statement is untrue and defamatory, it is not actionable since it is made in privileged circumstances. Some occasions are regarded as absolute privilege, for example, statements made in the Houses of Parliament or in judicial proceedings. Other occasions are considered to have qualified privilege. These include statements made in the performance of duty, in the protection of an interest, professional communications between solicitor and client or reports of parliamentary, judicial and certain other public proceedings. A statement that is subject to absolute privilege is not actionable, even though the speaker knows that what he is saying is untrue or he is acting out of malice. In contrast, an untrue statement made on a qualified occasion that is actuated by malice is actionable. Malice means the presence of an improper motive or even gross and unreasoned prejudice. The effect of malice is to destroy the privilege and if the statement is untrue and defamatory, then it is actionable. The Defamation Act 1996 established a summary procedure for claims under £10,000.

While Article 10 of the European Convention on Human Rights recognises the right of freedom of expression, this is qualified by the need to protect the reputation or rights of others.

Providing references

> ### Practical Dilemma 9.2   References
>
> A ward sister is asked to provide a reference for a staff nurse who has been working on her ward. The staff nurse came under suspicion of theft shortly before this request and the ward sister felt that she would not be honest or accurate if she omitted this fact. The staff nurse failed to get the job she was applying for and subsequently learnt of the contents of the reference. In the meantime, a cleaner was charged and found guilty of the theft. The staff nurse is threatening to sue the ward sister for defamation. Would she succeed?

There is no doubt that to say someone is guilty of theft would be a defamatory statement if it were untrue. However, writing a reference would probably be regarded as an occasion of qualified privilege. If the ward sister wrote the reference without any improper motive, she should have a good defence in an action for defamation. If, however, she made that statement for some other purpose, then the privilege is destroyed by malice. What if she merely stated that the nurse was under suspicion for theft, which would be true? If the words conveyed the impression that there were grounds for considering the nurse to be guilty of theft, then they could be regarded as defamatory and therefore actionable, unless protected by qualified privilege. The Defamation Act 1952 provides defences where an innocent defamation is made.

Liability for references

Any person asked to provide a reference owes a duty of care to both the subject of the reference and also to the recipient of the reference. In the case of *Hedley Byrne* v. *Heller*, the House of Lords[20] held that a duty of care was owed where a person gave advice that he knew would be relied on by the person seeking that advice. If the person suffered harm as a result of reliance on advice that was given negligently, then an action for compensation could be brought against the person who gave the advice. An employer who suffered harm from relying on a reference, which had been given negligently, could sue for compensation. Alternatively, if the reference contained inaccuracies and had been prepared negligently, the subject of the reference could sue the person providing the reference for harm, including financial loss, arising from the breach of the duty of care owed to him or her.[21] The Court of Appeal has held that an employer has a duty to undertake a reasonable inquiry into the factual basis of statements in a reference in order to discharge its duty to provide an accurate and fair reference.[22] The Information Commissioner's Office (ICO) has published a Data Protection Good Practice Note on access to employment references which is available on the ICO website.

Conclusions

It is inevitable that given the increase in litigation and complaints, greater and greater emphasis is placed on records and record keeping in the context of the nurse giving evidence and the nurse is increasingly likely to have to appear in court. However, it must not be forgotten that the most important aspect of record keeping is the fulfilment of the duty of care to the patient and ensuring that others who care for the patient are fully informed through the records of the action that has been taken or that still needs to be done. If the standard of record keeping meets the needs for patient care, then the records will be of sufficient quality to protect the practitioner should she have to defend her practice in any forum or court of law. Regular audit and monitoring are essential for standards to be set and maintained. If records are maintained at a high standard, then the making of statements and giving evidence in court are greatly facilitated. The NHS strategy for electronic patient records has had immense problems in keeping to its timetable, but eventually it should lead to a significant improvement in standards of documentation within the NHS. Constant audit and monitoring will continue to be essential.

Reflection questions

1 What errors have you noticed in record keeping? In what ways do you consider that standards of record keeping could be raised?

2 Consider the implications of electronic patient recording systems for your speciality and analyse its benefits for patient care.

3 Prepare a statement concerning an incident that has recently occurred. Read it through and consider if there are any errors.

4 What is meant by hearsay? Give several examples of it.

5 In defamation, information given on a privileged occasion without malice is not actionable, even though it is untrue and defamatory, provided that there is no malice. What is meant by this statement? What occasions do you consider could be privileged in this way?

Further exercises

1 Arrange a visit to court. Write up the points that any potential witness should be aware of in relation to the procedure, formality and language used. If you have the chance to visit more than one court (e.g. Crown or magistrates' or county or High Court), draw up a list of the differences between them.

2 What most concerns you about the possibility of giving evidence in court? Prepare a list of your concerns, then consider ways of meeting some of these anxieties.

References

[1] NMC Guidelines for Records and Record Keeping (reprint of UKCC 1998) 2002, updated in 2005 to take account of legislative changes

[2] NHS Training Directorate, Just for the Record, NHS Training Division, 1995; HSC 1998/ 217 Preservation, Retention and Destruction of GP Medical Services Records Relating to Patients; HSC 1999/053 For the Record: managing records in NHS Trusts and Health Authorities

[3] Audit Commission, Setting the Records Straight: a study of hospital medical records, Audit Commission, Abingdon, 1995

[4] Audit Commission, Update Setting the Records Straight, Audit Commission, Abingdon 1999

[5] *Deacon* v. *McVicar and Another*, 7 January 1984 QBD

[6] DH White Paper on the NHS, The New NHS – modern, dependable, The Stationery Office, London, 1997

[7] NHSE Information for Health, NHSE, Leeds, 1998

[8] Department of Health, Electronic Patients Records, DH, 3 October 2000; http://www.dh.gov.uk/gpepr

[9] Department of Health, Patients to Gain Access to New At-a-glance Electronic Health Records, DH, 4 February 2001

[10] www.connectingforhealth.nhs.uk

[11] Department of Health press release 2003/0502, Every Patient to get Electronic Patient Record, 8 December 2003

[12] Department of Health, Clear rules set for patients' electronic records, May 2005

[13] www.igt.connectingforhealth.nhs.uk/

[14] *BMJ*, 1979, 1232

[15] www.justice.gov.uk/civil/procrules_fin/menus/rules.htm

[16] Ibid.

[17] Ibid.

[18] Royal College of Nursing, Guidance for Nurse Expert Witnesses, Order No. 001084, RCN, January 2000

[19] *Meadows* v. *General Medical Council* [2006] EWCA Civ 1390, [2007] 1 All ER 1

[20] *Hedley Byrne* v. *Heller* [1963] 2 All ER 575 HL

[21] *Spring* v. *Guardian Assurance Co. Plc and Others*, The Times Law Report, 8 July 1994; [1995] 2 AC 296

[22] *Cox* v. *Sun Alliance* [2001] EWCA Civ 649; [2001] IRLR 448 CA

Chapter 10
The nurse and employment law

> ### This chapter discusses
>
> + Human rights
> + Contract of employment
> + Statutory provisions covering employment
> + Trade union rights
> + Public and private employees
> + Discrimination: The Equality and Human Rights Commission
> + Discrimination by race or sex
> + Discrimination on grounds of religion or belief or sexual orientation
> + Discrimination on grounds of age
> + Disability Discrimination Act 1995
> + Equality Act 2006
> + Agenda for Change

Introduction

The complexities of employment law can be bewildering, yet the nurse needs to know her way through the maze for two basic reasons: on the one hand, she is an employee and therefore should be acquainted with the rights of an employee; on the other hand, she may be or

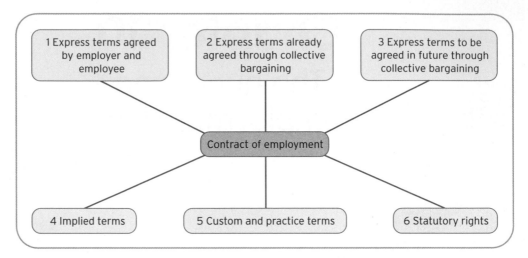

Figure 10.1 Sources of a contract of employment

become a manager in which case she will need to be able to advise her staff on their rights and also to understand the relevant employment law covering her role as manager. The areas discussed in this chapter are set out above. No attempt is made to give the full detail of all the employment statutes but instead the basic principles are set out together with the statutory framework. References are provided so that more detailed information can be obtained. Discussion on the NHS Institute for Innovation and Improvement which replaced the NHS University can be found in Chapter 11.

The legal relationship of employee/employer is composed of many terms drawn from a variety of sources. These are shown in Figure 10.1. First we look at human rights and then how the contract of employment comes into existence.

Human rights

Since October 2000 the European Convention for the Protection of Human Rights and Fundamental Freedoms has been directly enforceable in the UK courts. (See Schedule 1 to the Human Rights Act 1998 and Appendix A of this book.) All employees are entitled to have their rights as set out in the Schedule respected by their employers. Of particular significance to the employment situation are:

+ Article 3 and the right not to be subjected to inhuman or degrading treatment or punishment
+ Article 6, which gives a person a right to have their civil rights and obligations determined in a fair and public hearing within a reasonable time by an independent and impartial tribunal
+ Article 8, which gives a person a right to personal and family life, home and correspondence (subject to specified qualifications) and has implications for any monitoring by the employer of emails, telephone conversations and video surveillance (see below)
+ Article 9 and the right to freedom of thought, conscience and religion (subject to specified qualifications)
+ Article 10 and the right to freedom of expression (subject to specified qualifications)

+ Article 11 and the right to freedom of peaceful assembly and to freedom of association with others, including the right to form and to join trade unions for the protection of his interests

+ Article 14 and the right not to be discriminated against in the exercise of other rights (examples are given of forms of discrimination, but these are not intended to be exhaustive)

A claim before the European Court of Human Rights under Article 8 succeeded when a transsexual complained that the refusal by the Department of Social Security to pay her a state pension on reaching her 60th birthday violated her right to respect for her private life under the Charter Article 8.[1] (See Appendix A.)

If a court considers that any existing legislation is incompatible with the European Convention on Human Rights, it can make a declaration of incompatibility, so that Parliament can decide what action to remove the incompatibility is necessary. A court cannot overrule statutory provisions (see Chapter 1). The Equality and Human Rights Commission replaced the Commissions covering equal opportunities, disability rights and race equality on 1 October 2007 and its website[2] is a useful source of information about human rights and discrimination (see below). The Information Commissioner's website covers human rights and the duties of an employer in relation to data protection and freedom of information.[3]

Contract of employment

Formation of contract

Stages leading to formation of a contract of employment

When a nurse accepts the offer of a post, a contract then comes into existence and the nurse will be bound by its terms. In this sense the contract is an abstract concept; there may be nothing in writing but the relationship of the parties is radically altered by that agreement.

In any negotiation leading up to a contract of employment many documents may be circulated: an advertisement, an application form, perhaps a job description and certainly an interview.

All these stages are known as 'an invitation to treat'. Neither party is bound by them and can usually pull out of the negotiations at any stage. Thus an employer is not bound to appoint after advertising a post. Similarly, someone who has sent in an application form can withdraw at any stage from the field prior to acceptance of an offer. A contract only comes into being once an offer has been accepted. The offer is usually made by the employer. This could be in writing (for example, after holding interviews the applicants could be sent away without knowing the results and be told that they will be notified) or it could be at the actual interview when the applicants wait until the successful one is summoned and offered the post. Sometimes, this might be a conditional offer: it might, for example, be an offer dependent on a satisfactory medical examination or references or the selection panel might not have the power to offer the post but can only recommend to the authority that X be appointed. The candidate should be absolutely clear as to the nature of the offer since if it were subject to approval by a higher authority, which did not agree to that appointment or indeed to any appointment, the candidate would have no remedy if she has undergone expenses believing that she had a contract or has even terminated her existing job. If the candidate accepts an unconditional offer then and there, she is bound by that contract.

> ## Practical Dilemma 10.1   Better prospects
>
> A ward sister applies for, is offered and accepts a post in a neighbouring NHS trust. She then sees a nursing officer post advertised in her own trust, applies and is accepted before she has commenced work in the new post. What is her position in law?

Technically, she is in breach of contract with the neighbouring NHS trust. She is bound by the contract she has agreed with that trust. In practice, the trust is unlikely to take action against her; certainly the publicity that would arise would do little to enhance the reputation of that trust and the courts are unlikely to order the ward sister to commence work with the new trust, preferring to compensate by an order for damages to be paid rather than make what is known as an order for specific performance of the contract. The amount payable would be minimal, simply the loss incurred by the trust as a result of her breach of contract, taking into account the fact that she would have been entitled to give notice immediately.

Failure to declare a particular medical condition or criminal record

Pre-employment checks

It is for the prospective employer to ascertain the good and bad about any prospective employee. There is no obligation on the candidate to present her inadequacies. However, if the applicant is questioned about medical history or criminal record and lies or fails to disclose relevant information and if this information is later discovered after the applicant has been offered the post and accepted, then the employer is entitled to terminate the contract on the grounds of the misrepresentation provided that he would not have offered the post had he known of the facts. In addition, a lie can also be a criminal offence.

The Rehabilitation of Offenders Act 1974 protects those who have a past criminal record from being compelled to disclose it (for example, someone who has been imprisoned for between 6 and 30 months can regard this record as spent after a rehabilitation period of 10 years). However, this Act does not apply to most health service posts and thus the applicant would have to disclose a criminal record when asked. Where the appointment involves working with children or vulnerable adults, then the employer would be required to check that the person's name is not contained on lists of those considered unsuitable for such work. In addition, the police should be contacted to ensure that the individual is not on the POVA list or the Sex Offenders' Register (see page 225).

> ## Practical Dilemma 10.2   Undisclosed epilepsy
>
> An applicant for a post of nursing auxiliary is not asked and fails to disclose that she suffers from epilepsy. This is discovered subsequently when she has a fit at work. The employers send her a letter dismissing her. What are her legal rights?

The employers can either give her the requisite notice or they could dismiss her instantly on the grounds that she is not capable of performing the job safely. However, this is subject to the Disability Discrimination Act 1995, which is considered below. If the applicant had lied about her health, this would be taken into account in determining whether a dismissal would be fair. (For her rights to apply for unfair dismissal, see pages 231–6.)

Are terms agreed at an interview binding?

It sometimes happens that an applicant at an interview is given certain assurances about the conditions of work: shifts, hours, days off, holiday dates, location of the workplace etc. These terms can be made conditions of the contract. Thus an applicant who had already booked a holiday can obtain an agreement that one of the terms of the contract is that these dates can be retained. Failure to keep to this agreement would constitute a breach of contract by the employer. However, it is a question of fact as to whether the discussion leads to an agreed term or is merely a working arrangement that can be changed by the employer at a later date. In order to safeguard her position, the nurse, in accepting the post in writing, could confirm that certain terms have been agreed as part of the contract. A job description is not regarded in law as setting out terms of the contract. The list of duties contained therein can be changed unilaterally by the employer (within the overall contractual title) and the job description will usually end with a final requirement of 'and any other reasonable instructions of the employer'. This is perfectly lawful since it is an implied obligation on the part of the employee to obey the reasonable instructions of the employer. (See below for implied terms.)

Content of contract

Figure 10.1 shows sources of the various terms that comprise a contract of employment.

Express terms agreed between employer and applicant

These would include the starting date, the grade and title of post, the point on the salary scale at which the employee would start and many others. It is a matter of interpretation as to how many of the details in the advertisement become terms of the contract.

Express terms already agreed for the post

The bulk of the terms and conditions of posts in the National Health Service are nationally agreed and contained in the Whitley Council Agreements and the health service bodies were bound by these. The Agreements comprise the General Council Conditions and conditions relating to particular staff groups. The employee's contract should make it clear that it is subject to these nationally negotiated conditions. They should be available for inspection by any employee or applicant. NHS trusts have the power to negotiate terms locally.

Future terms agreed by Whitley Council or set by the review body

Even though an employee is not a member of a trade union and not represented on the Whitley Council, the changes and modifications to these terms will be binding on all employees and will usually be incorporated into the individual's contract of employment. At present, the Nurse Pay Review Body recommends revisions to the nurses' pay. NHS trusts can negotiate terms locally with their employees. The new NHS pay scheme, the Agenda for Change (see pages 250–1), envisaged the expansion of the remit of the Review Body for Nurses, Midwives, Health Visitors and the professions allied to medicine (the NPRB) to include a wider number of qualified health professionals and their support staff. The General Whitley Council and the separate functional Whitley Councils were replaced by a new NHS Staff Council which oversees the operation of the new pay system and has responsibility for NHS-wide terms and conditions of service. A Pay Negotiating Council negotiates pay for staff on the third pay spine.

Statutory terms

Additional terms are added by Act of Parliament and are discussed below. These are binding on the employer.

Implied terms

Additional terms are also implied in a contract of employment which place obligations on the employer or employee. Past court rulings by judges have decided whether certain specific terms should be implied and also what tests should be used to decide if a particular term is implied.

Box 10.1 sets out implied terms placing obligations on the employer. Box 10.2 sets out implied terms placing obligations on the employee.

Box 10.1   Implied terms binding on the employer

1 A duty to take reasonable care for the health and safety of the employee.
2 A duty to pay and to provide work.
3 A duty to treat the employee with consideration and support him.

Box 10.2   Implied terms binding on the employee

1 A duty to obey the reasonable orders of the employer.
2 A duty to act with reasonable care and skill.
3 A duty not to compete with the employer's enterprise.
4 A duty to keep secrets and confidential information.

Practical Dilemma 10.3   Implied terms

An emergency arises in Y Hospital following a multiple pile-up on the nearby motorway. A call is put out to those off duty in the nurses' home, which is on site, that help is urgently required. Mavis, a staff nurse who has just come off duty after an 8-hour shift, is asked to return. She refuses, saying she is too tired. She has actually arranged to go out with her boyfriend. Her absence is noted and she is subsequently disciplined. She argued that her off duty was her own time and she had no obligations to the employer during it. Also she was far too tired to be of any assistance and in fact would have been positively dangerous to the patients. The employers, in contrast, might argue that there is an implied term in the contract that even when the employee is off duty, she can still be summoned to assist in an emergency.

The outcome of such a case will hinge on whether such a term should be implied and also whether a nurse is correct in refusing to help when she is tired and therefore a potential hazard to the patient.

What tests are used to determine if a term will be implied? The courts have decided that the following tests are appropriate in determining whether a term will be implied. One is known as the officious bystander test. Imagine the following situation: nurse and NHS trust are discussing the possibility of establishing a contract between them. They are outlining the terms, hours, pay, holidays, etc., and someone overhearing them asks what happens in an emergency. Does the employer have the right to summon any nurse to return to work? If the negotiating couple were to turn to the questioner and say, 'Of course that goes without saying', then the term would be implied.

Another test used is whether the term is necessary to make business sense of the contract. There is no decided case on the question here, but most nurses would probably agree that such a term would be implied subject to the question of the physical and mental fitness of the nurse to continue to work. In addition, of course, the NMC states in its Code of Professional Conduct:[4]

> In an emergency, in or outside the work setting, you have a professional duty to provide care. The care provided would be judged against what could reasonably be expected from someone with your knowledge, skills and abilities when placed in those particular circumstances. (Paragraph 8.5)

What about Mavis's fitness to work? It is true that an employee who is unfit to work and is likely to be a danger to fellow employees and patients should stay away. However, in an emergency situation, risks might have to be taken and the risk of potential harm to the patient balanced against the value of that additional pair of hands. It would be a question of fact as to where the balance lay.

Terms resulting from custom and practice

This overworked phrase has been used by trade unionists to give contractual force to certain work practices and privileges that were not original terms of the contract. However, the judicial meaning is much narrower and is confined to special trades and works where the nature of the work has led to special terms being implied. To be legally recognised by the courts, a custom must be 'reasonable, certain and notorious'.

Can an employee see or have a copy of her contract?

A statutory right is given to employees to receive a written statement of particulars of employment. Previously, NHS employees, as Crown employees, were excluded from these provisions. However, by Section 60 of the NHS and Community Care Act, health service bodies lost the status of being Crown bodies and all NHS employees now have this statutory right. Employers are required within two months of the commencement of employment, and as soon as possible after any change in the contract, to give written particulars of the terms set out in Box 10.3. This statement is not the contract itself, but provides *prima facie* evidence of the contractual terms.

> ### Box 10.3   Written statement of employment particulars
>
> Name of employer and employee.
> Date when employment (and the period of continuous employment) began.
> Remuneration and the intervals at which it is to be paid.
> Hours of work.
> Holiday entitlement.
> Sickness entitlement.
> Pensions and pension schemes.
> Notice entitlement.
> Job title or brief job description.
> Period of employment, or date of ending fixed term, if post not permanent.
> Place of work or locations if more than one, and the employer's address.
> Details of collective agreements affecting employment.
> Additional detail if employee is expected to work abroad.
> Details of disciplinary and grievance procedures.

Changing the contract

> ### Practical Dilemma 10.4   Job title
>
> A staff nurse was appointed on the basis that she worked on the surgical ward at Roger Park Hospital. After two years, she was asked to work on the medical wards at Green Down Hospital. She was unwilling either to change her specialty or to move from the present hospital. Could she refuse to move?

The answer depends on whether the location and the specialty are terms of the contract. If they were, then it would be a breach of contract for the employer to change the contract unilaterally. This is because one of the basic principles of contract law is that one party cannot change the terms without the agreement of the other party to the contract. Thus, if these issues are seen to be contractual conditions, then the nurse is entitled to retain them. However, care must be taken in insisting on legal rights since it may be that a redundancy situation exists in which case a nurse who refused unreasonably to accept suitable alternative work would lose both her job and the right to obtain compensation. In addition, if someone has been unfairly dismissed, she has a duty to mitigate the loss (see section on unfair dismissal, pages 231-6).

Often, however, the location and ward are not contractual terms, but simply a working arrangement, in which case they can be reasonably altered by the employer without the consent or the right of refusal of the employee. How does one know if the issue in dispute is a contractual term or not? This would depend on the nature of the agreement between them, on the letter (if any) offering the post and on other evidence of the understanding between the parties as to the nature of the contract.

The employer: NHS trust and primary care trust

Most NHS nurses now work in NHS or primary care trusts. NHS Trusts were set up under the NHS and Community Care Act 1990 and contracts were transferred from health authorities and their directly managed units. Protection is given by Sections 6 and 7 of the 1990 Act to staff who are transferred to NHS trusts. In addition, Section 33 of the Trade Union Reform and Employment Rights Act 1993, in implementing the Transfer of Undertakings (Protection of Employment) Regulations 1981, makes it clear that protection is provided to the employee whatever the nature of the business or undertaking and there is a duty to consult with the employees. Section 218(8) of the Employment Rights Act 1996 states that:

> *If a person employed in relevant employment by a health service employer is taken into relevant employment by another such employer, his period of employment at the time of the change of employer counts as a period of employment with the second employer and the change does not break the continuity of the period of employment.*

Relevant employment includes where persons are engaged by a number of different health service employers while undergoing professional training.

Under Section 38 of the Employment Relations Act 1999, the Secretary of State has the power to extend the provisions of the EC transfer of undertakings rules to other employees not covered by the EC regulations.

Under the Health Act 1999, special provisions apply to protection of staff who are transferred from existing employers to work for primary care trusts.

Contracts cannot be changed unilaterally. Where, however, the employee seeks to obtain promotion or change her post she may be asked to accept new contractual provisions which may not be based on NHS terms and conditions of service.

Privity of contract

There used to be a rule of contract law known as privity of contract whereby only the parties to a contract could enforce it, even though the contract was agreed for the benefit of a third party. However, the Contracts (Rights of Third Parties) Act 1999, enables a third party to enforce the contract in either one of two situations: where the contract expressly provides that he may or where the contract purports to benefit him (unless there is clear provision to the contrary in the contract).

Breach of contract

By employee

The employee, as has been seen, has an implied duty to take reasonable care and skill in his work and to obey the reasonable orders of the employer. If he is in breach of these terms, he can be disciplined. In extreme cases, the employee's actions may justify summary dismissal by the employer. Other sanctions by the employer include suspension, demotion, warnings, etc.

By employer

The duty to abide by the contractual agreement is reciprocal and the employee is therefore entitled to expect that he will be treated with consideration and that there will be no unilateral change of contract conditions. If it is apparent that the employer is in fundamental breach of contract, then the employee may be able to consider himself constructively dismissed. This is considered below on page 233.

Statutory provisions covering employment

The Protection of Children Act 1999, the Protection of Vulnerable Adults scheme and the Sexual Offenders Act 1997 enable employers to establish if there are grounds for not employing prospective employees. Consequently at present there are three separate lists of persons who are barred from working with children or vulnerable adults. The lists operate under different legislation with different criteria and procedures. Following a public consultation[5] undertaken in the light of the Bichard Inquiry,[6] the Safeguarding Vulnerable Groups Act 2006 provides the legislative framework for a new vetting and barring scheme for people who work with children and vulnerable adults. It aims at minimising the risk of harm to children and vulnerable adults by barring unsuitable individuals not just on the basis of referrals but also at the earliest possible opportunity as part of a centralised vetting process that all those working with children and vulnerable adults must go through.

Protection of Children Act 1999

This legislation has four purposes.

1 It makes statutory the Department of Health's Consultancy Service Index list and it requires childcare organisations to refer the names of individuals considered unsuitable to work with children for inclusion on the list.
2 It provides rights of appeal against inclusion.
3 It requires regulated childcare organisations to check the names of anyone they propose to employ in posts involving regular contact with children with the list and not to employ them if listed.
4 It amends Part V of the Police Act 1997 to allow the Criminal Records Bureau to act as a central access point for criminal records information, List 99[7] and the new Department of Health list. In other words, the Criminal Records Bureau will act as a one-stop shop in the carrying out of checks.

The effect of the legislation is that organisations working with children, such as local authorities and health trusts, had a statutory duty from 2 October 2000 to vet prospective employees, paid or unpaid, for work involving contact with children.

Challenging the legal validity of the list

In a case in 1999,[8] a person challenged the inclusion of his name on the Consultancy Service Index held by the Department of Health to assist prospective employers in childcare to decide on a person's suitability to work with children. He had been employed as a childcare assistant, but was dismissed after allegations of sexually abusing a foster child and his own children. He lost his claim for unfair dismissal and his appeal. He claimed that the index was *ultra vires* (i.e. beyond the powers of the organisation), that the inclusion of his name was unreasonable since he had not been convicted and it was a breach of the Convention on Human Rights. The High Court held against him on all three points.

Protection of vulnerable adults

Provision was made in the Care Standards Act 2000 for a scheme to protect vulnerable adults. The Protection of Vulnerable Adults (POVA) scheme enables a list to be kept of any-one who has harmed or placed at risk of harm a vulnerable adult in their care, and providers of care are not able to offer employment to such individuals. Those on the list who seek employment in care positions will be committing a criminal offence. Checks against the POVA list will be requested as part of disclosures from the Criminal Records Bureau.[9] Care workers who had challenged their provisional placement on the POVA list as being contrary to their Article 6 and 8 rights won their case in the High Court which held that the provisions of the Care Standards Act 2000 in relation to provisional listings were not compatible with their human rights.[10] The Court of Appeal held that those who worked with vulnerable adults should be given the opportunity to make representations before being placed on the POVA list. That would prevent Section 82(4)(b) of the Care Standards Act being incom-patible with Article 6 of the European Convention on Human Rights. Further information on the Vulnerable Adults Scheme and the guidance produced by the Social Care Institute for Excellence can be obtained from the DH website. (See also Chapter 19 on the elderly and Chapter 13 on children.)

Safeguarding Vulnerable Groups Act 2006

As noted above, the Act sets up a new scheme for barring those unsuitable for work with children and vulnerable adults. Two barred lists are to be established: one for those who are barred from engaging in regulated activity with children and one for those who are barred from engaging in regulated activity with vulnerable adults. There will be an Independent Barring Board who will maintain a children's barred list and an adults' barred list. There will be right of appeal to the Care Standards Tribunal. Regulated activity covers a range of spe-cified activities that provide an opportunity for close contact with children or vulnerable adults. The Secretary of State has powers to make regulations relating to controlled activ-ities: defined activities where employers will have to put in place appropriate safeguards to manage the risk posed by barred individuals. Certain offences will lead to automatic inclusion on the barred lists; specified behaviour and evidence that there is a risk of harm can also lead to consideration for inclusion on either or both barred lists.

Sexual Offenders Act 1997

The Sexual Offenders Act 1997 was passed in order to ensure that once a sex offender had served his sentence and was about to be released, he would still be subject to some form of supervision to protect persons against the risk of his re-offending. Part I of the Act requires the notification of information to the police by persons who have committed certain sexual offences.

Statutory rights for employees

Certain Acts of Parliament provide additional rights to employees.[11] The most significant Acts are the Employment Rights Act 1996, Employment Relations Act 1999, Employment Act 2002, Employment Relations Act 2004 and the Equality Act 2006. Table 10.1 sets out some of the statutory rights and the minimum time of continuous service that the employee must

Table 10.1 Statutory rights

Right	Period of continuous employment
Guaranteed payment	4 weeks
Not to be dismissed because of medical suspension	4 weeks
Written statement of terms and conditions of employment	4 weeks
Written reasons for dismissal	1 year
Not to be unfairly dismissed	1 year
Maternity rights	
1 Paid time off work to receive antenatal care	No minimum period
2 Right to return to work after pregnancy	No minimum period
3 Not to be unfairly dismissed on grounds of pregnancy	No minimum period
Redundancy pay	2 years
Not to be dismissed because of trade union activities	No minimum period
Time off for trade union duties, trade union activities and public duties	No minimum period

have in order to claim these rights. They include medical suspension payments, guaranteed pay, rights for the pregnant employee, time off work provisions, rights in relation to trade unions and many others. In addition, after 2 October 2000, those employees working for a public organisation or an organisation that exercises public functions may have grounds for claiming a breach of their human rights if the employer does not respect the rights set out in the European Convention on Human Rights. (See Chapter 1 and Appendix A.)

The Employment Rights Act 1996 was aimed at consolidating the laws relating to employment rights and its provisions are shown in Box 10.4.

Box 10.4 **Statutory rights set out in the Employment Rights Act 1996**

1 Employment particulars
2 Protection of wages
3 Guaranteed payments
4 Sunday working for shop and betting workers
5 Protection from suffering detriment in employment
6 Time off work
7 Suspension from work
8 Maternity rights
9 Termination of employment
10 Unfair dismissal
11 Redundancy payments etc.
12 Insolvency of employers

Employment Relations Act 1999, Employment Act 2002 and Work and Families Act 2006

The 1999 Act made significant changes to the rights of the pregnant employee, introduced parental leave and provided time off for domestic emergencies and to care for dependants. In addition it provided a new statutory framework for collective bargaining and made changes in the law relating to trade unions (see below). The Act also gave rights to an employee to be accompanied in grievance and disciplinary disputes and abolished the offices of Commissioner for the Rights of Trade Union Members and Commissioner for Protection against Unlawful Industrial Action. The 2002 Act made further changes to maternity leave and introduced paid paternity leave and adoption leave. It also reformed the employment tribunal and ACAS procedures.[12] New statutory provisions relating to disciplinary and grievance procedures were implied into contracts of employment.

Rights of the pregnant employee

These rights have been strengthened by the implementation of the EC Pregnant Workers Directive and recent implementation of rights for parents and those with dependants. No continuous service is required to obtain these rights. New entitlements were introduced under the Work and Families Act 2006 and its consequent regulations for employees whose babies are due on or after 1 April 2007.[13] The rights include:

1 the right not to be dismissed on grounds of their sex, pregnancy or maternity leave
2 the right to receive 26 weeks' ordinary maternity leave and 26 weeks' additional maternity leave. Pregnant women who meet qualifying conditions may receive up to 39 weeks' Statutory Maternity Pay (those not entitled may receive 39 weeks' Maternity Allowance)
3 the right to return to work after confinement
4 the right to attend antenatal classes
5 the right to be offered suitable alternative work or be paid during suspension from work on maternity grounds
6 the right to have their health and safety protected when they are pregnant, have recently given birth or are breastfeeding (see Chapter 12).

Further details of the statutory maternity pay scheme are available.[14] In addition to the statutory rights, NHS conditions covering the same field often exist. The employee usually has the right to choose whichever benefits are more favourable to her. The RCN has provided guidance for nursing, midwifery staff and students.[15]

Right not to be unfairly dismissed on grounds of pregnancy

Practical Dilemma 10.5   **Morning sickness**

Barbara is two months pregnant and suffering very badly from morning sickness and hypertension. Her absence from the ward is causing considerable difficulties and she is not popular with the other staff. She has worked with the authority for three years. It has been agreed that she should be dismissed because of the continual absences. What are her rights?

She is pregnant, a full-time employee for three years and is therefore able to claim the right of not being unfairly dismissed on the grounds of pregnancy. The authority might argue that her pregnancy is making it impossible for her to do her job adequately, there is no suitable alternative work and therefore they are justified in dismissing her. This is, however, no longer an acceptable defence to an application for unfair dismissal on grounds of pregnancy and the employee would probably succeed in her application. No continuous service is required. Furthermore, the employee is entitled to receive pay during a time of suspension from work on maternity grounds, if suspension results from a health ground specified by statute (i.e. pregnancy, birth or breastfeeding) or to be offered suitable alternative work. If suitable alternative work is not available, the employee can claim pay during the time of suspension from work. Claims in relation to dismissal on grounds of pregnancy can also be brought under the Sex Discrimination Act (see pages 242-7).

Maternity right to return to work

In *Halfpenny* v. *IGE Medical System Ltd* 1999,[16] a woman who had left work to have a child exercised her statutory right to return to work after her maternity leave by giving the appropriate notice. She then sought to delay her return to work on grounds of sickness. The employers allowed a first extension, but then notified her that her job was no longer available. She lost her application for unfair dismissal, wrongful dismissal and unlawful sex discrimination before the industrial tribunal and her appeal before the employment appeal tribunal. Her appeal to the Court of Appeal, however, succeeded on the grounds that the exercise of her statutory right to return to work was made complete and effective by the giving of the appropriate notice at the appropriate time. The employers were guilty of unfair dismissal, wrongful dismissal and unlawful sex discrimination.

Dismissal of maternity leave replacement

The European Court in Luxembourg has ruled[17] that where an employee who was taken on to replace an employee during maternity leave herself became pregnant and was dismissed, it was an unfair dismissal on the grounds of pregnancy. The facts were that Mrs Webb was recruited with a view initially to replace Mrs Stewart who was to take maternity leave, but following a probationary period would probably continue when Mrs Stewart returned to work. Mrs Webb had not known that she was pregnant when the employment contract was entered into. When the pregnancy was confirmed, she was dismissed.

Her application on the grounds of direct or indirect discrimination on the grounds of sex failed before the industrial tribunal. Her appeals to the employment appeal tribunal and the Court of Appeal also failed. She then appealed to the House of Lords, which referred her case to the European Court of Justice for a preliminary ruling on the effect of Council Directive 76/207/EEC of 9 February 1976 on the implementation of the principle of equal treatment for men and women as to access to employment, vocational training, promotion and working conditions.

The European Court took into account the general context of the measures taken under Council Directive 92/85/EEC of 19 October 1992 to encourage improvements in the safety and health at work of pregnant workers and workers who had recently given birth and were breastfeeding and for special protection to be given to women, by prohibiting dismissal during the period from the beginning of their pregnancy to the end of their maternity leave. The European Court held that this protection of women could not be dependent on whether her presence at work during maternity was essential to the proper functioning of the under-taking in which she was employed. Any contrary interpretation would render ineffective the provisions of the Directive. Its decision was therefore that EEC Directive 76/207 precluded dismissal of an employee who had been recruited for an unlimited term with a view initially to replacing another employee during maternity leave and could not do so because, shortly after her recruitment, she was herself found to be pregnant.

Antenatal visits

There is a statutory right to attend antenatal examinations with paid leave. For the first visit, there is no requirement to show the certificate for the expected date of confinement or the appointment card, but for subsequent visits the employer can insist on seeing both. The right is not absolute, however. It depends on the reasonableness of the request and it may be reasonable to refuse such time off if an employee can reasonably make arrangements for an appointment outside normal working hours. There is no statutory right for the father to have paid leave to accompany his wife on antenatal visits, but the government is encouraging employers to adopt a flexible approach[18] and has published a fathers-to-be and antenatal appointments good practice guide.

Employment Relations Act 1999 and Employment Act 2002

Maternity leave, parental leave and time off for dependants came into force on 15 December 1999. Sections 7–9 and Schedule 4 provide new regulations on parental and maternity leave – a simplified framework of maternity rights and new rights to parental leave and to time off to deal with emergencies affecting dependants. Qualifying employees can exercise the right to parental leave subject to giving notice. The Employment Act 2002 has been updated by the Work and Families Act 2006 and regulations made under it so that pregnant employees whose expected week of childbirth is on or after 1 April 2007 benefit from the changes in maternity regulations. All pregnant employees are entitled to 52 weeks' maternity leave (26 weeks' ordinary maternity leave and 26 weeks' additional maternity leave). Statutory maternity pay is extended to 39 weeks provided the employee satisfies specified conditions. An employee who has contractual rights to maternity benefits which are superior to those granted by statute may select whichever is more favourable to her.

Parental leave for caring for a child (including adopted child)[19]

A right was given by the Employment Relations Act 1999 to enable either parent to be absent from work for the purpose of caring for a child or making arrangements for the child's welfare.[20] The right can be claimed by an employee who has a baby or adopts a child after 15 December 1999 and who has completed one year's continuous service with their employer by the time they wish to take leave. Anyone satisfying the conditions could have leave of up to 13 weeks per child. Parental leave can be taken any time up to the child's fifth birthday, five years after the adoption takes place or up to the 18th birthday for a disabled child.

The parent is entitled to return to the same job as before if the leave was for less than four weeks or a similar job if the leave was for longer than four weeks. Procedures can be agreed between employer and employees for the details of parental leave. An employee who has been refused parental leave can take a case to the employment tribunal.

Paternity leave and pay

Statutory paternity pay (SPP) is payable by employers to eligible employees to take paid leave to care for his baby or support the mother following birth. He can take either one week's or two consecutive weeks' paternity leave and during this time he may be entitled to statutory paternity pay.

Maternity pay

Statutory maternity pay scheme (SMP)

Pregnant employees who meet qualifying conditions based on their length of service and average earnings and who give the correct notice are entitled to receive from their employers up to 39 weeks' statutory maternity pay. The rate of SMP is 90 per cent of the average weekly earnings for the first six weeks, followed by the lesser of a flat rate of £112.75 a week from 1 April 2007 or 90 per cent of her average weekly earnings for the remaining 33 weeks. The flat rate is subject to review every April. Women who are not entitled to SMP but meet qualifying conditions based on their recent employment and earnings records may claim up to 39 weeks' maternity allowance (MA) from their Jobcentre Plus Office. Women may with the agreement of their employer undertake up to 10 days' work under their contract of employment without losing SMP or MA in order to keep in touch.

Time-off provisions

Paid or unpaid time off (depending on the benefit) is also a statutory right and can be seen in Box 10.5. Again, there are comparable Whitley Council rights and the employee is entitled to choose whichever is more advantageous.

Box 10.5 **Time-off provisions**

Time off for:

1 Trade union duties (officer): reasonable paid time off to carry out duties in connection with industrial relations and for training relevant to carrying out those duties (as a learning representative) (reasonable defined in ACAS Code of Practice No. 3).
2 Trade union activities (member): reasonable unpaid time off during working hours to take part in TU activities (see ACAS Code of Practice No. 3).
3 Public duties – local authority member, school governor, JP: reasonable unpaid time off (take into account time off given in relation to 1 or 2 above and other public duties).
4 To seek job in redundancy situation: reasonable paid time off to seek work or seek retraining.
5 Jury service: unpaid time off.
6 Health and safety representative: reasonable paid time off to perform function and train for it.
7 Time off for dependants.

In Practical Dilemma 10.6, below, Mary took the case to an industrial tribunal and won since it was held that rearranging a timetable was not giving time off. However, Mary was still receiving her full pay and the time-off provisions were only for unpaid time off. (The school could have reduced her workload, reduced her salary accordingly and then employed a locum to teach in Mary's place with the money saved. Mary might have preferred the existing arrangements!)

Practical Dilemma 10.6 **Rearranging a timetable**

Mary Briggs was a nurse tutor. She was also very involved in local government and had recently been elected as leader of the opposition on the county council. She was appointed to several subcommittees. She applied for time off to attend the meetings. The principal was extremely helpful and rearranged her timetable so that she would not have to teach in the afternoons when the council meetings took place. Mary complained that her workload had not decreased and she now found that she was having to spend several evenings doing work that normally she would have done during her free periods, which had now been lost.

Time off for dependants[21]

From 15 December 1999, reasonable time off is permitted where it is reasonable for an employee to deal with a domestic incident. This includes when a dependant is ill, gives birth or is injured; dies; unexpected disruption of arrangements for the care of the dependant; an incident at school. The employee must notify the employer of the reason for his absence as soon as is reasonably practicable and how long he is likely to be off. Dependant includes a spouse, a child, a parent, a person who lives in the same household as the employee (other than a tenant or lodger) and includes any person who reasonably relies on the employee for assistance when ill or injured. An employer's refusal to give time off for dependants could be followed by an application by the employee to an employment tribunal.

Flexible working

Section 47 of the Employment Act 2002 introduced a statutory right from April 2003 for an employee to request a variation in her contract. The right only arises for the purposes of the care of a child below six years or a disabled person below 18 years of age.[22] The employer has a statutory duty to consider the request and can refuse the request if one of the following grounds exist:

+ burden of additional costs
+ detrimental effect on ability to meet customer demand
+ inability to reorganise work among existing staff
+ inability to recruit additional staff
+ detrimental impact on quality
+ detrimental impact on performance
+ insufficiency of work during the periods the employee proposes to work
+ planned structural changes
+ such other grounds as the Secretary of State may specify by regulations.

Clear procedures for dealing with requests by employees for changes in their contracts are essential. Regulations which came into force in April 2007 extended the right to request flexible working cover by employees who cared for certain adults.[23]

Unfair dismissal

General principles

One of the most important of the statutory rights is the right not to be unfairly dismissed. Every employee has a right by virtue of his contract, statute or the common law (see below) to receive notice unless the employee is himself in breach of contract and is summarily dismissed. Thus, without a concept of unfair dismissal, a nursing officer who has worked for 20 years with that employer could lawfully be given her requisite notice under the contract with no particular reasons for the notice being specified and be lawfully dismissed. This would be contractually acceptable, but highly unjust. The right not to be unfairly dismissed protects employees who meet certain conditions against this unjust treatment. Sections 94 to 132 of the Employment Rights Act 1996 set out the provisions relating to unfair dismissal. There is also a right not to suffer a detriment or dismissal in health and safety cases. It is unfair to dismiss an employee in circumstances arising out of health and safety matters, e.g. carrying out health and safety activities at the request of the employer, being a safety representative or a member of a safety committee, bringing the employer's attention to harmful circumstances, refusing to work in dangerous conditions or taking appropriate steps to protect himself or others from damage.

The Public Interest Disclosure Act 1998 extends these provisions and protects an employee from victimisation where the employee has made a protective disclosure in accordance with the provisions of this Act (see Chapter 4).

The conditions that the employee must satisfy to bring an action for unfair dismissal are set out in Box 10.6. If these conditions are met, the employee can then, within three months of the dismissal, apply to the employment tribunal for an unfair dismissal hearing. The three months' time limit can be extended if the tribunal considers that it was not reasonably practicable for the employee to comply with it.

Box 10.6 Conditions for bringing an unfair dismissal action

1 One year's continuous service with that employer (except for example in cases of trade union activity or discrimination and dismissal on grounds of pregnancy or childbirth).
2 Eligibility under the legislation.
3 Being below retirement age.
4 Dismissal (i.e. termination by employer, expiry of fixed-term contract or constructive dismissal).

Unfair dismissal and long hours

Case 10.1 *Cowley v. S. African Airways* (1999)

Long hours[24]

Annette Cowley claimed unfair dismissal from her job as a cargo officer following her complaint of excessively long hours: she was required to work 16-hour shifts and claimed that she was unable to care for her baby properly. She said that working back-to-back shifts meant getting up at 5 a.m. to prepare her baby's food for the day, arriving for work at 7.45 a.m., finishing at 10 or 11 p.m., getting to bed at 1.00 a.m. and rising again at 5.00 a.m.

The employment tribunal found that she had been unfairly dismissed because the long hours discriminated against her on grounds of her sex. The airline was ordered to pay her three years' pay and was criticised over the wholly unreasonable demands over hours.

(Refer to the Working Time Directive, discussed on pages 237–9.)

Unfair dismissal and length of continuous service and compensation

The qualifying period for bringing unfair dismissal claims was reduced in 1999 from two years' continuous service to one year's continuous service. The compensation comprises a basic award based on a maximum week's pay of £330 in February 2008 (it is raised each year) times the number of years of continuous service (depending on age) (with a maximum of 30 years) and a compensatory award designed to compensate the employee for the financial results of losing his or her job. In February 2008 the ceiling was £63,000. This ceiling does not apply to awards under sex discrimination, equal pay and whistleblowing victimisation claims. Furthermore, an additional award can be made under Section 117 of ERA 1996 where the employer refuses a tribunal order to reinstate or re-engage the employee. The additional award is limited to between 26 and 52 weeks' pay with a ceiling on the maximum week's pay which can be used in the calculation. The ceiling is raised each year. Further information is available from the Department for Business, Enterprise and Regulatory Reform (DBERR, formerly the DTI).[25] The Court of Appeal reviewed the compensation payable to a nanny who had been unfairly dismissed while off sick and held that if she had not been dismissed she would have been paid statutory sick pay, so that was the measure of her loss. The Court of Appeal accepted that it was good employment practice for an employer who has dismissed an employee without notice to make a payment in lieu of notice which should not be subject to any deduction for sums earned elsewhere.[26]

Constructive dismissal

Practical Dilemma 10.7 **Dangerous conditions**

Kay was a nursing officer in charge of the acute wards of Roger Park Hospital. She had warned the senior managers that the situation was dangerous since, due to an acute shortage of nurses which coincided with a vigorous attempt to reduce the waiting lists, with extra beds being put up on all the wards, there was a danger that accidents could happen. No notice was taken of her warnings and, in fact, more patients were admitted. She advised the consultants that nurses would not be able to carry out certain tasks normally undertaken by doctors and that the junior doctors would be expected to add the drugs to intravenous transfusions. Her senior nurse manager was advised by the consultants that this was unacceptable and Kay was asked to withdraw that instruction and notify the nurses that they must continue to undertake such tasks. She pointed out that they did not have the time to do these. She was warned that she would face disciplinary proceedings if she continued to defy the managers. She said she would prefer to leave than endanger the lives of patients and stated that the managers were in breach of contract in failing to support her attempt to maintain professional standards. She left and subsequently brought an action for unfair dismissal.

Assuming that Kay qualifies as far as the conditions set out in Box 10.6 are concerned, she needs to establish as a preliminary point that she was dismissed and did not resign. The employers are likely to argue that they did not dismiss her, that she left work of her own free will and that she is therefore ineligible to bring an unfair dismissal action.

The question is: Have the managers acted in such a way that she is entitled to see the contract as at an end? It will be remembered that one of the implied terms in a contract of employment is that the employer will act reasonably towards the employee and support him. It could be argued here that in failing to support Kay's endeavours in this situation, the employers are in fundamental breach of contract. If this can be established, then Kay can argue that there is a constructive dismissal, she is entitled to bring her action before the tribunal and it is then for the managers to establish that the dismissal was fair. By the same token, the employers will be arguing that Kay was not dismissed, that she had failed to do all she could to work with them and that she had defied reasonable orders from them. Kay should also refer to the Public Interest Disclosure Act 1998 to show that her concerns about health and safety come under the disclosures protected by that Act and that she followed the procedure required by the Act (see Chapter 4 on whistleblowing). Ultimately, the outcome will depend on the evidence from both sides: Kay would have to show evidence, both documentary and through witnesses, of earlier attempts to persuade management that the situation was dangerous and that the managers were acting in fundamental breach of contract.

Case 10.2 *Atkin v. Enfield Group HMC (1975)*

Fair dismissal[27]

The Court of Appeal heard a case where a senior nurse had been dismissed for failure to wear the appropriate uniform. They held that the dismissal was fair.

Procedure in an application for unfair dismissal

The employee is normally expected to exhaust the internal appeal machinery set up by her employer before an application to an employment tribunal is heard. But owing to time limits (an application for unfair dismissal should be brought within three months of the date of dismissal, if reasonably practicable), the employee should instigate the application in any case and ask for an adjournment pending the outcome of the internal appeal. In this way, she will not be out of time. Following the application to the employment tribunal, there will be attempts by the Advisory, Conciliation and Arbitration Service (ACAS) to resolve the dispute. ACAS has published a new Code of Practice on the disciplinary practice and procedures in employment (revised 2004).[28] Employers must comply with the Code which requires that disciplinary rules and procedures are clearly set out and accessible to the employees. Failure by any employer to follow the ACAS guidelines will not make the employer liable to proceedings in itself, but evidence of this failure could be used against the employer in evidence before an employment tribunal. Since September 2000 employees have had a statutory right to be accompanied at any disciplinary or grievance hearing. Failure by the employer to permit the employee to be accompanied or to postpone (for up to five days) a hearing to enable the person to attend can lead to up to two weeks' compensation payable to the employee. Employees seeking to bring applications before an employment tribunal can brief a barrister direct without having to hire a solicitor first. It is estimated that the costs of bringing an action will be reduced by one third to a half. The Employment Relations Act 2004 Section 37 defines the rights of a companion at disciplinary or grievance hearings, which include addressing the hearing, summing up the case, responding on the worker's behalf and conferring with the worker during the hearing.

Dispute resolution

A statutory dispute resolution is set out in Schedule 2 to the Employment Act 2002. There are two forms: a standard three-step procedure and a modified two-step procedure. There are separate procedures for dealing with grievance issues and for disciplinary matters. Schedule 2 Part I sets out the dismissal and disciplinary procedures. In addition to the new procedures for disciplinary and grievance matters, Schedule 2 to the Employment Act 2002 sets out general requirements which must be followed by the parties. These are shown in Box 10.7.

Box 10.7 General requirements of the dispute procedures

+ Each step and action under the procedure must be taken without unreasonable delay.
+ Timing and location of meetings must be reasonable.
+ Meetings must be conducted in a manner that enables both employer and employee to explain their cases.
+ In the case of an appeal meeting that is not the first meeting, the employer should, as far as is reasonably practicable, be represented by a more senior manager than attended the first meeting (unless the most senior manager attended that meeting).
+ The employee has a right to be accompanied to these meetings (Section 10 of the Employment Relations Act 1999).

Automatically unfair dismissals

Some dismissals are automatically unfair and whether the employer acted reasonably or not is irrelevant. These have been expanded recently and include dismissals connected with: pregnancy or childbirth; parental leave and time off for dependants; jury service; health and safety; exercise of a right under the Working Time Regulations; making a protected disclosure; performing a function of an employee representative; assertion of a statutory right; membership or non-membership of a trade union; taking of protected industrial action; acting in connection with an employee's rights under the Part-time Workers (Prevention of Less Favourable Treatment) Regulations 2000; Fixed-term Employees (Prevention of Less Favourable Treatment) Regulations 2002; an application for flexible working; the Tax Credits Act 2002; the Information and Consultation of Employees Regulations 2004; a request not to retire and failure by the employer to comply with the relevant statutory disciplinary and dismissal procedures.

Unfair dismissal – time limit for applications

There is a time limit of three months from the dismissal within which an application must be made to the tribunal. However, the tribunal can dispense with this limit if to keep to the time limit was not 'reasonably practicable or feasible'. In one case,[29] the Court of Appeal held that reasonably practicable required that the full circumstances of the applicant's failure to apply within the time limit had to be taken into account, including the aim to be achieved. In the facts of this case, the applicant was suffering from depression and had been trying to avoid litigation by pursuing alternative remedies.

Hearing

If the employee is able to show that she satisfies the conditions set out in Box 10.6, the burden will be on the employer to show that the dismissal was based on a statutory reason. These are set out in Box 10.8. The tribunal must then decide if the employer has acted reasonably in treating this reason as sufficient to justify dismissal. The criteria that have been considered by the tribunals in determining the reasonableness of employers' actions are set out in Box 10.9. Every circumstance must be taken into account, and the fact that the tribunal might not have acted in the way in which the particular employer acted is not relevant. The crucial question is: Was *that* employer acting reasonably? One important point is whether the disciplinary Code of Practice and the guidelines prepared by ACAS were followed (see above).

Box 10.8   **Statutory reasons to dismiss**

1 Capability or qualifications.
2 Conduct.
3 Some other substantial reason.
4 Redundancy.
5 Statutory prohibition.
6 Lock out or participation in strike or industrial action.
7 National security.

Box 10.9   Criteria for the reasonableness of the employer

1 Code of practice.
2 Nature of employment situation, e.g. size and resources of organisation, type of work.
3 Consistency of employer.
4 Timing of dismissal.
5 Length of service of employee.
6 In cases of dishonesty and other misconduct:
   + the employer must show that he genuinely believes the employee to be guilty of the misconduct in question
   + he must have reasonable grounds on which to establish that belief
   + he must have carried out such investigation into the matter as was reasonable in all the circumstances
   British Home Stores v. *Birchell* 1978 IRLR 379.
7 Principles of natural justice.

Outcome

If the employee's application for unfair dismissal is upheld, the following remedies are available to the tribunal:

1 Reinstatement/re-engagement.

2 Compensation – basic award; compensatory award; special award.

In assessing compensation, the tribunal will take into account any fault on the part of the employee. In a case in 2004,[30] the House of Lords held that compensation for injury to feelings and other non-economic loss could not be awarded in unfair dismissal cases.

Dismissal and professional conduct and competence

Where a registered practitioner has been dismissed by his or her employer this will be reported to the NMC and the investigating committee or other practice committees may look into the situation with a view to deciding whether the practitioner is fit to practise (see Chapter 11). Other disciplinary action may or may not be reported to the NMC depending on the extent to which the fitness to practise of the practitioner is impaired. The NMC is concerned to ensure that employers take greater responsibility over the competence of their registered practitioners to practise and that issues relating to contractual matters are dealt with by employers rather than being referred to the NMC. The National Audit Office[31] has considered the management of suspensions of clinical staff in NHS hospital and ambulance trusts in England and suggested significant reforms, highlighting concerns about the length of suspensions of clinical staff on full pay and the fairness, openness and transparency of existing procedures. The National Clinical Assessment Authority (NCAA) is a division of the National Patient Safety Agency (see Chapter 12) and was established in April 2001 to review standards of medical and dental staff. It has suggested alternatives to suspension. It has also been suggested that its remit should be extended to other professions. One of the new powers introduced in 2002 for the NMC was to permit a registrant to remain on the Register subject to specified conditions (see Chapter 11). This would require monitoring of the practitioner, but there is no body comparable to the NCAA for practitioners registered with the NMC.

Statutory sick pay scheme (SSP)

Most NHS employees enjoy six months' full pay and six months' half-pay while absent on grounds of sickness. The employer is able to recover some of this from the statutory sick pay scheme. Details of the operation of the scheme are available from the Department for Business, Enterprise and Regulatory Reform.

All employers can offset any contractual liability to pay sick pay against their payments under SSP.

Redundancy

The NHS has its own redundancy scheme set out in the Whitley Council general conditions of service. It broadly follows the statutory scheme from the point of view of consultation when redundancies are envisaged. However, the NHS has a much wider definition of suitable alternative work. The Information and Consultation with Employees Regulations[32] came into force in April 2005 and require consultation with and information to be given by employers where there are decisions likely to affect future employment. Initially this applied to organisations where there are more than 150 employees. From 2008 the regulations will apply to organisations of 50 or more employees. Employees could also seek personal information about themselves from the employer under the Data Protection Act 1998 and general information under the Freedom of Information Act 2000. (See Chapter 8.)

Surveillance by employers

The European Court of Human Rights, in the case brought before it by Alison Halford, held that her rights of privacy had been invaded when her employers, the Merseyside Police Authority, intercepted the private telephone calls she made from the office. The court held, however, that provided that the employer warned the employees that their calls could be tapped, there would be no breach of the right to privacy as guaranteed by the European Convention.[33] Similar cases are likely to arise under Article 8 of the Convention and the right to respect for privacy and family life (see Chapter 1). The Information Commissioner has published, as part of its Employment Practices Data Protection Code, a code of practice relating to the monitoring of employees' emails by employers.[34] The Regulation of Investigatory Powers Act 2000[35] and the Telecommunications (Lawful Business Practices) (Interception of Communications) Regulations 2000[36] enable emails to be monitored without consent in specified circumstances such as the prevention or detection of crime or the investigation of unauthorised use of the system. The employer must have taken reasonable steps to inform users of the monitoring or have reasonable grounds to believe that employees are aware that this may happen. There are considerable advantages for employers to have a code of practice covering all aspects of surveillance and ensure that it is regularly updated, that employees are aware of its existence and that consent to the monitoring is a term of the contracts of employment.

Working Time Directives

A Directive had been adopted by the member states of the European Community on 23 November 1996, but implementation in the UK was delayed until 1 October 1998, when the Working Time Regulations[37] came into force.[38]

Main principles

The fundamental provision is that a worker's working time, including overtime, should not exceed an average of 48 hours for each 7 days over a specified period of 17 weeks. Regulations also specify provisions for rest breaks and annual leave. Night work should not normally exceed an average of 8 hours for each 24 hours. The employer has a duty to ensure that no night worker, whose work involves special hazards or heavy physical or mental strain, works for more than 8 hours in any 24-hour period. Before assigning a worker to night work, the employer has to ensure that the worker has the opportunity of a free health assessment before he takes up the assignment. There should be a weekly rest period of not less than 24 hours in each 7-day period, alternatively two rest periods each of not less than 24 hours in each 14-day period or one rest period of not less than 48 hours in each 14-day period.

Employers are required to keep records relating to the hours of work which can be inspected by enforcement agencies. The Health and Safety Executive and local authority environmental health officers are responsible for enforcing the working time limits. Individual employees can, if internal appeals mechanisms fail, apply to the employment tribunal for alleged infringements of their statutory rights. The application must be made within three months of the infringement and the Advisory, Conciliation and Arbitration Service (ACAS) will provide conciliation services. The European Court of Justice has held the UK requirement of 13 weeks' work before being eligible to have annual leave illegal.[39] In a later case the European Court of Justice held that UK guidelines on the Working Time Directive were incompatible with the Directive, in that the guidelines did not make clear that employers had to ensure that workers actually did take a rest break according to the regulations.[40]

NMC practitioners

Doctors in training and civil protection services (ambulance) were initially specifically excluded from the regulations, but junior doctors are gradually coming under the provisions which will apply in full by August 2009. NMC practitioners are not specifically excluded. However, they come within the definition of the group:

> [W]here the worker's activities involve the need for continuity of service or production, as the case may be, in relation to:
>
> i. services relating to the reception, treatment or care provided by hospitals or similar establishments, residential institutions and prisons.

The effect of this is that the regulations on night work, daily rest, weekly rest period and rest breaks do not apply to NMC practitioners where there is a need for continuity of service. However, Regulation 24 requires that where a worker is required to work during a period that would otherwise be a rest period or rest break, the employer shall wherever possible allow her to take an equivalent period of compensatory rest and, in exceptional cases, where this is not possible, the employer shall afford her such protection as may be appropriate in order to safeguard the worker's health and safety.

Working hours

The General Whitley Council (GWC) has agreed the implementation of the regulations for non-medical staff.[41] Section 44 of the GWC Handbook sets out the new provisions that apply to all non-medical staff. An NMC practitioner will normally not be expected to work more than 48 hours per 7-day period calculated over an averaging period of 17 weeks. Locally recognised unions could agree that the period of 17 weeks could be extended up to a maximum of 25 weeks.

Definition of working time

Working time means:

1 any period during which the employee is working at the employer's disposal and carrying out her activity or duties

2 any period during which she is receiving relevant training

3 any additional period that is to be treated as working time for the purpose of these regulations under a relevant agreement.

Working longer than 48 hours a week

Individual employees can, if they wish, agree to work more than the average of 48 hours a week. However, this must be an individual decision. It cannot be negotiated as part of the collective agreement and it must be agreed in writing by the employee. The employee should not be placed under pressure to agree to a longer time. The employee can end the agreement by giving notice to the employer, as specified in the agreement, or, if no notice time is specified, then seven days' notice must be given. The employer is required to keep records of this agreement and the term of notice and the number of hours worked since the agreement came into effect.

National Minimum Wage (NMW) Act 1998

From 1 April 1999, employers have been obliged to pay a minimum wage to employees, with those between 18 and 21 years receiving a lower figure. Employees can appeal to an employment tribunal without any continuous service requirement if they are dismissed because they qualify for the NMW or because they have attempted to enforce the NMW right.[42]

Part-time employees

On 1 July 2000 regulations came into force to prevent part-time workers being treated less favourably than full-time workers,[43] implementing the European Directive.[44] Paragraph 5 of these regulations gives the part-time worker:

> [T]he right not to be treated by his employer less favourably than the employer treats a comparable full-time worker as regards the terms of his contract, or by being subjected to any other detriment by any act, or deliberate failure to act of his employer.

The right applies only if the treatment is on the ground that the worker is a part-time worker and the treatment is not justified on objective grounds. The part-time worker has to compare himself with full-time workers working for the same employer. The right also applies to workers who become part time or, having been full time, return part time after absence, to be treated not less favourably than they were before going part time. It does not give an employee the right to insist on having part-time work.

The regulations (Paragraph 6) also entitle a worker, who considers that he has been treated in a manner that infringes this right, to request from his employer a written statement giving particulars of the reasons for the treatment. The worker must be provided with a statement within 21 days of his request. Failure to provide a statement at all or only in an evasive or equivocal way will enable the tribunal to draw any inference that it considers just and equitable to draw, including an inference that the employer has infringed the right in question. The regulations also protect the part-time worker from unfair dismissal and give a right not to be subjected to any detriment (Paragraph 7).

Any worker who considers that his rights have been infringed can present a complaint to an employment tribunal within three months of the day of less favourable treatment or detriment taking place. This is subject to the right of the tribunal to consider out-of-time cases, if in all the circumstances it is just and equitable to do so.

The European Union is proposing new rights for temporary workers, including workers hired through agencies. The proposals envisage that after a maximum of six weeks' work, a temporary employee would have the full rights of permanent employees.

Trade union rights

It is impossible in a work of this nature to be other than superficial in relation to the status and powers of trade unions. Reference should be made to the Further reading section for special books in this field. Box 10.10 illustrates some of the present rights of the independent trade union. The principal Acts are the Employment Relations Act 1999, and the Trade Union and Labour Relations (Consolidation) Act 1992 as amended by the Trade Union Reforms and Employment Rights Act 1993, the Employment Act 2002 and the Employment Relations Act 2004.

Box 10.10   **Trade union rights and the role of safety representatives**

1 A union is independent if it is not under the domination or control of an employer and not liable to interference by an employer. Its independence can be certified by the certification officer and his certificate is conclusive evidence that the union is independent.

2 Independence is an essential feature if the union is to enjoy the following statutory rights:
  + to take part in trade union activities
  + to be given information and be consulted over 'transfers of undertaking'
  + to gain information for collective bargaining
  + to secure consultation over redundancies
  + to insist on time off for trade union duties and activities
  + to appoint health/safety representatives.

3 A trade union is fully liable for any of its acts that constitute a tort (civil wrong) *except* where it acts in contemplation or furtherance of a trade dispute. The meaning of these words has been narrowed since 1980 so that, in general, secondary action (e.g. where employees of A go on strike to support the employees of B) is not covered and therefore the union would be liable for the damage that results from the unlawful action.

4 Safety representatives are appointed by a recognised trade union from among the employees. Names are to be notified to the employer in writing. They represent employees in consultation with the employer under Section 2(4) and (6) of the Health and Safety at Work Act 1974. Functions are set out in Regulation 4 of statutory instrument 1977 No. 500:
  + Investigate potential hazards and dangerous occurrences at workplace and examine cause of accidents at work.
  + Investigate complaints of employees relating to health, safety or welfare at work.
  + Make representations to employer under (a) and (b).
  + Make representations to employer on general matters affecting health, safety or welfare.
  + Carry out inspections under Regs 5, 6 and 7.
  + Represent employees in consultation with Health and Safety Inspectorate.
  + Receive information from inspectors under Section 28(8).
  + Attend meetings of safety committees.

  'No function given to a safety representative by this paragraph shall be construed as imposing any duty on him.'

Schedule 1 of the Employment Relations Act 1999 sets out details for the recognition of trade unions for collective bargaining purposes, including voluntary recognition, changes affecting the bargaining unit and derecognition. Part VII of the Schedule provides details of the right of a worker not to be subjected to any detriment by any specified act in relation to bargaining. Schedule 3 regulates the holding of ballots for union membership

Over the last 20 years, the power of the unions and employers to enforce a closed shop situation has decreased so that since the Employment Act 1988, the dismissal of a non-unionist in a closed shop situation is now automatically unfair. The 1992 Act gives protection to employees against exclusion or expulsion. The employer cannot prevent anyone from joining an independent trade union. The unions have the right to obtain information relevant to collective bargaining and also to receive notice of any redundancies. A union member should be allowed the presence of a union officer at any disciplinary proceedings. Under health and safety legislation, safety representatives appointed by trade unions have the right to visit the workplace and to inspect the site of any accident. Officials of trade unions have the right to reasonable paid time off for the purposes of their activities in relation to collective bargaining or representing their members and for training for such purposes. The members, however, only have the right of reasonable unpaid time off work for union activities. Employees have the right not to be dismissed for being, or refusing to be, union members or for taking part in union activities.[45]

The trade union officers do not have any management rights: they have no power as part of their function as union officials to give orders to the employees. Obviously, they might advise their members to follow a particular course, but it is up to the members' own judgement whether they follow the advice or not. The Employment Act 1988 gave additional protection to the employee: he has the right not to be denied access to the courts by union rules; the right not to be unjustifiably disciplined by a union; the right to complain to an employment tribunal and obtain compensation if this latter right is infringed. The Employment Relations Act 2004 implements the findings of a review of the Employment Relations Act 1999 which identified a number of areas where recognition procedures for trade unions could be improved. As a consequence of the 2004 Act, which came fully into force in October 2005, Codes of Practice on Access and Unfair Practices During Recognition Ballots and on Industrial Action and Notice to Employers have come into force. Further details are available on the DBERR website.[46]

Public and private employees

Those nurses who work as employees in the private sector enjoy much the same rights as those who work in the NHS. There are, however, some major differences. If the nurse is only one of a few employees, then she may not enjoy all those statutory rights enjoyed by those working for employers of large concerns. This also applies to those NHS nurses who work for single-handed general practitioners or group practices.

In addition, they may not be subject to NHS conditions of service. In this case, there will be other provisions relating to holidays, pay, sick pay, pensions, time off etc., which will either have been laid down in advance or which will have to be agreed with the employer. The nurse should make sure that she is aware of these provisions before she accepts the post.

Discrimination: The Equality and Human Rights Commission

The Equality and Human Rights Commission was established on 1 October 2007 under the Equality Act 2006, replacing the Equal Opportunities Commission, the Disabilities Rights Commission and the Racial Equality commissions. It also assumes responsibility for promoting equality and combating unlawful discrimination in three new areas: sexual orientation, religion or belief and age. It also has responsibility for the promotion of human rights. The Commission has a general duty under Section 3 to exercise its functions with a view to encouraging and supporting the development of a society in which

(a) people's ability to achieve their potential is not limited by prejudice or discrimination

(b) there is respect for and protection of each individual's human rights

(c) there is respect for the dignity and worth of each individual

(d) each individual has an equal opportunity to participate in society and

(e) there is mutual respect between groups based on understanding and valuing of diversity and on shared respect for equality and human rights.

More specific duties relate to equality and diversity (Section 8), human rights (Section 9), groups (Section 10), monitoring the law (Section 11) and monitoring progress (Section 12). It has powers to publish or disseminate ideas or information, undertake research, provide education or training, give advice or guidance, and issue codes of practice. It also has the power to carry out an investigation, to apply to court for an injunction against a person who it believes to be committing an unlawful act, to bring proceedings in its own name and to give legal assistance to an individual who alleges that he is a victim of behaviour contrary to the equality enactments. The following sections consider the basic provisions in law against discrimination and further information can be obtained from the EHRC website.[47] The EHRC supported a woman with a disabled son who claimed that she was discriminated against at work because of her child. The European Court of Justice in January 2008 held that there was direct discrimination where a person suffered discrimination and/or harassment because he or she is associated with a disabled person. It is described as a landmark case, which could bring new rights for the 6 million carers in the UK.[48]

Discrimination by race or sex

The Race Relations Act 1976 and the Sex Discrimination Acts 1975 and 1986 outlaw discrimination in employment, education, housing or the provision of goods, facilities and services on grounds of race, colour, nationality, or ethnic or national origins, sex and marital status. Referral can be made to the European Court of Justice if there is doubt over the application of its directives on equal pay and equal treatment to domestic law. (See the unfair dismissal and sex discrimination case of Seymour-Smith.)[49] The Race Relations (Amendment) Act 2000 was passed as a result of recommendations in the MacPherson report following the death of Stephen Lawrence and its finding that there was institutional racism within the police force. A new general statutory duty is created by Section 71 which requires specified public bodies (including NHS bodies) to have due regard to the need to eliminate unlawful racial discrimination and to promote equality of opportunity and good relations between persons of different racial groups. A statutory code of practice which the specified bodies must follow has been issued by the Commission for Racial Equality and is available from its successor, the Equality and Human Rights Commission website.[50] The Commission can also issue a compliance notice if satisfied that an organisation is failing to comply with the law or any order issued under Section 71. Each public authority is also required to publish a race equality scheme in accordance with the general and specific duties set out in the legislation. The Race Directive outlaws discrimination on grounds of racial or ethnic origin in the areas of training, goods, services, social protection, education and housing and came into force in July 2003. Further information on equality and diversity is available from the DBERR website and the Equality and Human Rights Commission.[51] The RCN has also issued guidance for employers and nurses on diversity in the workplace.[52] An inquiry set up following the death of David 'Rocky' Bennett, who died after being pinioned face down on the floor for 25 minutes in a medium secure unit for the mentally ill, reported that there was chronic institutional racism in the NHS and made radical recommendations for reform.[53]

Direct discrimination

This is where one person treats another less favourably on the grounds of sex, race or marital status than he would treat another person of another sex, race or marital status. The two questions that the tribunal would have to determine under the Act are: Has the person been discriminated against? And is the cause of that discrimination one of the forbidden grounds?

Indirect discrimination

This is where a condition* is applied to persons so that the following prevail:

1 The proportion of people of one race or sex who can comply with it is considerably smaller than the proportion of another.
2 The employer cannot show the condition is justifiable on other than racial or sexual grounds.
3 The condition is to the detriment of the complainant because he cannot comply with it.

Case 10.3   *Aina v. Employment Service (2002)*

Indirect racial discrimination[54]

A black African employee applied for the post of equal opportunities manager in his organisation. He was assessed as having the skills and ability for the job. However, his application was rejected because, unknown to him, the post was open only to permanent staff at higher grades than his. Monitoring data showed that the organisation had no permanent black African employees at the grades in question.

The employment tribunal held that there was no justification for the requirement, and that it amounted to indirect discrimination on racial grounds.

---

*The Sex Discrimination (Indirect Discrimination and Burden of Proof) Regulations 2001 which came into force on 12 October 2001 widened the definition of indirect discrimination so as to encompass a 'provision, criterion or practice', rather than merely a 'requirement or condition'. In addition the burden shifted to the employer to disprove sex discrimination once an applicant has proved that there is a case to answer.

Victimisation

This indirect form of discrimination is also prohibited under the legislation and covers the situation where a person is treated less favourably because he brings proceedings, gives evidence or information, alleges a contravention or otherwise under the Acts or intends to do any of these things. The House of Lords heard a case relating to school meals staff who claimed that they had suffered victimisation under the Sex Discrimination Act 1975 Section 4 when letters were sent to them because they had not settled their case under the Equal Pay Act 1970 as had other employees. The House of Lords held that the tribunal had applied the correct test of 'honest and reasonable' in determining whether the employees had suffered a detriment and the employees' appeal against the Court of Appeal ruling would be allowed.[55]

Segregation

It is unlawful to maintain separate facilities for members of different races. There is no such law in relation to different sexes.

The areas covered by the laws against discrimination are shown in Box 10.11. The discrimination laws are wider than much of the employment legislation. For example, they cover an applicant for a post, as well as independent contractors and the self-employed. Along with employers, the following are subject to the laws: trade unions, partnerships, qualification bodies for trades and professions and vocational training, employment agencies, the Training Agencies (formerly the Manpower Services Commission) and the Crown.

Box 10.11   **Areas covered by discrimination**

Arrangements for recruitment.

Advertisements.

Refusal or deliberate omission to offer employment.

Terms and conditions of service.

Access to transfer or promotion.

Access to training.

Fringe benefits.

Dismissal.

Any other detriment, e.g. full-time working is made a requirement.

Greater Manchester Police agreed to pay £30,000 to a black musician who said that he was twice beaten up by officers.[56] It has been held[57] that the words 'in the course of employment' in Section 32(1) of the Race Relations Act 1976 were not to be construed restrictively by reference to case law on the law governing vicarious liability. So an employee's racially abusive acts did not have to be connected with acts authorised to be done as part of his work so as to make the employer liable.

Exceptions to laws on discrimination

These are listed in Box 10.12 for discrimination on grounds of sex and Box 10.13 for discrimination on grounds of race. One of the most important is 'the genuine occupational qualification', i.e. that the employer can justify discrimination because of the particular characteristics of the post. For example, the employment of Chinese people in a Chinese restaurant may be justifiable.

Box 10.12 **Exceptions to unlawful discrimination on grounds of sex**

1   Sex of a person is a genuine occupational qualification for the job:
    + The essential nature of the job calls for a man because of his physiology.
    + A man is required for authenticity in entertainment.
    + The job needs to be held by a man or woman in order to preserve decency or privacy because:
        (i) it is likely to involve physical contact with a person in circumstances where that person may reasonably object to its being carried out by a person of the opposite sex
        (ii) persons of one sex might reasonably object to the presence of the other sex because they are in a state of undress or using sanitary facilities (e.g. lavatory attendants).
    + Job is at a single sex establishment – hospital, prison, etc.
    + Holder of post provides individuals with personal services promoting their welfare or education which can most effectively be provided by one sex.
    + Job needs to be held by a man because of restriction imposed by laws regulating the employment of women.
    + Job likely to involve work abroad which can only be done by men (e.g. Middle East).
    + Job is one of two that are to be held by a married couple.
    + Employee is required to live on premises.
2   Other exceptions:
    + Acts done to safeguard national security.
    + Undertakings with fewer than five employees.
    + Ministers of religion.
    + Sports and sports facilities.
    + Special treatment afforded to women in connection with pregnancy or childbirth.
    + Provisions in relation to death or retirement (subject to 1986 Act).

Box 10.13 **Exceptions to unlawful discrimination on grounds of race**

A genuine occupational qualification requires a particular race, e.g.:

1   Authenticity in entertainment.
2   Employee provides personal services towards the welfare or education of others.
3   A member of a particular race is required for reasons of authenticity in art or photography.
4   A bar or restaurant has a particular setting (e.g. Chinese restaurant) for which a person of that racial group is required for reasons of authenticity.
5   Immigration rules, civil service regulations that restrict those eligible for Crown employment.
6   Acts done to safeguard national security.

Applications for compensation for discrimination on grounds of sex or race can be made to the employment tribunal. In the case of discrimination on grounds of sex, the European Court held in the case of *Marshall* v. *Southampton AHA* (No. 2)[58] that the upper limit fixed by statute on the payment of compensation infringed the European Equal Treatment Directive which, since November 1993, applies to both public and private sector employees.

Subsequently, substantial sums have been awarded to women who have lost their jobs through dismissal on grounds of pregnancy. On 29 July 1994, the Employment Appeal

Tribunal held, in the case of the Ministry of Defence's appeal against the decision in *Cannock* (awarded £172,000 by a tribunal)[59] and other similar awards, that the assessment of awards in the future by industrial tribunals should assess the chances of a woman returning to work and make a percentage award on that basis.

However, the European Commission has not made comparable directives in relation to discrimination on race-related grounds and the upper ceiling on compensation still applies to those claims.

Discrimination in the NHS

A plan called 'Tackling Racial Harassment' in the NHS was launched in February 1999 by Alan Milburn, Health Minister. He described it as 'the most concerted drive the NHS has ever seen on the issue'. The Plan envisaged that by April 2000 every NHS employer would need to be in a position to tackle racial harassment whether committed by staff or by patients.

The NHS Executive has established an Equal Opportunities Unit. It holds regional seminars and is available to assist on equal opportunities policies and current practice.[60]

Male midwives

Originally midwifery was one of the exemptions to the Sex Discrimination Act 1975 and the employment and training of men as midwives was restricted. However, under Order 1983 SI No. 1202 the exemptions were brought to an end. The health authorities were notified that when implementing these legislative changes they must make appropriate arrangements to ensure that:

1 women have the freedom of choice to be attended by a female midwife

2 where male midwives are employed, provision is made for them to be chaperoned as necessary.

Equal pay

The Equal Pay Act 1970, as amended by subsequent legislation, aims at preventing discrimination as regards terms and conditions of employment between men and women. Central to its provisions is the concept of an equality clause which is to be implied into the contract of a woman who can show she is either employed in like work with a man at the same establishment, at an establishment where similar terms and conditions are applied or has been the subject of a job appraisal scheme or performs work of equal value.

The Act and Article 119 of the Treaty of Rome enable an employee to claim equal pay in comparison with a person of the opposite sex who is employed by the same employer at the same establishment if she or he is doing the same job or a job of equal value. Thus men as well as women can bring a claim under these provisions.

Domestics, cleaners, ward assistants and cooks, who did not receive bonuses paid to men who did comparable work at the Hartlepool and East Durham NHS Trust, won their case for lack of equal pay in April 1999.[61] They were to receive up to £3,000 each in an out-of-court settlement.

An employer can rely on the defence under Section 1(3) that there is a genuine material factor which justifies the unequal pay. The House of Lords has stated that this factor must be material in that it is not due to the difference in sex but is causally related to the difference in pay, and it must be genuine and not a sham or pretence.[62]

Speech therapist case[63]

Speech therapists had complained that their lower salaries in comparison with other health professionals, e.g. pharmacists, was a breach of the equal pay legislation. The Court of Justice of the European Communities held that it was for the employer to prove that the difference was based on objectively justified grounds unrelated to any discrimination on grounds of sex. The fact that the rate was arrived at by collective bargaining did not mean that it was not discriminatory. It was for the national court to determine, if necessary by applying the principle of proportionality, whether and to what extent the shortage of candidates for a job and the need to attract them by higher pay constituted an objectively justified economic ground for the difference in pay between the jobs in question.

The European Court of Justice can review the compatibility of the law in member states with EC Directives. For example, in the Boyle case it reviewed the validity of the maternity leave and pay conditions in the employment contracts of six women who were employed by the Equal Opportunities Commission.[64] The European Court of Justice held that the maternity scheme did not infringe the principles of equal pay or equal treatment, except in respect of the pension provision. The clause that limited the accrual of pension rights during maternity leave to those periods of paid leave was unacceptable. It should have covered unpaid leave. A Code of Practice on Equal Pay came into force on 1 December 2003, replacing the 1997 edition.[65] The Equal Pay Directive 1975 and the Equal Pay Treatment Directive 1976 were brought together in the Consolidated Equal Treatment Directive 2006.[66] Member states must implement it by 15 August 2009.

Discrimination on grounds of religion or belief or sexual orientation

New regulations came into force in December 2003 as a result of employment Directives from the European Community. The Employment Equality (Religion or Belief) Regulations[67] and the Employment Equality (Sexual Orientation) Regulations[68] protect employees and applicants and those in vocational training against discrimination, victimisation or harassment on the grounds of religion or belief or sexual orientation. Exceptions to equality in respect of religion or belief are recognised for national security, positive action and the protection of Sikhs from discrimination in connection with requirements as to wearing of safety helmets. Exceptions to equality in respect of sexual orientation are recognised for national security and positive action and also for benefits that are dependent on marital status. Enforcement in respect of both sets of regulations is through the employment tribunal. Employment Equality Regulations[69] came into force on 1 October 2005 which brought sexual indirect discrimination in line with racial discrimination. Article 9 of the European Convention on Human Rights gives a qualified right in respect of freedom of thought, conscience and religion.

The Equality Act 2006 makes further provisions in relation to discrimination on grounds of religion or belief, and discrimination on grounds of sexual orientation, by prohibiting discrimination when providing goods, facilities and services, education, using or disposing of premises and exercising public functions.

Discrimination on grounds of age

Protection from discrimination on grounds of age came into force in October 2006 as a result of a European Directive[70] which was implemented by the Employment Equality (Age) Regulations 2006.[71] The Regulations only apply to employment and vocational training and only protect employees up to 65 years who can be dismissed after that age provided the employer satisfies the specified procedure set out in the regulations. If the employer agrees to keep the employee on after that age, the employee is protected against other forms of discrimination in relation to discipline, pay, harassment and job classification. Employees have the right to request working beyond 65 years and in such a case employers have a duty to consider the request according to Schedule 6. Further regulations to ensure that the statutory sick pay scheme and other social security regulations were amended to take account of the age discrimination laws came into force in April 2007[72] and to ensure compliance with the EC Directive. In a case on 16 October 2007 involving a Spanish worker who challenged his forced retirement,[73] the European Court of Justice said that the EU states could introduce and enforce mandatory retirement ages as long as they are justified. Heyday, an offshoot of the charity Age Concern, had awaited this ruling before pursuing its own case. See the Age Concern website for further information[74].

Disability Discrimination Act 1995

The Disability Discrimination Act 1995 provides disabled people with protection from discrimination in the areas of:

1 access to goods, facilities and services
2 buying or renting land and property
3 employment
4 education
5 public transport.

The main sections of the Act are shown in the following Statute.

Statute   **Main provisions of Disability Discrimination Act 1995**

1 Definitions of disability and disabled person.
2 Employment: discrimination by employers, enforcement provisions, discrimination by other persons, occupational pension schemes and insurance services.
3 Discrimination in other areas: goods, facilities and services, premises, enforcement.
4 Education.
5 Public transport: taxis, public services vehicles, rail vehicles.
6 National Disability Council (superseded by the Disability Rights Commission).
7 Supplemental: codes of practice, victimisation, help.
8 Miscellaneous.

It has been illegal for businesses and organisations since 2 December 1996 to treat disabled people less favourably than other people for a reason related to their disability. From 1 October 1999 service providers had to take reasonable steps to change practices and procedures that make it unreasonably difficult for disabled persons to use a service. From 2004 service providers were required to take reasonable steps to remove, alter or provide reasonable means of avoiding physical features that make it impossible for disabled people to use that service. Schools, colleges and universities must provide information to disabled people.

Definition of disabled person

A person is disabled if they have a physical or mental impairment that has a substantial and long-term adverse effect on their ability to carry out normal day-to-day activities. Long term means 'lasting' or likely to last at least 12 months. There must be an effect on at least one of the following aspects:

1 mobility

2 manual dexterity

3 physical coordination

4 continence

5 ability to lift

6 ability to carry or otherwise move everyday objects

7 speech

8 hearing or eyesight

9 memory or ability to concentrate, learn or understand

10 perception of the risk of physical danger.

The Disability Discrimination Act 2005 Section 18 amended the definition of disability, removing the requirement that mental illness must be clinically well recognised if it is to be the basis of 'mental impairment' and adding that a person who has cancer (subject to specific conditions), HIV infection or multiple sclerosis is deemed to have a disability and thus be a disabled person. Section 3 places a general duty on every public authority to have regard to the need to eliminate unlawful discrimination, and harassment because of disability, and to the need to promote equality of opportunity, take steps to take account of disabled persons' disabilities, promote positive attitudes towards disabled persons and the need to encourage participation by disabled persons in public life.

Definition of discrimination of a disabled person

Discrimination occurs if a disabled person is treated less favourably.

Codes of practice have been published by the government covering:

1 Rights of access – goods, facilities, services and premises.

2 Elimination of discrimination in the field of employment against disabled persons or persons who have had a disability.

3 Duties of trade organisations to their disabled members and applicants.

4 Guidance on matters to be taken into account in determining questions relating to the definition of disability.

5 Discrimination in education: with separate codes for schools, for the over 16-year-olds and for special educational needs.

The Disability Discrimination Act 1995 also makes illegal harassment and victimisation of a disabled person. Harassment occurs where, for a reason which is related to a person's disability, another person engages in unwanted conduct that has the purpose or effect of violating the disabled person's dignity or creating an intimidating, hostile, degrading, humiliating or offensive environment for him or her. Victimisation is also prohibited under the DDA.

Further information can be obtained from the website[75] of the Equality and Human Rights Commission. In addition there are many guides issued by the Department for Business Enterprise and Regulatory Reform[76] and the Department for Children, Schools and Families on various parts of the legislation.

Any allegation of discrimination in employment can be taken to an employment tribunal. The Advisory, Conciliation and Arbitration Service provides conciliation services.

Equality Act 2006

The main provisions of the Equality Act 2006 are:

To establish the Commission for Equality and Human Rights (see above).

To make unlawful discrimination on the grounds of religion or belief in the provision of goods, facilities and services, education, the use and disposal of premises and the exercise of public functions,

To enable provision to be made against discrimination on the grounds of sexual orientation in the provision of goods, facilities and services, education, the use and disposal of premises and the exercise of public functions.

To create a duty on public authorities to promote equality of opportunity between women and men ('the gender duty') and prohibit sex discrimination and harassment in the exercise of public functions.

Agenda for Change

The Agenda for Change is a radical reorganisation of the NHS pay system and applies to most NHS staff with the exception of doctors, dentists and senior managers. Detailed information can be obtained from the Agenda for Change website.[77] An introductory booklet for staff explains how the new pay system will work, the new terms and conditions which will apply to all staff covered by the new scheme, basic pay and enhancements, overtime, annual leave and high cost areas and the premiums paid for long-term and short-term recruitment. The new scheme was tested out by pilot sites for early implementation (see Agenda for Change pay circular to the 12 early implementer sites[78]) and then covered the rest of the NHS, beginning on 1 October 2004. Monitoring of the new scheme is undertaken by the national implementation steering groups in England, Wales, Scotland and Northern Ireland in conjunction with the Pay Modernisation Implementation Steering Group (UK). A job evaluation handbook sets out how job evaluation will decide the points score which is to be used to match jobs to paybands and therefore levels of basic salary.[79] To support personal development and career progression, there will be a new NHS Knowledge and Skills Framework, which will enable each member of staff to have a personal development plan. Recent developments in Agenda for Change can be obtained from the Department of Health website.

NHS Professionals

NHS Professionals[80] was integral to the realisation of the NHS Plan and was established in November 2000 to link up healthcare staff who were seeking temporary work within the NHS with appropriate vacancies. In theory, instead of the NHS paying commercial firms to recruit staff for the NHS, NHS Professionals can undertake the work, saving NHS funds. The West Yorkshire Metropolitan Ambulance Service was appointed by the Department of Health to run much of the service. An Audit Commission report in 2003 criticised NHS Professionals as being underfunded, set up without a proper business plan and left to sink or swim by the Department of Health.[81] There were also criticisms from private nursing agencies for delays in paying staff and for creating a new layer of bureaucracy. As a result of such criticisms, NHS Professionals became a special health authority, set up under Section 11 of the National Health Service Act 1977 on 1 April 2004. It has an independent management board and chief executive who reports direct to the Department of Health. It is accountable for the management of the NHS temporary labour market and responsible for:

+ strategic oversight of temporary labour markets
+ management of agency framework contracts
+ setting standards and the policy framework for NHS temporary staffing
+ operational management of the NHS Professionals Services in partnership with the local NHS.

Recent years have seen both a shortage and an excess of staff in different areas with redundancies being made because of overspending. NHS Professionals has a major role in its work with the Department of Health and trade unions to maintain stability of employment for NHS staff.

Conclusions

Employment law is an area of law that is constantly changing with each government legislating to amend the rights of employer and employees, trade unions and the laws on discrimination. In addition, case law leads to better understanding on the interpretation of statutory provisions. The new European Union Treaty which was agreed in June 2007 may have further impact on the employment laws which apply in the UK. The Equality Act and the establishment of the Equality and Human Rights Commission should have a major impact on the protection of individuals from discrimination and the NHS, as the employer of the largest workforce in the UK, has a significant role to play in setting a non-discriminatory culture. An Employment Bill under discussion at the time of writing will, if enacted, make significant changes by replacing the statutory dispute resolution procedures, strengthening the enforcement of the national minimum wage and clarifying trade union rights over membership.

Reflection questions

1 If you have a letter that purports to be your contract of appointment, compare it with the particulars set out in Box 10.3.

2 Take any statutory right and contrast it with the comparable rights given in your contract of employment by national NHS conditions. Which right would be of most benefit to the employee?

3 A manager is both an employee and the representative of the employer. In what way, if any, is there likely to be a conflict between these two roles?

4 If you were preparing to interview prospective employees, what questions do you consider would be unlawful under the sex, race and disability and other discrimination legislation?

Further exercises

1 Obtain a copy of your employer's disciplinary procedure and apply the procedure to any of the situations of alleged negligence by a nurse set out in this book.

2 Visit an employment tribunal and prepare a brief guide for a potential applicant on the procedure and formalities.

References

1 *Grant* v. *United Kingdom* [2003] (32570/03) 44 EHRR 1
2 www.equalityhumanrights.com
3 www.ico.gov.uk
4 Nursing and Midwifery Council, Code of Professional Conduct: standards for performance, conduct and ethics, NMC, 2004
5 Department for Education and Science, Making Safeguarding Everybody's Business: A Post-Bichard Vetting Scheme, 1485-2005DOC-EN; www.dfes.gov.uk/consultations
6 www.bichardinquiry.org.uk/
7 List 99 is a list held by the Department for Children, Schools and Families of those considered unsuitable to work with children. It has always been a statutory list
8 *R* v. *Secretary of State for Health ex parte C* [1999] 1 FLR 1073
9 www.dh.gov.uk/vulnerableadults
10 *R (on the application of Wright and others)* v. *Secretary of State for Health and Another* [2006] EWHC 2888; [2007] 1 All ER 825; The Times Law Report, 16 November 2007 CA
11 Further details of statutory rights are available from the Department for Business, Enterprise and Regulatory Reform, www.berr.gov.uk
12 www.acac.org.uk
13 Department of Trade and Industry, Maternity entitlements and responsibilities: a guide, 2007, available from the DBERR website, www.berr.gov.uk
14 Department for Business, Enterprise and Regulatory Reform, www.berr.gov.uk
15 Royal College of Nursing, Your Rights and Safety: an A-Z guide, Order No. 001771, RCN, July 2002
16 *Halfpenny* v. *IGE Medical System Ltd* [1999] 1 FLR 944 CA
17 *Webb* v. *EMO Air Cargo (UK)*, The Times Law Report, 15 July 1994; [1995] IRLR 645, HL
18 www.dti.gov.uk/er/individual/fathers_to_be.pdf
19 Paragraphs 76-80 Part I Schedule 4 of Employment Relations Act 1999
20 Maternity and Parental Leave Regulations 1999, SI 1999 No. 3312
21 Part II Schedule 4 Employment Relations Act 1999
22 Flexible Working (Eligibility, Complaints and Remedies) Regulations 2002, SI 2002 No. 3236
23 Flexible Working (Eligibility, Complaints and Remedies)(Amendment) Regulations 2006, SI 2006 No. 3314
24 *Annette Cowley* v. *South African Airways*; Francis Gibb, Single mother wins fight over 16-hour shifts, *The Times*, 3 August 1999
25 Department for Business, Enterprise and Regulatory Reform, Dismissal Fair and Unfair: a guide for employers, 2007, www.berr.gov.uk
26 *Burley* v. *Langley* [2006] EWCA Civ 1778, [2007] 2 All ER 462
27 *Atkin* v. *Enfield Group Hospital Management Committee* [1975] IRLR 217

[28] Employment Protection Code of Practice (Disciplinary Practice and Procedures) Order 1998 SI 1998/44; see also ACAS Code of Practice, revised 2004

[29] *Schultz* v. *Esso Petroleum Co. Ltd* [1999] 3 All ER 338

[30] *Dunnachie* v. *Kingston upon Hull County Council* [2004] IRLR 727

[31] Report by the Comptroller and Auditor General on Management of Suspensions of Clinical Staff in NHS Hospitals and Ambulance Trusts in England, HC 1143, 6 November 2003

[32] Information and Consultation with Employees Regulations, SI 2004 No. 3426

[33] *Halford* v. *United Kingdom* (1997) 24 EHRR 523; [1997] IRLR 471; [1998] Crim LR 753

[34] www.ico.gov.uk

[35] Regulations of Investigatory Powers (Interception of Communications: Code of Practice) Order 2002, SI 2002 No. 1693

[36] Telecommunications (Lawful Business Practices) (Interception of Communications) Regulations 2000, SI 2000 No. 2699

[37] Working Time Regulations 1998, SI 1998 No. 1833

[38] NHS Executive, Working Time Regulations: implementation in the NHS, HSC 1988/204; DTI, A Guide to the Working Time Regulations, URN 1998/894

[39] *R* v. *S of S for Trade and Industry*, The Times Law Report, 28 June 2001

[40] *Commission of the European Communities* v. *UK* (C484/04) [2006] IRLR 888 ECJ

[41] NHS Advance letter (GC) 3/98, 18 November 1998

[42] Further information is available on 0845 8450 360

[43] The Part-time Workers (Prevention of Less Favourable Treatment) Regulations 2000, SI 2000 No. 1551

[44] Directive 97/81/EC, Part-time Work Directive as extended to the UK by Directive 98/23/EC

[45] See DTI booklet PL871 for details of union membership and non-membership rights

[46] www.berr.gov.uk

[47] *S. Coleman* v. *Attridge* [2008] ECJ Case C-303/06, 31 January 2008

[48] www.equalityhumanrights.com

[49] *R* v. *Secretary of State for Employment ex parte Seymour-Smith and Another*, The Times, 25 February 1999 (European Law Report)

[50] www.equalityhumanrights.com

[51] www.berr.gov.uk

[52] Royal College of Nursing, Diversity Appraisal Resource Guide, Order No. 001825, RCN, October 2002

[53] Sir John Blofeld, Inquiry into the Death of David 'Rocky' Bennett, February 2004

[54] *Aina* v. *Employment Service* [2002] DCLD 103D

[55] *Derbyshire and others* v. *St Helens Metropolitan Borough Council* [2007] UKHL 16; [2007] 3 All ER 81

[56] Russell Jenkins, Police pay singer £30,000 to settle race abuse claim, *The Times*, 14 April 1999

[57] *Jones* v. *Tower Boot Co. Ltd*, The Times Law Report, 16 December 1996

[58] *Marshall* v. *Southampton AHA (No. 2)* [1993] 4 All ER 586

[59] *Minister of Defence* v. *Cannock*, The Times Law Report, 2 August 1994

[60] NHS Confederation, Equal Opportunities Update, Issue No. 4, September 1998

[61] News item, Equal pay deal for NHS, *The Times*, 1 April 1999

[62] *Strathclyde Regional Council* v. *Wallace* [1996] IRLR 670

[63] *Enderby* v. *Frenchay HA and the Secretary of State for Health* [1994] 1 All ER 495

[64] *Boyle* v. *Equal Opportunities Commission* [1999] 1 FLR 119 European Court of Justice (Case 411/96)

[65] Code of Practice on Equal Pay Order 2003, SI 2003 No. 2865

[66] Directive 2006/54/EC

[67] The Employment Equality (Religion or Belief) Regulations, SI 2003 No. 1660

[68] The Employment Equality (Sexual Orientation) Regulations, SI 2003 No. 1661

[69] Employment Equality (Sex Discrimination) Regulations, SI 2005 No. 2467

[70] Council Directive 2000/78 ([2000] OJL303/16)

[71] Employment Equality (Age) Regulations 2006, SI 2006 No. 1031

[72] Employment Equality (Age) (Consequential Amendments) Regulations 2007, SI 2007 No. 825

[73] *Palacios de la Villa* v. *Cortefiel Servicios SA* [2007] ECJ C-411/05 16 October 2007; The Times Law Report, 23 October 2007

[74] www.ageconcern.org.uk; www.heyday.org.uk

[75] www.equalityhumanrights.com

[76] www.berr.gov.uk

[77] www.dh.gov.uk/agendaforchange

[78] Department of Health, Agenda for Change – (E1) pay circular, 24 July 2003

[79] www.dh.gov.uk/agendaforchange/jobevaluationhandbook.htm

[80] www.nhsprofessionals.nhs.uk

[81] Nigel Hawkes, NHS trust faces ruin over agency for nurses, *The Times*, 19 March 2003

Chapter 11
The nurse as a registered professional

This chapter discusses

+ Background to the establishment of the Nursing and Midwifery Council
+ Nursing and Midwifery Council
+ Registration and removal
+ Professional standards and codes of practice
+ Education and training
+ Post-registration education and practice (PREP)
+ Fitness to Practise Annual Report 2005-2006
+ Council for Healthcare Regulatory Excellence (CHRE)
+ NHS Institute for Innovation and Improvement
+ National Workforce Competence Framework

Introduction

It will be recalled from Chapter 1 that there were four fields of accountability to be faced by the nurse: the civil and criminal courts; the disciplinary proceedings of the employer; and the Conduct and Competence Committee (CCC) of the Nursing and Midwifery Council (NMC). This chapter considers the procedure for a hearing before the CCC and the other practice committees. First, however, the constitution of the NMC will be considered. Significant changes came into force in April 2002, when the United Kingdom Central Council for Nursing, Midwifery and Health Visiting was replaced by the NMC and in 2004 new procedures for Fitness to Practise were introduced.[1]

Background to the establishment of the Nursing and Midwifery Council

The Nurses, Midwives and Health Visitors Act 1979 had set up the previous framework for the United Kingdom Central Council, the national boards and the professional register and Statutory Instruments passed in the exercise of powers conferred by the principal Act provided the detail. At the request of the Department of Health, a review of the statutory regulation of nurses, midwives and health visitors was undertaken by JM Consulting. It reported in 1999[2] and made significant recommendations for a major reorganisation of the work, functions and organisation of the statutory regulation machinery. Its main recommendations were accepted by the government and the necessary legislative beginning was made in the Health Act 1999. In August 2000, the government issued a consultation paper[3] giving three months for feedback. The amending regulations were passed by order under Section 60 of the Health Act 1999, with a new Nursing and Midwifery Council replacing the UKCC and the four national boards, maintaining a professional register with some 640,000 entries. Contrary to initial suggestions, health visitors continued to have separate registration and representation within the new Council, but were absorbed into the new profession of specialist community public health nurses.

New procedures for Fitness to Practise, new rules for midwives and new regulations relating to the local supervising authorities came into force on 1 August 2004.[4] They can be downloaded from the NMC website or obtained from the website of the Office of Public Sector Information.

The Health Act 1999 Schedule 3 Paragraph 8 defines four fundamental functions of the new Council, which cannot be transferred by order to another body. These are:

1 keeping the register of members admitted to practise
2 determining the standards of education and training for admission to practise
3 giving guidance about standards of conduct and performance
4 administering procedures (including making rules) relating to misconduct, unfitness to practise and similar matters.

The covering letter to the consultation paper stated that the key objectives of the reorganisation were:

1 To reform ways of working, by requiring the Council to:
   + treat the health and welfare of patients as paramount
   + collaborate and consult with key stakeholders
   + be open and proactive in accounting to the public and the profession for its work.
2 To reform structure and functions by:
   + giving wider powers to deal effectively with individuals who present unacceptable risks to patients
   + creating a smaller council, comprising directly elected practitioners and a strong lay input, charged with strategic responsibility for setting and monitoring standards of professional training, performance and conduct

- streamlining the professional register
- providing explicit powers to link registration with evidence of continuing professional development.

Three statutory committees were suggested:

1 The Investigating Committee, dealing with initial complaints about individuals.
2 The Professional Conduct Committee, dealing with standards of conduct and disciplinary hearings.
3 The Health Committee, dealing with practitioners with health problems.

The Nursing and Midwifery Order 2001[5] provided detailed rules on the constitution of the Council and its functions and covers the following areas:

Part I General

Part II The Council and its Committees

Part III Registration

Part IV Education and Training

Part V Fitness to Practise

Part VI Appeals

Part VII European Economic Area (EEA) provisions

Part VIII Midwifery

Part IX Offences

Part X Miscellaneous

Schedules 1–5.

Following extensive consultation by the NMC, new rules were enacted in Statutory Instruments, which can be downloaded from the NMC or OPSI websites.

Nursing and Midwifery Council

The constitution of the NMC is given in Box 11.1 and its functions can be seen in Box 11.2. The Nursing and Midwifery Order requires the NMC to have specific statutory committees and these can be seen in Box 11.3.

Box 11.1 — **Constitution of the NMC (Schedule 1 of the Nursing and Midwifery Order 2001)**

The Nursing and Midwifery Council shall consist of:

(a) 12 members who are appointed by the Council on being elected under the election scheme (registrant members)

(b) 11 members who are appointed by the Privy Council (lay members)

(c) 12 members appointed by the Council on being elected under the election scheme (alternate members).

At least one registrant member and one alternate member shall be appointed from each part of the register and the number of members from each part shall be equal.

At least one member shall be elected from each of the national constituencies for each part of the register.

> ### Box 11.2 — Functions of the NMC
>
> *Article 3(2)* The principal functions of the Council shall be to establish from time to time standards of education, training, conduct and performance for nurses and midwives and to ensure the maintenance of those standards.
>
> *Article 3(3)* The Council shall have such other functions as are conferred on it by the Order or as may be provided by the Privy Council by order.
>
> *Article 3(4)* The main objective of the Council in exercising its functions shall be to safeguard the health and well-being of persons using or needing the services of registrants.
>
> *Article 3(5)* In exercising its functions, the Council shall –
>
> **(a)** have proper regard to the interests of all registrants and prospective registrants and persons referred to in paragraph (4) in each of the countries of the United Kingdom and to any differing considerations applying to the professions to which this Order applies and to groups within them, and
>
> **(b)** cooperate wherever reasonably practicable with –
> - **(i)** employers and prospective employers of registrants
> - **(ii)** persons who provide, assess or fund education or training for registrants or prospective registrants, or who propose to do so
> - **(iii)** persons who are responsible for regulating or coordinating the regulation of other health or social care professions, or of those who carry out activities in connection with the services provided by those professions or the professions regulated under this Order
> - **(iv)** persons responsible for regulating services in the provision of which registrants are engaged.

> ### Box 11.3 — Statutory committees of the NMC
>
> There shall be four committees of the Council, to be known as:
>
> 1. the Investigating Committee
> 2. the Conduct and Competence Committee
> 3. the Health Committee
> 4. the Midwifery Committee.
>
> These are referred to as the statutory committees.

The Investigating Committee, the Conduct and Competence Committee and the Health Committee are also referred to as the 'practice committees'. (The work of the Midwifery Committee and local supervising authorities is considered in Chapter 14.)

Registration and removal

Council has the duty of preparing and maintaining a register of qualified nurses, midwives and health visitors and setting out rules in relation to the entry on to, removal from, and restoration to the Register. These rules are set out in Part III of the Nursing and Midwifery Order 2001.

False representation

> ### Practical Dilemma 11.1   False qualifications
>
> Brenda had always wanted to be a nurse, but lacked the educational background. When she left school, she worked as a nursing auxiliary for many years and was given much responsibility. She then left the district when her husband moved jobs. She applied for the job of a night nurse in a private nursing home. At the interview, she was asked where she trained and she gave false information about her background. Because of her great experience, they were very impressed with her and failed to take up her references. After she had worked there for two years, a former colleague from her previous hospital came to visit a relative in the home and was surprised to discover that Brenda was referred to as 'sister'. The colleague made some enquiries and realised that Brenda was being treated as a registered nurse when in fact she was not one. She felt that it was her duty to point this out to the owners of the home because of the possibility that a patient could suffer harm. When the owners discovered the truth, Brenda was dismissed on the spot.

In a situation like this, as well as a loss of job, Brenda could face a criminal charge of falsely representing that she was on the Register or falsely representing that she possessed qualifications in nursing, midwifery or health visiting. These are offences under Article 44 of the Nursing and Midwifery Order 2001. The matter would not be one for the Nursing and Midwifery Council since she is not registered, but would be a matter for the criminal courts. An offence is committed if a person falsely represents herself as registered or uses a title set out in the Register indicative of different qualifications and different kinds of education or training, to which she is not entitled, or falsely represents herself as possessing qualifications in nursing or midwifery. In October 2003 it was reported that a person who had worked as a GP nurse for 15 years was convicted after pleading guilty to deception at the Crown Court and was given a 9-month suspended sentence. The deception came to light when she used false documents to gain a job as clinical coordinator.[6]

In such a case the Council would be required to provide evidence of the fact that she was not on the Register and not entitled. Of course, if she was on the Register for one purpose, e.g. a general nurse, it would be an offence for her to pretend that she was a midwife. This would then be a matter that could be heard before the CCC as well as the criminal court, since, as she is already registered, the Committee could decide if she should remain on the Register or if any other action should be taken against her.

The Statutory Instrument also sets out rules relating to registration, renewal of registration and readmission, lapse of registration and approved qualifications and EEA qualifications. Part IV of the order covers education and training, the appointment of visitors, information to be given by institutions, refusal or withdrawal of approval of courses, qualifications and institutions and post-registration training.

Removal from the Register

Under Article 21 of the Nursing and Midwifery Order 2001, the Council is required to establish and keep under review the standards of conduct, performance and ethics expected of registrants and prospective registrants and give them such guidance on these matters as it sees fit and to establish and keep under review effective arrangements to protect the public from persons whose fitness to practise is impaired.

(c) take such other steps as are reasonably practicable to obtain as much information as possible about the case

(d) consider, in the light of the information which it has been able to obtain and any representations or other observations made to it under sub-paragraph (a) or (b), whether in its opinion –

   (i) in respect of an allegation of the kind mentioned in Article 22(1)(a), there is a case to answer, and

   (ii) in respect of an allegation of the kind mentioned in Article 22(1)(b), whether the entry concerned has been fraudulently procured or incorrectly made.

The Investigating Committee, where it considers that there is a case to answer may:

1 undertake mediation or

2 refer the case:

   to screeners for them to undertake mediation

   to the Health Committee

   to the Conduct and Competence Committee.

If the allegation relates to an entry on the Register being fraudulently procured or incorrectly made, then the Investigating Committee can, if it is satisfied that the allegation is correct, make an order that the Registrar remove or amend the entry and it must notify the person concerned of her right to appeal under Article 38, but this order can be reviewed if new evidence comes to light (Article 26(7) and (12)).

The Investigating Committee also has the power to make an interim order at the same time or at any time before referring a case to the Health Committee or Conduct and Competence Committee.

If the Investigating Committee concludes that there is no case to answer or that the relevant entry was not fraudulently procured or incorrectly made, it must make a declaration to that effect, with reasons, if so required by the person concerned and can make a declaration with the consent of the person concerned.

Conduct and Competence Committee

It may be that, after scrutiny of the evidence in Janice's case (Practical Dilemma 11.2), the Investigation Committee or screeners decide that the case should be referred to the Conduct and Competence Committee.

The Conduct and Competence Committee has the function, after consulting the other practice committees, of advising the Council on:

1 the performance of the Council's functions in relation to standards of conduct, performance and ethics expected of registrants and prospective registrants

2 requirements as to good character and good health to be met by registrants and prospective registrants

3 and the protection of the public from people whose fitness to practise is impaired and to consider:

   any allegations referred to it by the Council, screeners, the Investigating Committee or the Health Committee and

   any application for restoration referred to it by the Registrar.

Rules to be followed in Fitness to Practise hearings were set out in a statutory instrument,[8] which can be downloaded from the NMC or OPSI websites.

The Rules cover the following topics in relation to the Conduct and Competence Committee and the Health Committee:

Action upon referral of an allegation
> Meetings and hearings
>> Notice of hearing
>> Procedure of the Conduct and Competence Committee and the Health Committee
>> Notice of decision
>> Referral of allegation from CCC to the Health Committee
>> Referral of allegation from the Health Committee to the CCC.

The hearing

The Rules also lay down the procedure which should be followed at a hearing covering preliminary meetings, public and private hearings, representation and entitlement to be heard, absence of the practitioner, witnesses, vulnerable witnesses, and the order of proceedings at the initial hearing, a review or restoration hearing or at an interim orders hearing and the notes and transcript of the proceedings. The details can be seen in the Statutory Instruments which are available from the NMC and OPSI websites.

The NMC consulted on whether the criminal standard of proof (beyond reasonable doubt) used in practice committees should be replaced by the civil standard of proof (on a balance of probabilities) (see Chapter 1) and concluded in the light of the response that the criminal standard should be kept, but that rules relating to civil procedures should be followed (see NMC website). It has subsequently been announced that from 2009 the civil standard of proof will be used for professional conduct proceedings for registered health professionals as a consequence of the Health and Social Care Bill 2007-8.

There are essentially two distinct stages to a hearing: the first is to determine whether the facts which have been alleged are proved and whether these facts mean that the registrant is guilty of misconduct and if her fitness to practise is impaired. The second stage is the determination of what action should be taken by the practice committee. Rule 24 was amended by SI 2007/893 changing the procedure to be followed from the initial hearing.

The outcome

Once there has been a decision that the nurse is guilty of misconduct and her fitness to practise is impaired, the Committee then has to decide what sanction to adopt. There are several choices (see Box 11.6).

Box 11.6 **Outcomes available to the Conduct and Competence Committee**

1 *Refer the matter to screeners for mediation or itself undertake mediation.*
2 *Take no further action.*
3 *Striking off the Register.*
4 *Suspension for a specified period from the Register (not exceeding one year): on expiry of this time, she shall be restored to the Register (a suspension order).*

> ### Box 11.6 continued
>
> 5 *Impose conditions with which the person must comply for a specified period which shall not exceed three years (a conditions of practice order).*
>
> 6 *Caution the practitioner and make an order directing the Registrar to annotate the Register accordingly for a specified period which shall not be for less than one year and not more than five years (a caution order).*
>
> 7 *Refer to another Committee.*
>
> 8 *Interim orders:* Article 31 enables an order to be made to suspend the person's registration or imposing conditions with which the person must comply for a period not exceeding 18 months, if it is necessary for the protection of members of the public or otherwise in the public interest, or is in the interests of the person concerned.

The professional screeners, the president or the Health Committee can refer a case back to the Conduct and Competence Committee. Under Article 30 any practice committee has power to vary the orders that it has made or refer the matter to another committee.

In all cases the respondent must be notified by recorded delivery of the decision of the CCC.

Criminal misconduct

If the charge relates to criminal misconduct, then slightly different rules apply. Evidence as to a conviction on a criminal charge can be put before the CCC and the respondent can adduce evidence to prove beyond reasonable doubt that she is not the person referred to in the certificate of conviction or that the offence referred to in the certificate of conviction was not that of which she was convicted (this prevents a second trial on the actual charge that was before the criminal courts).

The CCC will determine whether any conviction has been proved and after that the validity of the conviction will not be questioned. Proof of a conviction alone will not in itself be considered to be evidence of impairment of fitness to practise. However, proof of the conviction is evidence of the commission of the offence. It then has to be decided whether that offence constitutes impairment of fitness to practise.

In the case of Balamoody against the UKCC,[9] the court held that the terms of the professional conduct rules covered all criminal convictions regardless of either the seriousness of the offence or whether it was committed in the course of nursing. While a criminal conviction did not of itself constitute misconduct, some offences would almost certainly amount to misconduct and therefore, where a professional had failed to adhere to important statutory requirements whilst discharging functions of a senior and supervisory nature, resulting in a criminal conviction, the relevant professional body and the court would be forced to regard that person's actions as a cause for serious concern. In Practical Dilemma 11.2, if Janice were convicted of a criminal offence and the CCC were satisfied that the certificate of conviction applied to Janice, they would have to determine if her actions showed that she was unfit to practice and determine the action to be taken. Even if no criminal proceedings were brought, the Investigation Committee of the NMC would initiate proceedings to determine if there were a case to answer following the procedure set out in Rule 4 of the Statutory Instrument.

Practical Dilemma 11.3 **Breach of the peace**

A district nurse was very angry to discover that a traffic warden was standing by her car as she returned from visiting a patient. She pointed out her nurse's sticker and explained that she was visiting only for a few minutes to give an injection. The traffic warden was unimpressed by her pleading and took no notice of what she was saying. The nurse became very heated and an argument broke out during which the traffic warden said: 'You nurses are all the same. You all think the law does not apply to you.' The nurse lost her temper and pushed the warden. She was subsequently charged with conduct likely to cause a breach of the peace. She was found guilty and fined. She eventually found herself facing CCC proceedings.

A case such as that in Practical Dilemma 11.3 would be conducted under the procedure to be followed where a conviction is alleged. Rule 31 of the SI states that where a registrant has been convicted of a criminal offence a copy of the certificate of conviction shall be conclusive proof of the conviction and the findings of fact upon which the conviction is based shall be admissible as proof of those facts. The only evidence which may be adduced by the registrant in rebuttal of the conviction is evidence that she is not the person referred to in the certificate. If the district nurse in Practical Dilemma 11.3 fails to put forward such evidence, then the CCC would hold that the conviction had been proved, and decide if this was evidence of impairment of fitness to practise. It is then open to the nurse to submit that the charges are not in themselves proof of unfitness to practise.

Removal on grounds of health

At any time, the Investigating Committee, when investigating a case of alleged unfitness to practise or a complaint against a nurse, can refer the case to the Health Committee of the NMC.

The Health Committee is constituted to determine whether or not:

1 a practitioner will be removed from the Register or part of it
2 a person who has been removed from the Register or part of it may be restored
3 a practitioner's registration shall be suspended
4 the suspension of a person's registration shall be terminated.

The rules relating to membership of a practice committee and a panel are shown in Box 11.7.

Box 11.7 **Rules relating to membership of a practice committee and a panel**

The members of each practice committee shall include registered professionals and other members, of whom at least one shall be a registered medical practitioner.

The number of registered members on a practice committee may, but need not, exceed the number of other members on the committee and shall not in any case exceed that number by more than one.

The chairman of the committee shall be a Council member.

No one shall be a member of more than one practice committee and shall not be both a screener and a member of a practice committee.

> ## Box 11.7 continued
>
> When a panel of a practice committee are selected, there must be at least three members who are chosen with due regard to the former, current or proposed field of the person concerned and the nature of the matters in issue.
>
> The constitution of a panel hearing the matter is:
>
> One member of the panel must be registered in the same part of the Register as the person concerned.
>
> At least one member of the panel must be a lay member and not a registered medical practitioner.
>
> Where health of the person is relevant, there must be a medical practitioner.
>
> Non-Council members may be members of the panel.
>
> The number of registrants on the panel may exceed the number of lay members but not by more than one.
>
> The person chairing the panel may but need not be a member of the Council.
>
> Where there is a tie, the chairman shall have an additional casting vote but in fitness to practise decisions shall exercise his casting vote in favour of the person concerned.
>
> No person who is a member of Council or a committee may take part in proceedings of a practice committee while the subject of any allegations or investigations about her fitness to practise.

Screeners

Allegations may be referred to screeners in accordance with the Nursing and Midwifery Order or rules made under it (Article 23 applies). No person may be a screener if she is:

  a member of a practice committee

  a legal, medical or registrant assessor, or

  employed by the Council.

Detailed rules relating to the appointment and function of screeners are laid down in Article 24.

Procedure

Information, in writing and received by the Registrar, that raises any question of the practitioner's fitness to practise being seriously impaired by reason of her physical or mental condition shall be submitted to the professional screeners. Anyone wishing to lay information before the Registrar may make a statutory declaration:

1 If the professional screeners decide there is no reasonable evidence to support the allegations, they shall direct the Registrar to inform the complainant and, if they consider it necessary or desirable, the practitioner. The professional screeners may obtain the opinion of a selected medical examiner on the information and evidence that they have received.

2 If they feel that the matter should proceed further, they shall direct the Registrar to write to the practitioner by recorded delivery:

  + notifying her that information has been received that appears to raise a question as to whether her fitness to practise has become seriously impaired by reason of her physical or mental condition and indicating the symptomatic behaviour that gives rise to that question

+ inviting the practitioner to agree within 14 days to submit to examination at the Council's expense by two medical examiners to be chosen by the professional screeners and to agree that such examiners should furnish reports to the Registrar on the practitioner's fitness to practise

+ informing the practitioner that it is open to her to nominate other medical practitioners to examine her at her own expense and to report to the Registrar on the practitioner's fitness to practise

+ inviting the practitioner to submit to the Registrar any observations or other evidence that she may wish to offer as to her own fitness to practise.

If the two medical practitioners are not able to agree, a third can be appointed at the Council's expense.

The professional screeners can make their own enquiries before giving any of the above directions.

Action following reports received from the medical examiners

1 If the medical examiners are unanimously agreed that she is not fit to practise, then the Registrar shall refer the information, together with the medical examiners' reports, to the Health Committee. The solicitor may be directed to take all necessary steps for verifying the evidence to be submitted to the Health Committee and for obtaining any necessary documents and the attendance of witnesses.

2 If there is considered to be no sufficient evidence of illness, the practitioner and the complainant shall be informed.

Referral of case to professional screeners by Investigating Committee, president or Conduct and Competence Committee

The practitioner is invited:

1 to submit to examination by at least two medical examiners to be chosen by the professional screeners

2 to agree that such examiners should furnish to the Health Committee reports on the practitioner's fitness to practise and

3 the Registrar informs the practitioner that it is also open to her to nominate another medical practitioner at her own expense to examine her and report to the Health Committee.

If she refuses to submit to such an examination or nominate her own medical examiner, the professional screeners shall decide whether or not to refer the information received to the Health Committee, indicating the reason why no medical report is available.

Notice of referral

The procedure relating to the notice of a hearing is set down in Rule 11. The notice must be sent at least 28 days before the date of the hearing.

Health Committee

The Committee sits in private, unless the public interest of any third party outweighs the need to protect the privacy or confidentiality of the registrant. The procedure for the hearing is set down in Part 5 of the Rules.

The Committee can:

1 adjourn for further medical reports

2 find that the fitness to practise is not seriously impaired by reason of the practitioner's physical or mental condition

3 postpone judgment

4 find that the fitness to practise is seriously impaired by the practitioner's physical or mental condition (it can direct the Registrar to remove the practitioner from the Register and can specify a period or not). Following such a finding, the Health Committee can:
   (a) suspend registration for a specified period not to exceed one year
   (b) impose conditions of practice for a specified period not to exceed three years
   (c) issue a caution for a specified period between one and five years or
   (d) strike the person off the Register (if they have been continuously suspended or under Conditions of Practice for the previous two years).

In the event of a finding under point 2 above, the Committee must refer the matter back to the committee from which the case was referred or to the president (if she referred it) who shall refer it to the Conduct Committee.

Restoration to the Register

This is governed by Article 33: unless new evidence has come to light that enables a practice committee to review its order under Article 30(7), no application for restoration to the Register may be made:

+ before the end of the period of five years beginning with the date on which the order for striking off took effect or

+ in any period of 12 months in which an application for restoration to the Register has already been made by the person who had been struck off.

The Registrar shall refer the application for restoration to the committee that made the striking-off order or, where a previous application has been made, to the committee that last gave a decision on an application for restoration.

The Committee shall give the applicant an opportunity to appear before it and to argue her case in accordance with rules made by the Council.

The Committee may not grant an application for restoration unless it is satisfied that the applicant not only satisfies the educational requirements and that she is capable of safe and effective practice as a nurse or midwife and, having regard to the circumstances of the striking-off order, but also is a fit and proper person to practise the relevant profession. The Committee can, in granting the application for restoration, make it subject to the applicant satisfying such requirements as to additional education or training and experience as the Council has specified under its rules relating to return to work after an absence (Article 19(3)). When making an order for restoration to the Register, the Committee shall direct the Registrar to register the applicant in the relevant part, subject to payment of the prescribed fee and may also make a condition of practice order with respect to her.

The proceedings of the CCC and the Health Committee are subject to review by the High Court. For example, in *Slater* v. *United Kingdom Central Council for Nursing, Midwifery and Health Visitors*, *The Times*, 10 June 1987, the Queen's Bench Division quashed the decision of the PCC in removing Mr Stephen Slater's name from the Register of nurses and remitted the case to a freshly constituted Committee for a rehearing on the grounds that the practitioner's case had not been fully considered by the Committee and an injustice might therefore have been done. In a later case, *Hefferon* v. *Committee of the UKCC, Current Law*, May 1988, 221, the High Court quashed the decisions of the Committee on the grounds that there had been a breach of natural justice. With the establishment of the Council for the Regulation of Healthcare Professions, now known as the Council for Healthcare Regulatory Excellence (see below), it is now possible for a complainant to apply to the Council if they are aggrieved at a decision made by a health registration body, including the NMC.

Professional standards and codes of practice

The functions of the NMC set out in Box 11.2 include that of establishing and improving standards of training and professional practice and also providing, in such manner as it thinks fit, advice for nurses, midwives and health visitors on standards of professional conduct. In fulfilment of this duty, the NMC has issued a revised code of professional conduct and guidance on different aspects of professional practice. (At the time of writing consultation is taking place on a new code.) In addition the NMC is publishing a Library of Standards which will eventually replace its fact sheets, for example, *Standards to support learning and assessment in practice*,[10] as published by the NMC in 2006. The standards can all be found on the NMC website.[11]

Education and training

The statutory duty to establish and improve standards of training falls on the NMC. A team of professional officers works with members through specialist committees, including the Educational Policy Advisory Committee, the Midwifery Committee and a committee on research. The NMC published standards of proficiency for pre-registration midwifery education in March 2004.[12] Subsequently a consultation on the review of pre-registration midwifery education was held in spring 2006 and was followed by the publication of recommendations by the Midwifery Committee at its meeting in July 2006. The Nursing and Midwifery Council, the Health Professions Council and the Department of Health work in partnership with the NHS workforce development confederations (WDCs), higher education providers and other stakeholders to develop quality assurance arrangements for professional healthcare education. In its second joint statement the NMC and DH outlined the progress that has been made towards the development of a shared quality assurance framework and the planned outcomes associated with each element of the framework.[13] Five elements were identified as forming a quality assurance framework:

+ major review
+ ongoing quality monitoring
+ approval and re-approval processes
+ benchmarks and quality standards
+ evidence on which conclusions and judgements are based.

In 2006 the NMC announced a supplier to deliver a new Quality Assurance (QA) framework for nursing and midwifery education in England. HLSP, a UK and international professional services firm was to commence delivery of the new QA framework in time for the commencement of the new academic year in October 2006. The NMC stated that:

> *The new QA framework will support public protection through the application of professional standards. The NMC has developed the new QA framework in consultation with a range of stakeholders to provide a risk-based approach to monitoring the standards of delivery of NMC approved programmes. The level of monitoring activity will be targeted and proportionate to levels of risk. This could mean a reduced level of involvement with programme providers that are exceeding the standards required by the NMC.*[14]

Further information on the NMC Quality Assurance Framework for Nursing, Midwifery and Specialist Community Public Health Nursing is available on the NMC website.

Post-registration education and practice (PREP)

The UKCC set standards for the future of professional practice in 1994 which were known as PREP. These were subsequently revised by the NMC and the following are the current requirements for continuing professional development and practice. There are two separate PREP standards that affect registration:

+ The PREP continuing professional development (CPD) standard and
+ The PREP (practice) standard.

The PREP continuing professional development (CPD) standard

The PREP CPD standard requires registrants to:

+ Undertake at least 35 hours of learning activity relevant to their practice during the three years prior to their renewal of registration.
+ Maintain a personal professional profile of this learning activity.
+ Comply with any request from the NMC to audit compliance with these requirements.

The PREP (practice) standard

Registrants are required to have completed a minimum of 450 hours of practice during the three years prior to renewal of registration in each part of the register that they wish to renew.

+ Registrants wishing to renew ONE registration must have completed at least 450 hours of practice in their capacity as a nurse, or a midwife or a specialist community public health nurse.
+ Registrants wishing to renew TWO registrations, e.g. nursing AND midwifery or nursing AND specialist community public health nursing, must have completed at least 450 hours in each, making a total of 900 hours.
+ Registrants wishing to renew all THREE registrations must have completed at least 450 hours in each, making a total of 1,350 hours.

Those registrants who do not meet this standard must undertake an approved return to practice programme before they can renew their registration.

Registrants are required by law to renew their registration every three years by providing a signed 'notification of practice' form in which they declare that they have complied with the PREP standards. They must also pay the annual retention fee. Registration will be renewed only when the signed form and fee payment have been received and processed by the NMC. Since the NMC has moved to the annual payment of fees, registrants are required to pay a retention of registration fee at the end of the first and second years of the registration period.

The NMC has revised its guidance for employers on PREP.[15]

Midwives must also comply with PREP requirements as laid down in the new Midwives' Rules which were brought into force in 2004. In addition, in order to practise, midwives need to give notice of their intention to practise, in accordance with Rule 3 of the *Midwives' Rules and Standards*. This is done by submitting a completed annual 'intention to practise' form every year to their named supervisor of midwives. (See Chapter 14.)

Fitness to Practise Annual Report 2005–2006

During 2006/7, 1,624 new cases against nurses and midwives were alerted to the NMC, considerably higher than the previous year. Just under 50 per cent came from employers and just over 15 per cent from members of the public and 23 per cent from the police following convictions. For all cases reported after 1 August 2004 the new Fitness to Practise rules are used. During 2006/7 both sets of Rules were still used. Of the 144 hearings of the Conduct and Competence Committee using the new rules, 17 were cautioned, 6 given a Conditions of Practice order, 75 struck off, 13 no further action, 4 were given a suspension order and 29 cases were adjourned.

Of all the cases heard in 2006/7 (i.e under both old and new rules) 46 per cent occurred in the NHS. Over 19 per cent were concerned with dishonesty (which included theft, fraud, and false claim to registration, claiming sick pay fraudulently, falsification of records and dishonesty about previous employment and misappropriation of drugs); patient abuse (physical, sexual, verbal, inappropriate relationship) about 17 per cent; maladministration of drugs about 10 per cent; neglect of basic care about 10 per cent; failure to maintain adequate records almost 7.5 per cent; unsafe clinical practice almost 7.5 per cent; colleague abuse (physical, sexual, verbal, inappropriate relationship) over 4 per cent; failure to collaborate with colleagues over 4 per cent; failure to report incidents over 3 per cent; failure to act in an emergency over 3 per cent; pornography – adult over 2 per cent; violence (harassment, assault) almost 2 per cent; other (including absence without leave, motoring offences, drink and drugs related offences (other than maladministration), breach of confidentiality, bullying, manslaughter almost 9 per cent. Most cases involved more that one type of allegation.

The Health Committee met 20 times in 2006/7 and heard 43 cases of impairment to fitness practice due to ill health The outcome was 10 suspended, 2 removed, 5 conditions of practice order, 3 suspension order continued, 2 suspension terminated, 2 conditions of practice order continued, 8 case closed, 1 was withdrawn and 10 were adjourned. Almost 23 per cent of the allegations related to alcohol abuse, about 20 per cent to drug abuse, 6 per cent to depressive illness, over 37 per cent to other mental illness and over 14 per cent to physical illness.

The full Annual Report and the reports relating to the business plan, statistics and financial report can be downloaded from the NMC website.

Council for Healthcare Regulatory Excellence (CHRE)

Section 25 of the National Health Service Reform and Health Care Professions Act 2002 provided for the establishment of a body corporate known as the Council for the Regulation of Health Care Professionals (CRHCP). It subsequently changed its name to the Council for Healthcare Regulatory Excellence. Set up in the wake of the Kennedy Report into children's heart surgery at Bristol Royal Infirmary,[16] its remit covers nine regulatory bodies including the NMC. It is an independent body, which reports annually to Parliament. Its functions are set out under Section 25(2) of the Act as follows:

+ To promote the interests of patients and other members of the public in relation to the performance of their functions by the GMC, GDC, NMC, HPC and other health professional registration bodies and by their committees and officers.

+ To promote best practice in the performance of those functions.

+ To formulate principles relating to good professional self-regulation and to encourage regulatory bodies to conform to them.

+ To promote cooperation between regulatory bodies; and between them, or any of them, and other bodies performing corresponding functions.

It has 19 members – one representative from each of the 9 regulators and 10 public or lay members. It is accountable to Parliament and provides an annual report. Under Section 29 of the NHS Reform and Health Care Professions Act 2002, if the Council considers that a decision by one of the healthcare professions regulatory bodies under its jurisdiction (e.g. the NMC, GMC etc.) is unduly lenient, and it would be desirable for the protection of members of the public for the Council to take action, it can refer the case to the relevant court (i.e. High Court in England and Wales). The court then has the power to dismiss the appeal; allow the appeal and quash the relevant decision; substitute for the relevant decision any other decision which could have been made by the committee or person concerned; or remit the case to the committee or other person concerned to dispose of the case in accordance with the directions of the court. The referral must be within four weeks, beginning with the last date on which the practitioner concerned has the right to appeal against the decision. The High Court held on 29 March 2004 that the Council for the Regulation of Health Care Professionals had the right to refer cases to court even after an acquittal by the appropriate regulatory body. The GMC had challenged the CRHCP's right to refer the case of Dr Ruscillo to the court. This judgement, unless overturned on appeal, will apply to all those health registration bodies under the CRHCP, including the NMC.

In 2005/6 the CHRE considered 27 cases at case meetings of Council members and referred 10 cases to court. Of these 7 were from the GMC, 2 were from the GDC and 1 from the Health Professions Council. In a case where a GP was trapped by a journalist, posing as a patient wanting time off work, into providing a medical certificate even though she made it clear that she was not ill, the Fitness to Practise panel decided that the evidence of the journalist should be excluded as an abuse of process and no action should be taken against the GP. The CHRE appealed against that decision as unduly lenient. The High Court allowed the appeal, holding that the evidence obtained on the basis of entrapment should not have been excluded and the matter should be remitted to another hearing to determine the issue of serious professional misconduct.[17]

Reviews by the Department of Health and Chief Medical Officer led to the publication of a White Paper in February 2007 on the future of health professional regulation.[18] This envisages major changes for the CHRE including a smaller and more board-like Council with all members being appointed and the national regulators no longer nominating their presidents to the Council. In addition the CHRE will have a wider remit including the audit of the preliminary stages of the Fitness to Practice procedures of the regulators. The White Paper can be downloaded from the CHRE website.[19]

Public involvement

One of the main features of the new registration system was that public involvement should increase. In fulfilment of its statutory duties and in preparation for the new Council, the UKCC had issued in October 2000 a strategy for public involvement.[20] It developed an action plan identifying work to be completed by December 2000 and by September 2001 in ensuring that the public were fully involved. ('Public' is defined as patients, clients and their carers; organisations that support the interests of these groups; individuals with an interest in the delivery of healthcare and the registered practitioners, many professionals, employers, government and statutory organisations and professional and trade union organisations.) The strategy also identified the current public involvement in the work of the UKCC, including information leaflets, its website, press statements, exhibitions, conferences and seminars, UKCC membership of patient/voluntary groups and public sessions of the UKCC, public meetings, written public consultations, lay membership of the UKCC and regular meetings with consumer panel members for professional conduct. The NMC has continued to ensure good communications with the general public and its website is accessible not only to registered practitioners and health service employers, but also to the general public.

NHS Institute for Innovation and Improvement

The NHS Plan was published in July 2000[21] (see Chapter 5) and had the aim of increasing investment into the NHS and at the same time meeting the significant challenges of the NHS. One of these challenges was to ensure that those working within the NHS were competent to provide the necessary services. It was envisaged that health professions would increase in their flexibility, training and working practices and demarcations would be removed. In addition there would be a major expansion of the healthcare workforce. This demanded a huge human resource strategy. In October 2001 the Department of Health announced the publication of a prospectus for the NHS University.[22] It was to offer nationally recognised learning programmes for staff across the whole service. (This is estimated as more than 1.6 million people.) It was the intention that everyone in the NHS (from cleaners to consultants) would begin their career with the NHS University through induction courses and direct training. The NHSU would make training and development available for everyone at every level of the NHS, including those traditionally left out of workplace learning. A consultation paper, 'Learning for Everyone', was published in November 2002 to obtain feedback on how the NHSU should progress and develop.

In December 2003 the NHSU became a special health authority and published a draft strategic plan, which outlined its plans for 2004-2008.[23] The NHS University was dissolved on 31 July 2005 and its responsibilities for learning and skill development in the NHS taken over by the NHS Institute for Innovation and Improvement. Host organisations across the country are delivering the NHSU's programmes and services. Skills for Health is concerned with the development and use of integrated competency frameworks across healthcare (see below). Further information relating to the work of the NHS Institute for Innovation and Improvement, including its business plan for 2007/8, can be obtained from its website[24] and an information and advice helpline.[25]

National Workforce Competence Framework

Standards for those involved in specific specialities are being prepared to ensure that the workforce has the skills necessary in a particular care area. The first toolkit designed to assist staff was published in November 2003, when new guidelines were issued for coronary heart disease. The National Workforce Competence Framework for Coronary Health Disease sets out the core skills needed to deliver the best possible services for those with or at risk from coronary heart disease, concentrating on prevention, heart failure and rehabilitation.[26]

(The work of NHS Professionals is considered in Chapter 10.)

Conclusions

The new three-part Register opened in August 2004 and anyone can access the Register by logging on to the NMC website. A new NMC Council took office in July 2006, an induction programme has been completed and work is ongoing in developing an appraisal system for Council members. A review of the NMC Code of Professional Conduct: standards for conduct, performance and ethics began in January 2006 and following an extensive consultation exercise it is anticipated that the new Code should be in place in the spring of 2008. The NMC has developed a new UK-wide quality assurance framework for nursing and midwifery education and is in the course of reviewing Fitness to Practise at the point of registration. Essential 'skills clusters' for nursing are to become mandatory for pre-registration nursing programmes in September 2008. The CHRE identified the need to reduce the backlog of conduct and competence cases and the NMC is planning to reduce the waiting time to 6 months by 2010. Funding issues remain a challenge for the NMC, even with the increase in registration fees in 2007. Legislation implementing fundamental changes to the registration provisions of all healthcare professionals is awaited following the White Paper 'Trust, Assurance and Safety'.[27] The Health and Social Care Bill should be enacted in 2008.

Reflection questions

1 How would you define fitness to practise by a nurse? Would any of the following count as evidence of unfitness to practise by your definition?
   (a) a nurse has an illegitimate child
   (b) a nurse is convicted of shoplifting
   (c) a nurse is found guilty of a breach of the peace after being involved in an argument with a traffic warden
   (d) a nurse is fined for speeding
   (e) a nurse borrows money from a junior member of staff on her ward
   (f) a nurse is discovered to be drunk when off duty, but still in her uniform.

2 Since the decision as to whether there is misconduct or not and therefore whether there is impairment of fitness to practise depends on the detailed circumstances, what additional information would you need to answer question 1 and how would that information affect your answer?

Further exercises

1 The CCC sits in different parts of the country and is open to the public and members of the profession. Next time it meets in your vicinity, try to attend and write up the hearing from the point of view of the formality, the procedure followed, justice to the nurse defendant and justice to the general public.

2 In what ways does a hearing before the CCC differ from a hearing before a civil court? To what extent do you consider that the hearing and its procedure comply with Article 6 of the European Convention on Human Rights? (See Appendix A.)

3 What to you consider should be the time limit before a nurse who has been struck off can apply to be restored to the Register?

4 To what extent do you consider that the Council for Healthcare Regulatory Excellence (CHRE) influences and affects the professional status of the nurse or midwifery practitioner?

References

[1] The Nursing and Midwifery Council (Fitness to Practise) Rules, SI 2004 No. 1761

[2] J.M. Consulting Ltd, The Regulation of Nurses, Midwives and Health Visitors: report on a review of the Nurses, Midwives and Health Visitors Act 1997, J.M. Consulting Ltd, February 1999

[3] NHS Executive, Modernising Regulation: the new Nursing and Midwifery Council: a consultation document, DH, August 2000

[4] The Nursing and Midwifery Council (Fitness to Practise) Rules, SI 2004 No. 1761

[5] Nursing and Midwifery Order 2001, SI 2002 No. 253

[6] News item, Bogus nurse, *The Times*, 10 October 2003

[7] Nursing and Midwifery Order 2001, SI 2002 No. 253

[8] The Nursing and Midwifery Council (Fitness to Practise) Rules, SI 2004 No. 1761

[9] *Balamoody* v. *UKCC, The Independent*, 15 June 1998

[10] Nursing and Midwifery Council, Standards to support learning and assessment in practice, NMC, 2006

[11] http://www.nmc-uk/

[12] Nursing and Midwifery Council, Standards for proficiency for pre registration midwifery education, NMC, March 2004

[13] Department of Health and Nursing and Midwifery Council, Second Joint Statement: quality assurance of professional healthcare education (England), September 2003

[14] Nursing and Midwifery Council press release 42/2006, NMC announces new QA supplier

[15] Nursing and Midwifery Council, Employers and PREP, May 2006

[16] Bristol Royal Infirmary Inquiry (Kennedy Report), Learning from Bristol: the report of the public inquiry into children's heart surgery at the Bristol Royal Infirmary 1984–1995, Command Paper Cm 5207, July 2001; http://www.bristol-inquiry.org.uk/

[17] *Re Saluja (Reference of decision by General Medical Council in disciplinary proceedings) Council for the Regulation of Healthcare Professionals* v. *General Medical Council* [2006] EWHC 2784; [2007] 2 All ER 905

[18] White Paper, Trust, Assurance and Safety – The Regulations of Health Professionals in the 21st Century, 2007

[19] www.chre.org.uk

[20] UKCC, Strategy for Public Involvement, 2000

[21] Department of Health, The NHS Plan: a plan for investment, a plan for reform, Cm 4818-1, The Stationery Office, 2000; www.nhs.uk/nhsplan/contentspdf.htm

[22] Department of Health press release 2001/-480, Introducing the NHS University, 16 October 2001

[23] NHSU (Establishment and Constitution) Order 2003 SI 2003 No. 2772; NHSU Regulations 2003 SI 2003 No. 2773

[24] www.institute.nhs.uk/

[25] 08000 150 850

[26] Department of Health press release 2003/0435, November 2003

[27] White Paper, Trust, Assurance and Safety – The Regulations of Health Professionals in the 21st Century, 2007

Chapter 12
Health and safety and the nurse

This chapter discusses

+ Statutory provisions
+ Corporate manslaughter and corporate homicide
+ Common law duties: employer's duty and employee's duty
+ Remedies available to an injured employee
+ Special areas

Introduction

This chapter covers the basic principles of law relating to health and safety at work, taking examples from nursing practice. It covers both the statutes (Acts of Parliament and Regulations) and the common law (i.e. decided cases or judge-made law) that set out the legal requirements on health and safety. Statute law and common law work in parallel and cover similar duties (although statute law is more specific). The topics covered are shown above.

Statutory provisions

Health and Safety at Work Act 1974 (HASWA)

General principles

The Health and Safety at Work Act 1974 is enforced through the criminal courts by the Health and Safety Inspectorate, which has the power to prosecute for offences under the Act and under the regulations, also powers of inspection, and which can issue enforcement or prohibition notices.

The employer has two parallel duties – one under the civil law and enforced through the civil courts (see below), the other under the criminal law and enforced through the criminal courts. The Health and Safety at Work Act is an Act that is enforceable through the criminal courts and places on both employer and employee considerable duties in relation to health and safety. Some regulations made under the Health and Safety at Work Act 1974 (such as the manual handling regulations) can also be used as the basis for a claim for compensation in the civil courts. The Statute below sets out the general duties under Section 2 of the Act. The following Statute sets out the duties of the individual employee. A glance will show how comprehensive they are.

Statute | **Section 2 of the Health and Safety at Work Act 1974: Duty of employer**

General duties of employers to their employees

(1) It shall be the duty of every employer to ensure, so far as is reasonably practicable, the health, safety and welfare at work of all his employees.

(2) Without prejudice to the generality of an employer's duty under the preceding subsection, the matters to which that duty extends include in particular:

   (a) the provision and maintenance of plant and systems of work that are, so far as is reasonably practicable, safe and without risks to health;

   (b) arrangements for ensuring, so far as is reasonably practicable, safety and absence of risks to health in connection with the use, handling, storage and transport of articles and substances;

   (c) the provision of such information, instruction, training and supervision as is necessary to ensure, so far as is reasonably practicable, the health and safety at work of his employees;

   (d) so far as is reasonably practicable as regards any place of work under the employer's control, the maintenance of it in a condition that is safe and without risks to health and the provision and maintenance of means of access to and egress from it that are safe and without such risks;

   (e) the provision and maintenance of a working environment for his employees that is, so far as is reasonably practicable, safe, without risks to health, and adequate as regards facilities and arrangements for their welfare at work.

(3) Except in such cases as may be prescribed, it shall be the duty of every employer to prepare and as often as may be appropriate revise a written statement of his general policy with respect to the health and safety at work of his employees and the organisation and arrangements for the time being in force for carrying out that policy, and to bring the statement and any revision of it to the notice of all of his employees.

Statute continued

(4) Regulations made by the Secretary of State may provide for the appointment in pre-scribed cases by recognised trade unions (within the meaning of the regulations) of safety representatives from amongst the employees, and those representatives shall repres-ent the employees in consultations with the employers under subsection (6) below and shall have such other functions as may be prescribed.

(5) (Repealed.)

(6) It shall be the duty of every employer to consult any such representatives with a view to the making and maintenance of arrangements which will enable him and his em-ployees to co-operate effectively in promoting and developing measures to ensure the health and safety at work of the employees, and in checking the effectiveness of such measures.

(7) In such cases as may be prescribed it shall be the duty of every employer, if requested to do so by the safety representatives mentioned in subsections (4) and (5) above, to establish, in accordance with regulations made by the Secretary of State, a safety com-mittee having the function of keeping under review the measures taken to ensure the health and safety at work of his employees and such other functions as may be prescribed.

Statute | **Section 7 of the Health and Safety at Work Act 1974: Duty of employee**

(a) to take reasonable care for the health and safety of himself and of others who may be affected by his acts or omissions at work.

(b) as regards any duty or requirement imposed on his employer or other person by or under any of the relevant statutory provisions to co-operate with him in so far as is necessary to enable that duty or requirement to be performed or complied with.

Abolition of Crown immunity

Health authorities used to enjoy protection from the enforcement provisions of much legisla-tion on the grounds that, as Crown bodies, they were immune from prosecution. However, this immunity was removed by the National Health Service (Amendment) Act 1986 Sections 1 and 2 in respect of the food legislation and Health and Safety at Work Act 1974. Some immunities were, however, retained under Schedule 8 of the Act, including Employer's Li-ability (Compulsory Insurance) Act 1969 (see below).

Powers of the health and safety inspector and Healthcare Commission

Health and safety inspectors employed by the Health and Safety Executive have extensive powers to ensure that health and safety duties are implemented. These powers are set out in Section 20 of HASWA (see pages 279–80). The inspector is able to issue improvement or prohibition notices that order the recipient to make equipment or premises safe or to cease a particular activity until the danger is removed. He also has the power to prosecute the authority in the magistrates' or Crown Court for a breach of the duties or regulations or failure to comply with the notice. In October 2007 in a prosecution brought by the Health and Safety

Executive, a headmaster was fined £12,500 with legal costs of £7,500 following the death of a 3-year-old pupil who fell down unguarded steps. It was held there was inadequate supervision for the children at playtime.[1]

The Healthcare Commission also has powers under the Health and Social Care (Community Health and Standards) Act 2003 Section 53A (as added by the Health Act 2006 Section 16) to issue improvement notices in respect of hygiene failings (see Chapter 26).

Could an individual nurse be prosecuted?

Yes, under the Health and Safety at Work Act 1974 Section 7 (see page 278), which places a duty on all employees in respect of health and safety. First, a nurse who, for example, failed to follow the correct practice in disposing of pressurised cans as a result of which an incinerator blew up, injuring a porter, could be prosecuted for breach of her duty under Section 7 of the Act. Second, the nurse as manager will have responsibilities in advising on and implementing the NHS trust's duties under the Act and if she neglects these she could also be prosecuted personally. In Practical Dilemma 12.1 the ward sister and others responsible for failing to undertake a risk assessment and basic precautions could be prosecuted under Section 7 of the 1974 Act and the employer could be prosecuted for breach of its duties under Section 2 of the 1974 Act (see pages 277–8).

Practical Dilemma 12.1) Ward boiler

A ward kitchen has a water heater that is not fixed according to the regulations. The boiler is moved to a more convenient location. A lead from the boiler runs to a point a few feet away. A domestic trips over the lead, the boiler falls on her and she is severely scalded. The Health and Safety Inspectorate investigates and considers prosecuting the ward sister and others responsible.

It is also a criminal offence for any person to interfere with health and safety measures (see page 281).

General health and safety duty of employer to non-employees

Under Section 3 of the 1974 Act, the employer has a general duty of care to persons not in his employment. The employer has a duty to conduct his undertaking in such a way as to ensure, so far as is reasonably practicable, that persons not in his employment who may be affected thereby are not thereby exposed to risks to their health and safety. This duty would therefore cover patients, visitors and the general public.

Statute) **Section 20 of the Health and Safety at Work Act 1974**

An inspector may, for the purpose of carrying into effect any of the relevant statutory provisions within the field of responsibility of the enforcing authority which appointed him, exercise the powers set out in subsection (2) below.

Statute continued

(i) The powers of an inspector referred to in the preceding subsection are the following, namely:

(a) at any reasonable time (or, in a situation which in his opinion is or may be dangerous, at any time) to enter any premises which he has reason to believe it is necessary for him to enter for the purpose mentioned in subsection (1) above;

(b) to take with him a constable if he has reasonable cause to apprehend any serious obstruction in the execution of his duty;

(c) without prejudice to the preceding paragraph, on entering any premises by virtue of paragraph (a) above to take with him:

(i) any other person duly authorised by his (the inspector's) enforcing authority; and

(ii) any equipment or materials required for any purpose for which the power of entry is being exercised;

(d) to make such examination and investigation as may in any circumstances be necessary for the purpose mentioned in subsection (1) above;

(e) as regards any premises which he has power to enter to direct that those premises or any part of them, or anything therein, shall be left undisturbed (whether generally or in particular respects) for so long as is reasonably necessary for the purpose of any examination or investigation under paragraph (d) above;

(f) to take such measurements and photographs and make such recordings as he considers necessary for the purpose of any examination or investigation under paragraph (d) above;

(g) to take samples of any articles or substances found in any premises which he has power to enter, and of the atmosphere in or in the vicinity of any such premises;

(h) in the case of any article or substance found in any premises which he has power to enter, being an article or substance which appears to him to have caused or to be likely to cause danger to health or safety, to cause it to be dismantled or subjected to any process or test (but not so as to damage or destroy it unless this is in the circumstances necessary for the purpose mentioned in subsection (1) above);

(i) in the case of any such article or substance as is mentioned in the preceding paragraph, to take possession of it and detain it for so long as is necessary for all or any of the following purposes, namely:

(i) to examine it and do to it anything which he has power to do under that paragraph;

(ii) to ensure that it is not tampered with before his examination of it is completed;

(iii) to ensure that it is available for use as evidence in any proceedings for an offence under any of the relevant statutory provisions or any proceedings relating to a notice under Section 21 or 22;

(j) if he is conducting an examination or investigation under (d) to require any person ... to answer any questions as the inspector thinks fit and to sign a declaration of the truth of his answers ...

(k) to require production of, inspect and take copies of any entry in any books or documents ...

(l) to require any person to afford himself such facilities and assistance within that person's control or responsibilities as are necessary for him to exercise his powers;

(m) any other power which is necessary for the purpose of exercising any of the above powers.

> ### Statute — Section 8 of the Health and Safety at Work Act 1974
>
> No person shall intentionally or recklessly interfere with or misuse anything provided in the interest of health, safety or welfare in pursuance of any relevant statutory provisions.

The Court of Appeal has held[2] that, provided the employer has taken all reasonable care in laying down safe systems of work and ensuring that the employees had the necessary skill and instruction and were subject to proper supervision, with safe premises, plant and equipment, the employer was not guilty of an offence under Section 3 of the 1974 Act if the employee were negligent and caused harm to others.

Safety Representatives and Safety Committees Regulations 1977 (SRSC)

These regulations brought into force the requirement in HASWA 1974 that employers should permit the safety representative appointed by the recognised trade union to inspect the workplace, get information held by the employer relating to health, safety or welfare and have paid time off for training and carrying out their functions. Each employer is required to set up a health and safety committee to consider matters relating to health and safety.

Health and Safety (Consultation with Employees) Regulations 1996

These apply to those workplaces that are not covered by SRSC and require employers to consult with workers or their representatives on all matters relating to employees' health and safety.

Health and safety at work regulations

Regulations came into force on 1 January 1993 as a result of European Directives. These are shown in Box 12.1.

> ### Box 12.1 — Health and safety regulations that came into force on 1 January 1993
>
> 1 Management of Health and Safety at Work Regulations 1992 (updated 1999) (see below).
> 2 Provision and Use of Work Equipment Regulations 1992 (updated 1998).
> 3 Manual Handling Operations Regulations 1992 (as amended 2002) (see pages 312–17).
> 4 Workplace (Health, Safety and Welfare Regulations) 1992 (updated 1999).
> 5 Personal Protective Equipment at Work Regulations 1992 (updated 1999).
> 6 Health and Safety (Display Screen Equipment) Regulations 1992 (updated 1999).

The regulations shown in Box 12.1 are enforceable against all employers and employees (whether NHS or not). Codes of practice have been issued by the Health and Safety Commission. Failure to comply with the code is not in itself an offence, but can be used in evidence in criminal proceedings.

(For protection of the employee against dismissal in health and safety cases, see Chapter 10.)

The Environmental Protection Act 1990 creates duties in relation to waste management. Many of these have now been updated and reissued.

Management of Health and Safety at Work Regulations 1999

These regulations require each employer to undertake a suitable and sufficient assessment of the risks to the health and safety of his employees. A code of practice has been approved in conjunction with these regulations.[3] This code does not have legal force, but has special legal status.

If an employer is prosecuted for a breach of health or safety law and it is proved that he did not follow the relevant provisions of the code, he will need to show that he has complied with the law in some other way or a court will find him at fault.

The guidance

The guidance emphasises that risk assessment must be a systematic general examination of work activity with a recording of significant findings rather than a de facto activity.

The definition of risk includes both the likelihood that harm will occur and its severity. The aim of risk assessment is to guide the judgement of the employer or self-employed person, as to the measures they ought to take to fulfil their statutory obligations laid down under the Health and Safety at Work Act 1974 and its regulations.

Suitable and sufficient is defined in the guidance as:

+ able to identify the significant risks arising from or in connection with work

+ able to identify appropriate sources of information and examples of good practice

+ 'appropriate to the nature of the work and should identify the period of time for which it is likely to remain valid'.

Recording

The 'record should represent an effective statement of hazards and risks which then leads management to take the relevant actions to protect health and safety'. It should be in writing, unless in computerised form, and easily retrievable. It should include:

1 a record of the preventive and protective measures in place to control risks

2 further action required to reduce risk sufficiently

3 proof that a suitable and sufficient assessment has been made.

Principles that apply in risk assessment

The following principles apply in risk assessment:

1 If possible avoid the risk altogether.

2 Evaluate risks that cannot be avoided by carrying out a risk assessment.

3 Combat risks at source rather than by palliative measures.

4 Adapt work to the requirements of the individual.

5 Take advantage of technological and technical progress.

6 Implement risk prevention measures to form part of a coherent policy and approach. This will progressively reduce those risks that cannot be prevented or avoided altogether and will take account of the way work is organised, the working conditions, the environment and any relevant social factors.

7 Give priority to those measures that protect the whole workplace and all those who work there, and so give the greatest benefit.

8 Ensure that workers, whether employees or self-employed, need to understand what they must do.

9 The existence of a positive health and safety culture should exist within an organisation. This means that avoidance, prevention and reduction of risk at work must be accepted as part of the organisation's approach and attitude to all its activities. It should be recognised at all levels of the organisation, from junior to senior management.

Risk management and the nurse

For the most part, the nurse would share common health and safety hazards with other hospital, community or social services employees and thus models of risk assessment and management that applied to other health professionals would also apply to nursing. Thus hazards relating to the safety of equipment, cross-infection risks, safe working practices or to violence at work would all apply to nurses who should be involved in the system of the assessment of risk.

Each nurse should therefore be able to carry out a risk assessment of health and safety hazards in relation to colleagues, clients, carers and the general public. Manual handling and risk assessment is considered below on pages 312-17.

Reporting of Injuries, Diseases and Dangerous Occurrences Regulations 1995 (RIDDOR)

The regulations govern the reporting of injuries, diseases and dangerous occurrences. The 1985 regulations were replaced by new regulations that came into force on 1 April 1996.[4] There is now one set of regulations in place of the four sets under the 1985 regulations. The list of reportable diseases has been updated, as has the list of dangerous occurrences. It is legally possible for reports to be made by telephone to the Incident Contact Centre.[5] A pilot scheme was tested out in Scotland.[6]

Schedule 1 to the regulations lists the major injuries and Schedule 2 lists the dangerous occurrences that are reportable.

Regulation 7 of RIDDOR lays down the requirements in relation to record keeping of reportable events or diseases. These records must be kept for at least three years from the date on which they were made. The records must contain the details set out in Schedule 4 (see Box 12.2).

Box 12.2 **Contents of records kept under RIDDOR Schedule 4**

1 Date and time of the accident or dangerous occurrence.
2 Where accident suffered by a person at work: full name, occupation and nature of injury.
3 Where accident suffered by a person not at work: full name of person, status, nature of injury.
4 Place where the accident or dangerous occurrence happened.
5 Brief description of the circumstances in which the accident or dangerous occurrence happened.
6 Date on which the event was first reported to the enforcement authority.
7 Method by which the event was reported.

Schedule 4 also sets out the records required in the event of a reportable disease.

A new accident book (known as B1510) has been designed by the Department for Work and Pensions to take account of the Data Protection Act 1998 and the Human Rights Act 1998. Guidance on RIDDOR is provided by the Health and Safety Executive (HSE) and is available from its website.[7]

National Patient Safety Agency (NPSA)

The National Patient Safety Agency (NPSA) was established following a press release in June 2000[8] on the setting up of a national system for the NHS to learn from experience. A report, 'An Organisation with a Memory',[9,10] written by an expert group chaired by Professor Liam Donaldson, Chief Medical Officer, had recommended setting up a national reporting system. The Expert Committee was established in February 1999 with the brief to 'examine the extent to which the National Health Service and its constituent organisations have the capability to learn from untoward incidents and service failures so that similar occurrences are avoided in the future. To draw conclusions and make recommendations.'

The aim of the new NHS mandatory reporting system was to log all failures, mistakes, errors and near misses in healthcare and to be in place before 2001.

The recommendations of the report include:

1 the introduction of a mandatory reporting scheme for adverse healthcare events and 'near misses' based on sound, standardised reporting systems and clear definitions

2 the introduction of a single overall database for analysing and sharing lessons from incidents and near misses, as well as for litigation and complaints data that will identify common factors and consider specific action necessary to reduce risks to patients in the future

3 the encouragement of a reporting and questioning culture in the NHS that moves away from 'blame' and encourages a proper understanding of the underlying causes of failures

4 improving NHS investigations and inquiries and ensuring that their results are fed into the national database so the whole NHS can learn lessons.

Specific targets are set to reduce levels of litigation. The detailed proposals for a National Patient Safety Agency for running a mandatory national reporting system of all adverse incidents were published in April 2001.[11] The NPSA was created in July 2001 as a special health authority with the following functions:

+ collecting and analysing information on adverse events from local NHS organisations, NHS staff and patients and carers

+ assimilating other safety-related information from a variety of existing reporting systems and other sources in this country and abroad

+ learning lessons and ensuring that they are fed back into practice, service organisation and delivery

+ producing solutions to prevent harm where risks are identified

+ setting out national goals and establishing ways of tracking progress towards these goals.

The NPSA has identified ten key local requirements which include all individuals involved directly or indirectly in patient care being aware of what constitutes an adverse incident; that the incident is managed and reported to a designated person, or persons, in accordance with agreed arrangements and information is fast-tracked to relevant external stakeholders; the incidents are graded according to the actual impact on patients and on the organisation; there is an appropriate local investigation. The incidents which are graded as 'red' (i.e. where serious actual harm has resulted) should be reported to the NPSA within three working days of the day of the occurrence and should be subjected to a full root cause analysis. The local organisation must cooperate with the Department of Health in any necessary investigation. Lessons must be learnt from individual adverse patient incidents and the subsequent review and practice changed in order to improve the safety and quality of care. In 2003 the NPSA's remit was extended to primary care. In its annual report for 2006/7 the NPSA stated that in the year ending in March 2007 1,406,416 patient safety incidents had been reported. It had initiated a project to evaluate and identify ways to improve reporting and learning. Following a successful pilot, since May 2006 all reporting organisations had been able to access their incident data and compare their profile with similar NHS organisations.

The first patient safety alert of the NPSA was issued on 23 July 2002 and was about preventing accidental overdose with intravenous potassium.[12] The alert notice refers to the possible risks from treatment with concentrated potassium and the need for additional safety precautions in the way potassium solutions are stored and prepared in hospital. Details of all the NPSA's alerts are available on its website.[13] A recent alert issued in March 2007 is concerned with safe practice with epidural injections and infusions.[14] The remit of the NPSA was extended in 2005 to include safety aspects of hospital design, cleanliness, and food. It was also given the task of ensuring research is carried out safely through its responsibility for the National Research Ethics Service (NRES) (formerly the Central Office for Research Ethics Committees (COREC)). It is also responsible for the National Clinical Assessment Service (NCAS) which is concerned with the performance of individual doctors and dentists and has taken over from NICE (see Chapter 5) responsibility for the three confidential enquiries: into maternal death and child health; patient outcome and death; and suicide and homicide by persons with mental illness. In July 2007 the NPSA published a study which investigated the circumstances in a sample of deaths of patients admitted with acute illnesses. It stated that in 2005 1,804 serious incidents were reported as resulting in death and of these 576 were avoidable. It set out a series of recommendations including improvements in communication, training and the provision of appropriate equipment. The NPSA report came at the same time as new guidelines were issued by NICE on how health professionals should manage sudden declines in patients' health.

An open culture within the NHS

The NPSA has as one of its objectives to promote an open and fair culture in the NHS, encouraging all healthcare staff to report incidents without undue fear of personal reprimand. In furtherance of this aim it issued in September 2005 a safer practice notice advising NHS organisations to put in place local policies to improve communication with patients who are unintentionally harmed by their treatment.[15] The NPSA has also enabled patients to report incidents directly to it via its website through its National Reporting and Learning System. NPSA has set up direct web links with complaints organisations in England, Scotland and Wales for patients wishing to make a complaint or get advice. A patient safety incident is defined as 'any unintended or unexpected incident which could have or did lead to harm for one or more patients receiving NHS funded care'.

Protection of employees who report health and safety hazards

Additional protection for staff who report health and safety hazards has been given by the Trade Union Reform and Employment Rights Act 1993 against dismissal in health and safety cases and was consolidated in the Employment Rights Act 1996 (see Chapter 10). The Public Interest Disclosure Act 1998 is intended to strengthen protection given to employees who report health and safety hazards. This is considered in Chapter 4 under whistleblowing.

Occupiers' Liability Acts 1957 and 1984

General principles

If a nurse is injured as a result of the state of the premises, she may be able to bring an action against the occupier who has a duty under the Occupiers' Liability Act 1957 to ensure that the premises are safe. The statutory duty is set out below. The occupier's duty to trespassers comes under the Occupiers' Liability Act 1984, which is considered below.

Statute	Sections 2(1) and (2) of the Occupiers' Liability Act 1957

Section 2(1) An occupier of premises owes the same duty, the 'common duty of care', to all his visitors, except in so far as he is free to and does extend, restrict, modify or exclude his duty to any visitor or visitors by agreement or otherwise.

Section 2(2) The common duty of care is a duty to take such care as in all the circumstances of the case is reasonable to see that the visitor will be reasonably safe in using the premises for the purposes for which he is invited or permitted by the occupier to be there.

The duty under the Occupiers' Liability Act is owed to the visitor. This term 'visitor' includes the person who has express permission to be on the premises as well as the person who has implied permission to be there. Thus in the hospital context, the term 'visitors' will include employees, patients, friends and relatives visiting patients, contractors and suppliers and others who have a genuine interest in being there. If any of these persons were to be injured, for example, when plaster fell off the wall, they could claim compensation from the occupier.

Who is the occupier?

The occupier is the person who has control over the premises. This will usually be the owner of the premises, but not necessarily. There could be several occupiers, each having control over the premises and responsibilities for the safety of the building. For example, contractors might be working on hospital premises and both the NHS trust and the contractor could be regarded as occupiers for the purpose of the Act. A private house visited by a community nurse may be owner-occupied, in which case that person will be the occupier for the purposes of the Act. Alternatively, it could be under a tenancy agreement, in which case the landlord and the tenant will have different duties under this agreement regarding the upkeep and maintenance of the premises and could therefore be regarded as occupiers under the statutory provisions. Which occupier is liable for harm to a visitor will therefore depend on the cause of the injury.

Case 12.1	*Slade* v. *Battersea* (1955)

Slippery floor[16]

A visitor slipped on polish that had been put on the floor but not wiped off, which left the floor excessively slippery.

The visitor succeeded in obtaining compensation for the harm. The occupier had failed to take reasonable care for the safety of the visitor. (This was a case decided before the 1957 Act, but the result would be the same after 1957.) In a more recent case,[17] a woman sustained personal injuries when, late at night, she fell down a flight of stairs leading to a public lavatory for which the LA was responsible. The premises were locked and the stairway was unlit. She admitted that she had drunk a relatively small amount of alcohol. She sued the LA on the grounds that they were occupiers of the premises and owed a duty of care to her. She lost the case on the grounds that she had voluntarily accepted the risk of injury by using the stairs in the darkness (*volenti non fit injuria* - see Chapter 6, page 127) and without taking proper care for her own safety. Further, the evidence from the A&E department showed that she had consumed a greater amount of alcohol than she had admitted in evidence. Even if the court were wrong on the voluntary assumption of risk, she would be contributorily negligent to a high degree.

Statute | Section 2(4)(a) of the Occupiers' Liability Act 1957

Section 2(4)(a) In determining whether the occupier of premises has discharged the common duty of care to a visitor, regard is to be had to all these circumstances, so that (for example): where damage is caused to a visitor by a danger of which he had been warned by the occupier, the warning is not to be treated without more as absolving the occupier from liability, unless in all the circumstances it was enough to enable the visitor to be reasonably safe.

What is the effect of a warning notice?

Section 2(4)(a) of the Occupiers' Liability Act 1957 is set out above. The warning is not conclusive: if compliance with it is sufficient to prevent any harm to the visitor, then it will be effective as a defence in an action under the 1957 Act.

Practical Dilemma 12.2 | Warning

An NHS trust is undertaking major renovation work to a corridor and puts up a warning notice saying 'Danger'. As a nurse walks along, she is struck by a piece of plaster falling from the ceiling.

If there were other precautions that the NHS trust could reasonably have taken, e.g. a safety net cordoning off the work area, then the NHS trust would probably be seen to have been in breach of its duty of care to the visitor subject to the possibility of contributory negligence by her. If, contrariwise, the notice said, 'Corridor closed - diversion' and indicated a different route that was practicable, then the occupier would have satisfied the duty under the Act. If, of course, the nurse ignored the notice, continued along the dangerous corridor and was injured, then it is probable that there would be no breach of duty by the NHS trust, since the notice was in all the circumstances enough to enable the nurse to be reasonably safe.

Independent contractors

Where independent contractors are brought on to site, the usual occupier or owner of the premises will not normally be liable for their safety (see Statute, below).

Privatisation of cleaning and catering services

What is the effect of the privatisation of services on the occupier's liability? Privatisation may lead to some complications, since where services are contracted out, there is likely to be dual occupation of premises, i.e. by the NHS trust and by the private company. Thus in the case of a contract for cleaning services, if an injury is caused to a visitor by the conditions of the premises, e.g. an uneven surface or falling plaster and the NHS trust has retained responsibility for such conditions, then the NHS trust would be responsible for the visitor's injuries. If, by way of contrast, the injuries were caused by the carelessness of any of the contractor's employees, then the contractor would be responsible for compensating the person injured as a result of the negligence under the principles of vicarious liability previously discussed in Chapter 4. If, therefore, the employee of the cleaning firm has left the floor in a dangerous state and there are no warning notices and a nurse is injured as a consequence, she would sue the cleaning company because its employee had been negligent in the course of employment and had caused her foreseeable harm.

Statute	Section 2(4)(b) of the Occupiers' Liability Act 1957

Section 2(4)(b) When damage is caused to a visitor due to the faulty execution of any work of construction, maintenance or repair by an independent contractor employed by the occupier, the occupier is not to be treated without more as answerable for the danger, if in all the circumstances he had acted reasonably in entrusting the work to an independent contractor and had taken such steps (if any) as he reasonably ought in order to satisfy himself that the contractor was competent and that the work had been properly done.

Liability for children under the Occupiers' Liability Act 1957

It is expressly provided that all the circumstances must be taken into account in deciding whether the occupier is in breach of his duty of care under the Act (see Statute, below). The occupier can expect a lower standard of care from children and therefore additional precautions have to be taken where the presence of children can be foreseen.

Statute	Section 2(3) of the Occupiers' Liability Act 1957

Section 2(3) The circumstances relevant for the present purpose include the degree of care, and of want of care, which would ordinarily be looked for in such a visitor, so that (for example) in proper cases: an occupier must be prepared for children to be less careful than adults.

> ### Case 12.2   *Jolley* v. *Sutton LBC* (2000)
>
> **Playing about on a boat**[18]
>
> Sutton Borough Council were the owners and occupiers of the common parts of a block of council flats. A boat with trailer was brought on to the land and abandoned on a grass area where children played. The boat became derelict and rotten. The council put a notice on the boat that said: 'Do not touch this vehicle unless you are the owner.' Some boys planned to repair it in the hope that they could take it to Cornwall. They swivelled it round and lifted the bows on to the trailer so as to be able to get under the boat to repair the hull. They jacked the bows of the boat up. The boat fell on to the claimant, a boy of 14, as he lay underneath it attempting to repair and paint it. He sustained serious spinal injuries and became paraplegic.

The High Court judge awarded the claimant £633,770, taking into account contributory negligence of 25 per cent for the injuries he sustained. However, the Court of Appeal found in favour of the defendant since, although it was reasonably foreseeable that injuries could have occurred from playing on the boat, the injuries sustained were not reasonably foreseeable and therefore the defendants were not liable for them. The Council had not disputed that it was negligent, but argued that it was not liable because the accident was of a different kind from anything that it could have reasonably foreseen. The claimant appealed to the House of Lords, which upheld the appeal. The House of Lords held that ingenuity of children in finding unexpected ways of doing mischief to themselves and others should not be underestimated. Reasonable foreseeability was not a fixed point on the scale of probability. The Council was liable under the Occupiers' Liability Act 1957 and under Section 2(3) had to take into account the fact that children would be less careful than adults. The Council had admitted that it should have removed the boat and the risk that it should have taken into account was that children would meddle with the boat and injuries would thereby occur.

Clearly, following this judgment, liability depends on how the risk is framed.

Trespassers and Occupiers' Liability Act 1984

The Occupiers' Liability Act 1957 does not cover any duty towards trespassers. The courts recognised a limited duty of the occupier towards trespassers, particularly children, but subsequently statutory provision was made in the Occupiers' Liability Act 1984. Whether or not a duty is owed by the occupier to trespassers, in relation to risks on the premises, depends on the following factors (Section 1(3)):

+ if the occupier is aware of the danger or has reasonable grounds to believe that it exists
+ if the occupier knows or has reasonable grounds to believe that the other is in the vicinity of the danger concerned or that he may come into the vicinity of the danger (in either case, whether the other has lawful authority for being in that vicinity or not)
+ the risk is one against which, in all the circumstances of the case, he may reasonably be expected to offer the other some protection.

In applying these factors to decide if a duty is owed to a trespasser, it would be rare for a duty to be owed to an adult. There is, however, more likely to be a duty owed to a child trespasser. For example, on hospital premises, if a child is expressly told that he may not go through a particular door or into another section of the hospital and he disobeys those instructions, then he becomes a trespasser for the purposes of the Occupiers' Liability Acts. It is likely that a duty would then arise under the 1984 Act.

Nature of the duty owed to trespassers

Once it is held that a duty of care is owed to a trespasser, Section 1(4) of the 1984 Act defines the duty as shown in Box 12.3.

> ## Box 12.3 Duty of care to a trespasser under Section 1(4) 1984 Act
>
> 'The duty is to take such care as is reasonable in all the circumstances of the case to see that he does not suffer injury on the premises by reason of the danger concerned.'

The duty can be discharged by giving warnings, but in the case of children, these may have limited effect and depend on the age of the child.

The nurse and premises in the community

Where a nurse is visiting private homes, the occupier may be the owner of the house who is also in occupation or the occupier may be a tenant. If the nurse is injured on the premises, it will depend on how the injury occurred as to who would be liable: thus, if she is injured as the result of a frayed rug, the person in occupation, whether tenant or owner, would be liable; if she were injured as a result of a structural defect, then the owner or landlord would be liable depending on the nature of the tenancy agreement.

The occupier has the right to ask any visitor to leave the premises. Should the visitor fail to leave, then she becomes a trespasser and the occupier can use reasonable force to evict the trespasser. If, therefore, the nurse should be asked by a client or carer to leave, she should go. Should she be concerned for the well-being of the client, she should ensure that social services are notified so that appropriate action can be taken under the National Assistance Act 1948 or the Mental Health Act 1983. Where there is a clash between carer and client and the former asks her to leave and the latter for her to stay, the nurse has to decide on the basis of the specific circumstances: the rights of the client to occupation as compared with those of the carer and the specific needs of the client. Where she considers it prudent to leave the premises, she must discuss with her manager how best the client's needs can be met.

Consumer Protection Act 1987

Product liability

The Consumer Protection Act 1987 enables a claim to be brought where harm has occurred as a result of a defect in a product. It is a form of strict liability in that negligence by the defendant does not have to be proved. The Consumer Protection Act 1987 (Part 1), which came into force on 1 March 1988, gives a right of compensation against the producers and suppliers of products if a defect in the product has caused personal injury, death, loss or damage to property, without the requirement of showing that the defendant was at fault. This was introduced into this country following an EEC directive dated 25 July 1985 (No. 85/3741/EEC). The Act applies to the Crown. The NHS trust itself could be a defendant in a product liability action since it is a producer of many products; it could also be liable as a supplier.

A product is defined as meaning any goods or electricity and includes a product that is comprised in another product, whether by virtue of being a component part or raw material or otherwise.

Defect

The definition of defect is shown below. The defendant can rely on the fact that the state of scientific knowledge at the time was such that the defect could not have been discovered (i.e. 'the state of the art' defence or that the state of scientific and technical knowledge at the time the goods were supplied was not such that the producer of products of that kind might be expected to have discovered the defect).

Statute — **Sections 3 and 4 of the Consumer Protection Act 1987**

3. (1) Subject to the following provisions of this section, there is a defect in a product for the purposes of this part if the safety of the product is not such as persons generally are entitled to expect; and for those purposes 'safety', in relation to a product, shall include safety with respect to products comprised in that product and safety in the context of risks of damage to property, as well as in the context of risks of death or personal injury.

   (2) In determining for the purposes of subsection (1) above what persons generally are entitled to expect in relation to a product all the circumstances shall be taken into account, including:
   (a) the manner in which, and purposes for which, the product has been marketed, its get-up, the use of any mark in relation to the product and any instructions for, or warnings with respect to, doing or refraining from doing anything with or in relation to the product;
   (b) what might reasonably be expected to be done with or in relation to the product; and
   (c) the time when the product was supplied by its producer to another; and nothing in this section shall require a defect to be inferred from the fact alone that the safety of a product which is supplied after that time is greater than the safety of the product in question.

4. (1) In any civil proceedings by virtue of this part against any person ('the person proceeded against') in respect of a defect in a product it shall be a defence for him to show:
   (a) that the defect is attributable to compliance with any requirement imposed by or under any enactment or with any Community obligation; or
   (b) that the person proceeded against did not at any time supply the product to another; or
   (c) that the following conditions are satisfied, that is to say:
      (i) that the only supply of the product to another by the person proceeded against was otherwise than in the course of a business of that person's; and
      (ii) that Section 2(2) above does not apply to that person or applies to him by virtue only of things done otherwise than with a view to profit; or
   (d) that the defect did not exist in the product at the relevant time; or
   (e) that the state of scientific and technical knowledge at the relevant time was not such that a producer of products of the same description as the product in question might be expected to have discovered the defect if it had existed in his products while they were under his control; or

---

▶

> **Statute continued**
>
> **(f)** that the defect
>   **(i)** constituted a defect in a product ('the subsequent product') in which the product in question has been comprised; and
>   **(ii)** was wholly attributable to the design of the subsequent product or to compliance by the producer of the product in question with instructions given by the producer of the subsequent product.

How does product liability affect the nurse?

Practical Dilemma 12.3 Needle injury

A nurse is giving an injection to a patient when the needle snaps and she is injured.

Under the Consumer Protection Act 1987, the nurse would need to discover from the supplier of the needle in the NHS trust (probably the CSSD) the producer of that particular needle. The supplier has a duty under Section 2(3) to inform her of the name of the producer who will then be strictly liable to the nurse for causing her harm. If the CSSD is unable to provide her with that information, the CSSD could itself be liable to her. The nurse herself would have to show that there was a defect in the needle, i.e. that the safety was not such as persons generally are entitled to expect. This is defined in Section 3(2) as including the manner in which and purpose for which the product has been marketed, the instructions and warnings accompanying it and what might reasonably be expected to be done with or in relation to it at the time it was supplied (see Statute, above). In addition, the nurse has a remedy under the Employer's Liability (Defective Equipment) Act 1969 (see below). The nurse should also ensure that an adverse notice about the needles is made to the Medicines and Healthcare products Regulatory Agency (see page 295). A Needle Stick Injury Bill, which would have made it compulsory to report any such injuries, failed to become law in 2003.

Timing

There is a ten-year time limit from the date of the supply of the product. The individual plaintiff must bring the action within three years of suffering the harm or having knowledge of the relevant circumstances.

Naming the producer

What if the NHS trust department that supplied the goods cannot name the producer? The person who suffered the harm must ask the supplier to identify the producer or importer of the product in the EU and must make that request within a reasonable period after the damage has occurred and at a time when it is not reasonably practicable for the person making the request to identify those persons. If the health department supplying the goods fails to comply within a reasonable period after receiving the request, then the claimant is entitled to recover damages from the supplying department. All departments in an NHS trust that supply products to persons who suffer damage from them could thus become liable: the supplies department, pharmacy, cleaning, catering, CSSD, office equipment, works and buildings.

The implications of this are that department records must be sufficiently comprehensive and clear to provide the appropriate information to the person injured by the defect, in order that the claim can be made against the actual producer of the product rather than the supplier.

The nurse as supplier

Could the nurse ever be a supplier? In the course of her duty, a nurse certainly supplies many products to patients, other staff, visitors and contractors: drugs, food/drink, equipment, syringes, etc. Could she be a supplier for the purposes of this Act?

Practical Dilemma 12.4 Supplying defective products

The nurse gives a patient a high-protein food to take home with him, which is defective, e.g. it has glass in it, and the patient is injured.

In most similar circumstances, it will be clear to the person suffering harm who the producers or trademark user are and it will therefore be reasonably practicable for the person suffering harm to identify the potential defendant. In other cases, the nurse will have obtained the goods from another department in the hospital, which would become the supplier for the purposes of the Act.

Product liability (Consumer Protection Act 1987) and the Employer's Liability (Defective Equipment) Act 1969

The right of the employee to claim from the employer under the 1969 Act is unaffected by the provisions of the 1987 Act. Clearly, any person who has been injured by a defective product can use whichever remedy is likely to be most successful and in fact can bring an action using several different causes of action. The relationship between these two Acts is as follows:

1 The injured employee can obtain compensation from the employer under the 1969 Act only if there has been negligence by a third party.

2 The injured employee can obtain compensation from the employer as supplier only if he has not identified the producer under the 1987 Act.

3 The 1987 Act covers all persons suffering damage, i.e. patients, employees, visitors etc. The 1969 Act relates only to employees.

4 The 1987 Act covers damages in the form of personal injury, death, loss or damage to property; the 1969 Act covers only loss of life, impairment of a person's physical or mental condition and any disease, not loss or damage to property.

5 Fault need not be established under the 1987 Act – only a defect in the product. However, the defence of what is known at the time is available.

Defences

Certain defences are available under Section 4, which are shown in the Statute below.

> ## Statute — Defences under the Consumer Protection Act 1987 Section 4
>
> **a.** that the defect is attributable to compliance with any requirement imposed by or under any enactment or with any Community obligation; or
>
> **b.** that the person proceeded against did not at any time supply the product to another; or
>
> **c.** that the following conditions are satisfied, i.e.:
>   **i.** that the only supply of the product to another by the person proceeded against was otherwise than in the course of a business of that person's; and
>   **ii.** that Section 2(2) above does not apply to that person or applies to him by virtue only of things done otherwise than with a view to profit; or
>
> **d.** that the defect did not exist in the product at the relevant time; or
>
> **e.** that the state of scientific and technical knowledge at the relevant time was not such that a producer of products of the same description as the product in question might be expected to have discovered the defect if it had existed in his products while they were under his control; or
>
> **f.** that the defect:
>   **i.** constituted a defect in a product (the subsequent product) in which the product in question had been comprised; and
>   **ii.** was wholly attributable to the design of the subsequent product or to compliance by the producer of the product in question with instructions given by the producer of the subsequent product.

What damage must the claimant establish?

Compensation is payable for death, personal injury or any loss of or damage to any property (including land) (Section 5(1)). The loss or damage shall be regarded as having occurred at the earliest time at which a person with an interest in the property had knowledge of the material facts about the loss or damage (Section 5(5)). Knowledge is further defined in Section 5(6) and (7).

There have been few examples of actions being brought under the Consumer Protection Act 1987 in healthcare cases and only a handful of cases brought under it have been reported. One reported in March 1993[19] led to Simon Garratt being awarded £1,400 against the manufacturers of a pair of surgical scissors that broke during an operation on his knee, with the blade being left embedded. A second operation was required to remove it. Had he relied on the law of negligence to obtain compensation, he would have had to show that the manufacturers were in breach of the duty of care that they owed to him. Under the Consumer Protection Act 1987, he had to show the harm, the defect and the fact that it was produced by the defendant.

A report by the National Consumer Council[20] in November 1995 recommended that consumers should be assisted in using their rights under this Act.

In a recent case,[21] it was held that a claim brought under the Consumer Protection Act 1987 in respect of the infection by patients with hepatitis C contracted from blood and blood products used in blood transfusions could succeed. This decision may well lead to greater use of the Consumer Protection Act 1987 if personal injuries are caused, since negligence does not have to be established under the Act, only that there was a defect in the product that has caused the harm.

The General Product Safety Regulations 1994 require producers and distributors to take steps to ensure that the products they supply are safe, that they provide consumers with relevant information and warnings and that they keep themselves informed about risks. The Consumer Protection (Distance Selling) Regulations 2000 provide protection for the consumer where contracts are made on the Internet, through digital TV, by mail order, by phone or fax.

Medicines and Healthcare products Regulatory Agency (MHRA)

The Medicines and Healthcare products Regulatory Agency was established in April 2003 as an executive agency of the Department of Health and took over the functions formerly carried out by the Medical Devices Agency (MDA) and the Medicines Control Agency. It can be accessed via its website.[22] This section looks at its role in medical devices. Consideration of its role in medicines can be seen in Chapter 28.

Medical devices

The Medical Devices Agency (now superseded by the MHRA) was established to promote the safe and effective use of devices. In particular its role was to ensure that whenever a medical device is used, it is:

1 suitable for its intended purpose
2 properly understood by the professional user
3 maintained in a safe and reliable condition.

What is a medical device? Annex B to Safety Notice 9801 gives examples of medical devices.[23] It covers the following:

1 Equipment used in the diagnosis or treatment of disease, and the monitoring of patients: e.g. syringes and needles, dressings, catheters, beds, mattresses and covers, physiotherapy equipment.
2 Equipment used in life support, e.g. ventilators, defibrillators.
3 *In vitro* diagnostic medical devices and their accessories, e.g. blood gas analysers. (Regulations came into force in 2000 on *in vitro* diagnostic devices.)
4 Equipment used in the care of disabled people, e.g. orthotic and prosthetic appliances, wheelchairs and special support seating, patient hoists, walking aids, pressure care prevention equipment.
5 Aids to daily living, e.g. commodes, hearing aids, urine drainage systems, domiciliary oxygen therapy systems, incontinence pads, prescribable footwear.
6 Equipment used by ambulance services (but not the vehicles themselves), e.g. stretchers and trolleys, resuscitators.
7 Other examples of medical devices, including: condoms, contact lenses and care products, intrauterine devices.

Regulations[24] require that from 14 June 1998 medical devices placed on the market (made available for use or distribution even if no charge is made) must conform to 'the essential requirements' including safety required by law and bear a CE marking as a sign of that conformity. Although most of the obligations contained in the Regulations fall on manufacturers, purchasers who are positioned further down the supply chain may also be liable – for example, for supplying equipment which does not bear a CE marking or which carries a marking liable to mislead people.[25]

The CE marking is the requirement of the EC Directive on medical devices.[26] The manufacturer that can demonstrate conformity with the regulations is entitled to apply the CE marking to a medical device.

The essential requirements include the general principle that:

A device must not harm patients or users, and any risks must be outweighed by benefits. Design and construction must be inherently safe, and if there are residual risks, users must be informed about them. Devices must perform as claimed, and not fail due to the stresses of normal use. Transport and storage must not have adverse effects. Essential requirements also include prerequisites in relation to the design and construction, infection and microbial contamination, mechanical construction, measuring devices, exposure to radiation, built-in computer systems, electrical and electronic design, mechanical design, devices which deliver fluids to a patient, function of controls and indicators.

Exceptions to these regulations include the following:

1 *In vitro* diagnostic devices are covered by a separate directive.
2 Active implants (covered by the Active Implantable Medical Devices Regulations).[27]
3 Devices made especially for the individual patient ('custom made').
4 Devices undergoing clinical investigation.
5 Devices made by the organisation ('legal entity') using them.

In January 1998, the MDA issued a device bulletin[28] giving guidance to organisations on implementing the regulations. The bulletin covers the sections shown in Box 12.4.

Box 12.4   **Bulletin of the MDA January 1998**

Strategies for deploying, monitoring and controlling devices
Purchasing medical products
When a device is delivered
Prescription of devices
Record keeping
Maintenance and repair
Training
Community issues

The MHRA (formerly the MDA) has powers under the Consumer Protection Act 1987 to issue warnings or remove devices from the market.

Devices are divided into three classes according to possible hazards, Class 2 being further subdivided. Thus Class 1 has a low risk, e.g. a bandage; Class 2a has a medium risk, e.g. simple breast pump; Class 2b has a medium risk, e.g. ventilator; Class 3 has a high risk, e.g. intra-aortic balloon.

Any warning about equipment issued by the Medicines and Healthcare products Regulatory Agency should be acted on immediately. Notices from the Agency are sent to regional general managers, chief executives of HAs and NHS trusts, directors of social services, managers of independent healthcare units and rehabilitation service managers. Failure to ensure that these notices are obtained and acted on could be used as evidence of failure to provide a reasonable standard of care. Further guidance was issued on repair and maintenance of equipment in 2000.[29] It sets out good practice for the organisation responsible for carrying out repairs and maintenance. In February 2004 the MHRA issued a warning about equipment misuse. Doctors and nurses had carried out procedures with improvised equipment which had resulted in cases where two infants had died after a wooden tongue depressor was used as a splint, and led to an infection. In another case the wrong kind of cot sides were fitted to a bed, leading to the death of an elderly patient from asphyxiation.[30]

Adverse incident reporting procedures

In 1998, a safety notice[31] was issued requiring healthcare managers, healthcare and social care professionals and other users of medical devices to establish a system to encourage the prompt reporting of adverse incidents relating to medical devices to the MDA (now the MHRA). The procedures should be regularly reviewed, updated as necessary, and should ensure that adverse incident reports are submitted to MHRA in accordance with the notice.
    What is an adverse incident? The safety notice defines this as:

[A]n event which gives rise to, or has the potential to produce, unexpected or unwanted effects involving the safety of patients, users or other persons.

Such an event may be caused by shortcomings in:

[T]he device itself, instructions for use, servicing and maintenance, locally initiated modifications or adjustments, user practices including training, management procedures, the environment in which it is used or stored or incorrect prescription.

Where the incident has led to or could have led to the following:

Death; life-threatening illness or injury; deterioration in health; temporary or permanent impairment of a body function or damage to a body structure; the necessity for medical or surgical intervention to prevent permanent impairment of a body function or permanent damage to a body structure; unreliable test results leading to inappropriate diagnosis or therapy.

Minor faults or discrepancies should also be reported to the MHRA. The home site of the MHRA gives advice on reporting methods which can be online, or by email, post, fax or telephone.[32]

Liaison officer

The safety notice suggests that organisations should appoint a liaison officer who would have the necessary authority to:

1 ensure that procedures are in place for the reporting of adverse incidents involving medical devices to the MHRA

2 act as the point of receipt for MHRA publications

3 ensure dissemination within their own organisation of MHRA publications

4 act as the contact point between the MHRA and their organisation.

Single-use items

Where a supplier has labelled its product 'single use', then the official advice is that it should not be reprocessed and reused unless the reprocessor is able to ensure the integrity and safety in use of each reprocessed item and there is clear evidence of the effectiveness of the reprocessing operation.[33]

Medical devices and the community

The bulletin published in January 1998 gives specific guidance on equipment used in the community. It suggests that the delivery and collection of equipment procedures should include checks that:

1 the correct equipment has been delivered in good order

2 the end-user has received training or

3 the end-user has been told not to use the device until trained

4 the delivery and collection process does not risk cross-contamination.

The guidance emphasises that good device management is the same for hospitals and the community. It covers in particular: the delivery and commissioning of loan equipment; collection of equipment when no longer needed; checking and testing of returned equipment; adaptation of equipment; insurance; and device safety for medical and dental surgeries. Specific guidance on sterilisers, dental X-ray equipment and resuscitators is also provided. For the last, it suggests that the best practice is for the equipment to be checked daily, including the pressure in the oxygen cylinder and that the bag is working, any drugs are still in date, any sterile materials are in date and packaging is undamaged.

Regulations relating to medical devices were consolidated in 2002[34] and amended in 2003[35] to cover reclassification of breast implants. They are available from the Office of Public Sector Information website.[36]

Control of Substances Hazardous to Health 2002

The Control of Substances Hazardous to Health (COSHH) Regulations 1988 came into effect in 1989 and were replaced by amended regulations in 1996. New regulations came into force in November 2002[37] replacing the 1999 Regulations in order to comply with the EC Chemical Agents Directive, which set more detailed rules of compliance. The HSE has set up a COSHH website to provide guidance for employers[38] and has provided a brief guide to the Regulations.[39] This guide sets out the eight stages of a COSHH assessment which are shown in Box 12.5.

The regulations aim to control activities where exposure to substances could lead to disease or ill health, i.e. substances that are toxic, harmful, corrosive or irritant; the regulations also cover those that have delayed effects or are hazardous in conjunction with other substances. The employer must assess the risks and take appropriate action, e.g. providing protective clothing, information and training of staff. All health workers have responsibilities under the regulations relating to the Control of Substances Hazardous to Health. The nurse who uses different substances in her work should be specifically alert to the need to ensure that the regulations are implemented. New maximum exposure limits have been introduced. Further details of the regulations and guidance can be obtained from the HSC or from the COSHH website.

There must be clarity over who has the responsibility of carrying out the assessment. The guidance emphasises the importance of involving all employees in the assessment.

All potentially hazardous substances must be identified: these will include domestic materials such as bleach, toilet cleaner, window cleaner and polishes; office materials such

> ### Box 12.5 Stages in COSHH assessment
>
> 1 Work out what hazardous substances are used in your workplace and find out the risks from using these substances to people's health.
> 2 Decide what precautions are needed before starting work with hazardous substances.
> 3 Prevent people being exposed to hazardous substances, but where this is not reasonably practicable, control the exposure.
> 4 Make sure control measures are used and maintained properly and that safety procedures are followed.
> 5 If required, monitor exposure of employees to hazardous substances.
> 6 Carry out health surveillance where your assessment has shown that this is necessary or where COSHH makes specific requirements.
> 7 If required, prepare plans and procedures to deal with accidents, incidents and emergencies.
> 8 Make sure employees are properly informed, trained and supervised.

as correction fluids as well as the medicinal products in the treatment room and materials and substances used in nursing.

An assessment has to be made as to whether each substance could be inhaled, swallowed, absorbed or introduced through the skin or injected into the body (such as by needle).

The effects of each route of entry or contact and the potential harm must then be identified.

There must then be an identification of the persons who could be exposed and how.

Once this assessment is complete, decisions must be made on the necessary measures to be taken to comply with the regulations and who should undertake the different tasks. In certain cases, health surveillance is required if there is a reasonable likelihood that the disease or ill effect associated with exposure will occur in the workplace concerned. Nurses should be particularly vigilant about any substances used in their activities, including cleaning fluids, and ensure that a risk assessment is undertaken and its results implemented.

Managers should ensure that the employees are given information, instruction and training.

Records should show the results of the assessment, what action has been taken and by whom and regular monitoring and review of the situation.

Corporate manslaughter and corporate homicide

As a consequence of the Corporate Manslaughter and Corporate Homicide Act 2007 it is possible for an organisation to which the Act applies to be prosecuted in the case of a death under both Health and Safety legislation and the 2007 Act. The jury can be instructed to find the accused organisation guilty of both offences. An organisation can be found guilty of an offence under the 2007 Act only if the way in which its activities are managed or organised by its senior management is a substantial element in the breach of duty of care owed by the organisation. Senior management means the persons who play significant roles in (i) the making of decisions about how the whole or a substantial part of its activities are to be managed or organised, or (ii) the actual managing or organising of the whole or a substantial part of those activities (see page 31).

Common law duties: employer's duty

Direct duty of care for safety of the employee

Duty of the employer as an implied term of the contract of employment

As was seen in Chapter 10, some of the terms in the contract of employment are implied by the law. These include the obligation of the employer to safeguard the health and safety of the employee by employing competent staff, setting up a safe system of work and maintaining safe premises, equipment and plant. The employee must obey the reasonable instructions of the employer and take reasonable care in carrying out the work. Thus the employee may have a claim for breach of contract by the employer if her back has been injured as a result of failures on the employer's part in not providing the appropriate training or equipment. The employer's duty at common law is set out in Box 12.6.

Box 12.6 **Employer's direct duty of care**

At common law, the employer has an implied term in the contract of employment to look after the safety of the employee:

1 to ensure the premises, plant and equipment are safe
2 to provide competent staff
3 to establish a safe system of work.

The employer's duty at common law to take reasonable care to safeguard the employees against the reasonably foreseeable possibility of harm arising from work-related disorders is paralleled by the duties laid down in the Health and Safety at Work Act 1974 and under the regulations relating to Manual Handling, the Management of Health and Safety at Work, Display Screen Equipment and the other regulations discussed above. Where several employers are involved in causing harm to an employee the House of Lords ruled, in a case where employees alleged that asbestos had caused mesothelioma, that liability was several only, i.e. each defendant employer was only responsible for its own contribution to the claimant's injuries.[40] This led to the Compensation Act 2006 which states that liability in such circumstances is joint and several and the Act has retrospective effect.

Effect of failures by the employer

Failure by the employer to take reasonable care of the health, safety or welfare of the employee could result in the following actions by the employee:

1 Action for breach of contract of employment.
2 Action for negligence, where the employee has suffered harm. The employee could also use as evidence breach of specific health and safety regulations.
3 Application in the employment tribunal for constructive dismissal, if it can be shown that the employer is in fundamental breach of the contract of employment.

Examples of cases brought in relation to the employer's duty of care at common law are given in Cases 12.4 and 12.5, below, relating to stress and manual handling respectively.

There is an overlap between the direct duty of care of the employer for the safety of the employee and the duty of the employer as occupier under the Occupiers' Liability Act 1957 (see above). Thus in a case where a nurse is injured as a result of defects in the NHS trust's premises, she may have a cause of action under the Occupiers' Liability Act and also because of breach of the employer's common law duty to care for the employee.

Statute — **Employer's Liability (Compulsory Insurance) Act 1969**

Every employer carrying on any business in Great Britain shall insure against liability for bodily injury or disease sustained by his employees and arising out of and in the course of their employment.

'Business' includes a trade or profession and includes any activity carried out by a body of persons, whether corporate or unincorporate. There is a penalty for failure to insure.

Insurance by the employer

The Employer's Liability (Compulsory Insurance) Act 1969 (see Statute, above) obliges all non-Crown employers to be covered by an approved policy of insurance against liability for bodily injury or disease sustained by an employee and arising out of and in the course of employment. By Section 60 of the NHS and Community Care Act 1990, health authorities ceased to enjoy Crown immunity. However, Schedule 8 of the Act preserves immunity from this Act for health authorities and NHS trusts. The employers of a nurse working in the private sector or a practice nurse working for general practitioners are, however, bound by the Act.

Defective equipment

If an employee has been injured as the result of defective equipment, an additional remedy may be available under the Employer's Liability (Defective Equipment) Act 1969. This is set out below. The Act is binding on the Crown and enables the employee to obtain compensation from the employer if the injury has been caused by defective equipment supplied by the employer where a third party is to blame. Instead of the employee having the cost and hassle of obtaining compensation from the third party, that burden falls on the employer from whom the employee can obtain direct compensation.

Statute — **Employer's Liability (Defective Equipment) Act 1969**

Factors which must be present

1 Personal injury by employee in the course of employment.
2 As a consequence of a defect in equipment.
3 Equipment provided by his employer for purposes of his business.
4 Defect attributable wholly or partly to the fault of a third party (whether identified or not).

Action

1 Injury deemed to be also attributable to negligence on part of employer, i.e. employee can recover compensation from employer.
2 Contributory negligence by employee may be raised as a defence (either full or partial).
3 Employer can recover contribution from third party (in contract or negligence).

Applies to the Crown.

> **Practical Dilemma 12.5**   Faulty bed
>
> A nurse is injured when a recently supplied bed, which she is raising by the foot pedal, breaks and falls on to her leg. It is discovered that there was a defect in the bed mounting that should have been spotted by the manufacturers before it left the factory.

The nurse could claim compensation from the NHS trust under the provisions of the Employer's Liability (Defective Equipment) Act 1969. The costs, problems and time associated with suing the manufacturers would then fall on the shoulders of the NHS trust. She also has an additional remedy under the Consumer Protection Act 1987 (see above, pages 290-4).

Remedies available to an injured employee

The laws relating to health and safety are significant to nursing practice. The nurse herself may suffer from injuries at work and also she has a significant responsibility to protect the health and safety of others, including colleagues, patients and visitors. Back injuries are seen as almost an occupational hazard for nurses and midwives; publicity has recently been given to the number of staff who are injured by violence at work, including work in the community; the hazards that a nurse faces in administering carcinogenic substances such as cytotoxic drugs are only now being appreciated and precautions (such as protective clothing and masks) are being laid down. The nurse has always faced the problem of contamination from infectious diseases and the particular problems relating to AIDS and infectious diseases and the role of the Health Protection Agency are considered in Chapter 26. In this section, the remedies available to the nurse for injuries at work will be considered. The remedies can be seen in Figure 12.1. She may be able to sue several different defendants.

Injuries caused by another employee

Where a nurse has been injured as a result of the negligence of another employee, she can either sue the employee for compensation or she could bring an action against the NHS trust under the principles of vicarious liability.

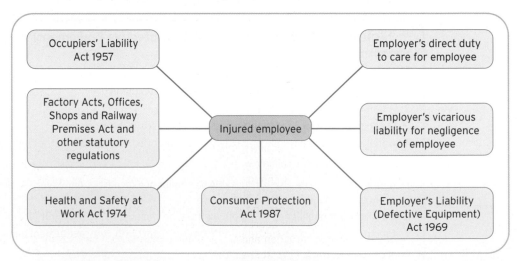

Figure 12.1 Remedies available to an injured employee

> ### Practical Dilemma 12.6   Wheelchair chaos
>
> Two nurses, Mary and Jean, are working together in a ward for elderly mentally infirm patients. They are moving a patient from a chair into a wheelchair. As they do so, the wheelchair moves and Mary, in her endeavour to save the patient, takes the full weight and falls to the floor. She suffers a severe injury to her back and shoulder. An investigation reveals that Jean was responsible for ensuring that the wheelchair brake was safely on and her carelessness was responsible for Mary's injuries.

Mary can take one of the following paths:

1 She could sue Jean personally, since Jean is probably in breach of the duty of care she owes to Mary to ensure that reasonable steps are taken to prevent foreseeable harm to Mary. However, such an action is likely to be pointless unless Jean is insured for such liability or has sufficient funds to pay compensation to Mary.

2 She could sue the NHS trust for its vicarious liability for harm caused by the negligence of an employee. Jean is an employee, has been negligent and is acting in the course of employment. Mary would still have to establish that Jean was personally negligent, but this action has the advantage over suing Jean personally since the NHS trust should have the funds to pay compensation.

3 In addition, Mary could sue the NHS trust for breach of its duty of care to look after her safety as an employee. In this action, Mary would have to establish that the NHS trust itself was at fault, e.g. if it had failed to provide Jean with adequate training in carrying out such a manoeuvre (see below).

In all three actions it will, of course, be a defence, complete or partial, that Mary was herself contributorily negligent (see Chapter 6).

Liability of the employer for work outside the premises

In the following case, a health authority was held liable for failing to give adequate instruction to a young resident support worker.

> ### Case 12.3   *Fraser v. Winchester HA* (1999)
>
> **Employer's liability for failing to give adequate instructions**[41]
>
> A resident support worker at a home for mentally and physically disabled residents was sent on a week's camping holiday with a patient without supervision or assistance. She had no training or instruction in the use of camping equipment. She suffered burns to her face and hands when, needing to cook an evening meal for the patient, she changed a cylinder on a gas cooker at the entrance to the tent and near to a lit candle. There was an explosion and the tent caught fire. The Court of Appeal agreed with the High Court finding that she should have been given instruction and better equipment, but held her one-third to blame because she realised the risk in what she did.

Special areas

Violence

The National Audit Office in 2003 reported an increase in violence within the NHS against health service employees not just from strangers in the streets, but also from carers and clients. Figures produced by the Department of Health in 2003[42] show that there was an estimated 116,000 violent incidents in the NHS (excluding general medical services) with 16 incidents per 1,000 ambulance staff per month. The rules relating to the terms of service of general practitioners were changed to enable them to arrange for the removal from their list of any patient who threatens them with violence. Several assaults on staff have led to criminal prosecutions and inquiries. For example in 1983,[43] a voluntary patient at a mental hospital was charged with assault occasioning actual bodily harm to an occupational therapist employed at the hospital. An occupational therapist was killed by a mentally ill patient in the Edith Morgan Unit at Torbay and an inquiry was set up.[44] A health care assistant was attacked in the grounds of a Bristol hospital,[45] in spite of the fact that there were security guards and improved lighting and closed circuit television as a result of a review four and a half years before. A young mental health worker, Ashleigh Ewing, was stabbed to death by a patient who had been discharged from psychiatric hospital. The patient was found guilty of manslaughter on the ground of diminished responsibility and ordered to be detained indefinitely in a secure unit. The North East Strategic Health Authority is to set up an inquiry.[46] Of all hospital staff working for NHS trusts, midwives experience more harassment than any other professional group including doctors, nurses and healthcare assistants.[47] The Court of Appeal held in 2006 that the NHS trust had failed in its duty of care to six nursing staff who were assaulted by a patient in Rampton Hospital. The hospital had failed to carry out a risk assessment in accordance with the recommendations of the Tilt Report into Security in High Security Hospitals and as a consequence the staff were injured.[48]

Zero tolerance

In October 2000, the DH announced new guidelines to tackle violence against NHS staff who are most at risk.[49] The guidelines cover risk assessment, crime prevention, protection of NHS staff in the community, techniques for dealing with abusive and potentially violent situations, training, reporting of incidents, the criminal justice system and support for victims.

The Department of Health has declared a zero-tolerance policy on violence and assaults on staff in the NHS and set up a website[50] to provide information and advice. Guidance has been issued for managers in reducing violence to NHS staff. The RCN and NHS Executive have also published guidance on reducing the risks from violence and aggression in the community.[51] The Crime and Disorder Act 1998 establishes local crime and disorder reduction partnerships (CDRPs), led jointly by police and local authorities. They have a statutory responsibility to develop and implement a strategy to tackle crime and disorder in their area in consultation with health, education and the voluntary and private sectors. The 1998 Act is amended by the Police Reform Act 2002 to extend responsibility for implementing the strategy to the fire and police authorities and includes PCTs in the partnerships. In spite of the efforts, the National Audit Office[52] reported in March 2003 that reports of violence against NHS staff had risen by 13 per cent over two years, costing the service at least £69 million annually. It estimated that about 40 per cent of incidents were not being reported. In the light of this report, the Secretary of State for Health announced[53] that if the Department of Public Prosecutions failed to take action against those attacking health workers, the victims could call on a new legal protection unit within the Department of Health to support private legal action against the attackers. The NHS Security Management Service reported that there were 58,695 physical assaults on NHS staff in England in 2005-6.

Remedies following violence

If a nurse has suffered harm as a consequence of violence, the remedies shown in Box 12.7 are available to her.

Box 12.7   **Remedies following violence**

1   Sue the aggressor personally for trespass to the person. (There is little point if they have no assets or income to pay the damages awarded.)
2   Sue the employer if she can establish that there has been a breach of the employer's duty of care to her.
3   Obtain compensation from the criminal courts following a successful prosecution of the assailant.
4   Claim compensation from the Criminal Injuries Compensation Authority (see Chapter 2, page 35).
5   Could receive, if eligible, statutory sick pay, Whitley Council sickness pay and DSS benefits.

Practical Dilemma 12.7   **Injuries in the A&E department**

A patient with lacerations to the face and severe bruising is brought into the department by two friends. All three have been drinking heavily. Two nurses take the injured man into the treatment room and ask the others to stay in the waiting room or leave the hospital. They insist on following the patient and in the ensuing fracas a nurse is injured.

Suing the patient

Could the nurse sue the patient if she has been injured by an assault? Yes, the nurse would have a right of action against anyone who assaults her, but there are difficulties where the defendant is mentally disordered. The magistrates' courts have thrown out such cases as being inappropriate. If the defendant is prosecuted, then the magistrate or judge can make an order for compensation to be paid by the defendant to the injured person. If the nurse decides to bring civil proceedings for trespass to the person, the defendant may not have the resources to pay any compensation awarded by the civil courts. Alternatively (and probably preferably), the nurse could seek compensation from the Criminal Injuries Compensation Authority (see Chapter 2, page 35).

Suing the NHS trust or employer

The employer's duty extends to protecting the employee against reasonably foreseeable attacks from violent patients or even from violent visitors and trespassers. If the employer has failed in this duty, then the injured employee could sue the employer. (See Practical Dilemma 12.8.)

> ### Practical Dilemma 12.8   Mixed ward
>
> A psychiatric nurse is on an acute mixed ward. Complaints have been made that, although this is a mixed ward, there are insufficient numbers of male nurses and thus the female nurses are often dealing with male patients on their own. A known aggressive male patient, without any warning or provocation, suddenly produces a razor and cuts a nurse badly on the face.

To obtain compensation from the NHS trust, the nurse must establish that another employee has been negligent in the course of employment and therefore the NHS trust is vicariously liable or that the NHS trust was itself directly at fault. To establish this, she would need to show that inadequate precautions were taken for her safety: that the risk of harm was reasonably foreseeable; that there were reasonable precautions that the authority could have taken and failed to take, e.g. male staffing, training in the handling of violent patients, special facilities for dealing with known aggressive patients, a special wing, an alarm system, a safe system for control of dangerous items. The injured nurse would also have to show a causal connection between the injuries she suffered and these failures on the authority's part, i.e. if she would still have been injured even had these precautions been taken, then the NHS trust would not be liable.

In its defence, the NHS trust would have to establish either that such reasonable precautions had been provided – a dispute on the facts – or that even if such precautions had been taken, the injury would still have occurred. In addition, it might be able to show that the nurse failed to take reasonable care of her own safety, i.e. she was contributorily negligent. Some employers have argued that being injured by aggressive mentally disturbed patients is an occupational hazard for the nurse working with the mentally ill or handicapped and that there is a voluntary assumption of the risk of injury by the staff concerned (see Chapter 6). However, it is not thought that this would provide a successful defence for an employer who was clearly at fault in respect of reasonable precautions in protecting the nurse from harm.

Criminal prosecution

Any aggression should be reported to the police and the Crown Prosecution Service will decide whether a public prosecution should commence. If the defendant is convicted, the magistrates or judge could make an order that criminal compensation is paid to the victim. The Department of Health will assist a victim if a private prosecution is contemplated but this could involve considerable expense and a successful outcome is dubious. It was reported in October 1998[54] that North West Durham Health Care Trust is to meet the full legal costs and provide emotional and professional support for all healthcare staff who take court action against an assailant in cases where the Crown Prosecution Service (CPS) fails to pursue the offender. It might be questioned, however, why the CPS is failing to prosecute; if the reason is the unlikelihood of securing a conviction, it may be therefore that the healthcare professional would not succeed. There is evidence that public prosecutions for assault on NHS staff are increasing. In its response to the Healthcare Commission's NHS staff survey on violence and abuse against NHS staff by patients and relatives, the NHS Security Management Service stated that there had been a 1,600 per cent increase in the number of prosecutions brought against those who assaulted NHS staff.

If the assault has been notified to the police, the victim would be able to obtain compensation from the Criminal Injuries Compensation Authority, which is considered in Chapter 2.

Self-defence

Can the nurse defend herself if attacked by a patient, visitor, trespasser or employee?

Every citizen has the right of self-defence. In the above example, therefore, the nurse could use reasonable means to defend herself against an aggressor. What is meant by reasonable?

Practical Dilemma 12.9   **Reasonable means**

A nurse is faced by a patient who is approaching her with a knife. He is a 6 feet tall, stockily built man of 35 years. There are no other staff or competent patients in the room and there is no call system available. As he comes forward, she picks up a chair and hits him over the head with it. He is severely concussed and requires stitches. Could she successfully defend an action for assault brought by the patient? Has she acted reasonably in defending herself?

Reasonableness means, first, that the force used should be no more than is necessary to accomplish the object for which it is allowed (so retaliation, revenge and punishment are not permitted) and, second, the reaction must be in proportion to the harm that is threatened. Thus, all the circumstances must be taken into account: the contrast between the strength, size and expertise of the assailant and the defendant and the type of harm with which the person is being threatened. Obviously, the greater the severity of the threatened danger, the more reasonable it is to take tougher measures. In assessing the reasonableness of the defence, account is taken of the fact that the defendant may have only a brief period to make up his mind what to do. Turning back to Practical Dilemma 12.9, if the nurse in question is tiny with no training in self-defence, the odds do seem to be stacked against her and may justify her use of the chair. All the circumstances must be taken into account, including the possibility of her retreating from the assault. Should the nurse be prosecuted and a trial take place in the Crown Court, it is for the jury to decide if the measures used in self-defence were reasonable in all the circumstances. Violence and the community health worker is discussed in Chapter 23.

Action by nurse and risk assessment

Monitoring of potentially violent situations is essential and the nurse should play her full part to bring any concerns to the attention of the management and ensure that action is taken. Steve McHale,[55] an aggression management coordinator, emphasises that nurses themselves must develop the skills to defuse rather than build up aggression. He states that: 'The main causes of aggression against nurses are the patient's loss of control or autonomy over a situation, a feeling of depersonalisation and a lack of communication.' If a nurse is involved in violence or witnesses a violent incident, she should make sure that a report and statement are completed.

The employer has a duty to take reasonable care of the nurse in relation to reasonably foreseeable violence. A risk assessment would therefore be required of this possibility and as a result any reasonable means to protect the employee should be adopted:

1   *Is it possible to remove the risk altogether*? If the answer to this is 'yes' but, for example, only by stopping all home visits by nurses, this would not be reasonably practicable.

2   *What preventive action or protective measures can be taken*? The answer to this might include the provision of two-way radios, personal alarms or, in very dangerous areas or on

visits to clients who present a threat, nurses going in pairs or accompanied by another person. In the institutional setting, protective measures may include more staffing, higher levels of supervision of difficult to manage patients and special security measures.

3 *Review the situation to ascertain if the nature of the risk has changed* (e.g. is the district more violent than it was formerly assessed to be? Has the nature and condition of patients in a hospital ward deteriorated?) and assess the extent of the success of the measures taken to prevent harm to nurses. Are any further measures necessary?

This type of analysis will relate not only to the nurses, but also could be part of a wider assessment of all health professionals into which the nurse could have an input.

Practical Dilemma 12.10 **Fear of violence**

A nurse visited a patient in his home following a stroke. She felt threatened by his attitude, but found difficulty in defining exactly the reason for her fears. Should she record her concerns?

This is a situation with which many nurses could identify. There is almost an intuitive feeling of fear. However, the nurse would have a duty to ensure that her colleagues were warned of potential dangers and she might therefore record in her notes that it might be advisable for a second person to accompany the nurse for the next house call. The duty of confidentiality owed to the patient (see Chapter 8) would be subject to an exception in the public interest where a nurse needed to warn colleagues about a fear of violence from a particular patient. Reference should be made to the guidance prepared by the Health and Safety Commission.[56] This gives practical advice for reducing the risk of violence in a variety of settings and emphasises the importance of commitment from the highest levels of management.

The NHS Security Management Service was established in April 2003 to take responsibility for all security management issues in the NHS, including violence to staff. It has published a strategy placing violence against staff as a top priority and has established mandatory reporting of incidents of violence. It is now incorporated into the NHS Counter Fraud and Security Management Service Division of the NHS Business Services Authority and has developed a programme of work from the Zero Tolerance Campaign.[57] In Wales the Welsh Assembly Government has launched the All Wales NHS Violence and Aggression Training Passport and Information Scheme and in Scotland the Scottish Executive is coordinating a Zero Tolerance Campaign. In September 2007 funding of £97 million was announced for further protection of NHS staff from violence: £29 million of this sum is to be used for safety alarms for lone workers and the remainder for training, additional local security management specialists, more prosecutions and a centralised reporting system to the NHS Security Management Service.[58] Reference can also be made to a practical guide on dealing with violence in the NHS by Paul Linsley.[59]

Domestic violence

It may sometimes come to the attention of nurses and particularly midwives that patients are possibly being subjected to violence at home. Clearly, if this involves a child, it is essential to ensure that child protection procedures are initiated and these are considered in Chapter 13. Where it is an adult who is the victim, the tendency in the past has been to respect the confidentiality of the victim and leave it to that person to report it to the police. However, attitudes are changing and domestic violence is no longer seen as a private matter between individuals but a criminal act where society has responsibilities.[60] In June 2003 the Home Office issued a consultation paper[61] on ways to prevent and follow up domestic violence. The paper looked at three elements: prevention, protection and justice and support for victims. The Domestic Violence, Crime and Victims Act 2004 followed and was aimed at facilitating prosecutions and convictions. It made breach of a non-molestation order a criminal offence, created a new offence of causing or allowing the death of a child or vulnerable adult and defined a common assault as an arrestable offence for the purposes of the Police and Criminal Evidence Act 1984, thereby increasing the powers of the police and citizens in relation to such an offence. Provisions under Part 3 of the Act relating to victims required a Victim's Code of Practice to be issued by the Secretary of State to cover the services to be provided to a victim of criminal conduct. Failure to comply with the Code, whilst not an offence in itself, could be used in evidence in civil and criminal proceedings.[62] See Chapter 19 for a discussion on elder abuse.

Stress

Concern with stress at work is now recognised as part of the employer's duty in taking reasonable care of the health and safety of the employee.

Case 12.4 *Walker* v. *Northumberland County Council* (1994)

Stress at work[63]

A social worker obtained compensation when his employer failed to provide the necessary support in a stressful work situation when he returned to work following an earlier absence due to stress. The employer was not liable for the initial absence, but that put the employer on notice that the employee was vulnerable and its failure to provide the assistance he needed was a breach of its duty to provide reasonable care for his health and safety as required to do under the contract of employment.

In order to establish grounds for compensation for stress induced by work, an employee would have to show:

1 that she was under an unacceptable level of stress at work

2 that the employer was aware of this situation

3 that there was reasonable action that the employer could have taken to relieve this pressure

4 that the employer failed to take that action

5 that as a result the employee has suffered a serious mental condition.

Advice on handling stress is given from experience in a Bristol hospital. Paul Bennett and colleagues emphasise the importance of looking at the work environment and personal skills as part of any stress management strategy.[64]

There are reports of more payments for compensation for stress across a wide range of employment. For example, in August 2000, it was reported that a bank manager was paid £100,000 in an out-of-court settlement by Lloyds TSB after suffering intolerable stress at work.[65] Claims are likely to be less successful following recent decisions of the Court of Appeal.[66] The Court of Appeal has clarified the law relating to compensation for stress at work. Four appeals were heard together by the Court of Appeal. In each one the employer appealed against a finding of liability for an employee's psychiatric illness caused by stress at work. Two of the claimants were teachers in public sector comprehensive schools, the third an administrative assistant at a local authority training centre and the fourth a raw material operative in a factory.

In determining whether the employer was liable or not, the Court of Appeal held that the ordinary principles of employer's liability applied to an allegation of psychiatric illness caused by stress at work. The threshold question was whether the particular kind of harm – an injury to health (as distinct to occupational health) that was attributable to stress at work (as distinct from other factors) – to the employee was reasonably foreseeable. Foreseeability depended on what the employer knew or ought reasonably to have known about the individual employee. Because of the nature of mental disorder, it was harder to foresee than physical injury, but might be easier to foresee in a known individual than in the population at large. An employer was usually entitled to assume that the employee could withstand the normal pressures of his job unless he knew of some particular problem or vulnerability. The test was the same whatever the employment: there were no occupations that should be regarded as intrinsically dangerous to mental health.

The relevant factors identified by the Court of Appeal in determining the reasonable foreseeability of stress were:

+ nature and extent of the work done by the employee
+ signs from the employee of impending harm to his health.

The employer was entitled to take at face value what he was told by an employee; he did not have to make searching enquiries of the employee or seek to make further enquiries of the employee's medical advisers.

If there were indications of impending harm to health arising from stress at work and these indications were plain enough for any reasonable employer to realise that he should do something about it, the duty of the employer to take steps would be triggered. The employer could only be in breach of duty if he failed to take the steps which were reasonable in the circumstances, bearing in mind the magnitude of the risk of harm occurring, the gravity of the harm which might occur, the costs and practicability of preventing it and the justifications for running the risk. The factors to be taken into account in determining what was reasonable action by the employer included:

+ size and scope of the employer's operation, its resources, and the demands it faced
+ interests of other employees
+ need to treat other employees fairly (for example, in any redistribution of duties).

An employer could be reasonably expected to take steps which were likely to do some good, and the court was likely to need expert evidence on that.

An employer who offered a confidential advice service, with referral to appropriate counselling or treatment services, was unlikely to be found in breach of duty. If the only reasonable and effective step would have been to dismiss or demote the employee, the employer would not be in breach of duty in allowing a willing employee to continue in the job.

In all cases, therefore, it was necessary to identify the steps that the employer both could and should have taken before finding him in breach of his duty of care. The claimant had to show that the breach of duty had caused or materially contributed to the harm suffered. It was not enough to show that the occupational stress had caused the harm. Where the harm suffered had more than one cause, the employer should only pay for that proportion of the harm suffered that was attributable to his wrongdoing, unless the harm was truly indivisible. It was for the defendant to raise the question of apportionment. The assessment of damages would take account of any pre-existing disorder or vulnerability and of the chance that the claimant would have succumbed to a stress-related disorder in any event.

On the actual facts of the appeals before it, the Court of Appeal allowed the appeals by the employers in three cases and dismissed the appeal in the case of *Jones* v. *Sandwell Metropolitan Borough Council*.

Subsequently, the House of Lords (in a majority decision) allowed an appeal from one of the employees,[67] holding on the facts of the case that the school's senior management team should have taken the initiative in making sympathetic enquiries about Mr Barber, head of the maths department, when he returned to work in June 1996 and in making some reduction in his workload to ease his return. In addition, his condition should have been monitored and, had it not improved, some more drastic action would have had to be taken. In a subsequent case it was held that the mere fact that the employers had provided counselling services did not relieve them of the duty to take reasonable care of an employee who was being subjected to considerable stress because of overwork and a lack of clear management controls. The Court of Appeal dismissed the employer's appeal against the finding of a breach of the duty of care and the award of £134,000.[68]

A university head of department, who claimed that he was subject to deliberate harassment by the university and his psychiatric illness was stress induced, failed in his claim because the judge held that the evidence did not support the contention that he was the victim of organised and deliberate harassment and that the risk of injury was not foreseeable until May 1997, when his symptoms became evident and the university had not failed to take reasonable steps to address the situation. He lost his appeal to the Court of Appeal.[69]

A Court of Appeal decision[70] dismissed an employer's appeal against a finding that it had breached its duty of care to the employee. The Court of Appeal held that the judge had been right to find that the Post Office owed a duty of care to Young, given its knowledge that Young's psychiatric problems were work related. The Post Office's failure to fully implement the agreed measures for Young's return to work were sufficiently serious to amount to a breach of that duty. Young was known to the Post Office to be both vulnerable, which meant that extra care should have been taken of him, and conscientious, which meant that he was likely to try to carry out his work without complaint. No finding of contributory negligence was therefore appropriate.

A mother of two who miscarried while under stress after her employer refused her flexitime working won her case against the City of London Corporation, owner of the Barbican Centre. Her compensation, which is likely to exceed £100,000, is to be awarded in March 2008.[71]

There is evidence that more concern is being paid to stress at work by the Health and Safety Inspectorate, which issued its first enforcement notice for failure to protect staff from stress in August 2003.[72] Failure to observe the enforcement notice could lead to prosecution. The notice was issued against the West Dorset Hospitals NHS Trust, which was given six months to assess stress levels among its 1,100 staff and introduce a new programme to reduce it. Stress reduction is one of eight key targets set by the HSE which has set up a stress website[73] covering the reasons why stress must be tackled, management standards and good practice. It has also provided a guide on improving efficiency which shows how tackling stress at work can improve an organisation's efficiency. Guidance is also provided on managing stress by the RCN for employees[74] and employers.[75]

Manual handling and back injuries

Where a nurse has injured her back at work, she may have a claim against her employer for breach of the duty of care owed to her at common law or failure to implement the Manual Handling Regulations. In addition, the employer may be vicariously liable for harm caused by another employee. Alternatively, if her back has been injured as a result of a defect in a product (e.g. a hoist or bed), she may be able to bring a case against the supplier under the Consumer Protection Act 1987. This section will first consider the regulations relating to manual handling, the decided cases and then consider specific situations that cause concern to the nurse.

Case 12.5 *Boag* v. *Hounslow* (1994)

Back injury[76]

On 24 July 1994 a nurse was awarded £205,000 for a back injury. The circumstances were that in November 1988, she and a colleague were trying to lift an elderly woman from a commode to a chair, when the patient's legs gave way. Owing to the lack of space, Mrs Boag was forced to twist her back to place the woman in the chair. The health authority, which admitted liability, agreed the out-of-court settlement shortly before the case was due to be heard. She was forced to give up her job and is regularly confined to bed. She attended a pain relief clinic and would probably never work again. Her husband had had to take time off work to help with the two children.

Manual handling regulations

Regulations were introduced in 1992 as a result of an EC Directive and were amended in 2002.[77] The Royal College of Nursing and the National Back Pain Association in their 'Guide to the Handling of Patients'[78] point out that there are discrepancies between the EC Framework Directive[79] and the UK regulations and that the former imposes a higher duty on employers closer to that of 'practicality' rather than 'reasonable practicability'. The regulations were amended in 2002 to add another paragraph on determining the appropriate steps to reduce the risk of injury.[80] Guidance on manual handling is given by the Health and Safety Executive.[81] The guidelines are not themselves the law and the booklet advises that the guidelines set out in Appendix 1 'should not be regarded as precise recommendations. They should be applied with caution. Where doubt remains a more detailed assessment should be made.' A short guide is provided by the HSE which can be downloaded from its website.[82]

A working group set up by the Health and Safety Commission has produced a booklet on 'Guidance on Manual Handling of Loads in the Health Services'.[83] This document is described as 'an authoritative document, which will be used by health and safety inspectors in describing reliable and fully acceptable methods of achieving health and safety in the workplace'. Part of this health services-specific guidance material relates to staff working in the community. The Health and Safety Executive has developed a manual handling assessment chart tool which can be downloaded from its website.[84] The HSE has also published case studies on how simple action can be taken to prevent back injuries. For example, the provision of bed rails enabled the best use of a patient's arm strength when being washed in bed.[85] The RCN has also published guidance on manual handling in a variety of settings.[86]

Summary of manual handling regulations

The duty placed on the employer under the regulations can be summed up as follows:

1 If reasonably practicable, avoid the hazardous manual handling.

2 Make a suitable and sufficient assessment of any hazardous manual handling that cannot be reasonably avoided.

3 Reduce the risk of injury from this handling so far as is reasonably practicable.

4 Give general indications of risk and precise information on the weight of each load and the heaviest side of any load, where the centre of gravity is not positioned centrally.

5 Review the assessment if there are any changes in the circumstances.

It is in the interests of all nurses to ensure that the employer is reminded when a review becomes necessary under the above provisions.

The duty that is owed by the employer is owed not only to employees, but also to temporary staff such as agency or bank staff who are called in to assist. All such employees are entitled to be included in the risk assessment process, since, as has been seen, the assessment must take into account the individual characteristics of each employee. Nurses who are unusually small in height or not so strong as the average might require special provisions in relation to manual handling.

Provision and Use of Work Equipment Regulations 1998 (PUWER)

PUWER (as amended by 2002 regulations) replaces the earlier Provision and Use of Work Equipment Regulations 1992 and applies to all equipment, including lifting equipment, used at work. There is a new requirement to inspect work equipment where significant risk could result from incorrect installation or relocation, deterioration or as a result of exceptional circumstances and to record the results of those inspections (Reg. 6). PUWER places requirements on duty holders to provide suitable work equipment for the task (Reg. 4), information and instructions (Reg. 8), and training to people who use it (Reg. 9). It also requires measures to be taken concerning dangerous parts of machinery (Reg. 11), controls and control systems (Regs 14–18), stability (Reg. 20) and mobility (Regs 25–9). The House of Lords held that there had been a breach of Regs 4(1) and 20 of the 1998 PUWER Regulations when a ladder to a bunk in a production platform was not fixed and had not been replaced properly so that a worker fell when descending from the top bunk. The incident was a foreseeable situation.[87]

Lifting Operations and Lifting Equipment Regulations 1998 (LOLER)

These regulations came into force on 5 December 1998 and apply in all premises and work situations subject to the Health and Safety at Work Act 1974 and build on the requirements of the Provision and Use of Work Equipment Regulations 1998.

In its guidance on the application of the LOLER regulations, the Health and Safety Commission note that (Paragraph 47): 'As hoists are used to lift patients, e.g. from beds and baths, in hospitals and residential homes, are provided for use at work and are lifting equipment to which LOLER applies, the duty holder, e.g. the NHS trust running the hospital or the owner of the residential home, must satisfy their duties under LOLER.'

Enforcement of regulations on manual handling

What action can be taken if the employer ignores these regulations? The regulations are part of the health and safety provisions that form part of the criminal law. Infringement of the regulations can lead to prosecution by the Health and Safety Inspectorate. The Inspectorate has the power to issue enforcement or prohibition notices against any corporate body or individual.

Court decisions on manual handling

Carrying a microwave   The Court of Appeal found in favour of an employee who had injured his back while carrying a microwave weighing between 15 and 20 kg.[88] The Court of Appeal found that:

+ the employers had failed to assess the specific risk in relation to the particular task to be performed by the employee and was therefore in breach of the Manual Handling Regulations (Reg. 4(1)(b)(ii))

+ the employers had failed to take appropriate steps to reduce the risk by failing to give the training recognised as being necessary to increase awareness of the risk and reduce instinctive responses

+ it was reasonably foreseeable that an employee would twist while supporting a lead

+ failure to provide the appropriate training was therefore, on the balance of probabilities, a cause of the accident.

Carrying by ambulance crew   The microwave case contrasts with another decision of the Court of Appeal in another manual handling case[89] where the Court held that the employers were not in breach of the directive or regulations on manual handling. King, an ambulance technician, suffered serious injuries carrying an elderly patient down the stairway of his home. He and his colleague had taken the patient down the stairway, which was narrow and steep, in a carry chair. He had been injured when forced for a brief moment to bear the full weight of the chair. The judge found in favour of the ambulance technician, holding that the employers were in breach of Council Directive (90/269 Article 3(2)) and the Manual Handling Regulations and that the employers had acted negligently by discouraging employees in circumstances such as those in this particular case from calling the fire brigade to take patients from their homes.

Sussex Ambulance NHS Trust appealed against the finding. The Court of Appeal held that the NHS Trust was not liable either under the directive or under the Manual Handling Regulations. There was nothing to suggest that calling the fire brigade would have been appropriate in the case. The evidence showed that such an option was rarely used because it had to be carefully planned, took a long time and caused distress to the patient. There might be cases where calling the fire brigade would be appropriate, but that would depend on the seriousness of the problem, the urgency of the case and the actual or likely response of the patient or his/her carers and the fire brigade. King had failed to show that, given that possibility, more emphasis in training would have avoided his injuries. The ambulance service owed the same duty of care to its employees as did any other employer. However, the question of what was reasonable for it to do might have to be judged in the light of its duties to the public and the resources available to it when performing those duties. While the risks to King had not been negligible, the task that he had been carrying out was of considerable social utility.

Furthermore, Sussex Ambulance NHS Trust had limited resources so far as equipment was concerned. There was no evidence of any steps that the trust could have taken to prevent the risk and the only suggestion made was that it should have called on a third party to perform the task for it. Since calling the fire brigade was not appropriate or reasonably practicable for the purpose of the directive and the regulations, the Sussex Ambulance NHS Trust had not shown a lack of reasonable care. Accordingly, it had not acted negligently.

Newham General Hospital In contrast to the ambulance case, a nurse aged 36 years was awarded £420,000 in damages by the High Court for a crippling back injury caused by her lifting a patient at Newham General Hospital, East London.[90]

East Sussex case and human rights and manual handling In February 2003 the High Court gave judgment on a case, where the claimants raised the issue of their human rights not to be hoisted.[91] A and B were sisters born in 1976 and 1980 who suffered from profound physical and learning disabilities. They lived in the family home which had been specially adapted and equipped for them and were looked after on a full-time basis by their mother X and their stepfather Y. A dispute arose between the claimants and East Sussex County Council (ESCC), which provided community care services, over the extent to which moving and lifting should be done manually. ESCC's policy on manual handling did not permit care staff to lift A or B manually. The claimants, supported by the Disability Rights Commission, argued that ESCC's manual handling policies, as applied to A and B, were unlawful and unjustifiable, on the basis that they improperly failed to take into account the needs of the disabled people involved. Its policy was subsequently amended to make it clear that ESCC did not operate a blanket no lifting policy. The claimants argued that the application of the policy to the specific circumstances of A and B's care and the draft protocols prepared by the independent handling adviser were unlawful.

The judge considered the effect of Sections 2 and 3 of the Health and Safety at Work Act 1974, the Manual Handling Operations Regulations 1992 and the Management of Health and Safety at Work Regulations 1999; decided cases on manual handling and the implications of the European Convention for Human Rights and the Charter of Fundamental Rights of the European Union. He emphasised that one must guard against jumping too readily to the conclusion that manual handling is necessarily more dignified than the use of equipment. Hoisting is not inherently undignified, let alone inherently inhuman or degrading. He identified the principles that applied and stated that, ultimately, the employer must balance the impact of the assessment on both carer and the disabled person.

This balancing exercise is to be resolved in the context of Article 8 by enquiring of each claimant whether the interference with his right to be respected is such as to be 'necessary in a democratic society'. Once the balance has been struck, if it comes down in favour of manual handling, then the employer must make the appropriate assessment and take all appropriate steps to minimise the risks that exist. The assessment must be properly documented and lead to clear protocols which cover all situations, including foreseeable emergencies and, in the case of patients such as A and B, events such as episodes of spasm and distress that might arise. The judge accepted that protocols developed by the employer cannot be too prescriptive. He emphasised that it was for ESCC to formulate its manual handling policy and to make the appropriate assessment in relation to A and B. Neither of those is a matter for the court. The making and drafting of the kind of assessments called for in a case such as this is outside the competence and expertise of the court. What the court can and should do is to assist ESCC by identifying the relevant legal principles.

The outcome of the case was that ESCC was required to complete with the assistance of the independent manual handling adviser the appropriate assessments and protocols. If these were not acceptable to the claimants, they could challenge them by way of judicial review.

Wolstenholme case In a case in Milton Keynes where Lorraine Wolstenholme, a disabled woman of 50, had slept in a wheelchair for 17 months after nurses stopped lifting her in case they were injured, a High Court judge ordered that arrangements for moving her should be made by 19 December 2003.[92]

What remedies exist for compensation?

Section 47 of the Health and Safety at Work Act 1974 prevents breach of a duty under Sections 2–8 of the Act being used as the basis for a claim in the civil courts. Breach of the regulations can, however, be the basis of a civil claim for compensation, unless the regulations provide to the contrary. Even where what is alleged is a breach of the basic duties, a nurse who suffered harm as a result of the failure of the employer to take reasonable steps to safeguard her health and safety could sue in the civil courts on the basis of the employer's duty at common law (see page 300). The statutory duty to ensure the Act is implemented is paralleled by a duty at common law placed on the employer to take reasonable steps to ensure the employee's health and safety. Contracts of employment should state clearly the duty on the employer to take reasonable care of the employee's safety and also the employee's duty to cooperate with the employer in carrying out health and safety duties under the Act and at common law. It is, of course, in the long-term interest of the employer to prevent back injuries, thereby avoiding payment of substantial compensation to his injured employees and also reducing the incidence of sickness and absenteeism.

Training in risk management and manual handling

This is essential to ensure that staff have the understanding to carry out the assessments and to advise on lifting and the appropriate equipment. Regular monitoring should take place to ensure that the training is effective and the policies for review are in place. There is also a duty on the employer to ensure that staff who are not expected to be regularly involved in manual handling are aware of the risks of so doing. This was the decision in the case of *Colclough* v. *Staffordshire County Council*,[93] where a social worker obtained compensation following a back injury caused by moving a client to safety. The council was liable because it failed to provide any training on risk awareness of the dangers of that situation. The implication of this decision is that even staff who are not expected to be involved in manual handling as part of their work, must be trained in risk awareness to protect them, should they ever be in the situation where they could be endangered through manual handling.

Lifting and instructing others

Nurses may be asked to instruct others such as carers, clients or other health or social service employees in the carrying out of the regulations on manual handling. Before they instruct others, they should be sure that they receive the necessary additional training to undertake the task of instruction, since failure to instruct competently could in itself give rise to an action in negligence, should harm occur as a result of negligent instructions.

Failures to instruct by agencies

Sometimes nurses become aware that agency staff have not been instructed in manual handling techniques. It would be reasonable practice in this situation for the nurses to ensure that senior management or the agency were informed so that steps could be taken to provide formal training for agency staff.

Therapeutic handling

It is sometimes argued that therapeutic lifting, e.g. in orthopaedic wards, to facilitate early mobilisation does not come under the manual handling regulations. There are, however, no grounds for this assertion. The definition of manual handling is:

[A]ny transporting or supporting of a load (including the lifting, putting down, pushing, pulling, carrying or moving thereof) by hand or by bodily force.

This would, therefore, include therapeutic situations.

No lifting policy and therapeutic handling

The first requirement of any manual handling policy is to avoid any manual handling that could reasonably practically be avoided. Clearly, if this were to be implemented in the thera-peutic regime, patients would never get mobilised following strokes and orthopaedic and other trauma. The nurse should ensure that a risk assessment is carried out that takes into account both the needs of the patient to become mobile and also dangers that staff face in promoting this mobilisation.

Lifting extremely heavy persons

This is of considerable concern to nurses. An extremely heavy person is defined by Fazel[94] as 25 stone (130 kg) or over. In a case study of the problems encountered following an emergency admission, the author analyses the possible action that could be taken, including reviewing the equipment that is available. The implications for other services such as the fire brigade and funeral directors and a protocol for the safe handling of extremely heavy patients are supplied. The legal issues arising are considerable. Staff cannot cease to provide services for such persons, but the consequences in terms of costs and effort in minimising the risk of harm are considerable. (See the case of the ambulance officer, above.)

Sexual and other harassment and bullying

It is essential that nurses are sensitive to the dangers of sexual harassment and make every effort to avoid potentially difficult situations. On the one hand, they must be aware of the sex discrimination laws (see Chapter 10) and must ensure that they do not discriminate either directly or indirectly. On the other hand, they must ensure that they are chaperoned in any situation that could lead to accusations of harassment by the nurse or where the nurse is herself (or himself) at risk.

Protection from Harassment Act 1997

The Protection from Harassment Act 1997 can also provide some protection in the work-place, if an individual considers that they are subject to unreasonable unwanted attention.
The Act creates:

1 *a criminal offence of harassment* (Section 1), which is defined as a person pursuing a course of conduct that amounts to harassment of another and that he knows or ought to know what amounts to harassment of the other (the reasonable person test is applied)

2 *a civil wrong*, whereby a person who fears an actual or future breach of Section 1, may claim compensation including damages for anxiety and financial loss

3 the right to claim an injunction to restrain the defendant from pursuing any conduct that amounts to harassment

4 the right to apply for a warrant for the arrest of the defendant, if the injunction has not been obeyed

5 *an offence of putting people in fear of violence*, where a person causes by his conduct another person to fear on at least two occasions that violence will be used against him

6 *restraining orders* can be made by the court for the purpose of protecting the victim of the offence or any other person from further conduct amounting to harassment or to fear of violence.

Certain defences are permitted in the Act including that an individual is preventing or detecting crime.

Bullying at work

Research into bullying in an NHS community trust found that, of the 70 per cent of staff who responded to a questionnaire on bullying, 38 per cent reported being bullied in the previous year and 42 per cent reported witnessing the bullying of others. It was concluded that bullying was a serious problem.[95]

In a case in 1998, £100,000 was accepted in an out-of-court settlement by a teacher who alleged that he had been bullied by the head teacher and other staff, when he was teaching in a school in Pembrokeshire.[96] Dyfed County Council denied negligence. He suffered a minor breakdown in October 1996 and was returned to the same school, although he had asked for a transfer. He claimed that he was isolated, ignored and subjected to a series of practical jokes. He then suffered a second nervous breakdown. It was claimed that a support plan worked out for him by the council was not properly implemented. Another teacher was awarded £86,000 after being bullied, harassed and being subjected to unacceptable professional conduct.[97] The Barber decision (see under Stress, page 311) was followed in a case where a police officer sued the Chief Constable for his vicarious liability for the actions of policemen who bullied and victimised the claimant. Since it was foreseeable that he could suffer psychological injury from their actions he was awarded £18,000 general damages for the physical and mental injury he suffered.[98] Failure by an employer to take adequate steps to control bullying by a group of women of another female employee which led to a foreseeable risk of psychiatric injury led to a finding that he was vicariously liable for his employees' actions under the Protection from Harassment Act 1997 and also at common law. The employee was awarded £60,000 plus past and future loss and expenses.[99] A former police officer succeeded in a claim for personal injuries caused by the bullying by officers employed by the Chief Constable who was held vicariously liable. The injuries were foreseeable as a consequence of the treatment he received.[100]

The lessons for managers from these cases are obvious. Advice is given by Claire Walker on how to deal with bullying[101] and Jacqueline Grove gives some practical advice on how to recognise the signs of stress from bullying and provides a survival guide.[102] In August 2000 a teacher was paid £15,000 compensation for unfair dismissal after an education authority had ignored medical reports that the teacher was being bullied into a breakdown, and then dismissed him while on long-term sick leave. The teacher stated that he planned to seek civil compensation for personal injuries.[103] An RCN guide on harassment and bullying at work[104] emphasises that nurses should not tolerate harassment, but challenge it by reporting it and keeping records. A review on the literature on bullying at work from the Health and Safety Laboratory is available from the HSE website.[105] The aim of the project is to enable the HSE to develop guidance for organisations on primary interventions in relation to bullying.

Repetitive strain injury (RSI)

This condition is also known as occupational overuse syndrome (OOS). Nurses should be aware, both for themselves and their patients, of the legal implications of RSI.

Even though, in an early case, a judge was quoted out of context as declaring that repetitive strain injury has no place in medical books,[106] RSI has been recognised for the purpose of compensation in health and safety cases. A House of Lords decision, however, may make it more difficult to obtain compensation for RSI.

On 25 June 1998 the House of Lords[107] rejected claims that a secretary, who was sacked after she developed a form of repetitive strain injury, should be able to sue her employers. It overruled the Court of Appeal decision that Ann Pickford should be allowed to make a claim against Imperial Chemical Industries. The Court of Appeal had found that ICI was negligent in failing to warn her of the need to take breaks during her work using a word processor and gave her the right to take her case back to the High Court for an assessment of damages, which she estimated at £175,000. In a majority judgment (4 to 1), the House of Lords decided that ICI did not need to warn her about the dangers of repetitive strain injury because typing took up only a maximum 75 per cent of her workload. To impose a warning that might cause more harm than good would be undesirable, since it might be counterproductive. The House of Lords questioned whether she had proved that the pain was organic in origin. She had been sacked in 1990 after taking long periods off work because of pain in both hands. She claimed that the injury had been caused by the very large amount of typing at speed for long periods without breaks or rest periods. The House of Lords said that it could reasonably have been expected that a person of her intelligence and experience would take rest pauses without being told.

It also held that RSI as a medical term was unhelpful. It covered so many conditions that it was of no diagnostic value as a disease. PDA4 (Prescribed Disease A4) had, however, a recognised place in the Department of Health and Social Security's list for the purposes of industrial injury, meaning a cramp of the hand or forearm due to repetitive movements such as those used in any occupation involving prolonged periods of handwriting or typing. The House of Lords held that the Court of Appeal should not have overruled the findings of the High Court judge, since he had ample evidence before him to justify his decision that in the plaintiff's case the giving of warnings was unnecessary, even though typists in another department had been given warnings.

Smoking

The dangers of smoking both to the smoker and to those passive smokers in the vicinity have led to an increase in the number of workplaces and public areas where smoking is prohibited. The government has been pursuing a policy to encourage people to give up smoking and to support them. It initiated smoking cessation services in health action zones in 1999/2000 following the White Paper, 'Smoking Kills'.[108] There were three key targets: young people, adult smokers and pregnant women. The results of the first monitoring of these services were published in February 2000. In December 2001, the government launched a new campaign, 'Don't Give Up Giving Up Smoking', and encouraged potential quitters to ring the NHS Smoking Helpline (0800 169 0169). In 2000 the Health and Safety Commission published guidance to employers on smoking in the workplace.

From July 2007 smoking has been banned in public places, which include hospitals. The RCN publication 'Clearing the Air'[109] points out that smoking remains the single biggest avoidable cause of death in the UK and aims to increase nurses' knowledge of the impact of smoking on public health and support their role as providers of smoking cessation advice. The RCN guide was updated in November 2002.[110] In November 2000, the results of a joint *Nursing Times*/Department of Health and Royal College of Nursing survey showed that 90 per cent of nurses who smoke wished to quit. The joint initiative of these organisations, called 'No

Butts', aims to give nurses the practical information and support they need to give up. A self-help booklet has been issued by the RCN.[111] The Royal College of Midwives (RCM) joined forces with the government in December 2001 to support pregnant women who smoke but want to give up. As part of this campaign, the RCM published an action guide for its members aiming to help midwives raise the issue of smoking with expectant mothers in order to improve the health of both women and their future children.[112] The DH provided £3 million to fund the appointment of persons to coordinate antenatal and post-natal smoking cessation services. In March 2001 the DH announced that nicotine replacement therapy (NRT) would be made available on prescription, subject to consultation.[113]

In April 2002 the National Institute for Health and Clinical Excellence (NICE) published guidance on the effectiveness of aids to smoking cessation. It advised that bupropion (Zyban) and NRT are not only clinically effective but also are among the most cost-effective of all healthcare interventions for giving up smoking. NICE has estimated that the annual demand for NRT or Zyban in 2003 will be between 500,000 and 1.4 million prescriptions, costing the NHS between £20 million and £56 million. The suppliers of NRT have agreed to give the NHS a rebate on their products once sales have exceeded a certain level. The Secretary of State for Health stated that this money would be passed to primary care trusts for stop-smoking programmes. 'Improvement, Expansion, and Reform. The next three years' priorities and planning framework 2003–2006', which set out a three-year plan for tackling smoking in the health service, was published by the Department of Health in 2003 and is available from the DH website.

Anti-smoking legislation

The Tobaccos Advertising and Promotion Act 2002, banning press and billboard advertising of tobacco products in the UK, came into force on 14 February 2003 and provisions prohibiting sponsorship of sporting and other events by tobacco companies were being brought into force between July 2003 and July 2005. On 30 September 2003 new more forceful warnings in black and white have been compulsory on cigarette packets covering at least 30 per cent of the front of the packet and at least 40 per cent of the back. The warnings also include the NHS Helpline number (0800 169 0169).[114] Evidence that a ban on smoking in public places can improve health is seen from evidence of its effects in the US town of Helena.[115] Smoking in public places was banned for six months and researchers showed that in comparison with earlier figures, the ban led to a 60 per cent reduction in heart attacks. The ban was lifted after a legal challenge. The European Commission is considering legislation to ban smoking in all public places including restaurants, bars and cafés. From July 2007 smoking in public places throughout the United Kingdom has been illegal. A consultation was launched in February 2007 to obtain views on raising the minimum legal age to purchase tobacco, and this was increased to 18 years in October 2007. The Chief Medical Officer has produced a series of video podcasts on smoking during pregnancy – these are available on the Department of Health website.[116]

Conclusions

A risk management strategy is at the heart of any policy relating to health and safety, not just for employees, but also for the clients and general public. Regular monitoring of the implementation of a risk management policy should ensure that harm is avoided and that a quality service is maintained for the public. This should be accompanied by clear, comprehensive documentation. The Health and Safety Commission has continued to implement its strategy for workplace health and safety in Great Britain to 2010 and beyond. However, there is still much room for improvement within the NHS. In April 2003 the National Audit Office reported that while there have been real improvements in the management of health and safety risks to staff in NHS trusts progress overall is patchy.[117] The number of reported accidents is increasing and the gap between the best and worst performing NHS trusts widening. In its report the NAO made specific recommendations for the NHS to improve its strategic approach to health and safety. It is clear that in the light of the evidence there is no room for complacency and there is a strong imperative for the NHS to improve the health and safety of the working environment as well as the health, safety and welfare of the workforce. Infection control is considered in Chapter 26.

Reflection questions

1 The Health and Safety at Work Act 1974 is enforced through the criminal courts. The employer's duty to care for the safety of his employees exists at common law. What is meant by these two statements and what is the difference in the enforcement provisions of each?

2 Who is the occupier of premises owned by the NHS trust and used by a primary care trust and general practitioners?

3 All the circumstances must be taken into account in deciding whether the occupier is in breach of his common duty of care. What does this mean? Explain the statement in relation to an accident caused to an infant patient who slipped on a pool of water on the floor in the ward.

4 A nurse is injured while lifting a patient because the nurse assisting her suddenly let go and the injured nurse was left supporting the whole weight. What remedies, if any, does the injured nurse have and how could she claim compensation?

5 If a nurse is injured as the result of defective equipment, in what ways could she obtain compensation and what action should be taken?

6 What records should be kept in relation to any health and safety incident or in connection with claims under Part 1 of the Consumer Protection Act 1987?

Further exercises

1 Ask to see (if you have not already received one) a copy of your NHS trust's or employer's health and safety policy. How is this policy reflected in your working conditions?

References

[1] Russell Jenkins, Head fined over fall that led to boy's death, *The Times*, 29 September 2007, p. 24

[2] *R v. Nelson Group Services (Maintenance) Ltd*, The Times Law Report, 17 September 1998 CA

[3] Health and Safety Commission, Management of Health and Safety at Work, Approved Code of Practice and Guidance, HMSO, London, 2000

[4] Health and Safety Executive, A Guide to the Reporting of Injuries, Diseases and Dangerous Occurrences Regulations 1995, HSE Books, 1999

⁵ 0845 300 99 23. The HSE information line is 0845 345 0055

⁶ Enquiries can be made to Health and Safety Executive Information Centre, Sheffield; Tel. 0114 289 2345; Fax 0114 289 2333

⁷ www.hse.gov.uk/riddor/

⁸ Department of Health, National System for NHS to Learn from Experience 2000/349, 13 June 2000

⁹ Department of Health, An Organisation with a Memory: report of an expert group chaired by Professor Liam Donaldson, Chief Medical Officer, Department of Health

¹⁰ Copies are available from The Stationery Office, PO Box 29, Norwich NR3 1GN or from the Department of Health website http://www.dh.gov.uk

¹¹ Department of Health, Building a Safer NHS for Patients, DH, April 2001

¹² National Patient Safety Agency, Patient Safety Alert PSA 01, London, NPSA, 2002

¹³ www.npsa.nhs.uk

¹⁴ National Patient Safety Agency, Patient Safety Alert No. 21: Safer Practice with epidural injections and infusions, NPSA, March 2007

¹⁵ NPSA, Being open when patients are harmed, available on the NPSA website

¹⁶ *Slade* v. *Battersea HMC* [1955] 1 WLR 207

¹⁷ *Dobell* v. *Thanet DC*, 22 March 1999, *Current Law*, August 2000, No. 527

¹⁸ *Jolley* v. *Sutton London Borough Council*, The Times Law Report, 24 May 2000; [2000] 3 All ER 409

¹⁹ B. Dimond, Protecting the consumer, *Nursing Standard*, March 1993, 7(243), pp. 18-19

²⁰ National Consumer Council, Unsafe Products: how the Consumer Protection Act works for consumers, National Consumer Council, November 1995

²¹ *A and Others* v. *National Blood Authority and Another (sub nom Re Hepatitis C Litigation)*, The Times Law Report, 4 April 2001; [2001] 3 All ER 289

²² www.mhra.gov.uk/

²³ MDA SN 9801, Reporting Adverse Incidents Relating to Medical Devices, January 1998

²⁴ SI 1994 No. 3017, Medical Devices Regulations 1994 came into force 1 January 1995, mandatory from 14 June 1998. Directive 93/42/EEC

²⁵ Medical Devices Agency Bulletin, Medical Device and Equipment Management for Hospital and Community-based Organisations, MDA DB 9801, January 1998

²⁶ Directive 93/42/EEC 1993 concerning medical devices

²⁷ Directive 90/385/EEC came into force 1 January 1993 and is mandatory from 1 January 1995

²⁸ Medical Devices Agency Bulletin, Medical Device and Equipment Management for Hospital and Community-based Organisations, MDA DB 9801, January 1998

²⁹ MDA, Medical Devices and Equipment Management: guidance on repair and maintenance provision, MDA DB 2000(02)

³⁰ www.mhra.gov.uk/; *Nursing and Midwifery Council News*, 5 February 2004

³¹ MDA SN 9801, Reporting Adverse Incidents Relating to Medical Devices, January 1998

³² MHRA Device Bulletin DB2007(01), Reporting Adverse Incidents and Disseminating Medical Device Alerts, available from www.mhra.gov.uk

³³ MDA, The Reuse of Medical Devices Supplied for Single-Use Only, MDA, London, 1995

³⁴ Medical Devices Regulations, SI 2002 No. 618

³⁵ Medical Devices (Amendment) Regulations, SI 2003 No. 1697

³⁶ www.opsi.gov.uk

³⁷ Control of Substances Hazardous to Health (COSHH) Regulations 2002, SI 2002 No. 2677

³⁸ www.coshh-essentials.org.uk

³⁹ HSE, COSHH: A brief guide to the Regulations, INDG136, revised April 2005

40 *Barker* v. *Corus (UK) Plc* [2006] UKHL 20; [2006] 3 ALL ER 785

41 *Fraser* v. *Winchester Health Authority*, The Times Law Report, 12 July 1999 CA

42 Department of Health, Survey of Violence, Accidents and Harassment in the NHS, 15 September 2003; www.dh.gov.uk/public/survey-violence-nhs0203.htm

43 *R* v. *Lincolnshire (Kesteven) Justices, ex parte Connor* [1983] 1 All ER 901 QBD

44 L. Blom-Cooper, H. Hally and E. Murphy, *The Falling Shadow – One Patient's Mental Healthcare 1978-1993*, Duckworth, London, 1995 (report of an inquiry into the death of an occupational therapist at Edith Morgan Unit, Torbay, 1995)

45 Chris Mahoney, Scene of HCA attack was secure, *Nursing Times*, 10 February 2000, 96(6), p. 5

46 Andrew Norfolk, Freed patient stabbed health worker to death on home visit, *The Times*, 23 October 2007, p. 13

47 Nursing and Midwifery Council News, 9 January 2004

48 *Bucks and others* v. *Nottinghamshire NHS Trust* [2006] EWCA Civ 1576

49 Department of Health, Guidance on Tackling Violence, October 2000; NHS Response Line 0541 555455

50 www.nhs.uk/zerotolerance/

51 Royal College of Nursing and NHS Executive, Safer Working in the Community, Order No. 000920, RCN and NHS Executive, September 1998

52 National Audit Office, A Safer Place to Work: protecting NHS hospital and ambulance staff from violence and aggression, NAO, 2003; www.nao.gov.uk/publications/nao reports/02-3/0203527es.pdf

53 Sam Lister, Ministers to fund action on abusive patients, *The Times*, 15 April 2003

54 Alexandra Frean, Funds for nurses who prosecute violent patients, *The Times*, 1 October 1998

55 Steve McHale, From insult to injury, *Nursing Times*, 8 December 1999, 95(49), p. 30

56 Health and Safety Commission, Violence and Aggression to Staff in Health Services, HSE Books, 1997

57 www.cfsms.nhs.uk/. Free phone line 0800 028 40 60

58 Department of Health press release, 25 September 2007

59 P. Linsley, *Violence and Aggression in the Workplace: A Practical Guide for all Healthcare Staff*, Radcliffe Publishing, Oxford, 2006

60 B. Dimond, Domestic Violence and the Midwife: can you report it?, *British Journal of Midwifery*, August 2003, 11(8), pp. 557-61

61 Home Office, Safety and Justice: the government's proposals on domestic violence, Home Office, June 2003; http://www.domesticviolence.gov.uk

62 B. Dimond, Protecting victims of domestic violence, *British Journal of Midwifery*, February 2005, 13(2), p. 105

63 *Walker* v. *Northumberland County Council*, The Times Law Report, 24 November 1994 QBD

64 Paul Bennett, Lindsey Scott and Kit Harling, Stress busters, *Nursing Times*, 15/22/29 December 1999, 95(50), pp. 28-9

65 Elizabeth Judge, Banker wins £100,000 stress payout, *The Times*, 10 August 2000

66 *Hatton* v. *Sutherland; Barber* v. *Somerset County Council; Jones* v. *Sandwell Metropolitan Borough Council; Baker* v. *Baker Refractories Ltd*, The Times Law Report, 12 February 2002, [2002] EWCA 76, [2002] 2 All ER 1

67 *Barber* v. *Somerset County Council*, The Times Law Report, 5 April 2004 HL

68 *Daw* v. *Intel Corp (UK) Ltd* [2007] EWCA Civ 70; [2007] 2 All ER 126, (2007) 104(8) LSG 36

69 *Foumeny* v. *University of Leeds* [2003] EWCA Civ 557; [2003] ELR 443

70 *Young* v. *Post Office* [2002] EWCA Civ 661; (2002) IRLR 660

[71] Steve Bird, Work-stress mother who miscarried wins her case against Barbican bosses, *The Times*, 22 December 2007

[72] Simon de Bruxelles, Oliver Wright and Helen Rumbelow, Bosses will be fined for workers' stress, *The Times*, 5 August 2003

[73] www.hse.gov.uk/stress

[74] Royal College of Nursing, Managing your Stress, Order No. 001481, RCN, March 2001

[75] Royal College of Nursing, Working Well – a call to employers, Order No. 001595, RCN, March 2002

[76] *Boag* v. *Hounslow and Spelthorne Health Authority*, *The Times*, 25 July 1994

[77] Health and Safety (Miscellaneous Amendments) Regulations, SI 2002 No. 2174

[78] Royal College of Nursing and the National Back Pain Association, Guide to the Handling of Patients, NBPA with the RCN, 4th edition, 1997

[79] EC Directive 90/269/EEC on the minimum health and safety requirements for the manual handling of loads (fourth individual directive within the meaning of Article 16(1) of Directive 89/391/EEC)

[80] Health and Safety (Miscellaneous Amendments) Regulations 2002, SI 2002 No. 2174, paragraph 4

[81] Health and Safety Executive, Manual Handling Operations Regulations 1992 (as amended), Guidance on Regulations, L23 (third edition), HSE, 2004

[82] HSE, Getting to grips with manual handling: A short guide, INDC143, revised June 2006

[83] Health and Safety Commission, Guidance on Manual Handling of Loads in the Health Services, HMSO, London, 1992

[84] www.hse.gov.uk/mac

[85] HSE, Handling Home Care: Achieving safe, efficient and practical outcomes for care workers and clients, HSG225, HSE Books (no date)

[86] RCN, Code of Practice for Patient Handling, Order No. 804 reprinted October 2007; RCN, Safer Staff, Better Care: RCN manual handling training guidance and competencies, Order No. 001975, February 2003; RCN, Introducing a Safer Patient Handling Policy, Order No. 000603, revised March 1999; RCN, Changing Practice, Improving Health – an integrated back injury prevention programme for nursing and care homes, Order No. 001255, August 2001

[87] *Robb* v. *Salamis (M&I) Ltd* [2006] EWHL 56; [2007] 2 All ER 97

[88] *O'Neil* v. *DSG Retail Ltd*, *The Times*, 9 September 2002; [2002] EWCA 1139; [2003] ICR 222

[89] *King* v. *Sussex Ambulance NHS Trust* [2002] EWCA 953; [2002] ICR 1413

[90] News item, £420,000 award, *The Times*, 17 October 2002

[91] *R (on the application of A and B, X and Y)* v. *East Sussex County Council (The Disability Rights Commission: an interested party)* Case No. CO/4843/2001, 10 February 2003

[92] News item, *The Times*, 19 November 2003

[93] *Colclough* v. *Staffordshire County Council*, 30 June 1994, *Current Law*, 208, October 1994

[94] E. Fazel, Handling of extremely heavy patients, *National Back Exchange Journal*, April 1997, 9(2), pp. 13–16

[95] Lyn Quine, Workplace bullying in NHS community trust: staff questionnaire survey, *British Medical Journal*, January 1999, 318(25), pp. 228–32

[96] Victoria Fletcher, Teacher 'bullied by staff' wins £100,000, *The Times*, 17 July 1998

[97] Tony Hatpin, Teacher bullied by head awarded £86,000, *The Times*, 18 November 2003

[98] *Clark* v. *Chief Constable of Essex* [2006] EWHC 2290; (2006) 103(38) LSG 32

[99] *Green* v. *DB Group Services (UK) Ltd* [2006] EWHC 1898; [2006] IRLR 754

[100] *Clark* v. *Chief Constable of Essex* [2006] EWHC 2290

[101] Claire Walker, Bullied to death, *Nursing Times*, 4 May 2000, 96(18), pp. 26–8

[102] Jacqueline Grove, Survival and resistance, *Nursing Times*, 4 May 2000, 96(18), pp. 26-8

[103] Paul Wilkinson, Teacher wins payout over school clash, *The Times*, 9 August 2000

[104] RCN, Bullying and harassment at work: a good practice guide for RCN negotiators and healthcare managers, Order No. 000926, reprinted October 2002; RCN, Dealing with bullying and harassment - guide for RCN members, Order No. 001301, January 2001; RCN, Dealing with bullying and harassment - guide for nursing students, Order No. 001497, August 2002

[105] Johanna Beswick *et al.*, Bullying at work: a review of the literature, WPS/06/04, Health and Safety Laboratory, 2006

[106] *Mughal* v. *Reuters Ltd* [1993] IRLR 571

[107] *Pickford* v. *Imperial Chemical Industries Plc*, The Times Law Report, 30 June 1998 HL

[108] DH, Smoking Kills - a White Paper on tobacco, The Stationery Office, London, 1998

[109] RCN, 'Clearing the air': a nurses guide to smoking and tobacco control, Order No. 001159, RCN, October 1999

[110] RCN, Clearing the air 2 - guide for nurses, Order No. 001945, RCN, October 2007

[111] RCN, How to stop smoking, RCN, 2000

[112] RCM, Helping Women Stop Smoking: a guide for midwives, RCM, 2002

[113] Department of Health press release, Nicotine replacement therapy products to be available on prescription and general sale, DH

[114] Department of Health press release 2003/0362, 30 September 2003

[115] News item, Smoking ban 'boosts health', *The Times*, 2 April 2003

[116] Chief Medical Officer, Smoking During Pregnancy, DH, June 2007

[117] National Audit Office, Report by Comptroller and Auditor General, HC 623, 30 April 2003

Part II

Specialist areas

Chapter 13
Children and young persons

Introduction

In addition to the basic principles of law discussed in the first part of this book, those who nurse children and young persons must also be aware of several special legal provisions that apply to those under 18 years. (In some hospitals, children over 16 years are cared for in adult wards, in others there are special adolescent units.) The Human Rights Act 1998 gives rights to the child (see Appendix A) as does the United Nations Convention on the Rights of the Child (1989).[1] While the UN Convention is not directly enforceable in the UK (unlike the

European Convention on Human Rights), the extent to which the UK complies with the Convention is monitored on a biannual basis. The Children Act 1989 has provided a framework for the provision of services for children in need and sets out the basic principles to be followed in determining the welfare of the child. There have been significant developments in the protection of children following the inquiry into the death of Victoria Climbié which led to the Children Act 2004. The Department of Health has provided guidance on the welfare of children and young people in hospital[2] and the Audit Commission investigated the care of children in hospitals in 1993.[3] The RCN has published the results of a study into children's nursing and acute healthcare service provision that found a high level of non-adherence to national recommendations.[4] It followed this with a report in July 2001[5] and also guidance for nurses of children on a philosophy of care[6] and a position statement on children and young people.[7] The British Medical Association has provided guidance on consent and the child.[8] A National Service Framework was published for children's services in 2004 and should have a major impact in ensuring good standards of care.

Consent to treatment

At age 18 and over, adults, if mentally competent, are able to make all decisions in relation to their medical care. They can also consent to being participants in research programmes and this applies whether the research is seen as being in their therapeutic interests or not. Prior to 18 years, several different provisions apply.

The 16- and 17-year-old

Treatment

Under Section 8 of the Family Law Reform Act 1969, the child of 16 or 17 can give a valid consent to treatment. The provisions of this section are set out below. These two subsections cover most eventualities as far as consent to treatment is concerned for the 16- and 17-year-old. Treatment is defined widely and would cover all nursing care. There is a presumption that, like the adult, the young person of 16 or 17 is capable of giving consent. This presumption is now contained in the Mental Capacity Act 2005 (which applies to those over 16 years) section 1(2), which states that a person must be assumed to have capacity unless it is established that he lacks capacity. Under Section 2(4) of the MCA any question whether a person lacks capacity within the meaning of this Act must be decided on the balance of probabilities.

Consent to research

It should be noted, however, that the above does not cover consent to take part in research unless it can genuinely be considered to be part of the treatment. Thus a 16-year-old suffering from a disorder where there is no clearly proven successful method of treatment might well be asked to consent to a new, untried form of treatment as part of a research project. If the presumption that the individual has the mental capacity to give consent stands and it is clearly in the patient's therapeutic interests and if there are no undue risks, then such a proposal would be covered by the words of the section. If, however, there was at hand a proven successful method of treatment, but the child was approached to see if he would agree to take part in a research programme where there were considerable risks that may or may not be of benefit to him, it is likely that such a treatment would not be covered by the Family

Reform Act (though it may be covered by the Mental Capacity Act 2005 and its provisions relating to research and mental incapacity (see Chapter 18)). Similarly, where a child or a young person of 16 and 17 is asked to participate in research which is of no benefit to him, consent cannot be given under the provisions of the Family Law Reform Act 1969, but could be given under the Mental Capacity Act 2005, if the young person were incompetent and over 16 years.

Statute — **Sections 8(1) and (2) of the Family Law Reform Act 1969**

Section 8(1) The consent of a minor who has attained the age of 16 years to any surgical, medical, or dental treatment, which in the absence of consent would constitute a trespass to his person will be as effective as it would be if he were of full age; and where a minor has by virtue of this section given an effective consent to any treatment, it shall not be necessary to obtain any consent for it from his parent or guardian.

Treatment is defined very widely (Section 8(2)). In this section, 'surgical, medical, or dental treatment' includes any procedure undertaken for the purposes of diagnosis and this section applies to any procedure (including in particular the administration of an anaesthetic) which is ancillary to any treatment as it applies to that treatment.

Refusal to have treatment

Case 13.1 — *Re W*

Anorexia nervosa and the 16-year-old[9]

A 16-year-old girl under local authority care suffered from anorexia nervosa. She refused to move to a specialist hospital. The Court of Appeal held that the Family Law Reform Act 1969 Section 8 did not prevent consent being given by parents or the court. While she had a right to give consent under the Act, she could not refuse treatment that was necessary to save her life.

Emergencies

The Act does not prevent any emergency action being taken to save the life of a child who is unconscious or unable to give consent. Thus a 16-year-old who is wheeled into the A&E department in an unconscious state can be given emergency treatment in the same way that a patient of any age would be treated. The professional providing this emergency treatment would be protected against any allegation of trespass to the person by the defence that he or she was acting in an emergency in the person's best interests under the Mental Capacity Act 2005.

Parallel consent

Section 8 of the Family Law Reform Act can also be interpreted as giving power to parents to give a valid consent on behalf of their child of 16 or 17. This is because a third subsection of this section states:

Section 8(3): *Nothing in this section shall be construed as making ineffective any consent which would have been effective if the section had not been enacted.*

One interpretation of this is that the fact that the child of 16 or 17 can now give a valid consent to treatment does not mean that consent by the parents on behalf of the child ceases to be effective. Prior to the 1969 Act, a parent could give a valid consent on behalf of his child up to adulthood and this right is not affected by the Act. Thus there exists a parallel right to consent: both the parents and the child of 16 or 17 could give consent. This is unlikely to cause difficulties except in those rare occasions where there is a dispute between the child and the parent. Whose views does the doctor or nurse take?

Practical Dilemma 13.1   Clash between parent and child

A girl of 17 who had recently become a Jehovah's Witness was involved in a car crash. She was just conscious as she was wheeled into the A&E department and made it clear that she did not wish to be given a blood transfusion. Her parents were notified of the crash and told of her statement. However, not sharing her religious views, they said they would give their consent if blood was necessary to save her life. The consultant wishes to know the legal situation.

The fact that Section 8(3) preserves the right of the parent to give consent means that, legally, the doctor could rely on that consent as a defence against any action for trespass to the person subsequently brought by the girl. Prior to Section 8 of the Family Law Reform Act being passed, parents had the right to give consent and this right continues. However, to go against the wishes of the young girl is a serious situation and ideally the dispute should be brought to court.

What if the doctor took notice of the girl's refusal, did not give blood and as a consequence the girl died? Could the parents then sue the doctor for negligence? The answer is that such a case would probably be unsuccessful, but much would depend on the circumstances, for example, the mental competence of the daughter in refusing blood; whether she understood the full implications; her general and specific capacity to give a valid consent.

Where there is a clash, the doctor has the choice of following the wishes of the child or the parents: if the position were reversed and the parents were Jehovah's Witnesses and the daughter consented to having blood, there would be no difficulties; he could rely on her consent under Section 8(1) and if the girl were unconscious he could act in an emergency to save her life, whatever the views of the parents. However, where it is the child of 16 or 17 who is withholding consent and the parents wish to give it, many would argue that it is the doctor's duty to save life and he should rely on the parents' consent under Section 8(3). The point was considered by the courts in *Re W*[10] where the court overruled the child's refusal (see Case 13.1). Were such a dispute to arise and where time permits, the best procedure to follow would be a reference to the court under the Children Act 1989.

A significant amendment to the law on the detention of young persons of 16 and 17 in psychiatric hospitals by the Mental Health Act 2007 (Section 43 amending Section 131 of the 1983 Act) will mean that from October 2008 parents will no longer be able to give consent to the admission of young persons of 16 and 17 who refuse to or are incapable of giving consent to admission. This may lead to a review of the law on the overruling of the refusal of consent by a young person of 16 or 17 years and cases such as *Re W* (see Case 13.1) will no longer be followed.

The Mental Capacity Act 2005 which came into force between April and October 2007 covers those over 16 years who lack the mental capacity to make decisions because of an impairment or a disturbance in the functioning of the mind or brain. It requires those who make decisions on behalf of those who lack mental capacity to act in the best interests of that person. Young persons of 16 or 17 who have the requisitie mental capacity would not come within the provisions of the Act and disputes over their care would be heard by the Family Court. The Court of Protection can make orders and directions in relation to those who lack mental capacity in relation to both property and financial matters as well as personal welfare. Where a person under 16 years is unlikely to have the requisite mental capacity after 16 years, then an order can be made in respect of such a person. For example, if a boy of 14 received compensation following a road accident which caused serious brain damage, the Court of Protection could give directions for the use of that compensation. There are provisions in the Mental Capacity Act 2005 to facilitate the transfer of cases between the Family Division of the High Court and the Court of Protection to ensure that cases are heard in the most appropriate forum.

Children under 16 years

The Children Act 1989 requires the court to have regard to 'the ascertainable wishes and feelings of the child concerned considered in the light of their age and understanding' (Section 1(3)(a)) in deciding whether to make specific orders under the Act. Certain sections require, if the child has sufficient understanding, the child's consent to be given, before the child can be asked to submit to a medical or physical examination.

Case 13.2   *Re E*

Refusal of blood by 15-year-old[11]

A youth aged 15 years 9 months was suffering from leukaemia and required a blood transfusion as part of his treatment. Both he and his parents were devout Jehovah's Witnesses and refused to give consent. The health authority applied for him to be made a ward of court and for a declaration that the treatment could proceed. The judge held that the lad was intelligent enough to take decisions about his own well-being, but that he did not have a full understanding of what the blood transfusions would involve. The welfare of the child was the first and paramount consideration. Although the court should be very slow to interfere in a decision the child had taken, the welfare of the child led to only one conclusion: that the hospital should be at liberty to treat him with blood transfusions. The judge therefore gave leave to the hospital authority to give treatment, including blood transfusion, and the consent of the patient and his parents was dispensed with.

In a case similar to *Re E*, a girl of 15½ years suffered from thalassaemia and had been kept alive by monthly blood transfusions and injections. She and her mother began to attend meetings of Jehovah's Witnesses and subsequently refused to accept blood transfusions. The judge decided that the treatment could be authorised on the grounds that it was in her best interests and the court had the power to overrule a competent child's refusal of treatment. He did, however, find that the girl was not Gillick competent (see below) because she lacked emotional maturity.[12] The High Court applied the Gillick principle to a case where parents were not informed that an abortion was to be carried out on a competent girl under 16 years[13] (see Chapter 15).

Non-parents

The Children Act 1989 Section 3(5) provides that a person who (a) does not have parental responsibility for a particular child, but (b) has care of the child, may (subject to the provision of this Act) do what is reasonable in all the circumstances of the case for the purpose of safeguarding or promoting the child's welfare. It is suggested that this would include giving consent to necessary emergency treatment in the absence of the parents. In addition, professional staff would have a duty of care to take action to save life in such circumstances.

Case 13.3   *Re R* (1991)

Compulsory treatment for mental disorder[14]

The court gave permission for psychiatric medication to be given to a girl aged 15 against her will. Her mental health had deteriorated and she was placed in an adolescent psychiatric unit. Her condition fluctuated between periods of lucidity. The Court of Appeal held that she was not mentally competent due to the fluctuating nature of her mental illness.

Kennedy and Grubb[15] have suggested in discussing the reasoning of the Court of Appeal that: 'It is more respectful of patients' autonomy to interpret incompetence so as to include the manic depressive and the anorexic (where appropriate) rather than regard them as apparently competent and then do wholesale violence to the law's commitment to the rights of decision-making of the competent.'

Children's rights: can children give consent themselves?

If the child is mature and capable of understanding the situation and it is not possible to contact the parents, the child can give a valid consent and this principle is emphasised in the Children Act 1989. This issue was considered in the Gillick case on the narrow issue of advice and treatment for family planning. However, the principles established by the House of Lords cover a much wider area.

Case 13.4   *Gillick* v. *West Norfolk and Wisbech AHA and the DHSS* (1985)

The Gillick case[16]

Mrs Gillick questioned the lawfulness of a DHSS circular, HN(80)46, which was a revised version of part of a comprehensive *Memorandum of Guidance* on family planning services issued to health authorities in May 1974 under cover of circular HSC(IS)32. The circular stated that in certain circumstances a doctor could lawfully prescribe contraception for a girl under 16 without the consent of the parents. Mrs Gillick wrote to the acting administrator formally forbidding any medical staff employed by the Norfolk AHA to give 'any contraceptive or abortion advice or treatment whatever to my . . . daughters whilst they are under 16 years without my consent'. The administrator replied that the treatment prescribed by a doctor is a matter for the doctor's clinical judgement, taking into account all the factors of the case. Mrs Gillick, who had five daughters, then brought an action against the AHA and

▶

Case 13.4 continued

the DHSS seeking a declaration that the notice gave advice that was unlawful and wrong and that did or might adversely affect the welfare of her children, her right as a parent and her ability properly to discharge her duties as a parent. She sought a declaration that no doctor or other professional person employed by the health authority might give any contraceptive or abortion advice or treatment to any of her children below the age of 16 without her prior knowledge and consent.

She failed before the High Court judge, succeeded in her appeal before the Court of Appeal and the DHSS and health authority then appealed to the House of Lords. The Lords decided by a majority of three to two against Mrs Gillick. The majority held that in exceptional circumstances a doctor could provide contraceptive advice and treatment to a girl under 16 without the parents' consent. The circular was therefore upheld.

Lord Fraser stated the exceptional circumstances, which are set out in Box 13.1. Mrs Gillick has subsequently requested that the phrase 'Gillick-competent child' should be replaced by 'a child competent according to Lord Fraser Guidelines'. Many questions still remain uncertain. Can it be assumed that a mature child under 16 can give a valid consent to any form of treatment and research? What efforts must be made to obtain the parents' consent? For what can a child give consent: a few stitches; an anaesthetic; an abortion? Clearly the competence of the child must match the nature of the decision to be made: a young child may be able to agree to having stitches in his leg, but not to brain surgery. It is an overwhelming requirement that decisions must be made in the best interests of the child. The paramount consideration is the welfare of the child.

Box 13.1   Exceptional circumstances set out in the Gillick case

1   The girl would, although under 16, understand the doctor's advice.
2   He could not persuade her to inform her parents or allow him to inform the parents that she was seeking contraceptive advice.
3   She was very likely to have sexual intercourse with or without contraceptive treatment.
4   Unless she received contraceptive advice or treatment her physical or mental health or both were likely to suffer.
5   Her best interests required him to give her contraceptive advice, treatment or both without parental consent.

What is the position where the child is a mother? If she has the mental capacity, does she have the legal capability of giving consent for her child to be treated or is it necessary to obtain the consent of her own parents, i.e. the baby's grandparents? As an example, many health visitors treating the child of an underage mother protect themselves by obtaining both the consent of the underage mother and also of a grandparent. From the cautious words of the majority judges sitting on the Gillick case in the House of Lords, it would appear that, provided the underage mother had the requisite mental capacity to consent to treatment on the child's behalf, this would be a valid consent.

Another interpretation of Section 8(3) of the Family Law Reform Act 1969 is that statutory powers given to a child of 16 or 17 to give a valid consent do not remove the ability of the mature child below 16 years to give a legally valid consent to treatment.

Where a child is refusing life-saving treatment, the test of Gillick competence will not be the only factor in determining the case, as Case 13.5 shows. In this case, the ruling in *Re W* (see Case 13.1) was followed.

Case 13.5   *Re L*

Refusal by 14-year-old Jehovah's witness[17]

A 14-year-old girl had sustained extensive and severe burns. Her life was considered to be at risk unless she underwent surgical treatment, which involved the possibility of a blood transfusion, although, as a practising Jehovah's Witness, she felt unable to consent to this. Her clearly expressed refusal was consistent with two earlier advance directive/release forms that she had completed, the last being only two months before her injuries. The hospital applied for leave to administer blood and blood products in the course of essential treatment without her consent.

The court granted the application on the grounds that:

1 She could not be said to be Gillick competent. (Information had been withheld from her about the horrible death brought on by the onset and spread of gangrene, if blood were not transfused; and she had led a sheltered life, very much under the influence of the family.)

2 Even had she been found to be Gillick competent, the extreme gravity of the case would, nevertheless, be sufficient basis for the order to be made.

The possibility of a young person under 16 years relying on Article 3 of the European Convention on Human Rights (see Appendix A) to justify their refusal of life-saving treatment or on Article 9 and his or her freedom to practise a specific religion has not yet been considered by the courts.

Clash between parents and child under 16

A case is considered in Chapter 17 where a 15-year-old child's refusal to have a transplant was overruled by the court.[18]

Overruling the parent

While parents have the power in law to give consent to the treatment of the child, this is not an absolute power. If their consent or their refusal to give consent is considered to be against the best interests of the child, then the court can intervene.

Case 13.6   *In re D* (1976)

Sterilisation of a mentally handicapped girl[19]

A girl of 11 years of age suffered from Sotos syndrome, the symptoms of which included accelerated growth during infancy, epilepsy, general clumsiness, an unusual facial appearance and behaviour problems, including emotional instability, certain aggressive tendencies and some impairment of mental function. The mother, taking the advice of the consultant paediatrician that her daughter would remain substantially handicapped and that she would always be unable to care for herself or look after any children, discussed with the obstetrician the possibility of her daughter being sterilised. An operation was arranged. However, before it was performed, the educational psychologist applied for the girl to be made a ward of court. Mrs Justice Heilbron, who heard the case, was not convinced that the operation was in the best interests of the girl and so ordered that the operation should not proceed.

It can be seen from this case how fortuitous it was that the case ever came before the courts. Had it not been for the strongly held views of the educational psychologist, the operation could well have gone ahead. This should not be so in the future. In a House of Lords case,[20] where the judges agreed to a sterilisation proceeding on 'Jeanette', they made it clear that, in future, every such case of a sterilisation on a mentally handicapped child should receive the approval of the court before it proceeded. In that case, they did not make the distinction between therapeutic and non-therapeutic sterilisation, which Mrs Justice Heilbron had made *In re D*. In theory, every case of sterilisation on a child should come before the courts, even though the operation is performed because of the presence of a malignancy. This is further discussed in Chapter 15.

The important point for children's nurses is that if they feel that a particular procedure or treatment agreed between the parents and the medical staff is not in the best interests of the child, then the nurse should raise it with her senior management who could, if necessary, arrange for the matter to be brought before the courts.

In a dispute between a family and the doctors, violence erupted on the wards as the family fought to prevent morphine, which would depress the respiratory functions, being administered to their child (see Case 13.7).

Case 13.7   *R v. Portsmouth Hospitals NHS Trust ex p Glass* (1999)

Dispute over treatment[21]

A boy of 13 was severely disabled with only a limited lifespan. The mother wished him to receive whatever medical treatment was necessary to prolong his life. Following an incident in which the hospital gave the child morphine against the mother's wishes, family members resuscitated the child and prevented him from dying. There was a complete breakdown of trust between the family and the hospital. The mother sought a declaration as to the course doctors in the hospital should take if the boy were admitted for emergency treatment and disagreements arose as to the treatment to be given to or withheld from the child. The judge refused the mother's application for judicial review and she appealed to the Court of Appeal.

The Court of Appeal held that it would be inappropriate to grant a declaration in anticipation and indicate to doctors at a hospital what treatment they should or should not give in circumstances that had not yet arisen. The best course was for the parents of a child and the medical staff to agree on the approach to be taken for the treatment of that child, but if that were not possible and a grave conflict arose, then the actual circumstances must be brought before the court so that the court could resolve what was in the best interests of the child in the light of the facts existing at that time. The principles recognised by the Court of Appeal were as follows.

1 sanctity of life
2 non-interference by the courts in areas of clinical judgement in the treatment of patients where that could be avoided
3 refusal of the courts to dictate appropriate treatment to a medical practitioner, subject to the court's power to take decisions in the child's best interests
4 treatment without consent, save in an emergency, was a trespass to the person
5 the court would interfere to protect the interests of a minor or a person under a disability.

The Court of Appeal dismissed the appeal.

Ms Glass subsequently appealed to the European Court of Human Rights, which held that the failure of the NHS trust to seek a declaration from the court before administering diamorphine to her son without her consent and in writing him up for DNR instructions without her knowledge was a breach of her Article 8 rights.[22]

Members of the family were prosecuted for their violence in the hospital.

Transplants and the interests of the child

Practical Dilemma 13.2   Sisterly transplants

Mary, aged 7 years, had an incurable blood disease and was found to be compatible only with her younger sister Janet, who was 4 years old. The parents therefore agreed that Janet would provide a bone marrow transplant for Mary. Staff Nurse Bryant was concerned by the legalities of the proposed transplant.

The parents have the right to consent to any treatment that is in the interests of the child (subject to any statutory limitations). However, in this case, there is a clash between the interests of Mary and the interests of Janet. Any operation, no matter how small, involves some risk to the patient and Janet would be put at risk for the benefit of Mary. In the case of a bone marrow transplant, it could be argued that the risk is so small and the psychological benefit for Janet when she becomes older so immense that it would be inhuman not to allow Janet to be a donor. If she were asked, she would probably agree herself, although her capacity to understand would be very limited. The situation would come under the legislation relating to transplants from live donors (see Chapter 16). The situation that would arise if Janet were mentally incapacitated and in an institution is discussed in Chapter 20.

A further extreme example of using one child for the benefit of another arose in October 2000 when it was reported from the USA that parents had had a baby selected by IVF who would provide compatible bone marrow for treating their daughter who suffered from a serious blood disorder.[23] The Human Fertilisation and Embryology Authority has decided that IVF is available for parents who wish to ensure that the selected embryo will be a match for an existing child. This is considered in Chapter 22.

In 1993 the court held that a blood transfusion should be given to a premature baby girl who suffered from respiratory distress syndrome and whose parents were Jehovah's Witnesses. The order authorising medical treatment was to be made under the court's inherent jurisdiction rather than pursuant to the Children Act 1989.[24]

In 2000 the future of twin Siamese girls came before the Court of Appeal.[25] The Court of Appeal decided that the operation could proceed. The case is discussed in Chapter 14.

Withholding consent by parents

Where the parents refuse to give consent to treatment, which the doctors determine is in the best interests of the child, then there is a well-tried procedure for taking the appropriate action. No child should die because the parents have unreasonably refused their consent to a necessary treatment.

> ## Practical Dilemma 13.3   Blood transfusion
>
> Eric, aged 3 years, is admitted with an operable tumour. The neurologist reassures the parents and says that Eric can be saved. The parents say that on religious grounds they could not agree to Eric's having a blood transfusion. Mr Sharpe, the neurosurgeon, replies that he would not be prepared to carry out such an operation with such a restriction, as it is highly likely that blood would be required in the operating theatre. The parents therefore refuse their consent to the operation. Since the tumour is operable, the neurosurgeon cannot let the child die, so he has two options. He can either proceed and justify his action on the basis that he is acting in the best interests of the child in an emergency; or he can arrange for an application to be made to the court for Eric to be made a ward of court, and for the operation to be ordered to proceed.

In the case of an emergency, when there is insufficient time to obtain a declaration from the court, essential action must be taken to save the life of the child, if that is clinically in the best interests of the child.

> ## Case 13.8   In re B (A Minor) (1981)
>
> ### Down's syndrome[26]
>
> A child who was born suffering from Down's syndrome and an intestinal blockage, required an operation to relieve the obstruction if she were to live for more than a few days. If the operation were performed, the child might die within a few months, but it was probable that her life expectancy would be 20–30 years. Her parents, having decided that it would be kinder to allow her to die rather than live as a physically and mentally handicapped person, refused consent to the operation. The local authority made the child a ward of court and, when a surgeon decided that the wishes of the parents should be respected, they sought an order authorising the operation to be performed by other named surgeons. The judge in the High Court decided that the wishes of the parents should be respected and refused to make the order. The local authority took the case to the Court of Appeal, which said that the operation should proceed.

The court decided that the question before it was whether it was in the best interests of the child that she should have the operation and not whether the parents' wishes should be respected. Since the effect of the operation might be that the child would have the normal lifespan of a person with Down's syndrome, and since it had not been demonstrated that the life of such a person was of such a nature that the child should be condemned to die, the court would make an order that the operation be performed. One significant case in which the courts did not follow the medical views was where parents refused to permit a liver transplant to take place on their toddler. The Court of Appeal held that in the very specific circumstances of the case (the parents lived abroad and as health professionals they believed the transplant not to be in the best interests of the child) the transplant would not be ordered against their wishes.[27]

The court will review any decision where parents are withholding consent or giving consent and decide whether the treatment should be given in the light of the best interests of the child. It is open to any interested party to ask the court to determine this question when he or she is concerned at what is proposed or not proposed.

Parents have a legal duty to care for their children. Where they fail to obtain medical treatment, they could be guilty of a criminal offence. A father was convicted of manslaughter and imprisoned and the mother given a suspended sentence for failing to give their diabetic daughter insulin.[28] The couple refused to allow their diabetic daughter to receive modern medicine because of their religious beliefs. In September 2002 a couple were jailed for starving their tortured two-year-old daughter to death.[29]

Letting die

The Down's syndrome case above raises the issue of whether it is permissible in law to allow a severely handicapped child to die or even assist him to die. In what circumstances does the doctor cease to have a duty to keep the child alive? Certainly, as the case of *In re B* shows, the views of the parents are not the deciding factor. The point was raised in the case of Dr Arthur, who was prosecuted for murder (later changed to attempted murder), since he prescribed, with the consent of the parents, the substance DF 118 for a Down's syndrome baby who also suffered from severe abdominal abnormalities. A jury acquitted him.[30]

The law does not recognise any form of euthanasia, but in practice it is left to the discretion of the medical staff to determine the extent of heroic medicine that is justified for severely handicapped babies. This discretion is reviewable in the courts. It is not an easy situation for medical staff and the Royal College of Paediatrics and Childhealth has published guidelines to assist practitioners,[31] as has the British Medical Association.[32] This issue is discussed further in Chapter 14 in the section on special care baby units.

Child protection

The children's nurse needs to be aware of the possibility that injuries or illness in a child may have been caused by another person. This applies not just to bruising or lacerations, but also to undernourishment and other ailments, including psychological damage. The possibility of sexual abuse must also be borne in mind if the relevant symptoms are present. The parents have a legal duty to provide care for their dependent children under Section 1(1) of the Children and Young Persons Act 1933.

The nurse is confronted by the following problems. What action should she take if she suspects a child of being the object of abuse of any kind? What are the potential consequences for her if she is mistaken? What powers does she have to prevent a parent removing a child from the ward when the child has been placed under an emergency section of the Children Act? What would her position be in relation to a court hearing? Does she have to make a statement to the police?

Practical Dilemma 13.4   Child abuse?

Jane, a girl of six months, was admitted to the children's ward with a suspected chest infection. She was immediately placed on antibiotics and sputum samples taken. While the nurse was changing her, she noticed some bruising to the upper legs and a possible burn mark on her back. The nurse pointed these marks out to the senior house officer, who suggested that the registrar should be called in, as it was possible that these marks were the result of abuse.

A procedure for dealing with suspected child abuse should be available on every ward. If child abuse is suspected, the nurse should be particularly vigilant in not leaving the child unattended with the parents. In addition, it is quite likely that she could be called on to give evidence to the court as to the nature of the relationship and interaction between the parents and the child in hospital and also as to the physical and mental state of the child on admission. It is essential, therefore, that her record keeping should be detailed and clear to enable her to answer questions at some later time. Where cot death is feared, a new procedure has been introduced since January 2004 following the acquittal of several mothers who were imprisoned for killing their babies. The consent of the Director of Public Prosecutions must be obtained where the prosecution of parents is contemplated in respect of the death of a young child, in order that the possibility of cot death can be ruled out. The acquittals resulted from the discrediting of evidence of Munchausen by proxy relied on by the expert witness Professor Sir Roy Meadows, a paediatrician (see page 209).

Statute | **Children Act 1989: protection of children**

A Part IV   Care and supervision order, Sections 31-42
D Part V   Protection of children, Sections 43-52
C Part XII   Miscellaneous and general, Section 100 Restriction of wardship; jurisdiction of High Court still exists in emergency situations
Section 43   Child assessment order
Section 44   Orders for emergency protection of children
Section 45   Duration of emergency protection orders
Section 46   Removal and accommodation of children by police in cases of emergency
Section 47   Local authority's duty to investigate
Section 48   Powers to assist in discovery of children who may be in need of emergency protection
Section 49   Abduction of children in care
Section 50   Recovery of abducted children
Section 51   Refuges for children at risk
Section 52   Risk and regulation relating to emergency protection order

---

The social services department of the local authority can apply for a child assessment order or an order for the emergency protection of the child under Part V of the Children Act 1989 to care for the child initially, pending the outcome of the full proceedings for the care of the child.

The orders that can be made in respect of a child suspected of being abused are contained in the Children Act 1989, set out in the Statute above. Failure by a local authority to take reasonable precautions to prevent abuse can lead to payment of compensation. In September 2007 Hackney agreed, in an out-of-court settlement, to pay £100,000 to a woman of 39 years and her two younger siblings, because it failed to remove them as children from their abusive home.[33] Jake Pierce won £25,000 compensation because of failures by social services. A social services department had returned him to the care of his parents without making a proper assessment and the court held that this fell short of the standard of practice to be expected of a reasonably competent local authority and it was therefore negligent. Pierce had been subjected to almost daily beatings by his parents and was kept in squalid conditions.[34]

Working together to safeguard children[35]

This is a guide to inter-agency working to safeguard and promote the welfare of children. It replaces the publication 'Working Together under the Children Act 1989' published in 1991. It highlights the duties in the Children Act 1989 that require inter-agency cooperation.

Section 27 enables a local authority to request help from: any local authority; any local education authority; any local housing authority; any health authority and any person authorised by the Secretary of State or, in Wales, the National Assembly. The request must be responded to.

Under Section 47, a duty is placed on such organisations or persons to help a local authority with its enquiries in cases where there is reasonable cause to suspect that a child is suffering or is likely to suffer significant harm. The guidance covers those topics shown in Box 13.2.

Box 13.2 — **Contents of inter-agency guidance**

Working together to support children and families
Some lessons from research and experience
Roles and responsibilities
Area child protection committees
Handling individual cases
Child protection in specific circumstances
Some key principles
Case reviews
Inter-agency training and development

Following the inquiry conducted by Lord Laming into the death of Victoria Climbié[36] the Department of Health published a detailed response, 'Keeping Children Safe',[37] and this was followed by a single source document for safeguarding children.[38] This document aims to provide a single set of advice for all those involved in the care of children, which replaces local guidance. It was followed by a Green Paper, 'Every Child Matters',[39] published in September 2003. The Green Paper focuses on four main areas:

1 supporting parents and carers

2 early intervention and effective protection

3 accountability and integration – locally, regionally and nationally

4 workforce reform

Five outcomes are considered as key to well-being in childhood and later life: being healthy, staying safe, enjoying and achieving, making a positive contribution and achieving economic well-being.

A Children's Commissioner (one is already appointed in Wales) has been established as an independent champion for children. In addition, legislation to create a Director of Children's Services accountable for local authority education and children's social services was proposed. A Minister for Children, Young People and Families has been created in the Department for Education and Skills (now the DCSF). The Children Act 2004 provides the legal underpinning for 'Every Child Matters' and its provisions are shown in Box 13.3. Significant features include the new Local Safeguarding Children Boards, and the duty on local authorities to appoint a director of children's services and a lead member for children's services.

Box 13.3 **Provisions of the Children Act 2004**

Part 1 Children's Commissioner

Part 2 Children's services in England: Co-operation to improve well-being
Arrangements to safeguard and promote welfare
Information databases
Local Safeguarding Children Boards: establishment, functions, procedure and funding
Children and young people's plans
Director of children's services
Lead member for children's services
Inspections of children's services

Part 3 Children's Services in Wales

Part 4 Advisory and support services for family proceedings

Following the Lord Laming Inquiry into the death of Victoria Climbié the Joint Chief Inspectors have reported on safeguarding arrangements for children and young people in England. The Healthcare Commission is contributing to the third Joint Chief Inspectors' Report on Safeguarding Children to be published in October 2008. The children's inspectorate is to be known as the Office for Standards in Education and Social Care and will review the work of Local Safeguarding Children Boards.

The RCN has published guidance on child protection and the nurse[40] and emphasises the need of each trust to have a designated or named nurse for child protection, have child protection procedures in place and have a defined policy on raising concerns about colleagues. A self-assessment tool for child protection arrangements for clinicians was updated and relaunched by the Healthcare Commission in 2004 and is available from its website. Guidance was provided in 2007 for practitioners and managers to help them identify and deal with abuse which may be linked to a belief in spirit possession. The guidance followed the research report on child abuse linked with accusations of possessions and witchcraft published in June 2006.[41] The establishment of children's trusts (see page 348) may assist in improving child protection provisions.

Any nurse must also be alert to the possibility of a colleague causing harm to a patient. This is considered in the section on whistleblowing in Chapter 4. Other issues that arise in relation to non-accidental injury include disclosure of confidential information (this is covered in Chapter 8) and giving evidence before the court (covered in Chapter 9).

Recent cases have held local authorities liable in respect of failures to take action to prevent abuse and in making negligent adoption and fostering arrangements. Thus two people who had been abused as children by their stepfather succeeded in their claim that the local authority had failed to provide an appropriate means of obtaining a determination of their allegations that the local authority had failed to protect them from serious ill treatment[42] and therefore were in breach of Article 13. (Article 13 is not included in Schedule 1 of the Human Rights Act 1998 (see Appendix A).) On the facts, there was no breach of Article 3. In contrast, in another case the European Court of Human Rights recently held that where the local authority failed to protect children from sexual abuse by the stepfather, the local authority was in violation of Article 3 and Article 13 and was held liable to pay damages.[43] In another case against a local authority, this time by a couple who adopted a violent child, the couple won their case that they should have been notified by the LA of the boy's serious and emotional behavioural difficulties.[44] The court held that the local authority could be held vicariously liable for negligence by its employees in failing to fulfil their duty of care owed to those who might foreseeably be injured if the duty was carelessly exercised.

Errors in identifying child abuse

There have been misdiagnoses of child abuse. For example, in one case,[45] following a case conference, a baby was taken into care on the basis of medical evidence that suggested that a spiral fracture of her femur was evidence of non-accidental injury. Subsequently, it was discovered that the baby suffered from brittle bone disease and the child was returned to the parents nine months after the hospital admission. The parents sued and action was also brought in the name of the child arguing a case of negligence, and breach of Article 8 of the European Convention of Human Rights. The claims failed on the grounds that the child had suffered no injury for which the law recognised a remedy; a duty of care was not owed by the defendants to the parents (the doctor owed a duty of care to the child and his obligations within the multidisciplinary process militated against the doctor owing any additional duty to the parents in relation to the diagnosis which commenced such a process) and to hold the doctor liable to the parents would cut across the statutory scheme set up for the protection of the child. The Human Rights Act came into force on 2 October 2000, was not retrospective and the cause of action arose in September 1998 and June 1999. In one case[46] in East Berkshire, a mother was suspected of Munchausen's syndrome by proxy when her son suffered from allergic reactions following birth and he was placed on the 'at risk' register. However, it was subsequently discovered that he did have allergy problems. The mother claimed compensation on the grounds that the original diagnosis was made negligently. The House of Lords held that it would not be fair, just or reasonable to impose a duty of care on a doctor in respect of a negligent clinical diagnosis where there was a concurrent and potentially conflicting duty of care towards a child patient. No duty of care was owed to the parents. This has been confirmed by the European Court of Human Rights. The Court of Appeal held that the Human Rights Act 1998 did not give rise to a duty of care to the parent of a child on the part of the local authority when exercising, through its social workers, its duty to protect children from abuse. The local authority's principal duty was to the child in need of protection, and there were powerful public policy reasons for not having a duty of care to the parents.[47] In this case the local authority had placed the claimant's four children on the Child Protection Register as being at risk from their parents. The mother had succeeded in her application to the Ombudsman who upheld a number of complaints of maladministration and recommended that she should be paid £5,000 for distress and damage to her reputation. However, the Court of Appeal, following the ruling by the House of Lords in the East Berkshire case, held that the local authority was not under a duty of care to the parents. The Court of Appeal has also held that a local authority owed no direct duty of care to a father in investigations carried out by social workers into allegations of sexual abuse by him of his daughter.[48]

Protection of Children Act 1999

This Act requires organisations to refer persons considered unsuitable to work with children to the Department of Health for inclusion on their list. It is discussed in Chapter 10.

Parental care and the nurse

> **Practical Dilemma 13.5**   **Mum knows best**
>
> The children's ward at Roger Park Hospital introduced a scheme for mothers and other relatives to undertake some of the tasks in caring for the children. This had many advantages: it put the child at ease, since the person most familiar to him was taking care of him as usual, albeit in a strange place; at the same time, there were savings in staff time. Originally, the scheme covered only the day-to-day routine care of dressing, feeding, bathing and amusing the child. Subsequently, however, it was extended to nursing and extended-role tasks, including the care of nasal-gastric feeding and intravenous medication. The reason for this extension was that several of the mothers of long-term chronically ill children undertook all these tasks in the community. The nurse or doctor had the task of ensuring that the mother had the appropriate training and the necessary equipment.
>
> Mrs Tait agreed to give her 4-year-old child, Robin, who had a chronic lung condition, the appropriate drugs intravenously every six hours. She had undertaken several such treatments on her own before and was familiar with the routine and procedure. On the ward, she was given the keys to help herself to the necessary drugs. This was contrary to the accepted practice, but was permitted because it was felt that she could be trusted. She gave Robin the 8.00 a.m. treatment without problems. She had to leave the hospital in the afternoon, but told another parent that she would be back for the afternoon treatment. Unfortunately, she did not return until 3.30 p.m. because of an unexpected traffic holdup. Robin was with some other children watching *Telly Tubbies*. She immediately went to the staff nurse to get the keys to draw up the drugs for the next treatment. She took the boxes from the cupboard and started to make up the syringes. She then took Robin into the single room to give him his treatment. As she was giving the medication, Robin became very ill and she called for help. It was then discovered that the afternoon dose had already been given to Robin and although this had been written up into his notes, the nurse who did so was at tea when Mrs Tait returned and she herself did not check Robin's notes as it was never her practice to do so. Robin suffered severe renal failure as a result of an overdose of an antibiotic. Is the accident entirely the mother's fault or does the nurse carry some responsibility?

What is the situation where responsibilities like this are divided between several people? In legal terms, it is probably true to say that the care of the child in hospital is primarily the responsibility of the nurse under the clinical supervision of the medical staff. In a sense, the nurse is delegating to the mother those duties that she is capable of performing and probably performs on her own at home. The nurse should only delegate those tasks that she feels the mother is competent to perform and, in addition, she should ensure that the mother (or, of course, any other relative, friend or volunteer) has the correct amount of training and supervision to undertake the task safely. The nurse would be responsible in negligence if she delegated an unsuitable task to the mother or failed to provide her with the appropriate instructions or gave her inadequate supervision. If, however, the nurse has satisfied all those requirements and something still goes wrong because the mother makes a mistake, then it would be the mother's responsibility for any harm caused to the child as a result of the mistake.

In the above situation, there is clearly a failure in communication between nurse and mother. It would have been preferable to set up a procedure whereby the mother was told to look at the drug chart, to fill it in when she gave the drugs to the child and also to check that the drugs had not already been given. She should also be supervised in her administration of the drugs. It is questionable whether the mother should have been allowed direct access to the medicines. Clearly, the nurse would be at fault in failing to set up this procedure and the supervision and the mother would bear some responsibility for failing to check that they had been given, although in mitigation it could be said that the person responsible for the ward at the time she returned should have known the child had already had his medication and informed the mother accordingly. The problems relating to supervision and instructing others are dealt with more fully in Chapter 4. The RCN has provided guidance on administering intravenous therapy to children in the community.[49] The Department of Health has published an NHS childcare strategy to provide affordable and accessible quality childcare and is attracting more staff to work in the NHS. Further information is available from the DH website.

Disciplining a child

> ### Practical Dilemma 13.6   The nurse *in loco parentis*
>
> Adam was a bright 7-year-old who appeared totally undaunted by his stay in hospital for a hernia operation. Unfortunately, his mother could spend very little time with him as she had two younger children and her husband was overseas. Once Adam had recovered from the immediate effects of his operation, he was uncontrollable. He wandered around the wards into the single-bed wards, ignoring all the nurses' instructions and delighting in disobeying them. In one of the single rooms, a child was being barrier nursed with suspected meningitis. Staff Nurse James saw Adam about to enter this room and in her anxiety and her impatience with him, she hit him hard on the leg. Adam screamed and other nurses came running. Staff Nurse James was disciplined by the nursing officer and Adam's mother said that she was going to make a formal complaint against the nurse and the hospital. Staff Nurse James argued that in the circumstances there was little else she could have done to prevent Adam entering that room and, in any case, she had the powers of a parent to discipline a child who needed to be controlled.

The European Court of Human Rights has ruled that severe corporal punishment to discipline children was a breach of Article 3 of the European Convention on Human Rights.[50] In the case, a stepfather had beaten a 9-year-old boy on several occasions with a garden cane. The stepfather had been prosecuted for assault occasioning actual bodily harm, but had been acquitted by the jury who accepted his defence that the caning had been necessary and reasonable to discipline the boy. The European Court of Human Rights held that ill-treatment must attain a minimum level of severity if it is to fall within the scope of Article 3. It depended on all the circumstances of the case, such as the nature and context of the treatment, its duration, its physical and mental effects and, in some instances, the sex, age and state of health of the victim. In finding that there had been a breach of Article 3, it awarded the boy £10,000 against the UK government and costs. The UK government acknowledged that the UK law failed to provide adequate protection to children and should be amended. Subsequently, guidance was issued by the government on the use of corporal punishment against children. Guidance for good practice in restraining, holding still and containing children has been issued by the RCN.[51] The Joint Committee of House of Lords and House of Commons,[52] in monitoring the UK compliance with the UN Charter on the Rights of the Child, considered that the retention in UK use of the defence of 'reasonable chastisement' is incompatible with the provisions of Article 19 of the Convention. Subsequently the Children Act 2004 was enacted. Section 58 states:

(1) In relation to any offence specified in subsection (2) below, battery of a child cannot be justified on the ground that it constituted reasonable punishment.

(2) The offences referred to in subsection (1) are:
   a. An offence under section 18 or 20 of the Offences against the Person Act 1861 (wounding and causing grievous bodily harm)
   b. An offence under section 47 of that Act (assault occasioning actual bodily harm)
   c. An offence under section 1 of the Children and Young Persons Act 1933 (cruelty to persons under 16).

(3) Battery of a child causing actual bodily harm to a child cannot be justified in any civil proceedings on the ground that it constituted reasonable punishment.

(4) For the purposes of subsection (3) 'actual bodily harm' has the same meaning as it has for the purposes of section 47 of the Offences against the Person Act 1861.

(5) In section 1 of the Children and Young Persons Act 1933, omit subsection (7)

(Section 1(7) made any parent or person having lawful control or charge of a child to administer punishment an exception of the offence of assaulting or wilfully ill-treating a child).

The effect of this section is that a parent who causes harm to her or his child and is prosecuted under the Offences Against the Person Act sections 18, 20 or 47 or under the Children and Young Persons Act 1933 Section 1 cannot use a defence that the battery constituted reasonable punishment. The same applies in civil proceedings where actual bodily harm is caused.

In 2007 the Children's Commissioner for England called for a complete ban on smacking children[53] as a consultation on the effect of the change in the law was initiated. As a result of the review the Children's Minister ruled out a total ban on smacking children on 26 October 2007.[54]

It therefore follows that corporal punishment should not be used when acting in the place of the parents. In the above example, Staff Nurse James has acted illegally and other methods of control would have been preferable. There were other ways of stopping him entering the room other than hitting him and, in the circumstances, it seems more likely that she lost her temper and was unreasonable.

A respect for the rights of the child and good nursing practice would advocate no use of physical force against a patient. A nurse faces both criminal and civil proceedings against her personally if she uses corporal punishment on a patient. She would, however, be entitled to use reasonable force to protect herself or other people by restraining the child if she or others were threatened with violence. The implications of this for staffing levels are clear and the degree of unruliness in children and the extent of parental help could affect the level of staffing required. Guidance on skill mix and staffing in children's wards and departments is provided by the RCN.[55] Training for staff in coping with unruly children is essential.

Education of children in hospital

It is estimated by the Department for Education and Skills (DfES) (now the Department for Children, Schools and Families – DCSF) that in any given year there are some 100,000 children and young people who require education outside school because of illness or injury. The special education of children in hospitals was provided for in the National Health Service Act 1946. Section 62 empowered regional hospital boards and teaching hospitals to arrange with a local education authority or voluntary body to use as a special school any premises forming part of the hospital. By 1955 there were 120 hospital special schools providing teaching for 8,476 pupils in addition to 1,425 children receiving individual or group tuition. In 1971 responsibility for the education of children in hospitals for the mentally handicapped was transferred to the education service (1975 in Scotland). Home tuition is an important part of the education service for ill or handicapped children and there are signs that demand is growing. The nurse should be aware that every child has a right to education, even when in hospital, and that, provided his medical condition permits it, every effort should be made to ensure that the child is receiving schooling, preferably off the ward area. The nurse has a positive role to play in encouraging the child to take part. The Special Educational Needs and Disability Act 2001 strengthens the general duty to provide a mainstream school place for a child with special educational needs, where their parents want that, and as long as that is compatible with the efficient education of other children. Codes of practice for special educational needs and under the Disability Discrimination Act 1995 are available from the Department of Health website. The DfES (now DCSF), in collaboration with the Department of Health, produced guidance, 'Access to Education for Children and Young People with Medical Needs,' in November 2001, which sets out the minimum national standard for the education of those unable to attend school because of medical needs. Further guidance is available from teachernet.[56]

Children's trusts

In a Department of Health press release in October 2002,[57] the Secretary of State announced the intention to set up children's trusts, which would be responsible for some of the following services: disabled children, children with special educational needs, child protection, identification, referral and tracking of children at risk, speech and language therapy, child and adolescent mental health services and areas where social care, health and education services needed to work together. In July 2003 the Children's Minister announced the creation of 35 children's trusts, which would unite children's social, education and health services in a single local structure. The aim was to break down professional rivalries and improve communication between different agencies responsible for child welfare. Each trust was given £100,000 a year for three years to get established. Many nurses working with children may find that their employment is transferred from a primary care trust or NHS trust to a children's trust.

National Service Frameworks (NSFs)

The NHS Plan[58] envisaged that National Service Frameworks would be established to improve services through setting national standards to drive up quality and tackle existing variations in care. The Children's NSF was published in September 2004. Five core standards are set in Part One for the NHS, local authorities and partner agencies to achieve high quality service provision for all children and young people and their parents or carers.

Standard 1: Promoting Health and Well-being, Identifying Needs and Intervening Early

The health and well-being of all children and young people is promoted and delivered through a coordinated programme of action, including prevention and early intervention wherever possible, to ensure long-term gain, led by the NHS in partnership with local authorities.

Standard 2: Supporting Parenting

Parents or carers are enabled to receive the information, services and support which will help them to care for their children and equip them with the skills they need to ensure that their children have optimum life chances and are healthy and safe.

Standard 3: Child, Young Person and Family-Centred Services

Children and young people and families receive high-quality services which are coordinated around their individual and family needs and take account of their views.

Standard 4: Growing Up into Adulthood

All young people have access to age-appropriate services which are responsive to their specific needs as they grow into adulthood.

Standard 5: Safeguarding and Promoting the Welfare of Children and Young People

All agencies work to prevent children suffering harm and to promote their welfare, provide them with the services they require to address their identified needs and safeguard children who are being or who are likely to be harmed.

Part Two sets standards for the following areas:

Children and young people who are ill

Children in hospital

Disabled children and young people and those with complex health needs

The mental health and psychological well-being of children and young people

Medicines for children and young people

Part Three, relating to maternity services, is considered in Chapter 14.

The NSF should have a major impact on children's services and the role of the children's nurse in ensuring that minimum standards are available in her department. Further information about the NSF is available from the Department of Health website.[59] The Healthcare Commission uses the Children's NSF as a measure of quality in the delivery of services to children and young people and carried out a major review of services for children in hospital in 2006, reporting on its findings in 2007 and outlining the improvements which need to take place to improve the quality of services. Further information on the Healthcare Commission's role in assessing these services and its reports can be found on its website.[60]

A Children Care Group Workforce Team (a multidisciplinary advisory body) supports improvements for children, young people and expectant mothers and collaborates with other CGWTs. An independent review of palliative care services for children and young persons was carried out in 2007 and is available on the DH website. A report providing guidance for the care of young persons with diabetes was published in 2007.[61]

Adolescents

Some hospitals have set up adolescent units for those between 13 and 16/17 years so that special provisions can be made for those in this group. Difficult problems can arise, as Practical Dilemma 13.7 illustrates.

> **Practical Dilemma 13.7**   **Refusal to obey the rules**
>
> David, aged 15, suffered from cystic fibrosis and required regular IV antibiotic treatment. Roger Park Hospital had set up a specialist unit for youngsters suffering from cystic fibrosis, and rules had been laid down about the conduct of the patients. David frequently took his own discharge from hospital, returning with alcohol, and staff also feared that he was taking soft drugs. They tried to reason with him but he was not cooperative. His parents said that he should be made to comply with the hospital regime. What is the law?

In Practical Dilemma 13.7, the managers of the unit are entitled to lay down the terms on which patients and visitors may enter. If David is Gillick competent, then he could agree an understanding with the unit that he will be admitted for treatment only on the basis of accepting the rules that have been laid down. If he refuses to agree to those conditions, including the prohibition on alcohol, then he could be told that he cannot be treated in the unit. In law his parents could give consent to his having treatment, but it is difficult for staff to maintain IV treatment if the young person is objecting to having it. In the long term, it may be possible for the CF patients and other patients with chronic conditions to agree on the 'house rules' and how they are to be implemented and thus bring peer pressure to bear on David. It is essential that the unit manager makes clear that the rules, especially relating to alcohol and illegal drugs, are enforced and those who do not accept the conditions cannot be cared for there. Where the adolescent is over 16 years and lacks capacity to give consent to a specific decision, the Mental Capacity Act 2005 would now apply. Action can be taken in the best interests of the young person. If there is a dispute about the lack of capacity or what is meant by 'best interests' an application could be made to the Court of Protection. (See Chapter 7 for further consideration of the Mental Capacity Act 2005.)

Teenage sexuality

There is considerable concern within the Department of Health at the rise in sexually transmitted diseases and at the high rate of teenage pregnancies in the UK. In November 2001 the Department of Health[62] announced the launch of a national information campaign to promote sexual health as part of its national strategy for sexual health and HIV. Subsequently a Teenage Pregnancy Unit website[63] has been set up as a cross-government unit located within the Department for Education and Skills (now the Department for Children, Schools and Families). The unit was set up to implement the Social Exclusion Unit's report on teenage pregnancy. The Teenage Pregnancy Unit website contains lists of other useful websites for teenagers and parents providing advice on sexual health and related issues. An Independent Advisory Group (IAG) on sexual health and HIV was established in 2003 as part of the implementation of an action plan for the national strategy for sexual health and HIV. In 2004 this IAG published its response to the Health Select Committee on Sexual Health.[64] It considered access to services, capacity, commissioning and prioritisation, funding prevention, education and sexual health promotion and the patient voice. It agreed with the select committee's conclusions on the six key factors that were the principal causes of the current situation:

+ A failure of local NHS organisations to recognise and deal with this major public health problem.

+ A lack of political pressure and leadership over many years.
+ The absence of a patient voice.
+ A lack of resources.
+ A lack of central direction to suggest that this is a key priority.
+ An absence of performance management.

It also believed that sexual health and HIV must be explicitly prioritised at both a local and national level. In reply to a request for information about abortions under the Freedom of Information Act 2000[65] the DH reported that the Teenage Pregnancy Strategy was working and between 1998 and 2004 the under-18 conception rate had fallen by 11.1 per cent and the under-16 rate by 15.2 per cent, with both rates at their lowest for 20 years. The Healthcare Commission in its findings on a review of data on sexual health in 2007[66] stated that in spite of these falling rates, the rate of under-18 conception in the most deprived 10 per cent of wards was still four times higher than the rate in the least deprived wards. The Healthcare Commission recommended improving data, information and planning and ensuring progress, standards and effectiveness are maintained through the national strategy for sexual health and HIV. It also found that chlamydia increased by more than 300 per cent between 1996 and 2005.

The Independent Advisory Group on Sexual Health reported in 2007 that the high rate of teenage pregnancy and sexually transmitted diseases were related to the culture of drinking and drug-taking among the young. It urged the government to do more to join up its campaigns on drugs, binge drinking and under-age sex.[67]

The British Medical Association published a report in December 2003 on adolescent health and highlighted weaknesses in controlling the epidemic of sexually transmitted infections. A ministerial letter was published giving guidance for local authorities and primary care trusts on teenage pregnancy in 2006.[68] The aim is to halve the under-18 conception rate by 2010. 'Every Child Matters' sets out the key features in the DH's strategy to reduce teenage pregnancy. It can be accessed on its own website.[69]

For some of the complex legal issues that can arise in this field, see the author's article.[70] Legal issues relating to abortion are considered in Chapter 15 and pregnancy in Chapter 14.

Litigation and the child or young person

Special rules relate to bringing or defending legal action in the name of a person under 18 years in order to protect the interests of the child or young person. The details can be found in Part 21 of the Civil Procedure Rules.[71] In addition, as noted in Chapter 6, where a child has been injured the time limit within which any claim for compensation must be brought does not commence until the person becomes 18 and if that individual suffers from a mental defect, the time limit does not start until the defect ends (usually not till death).

Conclusions

If the recommendations of the Kennedy Report[72] were to be implemented across the NHS there would be a change of culture of relationships between professionals and patients and parents: respect, honesty, openness and partnership would be in place. The NSF for children should ensure that minimum standards are in place for the care and treatment of children both in hospital and in the community. The incorporation of the UN Charter of the Rights of the Child into the law of the UK would make a fundamental difference to the recognition and enforcement of the rights of the child. In December 2007 the Children's Secretary Ed Balls published a ten-year Children's Plan which includes a comprehensive review of Child and Adolescent Mental Health Services, the primary school curriculum, speech and language therapy and Special Educational Needs, the development of masters-level qualifications for all new teachers, a national plan to tackle child obesity, a review of poor housing and a Youth Crime Action Plan.[73] This ambitious plan is likely to have a major influence on children's services over the next decade.

Reflection questions

1 What is the difference between a child of 15 and one of 16 years as far as consent to treatment is concerned? What is the effect of the Family Law Reform Act 1969 Section 8?

2 The occupier's duty of care for the safety of the visitor should take into account the possibility that children require greater care (see the second Statute on page 288). What is meant by this and how does it affect the work of the children's nurse?

3 Consider the extent to which your department allows parents to take part in the care of children in hospital. What additional responsibilities does this place on the nurse?

Further exercises

1 Examine the UN Charter of the Rights of the Child. What impact does this have on the care of the child in hospital?

2 Obtain a copy of your NHS trust's procedure on the care of suspected non-accidental injury cases and familiarise yourself with it.

3 If you were faced with a very disobedient child, how would you control him?

4 Does the law require that every effort be made to save every child no matter how handicapped? (See also Chapter 14 on special care.)

5 Access the procedures for child protection prepared by your organisation and familiarise yourself with their implications for your work.

References

[1] P.R. Ghandhi, *Blackstone's International Human Rights Documents*, Oxford University Press, 3rd edition, Oxford, 2003

[2] Department of Health, Welfare of Children and Young People in Hospital, HMSO, London, 1991

[3] Audit Commission, Children First: a study of hospital services, HMSO, London, 1993

[4] Royal College of Nursing, Children's Services: acute health care provision, Order No. 001055, RCN, June 1999

[5] Royal College of Nursing, Children's Services: acute health care provision, Order No. 001156, RCN, July 2001

6   Royal College of Nursing, Children and Young People's Nursing: a philosophy of care guidance for nursing staff, Order No. 002012, RCN, April 2003

7   Royal College of Nursing, Preparing Nurses to Care for Children and Young People, Order No. 001997, RCN, April 2003; Royal College of Nursing, Signpost Guide for Nurses Working with Young People, Order No. 002021, RCN, April 2003

8   British Medical Association, Consent, Rights and Choices in the Healthcare for Children and Young People, BMA, 2001

9   In re W (A Minor: medical treatment) [1992] 4 All ER 627

10 Ibid.

11 Re E (A Minor: wardship: medical treatment) [1993] 1 FLR 386 FD

12 Re S (A Minor: consent to medical treatment) [1994] 2 FLR 1065

13 R (On the application of Axon) v. Secretary of State [2006] EWHC 37 admin

14 In re R (A Minor: wardship: consent to medical treatment) [1991] 4 All ER 177 CA

15 Ian Kennedy and Andrew Grubb, Medical Law, Butterworths, London, 2000

16 Gillick v. West Norfolk and Wisbech AHA and the DHSS [1985] 3 All ER 402

17 Re L (Medical treatment: Gillick competency) [1999] 1 Med L Review 58; [1998] 2 FLR 810

18 Re M (Medical treatment: consent) [1999] 2 FLR 1097

19 In re D (A Minor: wardship, sterilisation) [1976] 1 All ER 327

20 In re B (A Minor: wardship, sterilisation) [1987] 2 All ER 206

21 R v. Portsmouth Hospitals NHS Trust ex p Glass [1999] 2 FLR 905; [1999] Lloyd's Law Rep Med 367

22 Glass v. United Kingdom, The Times Law Report, 11 March 2004, ECHR

23 Damian Whitworth, Joy of the family in front line of science, The Times, 5 October 2000

24 In re O (A Minor: medical treatment) [1993] 4 Med LR 272

25 In re A (Minors: conjoined twins: medical treatment), The Times Law Report, 10 October 2000

26 In re B (A Minor) [1981] 1 WLR 1421

27 Re C (a minor) (medical treatment – refusal of parental consent) [1997] 8 Med LR 166 CA known as Re T [1997] 1 All ER 906

28 The Times, 29 October 1993

29 Michael Horsnell, Couple jailed for starving tortured daughter to death, The Times, 21 September 2002

30 R v. Arthur (1981) 12 BMLR 1

31 Royal College of Paediatrics and Child Health, Withholding or Withdrawing Life Saving Treatment in Children: a framework for practice, RCPCH, September 1997 (reissued in 2004)

32 British Medical Association, Withholding and Withdrawing Life-prolonging Medical Treatment, 2nd edition, BMA, 2000

33 Clare Dyer, £100,000 for abused siblings council failed to take into care, The Guardian, 17 September 2007

34 Pierce v. Doncaster Metropolitan Borough Council, The Times Law Report, 27 December 2007

35 Department of Health, Home Office, Department for Education and Employment, the National Assembly for Wales, Working Together to Safeguard Children, Department of Health, 1999

36 http://www.victoria-climbie-inquiry.org.uk/

37 Department of Health, Keeping Children Safe, The Stationery Office, London, 2003

38 Department of Health, What To Do if You're Worried a Child is Being Abused, DH, 2003; www.dh.gov.uk/safeguardingchildren/index.htm

39 Department of Health, Every Child Matters, Green Paper, September 2003

[40] Royal College of Nursing, Child Protection: every nurse's responsibility, Order No. 002045, RCN, June 2003; available on www.rcn.org.uk

[41] Both reports are available from the website www.everychildmatters.gov.uk

[42] *DP and JC* v. *United Kingdom* (Application No. 38719/97), The Times Law Report, 23 October 2002 ECHR; [2003] I.F.L.R. 50

[43] *E and Others* v. *United Kingdom* (Application No. 33218/96), The Times Law Report, 4 December 2002 ECHR

[44] *A and Another* v. *Essex County Council*, The Times Law Report, 24 January 2003

[45] *RK and MK* v. *Oldham NHS Trust*, Lloyd's Rep Med 1 [2003] 1

[46] *JD* v. *East Berkshire Community NHS Trust, North Staffordshire Hospital NHS Trust and Others*, Lloyd's Rep Med 1 [2003] 9; [2005] UKHL 23; [2005] 2 All ER 443

[47] *Lawrence* v. *Pembrokeshire County Council* [2007] EWCA Civ 446

[48] *L (A Child) and Another* v. *Reading Borough Council and Another (No. 2)*, The Times Law Report, 27 December 2007

[49] Royal College of Nursing, Administering Intravenous Therapy to Children in the Community Setting - guidance for nursing staff, Order No. 001244, RCN, October 2001

[50] *A v. The United Kingdom* (100/1997/884/1096) judgment on 23 September 1998; (1999) 27 EHRR 611

[51] Royal College of Nursing, Restraining, Holding Still and Containing Children, Order No. 000999, RCN, March 1999

[52] Joint Committee on Human Rights, The UN Convention on the Rights of the Child, HL Paper 117 (incorporating HL Paper 98.i and ii of 2003), HC 81 (incorporating HC 1103-I of 2001-02 and 81-I of 2002-03), The Stationery Office, London, 2003

[53] Francis Elliott, Parents face total smacking ban as rules are reviewed, *The Times*, 16 June 2007, p. 11

[54] News item, Total smacking ban is ruled out, *The Times*, 26 October 2007

[55] Royal College of Nursing, Skill-mix and Staffing in Children's Wards and Departments, Order No. 001054, RCN, July 1999

[56] http://publications.teachernet.gov.uk Meeting the educational needs of children and young people in hospital

[57] Department of Health press release 2002/0432, 16 October 2002

[58] Department of Health, NHS Plan: a plan for investment, a plan for reform, Cm 4818-1 The Stationery Office, July 2000

[59] www.dh.gov.uk/nsf/children

[60] www.healthcarecommission.org.uk/

[61] Department of Health, Making every young person with diabetes matter, 2007

[62] Department of Health press release 2001/0579, 29 November 2001

[63] www.info.dh.gov.uk/tpu/tpu.nsf/vwwebhome?openview

[64] Independent Advisory Group on Sexual Health and HIV, Response to the Health Select Committee Report on Sexual Health, DH, January 2004

[65] Department of Health, Abortion: Numbers of previous abortions by age, 9 February 2007

[66] www.healthcarecommission.org.uk

[67] Rosemary Bennett, Alcohol and drugs fuel rise in dangers of teen sex, *The Times*, 15 June 2007

[68] Department of Health, Teenage Pregnancy next steps: guidance for local authorities and primary care trusts on effective delivery of local strategies, July 2006

[69] Every Child Matters (2007) Teenage pregnancy. www.everychildmatters-gov.uk/health/teenagepregnancy/

[70] B. Dimond, Teenage pregnancy and the law, *British Journal of Midwifery*, February 2002, 10(2), pp. 1005-8

[71] www.justice.gov.uk/civil/procrules_fin/index.htm

[72] Bristol Royal Infirmary Inquiry (Kennedy Report), Learning from Bristol: the report of the public inquiry into children's heart surgery at the Bristol Royal Infirmary 1984-1995, Command paper Cm 5207

[73] The Children's Plan. Building Brighter Futures. Department for Children, Schools and Families, December 2007. http://www.dfes.gov.uk/publications/childrensplan/downloads/The_Childrens_Plan.pdf (last accessed 25 January 2008)

Chapter 14
Midwifery

Introduction

The midwife has always been in a special position compared with the general nurse in relation to her powers and duties. She is recognised as an independent practitioner with considerable powers in the prescribing and administration of certain drugs that in the past were not possessed by the general nurse. (There have been recent extensions to the prescribing powers of the nurse and other professionals (see Chapter 28).) This section considers the special position of the midwife in law and the effects of some recent cases on midwifery practice.

Midwifery Committee

The Midwifery Committee is a statutory committee of the NMC required by Article 3 of the Nursing and Midwifery Order[1] (see Chapter 11). Its role is to advise the Council, at the Council's request or otherwise, on any matters affecting midwifery (Article 41(1)). The Council is required to consult the Midwifery Committee on the exercise of its functions insofar as it affects midwifery including any proposal to make rules under Article 42 (Article 41(2)). Under Article 42(1) the Council is required by rules to regulate the practice of midwifery and the aims of the rules are set out in Box 14.1.

The NMC identifies the role of the Midwifery Committee as including:

+ setting standards for LSAs (see below)
+ supervision of midwives in accordance with the Nursing and Midwifery Order
+ reporting to the NMC Midwifery Committee
+ compliance with Rule 44 of the midwives' rules and codes of practice
+ equity of access to a supervisor of midwives
+ communications between supervisors of midwives
+ record-keeping systems
+ supervisory systems
+ investigation of misconduct allegations
+ supporting and developing future leaders.

Midwives' rules and code of practice

Under Article 42 of the Nursing and Midwifery Order 2001,[2] the NMC must make rules regulating the practice of midwifery. Box 14.1 indicates the purpose of these rules. One of the most significant rules is set out in Box 14.2.

Box 14.1	Aims of the midwives' rules (Article 42(1) of the Nursing and Midwifery Order 2001)

1 To determine the circumstances in which and the procedure by means of which midwives may be suspended from practice.

2 To require midwives to give notice of their intention to practise to the local supervising authority (LSA) for the area in which they intend to practise.

3 To require registered midwives to attend courses of instruction in accordance with the rules.

> **Box 14.2**   Rule 6: responsibility and sphere of practice
>
> 1 A practising midwife is responsible for providing midwifery care, in accordance with such standards as the council may specify from time to time, to a mother and baby during the antenatal, intra-natal and post-natal periods.
>
> 2 Except in an emergency, a practising midwife shall not provide any care, or undertake any treatment which she has not been trained to give.
>
> 3 In an emergency, or where a deviation from the norm which is outside her current sphere of practice becomes apparent in a woman or baby during the antenatal, intra-natal or post-natal periods, a practising midwife shall call such qualified health professional as may reasonably be expected to have the necessary skills and experience to assist her in the provision of care.

In addition to the midwives' rules, a midwives' Code of Practice[3] has been prepared, originally by the UKCC but it has been reprinted by the NMC. This is complementary to the practice rules but, unlike the practice rules, it does not have the force of law. The NMC has consulted on changes to both the rules and the midwives' Code of Practice and two of the Statutory Instruments which came into force on 1 August 2004 SI 2004/1764 (Midwives Rules) and SI 2004/1654 (Fitness and Practise). They can be downloaded from the website of the NMC or the Office of Public Sector Information. Of course, the midwives would also be expected to comply with the NMC Code of Professional Conduct and other guidance from the NMC. It is not the intention to consider every one of these rules and codes in detail, but rather to consider some of the more common problems concerning the midwife. Every midwife should ensure that she has copies of all the relevant NMC guidance. The Midwifery Committee's recommendations of pre-registration training for midwifery are considered in Chapter 11.

Local supervising authorities (LSAs)

Midwives are subjected to statutory supervision that is regulated through local supervising authorities, which arrange for the appointment of supervisors of midwives. The NMC has the power to prescribe the qualifications of persons who may be appointed by the LSA to exercise supervision over midwives in its area and no one shall be appointed who does not comply with these. The Nursing and Midwifery Order 2001[4] Articles 42 and 43 provide detailed rules on the establishment and functions of the LSAs and the supervisor of midwives and these are supplemented by the Midwives' Rules[5] and the Midwives' Code of Practice. If rules are made requiring midwives to give the notice of intention to practise, the LSA must inform the Council of any notice that has been given to it (Article 41(2)). The Rules were amended in 2007 to require a local supervising authority to appoint supervisors of midwives and setting revised requirements for their appointment.[6] The local supervising authority has the following duties set by Article 43:

1 To exercise general supervision in accordance with the rules made under Article 42 over all midwives practising in its area.

2 To report to the Council where it appears that the fitness to practise of a midwife in its area is impaired.

3 To exercise power in accordance with the rules made under Article 42 to suspend a midwife from practice.

Under Article 43(3) the Council is required to set rules establishing the standards for the exercise by LSAs of their functions and may give guidance to LSAs on these matters.

New Fitness to Practise procedures came into force on 1 August 2004 – which can be downloaded from the NMC or Office of Public Sector Information websites.

Law relating to consent in midwifery care

Opposition to the midwife

> ### Practical Dilemma 14.1   Refusal to have a midwife
>
> Sharon Keene made it clear when her pregnancy was diagnosed that she wanted a natural birth and would not wish the midwife to attend. Sheila Armstrong, a community midwife, visited her and found her aggressive and hostile. She made it clear to Sheila that she did not want to be confined in hospital, but wanted her co-habitee, Jason, to deliver the baby. Sheila told her that if that were to occur, Jason would be acting illegally and Sheila attempted to explain to Sharon the help and assistance that could be made available from the midwifery services. As the pregnancy progressed, Sharon refused all antenatal care and failed to attend clinic appointments. Where does Sheila stand if she discovers that Sharon intends to proceed with Jason delivering the baby?

Midwives occasionally meet women who are keen to 'go it alone' and not receive help during the pregnancy and also wish to have the baby delivered at home. There is no legal action that can be taken to prevent this if the woman is a mentally competent adult. She can refuse treatment and help for a good reason, a bad reason or, indeed, for no reason at all (see *Re MB*, Case 14.1). In practice, however, Sheila cannot compel Sharon to receive help. Neither could Sharon be prevented from having a home birth. Even if this is not clinically desirable, there is no legal power to compel a mentally capacitated woman to come into hospital for the confinement.

Criminal offence

It is, however, a criminal offence for a person, other than a midwife or doctor, to attend at a confinement except in an emergency. The actual wording of Article 45 of the Nursing and Midwifery Order 2001[7] is as follows:

(1) A person other than a registered midwife or a registered medical practitioner shall not attend a woman in childbirth.

(2) This paragraph does not apply:
   a. Where the attention is given in a case of sudden or urgent necessity or
   b. In the case of a person who, while undergoing professional training with a view to becoming a medical practitioner or becoming a midwife, attends a woman in childbirth as part of a course of practical instruction in midwifery recognised by the Council or by the GMC.

(3) A person who contravenes paragraph (1) shall be liable of summary conviction to a fine not exceeding level 5 on the standard scale.

Thus if Jason (in Practical Dilemma 14.1) delivered the baby himself, he would be committing a crime. The only exception would be if there were an emergency and the baby arrived before they were aware of it. It is, of course, very difficult to prove that it was not an emergency and that there was no intention to call the midwife. Sheila would be able to warn the couple of the law and she would, of course, record this warning in her notes and also inform her supervisor of midwives. There have been some prosecutions under this section and its predecessor. For example, Rupert Baines from Bristol was found guilty of delivering a baby without assistance and Brian Radley from Wolverhampton was charged with attending a woman in childbirth otherwise than under the direction and personal supervision of a duly qualified practitioner and was fined £100 (August 1983). The difficulty confronting the midwife is in ensuring that she is aware of when the baby is imminent, since the aim is to protect the mother and child rather than take proceedings after the birth.

If she were obstructed by an aggressive partner during a home confinement, the midwife would be able to call on police powers to assist her.

Guidance on delegation of tasks by a midwife was provided by the NMC in January 2004 and is discussed in Chapter 24.[8]

Admission and treatment

Choice of treatment by mother

> **Practical Dilemma 14.2**   Consent
>
> Glenys Brown was expecting her first child. From the first moment the pregnancy was diagnosed, she was totally absorbed in her condition and the forthcoming event. She joined the local childbirth group and was very soon the local secretary. She attended psychoprophylactic and yoga classes and avidly read books, journals, leaflets and all available information. She had clear ideas on how her own baby was to be born and while she would have preferred total immersion in water, she accepted the fact that this would not be available in her local hospital. She was, however, adamant that she would not agree to an epidural, gas, an episiotomy or any other unnatural procedures. She was admitted to the delivery ward and after 12 hours of contractions the doctor set up a drip to speed the delivery as it was feared that the foetus was in danger. Glenys was eventually given an episiotomy despite her protests. She is now threatening to sue the midwife and doctor. Where do the midwife and doctor stand in law?

The basic principles relating to consent to treatment (set out in Chapter 7) apply to midwifery. There are no separate statutory laws covering the situation. The general principle is that the mentally competent patient has the right to refuse treatment and any touching or treatment without her consent is a trespass to her person. If the mother were to sue the midwife for assault, the only defence of the midwife would be that either the woman gave consent or the woman was mentally incompetent and that action was taken without her consent in her best interests in accordance with the provisions of the Mental Capacity Act 2005. There is no statutory right to compel a mentally capacitated mother to go into hospital for the birth of a child whatever the clinical indications. If the mentally capacitated mother refuses admission, then the midwife has to do all that is reasonable to support her at home.

Evidence suggests that many mothers, who would have wished to have had a home birth, are being discouraged from that in spite of the principles set out in the Cumberlege Report, 'Changing Childbirth'. The UKCC issued a position statement,[9] 'Supporting Women who Wish to Have a Home Birth', enabling more women to be able to opt for home birth. The position statement clarified the professional position of the midwife in respect of the provision of midwifery care for women who wish to have a home birth. In May 2005 the NMC Midwifery Committee approved a report provided by Julie Magill-Cuerdin on home births[10] which concluded that despite the lack of random controlled research:

> Nonetheless, the evidence for the safety of home birth is mostly consistent from the studies undertaken. The issue of trust between professionals and women and respecting their individual choices appears to be a key area in developing a home birth service.

The NMC in March 2006 published a circular on 'Midwives and home birth'.[11] This outlines the professional duty of the midwife to support the woman and the woman's right to a choice for care including the place of birth. It states:

> Should a conflict arise between service provision and a woman's choice for place of birth, a midwife has a duty of care to attend her.

It suggests that each LSA should have a plan of action in place to support home births.

The National Perinatal Epidemiology Unit is leading research into women's experiences of maternity services and the safety and quality of care. 'Birthplace' is an integrated programme of research designed to compare outcomes of births planned at home in different types of maternity units, and in hospital units with obstetric services. The results should provide evidence of the outcomes of the different places of birth. It is also intended to contribute to the implementation of Standard 11 of the National Service Framework (see below). Further information is available on the NPEU website. Current plans of the government, as outlined in 'Maternity Matters',[12] envisage that all women have the choice of a home birth (see page 381).

Consent to Caesarean section

There are no statutory powers to compel a mentally competent woman to receive treatment or admission against her will. In an early case, *In re S*,[13] a woman was compelled to have a Caesarean section against her will, but the basis for this decision is no longer acceptable. Subsequently, the High Court agreed that a Caesarean could be carried out without the consent of a woman who was suffering from mental disorder.[14] Section 63 Mental Health Act 1983 permitted treatment to be given to a detained patient for mental disorder and the Caesarean was considered to come within the definition of treatment for mental disorder. In a second case,[15] a compulsory Caesarean was declared lawful where a woman with a history of psychiatric treatment denied that she was pregnant. The judge held that there was evidence that the woman was mentally incapacitated and that there was power to act at common law in an emergency out of necessity to use reasonable force in her best interests. In a third case,[16] a woman was declared mentally incompetent and a Caesarean authorised against her will. These cases (two of which were heard by the same judge) led to considerable concern among midwives and women over the protection of the rights of the women.

Two decisions by the Court of Appeal have clarified the law on compulsion.

> ### Case 14.1 — Re MB (An Adult: medical treatment) (1997)
>
> **Capacity and compulsory Caesarean**[17]
>
> Miss MB required a Caesarean section in order to save her foetus. However, while she gave consent to the operation, she suffered from a needle phobia, which caused her to panic and refuse the preliminary anaesthetic. The trust applied for a declaration that the Caesarean could take place. The judge held that the woman was mentally incapacitated as a result of the phobia and the operation could therefore proceed in her best interests. The same day the Court of Appeal upheld that decision. In a reserved judgment it set out how capacity was to be determined (see Box 14.3) and the general principles that apply to the refusal of treatment (see Box 14.4).

> ### Box 14.3 — Determining capacity: Re MB
>
> A person lacks the capacity if some impairment or disturbance of mental functioning renders the person unable to make a decision whether to consent to or to refuse treatment. That inability to make a decision will occur when:
>
> **(a)** The patient is unable to comprehend and retain the information that is material to the decision, especially as to the likely consequences of having or not having the treatment in question.
>
> **(b)** The patient is unable to use the information and weigh it in the balance as part of the process of arriving at the decision.

> ### Box 14.4 — Principles laid down in Re MB and incorporated in guidance issued by the Department of Health[18]
>
> 1 The court is unlikely to entertain an application for a declaration unless the capacity of the patient to consent to or refuse the medical treatment is in issue.
> 2 For the time being, at least, the doctors ought to seek a ruling from the High Court on the issue of competence.
> 3 Those in charge should identify a potential problem as early as possible so that both the hospital and the patient can obtain legal advice.
> 4 It is highly desirable that, in any case where it is not an emergency, steps are taken to bring it before the court, before it becomes an emergency, to remove the extra pressure from the parties and the court and to enable proper instructions to be taken, particularly from the patient and, where possible, give the opportunity for the court to hear oral evidence, if appropriate.
> 5 The hearing should be *inter partes*.
> 6 The mother should be represented in all cases, unless, exceptionally, she does not wish to be. If she is unconscious she should have a guardian *ad litem*.
> 7 The Official Solicitor should be notified of all applications to the High Court . . .
> 8 There should in general be some evidence, preferably but not necessarily from a psychiatrist, as to the competence of the patient, if competence is in issue.
> 9 Where time permits, the person identified to give the evidence as to capacity to consent to or refuse treatment should be made aware of the observations made by the Court of Appeal in this judgment.
> 10 In order to be in a position to assess a patient's best interests the judge should be provided, where possible and if time allows, with information about the circumstances of any relevant background material about the patient.

The Court of Appeal emphasised that every person is presumed to have the capacity to consent to or to refuse medical treatment unless and until that presumption is rebutted. A competent woman who has the capacity to decide may, for religious reasons, other reasons, for rational or irrational reasons or for no reason at all, choose not to have medical intervention, even though the consequence may be the death or serious handicap of the child she bears, or her own death. In that event, the courts do not have the jurisdiction to declare medical intervention lawful and the question of her own best interests, objectively considered, does not arise.

The ruling in *Re MB* was followed by the Court of Appeal in a case brought against St George's Hospital.[19] In this case, the pregnant woman had refused treatment for pre-eclampsia. She was detained under Section 2 of the Mental Health Act 1983 and a declaration sought from the High Court that a Caesarean section could proceed. The declaration was given and the operation carried out. The patient subsequently appealed to the Court of Appeal and won on the grounds that she was wrongly detained under the Mental Health Act 1983 and the Caesarean section should not have been ordered. Guidelines were subsequently issued by the court where there were serious doubts about a patient's capacity to accept or refuse treatment.[20]

In *Re T* 1992,[21] which is discussed in Chapter 7 (Case 7.5), the Court of Appeal emphasised that professionals had a duty to check on the validity of a patient's refusal to have treatment to ensure that the patient is mentally capacitated and is not under an undue influence.

Acting in the best interests of a mentally incapacitated woman

While a woman who is deemed mentally capacitated can make a decision to refuse life-saving treatment, once it is determined that a woman lacks the requisite mental capacity to make decisions on her own behalf, then decisions have to be made in her best interests. In Scotland, the Adults with Incapacity (Scotland) Act 2000 covers the situation and since October 2007 the Mental Capacity Act 2005 makes provision for England and Wales, replacing the common law powers which had been recognised by the House of Lords in the *Re F* case.[22] Under the Mental Capacity Act 2005 action must be taken in the best interests of the adult who lacks the requisite mental capacity to make her own decisions. The Mental Capacity Act 2005 sets out the steps which must be taken in deciding what is in the best interests of the person who lacks the requisite capacity to make a specific decision (see Chapter 7, page 151). Where serious medical treatment is being considered and there is no informal carer or person to be consulted, an independent mental capacity advocate must be appointed who could report on the person's best interests.

Liability of the mother for harm caused to the baby

Civil liability

If a mother refuses treatment that is necessary in the interests of the child (for example, an episiotomy), does the child have a right of action for compensation against the mother because of the harm that she or he suffered? The only right of action for a child who was injured pre-natally is under the Congenital Disabilities (Civil Liability) Act 1976 (see page 369). This Act enables a child who is born injured as a result of negligence, which led to his or her suffering harm while a foetus, to sue the person responsible. However, under the Act, the mother can only be sued by the child's representative if she was driving a motor vehicle when she knew or ought reasonably to have known that she was pregnant and failed to take care for the safety of the unborn child. (In practice, the child would be suing the company that insured the mother as driver.) The Act, therefore, excludes the right of a child to sue for any harm that the mother may have caused the foetus, for example, by smoking, drinking, taking drugs or refusing treatment that is necessary in the best interests of the foetus.

Criminal liability

The mother could be liable in the criminal law under the Infant Life Preservation Act 1929. This makes it a criminal offence for any person who, with intent to destroy the life of a child capable of being born alive, by any wilful act causes a child to die before it has an existence independent of its mother (Section 11). There is a defence if the act that caused the death of the child was done in good faith for the purposes only of preserving the life of the mother. There are also criminal provisions relating to attempting to procure an abortion by administering drugs or using an instrument or supplying the same under the Offences Against the Person Act 1861 Sections 58 and 59. For further discussion on this, see Chapter 15.

However, in the context we are considering here, i.e. where a pregnant woman is smoking, addicted to drugs or drink or is refusing a Caesarean, it is not thought that she would have the necessary intent to be found guilty of a criminal act under these provisions. Similarly, a pregnant woman who refused to consent to an episiotomy in the circumstances outlined above would not be committing a criminal offence unless this refusal was made with the intention of causing the death of the child and unless this refusal to give consent could be defined as an offence under the 1929 Act.

Planning for the baby of a young teenage mother

Where the mother is very young, then both she and her baby may be the subject of proceedings under the Children Act 1989 (see Chapter 13 on children). In a case in 2000[23] the Family Division held that while there were no general principles that the babies of young teenagers should be adopted, it was not appropriate to concentrate on the welfare of the mother to the exclusion of the needs of the unborn baby. It was essential that the local authorities began planning for the baby as well as the mother as soon as possible. In this case, the mother, aged 13, and her baby were both living with a foster family where the foster mother was caring for the mother who had returned to full-time schooling. Mrs Justice Bracewell held that there was no general principle that the babies of young teenagers should be adopted, but each case had to be considered on its own facts. She laid down the following principles:

1 Planning for the baby as well as the mother should begin immediately. It was not appropriate to concentrate on the welfare of the mother to the exclusion of the needs of the child to be born.

2 There was a need to complete social work and expert assessments well before the birth to ensure that effective and timely planning could be undertaken.

3 If care proceedings under Section 31 of the Children Act 1989 were necessary, they should be issued on the day of birth and where the mother was very young should be transferred to the High Court and a separate guardian *ad litem* appointed for the mother and the child.

4 The baby's interim placement should be determined on the evidence before the court at an early hearing as a matter of urgency.

5 Early final determination of the case was vital.

6 Twin-track planning and/or concurrent planning was essential where one of the possible outcomes was adoption.

7 It was a misconception for social workers to consider that there was a prohibition on identifying suitable adopters before the final decision of the court, provided that decision was not pre-empted.

The advice of the Family Division is extremely helpful, but one of the usual difficulties in such pregnancies is that the pregnancy comes to light only at a very late stage, requiring very speedy action to be taken by health and social services professionals.

Taking the newly born into care

A child can be taken into care as soon as it is born, if the requirements of the Children Act 1989 are satisfied. This may be so if there is evidence of the woman's conduct in relation to other children in the family.

Case 14.2 *In re D (A Minor) v. Berkshire County Council* (1987)

Pre-birth conduct[24]

At birth (12 March 1985), the child was suffering from symptoms caused by withdrawal from narcotics. The mother had been a registered drug addict since 1982, had continued to take drugs in excess of those prescribed during her pregnancy and had known that by taking drugs while pregnant she could be causing damage to the child. The child was kept in intensive care in hospital for several weeks immediately following the birth. A place of safety order was obtained on 23 April 1985, followed by successive interim orders.

The House of Lords, in a unanimous judgment, stated that the provisions of Section 1.2(a) of the Children and Young Persons Act 1969 (which stated that if the court is satisfied that the child's 'proper development is being avoidably prevented or neglected or he is being ill-treated . . . and also that he is in need of care and control then . . . the court may, if it thinks fit, make such an order' (now re-enacted in the Children Act 1989)) should be given a broad and liberal construction that gives full effect to their legislative purpose. They saw no reason why the courts should not look back to the time before the child had been born. However, in this case, the mother was still a drug addict and there was thus a continuum between the pre-natal and post-natal period. The decision of the House of Lords against the mother cannot be used as a precedent for arguing that if the mother has failed to take care of herself and the foetus during pregnancy, this will constitute grounds for a care order irrespective of her post-natal care of the child. There is no recognition in law of a child's right to receive, pre-natally, a responsible standard of care from its mother. The Court of Appeal[25] has said that a care order is not available in respect of an unborn child (see Case 14.5).

Midwifery practice and standard of care

Midwives' Rule 6 (see Box 14.2) states that, except in an emergency, the midwife shall not provide midwifery care or undertake any treatment that she has not been trained to give. This general rule embraces a principle that applies to all NMC practitioners.

Midwife and doctor

Confidential information from the NHS Litigation Authority published by the *Observer* on 23 September 2007 revealed that current claims against the NHS for negligence amounted to almost £4.5 billion, of which £3.3 billion related to incidents alleging oxygen starvation at birth.[26] The standard of care provided by doctor and midwife is central to such allegations. The principles relating to the duty and standard of care discussed in Chapter 3 apply to the role of the midwife, but specific concerns can arise over the respective role of midwife and doctor. The midwife would be expected to follow the standard of care as defined by applying the Bolam Test. Research findings and publications by the National Institute for Health and Clinical Excellence (see below and Chapter 5) and recommendations from professional bodies such as the Royal College of Obstetricians and Gynaecologists and Royal College of Midwives also provide evidence for deducing what would be a reasonable standard of care. Rule 40 has been the subject of considerable debate and its successor Rule 6 is set out in Box 14.2 on page 358. It is at the heart of the debate of the respective roles and relationship of midwife and doctor.

In Case 14.3, although the time of gastric aspiration was uncertain, it was felt that the nursing staff had not adequately appraised the doctor of the patient's deteriorating condition and on this basis the hospital's solicitors accepted a proportion of liability. The inadequate attention paid to the patient by the general practitioner in the early post-operative period was thought to be of major significance. The MDU paid two-thirds of the agreed damages.[27] The acceptance of the nurse's partial liability in this case shows how important communication between the practitioners is in the care of the patient and the degree of responsibility that falls on the nurse's shoulders in ensuring that the doctor is adequately informed of the patient's progress or deterioration. The case also shows the importance of detailed and accurate records. In other circumstances, it could well be that the nurse appreciated the severity of the patient's condition, but that the doctor failed to respond to the entreaties to come. Accurate recordings of the times that phone calls were made, together with their content, will be partial evidence of the nurse's understanding of the situation. In serious cases, it may not be sufficient to rely on the judgement of one doctor and it may be necessary to take alternative action, which is a difficult dilemma for junior nursing and midwifery staff.

Case 14.3   Midwife and doctor mix-up[27]

A 25-year-old woman was delivered of a normal baby by Caesarean section in a small district hospital. The general practitioner who gave the anaesthetic had no specialist anaesthetic qualifications. The procedure lasted for two hours and was technically difficult because of adhesions from a previous Caesarean section. In the immediate post-operative period, the patient developed peripheral cyanosis with a drop in blood pressure (88/60) and was treated with intravenous fluids and oxygen. When she seemed to have improved, the doctor left the hospital.

An hour later, the patient developed a cough and tachycardia and the nurses gave linctus pholcodine. Ninety minutes later, the doctor was informed by telephone that the patient had a persistent cough and he ordered oral aminophylline. After another 90 minutes, he was summoned urgently because the patient had severe progressive respiratory distress and cyanosis. An X-ray confirmed Mendelssohn's syndrome and the patient was transferred to the main hospital where she required intensive resuscitation; she had sustained brain stem infarction with pseudobulbar palsy, spastic quadriparesis and cortical blindness. The Medical Defence Union (MDU) considered the claim for damages to be indefensible.

Litigation, time limits and record keeping

Litigation in obstetrics and midwifery is increasing more than in any other specialty and the levels of compensation are, because of the costs of keeping a severely brain-damaged person for 40 to 50 years, among the highest payments, which have reached over £3 million per case. In addition, although the usual time limit for adults bringing a civil action for compensation is usually three years from the date of the negligent incident or the knowledge of it or the harm suffered (see Chapter 6), where there is mental disability, the time limits do not come into force until the mental disability ends (which usually is not until death). The result is that many cases may not come to court for many years after the events, as the following case shows.

Case 14.4 — Midwife and health visitor mix-up[28]

When Sonja Taylor was born in 1974, both the midwife and the health visitor thought that the blood test for phenylketonuria had already been performed. The hospital records were not consulted. As a result, the child became seriously brain-damaged and the parents were not aware of the problem until it was too late to rectify it. Had the test been conducted, the child could have been placed on a diet and the harm prevented. In March 2000, £2.5 million was awarded in respect of this act of negligence.

Community midwife

Practical Dilemma 14.3 — Community midwifery

A very active community midwifery service existed in Roger Park District Health Authority. The midwives were proud of the fact that there was a much higher proportion of community confinements than in the rest of the country. In the community, medical support was provided by those general practitioners who had opted to care for obstetrical cases. Not all these GPs had received recent training in obstetrical practice. One such GP was Dr Marks, a 65-year-old doctor who had not attended a revision course in the last 30 years. He was a doctor of very fixed ideas. Grace Edwards had been practising midwifery for 18 years and had recently undertaken her statutory revision course at a large London hospital. She was called to Brenda Rice's home at 3.00 a.m. Grace realised that the birth was imminent. She phoned Dr Marks, advising him to come immediately and giving him details of the mother and foetal condition that were giving her cause for concern. On arrival, Dr Marks disagreed with Grace's view of the severity of the situation and refused to agree to an ambulance being called. He considered that a forceps delivery could be performed safely. Unfortunately, this proved not to be so and the baby was stillborn.

In a dilemma such as this, the midwife cannot avoid responsibility for her actions by saying that she obeyed the GP. If it is clear that his advice is mistaken and she fears for the health of the mother or baby, then she has a personal professional duty to them and would have to take further action. In extreme circumstances, this might mean summoning an ambulance or calling out an obstetrician from the hospital despite the objections of the GP. This example also illustrates the importance of ensuring that the community midwife should be experienced.

Breastfeeding

The Breastfeeding etc. (Scotland) Act 2005 made it an offence deliberately to prevent or stop a person in charge of a child from feeding milk to that child in a public place or on licensed premises. An exception to this offence is if the child at the material time is not lawfully permitted to be in the public place or on the licensed premises otherwise than for the purpose of being fed milk. Under Section 2 anything done by a person in the course of that person's employment shall be treated for the purposes of this Act as done also by that person's employer, whether or not it was done with the employer's knowledge or approval.[29] This Act only applies to Scotland and at the time of writing there are proposals for an Equality Bill which would introduce similar provisions for breastfeeding in a public place in England. The DH has stated that it is fully committed to the promotion of breastfeeding and has provided guidance on maternal and infant nutrition.[30]

Medicines and the midwife

In Chapter 28, the law relating to medicines and administration and prescribing is considered. Here the specific powers of a midwife in relation to medicines are considered.

Under the Misuse of Drugs Regulations 2001 Clause 11,[31] a registered midwife who has notified the local supervising authority of her intention to practise may possess and administer any controlled drug in so far as is necessary for the practice of midwifery and may surrender to her appropriate medical officer any stocks no longer required. A midwife may lawfully possess only those drugs that she had obtained on a midwife's supply order signed by the medical officer. The midwife's supply order must specify in writing:

1 name

2 occupation of midwife

3 purpose for which the drug is required

4 total quantity required.

Midwives' Rule 7 makes further regulations on the administration of any medicines in respect of her training and the type and safety of any apparatus for the administration of inhalation analgesic. Rule 7 is shown in Box 14.5.

Box 14.5 **Rule 7**

1 A practising midwife shall only administer those medicines, including analgesics, in which she has received the appropriate training as to use, dosage and methods of administration.

Paragraphs 15 to 25 of the midwives' Code of Practice give further guidance on the supply, possession and use of controlled drugs, destruction and surrender of controlled drugs, controlled drugs and home births, prescription-only and other medicines, administration of homeopathic or herbal substances and the administration of controlled drugs. In March

2003 the NMC issued a circular on the supply and administration of all non-prescription-only medicines and general sales list medicines by registered midwives in the course of their professional practice.[32] It stated that a registered midwife can supply and administer all non-prescription-only medicines and a student midwife, during the course of her programme of education, can administer those medicines under the guidance of a practising midwife, for which the registered midwife remains accountable. The midwife is able to supply and administer medicines from the categories of medicines specified in the Medicines (Pharmacy and General Sale Exemption) Order SI 1980 No. 1924 including nitrous oxide and oxygen without a patient group direction.

Congenital Disabilities (Civil Liability) Act 1976

The Congenital Disabilities Act 1976 was enacted because, following the thalidomide tragedy, it was not clear in law whether the child, once born, had a claim in respect of pre-birth injuries. The Act enables a child who is born alive to sue any person (except the mother, apart from one situation – see below) who has caused him to be born disabled as a result of an act of negligence. In order for an action to succeed under the Act, it must be established that the harm that occurred was caused by the wrongful act. For example, a pregnant woman could be assaulted and subsequently go into premature labour. The child might suffer from some mental and physical handicaps. It must be established that these disabilities were caused by the assault. Causation in brain damage is particularly difficult to trace, as vaccination cases show. The law does not recognise the foetus as having a legal personality and it therefore cannot have legal rights of its own until it is born and has a separate existence from its mother. Once born, it does then have the right to sue under the Congenital Disabilities (Civil Liability) Act for pre-birth injuries. The 1976 Act was amended by the Human Fertilisation and Embryology Act 1990 by adding Section 1A to the Act. This is shown below and gives a right of action to a child who is born disabled as a result of fertility treatment. The Act can be seen in Appendix B.

Statute — Section 1A of the Congenital Disabilities (Civil Liability) Act

In any case where:

(a) a child carried by a woman as the result of the placing in her of an embryo or of sperm and eggs or her artificial insemination is born disabled,

(b) the disability results from an act or omission in the course of the selection, or the keeping or use outside the body, of the embryo carried by her or of the gametes used to bring about the creation of the embryo and

(c) a person is under this section answerable to the child in respect of the act or omission, the child's disabilities are to be regarded as damage resulting from the wrongful act of that person and actionable accordingly at the suit of the child.

Liability of the midwife

If it can be shown that the midwife has failed without justification to follow the approved accepted practice and, as a consequence, the foetus is harmed and the child is born disabled, the mother has a right of action against her and also against the NHS trust for the injury she has suffered. In addition, the mother can bring a claim in the name of the child for any harm suffered by the child. This latter action can be brought under the Congenital Disabilities (Civil Liability) Act 1976.

Professional standards

Section 1(5) of the Act defines what is meant by professional standards and is set out below.

The working of the Act can be seen in another context. Imagine that another thalidomide-type situation were to occur. It might be possible that the mother had asked the midwife's advice in relation to a particular medicine/food during pregnancy. The midwife might re-assure her that the particular product was fine. If, in fact, it then caused defects to the baby, would the midwife be liable to the baby under the Congenital Disabilities (Civil Liability) Act? The answer is that, if, at the time, her advice was reasonable in relation to what was known about the product and she was following the approved practice in recommending it, she would be unlikely to be found negligent. (The mother might, of course, have other remedies such as against the manufacturers (see Chapter 12 and product liability).)

Statute	**Section 1(5) Congenital Disabilities (Civil Liability) Act 1976**

The defendant is not answerable to the child for anything he did or omitted to do when responsible in a professional capacity for treating or advising the parent, if he took reasonable care having due regard to then received professional opinion applicable to the particular class of case; but this does not mean that he is answerable only because he departed from received opinion.

Child's action is derivative

The child's right of action under the 1976 Act is derivative, i.e. only if the defendant would have been liable to one of the parents is the defendant then liable to the child. The father can be sued by the child. However, if the action concerns an occurrence that took place prior to conception, the defendant is not answerable to the child if at that time either or both of the parents knew of the risk of their child being born disabled. If, however, it is the child's father who is the defendant, the action can continue if he alone knew of the risk, but not the mother. To explain this provision, consider the following circumstance.

Practical Dilemma 14.4	HIV

Bill was aware that he was suffering from AIDS. He was unwilling to allow the special clinic to inform his wife and he refused to give them his address. However, he continued to have sex with her and she became pregnant. She was not aware that she might become HIV positive. The baby was found to be HIV positive.

In this situation, it is possible that the child could maintain a successful action against the father under the provisions of the Act. Bill was in breach of the duty of care owed to the mother in that he failed to warn her that he was suffering from AIDS and as a consequence the baby was born HIV positive. It could be argued, however, that the father's negligence was in failing to prevent the baby from being born, not in actually causing harm to the child and therefore the child would have no claim under the Act. This is discussed below in connection with the McKay case.

If both parents are aware of the possibility of the child being born disabled, no action can be commenced.

Mother's liability under the Act

The mother is liable to the child under the Act only if (Section 2) she is driving a motor vehicle when she knows (or ought reasonably to know) herself to be pregnant. Under this provision, she is to be regarded as being under the same duty to take care for the safety of her unborn child as the law imposes on her with respect to the safety of other people; and if, in consequence of her breach of that duty, her child is born with disabilities that would not otherwise have been present, those disabilities are to be regarded as damage resulting from her wrongful act and actionable accordingly at the suit of the child. In practice, of course, the child would be suing the company who insured the mother.

Rights of the child

An unborn child is not recognised in law as having a legal personality. At birth, however, he or she is able to bring an action in respect of any harm he or she has suffered.

The following case has made it clear that the courts have no power to make an unborn baby a ward of court.

Case 14.5 *In re F (in utero)* (1988)

The rights of the unborn[33]

The mother was aged 36 and had suffered from severe mental disturbance since 1977. Throughout 1982, she had led a nomadic existence, wandering around Europe. She had returned in 1983 and had been settled in a flat in south London. Her only means of support was supplementary benefit. The local authority was concerned about the baby expected towards the end of January. Early in January, the mother disappeared. The local authority instituted wardship proceedings.

The Court of Appeal was of the opinion that if it had the power to institute wardship proceedings it would do so, but did it have the power? It concluded that it did not. There was no jurisdiction for the court to make a foetus a ward of court. The court pointed out the difficulties of enforcing such an order against the mother: 'If the law was to be extended so as to impose control over the expectant mother, where such control was necessary for the benefit of the unborn child then it was for Parliament to decide whether such controls could be imposed and, if so, subject to what limitations. In such a sensitive field affecting the liberty of the individual it was not for the judiciary to extend the law' (per Lord Justice Balcombe).

Action for wrongful life

Case 14.6   *McKay v. Essex AHA* (1982)

German measles[34]

Mrs McKay was pregnant and suspected that she had contracted German measles in the early weeks of her pregnancy. Blood tests were arranged to see if she had been infected. Unfortunately, she was wrongly informed that she had not been infected. When the baby was born, it was found to be disabled as a result of the effect of German measles.

The Court of Appeal held that the child's claim for wrongful life (i.e. if there had been no negligence, the child would have been aborted) could not be sustained. Although this child was born before the Congenital Disabilities Act 1976 was passed, the court still held that an action for wrongful life could not stand, even under the provisions of the Act. This decision does not, of course, affect the rights of the mother to sue for damages resulting from the negligence in informing her of the results of the tests and Mrs McKay brought her own action on that point. The former decision was concerned solely with the rights of the child.

Nurseries within midwifery departments

Problems can sometimes arise within the midwifery department over the responsibility for the nursery nurse staff and those who are caring for the babies. It is essential that clear lines of accountability and responsibility are laid down so that there is no confusion on this point: local practices might differ.

Special care baby units

These units may or may not be under the control of the midwifery department. Some may be under the paediatric department. The nature of the control should not affect the standard of care. The shortage of staff in these units has received much publicity and undoubtedly the pressure on resources has created difficulties for staff. (Resource issues are considered in Chapter 4.)

Care of the grossly handicapped

Those who work in special care baby units face the problem of determining the extent to which heroic measures should be used to prolong the lives of grossly underweight or should be given to severely handicapped babies.

Case 14.7   *Re K* (2006)

Withdrawal of treatment of a 5-month-old child[35]

An NHS trust sought a declaration that a feeding tube could be removed from the abdomen of a premature baby who suffered from a severe congenital neuromuscular disorder. The parents agreed that life-prolonging treatment should cease.

The judge granted the declaration. It was in the child's best interests to cease the total parental nutrition at a time when she was clinically stable, so that she could die in peace and in a comparatively short space of time relieved by palliative care treatment. The situation came within categories 3 and 4 of the Royal College of Paediatrics and Child Health, see below.[36]

It is illegal for the doctors to prescribe, either intentionally or recklessly, a substance to bring about the infant's death. The courts have, however, ruled that there is a legal distinction between killing and letting die and have applied this principle in several cases relating to severely disabled babies.

The Court of Appeal made a declaration in the case of Re C[37] that an infant ward of court who was terminally ill, suffering irreversible and severe brain damage, was to be treated in accordance with the specialist's advice. The paragraph included by the trial judge relating to details of the treatment permitted, preventing the prescribing and administering of antibiotics and preventing the setting up of intravenous fusions or nasal-gastric feeding regimes, was deleted by the Court of Appeal.

In the case of Re J (1990),[38] the baby suffered from severe disabilities and was likely to develop serious spastic quadriplegia and be both deaf and blind. He was not, however, on the point of death or dying. In deciding whether he should be put back on to a mechanical ventilator, the Court of Appeal held that the test to be applied 'must be whether the child in question, if capable of exercising sound judgement, would consider the life tolerable'.

In the case of Re J (1992),[39] the baby suffered from a severe form of cerebral palsy with cortical blindness and severe epilepsy. The Court of Appeal held that the court will not exercise its inherent jurisdiction over minors by ordering a medical practitioner to treat the minor in a manner contrary to the practitioner's clinical judgement. In the practitioner's view, intensive therapeutic measures such as artificial ventilation were inappropriate. The Court of Appeal has declared that it would be lawful for doctors in their professional judgement to allow a severely disabled child to die. If a baby is born alive following an attempted abortion, then all reasonable care must be taken to ensure that the baby has a reasonable chance of surviving.

The Royal College of Paediatrics and Child Health has published guidelines on when it is appropriate to withhold or withdraw medical treatment.[40] The guidelines distinguish between the following clinical situations:

1 the brain-dead child

2 the permanent vegetative state

3 the 'no chance' situation

4 the 'no purpose' situation

5 the 'unbearable' situation.

In all these situations, the possibility of withholding or withdrawal of curative medical treatment might be considered. The guidance emphasises the importance of the fundamental principles of the duty of care and partnership of care and the respect for the rights of the child as set out in the United Nation's Convention on the Rights of the Child.[41] The guidelines of the Royal College of Paediatrics and Child Health represent its interpretation of the law, but are not the law itself. Further advice has been published by the British Medical Association.[42]

In Case 14.8 court held that the paramount consideration was the welfare of the child; the high respect for the sanctity of human life imposed a strong presumption in favour of taking all steps capable of preserving it; there could be no question of the court directing treatment that was contrary to the clinical judgement of the doctor; the court held that full palliative

---

Case 14.8   *NHS Trust* v. *D* (2000)

Death with dignity and human rights[43]

A child since birth had suffered from serious disabilities, in particular a severe, chronic, irreversible and worsening lung disease giving him a very short life expectation, coupled with heart failure, renal and liver dysfunction with a background of severe developmental delay. Doctors advised the NHS trust that it was not in the child's best interests to be resuscitated and the trust applied to court for a declaration. The child's parents opposed the application.

---

treatment was in the child's best interests and would allow him to die with dignity. There was no breach of the European Convention on Human Rights of either the right to life (Article 2) or the right not to be subjected to inhuman or degrading treatment (Article 3). A similar decision was reached in a case in 2006[44] where the parents of a severely disabled baby sought a declaration that it was lawful and in the baby's best interests for a tracheotomy to be carried out, and the trust sought a declaration that it was lawful to withdraw all form of ventilation from him. The Court applying the principle that his welfare was the paramount consideration, said considerable weight had to be given to prolongation of life but this was not absolute nor necessarily decisive. The Court considered that it was not in M's best interests to discontinue ventilation but certain procedures which involved the infliction of pain, such as CPR, electrocardiogram monitoring and IV antibiotics could be withheld in M's best interests.

Disputes over withdrawal of care

There are considerable advantages in seeking a declaration from the court before active treatment is withdrawn, especially where there are already allegations of negligence over what caused the disabilities. For example, parents accused a hospital of turning off their baby's life support to save care costs. The baby was born with considerable disabilities as a result of the alleged negligence of staff. However, the parents alleged that they were pressured into agreeing to the withdrawal of support treatment because the compensation for a dead baby was £10,000 whereas, had the baby been allowed to survive, compensation would be for the costs of care for the whole of his life.[45]

One example of frequent applications to court during a dispute between clinicians and parents over the care of a severely disabled child is that of the Wyatt case. See Case 14.9.

Case 14.9   *Wyatt* v. *Portsmouth Hospital NHS Trust* (2004–5)

Severely disabled baby[46]

The Portsmouth NHS Trust sought permission to decline to give invasive medical treatment to prolong the life of a profoundly disabled baby. Charlotte had been born at 26 weeks' gestation, weighing about 1 pound. She had chronic respiratory and kidney problems and brain damage that had left her blind, deaf and incapable of voluntary movement or response. She

---

Case 14.9 continued

was capable of experiencing pain. The dispute was over what should be done should she deteriorate and require artificial ventilation. The unanimous medical advice was that to give such treatment would not be in her best interests. However, her parents' view was that such treatment should at least be instituted and that the treatment could best be prepared for by the carrying out of an elective tracheotomy. They believed that it was their duty to maintain life as they did not believe that C was yet ready to die. The court granted the application, that any further aggressive treatment, even if necessary to prolong life, was not in C's best interests. There were two further applications by the parents to the court[47] and an appeal by the parents to the Court of Appeal was dismissed.[48] Subsequently, when she appeared to be making good progress, the parents asked the court to review its decision. The judge decided on 21 April 2005 that the decision should stand but it was subject to review.[49]

The Wyatt case illustrates the difficulties which arise when clinicians and parents are in dispute over what is in the best interests of the disabled child. The courts tend to follow the unanimous recommendations of the clinical staff and there are few cases on record where the court has supported the parents. In one such case the parents opposed a liver transplant recommended by the clinicians. The case is considered in Chapter 13.[50]

In contrast the court ordered that a desperately ill baby of 7 months should be treated against the wishes of the parents who were opposed to a bone marrow transplant and put their trust in God to heal the child.[51]

Case 14.10   In re A (Minors: Conjoined twins) (2001)

Separation of Siamese twins[52]

During the antenatal care of a woman in Gozo, an island near Malta, it was realised that she would need facilities for the birth of her baby that were not available locally. Under a quota arrangement between the Malta health authorities and the NHS, the mother came to Manchester where the Siamese twins were born by Caesarean section on 8 August 2000. The bodies of the two girls were fused together at the base of their spines, with their four legs splaying out sideways. They shared an aorta and a bladder and their circulatory systems, muscles and skull were joined together. The one girl, called Mary, had a primitive brain and her heart and lungs quickly failed and she depended on the heart and lungs of Jodie for her existence. The parents, both devout Catholics, had refused consent to any operation to separate them. The doctors applied to the High Court for a declaration that it would be lawful to separate the twins. Medical evidence presented to the court suggested that Jodie could have a reasonable chance of survival if they were to be separated, but such an operation would mean the death of Mary. If no operation were performed, there was a likelihood that Jodie would not survive for many months, because of the strain placed on her heart. Jodie's death would inevitably be followed by Mary's. The High Court judge issued a declaration that the operation should proceed. The parents appealed against this decision. The Court of Appeal asked for additional medical evidence and also received a submission from the Archbishop of Westminster that the operation should not proceed, but that the twins should be allowed to go to a hospice at Ravenna in Italy and should be treated there until they died.

The Court of Appeal held it was lawful for doctors to carry out the operation to separate the twins. The crucial questions to be answered were:

1 Was it in J's best interests that she be separated from M?

2 Was it in M's best interests that she be separated from J?

3 If those interests were in conflict, was the court to balance the interests of one against the other and allow one to prevail against the other and how was that to be done?

4 If the prevailing interest favoured the operation, could it be lawfully performed?

The court concluded that the operation would give J the prospects of a normal expectation of relatively normal life. The operation would shorten M's life, but she remained marked for death. M was alive because she sucked the lifeblood out of J. She would survive only as long as J survived. The operation could be carried out under the doctrine of necessity. The essential elements of that doctrine were all satisfied:

1 the act was needed to avoid inevitable and irreparable evil

2 no more should be done than was reasonably necessary for the purpose to be achieved

3 the evil inflicted must not be disproportionate to the evil avoided.

The court held that its decision was not in conflict with Article 2 of the European Convention on Human Rights (see Chapter 1).

The parents were given leave to appeal to the House of Lords, but decided not to do so. The operation was carried out: Mary died and Jodie recovered and returned to Gozo. The extent of her disabilities is not known.

In recent years, concerns have been expressed over resources in special care baby units and the number of places available. An additional £6.5 million was made available in October 2000 to provide or replace essential equipment such as incubators, resuscitation trolleys, ventilators and life system monitors in neo-natal intensive care units. In May 2000, £150 million was made available for critical care services. In September 2000, £10.5 million was provided for additional nurse training in critical care, including neo-natal intensive care. In 2007 the Healthcare Commission announced that, supported by the Department of Health, it has commissioned a national audit of neo-natal care, in response to the recognised need for auditing for national standards to inform good clinical practice. It will be led by the Royal College of Paediatrics and Child Health.

Cot deaths

In January 2004 the Solicitor General announced that a review of 528 women convicted of killing their babies would be carried out. The announcement followed the quashing by the Court of Appeal of the conviction of Angela Canning for murdering her two babies. The Court of Appeal quashed the conviction which was based on the evidence of Professor Sir Roy Meadows who put forward the theory that multiple cot deaths in the same family were likely to be murder. This theory has now been discredited. A review of previous cases included thousands of cases where children have been taken into care on the basis of the evidence of Professor Roy Meadows. Under new rules the Director of Public Prosecutions personally reviews all 'cot death' cases that have yet to come to trial and sanctions any prosecution.[53]

Registration of births and stillbirths

Births

There is a duty on the doctor or midwife attending a woman in childbirth to notify the prescribed medical officer of the birth or stillbirth within 36 hours. This applies whether the birth is at home or in an institution.

Under the Births and Deaths Registration Act 1953, it is the duty of the father or mother to give information to the registrar within 42 days. If either of them cannot, then there is a duty to do so on the occupier of the house, any person present at the birth or any person having charge of the child. This provision might well involve the midwife. If there is a failure to register within 42 days, the Registrar can compel any qualified informant to attend to give information and sign the Register. The Registrar must give 7 days' notice in writing. There are additional powers if there is no registration after that date.

Stillbirths

A stillbirth is a child that is stillborn, which issued forth from its mother after the 24th week of pregnancy and which did not at any time after being completely expelled from its mother breathe or show any signs of life (Section 41 of the Births and Deaths Registration Act 1953 as amended by the Stillbirth Definition Act 1992 Section 1). The stillbirth has to be registered and the informant has to deliver to the Registrar a written certificate that the child was not born alive. This would be signed by the registered medical practitioner or a certified midwife who was in attendance at the birth or who has examined the body.

A stillbirth should be disposed of by burial in a burial ground or churchyard or by cremation at an authorised crematorium.

What if the foetus is of less than 24 weeks' gestation?

If the foetus were delivered without any sign of life, then no registration is necessary. The foetus may be disposed of without formality in any way that does not constitute a nuisance or an affront to public decency. However, it is clear that even though the foetus is under 24 weeks, the bereaved parents should be given the sympathy and care that would be given if the baby were full term.

If the foetus is under 24 weeks' gestation and initially shows signs of life and breathing and then dies, it should be treated as a neo-natal death and be registered as a birth and death.

Use of foetal tissue

In its Code of Practice on Consent,[54] the Human Tissue Authority makes the following point:

> *The law does not distinguish between foetal tissue and other tissue from the living. Foetal tissue is regarded as the mother's tissue. However, because of the sensitivity attached to this subject, consent should be obtained for the pathological examination of foetal tissue or products of conception and for their use for all scheduled purposes, regardless of gestational age. REC approval is required for their use in research.*

Appendix B of the Code of Practice on the removal, storage and disposal of human organs and tissue[55] published by the Human Tissue Authority in 2006 provides guidance on the disposal of foetal tissue. It emphasises that pregnancy loss should always be handled sensitively and the needs of the woman or couple should be paramount and disposal policies should reflect this. The Code of Practice suggests that the information provided should explain who to contact to request a particular disposal option and the timescale for this. Any personal, religious or cultural needs relating to the disposal of the foetal tissue should be met wherever possible and should be documented in the woman's medical notes. It explains the various options for disposal including: burial, cremation and incineration and the rights of the woman to arrange the disposal. (See Chapter 16 on the Human Tissue Act 2004)

Record keeping and midwifery

The Sixth Annual Report of CESDI made many recommendations on record keeping. In particular, it noted that poor record keeping occurred in one-third of cases. The major problem was a failure to document events adequately and the report reiterated recommendations from earlier reports on record keeping:

1 All professionals should make clear and adequate notes. The standard should be that which enables a colleague coming new to the case to be properly informed.

2 The quality of maternity records needs to be improved to enable clear identification of risk factors and documentation of management plans for those during both ante-partum and intra-partum periods. These would be facilitated by a well-designed, universally used national maternity record.

There has been work on a national record for maternity services prepared by a national group.[56] They have prepared a personal maternity record that would be looked after by the mother and covers the antenatal stages. Work is progressing on other stages. There is no evidence that the antenatal record has had an extended take-up across the country. It may be that these developments will be overtaken by the development of electronic patient and health records, which are discussed in Chapter 9.

AIDS and the midwife

The possibility of a midwife contracting AIDS from an HIV-positive patient is a major concern, and midwives are worried about the possibility of protecting themselves by equipment, gloves, clothing and screening of patients so that midwives are warned of the potential dangers. These anxieties are part of the general dilemmas in relation to AIDS and are considered in Chapter 26.

National Institute for Health and Clinical Excellence (NICE)

NICE has issued several guidelines relating to obstetrics and midwifery practice. (See Chapter 5 for more details on NICE.) It published its antenatal care guidelines in 2003, covering the routine care for the healthy pregnant woman. They are available from the NICE website.[57] The first draft of its clinical guidance for England and Wales on Caesarean section was issued in September 2003 and the revised draft in November 2003. The final guidance was published in April 2004. Eventually NICE guidelines will become part of basic professional practice, but midwives will still have to use their professional discretion in deciding whether there are any exceptional circumstances that make the following of the guidelines for a particular woman inappropriate. (See Chapter 3 on policies, procedures and protocols.) Frequently NICE works in association with other national organisations in standard setting. For example, in November 2003 the Department of Health published guidance on more accurate tests for Down's syndrome screening that was based on advice from the UK National Screening Committee together with NICE guidelines on antenatal care. The guidelines are aimed at reducing the possibility of error in identifying high-risk pregnancies, increasing the detection rate of pregnancies most likely to have Down's syndrome and suggest the most effective way of having blood tests and ultrasound screening.[58] A recent NICE guideline for midwifery is that relating to routine post-natal care[59] published in 2006. Key competencies include maternal and newborn physical examinations; supporting breastfeeding women; recognising risks, signs, and symptoms of maternal mental health problems and recognising risks, signs, and symptoms of domestic and child abuse. The following year NICE published guidelines on antenatal and post-natal mental health.[60] The most common cause of maternal death is suicide and it is therefore important for midwives to incorporate the NICE guidelines into their practice, where appropriate, as part of the duty of care they owe to the woman. NICE clinical guidelines on intra-partum care were published in September 2007. The guideline supports normal birth as well as setting out what to do if labour does not progress normally. Its key recommendations include a woman in established labour receiving supportive one-to-one care. All NICE guidelines can be downloaded from its website.

National guidelines on midwifery practice

In April 1991, the House of Commons initiated an inquiry into maternity services because concerns had been expressed that the services did not meet the wishes of women. Its report was published in February 1992 (House of Commons Health Committee Session 1991–92, Maternity Services). It concluded that 'the policy of encouraging all women to give birth in hospitals cannot be justified on grounds of safety'. It made wide-ranging recommendations covering the development of midwife-managed units, involvement of midwives in junior doctors' training and emphasis on the rights and involvement of the mother. A joint committee supported its recommendations. The government set up an expert committee chaired by Lady Cumberlege to review policy on NHS maternity care and this committee reported in 1993.[61] 'Changing Childbirth' identified three key principles that should underlie effective woman-centred maternity services:

+ the woman must be the focus of maternity care

+ maternity services can be readily and easily accessible to all

+ services must be effective and efficient.

Recommendations were made on action to implement these principles. An implementation committee was established and health authorities and NHS trusts were required to implement the recommendations.[62]

While Cumberlege recommendations are still referred to, subsequent developments have to a certain extent overtaken them. The National Service Framework for Children and Maternity has been prepared (see Chapter 5) and can be accessed on the NSF website.[63] This NSF setting minimum standards for children and maternity care should have a major impact on the quality of care provided for pregnant women (see below). Under Section 46 of the Health and Social Care (Community Health and Standards) Act 2003 the Secretary of State has the power to set standards for the provision of healthcare.

In addition, following the NHS Plan,[64] the strategic document 'Delivering the Best' was published to identify midwives' contribution to the NHS Plan.[65] This document identified five challenges for midwives:

+ excellence in midwifery practice
+ dynamic leadership
+ partnerships with women
+ improving public health
+ working with others.

Furthermore, it outlined how they could be achieved. The document should be a useful resource for midwives, if they are not receiving the appropriate support from management to develop their skills, in providing the appropriate standards of care for women and generally implementing any national guidance for midwifery and maternity standards. Women may also make use of national guidelines in identifying shortfalls in the services provided and if they or their babies suffer harm may use these deficits as evidence of failures to follow a reasonable standard of care. 'Delivering the Best' can also be used as a training device and as a useful tool for discussions between supervisor and midwife.

In 2003 the House of Commons Health Committee looked at two aspects of maternity care: its eighth report[66] looked at inequalities in maternity services and its ninth report[67] considered choice in maternity services. Both reports make fundamental and significant recommendations for the future provision of services. The eighth report recommended that the government investigate the RCM's concerns about the recruitment of midwives from minority ethnic communities and its final recommendation was:

We recognise the potential of midwives and of maternity services to play an expanded role in promoting public health. However, maternity care staff must have access to appropriate levels of training and support if they are to be effective in this role. We recommend that the Department should facilitate the implementation of the proposals in 'Making a Difference' by making a detailed assessment of the training and support needs of staff who provide maternity care.

The ninth report on choice in maternity care suggested that the government should use the opportunity presented by the forthcoming NSF as an opportunity to recast maternity services to the advantage of both women and their carers, since the current delivery of maternity services over-medicalises birth. Barriers to home births were wholly unacceptable. Women should know that they have a right to have a home birth without seeking 'the GP's permission'. Its final recommendation was that the government should consider allocating some one-off resources to maternity units to make changes to their practice so that they could carry out the work recommended in the report, the money going to staff rather than buildings (in contrast to the 2001 allocation).

In 2005 Reform published an analysis of maternity services in the NHS.[68] It found that progress since the Cumberlege Report was modest, that centralisation of services had not produced the expected benefits and the service was under strain in terms of staffing. The report made significant recommendations for a modern framework for maternity services.

NSF for Children, Young People and Maternity Services[69]

Part 3 of the NSF is concerned with midwifery standards and Standard 11 is as follows:

Women have easy access to supportive, high quality maternity services, designed around their individual needs and those of their babies.

The expansion of that standard identifies: woman-centred care services; care pathways and managed care networks; improved pre-conception care; the identifying and addressing of mental health problems; choice of options in relation to place of birth; professional skilled in neo-natal resuscitation at every birth; post-birth care based on a structured assessment provided by a multidisciplinary team, breastfeeding information and support for mothers.

The National Perinatal Epidemiology Unit (NPEU) is carrying out a survey on the experience of maternity care to provide a benchmark of current practice and a baseline for measuring change over the period that the NSF is implemented.[70] The Healthcare Commission is responsible for monitoring the implementation of the NSF through its visits and inspections.

The DH has also revised guidance for parents in the form of the Pregnancy Book 2007 available on the DH website.

Maternity Matters

A report on maternity services was published in April 2007.[71] It aims to secure a service by the end of 2009 where all women will have choice over the type of care that they receive, together with improved access to services and continuity of care. The report includes advice for commissioners and providers of maternity services and also gives guidance to PCTs on the action which they should take to lay the foundations for future improvements, as documented in the NHS in England: operating framework for 2007/8 (www.dh.gov.uk).

Midwifery management

The Healthcare Commission carried out an investigation into the maternity services and the Northwest London Hospitals NHS Trust. As a result of its report special measures were instigated by the Secretary of State. A review team from the NMC made an extraordinary visit and its report is available on the NMC website.[72] This was followed by an action plan identifying objectives, action to be taken, whose responsibility, a completion date and the form of monitoring. In addition an action plan was devised by the Supervisor of Midwives for the Brent and Harrow Health Authority which was to be reviewed monthly by the Supervisor and the LSA Officer. Both documents can be accessed on the NMC website.

The Audit Commission published a comprehensive survey, A First Class Delivery, in 1995 and this survey was followed in 2006 by a survey by the NPEU on the clinical care and experience of mothers and contrasts the results with those obtained in 1995. It shows that there was an increase in the number of women who were offered home birth. The Caesarian rate had risen from 17 per cent to 23 per cent. It is available on the NPEU website.

A review of maternity services in England was launched by the Healthcare Commission in May 2007 looking at efficiency and capability, clinical focus and outcomes and the engagement of women. Its aim is to build up a comprehensive picture of maternity care. The report is to be published in 2008. Further information is available on the Healthcare Commission website.

Conclusions

Midwifery continues to be under pressure. The Royal College of Midwives estimated in 2007 that 5,000 more midwives are needed to meet the government's target for maternity services and also to meet the rising birth rate. The Cumberlege recommendations have still not been fully implemented across the country and the shortage of midwifery staff is making it impossible for every woman to have her choice of birth place. The Caesarean rate continues to rise. The strategic document 'Delivering the Best' sets clear aims for midwives, but this requires considerable support and resources from NHS trust boards and PCTs for them to be realised. Furthermore, the strategic document 'Building on the Best'[73] envisages that there will be direct access from woman to midwife, bypassing the GP, if the woman wishes to liaise directly with the midwife. It is to be hoped that the aspirations contained in the report 'Maternity Matters' and any recommendations resulting from the Healthcare Commission review on maternity services to be published in 2008 will attract the resources and managerial support essential to ensure their implementation across the UK.

Reflection questions

1 What is the legal status of a birth plan? In what circumstances can a mother refuse to give consent to life-saving treatment?

2 Analyse the principles set down by the Court of Appeal in the *Re MB* case (see Box 14.4) and consider the extent to which they have been incorporated into your practice. What are the implications of the Mental Capacity Act 2005 on treatment decisions in relation to those lacking the requisite mental capacity?

3 What are the implications of the Congenital Disabilities (Civil Liability) Act 1976 for the midwife?

4 What statutory duties does a midwife have in relation to the registration of a birth or stillbirth?

Further exercises

1 Consider the proposals in 'Maternity Matters' (2007) and analyse the extent to which they are implemented in your own unit. What are the legal implications for any deficiencies?

2 What specific powers and rights does the midwife have in relation to drugs that are not possessed by the registered general nurse? (See Chapter 28.)

References

[1] Nursing and Midwifery Order 2001, SI 2002 No. 253
[2] Ibid.
[3] UKCC, Midwives' Rules and Code of Practice, UKCC, 1998
[4] Nursing and Midwifery Order 2001, SI 2002 No. 253
[5] Nursing and Midwifery Council (Midwives) Rules, SI 2004 No. 1764
[6] Nursing and Midwifery Council (Midwives)(Amendment) Rules Order of Council, SI 2007 No. 2009
[7] SI 2002 No. 253 (re-enacting Section 16 of the Nurses, Midwives and Health Visitors Act 1997)
[8] Nursing and Midwifery Council Circular 1/2004, Guidance on Provision of Midwifery Care and Delegation of Midwifery Care to Others, 20 January 2004
[9] UKCC, Registrar's letter 21/2001, Supporting Women who Wish to Have a Home Birth - a position statement, UKCC, August 2001 (replacing Registrar's letter 20/2000, June 2000)

[10] Julia Magill-Cuerden, Report of issues arising from a document review to support recommendations for guidance for home births, NMC, 2004

[11] NMC, Midwives and home birth, NMC Circular 8-2006, March 2006

[12] Department of Health, Maternity Matters: choice, access and continuity of care in a safe service, 2007

[13] *In re S (An Adult: refusal of medical treatment)* [1992] 4 All ER 671

[14] *Tameside and Glossop Acute Services Trust v. CH* [1996] 1 FLR 762

[15] *Norfolk and Norwich (NHS) Trust v. W* [1996] 2 FLR 613

[16] *Rochdale NHS Trust v. C* [1997] 1 FCR 274

[17] *Re MB (An Adult: medical treatment)* [1997] 2 FLR 426

[18] Department of Health Circular EL (97)32, 1997

[19] *St George's Healthcare NHS Trust v. S* [1998] 3 All ER 673

[20] *St George's Healthcare NHS Trust v. S (Guidelines) (No. 2)* [1999] Fam 26

[21] *In re T (An Adult: refusal of medical treatment)* [1992] 4 All ER 649

[22] *F (re) (A Mental Patient: sterilisation)* [1990] 2 AC 1; *F v. West Berkshire HA and Another* [1989] 2 ALL ER 545

[23] *In re R (A Child: care proceedings)*, The Times Law Report, 19 July 2000 FD

[24] *In re D (A Minor) v. Berkshire County Council and Others* [1987] 1 All ER 20

[25] *In re F (in utero)* [1988] 2 All ER 193

[26] Denis Campbell, NHS is facing £4.5bn compensation bill over babies damaged at birth by hospital 'blunders', *The Observer*, 23 September 2007. http://observer.guardian.co.uk/uk_news/story/0,,2175218,00.html (last accessed 25 January 2008)

[27] Medical Defence Union Annual Report, 1982, 30

[28] Russell Jenkins, £2.5m payout for birth blunder after 26 years, *The Times*, 9 March 2000

[29] B. Dimond, Law for Midwives Step by step: 78 New Developments on infant feeding laws in Scotland, *British Journal of Midwifery*, June 2005, Vol. 13 No. 6, p. 386

[30] Department of Health, Maternal and infant nutrition, policy and guidance, 2007

[31] Misuse of Drugs Regulations, SI 2001 No. 3998

[32] Nursing and Midwifery Council Circular 8/2003, 31 March 2003

[33] *In re F (in utero)* [1988] 2 All ER 193

[34] *McKay v. Essex AHA* [1982] 2 All ER 771

[35] *K (A Child)(Medical Treatment: Declaration)* [2006] EWHC 1007; [2006] 2 FLR 883

[36] Royal College of Paediatrics and Child Health, Withholding or Withdrawing Life-Saving Treatment in Children, 2nd edition, RCPCH, 2004

[37] *In re C (A Minor: wardship, medical treatment)* [1989] 2 All ER 782

[38] *In re J (A Minor: wardship, medical treatment)* [1990] 3 All ER 930

[39] *In re J (A Minor: wardship, medical treatment)* [1992] 4 All ER 614

[40] Royal College of Paediatrics and Child Health, Withholding or Withdrawing Life-Saving Treatment in Children, 2nd edition, RCPCH, 2004

[41] United Nations' Convention on the Rights of the Child 1989

[42] British Medical Association, Withholding and Withdrawing Life-prolonging Medical Treatment, 2nd edition, BMA, 2000

[43] *A National Health Service Trust v. D,* The Times Law Report, 19 July 2000; [2000] 2 FLR 677

[44] *An NH Trust v. MB* [2006] EWHC 507; [2006] 2 FLR 319 Fam Div

[45] Lois Rogers, Baby's life support cut off 'to save care costs', *Sunday Times*, 30 July 2000

[46] *Wyatt v. Portsmouth Hospital NHS Trust* [2004] EWHC Civ 2247

[47] *Wyatt v. Portsmouth Hospital NHS Trust* [2005] EWHC 117; [2005] EWHC 693

[48] *Wyatt v. Portsmouth Hospital NHS Trust* [2005] EWCA Civ 1181

[49] *Wyatt* v. *Portsmouth NHS Trust* [2005] EWHC 2293

[50] *Re T* [1997] 1 ALL ER 906

[51] Helen Nugent, Sick baby must be treated, judge tells parents who put faith in God, *The Times*, 19 July 2007

[52] *In re A (Minors: conjoined twins: medical treatment)*, The Times Law Report, 10 October 2000; [2001] Fam 147 CA

[53] Sam Coates and Frances Gibb, Cot death cases to be reviewed before trial, *The Times*, 21 January 2004

[54] Human Tissue Authority Code of Practice on Consent, Code 1, January 2006

[55] Human Tissue Authority Code of Practice on removal, storage and disposal of human organs and tissue, Code 5, January 2006

[56] National Maternity Record Group, NMRP 6.97 V.P1 1997

[57] NICE, Antenatal Care: routine care for the healthy pregnant woman, Clinical Guideline 6, NICE, 2003; www.nice.org.uk

[58] Department of Health press release 2003/0438, Guidelines on Down's Syndrome Screening, November 2003

[59] www.nice.org.uk/CG037fullguideline

[60] www.nice.org.uk/CG45fullguideline

[61] Department of Health, Changing Childbirth: report of the expert maternity group, HMSO, London

[62] See Executive Letter (94)9, issued 24 January 1994 by the NHS Management Executive

[63] www.dh.gov.uk/NSF

[64] Department of Health, NHS Plan: a plan for investment, a plan for reform, Cm 4818-1, The Stationery Office, London, 2000

[65] Department of Health, Delivering the Best, DH, June 2003

[66] www.publications.parliament.uk/pa/cm200203/cmselect/cmhealth/696/69602.htm

[67] www.publications.parliament.uk/pa/cm200203/cmselect/cmhealth/796/79602.htm

[68] N. Bosanquet, J. Ferry, C. Lees and J. Thornton, Maternity Services in the NHS, Reform, 2005

[69] Department of Health, National Service Framework, Children, Young People and Maternity Services, October 2004

[70] www.npeu.ox.ac.uk/maternitysurveys/

[71] Department of Health, Maternity Matters: choice, access and continuity of care in a safe service, 2007

[72] www.nmc-uk.org;

[73] Department of Health, Building on the Best: choice, responsiveness and equity in the NHS, Cmd 6079 2003; www.dh.gov.uk

Chapter 15
The nurse on the gynaecology ward

This chapter discusses

+ Abortion
+ Sterilisation
+ Female circumcision

Introduction

This chapter considers the areas of particular concern to the nurse who works on the gynae-cology ward. For convenience, the chapter also includes the law relating to vasectomies within the topic of sterilisation. For issues relating to fertilisation and IVF, see Chapter 22. Reference should also be made to Chapter 13 for the law relating to consent by the young person to abortion, sterilisation and family planning.

Abortion

General principles

Although the unborn child is not a legal personality and cannot sue or be sued until it is born (see Chapter 14), its existence is protected in law by the Offences Against the Persons Act 1861, Section 58 of which makes it an offence to administer drugs or use instruments to procure a miscarriage and Section 59 prohibits other activities to procure a miscarriage. In addition, under the Infant Life Preservation Act 1929, it is an offence to destroy the life of a child capable of being born alive. The Infant Life Preservation Act 1929 provides that any person who, with intent to destroy the life of a child capable of being born alive, by any wilful act, causes a child to die before it has an existence independent of its mother, shall be guilty of felony, to whit, of child destruction. Twenty-eight weeks' gestation was *prima facie* evidence that the child is capable of being born alive. However, these acts are subject to the Abortion Act 1967 as amended by the Human Fertilisation and Embryology Act 1990. An abortion that satisfies the legal requirements laid down in this Act is not an offence. Under Section 5(1) of the Abortion Act, no offence under the Infant Life Preservation Act 1929 takes place if the abortion is carried out by a registered medical practitioner who terminates a pregnancy in accordance with the provisions of the Act. If these legal requirements are not satisfied, then abortion is an offence that carries a maximum sentence of life imprisonment. The provisions of the Act as amended are set out in the Statute below.

In 2006 a total of 193,700 abortions were performed on residents in England and Wales and 87 per cent of these were funded by the NHS; 89 per cent of these were carried out at under 13 weeks gestation; 68 per cent were under 10 weeks.[1]

Statute | **Provisions of the Abortion Act 1967 Section 1(1) (as amended by the Human Fertilisation and Embryology Act 1990)**

A person shall not be guilty of an offence under the law relating to abortion when a pregnancy is terminated by a registered medical practitioner if two registered medical practitioners are of the opinion, formed in good faith:

(a) that the pregnancy has not exceeded its 24th week and that the continuance of the pregnancy would involve risk, greater than if the pregnancy were terminated, of injury to the physical or mental health of the pregnant woman or any existing children of her family; or

(b) that the termination is necessary to prevent grave permanent injury to the physical or mental health of the pregnant woman; or

(c) that the continuance of the pregnancy would involve risk to the life of the pregnant woman, greater than if the pregnancy were terminated; or

(d) that there is a substantial risk that if the child were born it would suffer from such physical or mental abnormalities as to be seriously handicapped.

Account may be taken of the pregnant woman's actual or reasonably foreseeable environment in deciding whether there is a risk of injury to health under paragraph (a) (Section 1(2)). In December 2003[2] a curate was given approval to have a judicial review of a case where a woman had a late abortion because her foetus had a cleft palate. The curate, who herself had

had three operations to correct a congenital jaw defect argued that a cleft palate did not come within the provisions of Section 1(1)(d) of the Abortion Act (see Statute above). Subsequently the police carried out an investigation and in March 2005 the Crown Prosecution Service stated that they had decided not to prosecute because they were satisfied that the doctors involved had acted in good faith.

The abortion must be carried out in an NHS hospital or a place specifically approved by the Secretary of State or Minister of Health for the purposes of the Act. Emergency provisions are set out in Box 15.1.

Box 15.1 — **Emergency provisions**

The provisions set out in the above Statute, including the requirement to have two registered medical practitioners, do not apply in an emergency when a registered medical practitioner is of the opinion, formed in good faith, that the termination is immediately necessary to save the life or to prevent grave permanent injury to the physical or mental health of the pregnant woman.

Conscientious objection to participation in an abortion

The Abortion Act is one of the few examples where a professional can lawfully refuse to take part in an activity on the grounds of a conscientious objection. Thus Section 4 states that:

[N]o person shall be under any duty, whether by contract or by any statutory or other legal requirement, to participate in any treatment authorised by this Act to which he has a conscientious objection: Provided that in any legal proceedings the burden of proof of conscientious objection shall rest on the person claiming to rely on it.

This right is, however, subject to Section 4(2):

Nothing in subsection (1) of this section shall affect any duty to participate in treatment which is necessary to save the life or to prevent grave permanent injury to the physical or mental health of a pregnant woman.

The extent of the protection from being involved in an abortion was considered by the courts in Case 15.1.

Case 15.1 — *R v. Salford Health Authority ex parte Janaway* (1988)

The letter[3]

Mrs Janaway, a medical secretary, refused to type a letter referring a patient from a general practitioner to a consultant with a view to a possible termination of pregnancy. She was a Roman Catholic who believed strongly that abortion was morally wrong. The genuineness of her belief was never in dispute. She was asked to type the letter and refused on the basis that she was protected by Section 4 of the Abortion Act. She was dismissed by the health authority and subsequently applied for judicial review of the health authority's decision. This was refused and she therefore appealed.

The Court of Appeal held that she was not entitled to claim the protection of Section 4 of the Act. It could not be said that by typing the letter she was participating in any treatment authorised by the Act, neither could typing such a letter be regarded as a criminal offence prior to the Abortion Act so that it could be regarded as now being protected by the provisions of the Act. The House of Lords dismissed Mrs Janaway's appeal.

Nurses' participation in prostaglandin abortions

Case 15.2 | **RCN v. *The Department of Health and Social Security* (1981)**

Prostaglandin drip[4]

The Royal College of Nursing brought a case on behalf of its members against the DHSS because members had complained that they were often left on wards to supervise (sometimes for several days) a patient who was having a prostaglandin-induced abortion. The doctor would set up the drip and then the nurse would undertake the care of the patient. The RCN queried the legality of this in the light of the wording of the Act that the pregnancy should be terminated by a registered medical practitioner. The RCN questioned, in particular, advice given in a DHSS letter and circular relating to the procedures that might be performed by an appropriately skilled nurse or midwife.

In Case 15.2, the House of Lords decided on a majority of three to two that the DHSS advice did not involve the performance of unlawful acts by members of the RCN. Lord Diplock's views are set out in Box 15.2.

Box 15.2 | **Lord Diplock's view in the case of *RCN* v. *DHSS* [1981] 1 All ER 545**

In the context of the Act what was required was that a registered medical practitioner - a doctor - should accept responsibility for all stages of the treatment for the termination of the pregnancy. The particular method to be used should be decided by the doctor in charge of that treatment; he should carry out any physical acts, forming part of the treatment, that in accordance with accepted medical practice were done only by qualified medical practitioners, and should give specific instructions as to the carrying out of such parts of the treatment as in accordance with accepted medical practice were carried out by nurses or other hospital staff without medical qualifications. To each of them the doctor or his substitute should be available to be consulted or called in for assistance from beginning to end of the treatment. In other words, the doctor need not do everything with his own hands; the subsection's requirements were satisfied when the treatment was one prescribed by a registered medical practitioner carried out in accordance with his directions and of which he remained in charge throughout.

This decision has considerable significance for the scope of professional practice. It could be argued that even where a statute expressly places responsibilities on a registered medical practitioner, the law is still followed when that activity is delegated to another healthcare professional acting under the aegis of the registered medical practitioner. This is the view taken by those who argue that the legislation allows nurses to perform surgical abortions.[5] The possibility of extending the nurse's role in abortions is considered below under future reforms to the abortion law. The scope of professional practice is considered in Chapter 24.

When is an abortion illegal?

The simple answer is: under any circumstances other than those permitted under the 1967 Act as amended by the 1990 Act. It is specifically provided that no offence is committed under the Infant Life Preservation Act 1929 if the provisions of the 1967 Act are followed (Section 5 as amended by the 1990 Act) (see above). The amendments to the 1967 Abortion Act limit termination to 24 weeks or less, but only for Section 1(1)(a). Subsections (b), (c) and (d) give no time limit (see Statute on page 386). It was reported in May 2007[6] that a woman who had a backstreet abortion when she was 7½ months pregnant was convicted on a charge of child destruction under the Infant Life Preservation Act 1929 as re-enacted in the Crimes Act 1958. A body was never found.

Being born alive

> ### Practical Dilemma 15 1 Birth or abortion?
>
> Mavis Spencer was 15 and her pregnancy was discovered only at a late stage. From the information provided by her and from his own medical examination, the doctor judged her to be about 22 weeks pregnant. He agreed that a termination should proceed and he arranged for her to see a second doctor who agreed with him. Mavis was immediately admitted for a termination. However, because of unforeseeable delays on the ward, this was not commenced for another week. When the foetus was expelled it appeared to cry out and the nurse felt that it was breathing. She did not know what to do. The doctor told her to put the remains in the bucket for incineration. She was reluctant to do this, however, since she felt it to be a child capable of surviving. Where does the law stand?

If it is clear that there is a live birth, then all reasonable steps should be taken to preserve its life, otherwise there could be a prosecution for murder or manslaughter. A prosecution was brought against Dr Hamilton when an abortion produced a live foetus.[7] However, the case did not proceed beyond the committal proceedings. In the above situation, if it is apparent that the aborted foetus is breathing and viable, then he or she should be transferred to a special care baby unit. Failure to do so could be grounds for a charge of attempted murder. In addition, of course, even if the child were to die shortly afterwards, it would still have to be registered as a live birth (see registration provisions in Chapter 14 on midwifery). Whether or not the foetus had a right to life under Article 2 of the European Convention on Human Rights was considered in a French case heard before the European Court of Human Rights.[8] A doctor thought a woman (who was pregnant) was attending clinic for the removal of a contraceptive coil, and ruptured the amniotic sac as a result of which the pregnancy had to be terminated. The claimant alleged that the failure of France to have a criminal remedy for killing a foetus was a breach of the foetus's Article 2 rights. The ECHR held that the foetus was not a person and therefore not directly protected by Article 2, but it was left open as to whether the foetus could claim a version of right to life under the Article and the EU countries could decide the question themselves.

Negligence in failing to detect abnormality

In a case in 1991,[9] the plaintiff had an ultrasound scan when she was about 26 weeks' pregnant. The radiographer queried a possible abnormality of the spine, but the consultant decided that there was no firm evidence of abnormality justifying further action. The baby was born and found to be suffering from spina bifida. The mother claimed that the defendants were negligent in not ascertaining the possibility of abnormality and thus enabling her to have an abortion. Her claim failed since (under the Abortion Act 1967, i.e. prior to the 1990 amendments) it would have been illegal to have carried out an abortion at that stage, since the baby would have been capable of being born alive within the meaning of the 1929 Act.

If similar facts were to occur now, compensation would be payable if the mother were able to establish negligence, since there is no longer any time limit for securing a termination if there is a substantial risk that if the child were born it would suffer from such physical or mental abnormalities as to be seriously handicapped.

Challenge by the putative father

> ### Case 15.3   *C* v. *S* (1987)
>
> **Father's intervention**[10]
>
> An Oxford student whose girlfriend became pregnant sought to stop the abortion on the grounds that the foetus, of between 18 and 24 weeks, was viable and that the abortion would thus be an offence under the Infant Life Preservation Act 1929. In this case, the pregnant woman was given medication to terminate the pregnancy shortly after the time that conception must have occurred. It was assumed that the medication had been effective. She subsequently took anti-depressant drugs and underwent two chest X-rays, one of which was taken without any shielding to protect a foetus. Any of these treatments could have harmed the foetus. When she discovered that she was still pregnant, she obtained the two necessary signatures for abortion. The father brought the court action.

The Court of Appeal decided that the foetus was not capable of being born alive and therefore the termination of the pregnancy would not constitute an offence under the 1929 Act. The medical evidence showed that the cardiac muscle would be contracting and that there would be signs of primitive movement. It was said that these were real discernible signs of life. But the foetus would never be capable of breathing, either naturally or with the aid of a ventilator. Since the amendment to the Abortion Act 1967, the viability of the foetus is no longer in issue. In a more recent Scottish case,[11] a father was refused an injunction to restrain his wife from having an abortion.

Husband's attempt to stop an abortion

> ### Case 15.4   *Paton v. Trustees of British Pregnancy Advisory Service* (1978)
>
> **Husband's rights**
>
> In Case 15.3, the putative father was not married to the mother, but it might be asked whether, if he were married, it would give him any rights to prevent the abortion going ahead. This point came before the courts when Mr Paton asked the court to prevent his wife going ahead with a termination. Two doctors had signed that the termination should proceed. Mr Paton claimed that, as the father of the child, he had a right to apply to the court for the termination to be stopped.[12]

The court, however, disagreed. It held that, provided the requirements of the Act were met, then the husband did not have any right in law to prevent the abortion proceeding. He had no *locus standi* before the court. Mr Paton took his case to the European Commission on Human Rights[13] arguing that the life of the foetus is protected under Article 2 of the European Convention on Human Rights (right to life) and also the father's rights were protected under Article 8 (the right of respect for family life). He failed in both his arguments.

Right to an abortion

An abortion refused

> ### Practical Dilemma 15.2   An enforced child
>
> After having two children, Beryl Edwards considered her family to be complete. They moved to a larger house with a huge mortgage and Beryl took a part-time job to help pay for the additional loan and the extras: meals out and holidays. She was horrified when she discovered that she might be pregnant. Beryl became severely depressed and visited her GP. He was very reassuring, stating that she could have an abortion and within a few days she was referred to a consultant obstetrician. He listened to her case and then informed her that he did not consider that she satisfied the requirements of the Abortion Act and that he would therefore be unable to write a medical recommendation. Beryl's depression became worse and she was unable to work. Eventually, her husband suggested that she should seek another opinion. She was reluctant to do so, not believing that it would be of any value. Eventually, however, under pressure from her husband she paid privately to see another specialist, who informed her that in his opinion she did meet the Act's requirements. However, since she was now 23 weeks pregnant, he would be unwilling to propose an abortion since the pregnancy was too far advanced for an abortion to be performed safely and at this late stage he believed that it could constitute an offence under the Act. Beryl eventually had the child, but is seeking compensation against the first specialist. Is she likely to succeed?

Beryl does not have an absolute right to an abortion. To obtain compensation, she would have to prove that, in making his assessment of her present or foreseeable physical or mental health, the specialist was negligent in failing to take into account factors that approved medical practice would have expected him to have taken into account, and that his assessment had been made negligently. She may get some support from her GP but, of course, it was open to him to refer her to another doctor at an earlier stage. Indeed, the GP's failure to refer her to a second consultant might in itself give rise to a claim of negligence against the GP. However, if the first consultant's report had been adamant that there was no greater risk in proceeding with the pregnancy, then the GP could argue that there was no negligence on his part in accepting that view as the likely prevailing one and therefore a further referral was not justified.

Women may be dependent on the personal views of the doctors when they seek a termination of pregnancy. However, to establish negligence by a GP, there must be clear evidence that the GP failed to follow a reasonable standard of care in advising about arrangements for termination. In one case,[14] a woman visited her GP to seek a termination of pregnancy. She did not know that the GP was opposed to abortion on ethical and religious grounds. The woman alleged that the GP, by stating that it was too late and that it would not be recommended, effectively prevented her from having an abortion and was therefore in breach of the duty of care owed to her. The GP referred her to an abortion counsellor who told her of a private clinic at which an abortion could be obtained. She continued with the pregnancy and following an *antepartum* haemorrhage gave birth to a brain-damaged child. Her claim against the GP was dismissed on the grounds that in the light of the contemporaneous records and what she and her boyfriend had said in other contexts, the evidence showed that she had changed her mind and gone on to arrange antenatal care.

A woman who changed her mind about having an abortion was paid £27,500 in an out-of-court settlement by an NHS trust which ignored her attempts to withdraw her consent.[15]

There is concern that the availability of abortions varies according to where you live and therefore women who would satisfy the legal requirements of the Abortion Act 1967 may not receive a termination. A survey conducted by the Abortion Law Reform Association[16] in December 1999 showed that obtaining an abortion on the NHS depends on criteria such as whether you have had one before, your age, finances and whether you have been using contraception. The Royal College of Obstetricians and Gynaecologists[17] has recommended a maximum waiting time of 21 days from first doctor consultation to the surgical procedure and that 14 days should be the aim. This is clearly an area where NICE could make recommendations for uniformity of NHS provision across the country. (See Chapter 5 on the work of NICE.) The House of Commons Scientific and Technology Committee recommended in October 2007 that the inequality across the country should be eradicated.

In 2006 a total of 193,700 abortions were performed on residents of England and Wales: 87 per cent of these were funded by the NHS; 89 per cent of abortions were carried out under 13 weeks gestation and 68 per cent at under 10 weeks.[18] A study carried out by the Universities of Southampton and Kent found that half of those women who had an abortion after 12 weeks did not know that they were pregnant for at least 2 months and a further quarter only discovered their pregnancies at three months or later; 2 in 5 said that their periods had continued.[19]

Independent sector organisations that wish to provide abortion services must obtain registration from the Healthcare Commission and comply with the national minimum standards and regulations for independent healthcare and the procedures for the approval of independent sector places for the termination of pregnancy. In 2005 the Chief Medical Officer investigated a complaint that the British Pregnancy Advisory Service (BPAS) broke the law relating to late abortions by advising a Spanish clinic. His report[20] concluded that BPAS had not broken the law, but the investigation raised a number of issues around access to abortions, training of staff and information for women. Recommendations for primary care trusts are contained in a letter he wrote to PCTs and Strategic Health Authorities.[21]

Other related offences

The Offences Against the Person Act 1861 Section 58 makes it an offence to administer drugs or use instruments to procure an abortion. When a woman is charged, it must be shown that she is pregnant. This is not necessary when another person is charged with an offence. Section 59 of the 1861 Act makes it an offence to supply or procure any poison or any instrument or any other thing knowing that it is to be used with intent to cause a miscarriage whether or not the woman is with child. However, if the requirements of the Abortion Act are complied with, these provisions would not apply. Section 60 of the 1861 Act makes it an offence to conceal the birth of a child. Mr Reginald Dixon[22] was prosecuted under Section 58 of the Offences Against the Person Act 1861 when he continued carrying out a hysterectomy after discovering during the operation that the patient was pregnant. The patient subsequently said that had she known she would have wanted to keep the baby. He defended the charge on the grounds that he had acted in good faith to preserve the woman from grave permanent injury to her mental health within Section 1(1)(b) of the Act. He was acquitted by the jury.

Dr Bourne, a gynaecologist, was prosecuted under Section 58 of the 1861 Act after he had terminated the pregnancy of a 14-year-old girl who had been raped. He was found not guilty on the ground that his action was taken to preserve the life of the mother[23]. This situation is now covered by the emergency provisions of the Abortion Act 1967 (as amended).

The courts have considered whether the post-coital contraception pill came under the Abortion Laws. In *R* v. *Dhingra*[24] charges against a doctor under Section 18 of the Offences Against the Person Act 1861 for inserting an IUD were dismissed on the grounds that preventing implantation could not be interpreted as a miscarriage and in *R (Smeaton)* v. *Secretary of State for Health*[25] the claim by the Society for the Protection of Unborn Children that the sale of the morning-after pill without prescription was an offence under the 1861 Act was rejected.

Termination of one of multiple pregnancy

The Human Fertilisation and Embryology Act 1990 added a further amendment to the Abortion Act 1967 to cover the situation where one or more foetus(es) in a multiple pregnancy is terminated. The termination may be justified either to protect the health or life of the mother or where there is a substantial risk that if the child were born it would suffer from such physical or mental abnormalities as to be seriously handicapped (i.e. Section 1(1)(d)).

Confidentiality and illegal abortions

Practical Dilemma 15.3　　To tell or keep quiet

Pam Reynolds is admitted in an emergency to the A&E department with severe bleeding. She is transferred to the gynaecology ward where it is clear to nursing and medical staff that she had probably tried to obtain an illegal abortion, although Pam herself is silent as to what happened. It is the third time this month that there has been such an admission and the gynaecologist suspects that one person may be responsible. Does he or the nursing staff have any duty in law to inform the police?

The simple answer is that there is no statute that places a duty on anyone to report a crime of causing a miscarriage or an offence under the Infant Life Preservation Act. If, of course, the police had heard of the illegal abortion and had begun to investigate, then they would be able to subpoena witnesses or obtain information for their enquiries under the procedures laid down under the Police and Criminal Evidence Act 1984. What about notifying them before they are aware of the possible crime? Some would argue that the doctor has a public duty to inform the police in such circumstances; that it is in the public interest for him to disclose the information, but until the law is changed, this is not obligatory by law, but a nurse may have a professional duty to act in the public interest under NMC guidance. (For those offences that must be reported to the police, see Chapter 8.)

Notification

The Abortion Regulations 1968, as amended by the 1976, 1980 and 1991 regulations, place a duty on the practitioner to notify the Chief Medical Officer (CMO) on the appropriate forms, but restricts disclosure to anyone other than: an authorised officer of the DH; the Registrar General; the Director of Public Prosecutions; the police; for the purposes of criminal proceedings; bona fide scientific research; to any practitioner with the consent of the woman; or at the request of the president of the General Medical Council for the purpose of investigating whether there has been serious professional misconduct. Regulation 3[26] requires a certificate of opinion to be given in writing by the registered medical practitioners. Regulations which came into force in 2002[27] amend the notification provisions enabling it to take place by electronic means and enabling a person authorised by the CMO who is engaged in setting up, maintaining and supporting the computer system to be notified of the abortion. A new Schedule sets out the information to be supplied.

Consent by a pregnant person under 16 years

If a girl of 14 seeks an abortion, do her parents have to consent on her behalf? The answer depends on the competence of the girl and what is in her best interests. Assuming that the girl is not in the care of the local authority and is seeking an abortion, then provided that she has the capacity to make the decision, she could give a valid consent under the Gillick case principles discussed in Chapter 13 on children's nursing. In the Axon case the High Court upheld the right of a young person under 16 to keep information relating to a prospective abortion from the knowledge of the parents.[28] The High Court upheld the guidance given by Lord Fraser in the House of Lords in the Gillick case and maintained that it did not breach Article 8 of the ECHR (see Chapter 13). What, however, if the girl's own parents wanted her to have the child and promised that they would care for it; could they refuse to allow the termination to proceed?

> ### Case 15.5   In re P (A Minor) (1981)
>
> **Whose choice?**[29]
>
> The mother was 15. She already had a son of 12 months and had been in care since she was 13 following a conviction for theft. She lived in a mother and child unit with schooling facilities and was then 12 weeks pregnant. Her own parents objected to the abortion (as they had done during the first pregnancy). Her father offered to take care of his grandson and leave the daughter with the new baby. As a Seventh Day Adventist, he opposed the termination of life on religious grounds. He also thought that the girl would live to regret the decision she had taken. He was convinced that she was still a child and that she should not be allowed to take a decision that she could subsequently regret.

The child was placed under the wardship jurisdiction of the court and Mrs Justice Butler-Sloss ordered that the termination of the pregnancy should proceed. The judge was clearly influenced by the wishes of the girl, who had set her mind on the termination and had not, in fact, contemplated that it might not proceed. She discussed the matter with the girl and formed the opinion that she was of a strong personality and mature views. The judge also held that, on the facts, the risks to the health of the mother and the interests of the existing child satisfied the requirements of the 1967 Act. The grandparents' objections were thus overruled and they were accorded no rights in the matter. In this case, of course, the child was already in the care of the local authority. Where this is not so, it may be the practice for the parents of the pregnant girl to sign the consent form for a termination. Probably, too, if there is a clash between the rights of the mother and the grandparents, the latter may put pressure on the girl to agree to an abortion since she may well be dependent on their help in bringing up the child. Should a health professional become aware of such a conflict between an under-aged child and her parents, she could take action to ensure that the matter was determined by the court under the Children Act 1989.

Abortion and those lacking mental capacity

Under 18 years old

The parents have the right to make decisions on behalf of the minor provided that they are acting in the interests of the child. The principles discussed in relation to the sterilisation of the minor by the House of Lords in *In re B* (see Case 15.7) would thus apply. It is considered necessary to obtain the approval of the court. Where a young person is over 16 years and lacks the mental capacity to make his or her own decisions this situation would now come under the Mental Capacity Act 2005 (see below).

Adult person lacking mental capacity

Case 15.6 *T* v. *T* (1988)

The mother with learning disabilities[30]

The defendant was a woman aged 19 who was epileptic with severe learning disabilities. She was totally dependent on others and was cared for by her mother. She became pregnant and termination of pregnancy was recommended by the medical advisers on the grounds that there would be complications associated with that condition and that she would be incapable of providing and caring for a child. The doctors also recommended that she should be protected from any further pregnancies by being sterilised. The doctors were, however, unwilling to carry out the abortion or sterilisation operation without authorisation. The mother thus applied to the court for a declaration that the procedures could be carried out lawfully.

The court held that the situation was not covered by the Mental Health Act 1983 consent to treatment provisions (see Chapter 20), neither did a guardian under the Act have the power to give consent. The court was prepared to grant the declaration requested and declared the proposed treatment lawful and therefore a defence to any action for trespass to the person. The doctors would be carrying out the treatment in the interests of the patient as part of their duty of care to the patient. The court also held that it no longer had a power to act as *parens patriae* (a kind of wardship jurisdiction) and the court could therefore not give consent itself. (It held that this power had been repealed in 1959 and should be reinstated. A subsequent case,[31] however, has held that the courts did have the power to make decisions on the day-to-day care of mentally incapacitated adults. This case is considered in Chapter 19.)

Mental Capacity Act 2005

The situation is now changed as a result of the implementation of the Mental Capacity Act 2005 in October 2007. Where a person over 16 years lacks the capacity required to make a specific decision, the action must be taken in her best interests according to the statutory provisions. The new Court of Protection has jurisdiction over matters of personal welfare as well as property and finance. Were the situation in Case 15.6 to occur now, once it had been established that the pregnant woman lacked mental capacity, or where her capacity was disputed, an application would be made to the Court of Protection for a declaration as to what was in her best interests. If her mental capacity were in dispute, then the Court of Protection could determine whether she was able to make her own decisions. The Act is discussed in Chapter 7.

Future reforms to the abortion law

There are pressures at present to revise the abortion laws: there are those who maintain that the 24-week time limit should be reduced, and claim that their case is supported by the foetal scans; there are those who wish to facilitate earlier abortions and give more responsibility to nurses. The British Pregnancy and Advisory Service recommended in 2006 that there should be legal reforms to allow nurses to prescribe the abortion pill to women within the first nine weeks as a responsible back-up to contraception.[32] The BMA at its meeting in June 2007 was not prepared to support nurses and midwives being allowed to conduct early abortions but it did vote that only one doctor's signature should be required in the first nine weeks. In October 2007 the Science and Technology Committee of the House of Commons published a comprehensive report on the scientific developments relating to the Abortion Act 1967.[33] Among its recommendations it held that there was no evidence on the basis of foetal viability rates below 24 weeks which would justify the reduction of the abortion limit below 24 weeks; it considered that there were grounds for the enhancement of the nurse's role in relation to terminations, particularly in relation to signing the HAS 1 form and carrying out early surgical abortions; consideration could be given to amending the Act to enable the second stage of early medical abortion to be self-administered in a woman's home; NICE should be responsible for clinical guidelines on abortion provision including health risks associated with abortion; the government should consider ways of ensuring that all those who offer pregnancy counselling services make the guidelines available or indicate clearly in their advertising that they do not support referral for abortion. Legislation will be required to implement some of these recommendations.

Sterilisation

Sterilisation of a minor with learning disabilities

> ### Case 15.7   *In Re B (A Minor: Wardship Sterilisation)* (1987)
>
> **Sterilisation**[34]
>
> Jeanette was 17 years old, but was described as having a mental age of 5 or 6. Her mother and the local authority, which held a care order on her, advised by the social worker, the gynaecologist and a paediatrician, considered it vital that she should not become pregnant. She had been found in a compromising situation in her residential home. She could not be relied on to take or accept oral contraceptives. Jeanette was likely to move to an adult training centre at the age of 19 and it would not be possible to provide her with the degree of supervision she had at present.

The House of Lords decided that the paramount consideration was the interests of the girl and, taking account of all the medical evidence, decided that it was in her interests to be sterilised. They made no distinction between non-therapeutic and therapeutic care of the child and recommended that in future all such cases should come before the courts. The Mental Capacity Act 2005 applies to those over 16 years and from 1 October 2007 consideration of whether a sterilisation was in the interest of a girl of 17 years would come before the Court of Protection. Cases concerning children under 16 years would be heard under the Children Act 1989 by the Family Division of the High Court. However, the Mental Capacity Act 2005 facilitates transfers to and from the Court of Protection and High Court.

Sterilisation of an adult with learning disabilities

The House of Lords in the Jeanette case discussed above declared their decision before Jeanette reached 18, so they did not consider the law in relationship to the adult mentally handicapped person. This was considered in the case of *T* v. *T* (Case 15.6, page 395), but that decision was taken in the High Court. The view of the House of Lords on this situation was given in the case of *In re F* v. *West Berkshire Health Authority*.

In this case, the court had to decide whether the sterilisation of a mentally handicapped woman, F, aged 35, would be unlawful because of her lack of capacity to give her consent to the operation. Mr Justice Scott Baker in the Family Division granted a declaration that it was in the best interests of F to have the operation. He stated that there was a problem when, because of a mental condition, a patient was unable to give any meaningful consent to treatment for a physical condition. If he did nothing, a doctor could be said to be negligent; if he operated, he, *prima facie*, committed the tort of battery. The law's answer to this was that a professional was not liable if he acted in good faith and in the best interests of the patients. The Court of Appeal upheld this decision. The House of Lords confirmed the power at common law for a doctor to act in the best interests of the patient incapable of giving consent. The court also had an inherent jurisdiction to make declarations on the lawfulness of such treatment. Court involvement in cases of sterilisation was highly desirable as a matter of good practice.[35] A practice note was issued providing guidance on the procedure that should be followed for making medical and welfare decisions on behalf of adults lacking capacity.[36] The Mental Capacity Act 2005 would now apply.

There can be disputes over what the best interests of a patient are and in a more recent case the Court of Appeal held that it was in the interests of a woman of 29 with severe learning disabilities to be fitted with an intra-uterine device rather than undergo a subtotal hysterectomy. The judge had failed to give proper weight to the unanimous medical evidence that supported the less invasive coil treatment.[37] In a case involving male sterilisation, the Court of Appeal held that it was not in the best interests of a man with learning disabilities to have a vasectomy, which his mother wanted to take place.[38] The Court of Appeal held that the best interests of the patient encompassed medical, emotional and all other welfare issues. In relation to sterilisation, the best interests of a man were not the equivalent of the best interests of a woman because of the obvious biological differences.

The situation in Case 15.7 would now be covered by the Mental Capacity Act 2005. Where serious decisions have to be made on behalf of a person lacking the requisite mental capacity an application would have to be made to the new Court of Protection to determine the best interests of that person. The Mental Capacity Act requires decisions to be made in the best interests of an adult who lacks the requisite mental capacity. (The Act is discussed in Chapter 7.)

Unsuccessful sterilisations

Case 15.8	*Emeh* v. *Kensington and Chelsea and Westminster Health Authority* (1985)

Unwanted pregnancy[39]

Mrs Emeh, a mother of three children, underwent an operation for sterilisation in May 1976. In January 1977 she discovered that she was 20 weeks pregnant. She refused to have an abortion. She then gave birth to a child with congenital abnormalities who required constant medical and parental supervision. She claimed damages for the unwanted pregnancy and the birth and upkeep of the child. The trial judge held that the operation had been performed negligently and she could therefore recover damages for the time before she discovered the pregnancy, but since she refused to have an abortion, she was not entitled to the costs thereafter apart from the cost of undergoing the second sterilisation operation. Mrs Emeh appealed to the Court of Appeal and won.

The Court of Appeal held that since the avoidance of a further pregnancy was the object of the sterilisation operation, it was unreasonable after the period of pregnancy that had elapsed to expect the claimant to undergo an abortion. Her failure to do so was not unreasonable. She was therefore entitled to recover damages for her financial loss caused by the negligent performance of the sterilisation operation. She was awarded £7,000 for loss of future earnings, £3,000 for pain and suffering up to the trial and £10,000 for future loss of amenity and pain and suffering that will occur during the life of the child.

This decision is to be welcomed since it reverses an earlier decision.[40] The mother's refusal to have an abortion was not an unreasonable one and it could not be used as a reason to limit the damages payable. It has recently been confirmed in a decision of the House of Lords (see the McFarlane[41] case below) that arranging an adoption or abortion was not a requirement of the parents following the diagnosis of an unwanted child: 'There was no legal or moral duty to arrange an abortion or an adoption of an unplanned child.'

In another case,[42] a woman was sterilised when she was 4 weeks pregnant, a fact unknown to herself and the surgeon. The health authority accepted liability and damages of £96,631 were awarded, which included the future cost of caring for and educating the child. A pregnancy test should have been carried out before the operation for sterilisation was performed. Subsequently, the issue as to whether there should be compensation for bearing a healthy (but unplanned child) has come before the House of Lords.

Unplanned healthy baby

The House of Lords has stated that compensation is not payable for the costs in bringing up a healthy child. In *McFarlane and Another* v. *Tayside Health Board*[43] (see Case 15.9), the House of Lords laid down the principles that should apply to any assessment.

Case 15.9   *McFarlane and Another v. Tayside Health Board* (1999)

Unplanned pregnancy – compensation for healthy baby[44]

Mr and Mrs McFarlane had four children and Mr M agreed to have a vasectomy. Six months after the operation, he was advised that the sperm counts were negative and he could dispense with contraceptive precautions. Mrs M subsequently became pregnant and gave birth to a healthy daughter. They brought proceedings for damages for the cost of rearing the child and the pain and suffering by Mrs M in carrying and giving birth to her. Her claim was dismissed initially on the ground that such damages were irrecoverable in principle. The appeal succeeded and it was held that the couple should be given the opportunity to prove their loss and damage. The health board appealed to the House of Lords.

The House of Lords held that where medical negligence resulted in an unwanted pregnancy, and the birth of a healthy child, the parents were not entitled to recover damages for the costs of rearing that child, but the mother was entitled to recover damages for the pain and distress suffered during the pregnancy and in giving birth and for the financial loss associated with the pregnancy. Damages for the cost of bringing up a healthy baby were irrecoverable since it was not fair, just or reasonable to impose liability for such economic losses on a doctor or his employer. Lord Steyn held that it was morally unacceptable to allow such a claim having regard to the principle of distributive justice, which focused on the just distribution of burdens and losses among members of a society.

Unplanned baby with disabilities

In the McFarlane case, the House of Lords were considering the birth of an unplanned healthy baby. However, different considerations would arise if the unplanned baby were to be disabled. In the case of *Nunnerley and Another* v. *Warrington Health Authority and Another*[45] (held before the decision of the McFarlane case was known), the mother was given negligent advice that led to the unwanted birth of a disabled child. The High Court judge held that the claim for damages should not be limited to the costs of the care which they themselves had a legal duty to provide, but damages were payable for the cost of care beyond 18 years. The judge held that the normal principle of compensation should apply, i.e. the claimants were entitled to be put in the position that they would have been in but for the wrong done to them and they were therefore entitled to compensation beyond the child's 18th birthday.

In another case,[46] M gave birth to a Down's syndrome baby. The doctor had failed to inform her of the results of a routine scan that indicated that she was likely to give birth to a child suffering from Down's syndrome. M said that had she been informed of the results of the scan, then she would have chosen a termination. Liability was admitted and she was awarded £118,746. The High Court judge held that the ruling in *McFarlane* v. *Tayside Health Authority* was confined to the birth of a healthy baby. This principle was followed in *Hardman* v. *Amin*[47] where a doctor misdiagnosed rubella as tonsillitis in a pregnant woman, who therefore did not have a termination. The doctor subsequently admitted negligence. The mother successfully claimed the costs of the upbringing of a severely disabled baby. In *Gaynor and Vincent* v. *Warrington HA and Liverpool HA*,[48] where damages were sought for the birth of an unplanned child, who was disabled, the Court of Appeal held that it would be contrary to the general rules of the law of negligence and damages to enforce a cut-off when a child reached the age of 18 years. There was a considerable body of family law that indicated that the liability of the defendants towards a disabled child and the parents who cared for that child should continue beyond the age of 18. In another case a sterilisation operation was carried out when the claimant was pregnant and the defendant was deemed negligent in not carrying out a pregnancy test and advising about a termination. The baby suffered from disabilities following the mother's exposure to bacterium during childbirth. The defendant was held to be responsible for the foreseeable and disastrous consequences of performing her services negligently and therefore liable for the costs of bringing up a disabled child.[49] In the case of *Parkinson* v. *St James and Seacroft University Hospital NHS Trust*[50] the Court of Appeal held that the extra expenses associated with bringing up a child with a significant disability could be claimed.

Unplanned baby to a mother with disabilities

Case 15.10	*Rees v. Darlington Memorial Hospital NHS Trust* (2003)

Unplanned pregnancy – compensation for healthy baby to a blind mother[51]

Mrs Rees suffered a severe and progressive visual disability such that she felt unable to discharge the ordinary duties of a mother. She therefore wished to be sterilised and made her wishes known to a consultant employed by the defendants. The operation was performed negligently. She bore a healthy and normal child and sought damages for his upbringing. The Court of Appeal (in a majority decision) held that she was entitled to the additional costs attributable to her disability. The defendant appealed to the House of Lords.

The House of Lords allowed the appeal, and, following the unanimous decision in *McFarlane* v. *Tayside Health Board*[52] held that a disabled mother who gave birth to a normal, healthy child after a failed sterilisation operation could not recover by way of damages the extra costs of rearing him which were referable to her disability. However, she was a victim of a legal wrong which it was appropriate to recognise by the award of a conventional sum. This was put at £15,000 to be added to the award for pregnancy and birth.

Failure to warn of risks of pregnancy

There have been cases where no negligence in the performance of the operation has been proved, but compensation has been claimed on the grounds that the patient was not warned that there was a possibility of the operation being reversed and the patient becoming fertile or pregnant. This occurred in the following case.

Case 15.11   *Gold v. Haringey HA* **(1987)**

No warning[53]

Mrs Gold, who had two children, decided when she became pregnant again that she would not have any more children. She was referred to the consultant obstetrician who suggested sterilisation, but did not discuss the possibility of the husband having a vasectomy which had a slightly lower failure rate, neither did he discuss the risk of failure with her. The sterilisation operation was performed the day after the birth of the child, but was not a success and Mrs Gold gave birth to a fourth child. She sued the health authority for negligence because she had not been warned of the risk of failure and the statement that the operation was irreversible was a negligent misrepresentation.

Initially Mrs Gold was awarded £19,000 damages on the grounds that, although the operation had not been negligently performed, the defendants had been negligent in failing to warn her of the possibility of failure of the operation. The defendants appealed and the Court of Appeal allowed the appeal for the following reasons:

1 The standard of care required of the medical practitioner was the same as that required of members of the profession, i.e. the ordinary skilled member of that profession who exercised and professed that special skill (see Chapter 3 for further details on this standard). Where medical advice had been given, the standard of care required did not depend on the context in which it was given, but on whether there was a substantial body of doctors who would have given the same advice. Since, in 1979, a substantial body of responsible doctors would not have warned her of the risk of failure of the sterilisation operation, the health authority was not liable in negligence.

2 The statement that the operation was irreversible could not reasonably be constructed as a representation that the operation was bound to achieve its objectives. Mrs Gold therefore lost the case.

The Court of Appeal made it clear that it did not accept any distinction between advice given for a therapeutic procedure and that for a non-therapeutic procedure. The same standard should be applied to both, i.e. the Bolam Test.

Private healthcare

What if the case concerns an operation carried out in the private sector? Do any different principles apply? The significant difference between NHS care and private care is that there is a contract between patient and hospital in the provision of private care and failure to perform a satisfactory operation could lead to claims for breach of contract as well as a claim for negligence. In the case of *Thake* v. *Maurice*, the High Court awarded compensation for failure to warn the husband and the wife about the risks of the sterilisation failing. The Court of Appeal[54] decided that the standard of care required in the law of negligence would be the same as the standard to be given under a private contract for healthcare:

> *The reasonable man would have expected the defendant to exercise all the special care and skill of a surgeon in that specialty; he would not in my view have expected the defendant to give a guarantee of 100% success. (Neill LJ)*

Similar arguments could not be used in an NHS context since there is no contractual relationship between an NHS patient and the health authority or doctor. The possibility of action arising from failed sterilisations has led to much more meticulous wording of the agreement and warnings in relation to the possibilities of failure.

Where a child is born as a result of a failed sterilisation the legal situation is as follows:

(a) The costs of bringing up a healthy child are not payable. (*McFarlane* v. *Tayside Health Board*)

(b) Any extra costs directly due to the child being significantly disabled are payable. (*Parkinson* v. *St James and Seacroft University Hospital NHS Trust*)

(c) The mother can claim damages for the pain and suffering of the pregnancy and childbirth and financial loss. (*McFarlane* v. *Tayside Health Board*)

(d) A disabled mother is entitled to a set award of £15,000 as a recognition of the harm that she has suffered. (*Rees* v. *Darlington*)

(The sterilisation of a child under 16 is considered in Chapter 13, which also considers the law relating to contraceptive advice for the under-16-year-old.)

Rights of the spouse

There is no legal requirement that if a person wishes to be sterilised the agreement of his or her spouse or partner must be obtained. Clearly, however, joint discussion with the couple of the implications is desirable.

Practical Dilemma 15.4   **The husband says 'no'**

Audrey Rich was expecting her seventh child. Her eldest child was 10 years old and they lived with the husband in a four-bedroomed council house. She felt she could not cope with any further pregnancies and sought advice as to the possibility of being sterilised after the birth of the seventh. An appointment was arranged with the obstetrician for Audrey and Steve, but Steve refused to attend, claiming that he would never give his consent to Audrey's being sterilised. Audrey went on her own to see the obstetrician, who told her that he could not carry out the operation without her husband's consent.

There is no duty in law to obtain the consent of the spouse before sterilising the partner. In the past, there was a legal duty when the husband had a right of consortium and could sue any person who caused him to lose this right. However, this right to sue for loss of consortium was repealed by the Administration of Justice Act 1982 Section 2(a). The woman has never enjoyed such a right; the House of Lords refused to extend it to women in 1952.[55] There may be considerable advantages in obtaining a signature to say that the spouse knows of the intended operation, since if this is obtained the doctor is less likely to be summoned as a witness in divorce proceedings where one spouse is alleging that the operation was performed without his/her knowledge. However, a form signifying knowledge of the operation is very different from a form of consent.

In the situation outlined above, Audrey could obtain a solicitor's letter confirming the law, but this, of course, does not place any duty on the doctor to perform the operation. She could request referral to a doctor who would perform the operation or even apply to the health authority for assistance. Ultimately, she could seek a judicial review from the court of the refusal to perform the operation and obtain a declaration that such an operation could proceed without the husband's consent.

Female circumcision

Under the Prohibition of Female Circumcision Act 1985 female circumcision is a criminal offence. There was, however, evidence that some girls from ethnic minorities were being returned home to be circumcised. This led to the 1985 Act being replaced by the Female Genital Mutilation Act 2003, which strengthens the law against female genital mutilation. Under Section 1(1) of this Act it is a criminal offence for any person to:

> *[E]xcise, infibulate or otherwise mutilate the whole or any part of a girl's labia majora or labia minora or clitoris.*

The word 'girl' includes woman. Section 1(1) is subject to Section 1(2), which states no offence is committed by an approved person who performs:

(a) a surgical operation on a girl which is necessary for her physical or mental health, or

(b) a surgical operation on a girl who is in any stage of labour, or has just given birth, for purposes connected with the labour or birth by an approved person.

An approved person is defined as:

(a) in relation to an operation falling within subsection 1(2)(a) a registered medical practitioner

(b) in relation to an operation falling within subsection 1(2)(b), a registered medical practitioner, a registered midwife, or a person undergoing a course of training with a view to becoming such a practitioner or midwife.

There is also no offence if a person performs a surgical operation falling within Section 1(2)(a) or (b) outside the United Kingdom and exercises functions corresponding to those of an approved person.

Section 1(5) states that for the purpose of determining whether an operation is necessary for the mental health of a girl, it is immaterial whether she or any other person believes that the operation is required as a matter of custom or ritual.

Section 2 makes it an offence for a person to aid, abet, counsel or procure a girl to excise, infibulate or otherwise mutilate the whole or any part of her own labia majora, labia minora or clitoris.

Under Section 3, it an offence to aid, abet, counsel or procure a person who is not a United Kingdom national or permanent United Kingdom resident to do a relevant act of female genital mutilation outside the United Kingdom. An act is a relevant act of female genital mutilation if it is done in relation to a United Kingdom resident and it would constitute an offence under Section 1. Similar exceptions in relation to surgical operation and childbirth by approved persons apply. The Act also extends the offences to any act done outside the United Kingdom by a United Kingdom national or permanent resident.

Ann Clwyd, the Labour MP who introduced the legislation leading to the 2003 Act, complained at the lack of prosecutions under the legislation. A report suggested that African village elders were being flown into the UK to circumcise young girls.[56] The Metropolitan police have offered £20,000 to anyone giving information which leads to successful prosecution for female genital mutilation.[57] The House of Lords overruled a Court of Appeal decision that held that a 19-year-old from Sierra Leone was not protected by the asylum laws since she did not belong to a particular social group fearing prosecution. The House of Lords held that the fear of genital mutilation if she were to return enabled her to stay in Britain.[58] Baroness Hale stated that female genital mutilation is in breach of international human rights law and standards.

Conclusions

The Mental Capacity Act 2005 now covers the situation where an adult lacks the mental capacity to make their own decisions and would apply to abortion and sterilisation. This clarifies the law relating to the sterilisation or abortion and other decisions on behalf of those adults who lack the requisite mental capacity. The debate on changing the law on abortion is ongoing with those in favour seeking to remove the rule that two doctors are required to authorise the abortion and suggesting that a nurse should be able to prescribe an abortion pill and carry out early surgery for termination, and those against arguing that the 24-week time limit should be reduced to 21 weeks (Nadine Dorries presented a Bill to Parliament calling for the limit to be reduced to 21 weeks in November 2006). The latter group reinforce their arguments with the research that women are at greater risk of mental illness after an abortion.[59] Parliamentary discussions will follow the report in October 2007 from the Scientific and Technology Committee of the House of Commons on abortion and it is likely that amendments will be made to the Abortion Act to give a larger role to nurses in the termination of pregnancy, and secret trials to let GPs carry out abortions in their surgeries will be evaluated later in 2008.[60]

Reflection questions

1 What is the legal situation if an aborted foetus is found to be breathing?
2 What do you consider should be the registered nurse's role in the termination of pregnancy?
3 What information do you consider should be given to a patient before his or her consent is given to an operation for sterilisation? What are the legal requirements? (See also Chapters 7 and 22.)

Further exercises

1 Obtain a set of the documentation that has to be completed when an abortion is performed and examine the legal requirements as shown in these forms.

2 What forms are completed in your hospital when an operation for sterilisation is performed? Can you see any significant differences in the form completed by the patient and the form completed by the spouse?

References

[1] Department of Health, Abortion, March 2007; Numbers of previous abortions by age, DH, February 2007

[2] *Jepson v. Chief Constable of West Mercia* [2003] EWHC 3318

[3] *R v. Salford Health Authority ex parte Janaway, The Times*, 2 December 1988; [1988] 3 All ER 1079

[4] *Royal College of Nursing v. The Department of Health and Social Security* [1981] 1 All ER 545

[5] Nigel Hawkes, Law allows unsupervised nurses to carry out abortions, says surgeons, *The Times*, 27 March 2007, p. 27

[6] Nick Britten, Jury convicts mother who destroyed foetus, *Daily Telegraph*, 27 May 2007

[7] *R v. Hamilton, The Times*, 16 September 1983

[8] *Vo v. France* [2004] 2 FCR 577 (ECHR)

[9] *Rance and Another v. Mid Downs Health Authority and Another* [1991] 1 All ER 801

[10] *C v. S* [1987] 1 All ER 1230

[11] *Kelly v. Kelly* [1997] SLT 896

[12] *Paton v. Trustees of British Pregnancy Advisory Service* [1978] 2 All ER 987

[13] *Paton v. UK* (1980) 3 EHRR 408

[14] *Barr v. Matthews* (2000) 52 BMLR 217

[15] Clare Dyer, Cash Settlement for woman who changed her mind on abortion, *The Guardian*, 30 July 2007

[16] Kathryn Godfrey, Abortion by postcode, *Nursing Times*, 1 December 1999, 95(48), pp. 30-31

[17] Royal College of Obstetricians and Gynaecologists, Report on Abortions, RCOG, 2000

[18] www.dh.gov.uk/en/Policyandguidance/

[19] Rosemary Bennett, Half of late abortions are for women who didn't notice they were pregnant, *The Times*, 19 April 2007, p. 32

[20] Department of Health, An investigation into the British Pregnancy Advisory Service Response to Requests for Late Abortion, DH, September 2005

[21] Chief Medical Officer Letter, 21 September 2005, Gateway Reference 5463 DH

[22] *R v. Dixon (Reginald)* (1995) unreported

[23] *R v. Bourne* [1939] 1KB 687

[24] *R v. Dhingra* (1991) unreported

[25] *R (Smeaton) v. Secretary of State for Health* [2002] EWHC 610, [2002] 2 FCR 193

[26] Abortion Regulations 1991 SI 1999/490

[27] The Abortion (Amendment) (England) Regulations, SI 2002 No. 887

[28] *R (On the application of Axon) v. Secretary of State* [2006] EWHC 37 admin

[29] *In re P (A Minor)* [1981] 80 LGR 301

[30] *T v. T* [1988] 1 All ER 613

[31] *In re F (Adult: Court's Jurisdiction)*, The Times Law Report, 25 July 2000

[32] Lewis Smith, Abortion should be made easier for women says charity, *The Times*, 28 November 2006, p. 1

[33] Science and Technology Committee, Scientific developments relating to the Abortion Act 1967, 12th Report Session 2006-7, HC 1045-1, October 2007

[34] *In re B (A Minor: Wardship Sterilisation)* [1987] 2 All ER 206

[35] *In re F v. West Berkshire Health Authority* [1989] 2 All ER 545

[36] *Practice Note* [2001] 2 FCR 569, Adult lacking capacity; enquiries@offsol.gsi.gov.uk

[37] *Re S (Sterilisation: patient's best interests)* [2000] 2 FLR 389

[38] *Re A (Male sterilisation)* [2000] 1 FLR 549

[39] *Emeh v. Kensington and Chelsea and Westminster Health Authority* [1985] 2 WLR 233

[40] *Udale v. Bloomsbury AHA* [1983] 2 All ER 522

[41] *McFarlane and Another v. Tayside Health Board* [1999] 4 All ER 961 HL

[42] *Allen v. Bloomsbury Health Authority and Another* [1993] 1 All ER 651

[43] *McFarlane and Another v. Tayside Health Board* [1999] 4 All ER 961 HL; [2000] 2 AC 59

[44] Ibid.

[45] *Nunnerley and Another v. Warrington Health Authority and Another*, The Times Law Report, 26 November 1999; [2000] PIQR 069

[46] *Rand v. East Dorset HA* [2000] Lloyd's Rep Med 181

[47] *Hardman v. Amin* [2000] Lloyd's Rep Med 498

[48] *Gaynor and Vincent v. Warrington HA and Liverpool HA* [2003] 7 Lloyd's Rep Med 365 CA

[49] *Groom v. Selby* [2001] EWCA Civ 1522; [2002] PIQR P201 CA

[50] *Parkinson v. St James and Seacroft University Hospital NHS Trust* [2001] EWCA Civ 530

[51] *Rees v. Darlington Memorial Hospital NHS Trust*, The Times Law Report, 21 October 2003 HL; [2003] UKHL 52; [2002] 2 All ER 177 CA

[52] *McFarlane v. Tayside Health Board* [1999] 4 All ER 961 HL; [2000] 2 AC 59

[53] *Gold v. Haringey HA* [1987] 2 All ER 888

[54] *Thake v. Maurice* [1986] QB 644; [1984] 2 All ER 513

[55] *Best v. Samuel Fox and Co.* [1952] 2 All ER 394

[56] Nicola Woolcock, Parents fly in African village elders to circumcise their young daughters, *The Times*, 23 October 2006, p. 7

[57] Helen Pidd, Met's unique £20,000 reward to stop mutilation of women, 11 July 2007

[58] *Secretary of State for the Home Department (Respondent) v. Fornah (FC) (Appellant)* [2006] UKHL 46

[59] Rosemary Bennett, Women at greater risk of mental illness after an abortion, *The Times*, 27 October 2006, p. 40

[60] Sam Coates, Secret trial to let GPs carry out abortions, *The Times*, 5 December 2007

Chapter 16
Intensive care, transfusion and transplant surgery nursing

This chapter discusses

+ Definition of death
+ Importance of exact time of death
+ Legality of switching machines off
+ Not for resuscitation
+ Relatives and treatment of the patient
+ Patients refusing treatment
+ Living wills/advance decisions
+ Transfusions
+ Organ transplantation
+ Resource pressures
+ Review of critical care services

Introduction

Definition of death is of such concern to the intensive care nurse in relation to requests for organs for transplantation that it was thought best to discuss it here. Further aspects relating to death are considered in Chapter 29. Other concerns for the transplant nurse are the decision not to resuscitate a patient and consent for the use of organs and tissues and in what circumstances machines can be switched off. A telephone survey was conducted by the RCN[1] that provided an analysis of the role of the nurse in intensive care and illustrated considerable differences in the functioning of nurses in ICUs and considerable flexibility of roles between doctors and nurses. These findings were confirmed by the report of the Audit Commission, which is considered on pages 424-5.

Definition of death

The traditional method for the determination of whether life has ceased was to check whether breathing had stopped by checking the pulse, the heart beat and placing a mirror in front of the mouth, i.e. the cessation of circulatory and respiratory functions as evidenced by an absence of heart beat, pulse and respiration. For most cases, this was satisfactory. However, if the patient were on a ventilator where breathing was maintained artificially, this traditional definition was inappropriate. In addition, the advance in medical technology, particularly in transplant surgery, meant that it was essential to use the organs as soon as possible after respiration had ceased and, if there were likely to be a delay, to keep the body ventilated, i.e. artificially breathing until such time as the organs required for transplant could be taken. In these cases, 'brain death' became the criterion for whether death had taken place. If the traditional definition of death was used, there was an 88 per cent incidence of post-operative renal failure in kidney transplants, whereas if the criterion of brain death was used on a patient maintained on a ventilator, the post-operative failure rate was 10-20 per cent. The same percentage occurs when kidneys from living donors are used.

What is brain death?

A conference of the Royal Colleges in 1976 set out the diagnostic tests to be used for the determination of brain death; these were circulated in 1978 and also included in the code of practice, 'The Removal of Cadaveric Organs for Transplantation', which was distributed to doctors in January 1980. A subsequent conference in 1981 made the recommendations set out in Box 16.1.

In a case in 1992 where parents wished their child to be kept on a ventilator, the judge ruled that A, who had been certified as brain stem dead, was for all legal as well as all medical purposes dead and that a doctor who disconnected the ventilator was not acting unlawfully.[2] (See Section 47 of the Human Tissue Act 2004 for the law relating to the ventilation of a body for organ transplant, on page 420.)

The definition of brain stem death as set out in Box 16.1 was adopted by the Department of Health in 1998,[3] which accepted that while there was no statutory definition of death, 'irreversible loss of the capacity for consciousness, combined with irreversible loss of the capacity to breathe' should be regarded as the definition of death. A revised Code of Practice for the Diagnosis and Certification of Death was prepared by a working party on behalf of the Royal College of Anaesthetists in 2006. It sought to separate the diagnosis of death from any subsequent events, allowing patients in whatever situation to be diagnosed and treated appropriately. It also gave considerable more detail than the previous guidelines, in some areas, particularly in stating the relevant biochemical values and other data.[4]

Box 16.1   Definition of brain death

The diagnosis of brain death should be made by two medical practitioners who have expertise in this field. One should be the consultant who is in charge of the case and one other doctor (or in the absence of the consultant, his deputy who should have been registered for five years or more with adequate previous experience in the care of such cases and one other doctor). The two doctors may carry out their tests separately or together. If the tests confirm brain death they should still be repeated. It is for the doctors to decide how long the interval between the tests should be. It may not be appropriate for the doctors to carry out all the recommended tests. The criteria are guidelines, not rigid rules.

These criteria are as follows:

1   All brain stem reflexes are absent.
2   The pupils are fixed in diameter and do not respond to sharp changes in the intensity of incident light.
3   There is no corneal reflex.
4   The vestibular-ocular reflexes are absent.
5   No motor responses within the cranial nerve distribution can be elicited by adequate stimulation of any somatic area.
6   There is no gag reflex or reflex response to bronchial stimulation by a suction catheter passed down the trachea.
7   No respiratory movements occur when the patient is disconnected from the mechanical ventilator for long enough to ensure that the arterial carbon dioxide tension rises above the threshold for stimulation of respiration.

Additional recommendations are made as to how some of these tests should be undertaken.

Further guidance is given in the revised Code of Practice prepared by the Royal College of Anaesthetists in 2006.

The possibility of brain death is recommended where the patient is deeply comatose (but where depressant drugs, primary hypothermia and metabolic and endocrine disturbances can be excluded) or where the patient is being maintained on a ventilator because spontaneous respiration had previously been inadequate or had ceased (relaxants or other drugs should be ruled out as a cause of respiratory failure), or where there is no doubt that the patient's condition is due to irremediable structural brain damage.

Case 16.1   *Re A (1992)*

Definition of death[5]

An infant aged 19 months was placed on a ventilator following serious head injuries sustained at home. He showed no signs of recovery. The hospital followed the guidelines laid down by the Medical Research Council in carrying out various diagnostic tests and was satisfied that he was dead. It then applied to court for a declaration that the child could be removed from the ventilator. The family court judge, Judge Johnson, identified the results of the tests carried out by the doctors and stated that he had 'no hesitation at all in holding that A has been dead since Tuesday of last week, 21 January'. (It was then 27 January.)

Importance of exact time of death

The actual timing of death can be a significant feature in a variety of court actions. A few examples are set out in Box 16.2.

Box 16.2   **Causes of action where the time of death has considerable significance**

Civil law

A   Survivorship. The rules of inheritance depend on the order in which people die. If, therefore, there are incidents leading to multiple deaths, which victim died first can be very significant for inheritance. There are certain presumptions in law relating to the order of deaths in such circumstances, i.e. the oldest died first. However, if one of the victims is supported on a life support machine and kept 'alive' longer, the presumption would no longer operate.

B   Insurance policies often require that where death follows an accident it must be established that the death occurred within a fixed time limit in order to claim under the policy.

C   Where the machine is switched off this could lead to claims for compensation for negligence by professional staff especially where organs are used for transplantation.

(It used to be a requirement that to constitute the offence of murder, the victim had to die within a year and a day of the act leading to the death. This time limit was removed in 1996.)

Criminal law

In the past, to constitute murder the victim must have died within a year and a day of the act. In 1996, this time limit requirement was removed. However, issues of causation may still arise. If the victim is taken off the machine, is that the cause of death or is the cause of death the original assault on the victim? If he is kept on a machine for longer than that, is it murder? Several defendants have tried to argue that it was not.

Case 16.2   *R v. Malcherek; R v. Steel* (1981)

Causal link[6]

Malcherek was convicted of the murder of a victim of assault who had been connected to a life support machine that had been disconnected by medical practitioners. He was sentenced to life imprisonment. In a similar case, Steel was also convicted and sentenced to life imprisonment. Malcherek appealed against this decision and Steel applied for leave to put in further medical evidence as to the sufficiency and adequacy of tests by the doctors to determine brain death. They were both effectively challenging that there was a causal link between the assaults and the deaths of the victims. The judge in each case had withdrawn the issue of causation from the jury.

The Court of Appeal held that in each case it is clear that the initial assault was the cause of the grave head injuries in the one case and of the massive abdominal haemorrhage in the other. In each case, the initial assault was the reason for the medical treatment being

views of relatives and others should be obtained on what would have been the wishes of the patient. Nor can those making the decision about life-sustaining treatment be motivated by a desire to bring about the death in deciding what are the best interests.

Patients refusing treatment

Since the Suicide Act 1961, suicide has not been a crime (see Statute, below).

Statute — **Sections 1 and 2(1) of the Suicide Act 1961**

Section 1 of the 1961 Suicide Act states that 'the rule of law whereby it is a crime for a person to commit suicide is hereby abrogated'. This, coupled with the right of a person to consent to treatment, means that it is possible for a seriously ill person to refuse consent to, say, antibiotics and staff have to accept that refusal. Only where there is a doubt over the person's mental competence to refuse treatment could the medication be given under the provisions of the Mental Capacity Act 2005 (see Chapter 7). While it is no longer a crime for a person to decide on and bring about their own death, it is still, however, a crime for anyone to aid and abet in the suicide of another.

Section 2(1) states: 'A person who aids, abets, counsels or procures the suicide of another or an attempt by another to commit suicide, shall be liable on conviction on indictment to imprisonment.' (Up to 14 years.)

The position is clear for professional staff. Even though they sympathise with a patient's wish to die, they are prohibited by the criminal law in taking any steps or giving any advice to the patient to help him carry out this wish. Where a patient is clearly refusing medication because of this desire, it is essential for staff to record detailed accounts of the patient's attitude, his level of competence, the advice given to him and, preferably, where the patient takes his own discharge contrary to professional advice, to obtain the patient's signature to that effect. In a recent case the judge held that a woman, who had a degenerative brain condition, could not be prevented from travelling to Switzerland for her life to be ended, since she had the mental capacity to make that decision.[20] Clearly, however, anyone assisting such travel in this country is in danger of committing an offence under Section 2(1) of the Suicide Act 1961 (see Statute, above).

Euthanasia is not recognised by law in this country. The courts recognised that in law there is a distinction between letting die and killing a person, even though this is not accepted by some philosophers. Decisions sometimes have to be made in special care baby units and in intensive care or renal dialysis units, or over transplants, on who may be treated. This effectively means that those not selected for treatment may eventually die. This is, however, a very different matter from taking an action that will bring about or assist in bringing about another person's death. The House of Lords Select Committee on Medical Ethics in 1994[21] did not support any proposals to change the law that makes euthanasia illegal and several attempts to pass an Assisted Suicide law have failed. Supporters of euthanasia point to the situation in the Netherlands and Switzerland where assisted suicide is lawful. Lord Joffe has stated that despite the failures of his attempts to change the law, he has not given up.

Practical Dilemma 16.2   To let go

Harry Judd, aged 84, had told his daughter that if he became ill and suffered a cardiac arrest he did not want to be resuscitated. His wife had died two years before and he had become increasingly depressed and frail, with failing eyesight caused by his diabetes. He was still managing to cope on his own with a home help, but it was becoming more and more of a struggle. One day, the home help found him in a coma and he was rushed into hospital. He remained seriously ill for several days and then slowly improved. His consultant physician, Dr Jones, discussed Harry's prognosis with his daughter and son-in-law. It appeared unlikely that he would be able to manage on his own. The daughter reported Harry's views about not being resuscitated. The next evening, Harry suffered a cardiac arrest. The staff nurse summoned Dr Jones, who was unwilling to use resuscitative machinery. Is he obliged to do so?

From the above discussion, it will be evident that it is essential to clarify two issues: first, the mental capacity of Harry when he stated that he would not want to be resuscitated and, second, the medical prognosis of Harry. In addition, since 1 October 2007 the provisions of the Mental Capacity Act 2005 in relation to advance decisions must be complied with (see below). If Harry were mentally competent when he asked not to be resuscitated, his views should be respected. If, however, his wishes were the result of extreme depression caused by his bereavement and illness, then it may be concluded that he was not mentally capable when he made that request. He must then be treated according to his best interests. If it were absolutely clear that Harry's prognosis is hopeless, then there is no legal duty to resuscitate. If, however, there is any chance that Harry could recover and would have a reasonable prognosis, then Dr Jones's duty would require him to resuscitate him. If Harry is considered to lack the requisite mental capacity, the situation is covered by the Mental Capacity Act 2005.

The BMA have issued guidelines on withdrawing treatment.[22]

Living wills/advance decisions

In this country, the legality of a 'living will' (also known as an advance statement or an advance refusal or decision) was recognised at common law (i.e. judge-made law) and is now provided for in the Mental Capacity Act 2005. An 'advance decision' means a decision made by a person (P), who is over 18 years and has the capacity to make the decision, that if at a later time and in such circumstances as he may specify, a specified treatment is proposed to be carried out or continued by a person providing healthcare for him, and at that time he lacks the capacity to consent to the carrying out or continuation of the treatment, then the specified treatment is not to be carried out or continued.[23] The advance decision can be written in layman's language and no formalities are required unless it is intended to cover a situation where life-sustaining treatment is necessary. These formalities require the person to make it clear that the advance decision is intended to apply to life-sustaining treatment and that:

(a) it is in writing;

(b) it is signed by P or by another person in P's presence and by P's direction;

(c) the signature is made or acknowledged by P in the presence of a witness; and

(d) the witness signs it, or acknowledges his signature, in P's presence.

As long as the maker of the decision has the requisite mental capacity to make decisions, the advance decision remains inapplicable. The effect of a valid advance decision which applies to the treatment in question is that any person who carried out the treatment contrary to the advance decision could be guilty of an offence or civil wrong. An advance decision can be withdrawn or altered without any formality unless it relates to life-sustaining treatment. The minimum age for being able to create an advance decision is 18 years because a young person under 18 years cannot refuse life-sustaining treatment if such treatment is in his or her best interests. If there are doubts as to the validity or relevance of an advance decision, then an application can be made to the Court of Protection to determine such questions. In the meantime any necessary action can be taken to keep the person alive.

It is not possible by means of a living will or advance decision to compel health service professionals to provide treatment at a later time when the patient lacks the mental capacity to make his or her own decisions. A living will can therefore only legally be a refusal of treatment. This is the ruling in the case brought by Mr Burke, who challenged the guidance provided by the GMC on withholding or withdrawing treatment in respect of a mentally incapacitated adult and claimed the right to insist that specific treatment were provided for him, even though it was contrary to the professional discretion of the medical staff.[24] The Court of Appeal upheld the GMC's appeal against the High Court decision. The result is that a person has no legal right to insist on specific treatment being given at a later time, when he lacks the requisite mental capacity. Whilst a person can refuse specific treatments, a person cannot insist on specific treatments being given.

Transfusions

In an attempt to reduce transfusion errors, the British Committee for Standards in Haematology, Blood Transfusion Task Force, RCN and the Royal College of Surgeons of England[25] produced the first clinical guidelines on blood transfusion. If hospitals implement them and provide the necessary resources and training, transfusion errors should be reduced. Guidance has also been provided by the National Patient Safety Agency.[26] An NHS Blood and Transplant (NHSBT) organisation was set up in 2005 as a special health authority. It combines the roles of the National Blood Authority and UK Transplant with a remit of increasing the quality, safety and supply of donated blood, organs and tissues and increasing the effectiveness of blood and transplant services. New regulations on blood safety require annual reports on serious adverse events and reactions to be made by blood establishments, hospital blood banks and facilities where blood transfusions take place.[27]

Those haemophiliac patients who were infected with HIV in the early 1980s would have been unable to succeed in obtaining compensation through the civil courts, since at that time AIDS/HIV was not recognised and blood for transfusions was not tested for it. The government paid compensation to them, but the agreement included a waiver to prevent them from taking action over other blood-borne viruses that they might contract in the future. This waiver is now being challenged by a haemophiliac who claims that he was infected with hepatitis C virus from a blood transfusion. It has been held that a claim brought under the Consumer Protection Act 1987 in respect of the infection by patients with hepatitis C contracted from blood and blood products used in blood transfusions could succeed (see page 294).[28] The government has set up a scheme for haemophiliacs to be compensated for being given contaminated blood (see Chapter 26, page 610). The Skipton Fund handles claims (www.skiptonfund.org/Eng). An inquiry into the circumstances surrounding the supply to patients of contaminated blood and blood products has been established under the chairmanship of Lord Archer of Sandwell. It will also look at the consequences to the haemophilia community and others afflicted and suggest further steps to address their needs. Further information can be obtained from the inquiry website.[29]

Organ transplantation

Transplants from deceased persons

The Human Tissue Act 2004 now covers the use of organs from living or dead donors.

Practical Dilemma 16.3   **A transplant opportunity?**

A youth of 23 years is knocked down in a road traffic accident. He has no identification on him and appears to be unaccompanied. He is brought into hospital by the ambulance crew and is resuscitated. He is maintained on the ventilator, but the prognosis is poor. Transplant teams are anxious to remove his lungs, heart, kidneys and liver and an ophthalmologist would like to make use of his eyes. The police are asked to notify the relatives as soon as possible. They are advised by the surgeon that the organs should be removed within half an hour of death. The youth is kept on a positive pressure ventilator. Can his organs be used for transplant on diagnosis of death before the relatives are contacted? What difference would it make if he were found to be carrying a donor card?

The Human Tissue Act 2004 now applies to the situation in Practical Dilemma 16.3. Where the dying person has not indicated his wishes, then any person whom he has nominated to act on his behalf can give consent to the organ donation. Where there has been no such nomination, then a person in a qualifying relationship such as a partner or other relative or friend can give consent. If, however, the dying person has been registered as an organ donor with the NHS organ donor register[30] or is carrying a donor card, then that would count as a valid consent for the removal of the organs. If none of the conditions listed above can be met, the person in charge of the body could give consent.

Transplants from living donors

Special provisions apply to a situation where a potential donor is alive, as Practical Dilemma 16.4 illustrates.

Practical Dilemma 16.4   **Live donation**

A nurse cares for a renal patient aged 23. She has been on dialysis for a number of years, but has been advised that a kidney transplant is urgently required. Her mother has offered to be a donor and seeks the advice of the nurse over whether such an offer would be accepted.

Under Section 33 of the Human Tissue Act 2004 it is a criminal offence to remove any transplantable material from the body of a living person intending that the material be used for the purpose of transplantation. However, in certain circumstances approval can be given by the Human Tissue Authority to the transplantation of organs (or part of organs), bone marrow and peripheral blood stem cells from living persons. Regulations drawn up under the Human Tissue Act specify the strict conditions which must be satisfied.[31] The prohibition on transplants from a live donor is lifted under Regulation 11 if specific conditions are satisfied. The conditions which must be satisfied include the following:

1 A registered medical practitioner who has clinical responsibility for the donor must have caused the matter to be referred to the Human Tissue Authority.

2 The Authority must be satisfied that no reward has been or is to be given and consent has been given for the removal of the transplantable material or it is otherwise lawful.

3 The Authority must take into account the report of the interviews with the donor (or person who gave consent) and the recipient when making its decision.

4 The authority must give notice of its decision to:
   (a) the donor (or any person acting on his behalf);
   (b) the recipient (or any person acting on his behalf); and
   (c) the registered medical practitioner who referred the matter to the Authority.

5 One or more qualified persons must have conducted separate interviews with each of the following:
   (a) the donor;
   (b) if different from the donor, the person giving consent, and
   (c) the recipient;
   and (unless the transplant is the result of a court order) reported to the Authority on the following matters:
   (a) any evidence of duress or coercion affecting the decision to give consent;
   (b) any evidence of an offer of a reward; and
   (c) any difficulties of communication with the person interviewed and an explanation of how those difficulties were overcome.

6 The following matters must be covered in the report of the interview with the donor and, where relevant, the other person giving consent:
   (a) the information given to the person interviewed as to the nature of the medical procedure for, and the risk involved in, the removal of the transplantable material;
   (b) the full name of the person who gave that information and his qualification to give it; and
   (c) the capacity of the person interviewed to understand:
      (i) the nature of the medical procedure and the risk involved, and
      (ii) that the consent may be withdrawn at any time before the removal of the transplantable material.

7 A person is qualified to conduct an interview if:
   (a) he appears to the Authority to be suitably qualified to conduct the interview;
   (b) he does not have any connection with any of the persons to be interviewed, or with a person who stands in a qualifying relationship to any of those persons, which the Authority considers to be of a kind that might raise doubts about his ability to act impartially; and
   (c) in the case of an interview with the donor or other person giving consent, he is not the person who gave the information to those people.

In Practical Dilemma 16.4 the mother of the renal patient should make known her intention to the doctor in charge of the patient, who can ensure that the appropriate referral is made

419

to the Human Tissue Authority and the procedure would then be set in place. She may of course not prove to be a match. However, it is possible for her to take part in a paired or pooled donation. In October 2007 there was a report of a paired donation, i.e. twinned kidney transplant between couples, where a potential donor from couple A was matched with a recipient from couple B and the partner of the recipient was matched with the partner of the donor A. It is therefore possible for the mother to be matched with another recipient whose relative was a potential donor and match for her child. Regulation 13 requires that where the donor is a child, an adult who lacks the capacity to give consent or the case involves a paired donation, pooled donation or non-directed altruistic donation, then a panel of no fewer than three members of the Human Tissue Authority must make the decision on whether approval should be given. Procedures are in place for requiring the HTA to review its decision over a transplant (Regulations 13 and 14). Transitional provisions cover organ transplants between genetically related persons.[32]

Keeping the patient ventilated

Section 47 of the Human Tissue Act 2004 states that where part of a body (i.e. of a deceased person) lying in a hospital, nursing home or other institution is or may be suitable for use for transplantation, it shall be lawful for the person having the control and management of the institution:

(a) to take steps for the purpose of preserving the part for use for transplantation, and

(b) to retain the body for that purpose.

However, the authority given under this section only extends to the taking of the minimum steps necessary for the purpose mentioned in that provision, and to the use of the least invasive procedure.

Once it has been established that consent making removal of the part for transplantation lawful has not been, and will not be, given, then the authority under this section ceases to apply.

Transplant and consent provisions

Transplants and children

The principles of consent, which are considered in Chapter 7, apply to the recipient of the transplant. If the person is mentally competent and over 18 years, then they can give consent or refuse. If the person is under 18 years, then the principles that are discussed in Chapter 13 on children apply. In the following case, the mother consented to the child's transplant, but the child refused.

Case 16.5   *Re M (Medical Treatment: consent) (1999)*

Child refusing a transplant[33]

A 15-year-old girl refused to consent to a transplant that was needed to save her life. She stated that she did not wish to have anyone else's heart and she did not wish to take medication for the rest of her life. The hospital, which had obtained her mother's consent to the transplant, sought leave from the court to carry out the transplant.

> ### Case 16.5 continued
>
> The court held that the hospital could give treatment according to the doctor's clinical judgement, including a heart transplant. The girl was an intelligent person whose wishes carried considerable weight, but she had been overwhelmed by her circumstances and the decision she was being asked to make. Her severe condition had developed only recently and she had had only a few days to consider her situation. While recognising the risk that for the rest of her life she would carry resentment about what had been done to her, the court weighed that risk against the certainty of death if the order were not made.

Transplants from mentally incompetent persons

Chapter 13 on children considered the rights of the parent to give consent to a donation of tissue from one child to another and the question of whether this would be lawful if one person were mentally incapacitated was considered. The sole question for the courts is what is in the interests of the donor where the donor lacks the mental capacity or capability in law to give consent in his own right. This situation arose in the American case of *Hart* v. *Brown* where the donor and recipient were identical twin girls. The court approved the parental request to transfer a kidney from one to the other. One of the main justifications was that, medically, such a graft was more likely to be successful and another justification was that, if they refused to allow the donation, the donor might, in later life, feel guilty at not being allowed to be a donor.[34] In another American case (*Strunk* v. *Strunk*),[35] a kidney transplant was authorised to proceed from an institutionalised adult with the mental capacity of a 6-year-old to his brother who was terminally ill with kidney trouble. The court accepted the medical evidence that there was a strong emotional bond between the brothers and the mentally incompetent would suffer a severe traumatic experience if the brother died.

In England, the courts have discussed whether a mentally and physically impaired younger sister could give bone marrow to her older sister who was suffering from a serious blood condition[36] (*Re Y 1996*). The court held that it was in the younger sister's best interest for her to give bone marrow to her older sister and the risks to her were minimal. The important issue was that it is the interests of the donor that have to be considered, not the interests of the recipient. It can be a criminal offence for parents to fail to take appropriate action for the care of their children. The situation of transplants from a person lacking the requisite mental capacity is now covered by the Human Tissue Act 2004 and the Regulations made under that Act.[37] The transplant could only take place if it were clearly in the best interests of the proposed donor and if were approved by a panel of at least three members of the Human Tissue Authority.

Liability arising from transplants

> ### Practical Dilemma 16.5   Diseased organs
>
> A patient received a kidney transplant and was subsequently told that it was HIV infected. It was discovered that this was unknown to the doctors and family of the deceased patient. Does the patient who received the kidney have any rights of action?

In the above situation, there is a duty of care, according to the reasonable professional standard for the transplant team, to ensure that the kidney is reasonably safe for transplant. In determining whether this duty of care had been fulfilled, note would be taken of the timescale within which any tests would have to take place. The possibility of the patient being able to sue under the Consumer Protection Act 1987 depends on whether the organ could be defined as 'goods' under that Act and whether the transaction could be seen as in the course of business. Since the Human Organ Transplant Act 1989 (now consolidated in the Human Tissue Act 2004) prohibits commercial dealings, it could be argued that organ transplantation is not in the course of business. However, the activities of hospitals and health organisations would be defined as in 'the course of business'. National heart and lung transplant standards have been published by the National Specialist Commissioning Advisory Group[38] in 2006 to ensure that patients receive services that match the evidence on best care available. These standards replace those issued in September 2002.

The government launched Saving Lives, Valuing Donors in July 2003 which was a 10-year framework to encourage people to donate organs and tissues. The progress was reviewed in 2004.[39] In 2007 the Chief Medical Officer suggested that the possibility of introducing 'opt-out provisions' for organ and tissue donation should be placed on the political agenda in order to increase the number of organs available. A task force appointed by the Department of Health to investigate improvements to the transplant services reported in January 2008. It made recommendations on increasing the number of transplant coordinators, strengthening the network of retrieval teams, identifying potential donors sooner and mandatory training of critical care staff. It set up a sub-committee to look at the issue of presumed consent which will report in the summer of 2008. The implementation of its recommendations may lead to an increase in the number of donors and conclusions that no change in the law on consent is required.

Retention of organs

Considerable public concern was raised when it was learnt that human organs from children who had died had been retained at Bristol Royal Infirmary. New guidance was considered necessary when, during the inquiry into allegations of professional misconduct in carrying out paediatric heart surgery, it was learnt that more than 11,000 children who had died in the past 40 years had had their organs used for research in British hospitals without the explicit consent of their parents.

At the same time, concerns were raised about the retention of human brains and spinal cords at the Walton Centre, Liverpool, and of children's organs at Alderhey Hospital. The Report of the Royal Liverpool's Children's Inquiry (chaired by Michael Redfern QC)[40] on the retention of organs and body parts was published on 30 January 2001. Its publication coincided with three other publications:

1 A report of a census of organs and tissues retained by pathology services in England carried out by the Chief Medical Officer.[41]

2 The removal, retention and use of human organs and tissue from post mortem examination: advice from the Chief Medical Officer.[42]

3 Consent to organ and tissue retention at post mortem examination and disposal of human materials.[43]

The inquiry found that thousands of children's body parts had been collected at the hospital, some going back to before 1973. Most, however, were retained after 1988 when Professor

Richard Van Velzen was appointed to the Department of Pathology and there was a huge increase in the number of organs removed and retained.

In response to the Redfern Report, the Secretary of State set up a Retained Organs Commission under the chairmanship of Professor Margaret Brazier. It was a special health authority which had the responsibility of overseeing the return of tissues and organs from collections around the country, ensuring that collections were accurately catalogued, providing information on collections throughout the country, ensuring that suitable counselling was available, acting as an advocate for parents if problems arose, advising on good practice in this area and handling enquiries from families and the public. On completion of its work it ceased to exist in March 2004.

Legal action by parents who had suffered as a result of the removal and retention of organs from their dead children in a group litigation action was initiated and the court agreed that the legal costs would be capped at £506,500.[44] On 26 March 2004 the High Court ruled, in respect of three test cases, that where hospitals had illegally removed the organs in post mortem examinations without the parents' consent, parents could claim damages if they had suffered psychological injury.[45] Damages of £2,750 were awarded in one of the test cases; the other two lost.

As a consequence of these developments the Human Tissue Act 2004 was passed which made it an explicit requirement that the informed consent of the parents or relatives must be obtained for the post mortem to be carried out (unless required by a coroner) and for the removal and retention of organs or tissues and the introduction of criminal offences for failure to obey the laws. These are discussed below, pages 423-4.

'Human Bodies, Human Choices'

A consultation paper, 'Human Bodies, Human Choices', was published in July 2002,[46] which invited feedback on the principles to apply to the removal, retention and storage and use of organs. It was followed by proposals for new legislation on human organs and tissue, which were published in September 2003.[47] These would include:

+ Explicit consent to be the fundamental principle underpinning the lawful removal, storage and use of bodies, body parts, organs and tissue.

+ The principle that the human body and its parts should not, as such, give rise to financial gain.

+ A regulatory framework within an overarching authority, the Human Tissue Authority, would be responsible for licensing and inspecting regulated activities, including public display.

+ Penalties for undertaking certain activities (including DNA testing) without consent or without a licence.

+ Statutory codes of practice issued in relation to matters such as the conduct of post mortems and anatomical examinations; the import and export of human body parts; communication with families about post mortem examinations; definitions of death; and disposal of human tissue.

+ Human organ transplantation to continue to operate broadly under current arrangements, but within the new legislative framework.

Human Tissue Act 2004

The Human Tissue Act 2004 gave legal effect to these proposals and to the Tissue Directive of the EC,[48] which was implemented in 2007.[49] The Act regulates the removal, storage and use of human organs and other tissues for specified purposes, specifies the appropriate consent for children and adults; creates a criminal offence in relation to the removal without appropriate consent; establishes a Human Tissue Authority and a licensing regime, arranges for the publication of codes of practice and sets up inspectorates for anatomy and pathology and of organ and tissue for human use. In addition it makes provision for the use of DNA and creates an offence relating to non-consensual analysis of DNA, with specified exceptions. The government did not support any legal change to allow a person's organs to be donated automatically on their death unless they or their family had specifically asked otherwise, i.e. presumed consent for organ donation was not included in the Act. However, the Chief Medical Officer of the DH called in July 2007 for the introduction of an 'opt-out' system and a review is being carried out (see page 422). Further information is available from the website[50] of the Human Tissue Authority on which the codes of practice can be found.

Resource pressures

There is national concern over the pressure placed on intensive care beds, often highlighted during flu epidemics. Thus in the winter of 2003/4 a warning was given by the Intensive Care Society in its report 'Critical Insight' that critical care units across the country would face an inevitable bed shortage as the flu season began.[51]

An Audit Commission report[52] on intensive care units pointed out: 'It does not make sense to respond to pressures created in cheaper areas of the hospital by increasing the number of the most expensive beds.' The report found that critical care beds were not always used appropriately and 'critical care units can become the backstop of a poorly performing hospital'. It gave as an example of inappropriate use the fact that almost one-third of hospitals place extra strain on critical care beds, and bear unnecessary extra costs, by nursing patients with epidurals for pain relief after major surgery within critical care units. The Audit Commission report found that there were great variations in the resources deployed: 'Some units employ twice as many nurses as others have in order to have, for example, five direct care "bedside" nurses on duty at any time . . . Yet the cost of neither nurses nor doctors is related to mortality differences between units.' It suggests that there should be national research to record more scientifically the benefits offered by one-to-one nursing.

Practical Dilemma 16.6   Inadequate staffing

During a flu epidemic, there was considerable pressure on ITU beds and operations were being postponed because of the inability to offer patients follow-up in ITU. During this crisis, an extra bed was used in ITU, although the staffing numbers were not increased. Sarah Roberts was attempting to look after her own patient as well as cover for another patient, when the nurse was on break. Unfortunately, she administered the wrong dose of a drug and the patient died.

Sarah could face criminal proceedings for acting with a lack of professional care. If it can be shown that she is guilty of such gross professional recklessness and negligence that it amounts to a criminal offence, she could be found guilty of the manslaughter of the patient. Account would be taken of the pressure she had been placed under and the extent to which she had fulfilled her professional duty to the NMC under its Code of Professional Conduct by drawing the crisis situation to the notice of senior management and taking other appropriate action. The legal issues relating to resources are considered in Chapter 4.

Review of critical care services

Following the Audit Report, an expert group was set up to review critical care services. Its report,[53] 'Comprehensive Critical Care', was published in 2000 along with a review of adult critical care nursing.[54] The Comprehensive Critical Care Report recommended a modernisation programme to develop consistent and comprehensive critical care services. Four levels of care were identified:

Level 0 normal acute ward care

Level 1 acute ward care, with additional advice and support from critical care team

Level 2 more detailed observation or interventions, e.g. patients with a single failing organ system

Level 3 advanced respiratory support alone or basic respiratory support together with support of at least two organ systems.

The Report highlighted the need for action in four areas.

1 a hospital-wide approach to critical care

2 a networked service

3 workforce development

4 better information with all critical care services, collecting reliable management information and participating in outcome-focused clinical audit.

A health service circular[55] required the setting up of local plans to implement a modernisation programme. It also stated that any plans put in place by NHS trusts for additional capacity or reconfiguration of services should include robust plans for the recruitment and education or training of nurses. Trusts should put in place high-dependency training for ward staff as an early measure. An additional £145 million was made available for adult critical care, including £2.5 million to support local service redesign in 2000/1. Details of the progress of these developments are available from the Department of Health.[56] The Chief Nursing Officer at the Department of Health has also published a strategic programme for action for the nursing contribution to the provision of comprehensive critical care.[57] The document emphasises that although it provides direction for nurses, it should be read and worked through in the context of the multi-professional clinical team. A critical care information advisory group (CCIAG) has been established and has developed a strategy to review and enhance critical care information standards, needs and data collection. A Critical Care Stakeholders Forum has published examples of good practice in the delivery and organisation of adult critical care services.[58] The Forum also published clinical indicators for critical care outreach services in March 2007 (see reference 52).

Other major concerns of relevance to the intensive care nurse include definition of the scope of her professional practice. The DH launched a document called the 'Recruitment and Retention of Staff in Critical Care' on 4 June 2004. This is considered in Chapter 24 and the same basic principles that are discussed there apply to the intensive care nurse. Other aspects relating to death are considered in Chapter 29.

Conclusions

Despite the work of Lord Joffe and supporters for the introduction of laws permitting voluntary euthanasia, aiding or abetting a suicide attempt is still a criminal offence in this country. The Human Tissue Act 2004 has made significant changes to the laws relating to many of the issues covered in this chapter. The introduction of a criminal offence for failure to obtain the consent of the relatives to the removal of human tissue should ensure that the new laws are followed and the Human Tissue Authority has a major responsibility in monitoring this area. The shortage of organs for transplant continues to be of major concern and the possibility of enacting laws which presume consent to donation is once again on the political agenda. The proposal that the Human Tissue Authority should be amalgamated with the Human Fertilisation and Embryology Authority into the Regulatory Authority for Tissue and Embryos (RATE) has been dropped by the government following criticism by the Joint Parliamentary Scrutiny Committee reviewing the Human Tissue and Embryos (Draft) Bill (see Chapter 22). This should mean that the HTA is able to continue the development of its strength and influence in this significant area.

Reflection questions

1 What are the main provisions of the Human Tissue Act on the law on consent to donate organs? What are the advantages and disadvantages of introducing an opt-out system?

2 What is meant by brain death? What problems arise from recognising this as opposed to the traditional definition of death?

3 Examine the role of the consultant nurse in ITU. What safeguards should exist to protect the patient?

4 A patient who is being ventilated asks you to switch off the machine. What is the legal position?

Further exercises

1 Over a period of two weeks, list the legal problems that you have encountered in your work in an intensive care unit or transplant unit and refresh your memory of the basic principles of accountability.

2 Relatives often have very fixed views on the outcome they wish for the seriously ill patient. Prepare a short paper outlining the basic principles of consent that apply in order to clarify the situation for relatives. Refer to the Mental Capacity Act 2005 (see Chapter 7).

3 Look back over the records that you have made on a patient who was in hospital several weeks before. If you were now to be challenged on any aspect of your care in that case, how useful and comprehensive would your notes be? Are there any obvious gaps on which you should have kept a record and are there any faults in the record keeping? (Refer to Chapter 9.)

References

[1] Royal College of Nursing, The Nature of Nursing Work in Intensive Care, Order No. 000728, RCN, May 1997

[2] *Re A* [1992] 3 Med LR 303

[3] Department of Health, Code of Practice for the Diagnosis of Brain Stem Death, DH, March 1998

[4] Royal College of Anaesthetists Letter dated 14 May 2006, Code of Practice for Diagnosis and Certification of Death and Guidelines for the Management of Potential Organ and Tissue Donors, 2006

[5] *Re A* [1992] 3 Med LR 303

[6] *R* v. *Malcherek*; *R* v. *Steel* [1981] 2 All ER 422 CA

[7] *Criminal Law Report*, 1977, p. 443

[8] *B (re) (Consent to treatment: capacity)*, The Times Law Report, 26 March 2002, [2002] 2 All ER 449

[9] Ibid.

[10] *AK (Adult Patient: medical treatment: consent) Re* [2001] 1 FLR 129

[11] *Airedale NHS Trust* v. *Bland* [1993] 1 All ER 821

[12] *Frenchay NHS Trust* v. *S*, The Times Law Report, 19 January 1994 CA

[13] *A Hospital* v. *W; sub nom A Hospital* v. *SW* [2007] EWHC 425

[14] *An NHS Trust* v. *D* [2005] EWHC 2439, [2006] 1 FLR 638

[15] *An NHS Trust* v. *X* [2005] EWCA 1145; [2006] Lloyd's Rep Med 29

[16] British Medical Association, Resuscitation Council (UK) and the Royal College of Nursing, Decisions Relating to Cardiopulmonary Resuscitation, BMA, 1999; updated March 2001 and October 2007

[17] NHS Executive, Resuscitation Policy, HSC 2000/028, September 2000

[18] British Medical Association, Resuscitation Council (UK) and the Royal College of Nursing, Decisions Relating to Cardiopulmonary Resuscitation, BMA, October 2007, Paragraph 13, p. 19

[19] Michael Horsnell, Doctors call for death inquiry, *The Times*, 7 December 1999

[20] *Re Z* [2004] EWHC 2817

[21] House of Lords Select Committee on Medical Ethics, HL Paper No. 21, 1, HMSO, London

[22] BMA, Withholding and Withdrawing Life-prolonging Treatment guidelines, BMA, updated March 2007

[23] Mental Capacity Act 2005 Section 24(1)

[24] *R (on the application of Burke)* v. *General Medical Council and Disability Rights Commission and the Official Solicitor to the Supreme Court* [2004] EWHC 1879, [2004] Lloyd's Rep Med 451

[25] British Committee for Standards in Haematology, Blood Transfusion Task Force, RCN and the Royal College of Surgeons of England, The administration of blood and blood components and the management of transfused patients, *Transfusion Medicine*, 9(3), 227–38, 1999

[26] National Patient Safety Agency, Right patient, right blood – new advice for safer blood transfusions, November 2006

[27] Blood Safety and Quality Regulation, SI 2005 No. 50 (amended SI 2006 No. 2013 and SI 2007 No. 604)

[28] *A and Others* v. *National Blood Authority and Another (sub nom Re Hepatitis C Litigation)*, The Times Law Report, 4 April 2001; [2001] 3 All ER 289

[29] www.archbbp.com

[30] www.uktransplant.org.uk/ukt/

[31] Human Tissue Act 2004 (Persons who Lack Capacity to Consent and Transplants) Regulations 2006, SI 2006 No. 1659

[32] Human Tissue Act 2004 (Commencement No. 5 and Transitional Provisions) (Amendment) Order 2006 No. 2169

[33] *Re M (Medical Treatment: consent)* [1999] 2 FLR 1097

[34] *Hart* v. *Brown* 289 A 2d 386 Conn 1972

[35] *Strunk* v. *Strunk* 445 SW 2d 145 (Ky App) 1969

[36] *Y (Adult Patient: transplant: bone marrow) Re* (1996) BMLR 111; (1996) 4 Med LR 204

[37] Human Tissue Act 2004 (Persons who Lack Capacity to Consent and Transplants) Regulations 2006, SI 2006 No. 1659

[38] Available on the DH website

[39] Department of Health, Saving Lives, Valuing Donors: A transplant framework for England – one year on, DH, 2004

[40] Department of Health, The Royal Liverpool's Children's Inquiry Report, DH, 30 January 2001

[41] Chief Medical Officer, A Report of a Census of Organs and Tissues Retained by Pathology Services in England, DH, January 2001

[42] Department of Health, The Removal, Retention and Use of Human Organs and Tissue from Post-Mortem Examination: advice from the Chief Medical Officer, DH, January 2001

[43] Department of Health, Consent to Organ and Tissue Retention at Post-Mortem Examination and Disposal of Human Materials, DH, January 2001

[44] *AB and Others* v. *Leeds Teaching Hospitals NHS Trust and in the Matter of the Nationwide Organ Group Litigation* [2003] Lloyd's Rep Med 7 355

[45] *AB and Others* v. *Leeds Teaching Hospitals NHS Trust and Another*, The Times Law Report, 12 April 2004

[46] Department of Health and Welsh Assembly, Human Bodies, Human Choices: a consultation report, July 2002

[47] Department of Health and Welsh Assembly, Proposals for New Legislation on Human Organs and Tissue, September 2003; www.dh.gov.uk/tissue

[48] Tissue Directive 2004/23/EC

[49] Human Tissue (Quality and Safety for Human Application) Regulations, SI 2007 No. 1523

[50] www.hta.org.uk

[51] Oliver Wright and Christian Barby, Critical care beds shortage 'certain' when flu strikes, *The Times*, 26 November 2003

[52] Audit Commission, Critical to Success: the place of efficient and effective critical care services within the acute hospital, Audit Commission, 1999

[53] Department of Health, Comprehensive Critical Care Report of an Expert Group, DH, 2000

[54] Department of Health, The Review of Adult Critical Care Nursing Report to the Chief Nursing Officer, DH, 2000

[55] NHS Executive, Modernising Critical Care Services, HSC 2000/017, May 2000

[56] Critical Care Outreach 2003, Progress in Developing Services, Department of Health, October 2003

[57] www.dh.gov.uk.cno./criticalcarenurs.htm

[58] Department of Health, Quality Critical Care: Beyond 'Comprehensive Critical Care', October 2005

Chapter 17
Theatre and anaesthetic nursing and the recovery ward

Introduction

Like the ward nurse, the theatre nurse is constantly concerned with the possibility of litigation and also with the problems of her role in relation to the surgeons and the anaesthetists. Reference should also be made to Chapter 29 on the law relating to death and inquests and the need to report to the coroner if a patient dies on the operating table or shortly afterwards. Another concern for theatre staff, when an aborted foetus shows signs of life, is considered in Chapter 15.

Civil liability procedures and practices in theatre

Professional liability

Practical Dilemma 17.1   **Lost swab**

Staff Nurse French was the scrub nurse for a hernia operation performed by a registrar. They were running late and still had two patients left on the morning list. The afternoon list was due to start in 10 minutes. Just before the registrar sutured the patient's wound, he asked for a swab count. Staff Nurse French checked the 34 used swabs, which had been hung on the rack, and six unused swabs and two unopened packs with the operating department practitioner. She confirmed that those were the only ones in use and the patient was sewn up. A few days later, just before the patient would normally have been discharged, he reported violent pains and became seriously ill. It was decided to X-ray the patient prior to returning him to theatre. The X-ray showed up a swab. The relatives of the patient were told what had happened and they made it clear that they would seek compensation. An internal investigation was commenced to see if the cause of this error could be found. The conclusions were that there was an extra swab in one of the packs and this had not been spotted when the staff nurse opened and counted them. A dispute then ensued between the registrar and the staff nurse over liability for the incident. The staff nurse claimed that, as she had checked the swabs in front of the registrar, he should accept responsibility for it; the registrar stated that as the staff nurse had clearly counted wrongly, it was entirely her responsibility and, in addition, the unscrubbed runner nurse had made a second check.

In a dispute like this, the patient would be able to argue that this is a case of *res ipsa loquitur* and the burden should pass to the NHS trust to show that they were not negligent. (This is discussed in Chapter 6.) It will be recalled from the case of *Wilsher* v. *Essex Area Health Authority*[1] that the courts do not accept any concept of team liability (see Case 4.3, pages 61-3). The NHS trust itself could be directly liable and, in addition, each individual professional could be liable for what he personally did or failed to do and would be judged according to the standards expected of him, but the employer would accept vicarious liability.

The actual proportion of responsibility in a case like the above would obviously depend on the actual facts of what went wrong. When the swabs were unpacked, were they properly checked to ensure that none were stuck together? What was the accepted approved practice that the doctor and the nurse should have followed? Were there any justifiable reasons why this need not have been followed? In addition, there might be some liability on the part of the manufacturer. Since 1 January 1990, health authorities have accepted responsibility for the negligence of doctors and dentists while acting in the course of employment. This also applies to NHS trusts. It is, therefore, less important how liability between nurse and doctor is shared, since the compensation will be paid to the patient by the employer, because of its vicarious liability for the negligence of its employees. It is important, however, to allocate responsibilities through procedures and policies to ensure that similar harm does not occur again. It is essential that procedures are in place to prevent such incidents arising.

There have been some very rare cases where, although the scrub nurse points out that a swab is unaccounted for, the surgeon still proceeds with stitching up the patient. This may be justifiable in particular cases if the patient's condition is deteriorating and there is a greater risk in keeping him under the anaesthetic than in taking the risk of the swab still being inside him. It would be very different if the surgeon were simply ignoring the nurse's count without any justification.

The proportion of liability between nurse and surgeon thus depends entirely on the individual facts of the case.

Policies and practices

Practical Dilemma 17.1 illustrates the importance of having clear policies and codes of practice as to the responsibility of each person in theatre, so that there is no overlap. In a situation where the patient is unable to correct any wrong assumptions, it is essential that these codes cover every possible danger. The responsibility for the identification of the patient, the nature of the operation to be performed, including the identification of the part of the body or limb to be operated on, must all be clearly allocated so that there can be no errors. Many of these procedures may be repeats of checks already made at ward level, but they cannot be omitted on that account in theatre. If any such cases came to court, the judge would expect evidence on what the procedure should have been and what in fact took place.

There are many implications for theatre nurses: they should clearly be familiar with the procedures and implement them, resisting any unjustifiable shortcuts whatever the pressure. In addition, their records should be detailed and meaningful so that if there is a query about the care in the theatre, then they are able to refer to a comprehensive account of what took place. Booklets produced by the defence societies, the Royal College of Nursing and the National Association of Theatre Nurses on theatre safeguards cover procedures for admission, labelling and ward procedure, lost swabs and instruments and other causes of potential hazards (see Box 17.1). A Step Guide to Improving Operating Theatre Performance,[2] prepared by the NHS Modernisation Agency, was sent to all NHS trusts in 2006 to reduce cancelled operations and optimise theatre use. It draws on best practice across the country.

Box 17.1 **Potential hazards in the operating theatre**

Allergies not marked on notes.

Units of blood not checked.

Nerves over bony surfaces damaged.

Eyes exposed to harm.

Sharp and powered tools used dangerously.

Faulty gauges on pneumatic cuffs, faulty monitors.

Tourniquets left on too long and skin necrosis beneath tourniquet cuffs.

Spirit solutions used with cautery.

Hot instruments and hot water in tubing.

Water mattresses overheating.

Diathermy burns.

Uninsulated electrodes.

Misplaced footswitch.

Faulty alarms and faulty equipment.

In 2003 the National Institute for Health and Clinical Excellence published interventional procedures guidance covering eight clinical areas to protect patients and support health professionals when performing innovative surgical procedures. For four of the procedures, NICE advised that the data appear adequate to support their use; in the other four, there is uncertainty and in such cases NICE advises that patients are kept fully informed and that clinicians monitor and audit the results of the procedures they undertake carefully. Details are available from its website[3] (see Chapter 5). Guidelines issued by NICE in respect of specific surgical procedures are available on its website.

In 2000 the wrong kidney was removed from a patient in Prince Philip Hospital, Llanelli. In the subsequent report of the inquiry by the Commission for Health Improvement[4] into that incident, it was found that there were serious faults in the marking of X-rays and significant recommendations were made. A trial of the two surgeons involved began at Cardiff Crown Courts, but the prosecution failed to establish that the removal of the wrong kidney caused the death of the patient and the jury were ordered by the judge to acquit the defendants. Subsequently, professional conduct proceedings were held by the General Medical Council. Action Against Medical Accidents reported that since 2004 there had been 283 claims against NHS trusts after surgical instruments or other foreign bodies had been left inside patients following surgery: £4 million was paid in compensation for such incidents.[5] The National Patient Safety Agency issued a patient safety alert on correct site surgery with recommended action to be taken by the NHS in March 2005[6] and a fact sheet on patient safety in anaesthetics and theatres is available on its website.

The theatre nurse and the scope of professional practice

There is little uniformity in the tasks that nurses are expected to perform in theatre. The duties of a scrub nurse can depend on the personal preferences of an individual surgeon and on whether the hospital is a teaching hospital. Anaesthetic nurses may also have a variety of duties: for example, in some theatres they may be expected to draw up the drugs in syringes for the anaesthetist to check; in others, the anaesthetist might do this himself. The nurse's role will also depend on the existence of and the duties performed by the operating depart-ment practitioner. Some of the tasks she performs will be regarded as expanded-role duties in which she might have been trained on a post-registration training course. In its report 'Anaesthesia under Examination',[7] the Audit Commission made significant recommendations on anaesthetic and pain management services and suggested that there was considerable scope for the role expansion of many of the different professional groups who work in theatres. The report illustrates how problems can arise when interdisciplinary teamworking breaks down. It puts forward practical suggestions on how trusts can improve anaesthetic and pain relief services. (See Chapter 24 and page 575–6 on the scope of professional practice and the theatre nurse.) The National Association of Theatre Nurses has provided guidance on principles of safe practice in theatres.[8] It recommends that demonstrations of new technol-ogy should take place in a workshop or laboratory setting and perioperative staff should be familiar with the technology prior to direct patient use. Operating department practitioners are now a registered profession under the aegis of the Health Professions Council. In Chapter 28 their role in relation to medication is discussed. The scope of professional practice of the theatre nurse should take into account the role of the ODP (see Chapter 24). The NPSA has published a safety leaflet on teamwork including teamwork in surgery which is available on its website.[9]

Accidents in the theatre

An incident book should be kept to record accidents and other mishaps in theatre and the recovery room and accidents and other untoward incidents should be reported to the chief executive or his/her assigned officer. There may be opposition from some medical staff over the necessity to record untoward incidents, but the nurse has a duty to ensure that records are maintained on incidents that cause harm: diathermy burns, an unintentional cut and the more serious incidents such as operating on the wrong side of the patient or even on the wrong patient. A policy of disclosure to the patient should be encouraged. However, it is not for the nurse to notify the patient; this is the consultant's or manager's duty. The National Patient Safety Agency (NPSA) was established in 2001 to set up a national reporting system of adverse healthcare incidents so that lessons could be learnt and accidents prevented. The NPSA is discussed in Chapter 12. Proposals for a new NHS redress scheme recommended the introduction of a duty of candour but this was not included in the NHS Redress Act. This is discussed in Chapter 6. The Kennedy Report[10] following the inquiry into the children's heart surgery at Bristol also emphasised the need for openness and honesty between health professionals and patients (see Chapter 4). An association has been established for assistants in surgical practice, which has set up a website to support members.[11] It also runs workshops and conferences to provide professional development to assistants in surgical practice, including non-medically qualified practitioners. Its Code of Practice and clinical milestones for the surgical care practitioner can be seen on its website.

Consent in the theatre

Some particular problems arise in relation to consent in the theatre. One is the failure of ward staff to ensure that the appropriate forms have been filled in before the patient is sent to theatre. Consider Practical Dilemma 17.2.

Practical Dilemma 17.2   **Validity of consent**

Paula Green was admitted to hospital for a biopsy of the breast. It was intended that, should there be any malignancy, a mastectomy would be carried out immediately. Paula was given the pre-medication by the ward staff and brought to theatre. When the theatre sister was checking through the records, she noticed that there was no consent form. The anaesthetist, who had begun to prepare Paula for the operation, said that he had seen Paula on the ward the previous day and knew there was no doubt that she wanted this to be carried out and that she might still be able to put her signature to a form. The theatre sister was very concerned about this. The surgical registrar then apologised and said that he had spoken to Paula about the operation and that she knew the implications of it. However, when he had visited the ward, he had run out of consent forms. He had intended returning to the ward to get Paula's signature but had been distracted and had completely forgotten about it. He saw no reason not to proceed with the operation and argued that Paula would be far more upset if the operation did not proceed and she returned to the ward without it than for the operation to go ahead without her signature. What should the theatre sister do?

Consent after pre-medication

In Chapter 7, it was pointed out that consent can be given in a variety of forms: in writing, by word of mouth, by implication. These are all equally valid in law. It could be argued, therefore, that the fact that Paula had given her consent to the registrar means that that can be relied on and therefore the operation can proceed. However, consent in writing is infinitely superior as a form of evidence. Imagine that Paula's operation proceeded. When the biopsy was analysed, a malignancy was discovered and the surgeon therefore proceeded with a mastectomy. On recovery, however, Paula denied that she had any idea that this was a likely possibility and had she known she would have preferred to have had radiotherapy. This possibility cannot be discounted and in such a situation it would be far better for Paula to return to the ward and, when the pre-medication has worn off, to agree in writing that the operation can proceed. One can imagine certain circumstances where there would be such considerable risks in postponing the operation that, on balance, the advantages to the patient are in favour of proceeding rather than returning the patient to the ward. In such cases, there could be an action for negligence if harm were caused by this delay. However, these would be unusual circumstances. In general, it would be wiser to ensure that the patient has signed a consent form and has had all the risks and implications explained to her. Sending the patient back to the ward, although undoubtedly leading to a furious complaint from a rightly indignant patient, has several long-term advantages: the ward staff will be less likely to give the patient a pre-medication before checking whether the consent forms have been signed and the doctors will know that they cannot get by with a casual approach to patients' rights.

A more difficult situation which occasionally occurs is where the patient himself, after pre-medication and prior to the general anaesthetic, asks the surgeon if something else could be 'sorted out', e.g. an ingrowing toenail, a cyst, etc. What is the surgeon to do? It would seem churlish for him to say, 'No. I must have your consent in writing for that and since you have been pre-medicated you are incapable of giving a valid consent.' Contrariwise, if he agrees to proceed and undertakes the additional task and there are some unforeseen or unmentioned side effects, then litigation may result. Compensation was paid to a patient when she changed her mind about an abortion, but this was ignored and the termination was carried out (see Chapter 15).[12]

Consent refused

> **Practical Dilemma 17.3**   **What the eyes don't see . . .**
>
> An adult Jehovah's Witness patient makes it clear that he will agree to a particular operation only on the understanding that he will not be given blood (see Figure 7.1). The surgeon agrees to operate on that basis, but does intend that, if blood is needed, the patient will be given it anyway and will be none the wiser. The operation proceeds. The patient begins to haemorrhage and the surgeon instructs that blood should be given. Somehow the patient discovers what has happened and sues the NHS trust for trespass to the person.

In this case, it is clear that there has been a trespass to the person since the patient was given blood contrary to his express instructions and any deliberate intention to mislead the patient by the surgeon was a breach of professional conduct. The patient should, therefore, be entitled to substantial damages. Only if there were any doubt about the mental capacity of the patient, and therefore the possibility that he was incapable of making a decision, could the judge consider that the actions were justified in the best interests of the patient under the Mental Capacity Act 2005. (See the case of *Re MB*, which is considered in Chapter 7 and Chapter 14.) To avoid the possibility of court action, a surgeon could advise that he is not prepared to operate with restrictions on his discretion and if the patient refused to give an unrestricted consent, then he would not be operated on. (Note the case of *Malette* v. *Shulman*, where blood was given to an unconscious card-carrying patient (see Case 7.6).)

Other restrictions that the patient may also wish to impose on the surgeons are often refused; thus it should be made clear that the operation will not be performed by a particular surgeon or that there will be a specified anaesthetist or that any particular procedure will be followed. It is now recommended that the forms contained in the Department of Health's guidance on consent to examination and treatment[13] should be used prior to any operation. (These are discussed in Chapter 7.)

Even though the patient has consented to a particular operation and is therefore prevented from bringing an action for trespass to the person, it might well be that, if harm occurs, the patient will complain that he has not been informed of this possibility and side effects and that, had he known, he would not have gone ahead with it. This possibility is discussed in connection with the Sidaway case (see Chapter 7).

One important point must be emphasised, however. The patient, in signing the consent form, is consenting to an action that without his consent would count as a trespass to his person. He is also consenting to undergo the risks of those unforeseen chances that, no matter how much care is taken, can still occur. He is not consenting to negligence or to the possibility that harm could occur to him because a nurse or doctor is careless or because the procedures are not followed correctly or inadequate precautions are taken to ensure that he will be safe.

Sometimes it might be pointed out to the patient that a particular operation is experimental and he might expressly agree to undergo the additional risk of this unknown procedure, but he still does not consent to the possibility of a failure to follow approved accepted practice.

Other difficulties in relation to consent to treatment are considered in the chapters relating to consent generally (Chapter 7), children's nursing (Chapter 13), gynaecology (abortion and sterilisations) (Chapter 15), psychiatric nursing (Chapter 20) and A&E departments (Chapter 21).

There have recently been successful claims by patients who have brought action on the grounds that, while under the anaesthetic, they were conscious of activities around them and suffered agonising pain, but were unable to move. It was reported that the Royal College of Anaesthetists[14] in a survey of doctors suggested that at least 7,750 patients are conscious during operations each year. Of these, about 250 feel their bodies being opened and internal organs manipulated by doctors. In 1985 £15,000 was awarded to Margaret Acters by Wigan. Clearly, nurses should be vigilant for any sign that the patient is not properly anaesthetised. The role of the operating department practitioner in relation to medicines is considered in Chapter 28.

Recovery room nursing

This is often under the control of the consultant anaesthetist. Recovery nurses would usually have post-registration training in recovery nursing. The training would include developing the skills, expertise and knowledge to detect possible adverse side effects resulting from the anaesthetic drugs. They must be trained to act speedily in an emergency and staffing ratios assume even greater importance than elsewhere in the hospital. It is essential that they are clear as to their competence in a wide area.

Another interesting facet of the law in this area is the fact that nurses may hear confidential information from the semi-conscious patient that would come under the principles discussed in Chapter 8. Similarly, it is essential that the nurses do not discuss the patient or any other patient in front of any of the semi-conscious patients in the recovery room since there are many accounts of patients who have overheard what staff have said and have been very upset by this. The nurse's duty of care obviously includes the duty of foreseeing what could harm a patient in this context and taking reasonable precautions to prevent that occurring.

Conclusions

This chapter has covered an area that is central to any major success in the reduction of waiting lists and the decrease of litigation. The work of theatre and related staff is subject to inspection by the Healthcare Commission (CHAI) and theatre staff must be aware of recommendations from the National Institute for Health and Clinical Excellence. Significant changes have resulted from developments in the scope of professional practice of the nurse and from the recognition of the operating practitioner as a health professional registered under the Health Professions Council.

Reflection questions

1 How do the provisions of the Health and Safety at Work Act (see Chapter 12) affect the theatre manager?

2 Procedures do not provide the solution to every eventuality. In what circumstances do you consider a nurse would be justified in deviating from a specified procedure (see Chapter 3)?

3 How do the basic principles of consent to treatment affect the work of the theatre nurse (see Chapter 7)?

4 How do the principles relating to the scope of professional practice affect the theatre nurse (see Chapter 24)?

Further exercises

1 Obtain a copy of the incident book that is kept in the theatre in which you work and consider how some of these incidents could have been avoided.

2 Access the NPSA website and study their hazard reports on incidents in operating theatres. To what extent is your department taking all appropriate steps to prevent such occurrences?

References

[1] *Wilsher* v. *Essex Area Health Authority* [1986] 3 All ER 801 CA

[2] Department of Health, A Step Guide to Improving Operating Theatre Performance, 2002 case studies published in 2005

[3] www.nice.org.uk

[4] Commission for Health Improvement, Report on Prince Philip Hospital Llanelli, 15 November 2000

[5] Surgical instruments left inside patients, News item, *The Operating Theatre Journal*, Issue 201, June/July 2007

[6] National Patient Safety Agency, Patient safety alert No. 06, March 2005

[7] Audit Commission, Anaesthesia under Examination: the efficiency and effectiveness of anaesthesia and pain relief services in England and Wales, Audit Commission, 17 December 1997

[8] National Association of Theatre Nurses, Principles of Safe Practice in the Perioperative Environment, NATN, Harrogate, 1998

[9] National Patient Safety Agency, Patient Safety Division, Teamwork for safety: why we need it, and how we do it (no date)

[10] Bristol Royal Infirmary Inquiry (Kennedy Report), Learning from Bristol: the report of the public inquiry into children's heart surgery at the Bristol Royal Infirmary 1984-1995, Command Paper Cm 5207, July 2001; http://www.bristol-inquiry.org.uk/

[11] www.nassp.org.uk/about_nassp.

[12] Clare Dyer, Cash Settlement for woman who changed her mind on abortion, *The Guardian*, 30 July 2007

[13] Department of Health, Good Practice in Consent Implementation Guide, DH, November 2001

[14] *Sunday Times*, 31 July 1994

Chapter 18
Nurse educator and researcher

This chapter discusses

+ Record keeping by teachers
+ Liability for instructing others
+ Hearing about unsound practices
+ Employment law
+ Legal aspects of research

Introduction

Law is relevant to the role of the nurse educator in several respects. Tutors have recently been involved in litigation in respect of what they have taught, how it was taught and when. NHS employees and nurse lecturers should be familiar with the differences and implications. The legal issues arising from research are also relevant to the lecturer. They need also to be concerned with all the general aspects of the law covered in the first part of this book: not only in relation to their own position, but also because they might have to teach some of it!

Guidance on the standards for the preparation of teachers of nursing, midwifery and health visiting was provided by the UKCC[1] and developed by the NMC[2] with revised arrangements for the introduction of standards for practice teachers. The Higher Education Academy developed a national professional standards framework for teaching and supporting learning in higher education in 2006 which complements the NMC standard to support learning and assessment in practice which applies from 2007. The HE Academy is being asked to accredit the NMC standard so that NMC treachers may be recognised by the HE Academy. From 2006 all teachers new to teaching in HE must have a teaching qualification.[3] In order to obtain registered status, students must not only pass the academic and practical requirements of the course,[4] but there must also be a declaration by the head of the college (or department) of nursing that there is no reason why the student is not eligible to be placed on the NMC Register. This places a clear duty on the lecturers to ensure that any information that indicates that the person would be unsuitable should be brought to the attention of the head of the college or department of nursing. This requirement is particularly important in the light of the recommendations of the Clothier Inquiry into Beverly Allitt. The report[5] recommended that those with a history of personality disorder should not be taken into nursing (see Chapter 5). The NMC conducted a consultation on how registrants should certify their character and health for the purposes of re-registration and published guidance on good health and good character in 2006 as an appendix to annexe 2 of circular NMC 06/16. The NMC defines good health and good character as:

> Such that they are capable of safe and effective practice as a nurse or a midwife.

Each person must be assessed on an individual basis and any disabilities they have are assessed in the light of their capacity to provide safe and effective practice. The NMC cites the Department of Health definition of character as:

> Character is a combination of personal qualities which are relevant to a person's fitness to practise. Conduct is that part of a person's behaviour which is relevant to her fitness to practise.

The NMC states that the assessment of good character includes consideration of any conduct, behaviour or attitudes that are not compatible with professional registration as well as convictions and cautions.

Record keeping by teachers

Practical Dilemma 18.1   **Instruction in lifting – the evidence**

Beryl Sharp, a nurse tutor, received a request from her hospital claims manager to provide her with the information she had given to a staff nurse on a lifting course. It appeared that this staff nurse had sustained a serious back injury at work and was suing the NHS trust for a breach in its direct liability to take care of her safety. The claim was likely to amount to a considerable sum, since the prognosis was poor and she was unlikely to be able to return to work in the foreseeable future. The NHS trust was defending the claim on the grounds that the ward was adequately staffed and that the staff nurse had been given instruction in lifting. It now required evidence of that fact from Beryl. Fortunately, Beryl was a hoarder – a fact frequently greeted with derision by her colleagues. She never threw anything out and was able to go through her records and find the series of seminars that had been organised on lifting. She had both the dates and the names of participants, including the names of those who had failed to attend. She had not given the seminar herself: a physiotherapist had done the teaching. Beryl had simply organised it as part of her work as an organiser for continuing education. She checked her records and could find no record that the particular staff nurse had attended. In fact, she was able to see that she was included in the list of those who were supposed to attend, but was not present at a seminar and that 'sick' had been written against her name. There was no evidence that she had been invited to attend a subsequent seminar, although another three were held in the following months.

One can imagine that this information would disappoint the hospital claims manager in providing information to defend the staff nurse's claim. However, it is not completely fatal to any defence of the claim, since it might well be that the staff nurse had received appropriate training in lifting during her basic training. In addition, there may be some element of contributory negligence in that the staff nurse herself failed to ensure that she was included on another seminar once she had returned from sick leave.

Such a request gives rise to many further questions for the nurse lecturer. How long must records be kept? What sort of detail is necessary? It will be recalled from the section in Chapter 6 dealing with the time limits for bringing a court action that in a case of negligence the action must be brought within three years of the negligent incident (unless the victim is under 18 years old, under a disability or, in cases where she was not aware of the fact of the negligence or the existence of harm, within the three years of such information becoming available). A period of retention of seven years is therefore likely to cover most eventualities apart from these exceptions. In addition, it could be argued that in those areas where regular retraining and revision study days are necessary, if several years have elapsed since the opportunity to go on to a course, then the authority is at fault in not providing a revision course. The information that should be retained is set out in Box 18.1.

Box 18.1   **Information that should be kept by the nurse tutor**

Names of those who should have attended the sessions.

Names of those who did attend.

Times and dates of the sessions.

Content of the sessions and who did the teaching.

Grades of achievement where there was any assessment.

Records are, of course, kept of the content, standard and timetable of learners, and it is not difficult to extend this to the post-basic courses.

Liability for instructing others

In Chapter 3, there is an explanation of the duty of care owed by those who are instructing others so that if harm were to occur as a result of negligent instructions, the tutor can be sued by the person who has suffered the harm. This applies not just to the classroom situation, but also to all those situations where advice is given in circumstances where the person receiving it can be expected to act on it. If the advice has been given negligently, then an action in negligence for breach of a duty of care may follow.

> ### Practical Dilemma 18.2   Negligent instructions
>
> Beryl Sharp acted as the course tutor on some of the post-basic courses. She ran one course, that of training nurses in the adding of drugs to IVs, and failed to mention that the first dose of the drug to be added to the IV should always be given by a doctor. One of the staff nurses who had been at that session and had been deemed competent to give IV drugs returned to the ward and was instructed that a patient who was already on an intravenous drip had been written up for an IV drug. At the appropriate time, the staff nurse prepared the drug, checked it with another nurse, and added it to the drip according to the instructions she had been taught on the course. The patient reacted violently against the drug and a doctor was summoned urgently. An inquiry was then held to find out why the first dose of this drug had been administered by a nurse and not by a doctor. It was the local policy for the doctor to administer the first dose of a drug intravenously. It then emerged that Beryl Sharp had failed to point out this requirement in her teaching on the course.

In this situation, the victim is a patient. In other cases, the victim could be the person who received the negligent information or advice. Where a patient is the victim, the claim is relatively simple: he would show that he has suffered harm as a result of a negligent act of an employee acting in the course of employment and therefore that the employer is vicariously liable for the harm. Alternatively, the individual employee could be sued as personally liable for the harm. In such a case, the employee may bring her own action against the tutor who was negligent in the instructions that she gave. In this type of action, the following facts would have to be shown:

1 A duty of care was owed by the instructor to the instructee.
2 There was a breach of this duty since the instructions were given negligently.
3 As a reasonable foreseeable consequence of this breach, the person has suffered harm (this might be personal injury, but it could also include financial loss or loss or damage to property).

It is essential that the person harmed can show that this harm was caused by the negligence of the tutor. If it were unreasonable for the person to rely on the instruction by the tutor, then compensation would not be payable on the basis of the tutor's negligence.

Hearing about unsound practices

If a lecturer in the college of nursing discovers from his/her learners about staff who are guilty of unacceptable practices or ill treatment of patients, what action should the nurse lecturer take? Should she investigate the allegation and, if challenged, say why? Should she keep her source secret? Should she report her suspicions to nurse management? Obviously, there can be no single answer since much depends on the circumstances. If, for example, the learner has witnessed ill treatment of a patient by a member of staff on a ward, then the learner should be encouraged to write a statement setting out exactly what she has seen and the nurse lecturer should ensure that appropriate action is taken by nurse management, at the same time protecting the learner from any victimisation. (Refer to whistleblowing and the Public Interest Disclosure Act 1998 considered in Chapter 4.) If the nurse witnesses a procedure being carried out on the wards that is not in line with present-day safe practices, the nurse lecturer could arrange appropriate revision courses with the in-service training officer colleagues.

Conflicts could also arise where the college has been teaching learners the basic principles of patients' rights, e.g. consent to treatment, and as a result the learner encounters difficulties with some medical staff. There could be criticism of the lecturers and of the college for its teachings. Such a situation indicates the importance of very close contact between the college and the NHS trust. The college of nursing should not, however, be seen as a policing machine for the hospital. By the same token, it has an essential part to play in maintaining the highest standards of nursing care in cooperation with the managers. Close integration of nurse clinical teaching and practice is essential. The Kennedy Report on children's heart surgery in Bristol[6] recommended that there should be a duty of candour owed by health professionals to the patient and this idea was taken up in the proposals for a new NHS redress scheme[7] to provide compensation for clinical negligence. However, the eventual NHS redress scheme did not include this duty, but such a duty can be read into the Code of Professional Conduct of the NMC.[8] Consultation is taking place on a new Code at the time of writing. The National Patient Safety Agency has provided guidance on being open in relation to hazards (see Chapter 12).

Employment law

Students

Learners were once both employees and students. Following the introduction of Project 2000, learners are students, usually attached to a college of education. They are entitled to receive student bursaries and the college negotiates an agreement with accredited hospitals for the clinical placements. In theory, students are supernumerary to the workforce, but inevitably, especially in the last years of training, the hospitals and community services may exploit their services. There is no right in the learning contract for the student to insist on employment once she is qualified.

Dismissal on grounds of absenteeism or course failure

Since the student is not an employee, if she should be dismissed during the course on the grounds of absenteeism or failing course assessments or examinations, then the student's remedy is an appeal through the appeal mechanisms of the college. These should have clear guidelines on the rules that operate in these circumstances and these procedures should be carefully followed. There is a contractual relationship between the student and the college that is enforceable in law.

Clinical placements

There is normally a memorandum of agreement between colleges providing clinical training and the hospitals and community trusts providing clinical placements. This agreement should cover the issue of liability for the actions of the students if they cause harm to others through negligence. Since the students are not employees of the unit providing clinical placements, the latter can argue that they are not vicariously liable for the actions of students.

In addition, the agreement should cover liability for harm to the student. Prior agreement between the college and the organisation providing the clinical placement can resolve such issues and also cover the topic of supervision of the student and clinical instruction.

Contractual rights of lecturers

Lecturers, tutors and clinical instructors are, of course, under a contract of employment whether their employer is a university/higher education institution or an NHS organisation and they are obliged to observe the express and implied terms of the contract of employment (see Chapter 10). In addition they are entitled to expect that their employer will recognise its contractual obligations under the contract of employment. A memorandum of understanding for joint staff of universities and NHS organisations was agreed in March 2007 and can be downloaded from the Department of Health website. It was prepared in response to the VAT tribunal ruling in April 2005 in a case involving the University of Glasgow and HM Revenue and Customs. The memorandum sets out the NHS and university understanding of the role of joint staff, clarifies selected duties and responsibilities of their employers, documents established practice in respect of these staff and confirms that such arrangements are outside the scope of VAT.

Legal aspects of research

Research-based practice is an essential requirement of professional care. The National Institute for Health and Clinical Excellence (see Chapter 5) is seeking to identify and publish recommended clinically effective practice that has a strong research basis. The Department of Health has initiated a new programme for research in the NHS called Best Research for Best Health.[9] The strategy and its implementation plans prepared by the new National Institute of Health Research (NIHR) can be downloaded from the DH website. The Code of Professional Conduct of the NMC[10] has an explicit requirement that practitioners should follow research-based practice. Paragraph 6.5 of the Code states:

> *You have a responsibility to deliver care based on current evidence, best practice and, where applicable, validated research when it is available.*

The nurse is therefore increasingly likely to be involved in research: either conducting it herself or being involved in the care of patients who are the subjects of a research project. Often a research project is an integral part of a management course or post-registration qualification and she will be expected to prepare a dissertation or project that shows some original material and analysis. In addition, there may well be researchers coming into her department or ward: she should in either case be aware of the many legal issues that arise. Some of the basic problems relate to consent by the patient, confidentiality and disclosure of the findings, safety of the researcher and liability for any volunteer in a drugs research programme. The conduct of research and the rights of the research subject are set out in the Declaration of Helsinki, which was reproduced as an appendix in the Department of Health's guidance for local research ethics committees, originally issued in 1991.[11] New guidance on research ethics committees was issued in July 2001[12] (see below). A Central Office for Research Ethics Committees (COREC - now NRES, see below) was set up to work on behalf of the Department of Health, which coordinates the development of the research ethics committees, manages multi-centre research ethics committees (MRECs) and provides advice on policy, operational matters and training. A European Directive[13] on clinical trials has been incorporated into legislation.[14] A summary of the Directive is shown in Box 18.2. A United Kingdom Ethics Committee Authority (UKECA) will be set up with responsibilities for establishing, recognising and monitoring research ethics committees (see below).

Box 18.2   **EC Directive 2001/20/EC**

On the implementation of good clinical practice in the conduct of clinical trials on medicinal products for human use

Article 1 Aim of the Directive:

+ To establish specific provisions regarding the conduct of clinical trials, including multi-centre trials on human subjects involving medicinal product as defined by Article 1 of Directive 65/66/EEC

+ Good clinical practice to be identified and complied with

+ To adopt and if necessary revise principles of good clinical practice and detailed guidance to be published by the Commission

+ All clinical trials to be designed, conducted and reported in accordance with the principles of good clinic practice.
Article 2 Definitions
Article 3 Protection of clinical trial subjects
Article 4 Clinical trials on minors
Article 5 Clinical trials on incapacitated adults not able to give informed legal consent
Article 6 Ethics Committee
Article 7 Single Opinion
Article 8 Detailed guidance to be published by Commission
Article 9 Commencement of a clinical trial
Article 10 Conduct of a clinical trial
Article 11 Exchange of information
Article 12 Suspension of the trial or infringements
Article 13 Manufacture and import of investigational medicinal products
Article 14 Labelling
Article 15 Verification of compliance of investigational medicinal products with good clinical and manufacturing practice
Article 16 Notification of adverse events
Article 17 Notification of serious adverse reactions
Article 18 Guidance concerning reports
Article 19 General provisions
Article 20 Adaptation to scientific and technical progress
Article 21 Committee procedure
Article 22 Application
Article 23 Entry into force 4 April 2001

In addition, a researcher would be required to observe the rights set out in the European Convention on Human Rights, which, since 2 October 2000, are actionable in this country (see Chapter 1 and Appendix A). Where the nurse becomes aware that the rights of the patient are not being protected by the researchers, she would have a professional duty to raise this with senior management and, if no action were taken, to make use of the whistle-blowing provisions of the Public Interest Disclosure Act 1998 (see Chapter 4). Reference can be made to the author's chapter exploring the legal implications of research.[15]

Control of a research programme

> ### Practical Dilemma 18.3   Gagged
>
> Ann Jones, a ward sister, was on a management course that required her to complete a dissertation. She chose as her subject the consequences of the privatisation of cleaning services and studied one hospital where the services were contracted out to a private firm and another hospital where direct labour ancillary staff were used. Her conclusions were that privatisation led to a lower standard of cleaning, a less hygienic environment for patients and nursing staff undertaking more cleaning work because the private firm sent cleaners to the wards for only a short proportion of the day. Just before she was due to submit the dissertation for her diploma, her nursing director heard of it and asked to see it. She has now been told that her findings are politically unacceptable, that she cannot present it to the college and that she must commence a totally different topic of research.

This situation gives rise to many legal issues. In this situation, the researcher is also an employee. She therefore has responsibilities to her employer. Even if she were an independent researcher funded from outside the institution that is the subject of the research, she might well have had to agree to a clause that the research findings have to have the prior approval of the institution before the research results can be published. As an employee, she would be expected to obey the reasonable orders of the employer. Is it reasonable in these circumstances for the researcher to be silenced? The answer would depend on more detailed facts: for example, was it only because the results were unwelcome that they are being suppressed? Was the basis of her data collection and statistical analysis sound? If there is no criticism to be made of her method and findings other than that they are embarrassing, it could be argued that the same principles apply here as apply in the situation discussed in Chapter 7 relating to reporting on negligence by a colleague or some other form of unacceptable practice. Where management itself fails to take action, i.e. when all the internal procedures for improving the situation have been used to no avail, then it would not be considered unreasonable to take the matter to a higher authority, initially within the organisation and, if necessary, ultimately outside, but this obviously depends on the findings and the reasons for prohibiting publication.

The Public Interest Disclosure Act 1998 can be used to ensure that any person properly reporting health and safety concerns or criminal matters is protected from victimisation (see Chapter 4). In November 2003 a university criminologist, who was conducting research into assisted suicides by people with AIDS, was awarded £62,000 by a committee of academic enquiry into the actions of Exeter University because Exeter University withdrew a written promise to give him legal backing should a court order him to disclose the names of those to whom he had spoken.[16] He had been forced to abandon his research, because he promised those involved in helping him that he would protect their identities.

Research ethics committees (RECs)

The researcher must ensure that she receives the proper approval before beginning any research. In some cases, this might mean obtaining the approval of a local ethics committee. Where this authority is received, it would be more difficult to prohibit publication of the results purely on the grounds of embarrassment at the findings. The Department of Health issued advice on the establishment and operation of local research ethics committees and any research involving NHS patients, access to their records or use of NHS premises or facilities must be referred to the LREC.[17] New guidance was issued by the Department of Health in 2001[18] and the new arrangements came into force in April 2002. The governance statement defines the purpose of an REC in reviewing the proposed study:

> Is to protect the dignity, rights, safety and well-being of all actual or potential research participants. It shares this role and responsibility with others, as described in the 'Research Governance Framework for Health and Social Care'.[19]

Research may not be started until ethical approval has been obtained. It is the personal responsibility of the person named as principal investigator to apply for approval by the REC and this person retains responsibility for the scientific and ethical conduct of the research.

Section A of the guidance provided by the Department of Health sets out a statement of general standards and principles and covers the following topics:

+ role of research ethics committees
+ remit of an NHS REC
+ establishment and support of NHS RECs
+ membership requirements and process
+ composition of an REC
+ working procedures
+ multi-centre research
+ process of ethical review of a research protocol
+ submitting an application
+ glossary.

Section B provides more detailed guidance on operating procedures and the requirements for general support for RECs. Section C provides a resource for RECs and collates current advice on ethical issues and is to be regularly updated.

The Department of Health set up a Central Office for Research Ethics Committees (COREC) in 2000 which issued guidance for NHS research ethics committees in 2001. COREC was placed under the National Patient Safety Agency in 2005 and relaunched as the National Research Ethics Service (NRES) in March 2007. In NPSA's annual report for 2006/7 it stated that the NRES had developed updated standard operating procedures to meet the implementation of the Human Tissue Act 2004, new guidance on the ethical review of medical devices, and a memorandum of understanding with the MHRA (Medicines and Healthcare products Regulatory Agency) and the Gene Therapy Advisory Committee (GTAC).

An ad hoc advisory group was set up to review the operation of NHS research ethics committees. Its report[20] was published in June 2005. Its conclusions ranged widely over the need to change the system of RECs, the need to address perceived weaknesses in the REC system, and provide better support for chairs, members and administrative staff. The aim of its recommendations was to raise the status and profile of RECs, and lay the firm foundation for an REC system that can be more responsive to changing requirements in the future in a UK-wide context. It recommended that significant changes to the NHS research ethics committee system should be made. At the time of writing these recommendations are still to be implemented.

Confidentiality

Where use is made of personal information, access to it and disclosure of it in such a form that the individuals can be identified is subject to the provisions of the Data Protection Act 1998 (see Chapter 8). This means that if the data are not exempt from any of the provisions of the Act and if they are to be used in addition for research, then they must also be registered for research use. Even where the data are not automated, they would still come under the provisions of the Data Protection Act 1998, which applies to both computerised and manually held data. This means that they may be disclosed only in those exceptional circumstances outlined in Chapter 8.

Difficulties can arise for the researcher where information is obtained that has nothing to do with the research, i.e. it is simply doing the research that has given the opportunity to gain this information. The General Medical Council states that information can be given by practitioners about their patients for the purpose of research, but the patient's consent should be sought or the information provided in an anonymous form.[21] The Patient Information Advisory Group (PIAG), set up under Section 61 of the Health and Social Care Act 2001, considers proposals for the use of patient-identifiable information (see further in Chapter 8). The PIAG works in partnership with the United Kingdom Clinical Research Collaboration's (UKCRC) Regulatory and Governance Advice Service to provide practical help with the legislative and good practice requirements that govern clinical research in the UK. Further information can be obtained from its website.[22]

Practical Dilemma 18.4　　**Silence or disclosure?**

Sandra James, a staff nurse, was conducting a research project into the care of the post-operative surgical patient. She was interested in the rate of infection, length of stay, convalescent care and the nature of community care. Her research therefore required visits to the patients' homes. One of her patients, Glenda Mitchell, had been operated on for gallstones. She was in hospital for seven days and was then discharged to her home. Her cohabitee had taken a few days off work to care for their 3-year-old daughter. While Sandra was visiting the home, she was surprised to see that the child was very frightened of her and was withdrawn and hostile. Sandra tried to talk to her and touch her and noticed severe bruising and pinch marks on the child's legs.

In a suspected case of non-accidental injury, there is a clear justification for disclosing confidential information in the interests of the child. In a case like this, Sandra might try to persuade the mother to explain the child's bruising and, if this were unsatisfactory, she should ensure that appropriate action is taken to protect the child, e.g. arranging for the health visitor to visit, initiating the non-accidental injury (NAI) procedure or even bringing in the NSPCC.

Whatever action she takes along these lines would be protected from any action for breach of confidentiality on the grounds that the public interest justified it. In one case,[23] the House of Lords stated that the NSPCC was entitled to maintain the secrecy of the names of its informants, even if they had been malicious. This decision is based on public policy because it is essential that people are prepared to report potential incidents of child abuse. If, however, the facts of this situation are changed slightly and instead of a potential NAI case a potential crime against property is suspected, e.g. stolen goods are seen in the house, many professionals would feel that their professional duty of confidentiality must be maintained.

Consent

Unfortunately, not all research subjects are notified that they are to be included in a research project and their consent is not always obtained to the participation. Even in randomised controlled trials of drugs, patients should be informed that they have the right to refuse to take part. If the treatment is therapeutic rather than pure research, then in exceptional circumstances it could be argued that the doctor's right of therapeutic privilege (discussed by the House of Lords in the Sidaway case (see Chapter 7)) applied and there are special circumstances to justify not informing the patient of that fact. The right of therapeutic privilege could be relied on only in exceptional circumstances and the presumption is that the patient's consent should be obtained.

The basic legal principles are as follows: consent to participate in research should be given freely by an adult, mentally competent person and should be preceded by sufficient relevant information about serious harmful side effects as approved practice would require the professional to give the patient. Where research is contemplated on minors, it should proceed only if it is in the subject's interests and the benefits substantially outweigh any potential harm and the research is approved by the REC. The question as to whether parents have the right to consent to non-therapeutic research on their children is discussed in Chapter 13.

Consent and the mentally incapacitated adult

Research on those lacking the requisite mental capacity to give consent is now covered by the Mental Capacity Act 2005 (apart from clinical trials, see page 444). The Act enables research to be carried out, but only if stringent conditions are met. These are set out in Sections 30-34 of the Act and shown in Box 18.3.

Box 18.3

Conditions for research on those lacking mental capacity set by the Mental Capacity Act

+ The research is connected with an impairing condition affecting P (the person lacking mental capacity) or its treatment

+ An impairing condition is defined in Section 31(3) as a condition which is (or may be) attributable to, or which causes or contributes to, the impairment of, or disturbance in the functioning of, the mind or brain

+ There must be reasonable grounds for believing that the research would not be as effective if carried out only on, or only in relation to, persons who have the capacity to consent to taking part in the project

+ 5a The research must have the potential to benefit P without imposing on P a burden that is disproportionate to the potential benefit to P or

+ 5b be intended to provide knowledge of the causes or treatment of, or of the care of persons affected by, the same or a similar condition

+ If 5(b) applies and not 5(a), there must be reasonable grounds for believing: (a) that the risk to P from taking part in the project is likely to be negligible, and (b) that anything done to, or in relation to, P will not: (i) interfere with P's freedom of action or privacy in a significant way, or (ii) be unduly invasive or restrictive

+ There must be reasonable arrangements in place for ensuring that the requirements of consulting carers and additional safeguards are met

Regulations[24] cover the situation where an adult who had given consent to participation in research lost the requisite mental capacity during the research project. The Department for Constitutional Affairs (now absorbed in the Ministry of Justice) has provided a Code of Practice on the implementation of the Mental Capacity Act 2005[25] which is available on the Ministry of Justice website.[26] The provisions of the Mental Capacity Act 2005 do not apply to research which comes under the Clinical Trial Regulations.

Consent to research and statutory provisions

The Department of Health has prepared guidance on consent by a legal representative on behalf of a person not able to consent under the Medicines for Human Use (Clinical Trials) Regulations 2003. Where there are any risks to the adult, an application to court would probably have to be made. Where there are no risks, the local research ethics committee should be made aware of the lack of mental capacity of the research subjects. Failure to obtain consent to research or to give the necessary information could render the researcher liable to action. The Human Fertilisation and Embryology Act 1990 prevents research taking place on an embryo after the first 14 days from fertilisation, neither can a human embryo be placed in a non-human animal or the nucleus of a cell of an embryo be replaced. Significant changes to the 1990 Act are, at the time of writing, being debated in Parliament (see pages 532–3). The law was changed as the result of the scandal at Bristol Royal Infirmary when, during an inquiry into allegations of professional misconduct in carrying out paediatric heart surgery, it was learnt that more than 11,000 children who had died in the past 40 years had had their organs used for research in British hospitals without the explicit consent of their parents. (The law relating to the removal, retention and storage of organs and tissue is discussed in Chapter 16.)

Liability for volunteers in research

Practical Dilemma 18.5   Guinea-pig

Benjamin Robinson was a medical student who was very short of money because he sent part of his grant home to his family each week. He heard of a research project being undertaken in the pharmaceutical department and offered his services. Because he was anxious to be accepted, he failed to tell the medical officer in charge of the research that he had suffered from glandular fever as a child. He subsequently took drugs to test out the toxicity of a drug for migraine. A few weeks later, he had a heart attack and died. Is there any liability for his death by the NHS trust and/or the research team?

At present there is no law that the volunteer should automatically obtain compensation for harm that occurs as a result of the research participation. The Pearson Report of 1978[27] recommended that volunteers in medical research should be compensated on a no-fault basis, but this has not been implemented through legislation. At present, the Association of the British Pharmaceutical Industry (ABPI) has prepared guidelines for the provision of compensation to victims of research and supports through a written agreement with each research subject that any subjects who have been harmed as a result of participation in a drugs trial will be compensated on a strict liability basis without proof of negligence. This is a voluntary agreement, but would normally be a part of the protocol of the research project approved by the local research ethics committee. Apart from this scheme, as the law stands at present, the volunteer who is harmed as a result of participation in a research project can obtain compensation only on the basis of negligence, i.e. he must establish that a duty of care was owed to him, this has been broken, and as a reasonably foreseeable result of this breach the subject has suffered some harm.

Applying these principles here, it is hoped that the pharmaceutical company undertaking the research would compensate Benjamin's family on a strict liability basis. If the pharmaceutical company failed to pay up, then the family would have to show that in one way or another the researchers were negligent. For example, the researchers failed to give Benjamin a proper medical examination or the design of the research was faulty and reasonably foreseeably dangerous to the volunteers. There is little evidence of that here and, in addition, Benjamin, by concealing his previous illness, would have been contributorily negligent and therefore considered to a certain extent to be responsible for what happened.

It is possible that if it can be established that Benjamin was harmed as the result of a defect in a product, then the Consumer Protection Act 1987 applies and Benjamin's family can obtain compensation under these provisions against the producer or supplier. This is considered at greater length in Chapter 12. Much of the debate on liability would hinge on whether at the time of production the producer should have realised that there was a defect in the product.

Another possible defence against such a claim is the possibility of alleging that Benjamin, by volunteering willingly, assumed the risks of such an event occurring. This is known as the defence of *volenti non fit injuria* and is explained in more detail in Chapter 6. In order to rely on this as a defence, it would have to be shown not only that Benjamin knew of the risks, but also that he consented willingly to run them and agreed to waive all claim for compensation as a result.

Fraud in research

There is a danger that the pressure to undertake research and provide significant results could lead to fraudulent research practices. For example, it was discovered that a cancer specialist had fabricated the results of his research into the efficacy of a chemotherapy drug.[28] Failure by a practitioner registered with the NMC to follow sound and honest research principles could be seen as evidence of unfitness to practise and lead to her being struck off the Register.

Health and safety of the researcher

Exactly the same principles of health and safety apply to the researcher as apply to other employees, i.e. the employer owes a duty of care at common law to ensure that they are provided with a safe environment, a safe system of work and competent staff. Where the researchers are not employees, the occupier of the premises on which they are working would still be expected to uphold the duty of care for their safety under the Occupiers' Liability Act 1957. It could be, however, that as specialists they would be expected to be aware of those risks that arise from their particular tasks and the NHS trust would not be liable for harm resulting from that. The provisions of the Health and Safety at Work Act 1974 would also apply (see Chapter 12).

Conclusions

Recent cases and the Human Rights Act 1998 suggest that the nurse tutor and the nurse involved in research are more likely to be facing legal scrutiny about their practice. There is increasing pressure by the public for open and robust guidelines to protect the rights of the patient in the conduct of research. In addition, the NHS Plan and its recommendations for a substantial increase in the numbers of NMC-registered practitioners will increase the pressure on nurse lecturers to provide pre-registration training for nurses. PREP requirements dictate that to remain on the Register the nurse must have at least five days' training and development every three years and post-registration tutors have come under increasing pressure. The Department of Health has given priority to the proper organisation and management of research within the NHS and its proposed action in the light of the recommendations of the ad hoc advisory group on the operation of NHS research ethics committees is awaited. It remains to be seen how effectively the new provisions under the Mental Capacity Act protect those who are incapable of giving consent to participation in research. The registered nurse is likely to have a major role in the implementation of the new legislative provisions.

Reflection questions

1 How could a nurse tutor defend herself if a nurse who is accused of causing harm to the patient blamed the teaching that she had received in the nurse training college?

2 What records do you currently keep on your teaching programmes? Review the period for which you keep them and their content in the light of this chapter.

3 What records do you keep in respect of external lecturers who are invited to teach in your department? How would you defend a case where an employee was suing for back injury and the manual handling training was carried out in your department?

4 In what ways does cooperation exist between the nurse training school and the wards and departments to ensure that the nurses' training meets the standards of approved accepted practice?

5 Researchers state that they are carrying out research on those who are unable to give consent. What protection does the Mental Capacity Act 2005 apply to such participants?

Further exercises

1 Prepare a procedure for initiating a research proposal, for obtaining the necessary approvals, for envisaging any possible difficulties in carrying it out and for publishing the results.

References

[1] UKCC, Standards for the Preparation of Teachers of Nursing, Midwifery and Health Visiting, UKCC, March 2000

[2] Nursing and Midwifery Council, Revised arrangements for the introduction of standards for practice teachers, Circular 08/2007

[3] Nursing and Midwifery Council, Higher Education Academy Membership A–Z, advice sheet, NMC, March 2006

[4] Nursing and Midwifery Council, Standards of proficiency for pre-registration nursing education (02.04), for midwifery education (03.04) and specialist community public health nursing education (04.04), NMC 2004

[5] Clothier Report, The Allitt Inquiry: an independent inquiry relating to deaths and injuries on the children's ward at Grantham and Kesteven General Hospital during the period February to April 1991, HMSO, London, 1994

[6] Bristol Royal Infirmary Inquiry (Kennedy Report), Learning from Bristol: the report of the public inquiry into children's heart surgery at the Bristol Royal Infirmary 1984–1995, Command Paper Cm 5207, July 2001; http://www.bristol-inquiry.org.uk/

[7] Department of Health, Making Amends: a consultation paper setting out proposals for reforming the approach to clinical negligence in the NHS, CMO, June 2003

[8] Nursing and Midwifery Council, Code of Professional Conduct: standards for performance, conduct and ethics, NMC 2004

[9] Department of Health, Best Research for Best Health, DH, 2006

[10] Nursing and Midwifery Council, Code of Professional Conduct: standards for performance, conduct and ethics, NMC 2004

[11] Department of Health, Guidance for Local Research Ethics Committees, DH, 1991 (HSG(91)5)

[12] www.dh.gov.uk/research/rd1/researchgovernance/corec.htm

[13] EC Directive 2001/20/EC

[14] Medicines for Human Use (Clinical Trials), SI 2004 No. 1031 (Amended SI 2006 No. 1928 and SI 2006 No. 2984)

[15] B. Dimond, Legal issues, Chapter 9 in Louise de Raeve (ed.) *Nursing Research: An Ethical and Legal Appraisal*, London and Philadelphia, Baillière Tindall, 1996

[16] Simon de Bruxelles, Academic awarded £62,000 for broken promise, *The Times*, 21 November 2003

[17] Department of Health, Guidance for Local Research Ethics Committees, DH, 1991 (HSG(91)5); Department of Health, Standards for Local Research Ethics Committees: a framework for ethical review, DH, 1994 (replaced by Department of Health, Governance Arrangements for NHS Research Ethics Committees, DH, 2001); www.dh.gov.uk/research/rd1/researchgovernance/corec.htm

[18] Department of Health, Governance Arrangements for NHS Research Ethics Committees, DH, 2001 (replaces HSG(91)5 (The Red Book) and HSG(97)23 on multi-centre research ethics committees); www.dh.gov.uk/research/rd1/researchgovernance/corec.htm

[19] Department of Health, Research Governance Framework for England, DH, 1st edition 2001; draft 2nd edition 2003; www.dh.gov.uk/research/rd3/nhsandd/researchgovernance.htm

[20] Department of Health, Report of the Ad Hoc Advisory Group on the Operation of NHS Research Ethics Committees, June 2005

[21] General Medical Council, Confidentiality, GMC, London, 1995

[22] www.ukcrc-rgadvice.org/

[23] *In re D v. NSPCC* [1977] 1 All ER 589

[24] The Mental Capacity Act 2005 (Loss of Capacity during Research Project) (England) Regulations 2007, SI 2007 No. 679

[25] Code of Practice, Mental Capacity Act 2005, Department of Constitutional Affairs, February 2007

[26] www.justice.gov.uk

[27] Pearson Report, Royal Commission on Civil Liberty and Compensation for Personal Injury, Cmnd 7054, HMSO, London, 1978

[28] Lois Rogers, Cancer 'cure' doctor admits bogus research, *Sunday Times*, 13 February 2000

Chapter 19
Legal aspects of the care of older people

This chapter discusses

+ Rights to care
+ National Service Framework for Older People
+ Intermediate care
+ Force, restraint and assault
+ Medication and the confused older patient
+ Multidisciplinary care of older people
+ Standard of care
+ Abuse of older people
+ Long-term funding of care for older people
+ Filling the vacuum on decision making for the mentally incapacitated adult

Introduction

It is a truism that every elderly person is different. The fact that a person is over 60 or 70 or 80 or 90 says absolutely nothing else about them. Standards of health, loneliness, housing, finance, mobility and capability are as varied as with any other age group. All that can be said of them as a group is that it is more likely than not that they will be faced with some problems – social, economic, health or others – and that these are more likely to be multiple problems, interrelated, with one triggering off another. For example, it might be that an old person living on his own has limited mobility and therefore finds it difficult to get to the shops. He thus does not feed himself properly and comes under the hospital's care as a result of lack of proper nourishment. It is equally true that in itself there are no basic principles of law purely for older patients, apart from the age discrimination laws which relate mainly to employment and are discussed in Chapter 10. They can also claim against any discrimination in respect of their human rights as set out in the European Convention on Human Rights as a result of Article 14 (see Appendix A to this book). All that has been said of the general principles of negligence and vicarious liability applies equally to the nurse who cares for older people. Discrimination issues may also arise in the care of older people from black and minority ethnic communities or from ageism, and these must also be addressed.[1] Age Concern noted in February 2007 that ageism is the most common form of discrimination in the UK. Its survey revealed that more than three times more people have been the victims of ageism than any other form of discrimination.[2] Older people are the highest users of acute services in the NHS.[3] There are particular difficulties that the nurse who cares for older people is more likely to encounter than other nurses and it is to these that we now turn.

(There are, in addition, problems relating to the property and possessions of older people and these will be dealt with in Chapter 25. In Chapter 29, there is a discussion on the law relating to the making of wills and other aspects of dealing with death. Those nurses who care for older people in the community should refer to Chapter 23 for coverage of that topic. Those caring for older people who are mentally infirm should refer to Chapter 20.)

Rights to care

There are no laws that set a cut-off point at which interventions for older people are not justified. On the contrary, the human rights legislation would prohibit discrimination on the grounds of age. In the past, for example, there have been occasions where ambulances have been told to take patients over 65 to a geriatric ward rather than to a coronary care unit; where a non-resuscitation policy has been based on the age of the patient rather than their physical condition and prognosis; where they have been refused surgical treatment because of their age. Such discrimination has no legal basis. There are in law no age limits for accessing treatment. The only criteria are the prognosis of the patient and the extent to which further investment in their health is justified in terms of the benefit that it would bring to that individual. Age discrimination legislation has been brought into force that makes it illegal for an older person to be discriminated against on the basis of age (see above). A tool has been designed to identify whether or not age discrimination is occurring in hospital, primary care and social care.[4] Discrimination of the grounds of age would be a breach of Article 14 of the European Convention on Human Rights (see Appendix A) when linked with violation of another Article. However, in one case the High Court held that it was not a breach of Article 8(1) of the ECHR, or if it was it was justified under Article 8(2), when a local authority closed a day centre, because it was working well below full capacity and the cost savings would release resources for domiciliary care. The local authority had not acted irrationally.[5]

National Service Framework for Older People

The SSI report on improving older people's services[6] in 2001 showed that local authorities were expanding their services to promote independence through prevention and rehabilitation. This was in accordance with the philosophy of the National Service Framework (NSF) for

Older People[7] published by the Department of Health in 2001. Guidance was issued in March 2001.[8] (See Chapter 5 for further details on NSFs.)

The NSF for Older People is:

A strategy to ensure fair, high quality, integrated health and social care services for older people. It is a 10-year programme of action linking services to support independence and promote good health, specialised services for key conditions, and culture change so that all older people and their carers are always treated with respect, dignity and fairness.

The eight standards cover the following areas:

Standard 1   Rooting out age discrimination

Standard 2   Person-centred care

Standard 3   Intermediate care

Standard 4   General hospital care

Standard 5   Stroke

Standard 6   Falls

Standard 7   Mental health in older people

Standard 8   Promotion of health and active life in older age.

Each standard sets out its aim, defines the standard and identifies its rationale and the key interventions. In addition, a timetable of milestones is set by which specific targets must be achieved. A booklet on medicines and older people is also published to ensure that older people gain maximum benefit from medication and do not suffer unnecessarily from illness caused by excessive, inappropriate or inadequate consumption of medicines. The NSF also identifies how the standards are to be implemented at local level and the national support that will underpin the standards. NICE (see Chapter 5) has an important role to play in ensuring that the standards are based on clinically effective research based practice. The NSF for Older People is underpinned by a programme of research commissioned by the Policy Research Programme and Service and Delivery Organisation Programme.[9] The Healthcare Commission (i.e. CHAI) and the Commission for Social Care Inspection (CSCI) ensure through inspections that the standards are implemented across health and social services. In addition, progress overall is overseen by the NHS Modernisation Board and the Older People's Taskforce. A progress report on the NSF was issued by the National Director for Older People's Health in November 2004, entitled Better Health in Old Age.[10] A resource document is also published. Additional guidance has been issued on specific standards.

Thus a booklet on Standard 4 General Hospital Care was published in April 2006 to collate the information on projects supporting its implementation and to identify their achievement to date.[11] The priorities for the second phase of the 10-year programme for the NSF for Older People were set out by the Department of Health in April 2006 and can be downloaded from the DH website.[12]

Other initiatives to improve the services for older people include Dignity in Care Campaign, launched in November 2006, which aims to ensure that older people are treated with dignity when using health and social care services. It wishes to create a zero tolerance of lack of dignity in the care of older people in any care setting. In 2007 the Healthcare Commission carried out a review of acute services to ensure that older people are treated with dignity and respect. Further information can be obtained on the Healthcare Commission and on the DH websites. The Care Services Improvement Partnership (CSIP) set up an initiative for older people and physical disabilities and its change agent team (now merged with the integrated community equipment services team) works with social care, health and housing to promote independence, extend choice and improve people's quality of life. Further information can be obtained from the CSIP website.[13] The Older People's Care Group Workforce Team (CGWT) links with the care group workforce teams for access, cancer, coronary heart disease, long-term conditions and mental health to ensure older people's issues are considered in all these areas of workforce development. Information on all these CGWT sites can be obtained from the Department of Health website.

In November 2000 the government announced the appointment of a national director of older people's services with a remit to stamp out any signs of ageism in the NHS as part of the overall plan to modernise services for older people. The appointee, Professor Ian Philip, stated that his three priorities were:

1 to make sure that everyone, regardless of age, has fair access to services and receives treatment on the basis of need

2 to treat each older person as individual with their own specific and often complex needs

3 to ensure that there is an integrated approach where agencies work together rather than separately, to provide the highest levels of care.

Nurses caring for older people will without doubt share these principles and will benefit from the existence of a national director with these responsibilities.

Intermediate care

Intermediate care has been described[14] as a core element of the government's programme for improving services for older people. In conjunction with improvements to community equipment services, home care support and related services, it will enable increased numbers of older people to maintain independent lives at home.

To come within the definition of intermediate care, services must meet *all* of the following criteria:

+ are targeted at people who would otherwise face unnecessarily prolonged hospital stays or inappropriate admission to acute inpatient care, long-term residential care or continuing NHS inpatient care

+ are provided on the basis of a comprehensive assessment, resulting in a structured individual care plan that involves active therapy, treatment or opportunity for recovery

+ have a planned outcome of maximising independence and typically enabling patients/users to resume living at home

+ are time limited, normally no longer than 6 weeks and frequently as little as 1-2 weeks or less

+ involve cross-professional working, with a single assessment framework, single professional records and shared protocols.

Intermediate care is covered in Standard 3 of the NSF for Older People (see above).

Various models are envisaged including rapid response, hospital at home, residential rehabilitation, supported discharge and day rehabilitation. Guidance on the responsibilities for intermediate care and charging, planning its development, the role of the independent sector, the funding of intermediate care and community equipment services and the evaluation of the service has been provided by the Department of Health.[15] Sanctions against local authorities that fail to provide discharge arrangements for an older person in hospital, thereby blocking a bed, are provided under the Community Discharge (Delayed Discharges) Act 2003, which is discussed in Chapter 23.

Consent to treatment

Practical Dilemma 19.1   **An operation at 90?**

Amy Ash was admitted to a long-stay geriatric hospital because she had reached the stage where she could not care for herself. Her daughter was unable to look after her as she was coping with her son who had learning disabilities. Amy was intermittently competent. There were days when she recognised Gwen, her daughter, and others where she did not, but instead abused Gwen when she came to visit her. She had been complaining increasingly of a pain in her chest. The ward sister arranged for the physician to see her and he diagnosed a hiatus hernia. There was considerable debate over the best method of treatment. Initially, a strict diet and medication were proposed, but there were signs that this was not working when Amy started bleeding internally. The physician asked Gwen to come in and see him to talk about Amy's future care. He said that possibly the only long-term course of treatment was an operation. However, at Amy's age there were considerable risks in undertaking this. Although she was in a reasonably good state of health, she might not withstand the operation. Gwen was in a dilemma, not knowing whether to sign the form of consent on Amy's behalf. She attempted to explain the position to Amy. Amy grasped the fact that she would have to have an operation. She made it clear to Gwen that she had had a good life and did not want to be cut open now. Gwen also spoke to the ward sister who explained that Amy was in very good health and would probably survive the operation, but, of course, one could not be 100 per cent sure. What should Gwen do?

In Practical Dilemma 19.1, the Mental Capacity Act 2005 would now apply, if it is determined that Amy lacks the requisite mental capacity to make a decision about the operation. Does she lack mental capacity?

It could well be that in her saner moments she is fully capable of understanding what is happening to her and of giving a valid consent or refusal. At other times, she may well be far removed from reality. If the doctor obtains her signature on a form consenting to the operation in one of these sane spells, can he rely on it when she becomes insane? The answer is probably yes. Section 2(2) of the Mental Capacity Act 2005 states that 'It does not matter whether the impairment or disturbance is permanent or temporary'. Provided that Amy has the mental capacity at the time she gives consent to the operation, that would be a valid consent. It is essential, however, that only a reasonable time elapses between the signing of the form and the operation being carried out and the operation must clearly be in the interests of the patient. What is reasonable? Certainly not as long as a year, but possibly up to three months. It depends on the operation to be performed and whether the circumstances remain exactly as they were when the patient signed the form.

If Amy is incapable of making a decision when the operation is required, then the Mental Capacity Act 2005 applies. In the absence of an advance decision (in which Amy when mentally capable set out her wishes as to what should happen in this situation), action must be taken in her best interests and the steps set out in the Mental Capacity Act 2005 followed (see Chapter 7). Relatives and others who may have been aware of what Amy would have wished, and what her feelings, views, values and beliefs would have been, should be consulted to determine her best interests. Advance decisions or living wills are considered in Chapter 17.

Force, restraint and assault

Caring for confused older patients raises concerns about what action can be taken in fulfilment of the duty of care, when treatment is being refused contrary to the best interests of the patient or when they are at risk of harm and need to be restrained. Guidance is provided by the RCN on restraint and the care of older people.[16] Anyone using restraint of any sort must ensure that their actions are compatible with Article 3 of the Human Rights Convention, which is discussed in Chapter 1 and can be found in Appendix A. Advice is also given by Counsel and Care on minimising the use of restraint in residential and nursing homes for older people.[17] It includes flowcharts to assist in assessing the level of risk and making decisions on the use of restraint. Counsel and Care has also published a discussion document[18] that considers the meaning of restraint, examples of why restraint is used and suggests some working principles. Reference should also be made to publications of the Social Services Inspectorate, such as 'No Longer Afraid'.[19] Where an adult lacks the mental capacity to make their own decisions a limited form of restraint can be used under the Mental Capacity Act 2005. Under Section 5 of the MCA restraint cannot be used unless two conditions are satisfied. These are:

+ that the decision maker must reasonably believe that it is necessary to do the act in order to prevent harm to the client/patient and

+ that the action is a proportionate response.

Proportionate means that the act of restraint is proportionate to both the likelihood of harm to the client/patient and the seriousness of the harm.

The use of restraint is defined as including both the decision maker using or threatening to use force to secure the doing of an act which the client/patient resists and also restricts the mentally incapacitated person's liberty of movement, whether or not he or she resists.

Examples of justified restraint might include pulling a person back from crossing in front of a car or moving a person away from an open window. The Mental Capacity Act was amended to enable a person's liberty to be restricted in circumstances where the use of mental health legislation was not justified or possible. These amendments were made to fill what was known as the Bournewood gap and they are considered in Chapter 20.

Restless patients

> **Practical Dilemma 19.2**   **The wanderer**
>
> One further difficulty that the staff had with Amy (described in Practical Dilemma 19.1) was that she could never stay in one place. She always liked to be on the move. Her restlessness took her all round the hospital where she was well known and those with time on their hands would eventually bring her back to the ward. Unfortunately, building work started on site and the contractors were asked to take special care in crossing hospital roads. The nursing officer instructed Amy's ward sister to keep her on the ward because of the danger. The ward sister could not be sure that someone was always available to keep an eye on Amy and, rather than lock the ward door and imprison all the patients, she decided to use a restrainer on Amy so that every time Amy tried to get out of her chair a belt, which was fastened around Amy and to the chair, rang a bell and prevented Amy from leaving the chair. Gwen visited Amy and was distressed to see this form of restraint; Amy herself protested about it. What is the legal position?

To restrict a person's movement without lawful authority so that they have no way of escape is a form of false imprisonment. This effectively is what Amy is – imprisoned. Limited restraint could be used under the Mental Capacity Act, as described above. However, any form of restraint which could be seen as a breach of Article 5 and a person's right to liberty and security of person must comply with either the Mental Health Act 1983 (as amended) or the amendments to the Mental Capacity Act 2005 introduced to fill the Bournewood gap. These are both considered in Chapter 20.

The form of restraint used by the ward sister would appear to be neither temporary nor reasonable. What alternatives are available to the ward staff, given that they have a duty to care for Amy and to prevent her exposure to danger? Adequate staffing to keep an eye on each person is obviously one possibility, but given present-day economic constraints and nurse staffing levels it may not be a realistic option. Another possibility is the use of more volunteers to supervise certain patients. One suggestion is to change the locks so that it takes some ingenuity to open the door without the help of the ward staff, although this is not a happy compromise. Electronic tagging devices are also used, so that if a patient wearing such a device goes through an exit, then a bell warns the staff. Even if there are no contractors on site, there may be other dangers such as a main road nearby, a stream in the grounds, etc. If unreasonable methods of restraint are used, this could be a violation of their Human Rights as set out in Article 3: 'No one shall be subjected to torture or to inhuman or degrading treatment or punishment.'

Where staff consider that some form of restraint is necessary in order to control very aggressive older patients, they should obtain advice on the application of the Mental Capacity Act 2005 or the Mental Health Act 1983 (see Chapter 20). The Alzheimer's Society suggested in December 2007 that electronic tagging should be offered to dementia sufferers to allow their relatives to locate them quickly should they wander off. The Society advised that where possible permission should be sought from the sufferer, perhaps in advance, before he or she has reached the later stages of dementia.[20]

Control at night

At night, cot sides are often used to prevent patients climbing or falling out of bed. In one sense, where the older person is clearly struggling against them, these represent a form of restraint. By the same token, they may in some circumstances be justified and indeed necessary where the patient is very confused and restless. Failure to use them might lead to action against the authority for failing in its duty of care for the patient. However, the potential danger of the patient trying to climb over the cot sides and causing himself harm must always be borne in mind. A risk assessment has to be carried out on whether the use of cot sides in each individual situation is justified.

Records should be kept of this risk assessment. Information is available from the Medicines and Healthcare products Regulatory Agency (MHRA, see Chapter 12) on the use of bed safety rails.[21] Its Device Bulletin in 2006[22] provides guidance on the use of bed rails which are not supplied by the bed manufacturer, the need for a full risk assessment on the suitability of using a bed rail and general guidance on their use.

Daily care

> **Practical Dilemma 19.3** Chiropody case
>
> One form of treatment that Amy could not tolerate was having her toenails cut. She was abusive to the podiatrist who found it very difficult to keep her nails in reasonable order. The podiatrist asked the ward sister if she would hold Amy down while she attempted to cut her nails. The ward sister was not happy with this suggestion and felt that they should first seek medical guidance as it might be preferable to cut the nails when Amy was mildly sedated. What is the legal position?

Chapter 7 discusses consent to treatment where it is stated that touching another person without their consent or some other lawful authority is a trespass to their person. Does the fact that Amy needs to have her toenails done constitute lawful authority? The answer to this is, in general, no. However, the fact that Amy lacks the capacity to give a valid consent may well justify the professionals taking some action to care for her. As has been seen earlier, professionals are justified in taking care of a patient out of necessity to save his life. This is quite clear if the patient is unconscious. However, in considering podiatry, we are not talking of something that is, at least initially (although it may well be ultimately), a life-saving procedure. In addition, there are numerous nursing tasks and social tasks such as bathing, hairwashing and brushing to which patients like Amy may well object. In theory, of course, to brush Amy's hair without her consent is a trespass to her person. There may be occasions when Amy can be persuaded to have it done and will not struggle against it. However, inevitably, there may come a time when Amy needs to have something done despite her protests. In such cases restraint may be used, providing the conditions set out in the Mental Capacity Act as described above are satisfied. If the level of restraint required is such that it could infringe her rights under Article 5 of the European Convention on Human Rights, then it may be necessary to consider using the limited deprivation of liberty envisaged by the Bournewood safeguards (see Chapter 20).

Medication and the confused older patient

The above principles apply equally to the administration of medication. The majority of patients in psychiatric hospitals are on some form of medication, but only a few of them are under a section (about 5 per cent). There are many occasions when, through a variety of reasons ranging from justifiable ones to pure cussedness or confusion, they reject the tablets, injections or liquid. What does the nurse do? Obviously, where the patient is capable of making that decision, his refusal should be respected. But this is rarely the case. Often the patient is in Amy's situation: intermittently or permanently confused and mentally infirm. The provisions of the Mental Capacity Act which enable action to be taken in the best interests of the person lacking the capacity to make decisions can be applied (see Chapter 7).

The UKCC published in 2001[23] a position statement on the administration of medicines by covert means. This is discussed in Chapter 28 on medicines.

Medication may sometimes be used as a form of restraint. There are considerable dangers in so doing and the practice may be declared illegal under Article 3 of the Human Rights

Convention (see Chapter 1 and Appendix A) on the grounds that it is degrading or inhuman treatment. A line has to be drawn between medication that is in the best interests of a mentally incompetent patient (and could therefore be given under the Mental Capacity Act) and medication that is for other purposes. The latter would be unlawful. In January 2004 a House of Commons Health Committee Investigation into elder abuse reported that more than half of the care homes for older people are failing to administer old people's medication properly. Only 45 per cent of homes met minimum standards. (The situation found by the Joint Committee in August 2007 on elder abuse in care homes suggested that standards had not improved – see page 463, below.)

Multidisciplinary care of older people

Many health and social services professionals are involved in the care of older people and liaison across the organisational divide of health and social services is essential in order to ensure that a high standard of care is provided. The Audit Commission recommended innovative practice and close communication in preventing bed blocking and poor standards of care in its report 'The Coming of Age',[24] and In a report In 2000 it made strong recommendations on the care of the confused older person.[25] In this latter report, it emphasises the range of services that those suffering from dementia require and the need for health and social services to work closely together to make the best use of available resources. However, the National Audit Office reported in 2007 that too little is being done to deal with the growing problem of dementia care. Its report stated that Britain is slow to diagnose cases and lags behind other European countries in providing care. There are estimated to be about 500,000 persons with dementia in England.

The NHS Plan[26] (see Chapter 15 of the NHS Plan) has recommended closer cooperation between health and social services in order to ensure that patients are not blocking hospital beds because of a lack of funds held by social services. Its recommendations included: by April 2002, a single assessment process for health and social care (advice on the single assessment process (SAP) for older people is available on the DH website),[27] with protocols to be agreed locally between health and social services; each older patient and where appropriate their carers would be involved in agreeing a personal care plan; Care Direct would be established to provide a faster access to care, advice and support. This new service would provide information and advice about health, social care, housing, pensions and benefits by telephone, drop-in centres, online and through outreach services. Chapter 7 of the NHS Plan envisaged the establishment of a new level of primary care trusts that would provide for closer integration of health and social services. These bodies are known as care trusts and are able to commission and deliver primary and community healthcare as well as social care for older people and other client groups (see Chapters 5 and 23).

Standard of care

> **Practical Dilemma 19.4** **An unknown break**
>
> Fred, a patient, aged 75, recovering from an orthopaedic operation, was occasionally restless in the night. On one such occasion, he fell out of bed. The night sister rushed to his aid and with the help of the other night nurses, she put him back in bed. Fred appeared none the worse, was happy to have a cup of tea and then he settled down. The next morning, the night sister was about to mention to the day shift that Fred had had a disturbed night, but did not give them the details as they were distracted by a patient with a query. A few days later, Fred was seen to be avoiding putting any weight on his left leg. He was examined, sent for X-ray and a fracture diagnosed. His son asked how this had happened. However, no one could recall any incident in the day and the night staff had not entered the earlier incident in the records or reported an accident. An investigation was then initiated.

Even if the night nurse considered on reasonable grounds that there was no need to call the doctor out in the night, her failure to ensure that the incident was reported to the doctor on the following morning and her failure to arrange for a doctor to examine Fred was clearly not in accordance with approved practice. In addition, she failed to give to the day staff a full account of the night's events so that they were unable to ensure that the appropriate action was taken. The night sister compounded these omissions by failing to fill in an accident report. Unless there are any other mitigating factors in an incident like this, Fred would undoubtedly have a possible claim for compensation against the negligent night nurse and therefore against the NHS trust for its vicarious liability for their employee. Compensation is unlikely to amount to very much, since it would cover only the additional days of pain and suffering because the fracture had not been diagnosed earlier (unless, of course, the nurses were negligent in failing to put cot sides up and prevent the original fall). However, if it is discovered that those few days' delay have had considerable effects on the long-term prospects for Fred's recovery, then, clearly, compensation would be greater. The night sister would obviously face disciplinary proceedings and also fitness to practise investigations. In its annual report for 2002–2003, the NMC highlights the fact that many cases heard by its Professional Conduct Committee relate to poor practice in the care of older people and vulnerable patients. This category made up almost 30 per cent of complaints during 2002–2003. Two of the four cases it describes in detail in its report are concerned with practitioners' failure to deal appropriately with older patients who had falls.

Pressure ulcers

It is accepted that the breakdown of tissue is not confined to older patients, but since they may be more vulnerable to pressure sores, this subject is discussed in this chapter. Many years ago the possibility of suffering from pressure sores was believed to be an inevitable result of long-term immobilisation. Now, however, they are seen as evidence of negligence by those providing the care and inevitably are therefore likely to result in litigation. In recent years awards have been made of £32,000[28] and £14,000[29] and where death results from the inadequate care that leads to pressure sores, manslaughter charges could be brought[30] (see Chapter 2, page 30). Disciplinary proceedings by the employer and fitness to practise proceedings could also be brought against those who have failed to act according to appropriate standards. NICE has prepared guidelines on pressure ulcer risk management and prevention[31] that will be updated as the research basis for best practice improves. (It was due to be reviewed in April 2005 but this has not yet taken place.) Eventually NICE guidance is likely to be incorporated into the Bolam Test of reasonable professional practice. There may be disputes over which hospital, care home or other establishment is responsible for the breakdown of tissue and documentation of the examination of a patient on admission (or discharge) and of the risk assessment and management undertaken would be essential to establish which institution and staff were to blame for the patient's condition.

Abuse of older people

Research suggests that abuse of older persons, or other vulnerable persons, is a significant issue. Claudine McCreadie of the Institute of Gerontology has published an extensive analysis of research[32] on elder abuse that should be essential reading for every health professional caring for older people. She concludes that the term 'elder abuse' covers a diversity of situations; that the extent of the problem is still unknown, but sufficient to make the case for a service response; that research and training are essential; and she points to the danger that older people who are being abused will fall between existing service provisions and their needs will remain unaddressed unless action is taken. Her paper written in 2001 on learning the lessons from SSI reports ('Making connections: good practice in the prevention and management of elder abuse') is available from the DH website.[33] A House of Commons Health Committee investigation into elder abuse reported in January 2004 and found less than half of care homes for older people complied with standards on the administration of medication. In 2007 the National Centre for Social Research and King's College London reported on a two-year study which showed that almost 350,000 pensioners were abused or neglected in their own homes by carers (family members were responsible for 51 per cent). Campaigners called for new laws to give social workers the same rights of entry as they have where child abuse is suspected.[34]

Information has come to light on the extent of financial abuse and exploitation. Ginny Jenkins, Director of Action on Elder Abuse, stated that it is estimated that one in ten of those granted powers under enduring powers of attorney abuses the trust.[35] The Protection of Vulnerable Adults Scheme (POVA) enables a check to be made on those who have abused, neglected or otherwise harmed vulnerable adults in their care before they are given employment in care positions. Fresh guidance on POVA has been issued by the DH and the Social Care Institute for Excellence (SCIE) has provided a good practice guide on making referrals to the Protection of Vulnerable Adults list. The Parliamentary Joint Committee on Human Rights in August 2007[36] found that more than a fifth of care homes have been found to be failing basic standards of care for privacy and dignity. Its recommendations are considered in Chapter 23.

Code of practice

Each local authority should have in place a code of practice to protect older people from abuse. An agreed procedure should be followed where there are concerns that an older person may be subject to abuse. Community nurses should obtain a copy of their local code of practice if they have reason to fear that one of their patients is subject to abuse, whether physical, sexual, emotional or financial. Box 19.1 sets out the steps that a community nurse should follow. Help the Aged has been running a campaign to prevent elder abuse and further details and leaflets can be obtained from its website.[37] A confidential helpline has been set up by Action on Elder Abuse[38] which also provides guidelines for health and social workers in detecting and preventing elder abuse, available on its website.[39]

Box 19.1 — Guidelines for action in abuse of older people

1 Find out if the local authority has a procedure for the protection of vulnerable adults where abuse is suspected. If so, follow this procedure. Ensure you document your concerns and action.

2 In the absence of a procedure, seek the advice and guidance of senior management. Information can also be obtained from the Action on Elder Abuse helpline.

3 Keep clear records of the facts on which your suspicions are based.

4 Check if the circumstances set out in Section 47 of the National Assistance Act 1948 or Section 135(1) of the Mental Health Act 1983 (see Chapter 20) appear to be present.

5 Report your concerns to the appropriate social worker, suggesting, if appropriate, a community care assessment under Section 47 of the NHS and Community Care Act 1990.

6 Ensure that the patient's general practitioner is also notified of your concerns.

Long-term funding of care for older people

'With Respect to Old Age',[40] the Royal Commission Report, made radical recommendations for their future care. It suggested that: 'The costs of long-term care should be split between living costs, housing costs and personal care. Personal care should be available after assessment, according to need and paid for from general taxation; the rest should be subject to a co-payment according to means.' A minority of two members of the Royal Commission, in a note of dissent, stated that they could not support the majority view that personal care should be provided free of charge, paid for from general taxation, on the basis of need. The government did not accept the Royal Commission's recommendation that personal care should be met from public funds, although it made various recommendations to reduce the hardship of means-tested payment of fees. The disputes between the demarcation of NHS-funded care (and therefore free at the point of delivery) and means-tested social services care continued to give rise to many concerns and complaints.

Following the Coughlan judgement[41] (where the Court of Appeal held that a person in a nursing home who had been promised that she could stay there for life was entitled to enforce that promise), the Ombudsman issued a report on continuing care on 20 February 2003 after which the Department of Health issued instructions[42] that strategic health authorities should agree with local councils one set of criteria for continuing care in keeping with the Coughlan judgment (this is discussed in Chapter 23). Subsequently, in 2007, the DH announced that a National Framework for continuing care would be implemented in October 2007. Assessments for continuing NHS care are to be carried out by a multidisciplinary team using the concept of 'a primary health' need as the criteria for the receipt of continuing healthcare.[43] This initiative should resolve the issues which were raised by the High Court decision in the Grogan case[44] (see Chapter 23).

The Royal Commission also recommended that a National Care Commission should be set up to monitor trends, including demography and spending, to ensure transparency and accountability in the system, to represent the interests of consumers and set national bench-marks, now and in the future. The Care Standards Act 2000 set out a new framework for regulation of the independent healthcare sector and most social care. A National Care Standards Commission was established. This was subsequently abolished and its health registration and inspection functions transferred to CHAI (i.e. the Healthcare Commission) and its social services registration and inspection functions transferred to CSCI (see Chapters 5 and 23). From April 2009 the Government intends that there will be one regulatory authority, with enhanced powers, combining the Healthcare Commission, the Mental Health Act Commission and the Commission for Social Care Inspection.

(Court decisions concerning the assessment of means-tested payments for nursing and residential care homes and community care are considered in Chapter 23.)

In December 1997, the UKCC published a policy paper on the continuing care of older people.[45] Among its recommendations are: that the UKCC should recognise that the central features of the nursing role in continuing care are holistic assessment, health promotion and the ability to work in multi-professional partnership with clients, their carers and other agencies; that specialist practitioners, in particular community nurses and health visitors, be actively involved in all continuing care settings; and community nurses and health visitors have a key role in the assessment of older people for continuing care services and in ongoing assessment and review following placement. The NMC in its professional conduct annual report for 2002-2003 placed emphasis on the practitioners' duty of care to older patients and clients.

Filling the vacuum on decision making for the mentally incapacitated adult

For a long time we have waited for legislation to fill the gap on decision making on behalf of the mentally incapacitated adult. The House of Lords decision in Re F[46] enabled a professional to act in the best interests of the patients according to the approved accepted standard of care (i.e. the Bolam Test). In the absence of consent and where major surgery or treatment was contemplated (e.g. sterilisation), a declaration was sought from the courts. The Law Commission in 1991 issued a consultation paper on decision making and the mentally incapacitated adult.[47] Following feedback, three further papers were published covering private and public law issues and treatment decisions. The Commission recommended that legislation covering advance directives should be passed in order to clarify their validity, formation, revocation and status. It also recommended that there should be a statutory power to treat those who lack the mental capacity to make their own decisions. Its proposals were considered by the House of Lords Select Committee on Medical Ethics (1994). The Law Commission published in 1995 its final proposals for decision making on behalf of the mentally incapacitated adult.[48] Subsequently, the Lord Chancellor published a consultation paper[49] and proposals were put forward by the government.[50] These culminated in the Mental Capacity Act 2005. Under this act, a statutory definition is provided for mental capacity and those acting on behalf of those lacking the requisite mental capacity must act in those persons' best interests. The Act also makes provision for advance decisions or living wills. The Act also provides for a lasting power of attorney to be granted to a donee, which can include the power to make decisions on treatment and care, once the donor loses the requisite mental capacity. A new Court of Protection has been established which will have a wider jurisdiction than the old and can make decisions on personal welfare and appoint deputies to make decisions. In Scotland the Adults with Incapacity (Scotland) Act 2000 is in force and covers the situation of decision making on behalf of incapacitated adults.

Conclusions

Significant legal developments have taken place recently which should impact upon the care and treatment of the older person. The Mental Capacity Act 2005 enables decisions to be made on behalf of those who lack the mental capacity to make their own decisions. The Act also enables those who are mentally capable to create an advance decision covering treatments they would not wish to receive at a later time when they lack the requisite mental capacity to make decisions (see Chapter 16). In addition the Act enables a mentally capacitated person to set up a lasting power of attorney whereby a donee or attorney is empowered to make decisions on personal welfare matters at a later time, when the donor lacks the requisite capacity to make his or her own decisions. These powers are considered in Chapter 7 and their impact upon the care of the older person should be immense. In addition, as a consequence of a much debated decision by the House of Lords in the Birmingham case,[51] the government is considering amending the Human Rights Act so that those non-public organisations which at present are not seen as exercising functions of a public nature and are therefore outside the scope of the Human Rights Act would come within its aegis. Changes are also taking place in the organisation of those bodies which inspect and regulate the standards in care homes and Department of Health policies appear at present to be moving in favour of providing care to individuals in their own homes rather than care for them in residential settings. In September 2007 the Healthcare Commission called upon NHS hospitals to step up efforts to provide dignity in care to older people.[52] It remains to be seen how far these major changes will contribute to an improvement in and greater respect for the dignity and privacy of the older person.

Reflection questions

1 A crucial factor in the care of older people is the extent to which the patient is mentally capable and able to make decisions. Look at the Mental Capacity Act 2005 and determine how the definition of capacity can be applied to your patients (see also Chapter 7).

2 What particular precautions should you take when caring for older patients who are disturbed?

Further exercises

1 To what extent do you consider the nurse should be the advocate for the patient and to what extent do you think that this role can be left to relatives?

2 Obtain a copy of your NHS trust's summary of accidents to patients and analyse those relating to older patients. To what extent do you consider some of these accidents could have been prevented if different procedures had been adopted by the carers or by the NHS trust itself?

3 Obtain a copy of the NHS National Service Framework for Older People. Take one of the standards and analyse the extent to which they are implemented within your department/ organisation. What action would need to be taken to ensure full implementation?

References

[1] Royal College of Nursing, The Nursing Care of Older Patients from Black and Minority Ethnic Communities, Order No. 000860, RCN, April 1998

[2] www.ageconcern.org.uk

[3] Healthcare Commission, Review of dignity in care 2007, available on website: www.healthcarecommission.org.uk/

[4] Department of Health, NSF for Older People: Age Discrimination Benchmarking, 2003; www.dh.gov.uk/nsf/agediscrim.htm

[5] *R (On the application of Bishop)* v. *Bromley LBC* [2006] EWHC 2148; (2006) 9 CCL Rep 635

[6] Department of Health Social Services Inspectorate, Improving Older People's Services, DH, 2001

[7] Department of Health, National Service Framework for Older People, DH, 2001; www.dh.gov.uk/NSF/olderpeopleexec.htm (executive summary)

[8] HSC 2001/007; LAC(2001)12, National Service Framework for Older People

[9] www.dh.gov.uk/research/rd1/strategicresearch/ageing/olderpeople.htm

[10] Professor Ian Philip, National Director for Older People's Health, Better Health in Old Age, DH, November 2004

[11] Department of Health, National Framework for Older People: Standard 4 General Hospital Care 2004/6 Project, DH, April 2006

[12] Department of Health, A new ambition for old age: Next steps in implementing the National Service Framework for Older People, DH, 2006

[13] www.csip.org.uk/our-initiatives/older-people-and-physical-disabilities

[14] HSC 2001/01; LAC(2001)1, Intermediate Care

[15] Ibid.

[16] Royal College of Nursing, Restraint Revisited: rights, risk and responsibility, Order No. 000998, RCN, October 1999

[17] Counsel and Care, Residents Taking Risks: minimising the use of restraint. A guide for care homes, Counsel and Care, no date

[18] Counsel and Care, Showing Restraint: challenging the use of restraint in care homes, Counsel and Care, no date

[19] Social Services Inspectorate, No Longer Afraid, HMSO, London, 1993

[20] Rosemary Bennett, Electronic tags to track dementia patients, *The Times*, 27 December 2007. http://www.timesonline.co.uk/tol/life_and_style/health/article3097496.ece (last accessed 25 January 2008)

[21] www.mhra.gov.uk/; Are You Sleeping Safely? An event to help you use bed safety rails wisely

[22] Medicines and Healthcare products Regulatory Agency, Safe Use of Bed Rails, DB 2006(06), 2006

[23] UKCC Registrar's letter 26/2001, Position Statement on the Covert Administration of Medicines – disguising medicine in food and drink

[24] Audit Commission, The Coming of Age: improving care services for elderly people, The Stationery Office, London, 1997

[25] Audit Commission, 'Forget Me Not': mental health services for older people, The Stationery Office, London, 2000

[26] Department of Health, The NHS Plan: a plan for investment, a plan for reform, Cm 4818-1, The Stationery Office, London, July 2000

[27] www.dh.gov.uk/sap/index.htm

[28] *Castle* v. *Kings Healthcare NHS Trust* (2000) AVMA Medical Legal Journal, 6(6), pp. 251-2

[29] *P* v. *Hillingdon Hospital NHS Trust* (2000) AVMA Medical Legal Journal, 6(6), p. 253

[30] www.nmc-uk.org/nmc/main/news/nurses_guilty_of_manslaughter

[31] National Institute for Health and Clinical Excellence, NICE Guideline on Pressure Ulcer Risk Management and Prevention, NICE, April 2001

[32] Claudine McCreadie, Elder Abuse: update on research, Institute of Gerontology, 1996

[33] http://www.dh.gov.uk/scg/makingconnections.htm

[34] National Centre for Social Research and King's College London, The UK Study of Abuse and Neglect, June 2007

[35] Speaking on 'Law In Action', BBC Radio 4, 22 October 1998

[36] House of Lords and House of Commons Joint Committee on Human Rights of Older People in Healthcare, 18th Session, 2006–7, HL 156-1/HC 378-1, August 2007

[37] www.helptheaged.org.uk

[38] Action on Elder Abuse Helpline, Freephone 0808 808 8141

[39] www.elderabuse.org.uk

[40] Royal Commission, With Respect to Old Age, The Stationery Office, London, March 1999

[41] *R* v. *North and East Devon Health Authority ex parte Coughlan* [2000] 3 All ER 850; [2000] 2WLR 622

[42] DH response to the Ombudsman's report on continuing care, last modified February 2007

[43] DH, The National Framework for NHS Continuing Healthcare and NHS-funded Nursing Care, June 2007

[44] *R (Grogan)* v. *Bexley NHS Care Trust* [2006] EWHC 44; (2006) 9 CCL 188

[45] Abigail Masterson, UKCC Policy Paper No. 1: the continuing care of older people, UKCC, London, December 1997

[46] *Re F (Mental Patient: sterilisation)* [1990] 2 AC 1

[47] The Law Commission Consultation Paper No. 119, Decision Making and the Mentally Incapacitated Adult, HMSO, London, 1991

[48] Law Commission Report No. 231, Mental Incapacity, The Stationery Office, London, 1995

[49] Lord Chancellor's Office, Who Decides? The Stationery Office, London, 1997

[50] Lord Chancellor's Office, Making Decisions, The Stationery Office, London, 1999

[51] *YL* v. *Birmingham City Council and others* [2007] UKHL 22, The Times Law Report, 21 June 2007

[52] Healthcare Commission, Caring for Dignity: A national report on dignity in care for older people while in hospital, 27 September 2007

Chapter 20
Nursing the mentally disordered

Introduction

This chapter cannot cover all the law relevant to the nursing of the mentally ill and those with learning disabilities.[1] The intention is to deal with some of the more common dilemmas faced by these nurses through the case study approach and to include in the diagrams a summary of some of the main points of the Mental Health Act 1983 (as amended by the Mental Health Act 2007). This Act is the main legislation covering the detention of the mentally disordered and for the most part replaces the Act of 1959, which, by the end of the 1970s, was seen as failing to protect the rights of the mentally disordered. The chapter also considers the amendments introduced by the Mental Health Act 2007. The chapter will also consider the amendments to the Mental Capacity Act 2005 which were introduced as a result of the Bournewood case where the European Court of Human Rights criticised the reliance on common law for restricting the liberty of those unable to give a valid consent (the Bournewood gap). Reference should be made to the Code of Practice of the Department of Health on the Mental Health Act.[2] The UKCC has provided guidelines for mental health and learning disabilities nursing[3] and also guidance for the nursing, midwifery and health visiting contribution to the continuing care of people with mental health problems.[4] The legislation must be read in conjunction with the Articles of the European Convention on Human Rights (see Chapter 1 and Appendix A). For example, in 2003 the House of Lords ruled that conditional discharge under Section 73 of the Mental Health Act 1983 was not incompatible with the European Convention on Human Rights.[5] Those with learning disabilities have exactly the same rights as others if they are assessed as having the requisite mental capacity to make a specific decision. Where a person with learning disabilities also has a mental illness or personality disorder, then he or she may come within the provisions of the Mental Health Act 1983. Where a person with learning disabilities lacks the requisite mental capacity to make his or her own decisions, then he or she would come under the provisions of the Mental Capacity Act 2005. Article 2 and the right to life came under scrutiny in relation to the duties of NHS trusts when the daughter of a detained patient who had committed suicide on a railway line claimed that the trust was in breach of Article 2. The case was heard on the preliminary issue as to the proper test to be used to establish a breach of Article 2. The court held that the correct test was one of gross negligence of the kind sufficient to sustain a charge of manslaughter. Using this test the daughter had no reasonable chance of succeeding in her claim and the trust's application for summary judgment striking out the claim succeeded.[6]

Informal patients

The vast majority (well over 90 per cent) of patients who are cared for in psychiatric hospitals are not detained. They have either given consent to admission or, if they lack the mental capacity to consent to admission, they are treated under the provisions of the Mental Capacity Act 2005 which replaces the common law powers recognised by the House of Lords in the *Re F* case[7] (see Chapter 7). The House of Lords in the Bournewood[8] case considered the question of whether a mentally incapacitated person, incapable of giving consent to admission, could be held at common law in a psychiatric hospital and not placed under the Mental Health Act 1983 (see Case 20.1). It decided that Section 131 of the Mental Health Act 1983 did not require a mentally disordered person to have the capacity to consent to admission as an informal patient. However, the application against this decision to the European Court of Human Rights succeeded and the UK government was required to introduce changes. The result was that the Mental Capacity Act 2005 was amended to make provision for the restriction of liberty of such persons.

> ### Case 20.1   *L* v. *United Kingdom* (2004)
>
> **Lack of capacity to consent to admission**[9]
>
> L, an adult with learning disabilities, was informally admitted to a mental health unit. He was not detained under the Mental Health Act 1983. His carers asked for his discharge, but his psychiatrist considered that it was not in his best interests to be discharged and that he should remain in hospital. The carers challenged the legality of this decision. They lost in the High Court, but the Court of Appeal held that Section 131 of the Mental Health Act required a person to have the mental capacity to agree to admission; a person lacking the requisite capacity should be examined for compulsory admission under the Act. The House of Lords upheld the appeal of the NHS trust, holding that an adult lacking mental capacity could be cared for and detained in a psychiatric hospital, using common law powers. Subsequently an application was made to European Court of Human Rights which held that there was a breach of his Article 5 right to liberty.

Revision was therefore necessary to ensure compliance with the Human Rights Act 1998 (see Chapter 1 and Appendix A). Article 5 of the European Convention on Human Rights, which is set out in Schedule 1 in the Human Rights Act 1998, states:

> *Everyone has the right to liberty and security of person. No one shall be deprived of his liberty save in the following cases and in accordance with a procedure prescribed by law.*

Included in the 'following cases' under (e) are 'persons of unsound mind'. However, the fact that mentally incapacitated adults can under the Bournewood ruling be detained without being placed under the Mental Health Act 1983 was not a procedure prescribed by law. The Bournewood amendments to the Mental Capacity Act 2005 were therefore necessary to provide protection for such persons, when a restriction of liberty was required in their best interests.

Bournewood safeguards

The Mental Health Act 2007 amended the Mental Capacity Act 2005 to introduce the safeguards necessary to justify loss of liberty of residents in hospitals and care homes These are known as the 'Bournewood safeguards'. They are set out in the new Schedule A1 to the MCA as introduced by the Mental Health Act and can be found in a briefing paper available from the Department of Health.[10]

Who are covered by the Bournewood provisions?

+ Those over 18 years
+ Who suffer from a disorder or disability of mind
+ Who lack the capacity to give consent to the arrangements made for their care and
+ For whom such care (in circumstances that amount to a deprivation of liberty within the meaning of Article 5 of the European Convention on Human Rights) is considered after an independent assessment to be a necessary and proportionate response in their best interests to protect them from harm

What procedures are required?

1 Application for authorisation

The care home, i.e. the managing authority, must identify a client/patient as lacking capacity and who risks being deprived of his/her liberty. It must apply to the supervisory body, i.e. the local authority in which the client/patient was ordinarily resident, for the authorisation of deprivation of liberty.

2 Assessments required

1 Age assessment - client/patient must be over 18 years

2 Mental health assessment - client/patient must be suffering a mental disorder

3 Mental capacity assessment - client/patient must lack the capacity to decide whether to be admitted to or remain in the hospital or care home

4 Eligibility assessment - the client/patient must:
   (a) Not be detained under the Mental Health Act
   (b) Not be subject to a conflicting requirement under the Mental Health Act
   (c) Not be subject to powers of recall under the Mental Health Act
   (d) Not be subject to a treatment order in hospital to which the client/patient objects

5 Best interests assessment - the authorisation would be in the client/patient's best interests and is a proportionate response to the likelihood of suffering harm and the seriousness of that harm

6 There is no conflict between the authorisation sought and a valid decision by a donee of a lasting power of attorney or a deputy, nor with a valid and applicable advance decision made by the client/patient.

3 Appointment of representative for the client/patient

If the best interests assessor concludes that the client/patient has the capacity to appoint his/her own representative, then he/she can do this. Otherwise the best interests assessor can appoint a representative. If the assessor notifies the supervisory body that a representative has not been appointed for him/her then it can appoint a representative who can be paid to act as the client's/patient's representative.

4 Authorisation granted

If all the assessments are satisfactory then authorisation by the supervisory body can be granted for the deprivation of the client's/patient's liberty for up to 12 months.

5 Review and Monitoring

The supervisory authority should keep under review the client's/patient's deprivation of liberty and the whole process of the assessments and authorisation will be monitored to ensure that all the required procedures were followed.

In the example given in Practical Dilemma 20.1, there would appear to be no justification for locking the ward and preventing everyone leaving simply to control Maud. It could therefore be argued that this is a false imprisonment of everyone in the ward. What about Maud? There may be justification in detaining Maud because she is a danger to herself were she allowed to wander away. As a consequence of the amendments to the Mental Capacity Act

> ### Practical Dilemma 20.1   Resistance in the elderly (1)
>
> Maud, a frail 85-year-old, was a 'wanderer' and occasionally resisted the efforts of the nursing staff to give her medication. She was an informal inpatient on a psychogeriatric ward. One day she attempted to wander off the ward and, because they were short staffed and could not keep an eye on her all the time, the ward door was locked. A visitor to another patient complained that it was illegal for the door to be locked when the patients were not under section. What is the legal position?

2005, introduced to provide safeguards in the Bournewood situation, it would now be possible to consider an application to the local authority as set out above. If long-term detention of Maud were required she should be assessed for detention under the Mental Health Act 1983 as amended by the 2007 Act.

> ### Practical Dilemma 20.2   Resistance in the elderly (2)
>
> On one occasion, Maud made it clear that she would not have her medication, which was prescribed as a sedative and for her heart condition. As an informal patient, could she be forced to take the medication since it was for her benefit and she lacked the mental capacity to make a reasoned judgement over whether she should be taking it?

It is necessary in a situation such as Practical Dilemma 20.2 for a clear assessment to be made of Maud and whether she lacks mental capacity to make a decision about her medication and whether or not she is suffering from mental disorder. If Maud is assessed as lacking the mental capacity to decide whether she should take medication, then she would come under the provisions of the Mental Capacity Act 2005 and action must be taken in her best interests. The provisions of the Act are set out in Chapter 7. If she is assessed as suffering from mental disorder then consideration should be given as to whether she should be detained under the Mental Health Act 1983 (as amended) and given compulsory treatment under Part 4 of the Act. The answer to the question in Practical Dilemma 20.2 is that as an informal patient lacking the requisite mental capacity to determine whether or not to take medication, she could be compelled to take medication if it was considered to be in her best interests.

> ### Case 20.2   *In re F (Adult: Court's jurisdiction) (2000)*
>
> **Care of incapable adults at risk of harm**[11]
>
> T, an 18-year-old girl with an intellectual age of 5 to 8 years, lacked the capacity to make decisions about her future. The local authority sought to invoke the inherent jurisdiction of the court under the doctrine of necessity to obtain directions as to where T should live and to supervise her contact with her natural family, principally her mother. The mother challenged the power of the court to make such a ruling, on the grounds that its former *parens patriae* jurisdiction had lapsed in 1959. The Court of Appeal held that in the present conflict,

> **Case 20.2 continued**
>
> where serious questions hung over the future care of T if returned to her mother, there was no practicable alternative to intervention by the court. It was held that it was essential that T's best interests should be considered by the High Court and there was no impediment to the judge hearing the substantive issues involved in the case. Lord Justice Sedley specifically stated that this conclusion did not conflict with the European Convention for the Protection of Human Rights and Fundamental Freedoms[12] (see Appendix A).

Acting in the best interests of a mentally incapacitated adult

Prior to the implementation of the Mental Capacity Act 2005, powers were recognised at common law which enabled professionals and carers to make decisions on behalf of those lacking the mental capacity to make decisions in their best interests.[13] Thus in one case,[14] a young man, (S) born in 1984 with velo-cardio-facial syndrome with severe global development delay and bilateral renal dysplasia, was assessed as having a cognitive functioning age of about 5–6 years. His dialysis catheter became infected and there was concern over what treatment would be in his best interests. The President of the Family Division, Dame Elizabeth Butler-Sloss, held that:

+ The fundamental principle of the sanctity of life was of particular relevance in this case where the existing and proposed treatment options were crucial to sustain S's life.

+ As S lacked capacity to make decisions about his medical treatment and there was disagreement between S's family and the treating clinicians, it was the duty of the court to decide, in an exercise addressing medical, emotional and all other welfare issues, what was in his best interests.

+ Just because a person could not understand treatment it was wrong to say that he could not have it: it was crucial that S, who suffered from serious mental in addition to physical problems, should not be given less satisfactory treatment than a person who had full capacity to understand the risk, pain and discomfort inseparable from major surgery.

+ It was in S's best interests that he should continue to receive dialysis as long as some form of that treatment was working and providing him with a reasonable quality of life; when haemodialysis was no longer effective, he should move to peritoneal dialysis; dialysis via an AV fistula should not be ruled out but should be considered in consultation with learning disability experts once S had settled into the adult renal unit and an adult way of life; a kidney transplant should not now be carried out as it was not clear that he would enjoy a longer lifespan with a transplant; but if, in future, medical reasons were in favour of a transplant, it should not be rejected on the grounds that S's inability to understand the purpose and consequences of the operation or concerns about his management.

Mental Capacity Act 2005

This Act, which came fully into force in October 2007, replaces the common law provisions by providing a statutory definition of capacity and setting out the steps to be taken in determining the best interests of a person who lacks the requisite mental capacity. It is discussed in Chapter 7. It requires, in the absence of informal carers or others who can be consulted about a person's best interests, the appointment of an independent mental capacity advocate to be appointed where decisions relating to serious medical treatment or accommodation are being considered.

Patients detained under mental health legislation

As stated earlier, only about 5-10 per cent of psychiatric patients are at any one time detained under the mental health legislation. The next section gives an account of the main statutory provisions of the Mental Health Act 1983 (as amended by the Mental Health Act 2007) that apply to the detention and treatment of such patients.

Fundamental principles

The Mental Health Act 2007 amends the Mental Health Act 1983 to require the Secretary of State to include in the Code of Practice (prepared under Section 118 of the 1983 Act) a statement of principles. Each of the following matters must be addressed in this statement:

(a) respect for patients' past and present wishes and feelings

(b) respect for diversity generally including, in particular, diversity of religion, culture and sexual orientation (within the meaning of Section 35 of the Equality Act 2006)

(c) minimising restrictions on liberty

(d) involvement of patients in planning, developing and delivering care and treatment appropriate to them

(e) avoidance of unlawful discrimination

(f) effectiveness of treatment

(g) views of carers and other interested parties

(h) patient well-being and safety and

(i) public safety

The Secretary of State shall also have regard to the desirability of ensuring the efficient use of resources and the equitable distribution of services.

Definition of mental disorder

No person may be compulsorily detained under the Mental Health Act 1983 unless he or she is suffering from mental disorder as defined in the Act. The definition as revised by the 2007 Act is as follows:

any disorder or disability of the mind.

(The previous classifications of mental illness, mental impairment and psychopathic disorder are no longer used in the statutory definition.)

Learning disability (which is defined as 'a state of arrested or incomplete development of the mind which includes significant impairment of intelligence and social functioning') is not considered to be mental disorder unless the disability is associated with abnormally aggressive or seriously irresponsible conduct on the person's part.

Dependence on alcohol or drugs is not considered to be a disorder or disability of the mind for the purposes of the definition of mental disorder.

Holding power of the nurse

Practical Dilemma 20.3   To stop or let go

Bill Smith, an informal patient in a psychiatric hospital, admitted three weeks ago, wakes up at 3.00 a.m. and starts abusing nursing auxiliary Mavis Jones who is on her own, Staff Nurse Rachel Robinson having just gone for her break. Bill starts throwing furniture around and is threatening to leave the ward. Mavis contacts the night operator and asks for immediate help. What is her legal position in relation to Bill? Rachel Robinson returns with a charge nurse. They telephone for the responsible medical officer and are informed that he will not be able to arrive until 9.30 a.m. What are their legal powers?

The Statute below sets out the main points of the holding power of the nurse laid down by Section 5(4) of the Act. As a nursing auxiliary, Mavis is not a prescribed nurse for the purposes of using the holding power under the Mental Health Act. The only nurses designated as prescribed nurses under the Act are those who have been trained in mental illness or mental handicap. She does, however, have the health carer's duty to act in an emergency to save life. She also has the powers of the citizen to effect an arrest on the limited occasions set out in the Police and Criminal Evidence Act. If she feared for the life of Bill were he to be allowed to leave hospital immediately or for the life of anyone else, she could legally prevent his leaving the ward in an emergency. Rachel Robinson would be regarded as a prescribed nurse if she were registered as a nurse trained in mental health.[15] She can exercise the holding power set out under Section 5(4) of the Mental Health Act 1983 if the conditions set out in the Statute below are present. If all these requirements are present, then Rachel has the power to detain Bill for up to six hours. As soon as the appropriate medical practitioner arrives, however, the holding power will cease.

Statute   Section 5(4) of the Mental Health Act 1983

1 The patient is receiving treatment for mental disorder.

2 The patient is an inpatient.

3 It appears to the prescribed nurse that the patient is suffering from mental disorder to such a degree that it is necessary for his health or safety or for the protection of others for him to be immediately restrained from leaving the hospital.

4 It is not practicable to secure the immediate attendance of a practitioner who could exercise the powers under Section 5(2).

Rachel must fill in the appropriate forms and ensure that these are taken to the managers of the hospital immediately. Procedures vary: in some hospitals, it is the practice for the hospital manager to be on call for such purposes; in others, this duty is delegated to the nurse manager on duty at night and weekends. If the doctor arrives and decides that Bill should be detained under Section 5(2), then whatever part of the holding power has elapsed before his arrival will become part of the 72 hours' detention.

From the situation described here, it is apparent that the appropriate doctor will not be able to arrive within the six hours. In this case, it is essential for the doctor to exercise his powers of nomination under Section 5(3) so that another medical practitioner (or approved clinician) can act as nominee and see Bill at the earliest possibility.

This situation gives rise to other questions. Must Rachel remain with Bill personally even though she is due off duty at 7.30 a.m.? There is no requirement in the Act that Rachel should stay. The fact that Bill is under a holding power should, of course, be made clear to the senior nurse on the shift that takes over from Rachel. In particular, she should be informed of the time of commencement of the holding power and, if a doctor fails to arrive, the time when the holding power is due to end.

What powers does Rachel have in relation to Bill? Could Bill, for example, forcibly be given some medication for which he has been written up? The Act gives Rachel the power to restrain Bill from leaving hospital. She does not have power under the Mental Health Act to compel Bill to have treatment. Informal patients or those who have been placed under short-term detention orders covered by Sections 5(2), 5(4) and Section 4 are specifically excluded from the compulsory treatment provisions of Part 4 of the Act. Many feel that it is kinder to control Bill through medication than through physical restraint. There is no power to do this under the Act, however, and any such use of compulsory treatment can be lawfully justified only under the common law powers to act out of necessity. The legality of using them for this purpose is in doubt and practice varies.

What if Bill runs off during the period of the holding power – can he be brought back? Section 18(5), by implication, allows Bill to be brought back as long as the time limit for the holding power has not elapsed. Section 18(1) (as amended by the 2007 Act) enables a patient who is absent without leave to be taken into custody and returned to the hospital by any approved mental health professional, by any officer on the staff of the hospital, by any constable or by any person authorised in writing by the managers of the hospital.

Could the holding power be used if Bill were an inpatient in a general hospital? From the requirements listed above, it is clear that Bill must be receiving treatment for mental disorder. It is, of course, possible for Bill to be admitted for surgery while still under treatment for a mental disorder and in this case the holding power could be exercised, but only if the nurse had the appropriate registration.

Compulsory detention of an informal inpatient

What would happen in a general hospital if a patient became severely mentally disordered? Temporary emergency measures could be taken to save life: either the life of the patient or of others. In addition, it is possible for any registered medical practitioner or approved clinician in charge of the patient to exercise the powers under Section 5(2).

This section applies to an inpatient in a hospital. There is no requirement that he should be having treatment for mental disorder. The registered medical practitioner or approved clinician in charge of the patient's treatment must consider that an application ought to be made under the Act for the admission of the patient to hospital. He then furnishes the managers with a report to that effect and the patient may then be detained in the hospital for a period of 72 hours from the time the report is furnished.

In such circumstances on a general ward, it would also be possible to make use of the powers under Section 4. In this case, it would be necessary for the nearest relative or an approved mental health professional to make the appropriate application for admission.

Compulsory admission

Table 20.1 sets out the section numbers and requirements for each section that enable compulsory admission to take place and the length of detention. The requirements in relation to the two medical recommendations are set out in Box 20.1.

Box 20.1 | **Requirements for the two medical recommendations**

1 Practitioners must have personally examined the patient either together or separately, but where they have examined the patient separately not more than 5 days must have elapsed between the days on which the separate examinations took place.

2 One of the medical recommendations must be from a practitioner approved by the Secretary of State for such purposes as having experience in the diagnosis or treatment of mental disorder and unless that practitioner has previous acquaintance with the patient, the other practitioner should have, if practicable.

3 One (but not more than one) of the medical recommendations should be given by a practitioner on the staff of the hospital to which the patient is to be admitted.

4 3 above does not apply, i.e. both medical recommendations can be given by staff of the hospital in question, if:
+ compliance with 3 above would result in delay involving serious risk to the health and safety of the patient
+ one of the practitioners works at the hospital for less than half of the time which he is bound by contract to devote to work in the health service
+ and where one of the practitioners is a consultant, the other does not work in a grade in which he is under that consultant's directives.

5 A medical recommendation cannot be given by:
+ the applicant
+ a partner of the applicant or of a practitioner by whom another medical recommendation is given for admission
+ a person employed as an assistant by the applicant or by any such practitioner
+ a person who receives or has an interest in the receipt of any payments made on account of the maintenance of the patient
+ except as set out in 3 and 4 above a practitioner on the staff of the hospital to which the patient is admitted or by specified relatives of the other practitioner giving the medical recommendation.

6 A general practitioner who is employed part time in a hospital shall not be regarded as a practitioner on its staff.

These provisions also apply to the two medical recommendations for guardianship.

Statute | **Section 26(i) of the Mental Health Act 1983**

Definition and powers of the nearest relative

Definition: the highest in the following hierarchy:

relative who ordinarily resides with or cares for the patient

husband or wife or civil partner

son or daughter

father or mother

Statute continued

brother or sister

grandparent

grandchild

uncle or aunt

nephew or niece.

Preference is given in relatives of the same description to the whole blood relation over the half-blood relation and the elder or eldest regardless of sex.

Husband and wife include a person who is living with the patient as the patient's husband or wife and has been so living for not less than 6 months. A person other than a relative with whom the patient ordinarily resides for a period of not less than 5 years shall be treated as if he were a relative. However, such a person is at the bottom of the above hierarchy.

Power of nearest relative:

1 To apply for the admission of the patient for assessment, for assessment in an emergency, for treatment and for guardianship.

2 To be informed about the approved mental health professional's application to admit patient for assessment.

3 To be consulted about the approved mental health professional's proposed application for treatment and to object to it.

4 To be given information about the details of the patient's detention, consent to treatment, rights to apply for discharge, etc. (but subject to the patient's right to object to this information being given).

5 To discharge the patient after giving 72 hours' notice in writing to the managers.

6 To apply to a mental health review tribunal under Sections 16, 25 and 29.

Definition and role of nearest relative

The nearest relative has an important role to play and has to be given specific information; this task often falls on the nurse. The definition of nearest relative and the hierarchy is given in the Statute above, which also illustrates the powers of the nearest relative.

Role of the approved mental health professional

Table 20.2 sets out the main tasks of the approved mental health professional (which replaces the approved social worker as a result of the amendments in the Mental Health Act 2007). Only mental health professionals who have completed the appropriate training (and are not registered medical practitioners) can be recognised as approved for the purposes of the Act. While the Act allows the nearest relative to be an applicant for compulsory admission under Sections 2, 3, 4 and 7, in practice the applicant will usually be the approved mental health professional and this is the preferred procedure.

Table 20.1 Compulsory admission provisions

Section	Duration (up to)	Applicant	Medical requirements	Other requirements
4 Emergency admission for assessment	72 hours	Approved mental health professional or nearest relative	1 recommendation only stating that patient is suffering from mental disorder and stating the provisions of Section 2 exist (see below)	Applicant must have personally seen patient within 24 hours before the application. Admission must be of urgent necessity
2 Admission for assessment	28 days	Approved mental health professional or nearest relative	2 medical recommendations: (a) patient is suffering from mental disorder of a nature or degree which warrants detention in hospital for assessment and (b) he/she ought to be so detained in the interests of his/her own health or safety or with a view to the protection of others	Applicant must personally have seen patient within the period of 14 days ending with the date of the application
3 Admission for treatment	6 months, renewable for a further 6 months, then for a period of 1 year	Approved mental health professional or nearest relative	2 medical recommendations: (a) patient is suffering from mental disorder of a nature or degree which makes it appropriate for him/her to receive medical treatment in hospital and, (b) repealed by 2007 Act	As above under Section 2. Approved mental health professional must consult with nearest relative before making an application unless this would not be reasonably practicable or would involve unreasonable delay. The application cannot be made if the nearest relative objects

(c) it is necessary for the health or safety of the patient or for the protection of others that he/she should receive such treatment and it cannot be provided unless he/she is detained under this section and

(d) appropriate medical treatment is available

Section	Duration	Grounds	Medical evidence
37 Hospital order without restrictions	6 months, renewable for a further 6 months, then for a period of 1 year	Order can be made by Crown Court in case of person convicted of an offence punishable by imprisonment or by magistrates: (a) if convicted of offence punishable on summary conviction with imprisonment or (b) if person is suffering from mental disorder and magistrates are satisfied that he committed the crime	2 doctors required to give oral or written evidence that: (a) offender is suffering from mental disorder of a nature or degree which makes it appropriate for him/her to be detained for medical treatment and appropriate medical treatment is available for him (b) repealed by 2007 Act (c) the court is of the opinion, having regard to all the circumstances, that the most suitable method of disposing of the case is by means of a hospital order
41 Restriction order (imposed in conjunction with hospital order Section 37)	For a specified period	Crown Court that has made a hospital order can impose a restriction order. Magistrates' court cannot make a restriction order but can send offender over 14 to Crown Court for a restriction order to be made	As for Section 37; at least 1 of the 2 doctors must give evidence orally before the court

Table 20.2 Role of the approved mental health professional

Duty	Details
Duties of the approved mental health professional	
Section 11(3) Inform nearest relative of admission of patient and of nearest relative's right to discharge	1 In admission for assessment (Sections 2 and 4) 2 Before or within a reasonable time after an application for admission for assessment is made 3 Such steps as are practicable to inform the person appearing to be the nearest relative
Section 11(4) Consult nearest relative on admission for treatment or guardianship and discontinue application if nearest relative notifies objection	1 Consultation with person appearing to be the nearest relative of the patient 2 Unless it appears that in the circumstances such consultation is not reasonably practicable or would involve unreasonable delay
Section 13(1) To apply for admission or guardianship order if satisfied application ought to be made and is of the opinion that it is necessary or proper for application to be made by him	1 In respect of patient within the area of local social services authority by whom he is appointed 2 Must have regard to wishes expressed by relatives of patient or any other relevant circumstances that are necessary or proper for application to be made by him
Section 13(2) To interview patient in suitable manner and satisfy himself that detention in a hospital is in all the circumstances of the case the most appropriate way of providing the care and medical treatment of which the patient stands in need	1 Before making application for admission to hospital
Section 13(4) To take patient's case into consideration with a view to making an application for admission. If he decides not to make an application he will inform the nearest relative in writing of his reasons	1 If nearest relative so requires local social services authority of area in which patient resides, authority must direct approved mental health professional as soon as practicable
Section 14 To provide report on social circumstances	1 Where patient admitted to hospital an application by nearest relative other than Section 4 2 Managers must as soon as practicable give notice of that fact to local social services authority for area in which patient resided immediately before his admission

Table 20.2 *continued*

Duty	Details
Section 117 Duty of district health authority and of local social services authority to provide aftercare services	1 Applies to patients detained under Section 3 or admitted under hospital order (Section 37) or transferred under transfer direction (Sections 47 or 48) who cease to be detained and leave hospital 2 Authorities must cooperate with relevant voluntary agencies 3 Aftercare services to be provided until such time as the authorities are satisfied that the person concerned is no longer in need of such services

Informing the patient and relatives

Informing the patient

The task of explaining his legal rights to the patient once a detention order has been imposed often falls on the nurse (see Statute, below).

Statute | **Section 132 of the Mental Health Act 1983: informing the patient**

The managers of the hospital in which a patient is detained under the Act must:

1 Take such steps as are practicable to ensure the patient understands:
+ under which provisions of the Act he is for the time being detained and the effect of that provision
+ what rights of applying to a mental health review tribunal are available to him in respect of his detention under that provision and
+ the effect of certain provisions of the Mental Health Act including the consent to treatment provisions, the role of the Mental Health Act Commission and other provisions relating to the protection of the patient.

2 The steps to inform the patient must be taken as soon as practicable after the commencement of the patient's detention under the provision in question.

3 The requisite information must be given to the patient in writing and also by word of mouth.

> ### Practical Dilemma 20.4   Information
>
> Edna Johns, an informal patient in a psychiatric hospital, became very disturbed and aggressive in the early hours of the morning, threatening to kill herself and wishing to leave hospital. Staff Nurse Thomas, an RMN, on learning that the responsible medical officer would take at least 30 minutes to arrive on the ward, decided to exercise the holding power under Section 5(4). When the appropriate doctor arrived, he decided to detain Edna under Section 5(2). Within the next 48 hours, the approved mental health professional applied for admission under Section 3 on the recommendation of Edna's doctor and a second recommendation. What duties exist in relation to informing Edna?

The duties set out under Section 132 are illustrated in the above Statute. Forms are available covering the information to be given under each section. Often the nursing staff have the task of giving out the forms and telling the patient about the provisions. It is vital that it is recorded that the patient has been informed since it is a statutory duty and there should be evidence that the statutory duty has been carried out.

In Edna's case, she will have been placed under three separate sections in less than 72 hours. She must be given the relevant information each time the section is imposed and will be given a different form each time. Section 132 requires the information to be given as soon as practicable after the commencement of the section. 'Practicable' must take into account the patient's physical and mental ability to take in what is said. To stand over a screaming or even unconscious patient reading him his rights would not seem to be a proper fulfilment of the statutory duty.

Informing the relatives

Where the patient is too disturbed to take in the information, the statutory duty to inform the nearest relative assumes even greater importance. Section 132(4) requires the managers to furnish the person appearing to them to be the patient's nearest relative with a copy of any information given to the patient, in writing, under the duty outlined above. The steps for this must be taken when the information is given to the patient or within a reasonable time thereafter. The patient has the right of veto and can request that this information is not given. Reasonable time here would seem to imply that it is not necessary to phone Edna's relative in the middle of the night to inform them of the exercise of the holding power, but this should be done as soon as possible the next day.

Consent to treatment provisions

See the following Statute and Box 20.2.

Long-term detained patients

Under the provision of Part 4 of the Mental Health Act 1983, those patients who are detained under long-term detention provisions (e.g. Sections 2, 3, 37 and 41) can in certain circumstances be given compulsory treatment. For these patients, the Act covers all possible treatments for mental disorder, both in emergency and non-emergency situations. The provisions are set out in the Statute below.

Statute | **Sections 57, 58 and 63 of the Mental Health Act 1983**

1 Treatments involving brain surgery or hormonal implants can only be given with the patient's consent, which must be certified and only after independent certification of the consent and of the fact that the treatment should proceed (Section 57).

2 Treatments involving electroconvulsive therapy or medication where 3 months or more have elapsed since medication was first given during that period of detention can only be given either (a) with the consent of the patient and it is certified by the patient's own approved clinician in charge of the treatment or another registered medical practitioner appointed specifically for that purpose that he is capable of understanding its nature, purpose and likely effects, or (b) the registered medical practitioner appointed (not being the responsible clinician or the approved clinician in charge of the treatment in question) has certified in writing that the patient is not capable of understanding the nature, purpose and likely effects of that treatment or has not consented to it, but that ... the treatment should be given (Section 58) (as amended by the 2007 Act, see page 486 and Box 20.3).

3 All other treatments: these can be given without the consent of the patient provided they are for mental disorder and are given by or under the direction of the approved clinician in charge of the treatment (Section 63).

Box 20.2 | **Consent to treatment: urgent treatments**

These can be given according to the degree of urgency and whether they are irreversible or hazardous.

Any treatment	which is immediately necessary	to save the patient's life
Treatment which is not irreversible	if it is immediately necessary	to prevent serious deterioration
Treatment which is not irreversible or hazardous	if it is immediately necessary	to alleviate serious suffering
Treatment which is not irreversible or hazardous	if it is immediately necessary and represents the minimum interference necessary	to prevent the patient from behaving violently or being a danger to himself or others

Irreversible is defined as 'if it has unfavourable irreversible physical or psychological consequences' and hazardous is defined as 'if it entails significant physical hazard'.

A new Section 62A has been added to the Mental Health Act 1983 to enable treatment to be given to those community patients who have been recalled. The patient is to be treated as if he had remained liable to be detained since the making of the community order.

Electro-convulsive therapy (ECT) and other specified treatments

Amendments were made to Section 58 of the Mental Health Act 1983 by Section 27 of the Mental Health Act 2007 to cover ECT and other treatments specified in regulations. A person shall not be given such treatments unless he or she falls within certain specified conditions. These conditions include those listed in Box 20.3.

Box 20.3 Specified conditions for treatments Section 58A

1   The patient is at least 18 years, has consented to the treatment and his capacity to consent has been certified by the approved clinician in charge of it or by the appointed registered medical practitioner

2   The patient is below 18 years, has consented to the treatment and an appointed registered medical practitioner (not being the approved clinician in charge of the treatment) has certified in writing the patient's capacity to consent and that it is appropriate for the treatment to be given, or

3   an appointed registered medical practitioner (not being the responsible clinician or approved clinician in charge of the treatment) has certified in writing:
    (a) that the patient is not capable of understanding the nature, purpose and likely effects of the treatment; but
    (b) that it is appropriate for the treatment to be given and
    (c) that giving him the treatment would not conflict with:
        (i) an advance decision which the registered medical practitioner concerned is satisfied is valid and applicable or
        (ii) a decision made by a donee or deputy or by the Court of Protection.

Before a certificate is given in circumstance 3, the appointed registered medical practitioner must consult two persons who have been professionally concerned with the patient's medical treatment; one must be a nurse and the other neither a nurse nor a registered medical practitioner. In addition neither shall be the responsible clinician or the approved clinician in charge of the treatment in question.

Role of the nurse

What is the role of the nurse in consent to treatment provisions? Under the provisions of Sections 57 and 58, the independent registered medical practitioner, in determining whether the treatment should proceed, must consult with a nurse and another professional who have been professionally concerned with the patient's medical treatment. The independent doctor must record the fact that he has consulted these two persons. Interestingly, however, there is no requirement on the form that he should actually record their opinions, so it could well happen that both the nurse and the other professional counselled against, say, ECT, but that the doctor still recommended ECT. A disagreement is unusual, but it is advisable for the nurse, whether there is agreement or not with her views, to ensure that the advice she gave is recorded clearly and comprehensively.

Challenges to compulsory treatment

A detained patient challenged the fact that she had been given treatment against her will, arguing that the judge should not have concluded that although there was a body of responsible medical opinion that the statutory test for medication had not been satisfied, it was in her best interests and necessary for the purposes of Article 3 that the proposed treatment should be administered. The Court of Appeal dismissed her appeal, holding that the standard of proof that medical necessity was shown is not the criminal standard, but it has to be convincingly shown, and whether the treatment satisfies the Bolam Test is a necessary but not a sufficient condition of treatment in a patient's best interests. Determining best interests may involve choosing the best option between what may be a number of options, all of which satisfy the Bolam Test. Even where there is a responsible body of opinion that the proposed treatment is not in the patient's best interests and is not medically necessary, it does not follow that it *cannot* be convincingly shown that the treatment proposed is in the best interests or medically necessary.[16]

Ian Brady, a detained patient at Ashworth Hospital, wished to go on hunger strike and challenged the responsible medical practitioner's decision that he could be force-fed[17] on the grounds that it was contrary to his human rights. In the judicial review hearing the court held that his decision to go on hunger strike was a symptom of his personality disorder. He was therefore mentally incapacitated and his doctor had a duty to act in his best interests by feeding him. Unlike the Broadmoor patient C[18] (see Chapter 7), he was incapable of weighing up risks and benefits.

Seclusion

There is no provision in the Mental Health Act 1983 relating to seclusion. Placing a detained patient under seclusion was challenged by judicial review as being contrary to Article 3 of the European Convention on Human Rights, i.e. 'inhuman and degrading treatment or punishment'.[19] The High Court held that seclusion is capable of infringing a patient's rights under Article 3; it did not per se amount to a breach of those rights. Seclusion could also be negligent, Wednesbury unreasonable (see Glossary) or a breach of Article 8 of the European Convention on Human Rights. Whether in fact seclusion amounts to inhuman or degrading treatment will depend on the circumstances of the particular case and will involve consideration of any intention to humiliate or debase the position of the alleged victim, the consequences of the treatment and the availability of resources. A power to seclude can be implied within the provisions of the Mental Health Act 1983 if there is a 'self-evident and pressing need' for that power. Seclusion did not amount to false imprisonment or a breach of Article 5 of the European Convention on Human Rights. Seclusion was not medical treatment for the purposes of the Act since it is not used to alleviate or prevent the deterioration of an illness or its symptoms or to enable treatment to be given, but its use is authorised to ensure that control is maintained over patients. The court held that there was no infringement of the patient's rights when he was secluded and the fact that there was a departure from the Code of Practice on the Mental Health Act did not affect the duration or conditions of the claimant's seclusion, which was not unlawful.

Physical illness

These provisions on consent to treatment would thus appear to cover all eventualities concerning the long-term detained patient. However, there is a gap in relation to treatment for physical illness.

Practical Dilemma 20.5   Appendicitis

Paul, a severely depressed patient, had been detained under Section 3 for two months. One morning, he complained of severe stomach pains. He was sick, with a high temperature. Paul was taken to the 'sick' ward for the treatment of physical illnesses within the mental hospital and was diagnosed as suffering from appendicitis. It was recommended that an operation be performed immediately. When Paul heard this, he immediately said there was no way in which he would agree to the operation. What is the legal position?

If Part 4 of the Act is seen as applying only to the treatment of mental illness, then its provisions are irrelevant in these circumstances. Alternatively, it could be argued that if brain surgery can be undertaken under Section 62 to save the life of a patient (and this may cover informal patients, since they are covered by the provisions of Section 57), where the treatment is given for a mental disorder, then the words 'any treatment' in Section 62 can cover not only treatment for mental disorder, but also treatment for physical disorders. If the purpose is to save life, then Section 62(1)(a) covers the situation. This is a logical view, but it has not gained universal acceptance. The alternative is to say that the situation is not covered by Part 4 of the Act and therefore the provisions of the Mental Capacity Act 2005 would apply. These provisions enable treatment to be given without the patient's consent as part of the doctor's duty of care to the patient. In cases prior to the implementation of the MCA, *In re C* 1994 (see Case 7.3), a Broadmoor patient's refusal to have an amputation was upheld by the court. In the case of *B* v. *Croydon Health Authority*, the Court of Appeal held that compulsory feeding by tube came under Section 63 (TLR 1 December 1994). There have also been several cases where a pregnant woman detained under the Mental Health Act 1983 has been compelled to undergo a Caesarean section under Section 63 of the Act.[20] This has been disputed by the Court of Appeal in *Re MB*[21] (see Chapter 14, pages 361-3). It is clear that if a detained patient, suffering from mental disorder, has the mental capacity to understand the proposed treatment and the implications of his or her refusal, then the court would not order the treatment to proceed unless it could clearly be seen to be treatment for the mental disorder and therefore comes within Section 63. If, however, the patient lacks the mental capacity to refuse treatment in his or her best interests, treatment could lawfully be given under the Mental Capacity Act 2005. There are considerable advantages in securing a declaration of the Court of Protection that it is lawful to provide the treatment.

Independent mental health advocates (IMHA)

The Mental Health Act 2007 amends the Mental Health Act 1983 to make provision for independent mental health advocates to be available to help qualifying patients. Regulations are to be drawn up to specify the circumstances in which the IMHAs should be appointed and the conditions for their approval. New Sections 130A, B, C and D are inserted into the 1983 Act to cover the details of these appointments, the qualifying patients and the information to be given to the IMHA.

Short-term detained patients and informal patients

Short-term detained patients and informal patients are not covered by the Part 4 treatment provisions of the Mental Health Act. There is only one exception to this: informal patients are specifically covered by the provisions of Section 57 relating to brain surgery and hormonal implants and by the relevant provisions of Sections 59, 60 and 62. As far as Section 57 is concerned, this means that brain surgery for mental disorder or hormonal implants cannot be given without the safeguards set out above. The short-term detained patient is not explicitly covered, but there would appear to be no reason why he should not receive the same protection.

As far as all other treatments are concerned, one has to look outside the Act for the law relating to consent to treatment and this is set out in Chapter 7. Since only some 5 per cent of mentally ill and mentally handicapped patients are under the detention of the Mental Health Act 1983, the vast majority of patients are outside the basic provisions of the Act. Those who lack the requisite mental capacity to make specific decisions would come under the provisions of the Mental Capacity Act 2005 (see Chapter 7).

Community provisions

The philosophy behind the Mental Health Act 1983 is that a patient should be compulsorily detained in hospital only if informal admission is not an option and if alternative services in the community cannot be provided. There are very few community provisions in the 1983 Act except for guardianship, Section 17 (leave), and Section 117 (aftercare). The Mental Health Act 2007 amended the Mental Health Act 1983 to make provision for a community treatment order which replaces aftercare under supervision (supervised discharge).

Guardianship

> **Practical Dilemma 20.6**   **How much control?**
>
> Paul has been under a guardianship order for three months. He lives with his mother, the guardian, and attends a day centre three times each week. He sees the community psychiatric nurse regularly, both at the centre and also at home, and is on substantial levels of medication. One day, he decides not to take the drugs. His mother pleads with him, but is unable to persuade him to take them. She informs the CPN who also attempts to persuade Paul, but is unsuccessful. His behaviour deteriorates and he becomes more aggressive. His mother asks if there is any way in which he could be compelled to take the drugs as she fears that he will ultimately have to be readmitted. Is there a way?

The answer is that the Mental Health Act 1983 excludes from its provisions relating to consent to treatment those patients on guardianship orders. There are three statutory powers in relation to guardianship and these are set out in Section 7 on page 490.

There are no means of enforcing the guardianship powers over the patient other than the right of returning the patient to the specified place if he absconds. The ultimate sanction is possibly the knowledge that if the patient does not cope in the community, then he is likely to be admitted to hospital. It is not, however, good professional practice to use this as a threat. Apart from gentle professional persuasion, there is no way to force a patient to take drugs. Following the introduction of the community treatment order following the Mental Health Act 2007 (see page 491), this will be considered for patients who have been detained under Section 3.

> ### Statute — Statutory powers of the guardian under the Mental Health Act 1983 Section 7
>
> 1 The power to require the patient to reside at a place specified by the guardian.
>
> 2 The power to require the patient to attend at places and times specified for the purpose of medical treatment, occupation, education and training.
>
> 3 The power to require access to the patient to be given at any place where the patient is residing to any responsible clinician, approved mental health professional or any person specified.

Section 17 Leave

A detained patient can be given leave of absence by the responsible medical officer in charge of the patient. The leave does not have to be in writing, but good practice as recommended by the Code of Practice of the Department of Health[22] suggests that there should be a written record of the leave granted and the terms on which it is granted. Section 17 leave can be used as part of the care plan of the patient towards ultimate discharge from the section and from the hospital. Thus a patient on Section 17 leave can be required to stay in residential accommodation. (The patient cannot be charged for residential accommodation he is required to stay in as a condition of Section 17; see below). Section 17 leave can be withdrawn at any time on the written instructions of the RMO. Any nurse responsible for a patient would have to assess the patient prior to leave commencing, so that there were no grounds for preventing the leave taking place. The Mental Health Act 2007 supplements Section 17 to provide for community treatment orders (see below) and inserts after Section 17(2) the following (2A): 'But longer-term leave may not be granted to a patient unless the responsible clinician first considers whether the patient should be dealt with under section 17A instead.'

Section 117 Aftercare services

A statutory duty is placed on the health authority and local authority in conjunction with the voluntary sector to arrange for the provision of aftercare services for the patient. This duty continues until such time as the health and local authority consider that the patient is no longer in need of the services that they can provide. (The duty cannot end if the patient is in under a community treatment order; see below.) The section applies to patients who have been detained under Sections 3, 37, 47 and 48. However, the duty to provide a community care assessment under Section 47 of the National Health Service and Community Care Act 1990 applies to these patients and also to patients detained under other sections of the Act (e.g. Sections 2, 4, 5(2) and 5(4)) and to informal patients.

The duties under Section 117 cannot be forced on the patient who may refuse to accept the treatment plan or services provided. This therefore led to concerns that patients were being released from psychiatric care without adequate supervision in the community. The cases of Christopher Clunis, who killed Jonathan Zito, and Ben Silcock, who was mauled in the lion's den, reinforced these fears. Some local authorities had been charging patients on a means-tested basis for residential accommodation provided under Section 117. The Court of Appeal[23] made it clear that where accommodation is provided under Section 117 for a patient, then a local authority may not provide it under Section 21 or charge for it under Section 22 of the National

Assistance Act 1948. Where patients are required to live in residential accommodation under Section 17, then they are entitled to this accommodation as an aftercare service under Section 117 when discharged from detention under the Act and cannot therefore be charged for it.

Community treatment order

The provisions on aftercare under supervision, or supervised discharge introduced by the Mental Health (Patients in the Community) Act 1995 were replaced by the community treatment order introduced by Section 32 of the Mental Health Act 2007 which added new sections 17A, 17B, 17C, 17D, 17E, 17F and 17G into the Mental Health Act 1983.

Statute | **New Sections 17A, 17B, 17C, 17D, 17E, 17F and 17G of the Mental Health Act 1983**

Under the Section 17A the responsible clinician may by order in writing discharge a detained patient from hospital subject to his being liable to recall in accordance with Section 17E. Under **17A(4)** the responsible clinician may not make a community treatment order unless—

(a) in his opinion, the relevant criteria are met; and

(b) an approved mental health professional states in writing—
    (i) that he agrees with that opinion; and
    (ii) that it is appropriate to make the order.

(5) The relevant criteria are—
    (a) the patient is suffering from mental disorder of a nature or degree which makes it appropriate for him to receive medical treatment;
    (b) it is necessary for his health or safety or for the protection of other persons that he should receive such treatment;
    (c) subject to his being liable to be recalled as mentioned in paragraph (d) below, such treatment can be provided without his continuing to be detained in a hospital;
    (d) it is necessary that the responsible clinician should be able to exercise the power under Section 17E(1) below to recall the patient to hospital; and
    (e) appropriate medical treatment is available for him.

(6) In determining whether the criterion in subsection (5)(d) above is met, the responsible clinician shall, in particular, consider, having regard to the patient's history of mental disorder and any other relevant factors, what risk there would be of a deterioration of the patient's condition if he were not detained in a hospital (as a result, for example, of his refusing or neglecting to receive the medical treatment he requires for his mental disorder).

17B Conditions for a community treatment order

(1) A community treatment order shall specify conditions to which the patient is to be subject while the order remains in force.

(2) But, subject to subsection (3) below, the order may specify conditions only if the responsible clinician, with the agreement of the approved mental health professional mentioned in Section 17A(4)(b) above, thinks them necessary or appropriate for one or more of the following purposes—
    (a) ensuring that the patient receives medical treatment;
    (b) preventing risk of harm to the patient's health or safety;

Statute continued

(c) protecting other persons.

(3) The order shall specify–

(a) a condition that the patient make himself available for examination under Section 20A below; and

(b) a condition that, if it is proposed to give a certificate under Part 4A of this Act in his case, he make himself available for examination so as to enable the certificate to be given.

(4) The responsible clinician may from time to time by order in writing vary the conditions specified in a community treatment order.

(5) He may also suspend any conditions specified in a community treatment order.

(6) If a community patient fails to comply with a condition specified in the community treatment order by virtue of subsection (2) above, that fact may be taken into account for the purposes of exercising the power of recall under Section 17E(1) below.

(7) But nothing in this Section restricts the exercise of that power to cases where there is such a failure.

17C Duration of community treatment order

A community treatment order shall remain in force until–

(a) the period mentioned in Section 20A(1) below (as extended under any provision of this Act) expires, but this is subject to Sections 21 and 22 below;

(b) the patient is discharged in pursuance of an order under Section 23 below or a direction under Section 72 below;

(c) the application for admission for treatment in respect of the patient otherwise ceases to have effect; or

(d) the order is revoked under Section 17F below,

whichever occurs first.

17D Effect of community treatment order

(1) The application for admission for treatment in respect of a patient shall not cease to have effect by virtue of his becoming a community patient.

(2) But while he remains a community patient–

(a) the authority of the managers to detain him under Section 6(2) above in pursuance of that application shall be suspended; and

(b) reference (however expressed) in this or any other Act, or in any subordinate legislation (within the meaning of the Interpretation Act 1978), to patients liable to be detained, or detained, under this Act shall not include him.

(3) And Section 20 below shall not apply to him while he remains a community patient.

(4) Accordingly, authority for his detention shall not expire during any period in which that authority is suspended by virtue of subsection (2)(a) above.

17E Power to recall to hospital

(1) The responsible clinician may recall a community patient to hospital if in his opinion–

Statute continued

   (a) the patient requires medical treatment in hospital for his mental disorder; and

   (b) there would be a risk of harm to the health or safety of the patient or to other persons if the patient were not recalled to hospital for that purpose.

(2) The responsible clinician may also recall a community patient to hospital if the patient fails to comply with a condition specified under Section 17B(3) above.

(3) The hospital to which a patient is recalled need not be the responsible hospital.

(4) Nothing in this Section prevents a patient from being recalled to a hospital even though he is already in the hospital at the time when the power of recall is exercised; references to recalling him shall be construed accordingly.

(5) The power of recall under subsections (1) and (2) above shall be exercisable by notice in writing to the patient.

(6) A notice under this Section recalling a patient to hospital shall be sufficient authority for the managers of that hospital to detain the patient there in accordance with the provisions of this Act.

17F Powers in respect of recalled patients

(1) This Section applies to a community patient who is detained in a hospital by virtue of a notice recalling him there under Section 17E above.

(2) The patient may be transferred to another hospital in such circumstances and subject to such conditions as may be prescribed in regulations made by the Secretary of State (if the hospital in which the patient is detained is in England) or the Welsh Ministers (if that hospital is in Wales).

(3) If he is so transferred to another hospital, he shall be treated for the purposes of this Section (and Section 17E above) as if the notice under that Section were a notice recalling him to that other hospital and as if he had been detained there from the time when his detention in hospital by virtue of the notice first began.

(4) The responsible clinician may by order in writing revoke the community treatment order if—

   (a) in his opinion, the conditions mentioned in Section 3(2) above are satisfied in respect of the patient; and

   (b) an approved mental health professional states in writing—

      (i) that he agrees with that opinion; and

      (ii) that it is appropriate to revoke the order.

(5) The responsible clinician may at any time release the patient under this Section, but not after the community treatment order has been revoked.

(6) If the patient has not been released, nor the community treatment order revoked, by the end of the period of 72 hours, he shall then be released.

(7) But a patient who is released under this Section remains subject to the community treatment order.

(8) In this Section—

   (a) 'the period of 72 hours' means the period of 72 hours beginning with the time when the patient's detention in hospital by virtue of the notice under Section 17E above begins; and

   (b) references to being released shall be construed as references to being released from that detention (and accordingly from being recalled to hospital).

> **Statute** — **Sections 20A and 20B of the Mental Health Act**
>
> **Section 20A Community treatment period**
>
> A community treatment order shall cease to be in force on expiry of the period of six months beginning with the day on which it was made and this period is referred to in this Act as 'the community treatment period'. The community treatment period may be extended for a period of six months and then on for further periods of up to one year at a time. Section 20A sub-sections 4–10 set out the conditions for renewal and the procedure to be followed.
>
> **20B Effect of expiry of community treatment order**
>
> When the community treatment order expires, the community patient shall be deemed to be discharged absolutely from liability to recall under this Part of this Act, and the application for admission for treatment ceases to have effect.

Treatment provisions for those on a community treatment order

The Mental Health Act 2007 inserts into the Mental Health Act 1983 a new Part 4A which sets out the provisions for the treatment of community patients who are not recalled to hospital. Sections 64A–K set out the conditions on which treatment can be given in the community: 64D enables treatment to be given to an adult who lacks the requisite capacity, if specified conditions are met, but force may not be used; 64G enables emergency treatment to be given to patients lacking the capacity or competence to give consent and under this Section force can be used provided certain conditions are met and the treatment is to prevent harm to the patient and the force must be a proportionate response to the likelihood of the patient suffering harm and to the seriousness of that harm.

Section 135(1) Removal to place of safety

The Statute below sets out the basic provisions of this power of the approved mental health professional. The Section has been amended by the Police and Criminal Evidence Act 1984, so it does not now have to be a named constable who accompanies the approved mental health professional to the house.

> **Statute** — **Mental Health Act 1983 Section 135(1) and (4)**
>
> (1) If it appears to a justice of the peace, on information on oath laid by an approved mental health professional, that there is a reasonable cause to suspect that a person believed to be suffering from mental disorder
>   **(a)** has been, or is being, ill treated, neglected or kept otherwise than under proper control, in any place within the jurisdiction of the justice; or
>   **(b)** being unable to care for himself, is living alone in any such place
>   the justice may issue a warrant authorising any constable to enter, if need be by force, any premises specified in the warrant in which that person is believed to be, and, if thought fit, to remove him to a place of safety with a view to the making of an application

Statute continued

in respect of him under Part 2 of this Act, or of other arrangements for his treatment or care.

Section 135(4) In the execution of a warrant issued under Section 135(1) a constable shall be accompanied by an approved mental health professional and by a registered medical practitioner (as amended by Police and Criminal Evidence Act 1984 Schedule 6 para 26 and the Mental Health Act 2007).

Section 136 Removal from a public place by police

The basic provisions of this section are set out in the Statute below. There has been considerable concern over the use of the Section since the documentation has been inadequate; the police have not always recorded the details as to when they have used this Section; and when the patient has been brought to hospital, the details have not always been recorded by the hospital staff and managers. Many hospitals have now designed their own forms for this purpose that record the date and time the patient arrives and the number and name of the constable who brings the patient in.

Statute | **Police Powers Section 136 of the Mental Health Act 1983**

(1) If a constable finds in a place to which the public have access a person who appears to him to be suffering from mental disorder and to be in immediate need of care or control, the constable may, if he thinks it necessary to do so in the interests of that person or for the protection of other persons, remove that person to a place of safety within the meaning of Section 135.

(2) A person removed to a place of safety under this Section may be detained there for a period not exceeding 72 hours for the purpose of enabling him to be examined by a registered medical practitioner and to be interviewed by an approved mental health professional and of making any necessary arrangements for his treatment or care.

Time limits for mental health review tribunals

Table 20.3 illustrates the time limits for applying to the tribunal, the powers of the tribunal, and the applicants. A major innovation of the 1983 Act was that the managers must automatically refer a patient to the tribunal if he has failed to apply himself. There must be a tribunal hearing at least once every three years. Every child under 16 must be referred by the managers every year if he has not himself applied.

Table 20.3 Applications to mental health review tribunals

Section	Patient	Nearest relative	Manager
2 or 4	Applications by patients within first 14 days of detention	No application by nearest relative	Application by manager under 2007 Act amendments
3	Application by patient within first 6 months of detention, once within second 6 months, then annually	Yes, within 28 days of being informed that responsible medical officer has issued report barring discharge of patient When an order is made appointing a nearest relative under Section 29 On reclassification of patient under Section 16	Automatic referral if tribunal has not considered case within first 6 months of detention, thereafter if tribunal has not considered case within previous 3 years (1 year if patient is under 18)
37	Yes, once within second 6 months of detention, then annually	Yes, once within second 6 months of detention, then annually	Automatic if the case has not been considered by tribunal within previous 3 years (1 year if patient is under 18)
41	Yes, once within second 6 months of detention, then annually	No application by nearest relative	Automatic referral by Home Secretary if tribunal has not considered case within the preceding 3 years

Role of managers

The managers are given certain statutory duties under the Act. These are set out in Box 20.4. Of these, all can be delegated by the NHS trust board, except the duty to hear an application from a patient for discharge. In this case, the NHS trust is empowered to appoint a subcommittee for hearing such applications.

Box 20.4 **Role of managers**

1 To accept a patient and record admission (Section 140).

2 To give information to detained patient (Section 132) and community patient (Section 132A).

3 To give information to nearest relative (Section 132(4)) and inform him of discharge (Section 133(1)) or of detention (Section 25(2)).

4 To discharge patient (Section 23(2)(b)). Powers may be exercised by any three or more members of the authority (Section 23(4)).

5 To refer patient to mental health review tribunal (Section 68 as amended by the Mental Health Act 2007).

6 To transfer patient (Section 19(3), Section 19(1a) Reg. 7(2) and Reg. 7(3)).

Box 20.4 continued

7   To give notice to local social services authority specifying hospitals in which arrangements are made for reception in case of special urgency of patients requiring treatment for mental disorder (Section 140).

Definition of managers

NHS Trust, PCT or NHSFT or special health authority responsible for the administration of the hospital (Section 145).

All powers can be delegated by manager to the officers except for (4) above: discharging the patient. Special provisions apply to NHS Foundations Trusts.

Mental Health Act Commission

Box 20.5 illustrates the powers and constitution of the Mental Health Act Commission. From April 2009 it is to be merged with the Healthcare Commission and the Commission for Social Care Inspection into a new regulatory body with enhanced powers.

Box 20.5   **Powers and constitution of the Mental Health Act Commission**

1   Composition: chairman and about 90 members (doctors, nurses, lawyers, social workers, academics, psychologists, other specialists and lay members).
2   Headquarters in Nottingham.
3   Ten national standing committees.
4   Duty to draft and monitor Code of Practice.
5   Prepare a biennial report to Parliament.
6   Review any decision at a special hospital to withhold a postal packet or its content.
7   Carry out on behalf of the Secretary of State duties in relation to the review of the exercise of powers and discharge of duties under the Act, visiting and interviewing detained patients and hearing complaints from detained patients.
8   Exercise duties and appointment of second-opinion doctors in relation to Part 4. Consent to treatment provisions.

Mentally ill patients and the European Convention on Human Rights

Several patients have won cases in Strasbourg for breach of their rights as set out in the European Convention on Human Rights, including the case of Bournewood, discussed above. In one case,[24] the European Court of Human Rights held that the UK was in breach of Article 5 of the European Convention on Human Rights because for a considerable period of time the patient was not lawfully detained. Several mental health review tribunals had given the patient a deferred conditional discharge under Section 73 of the Act, but discharge had been delayed because the local authority had been unable to find suitable supervised hostel accommodation. After 2 October 2000, those who allege that their human rights have been infringed have been able to bring action in the courts of the UK, instead of going to Strasbourg (see Chapter 1 and Appendix A).

National Service Frameworks

As envisaged in the White Paper on the NHS,[25] the government has published National Service Frameworks for different specialties to ensure that there is a minimum standard of provision across the country. The National Service Frameworks for Mental Health were published in 1999 and set standards in five areas:

Standard one: mental health promotion

Standards two and three: primary care and access to services

Standards four and five: effective services for people with severe mental illness

Standard six: caring about carers

Standard seven: preventing suicide.

The Frameworks document describes the standards as 'realistic, challenging and measurable, and are based on the best evidence available':

They will help to reduce variations in practice and deliver improvements for patients, service users and their carers, and for local health and social care communities – health authorities, local authorities, NHS trusts, primary care groups and trusts, and the independent sector.

NMC practitioners working in mental health services should ensure that they obtain a copy of these standards, and their updates, in order that they can ensure that the services they are providing are comparable with these national standards.

Conclusions

The implementation of the Mental Capacity Act 2005 from 1 October 2007 and the implementation of the amendments to the Mental Health Act 1983 by the Mental Health Act 2007 should effect considerable changes in the care of those lacking the requisite mental capacity to make decisions and/or suffering from mental disorder. Whilst the amendments to the Mental Health Act 1983 are not as radical as those proposed by the Expert Advisory Group chaired by Professor Robinson in 1999, they will make significant differences to the care of those in the community, particularly with the introduction of the community treatment order. It remains to be seen if the Bournewood safeguards which amend the 2005 Act provide the necessary protection for those who lose their liberty. From April 2009 the Mental Health Act Commission is due to be merged with the Healthcare Commission and the Commission for Social Care Inspection into a new regulatory body with enhanced powers. It is to be hoped that this will provide greater protection for the human rights of those who lose their liberty because of mental disorder.

> ## Reflection questions
>
> 1 Contrast the rights of the informal patient and compare these to the statutory rights of the patient detained under mental health legislation.
>
> 2 Analyse the provisions for giving compulsory treatment to those patients detained under the Act.
>
> 3 Discuss the new community treatment order and the benefits which it could bring to patients and carers.

Further exercises

1 Study the restraint and seclusion policy in your hospital and consider the extent to which its implementation can remain within the law, in particular the Human Rights Act. (See Appendix A.)

2 Ask to see the latest report of the Mental Health Act Commission in your hospital.

3 In what ways would informal patients benefit from coming under the jurisdiction of the Mental Health Act Commission?

References

[1] See B. Dimond and F. Barker, *Mental Health Law for Nurses*, Blackwell Scientific Publications, Oxford, 1996

[2] Department of Health, Code of Practice on the Mental Health Act 1983, HMSO, 3rd edition, London, 1999

[3] UKCC, Guidelines for Mental Health and Learning Disabilities Nursing, UKCC, April 1998

[4] UKCC, The Nursing, Midwifery and Health Visiting Contribution to the Continuing Care of People with Mental Health Problems: a review and UKCC action plan, UKCC, 2000

[5] *R (H)* v. *Secretary of State for the Home Department and Another* [2003] UKHL 59

[6] *Savage* v. *South Essex Partnership NHS Foundation Trust* [2006] EWHC 3562; *The Times*, 16 February 2007

[7] *In re F* v. *West Berkshire Health Authority* [1989] 2 All ER 545

[8] *R* v. *Bournewood Community and Mental Health NHS Trust ex p L* [1998] 3 All ER 289; [1999] AC 458

[9] *L* v. *United Kingdom* (Application No 45508/99) [2004] ECHR 720, Times Law Report, 19 October 2004

[10] Department of Health Briefing Sheet, Bournewood, November 2006, Gateway Reference 6794

[11] *In re F (Adult: court's jurisdiction)*, The Times Law Report, 25 July 2000

[12] European Convention for the Protection of Human Rights and Fundamental Freedoms 1953, Cmd 8969

[13] *F* v. *West Berkshire Health Authority* [1989] 2 All ER 545

[14] *A Hospital NHS Trust* v. *S, DG (S's father) and SG (S's mother)* [2003] Lloyd's Rep Med 3 137

[15] Mental Health (Nurses) Order 1998 SI 1998 No. 2625

[16] *R (on the application of N)* v. *Doctor M and Others* [2003] Lloyd's Rep Med 2 81

[17] *R v. Collins ex p Brady* (2001) 58 BMLR 173; [2000] Lloyd's Rep Med 355

[18] *Re C (Adult: refusal of medical treatment)* [1994] 1 All ER 819; (1993) 15 BMLR 77

[19] *S v. Airedale National Health Service Trust* 1 [2003] Lloyd's Rep Med 21

[20] *Tameside and Glossop Acute Services Trust v. CH* [1996] 1 FLR 762; *Norfolk and Norwich (NHS) Trust v. W* [1996] 2 FLR 613

[21] *Re MB (An Adult: medical treatment)* [1997] 2 FLR 426

[22] Department of Health, Code of Practice of the Mental Health Act 1983, The Stationery Office, London, 1999

[23] *R v. Richmond LBC ex parte Watson and Other Appeals* [2001] 1 All ER 436

[24] *Stanley Johnson v. The United Kingdom* [1997] series A 1991 VII 2391

[25] White Paper, The New NHS – modern, dependable, The Stationery Office, London, 1997

Chapter 21

Accident and emergency, outpatients, genito-urinary departments and day surgery

This chapter discusses

+ Accident and emergency department
+ Outpatients department
+ Genito-urinary medicine
+ Day surgery

Accident and emergency department

In recent years, the role of the nurse in the A&E department has undergone a fundamental change, not just as a result of the transfer of many activities formerly undertaken by medical staff to nurses, but as a result of the nurse taking on a wider sphere of responsibility and working within new parameters and developing a new specialty of A&E nursing. The role of the clinical nurse specialist includes the provision of immediate care to patients and the determination of priorities for care (triage). The legal implications of the expanded role of the nurse are considered in Chapter 24. The RCN provided in 1994 a framework for the safe development of A&E nursing at specialist and advanced level.[1] In 2003 the RCN in conjunction with the Department of Health published a joint report, 'Freedom to Practise: dispelling the myths'.[2] The report aims to dispel the myths about what the nurse and other healthcare professionals can or are entitled to do within their codes of conduct. At the launch of the report, the Health Minister stated that the NHS is still not maximising the nursing expertise we have in the health service and this means we are, in effect, wasting NHS resources. The booklet also provides practical fact sheets about the legal and professional frameworks that support practice and enable the development of practice. Another initiative introduced to speed up the treatment of patients and avoid extensive waiting times is the 'See and Treat' initiative from the Modernisation Agency's Emergency Services Collaborative. The aim of this is to assess and treat patients with minor complaints as soon as they arrive, rather than asking them to wait. The key principle is that the first clinician to see the patient is able to assess, treat and discharge them safely.[3] The legal implications of delegation to nursing staff are considered in Chapter 24. The Department of Health has set a target of four hours for emergency care, but recognises that there are clinical exceptions to this. They can be found on the DH website.[4] The target setting was followed by a joint document prepared by the Royal Colleges of Surgeons and Physicians, the Faculty of Accident and Emergency Departments, the British Association for Emergency Medicine and the Department of Health's Clinical Director for Emergency Access on reforming Emergency Care.[5] An Emergency Care Practitioner (ECP) Report has been prepared by the DH which sets out the role of the ECP in the management of patients who require emergency (unscheduled) care.[6] A major plan for many A&E units to be closed is, at the time of writing, being considered by the Department of Health.[7] A minimum population of 450,000 patients per A&E would lead to the closure of those departments with smaller catchment areas.

Pressure of work

> ### Practical Dilemma 21.1   Priorities under pressure
>
> The A&E department was unusually pressurised one weekend: staff shortages due to a flu epidemic and cutbacks because of an attempt to reduce overspending left only a skeleton staff. Unfortunately, there was a particularly horrific pile-up on the motorway in the fog. Twelve people were brought in with varying levels of seriousness. One of them, David Lewis, a boy of 10, appeared to be suffering mainly from shock and bruises. He complained of a sore wrist. His mother was advised to take him home and give him a few paracetamol, a hot drink and, after a good night's sleep, he would be fine. The next day, however, it was learnt that he had died during the night after inhaling vomit.

There is every possibility in this case that the mother will make an official complaint and possibly take legal action. Normally, it is not a successful defence to an action for negligence that the staff were under pressure (see Case 4.10), if it can be established that they failed to follow the approved accepted practice in relation to the care of the patient. Dealing with children is particularly difficult, since they cannot always correctly identify the site of any pain and discomfort. The possibility of head injury does not appear to have been considered in this case and this would be subject to investigation. Was the mother told the correct way of caring for the boy? The legal position is as follows:

1 There is a duty to care for the boy.

2 It must be established by the parents that the staff failed to follow the accepted approved practice.

3 This failure reasonably foreseeably led to the death of the boy.

The workload in an A&E department is extremely erratic. One moment there can be few demands, the next there may be a major incident or a sudden influx of patients and the pressure is on. What is the standard of care in such circumstances? Even though the nurses and doctors are under extreme pressure, each patient is still entitled to expect the appropriate standard of care. Thus it would still be actionable if a fracture remained undiagnosed or if a head injury were to be missed. However, the courts would take into account the pressure on the staff if priorities had to be set over who should be treated first. It would be open to the court to examine the basis of these priorities. In Chapter 4, the case of *Deacon v. McVicar*[8] (Case 4.11) is considered. In this case, a patient alleged that she should have been seen earlier and the court was prepared to examine the records of other patients who were in the ward at the time to see if they were making demands on the staff at that time. The policy of triage has not yet been brought before the courts, but there is no reason to doubt that the above principles would apply, i.e. the professional staff have to take all due care in treating the patients and, where priorities have to be decided on, this must be according to approved accepted practice. There is no doubt that, in general, pressure of work does not justify a lower standard of care for the patient. It may, in addition, lead to a successful action against the NHS trust itself if it can be established that the authority failed to provide adequate resources and training for the patients to be cared for safely. It may be necessary in emergencies for staff to undertake tasks that they are not properly trained to do. If so, it is a question of balancing one risk against another, i.e. the risk of not being treated at all against the risk of harm arising because the only available person to treat the patient has not had sufficient training. Inevitably, the only way of coping with wide variations in demand is either to bring in additional staff to meet peaks of demand or for patients with less severe conditions to wait till staff are available to assist. Even though successful legal action would probably not lie for a long wait, the complaints procedure might be used for those who consider that they have waited an unacceptable length of time. To prevent such claims, clear standards of communication with patients must be drawn up and implemented to ensure that patients are fully apprised of the situation.

In 1999 the Department of Health announced an A&E modernisation programme, which was given targeted funding and consisted of three strands:

+ overseeing a capital investment programme
+ recommending short-term interventions to ease emergency and millennium pressures
+ producing a strategic view for the development of A&E services.

This programme is still ongoing and the waiting times within A&E departments are closely monitored. A significant development in the A&E modernisation programme is the appointment of clinical nurse specialists (see Chapter 24). In January 2004 the Department of Health published guidance on handling major incidents,[9] which sets out the general principles to help the NHS develop its existing emergency plans to respond to new potential threats. As part of the work of the NHS Modernisation Agency, a national programme (the Emergency Services Collaborative) was established to reduce waiting times in emergency departments and improve the experience of patients and carers. The NHS Modernisation Agency works with local teams in A&E departments across the country to learn from best practice and share examples of how they have improved.[10] In 2003 Jonathan Asbridge was appointed as the first National Director for Patient Experience in A&E. The Healthcare Commission reported on accident and emergency services in 2005 following a major review. Its recommendations include continued attempts to monitor and improve waiting times, and that extra funds should be made available to employ additional staff to fulfil specific purposes so that they can be deployed efficiently and effectively. NHS Trusts should review their services for children. The Emergency Workers (Obstruction) Act 2006 makes obstructing or hindering certain emergency workers (or those persons assisting emergency workers) responding to emergency circumstances a criminal offence. The definition of emergency worker includes a person employed by (or by an organisation supplying services to) an NHS body in the provision of ambulance services or of a person providing services for the transport of organs, blood, equipment or personnel made at the request of an NHS body.

NICE issued in September 2007 a clinical guideline on the triage, assessment, investigation and early management of head injury in infants, children and adults which is available on its website.

Giving information to patients

Additional precautions must thus be taken to ensure that, where the patient is not detained overnight, he has sufficient information to recognise any signs and symptoms that suggest a return to the hospital or to the general practitioner for further consultation and examination. Most hospitals already have pre-printed leaflets covering warnings in relation to head injuries, care of plaster, the need for anti-tetanus and other potential dangers. There is a need to stress, by word of mouth also, the importance of a patient following these instructions. If a patient ignored the instructions, having had clear advice from the staff, there is unlikely to be any blame on the part of the staff and certainly there may be a large element of contributory negligence on the part of the patient. Where information is given by word of mouth to the patient, one frequent concern of the staff is, 'How can I prove what I said since it is only the patient's word against mine?' This is always a dilemma in negligence cases, since no matter how strong the defendant's case would appear to be on paper, it still has to be proved through witnesses to the satisfaction of the courts. It is here that good record keeping is extremely important. If the nurse notes that the patient was given the relevant information, this does not in itself prove that he was since the records do not necessarily reflect what actually took place, but it does indicate the existence of a system where the nurse is more likely than not to have given the requisite information. In addition, of course, any witness who can recall the events and substantiate what the nurse was saying will undoubtedly help her. An additional precaution where it is essential to emphasise the importance of following the correct advice is for the patient himself to be asked to sign that he has understood the importance of obeying the instructions and has received written instructions (see also Chapter 4).

Relationship between duty of care owed by the GP and by the A&E department

Another difficulty that arises in the A&E department is the extent to which the department is used, inappropriately as far as the operational policy of the A&E department is concerned, as a GP surgery or health centre.

Practical Dilemma 21.2   **Minor ailments**

A patient came into the A&E department complaining of a pain in his ear. He was registered by the admission clerk and seen by a nurse, who then told him to wait to see the doctor. The doctor asked him how long he had had the pain and the man said that he had had it for about three days. He was asked if he had been to see his GP and he said that he was not sure who his GP was. The house officer suggested that he should go to see his GP and that he should not have come to the A&E department which was for emergency treatment of a serious kind. The man was very reluctant to go and very upset. It was subsequently learnt that he was admitted to the district general hospital with mastoid meningitis and an inquiry was established to find out why he had not been diagnosed in the A&E department.

The general principle would appear to be that once a patient comes through the doors, a duty of care is owed and the patient should not be sent away without an adequate examination. The words 'through the doors' are important, since a duty of care is not owed in a vacuum. It is perfectly possible for a hospital to say 'we do not accept A&E patients here' and refuse to treat a patient. However, once a hospital accepts a patient for attention, then a duty of care would arise to ensure that this patient receives the appropriate standard of care, even though it might mean arranging the transfer of the patient to another hospital or advising the patient to see his own GP. The new arrangements for deputising services and out of hours centres should ensure that A&E departments are not misused, but are kept for emergency treatments not appropriate for primary care services. Yet there is evidence that too many people are attending emergency service departments because of the reduced out-of-hours service provided by GPs.

Extent of duty of care

Practical Dilemma 21.3   **Referral for what?**

A patient was referred to the A&E department by the GP for X-ray because she had fallen and sustained a severe injury and considerable bruising to her leg. The house officer arranged for her to be X-rayed and it was found to be negative. The patient mentioned to the doctor that she was very short of breath and thirsty. However, only her leg was examined. She subsequently discovered that she was suffering from diabetes and claimed that the casualty officer should have diagnosed this.

This is another situation that raises the extent of the duty of care owed by the hospital staff to the patient. If the GP refers a patient for a very specific purpose, which is carried out, can it then be said that the patient should have been given a full examination so that other significant defects could have been detected? The answer must obviously depend on the particular circumstances and what the reasonably accepted approved practice is.

The clinical nurse specialist in the A&E department

Increasingly, protocols are being developed for a nurse specialist to work within the A&E department, seeing patients who are not examined by a doctor, prescribing on a limited scale and performing an expanded range of activities. The legal issues arising from this scope of professional practice are considered in Chapter 24. For the appointment of modern matrons in A&E departments, see Chapter 24.

Pressure to disclose confidential information

The basic principles relating to the disclosure of confidential information are discussed in Chapter 8. In that chapter, two examples are given of requests for information in A&E departments. Staff are under particular pressure in this respect, since they are likely to be hounded by both the police and the press in order that sensitive and personal information can be disclosed. The professions owe a duty to society, i.e. to act in the public interest, which may take precedence over any duty of confidentiality owed to the patient. However, the codes of professional conduct are couched in general terms and do not cover specific examples. The advice is that, where in doubt as to where the individual's duty lies, advice should be taken from the professional associations and the NMC. The statutory powers of the police under the Police and Criminal Evidence Act enable, in cases of serious arrestable offences, a special procedure to be followed to compel the production of personal information and human tissue which would otherwise be protected from disclosure. Some hospitals have different policies and procedures relating to disclosure in different circumstances and these vary in the degree of readiness with which this confidential information is disclosed. Whatever the policy, in the end it must be the individual professional's decision, since that individual may have to justify to the patient why confidentiality was not maintained.

Practical Dilemma 21.4   Road traffic accidents

The police are entitled to know the names and addresses of those who have been involved in a road traffic accident. This does not mean, however, that the media are also entitled to know these names or to know the condition of the patient. If the patient gives consent (and possibly the relatives, although this is more doubtful), then the information can be disclosed. If, however, this consent is refused, the hospital spokesman must remain silent as far as the disclosure of any confidential information is concerned. Once again, practice varies and there is an absence of court cases to settle the issue. For example, some hospitals allow a condition report to be given to the press without obtaining the consent of the patient, e.g. 'Of the ten persons injured in the motorway pile-up on Tuesday, one has since died, three have been discharged, four are comfortable and two are on life support machines.' There are few who would see this as a breach of confidence. Anyone (and this includes medical staff) who is aware of information about people involved in a road accident where personal injuries occurred has a duty to ensure that the police are notified.[11]

Patients' records come under the provisions of the Data Protection Act 1998 and are, of course, subject to close controls over disclosure. NHS trusts, PCTs and strategic health authorities should appoint a Caldicott Guardian to oversee standards of confidentiality within the organisation (see Chapter 8). Any concerns could be raised with that person, who should be on the board.

Aggression and violence in A&E

One major headache for A&E staff is the increasing problem of dealing with aggressive drunken patients and the rights of the staff either to claim compensation from the criminal courts (if there is a successful prosecution of the assailant) or claim from the Criminal Injuries Compensation Authority. These topics are considered in Chapter 12.

Problems relating to the unconscious patient and the patient who has attempted to commit suicide have been considered in Chapter 7 on consent to treatment.

Outpatients department

Excessive waiting

> **Practical Dilemma 21.5** **Waiting**
>
> Bruce was self-employed and time was money. He had been suffering from a severe pain and his doctor had referred him to the consultant surgeon querying gallstones or cholecystitis. He was sent an appointment to see the surgeon at 9.30 a.m. in outpatients. Because he had an important meeting that afternoon, which could involve him in a lot of valuable work, he phoned the clerk who assured him that the clinic ended at lunchtime. When he got to the clinic, he discovered that 30 people had been booked in for 9.30, most of whom had arrived before him. As he sat chatting, he discovered that others who had been booked in for 12.00 noon had come early, since they were seen in the order of arrival and not according to appointments. He settled down for a long wait and then was told at 1.00 p.m. that the surgeon had had to rush off to theatre to cover for a colleague who had been taken ill, but that if Bruce waited, the doctor would see him when the operation was over. Bruce said that he could not wait as he had a very important meeting. The clerk replied that if he went away he would be treated as a 'did not attend' and would have to take his place in the queue being seen in outpatients. He would not be able to give him an appointment for at least another three months. Bruce insisted on seeing the sister in charge.

Oddly enough, there seems to be no legal grounds for bringing an action against an NHS trust for causing excessive waiting in outpatients or in A&E departments. The Department of Health has set down targets to reduce waiting in A&E departments, but these are enforced through the complaints system, rather than through legal action. In private practice there would be a contract between professional and client and it could be more clearly argued that there was a breach of contract when a client was kept waiting an unreasonable length of time. However, in NHS care, there is no contract between the patient and the NHS trust or between the patient and the professional and the patient who is aggrieved at having to wait an unreasonably long time would have to argue that there was a breach of the duty of care owed to the patient under the laws of negligence that has caused him some loss or harm - a loss or harm that is compensateable under the law. There have been actions when patients have waited excessively long periods of time for inpatient treatment. However, no action has been brought in relation to a long wait within the department itself. Such a complaint is more likely to be investigated by the hospital management and be reviewed by the Healthcare Commission (CHAI) (see Chapter 27) or the Health Service Commissioner (i.e. ombudsman). The Health Service Commissioner has investigated many complaints of unreasonable waiting times in A&E, outpatients and other departments. The procedure for handling complaints is considered in Chapter 27. The Patient's Charter and local charters set targets for maximum waiting times. Compliance with these targets cannot be enforced in a court of law, but complaints can be made through the complaints procedure.

In the above practical dilemma, when the sister is confronted by a very disgruntled patient, she should ensure that the facts given by the clerk are accurate. It is unlikely, for example, that a patient who has been kept waiting in the way in which Bruce has should be treated as a 'did not attend'. If so, the system is manifestly unjust. The sister should be able, with cooperation from the doctor, to arrange for Bruce to be seen much earlier. In addition, she may be able to arrange a compromise by asking Bruce to attend the meeting and to return that same day. Certainly she should be able to take the heat out of the situation, explain the problems fully to Bruce, work out some acceptable solution and, of course, apologise to him for what has happened. This is not law, but it is good practice. However, there are many such occasions where the patient may or may not have a right of action in law where skilled counselling and cooperation with the patient prevents a situation developing into a court action or Health Service Commissioner's inquiry. The RCN has provided a guide to the competencies required by outpatient nurses.[12]

Mistaken identity

> ### Practical Dilemma 21.6   The wrong notes
>
> Sister Bailey was short staffed in the outpatients department and the situation was made worse by a strike among the coordinators. However, the consultants were adamant that the clinics should continue. She called out for one patient, Handel Thomas, to come to the diabetic clinic. She checked that he was from The Marina, Fish Street, and he said he was. He was asked if he had brought any samples with him and he replied: 'No, no one told me to.' He was then taken in to see the consultant. He was given a very full investigation and was asked how often he injected his insulin. He was a little surprised at this and replied that he had never been told to use insulin.
>
> After considerable confusion, during which time Handel was getting very disturbed, it emerged that there was another Handel Thomas in Fish Street. This Handel James Thomas lived at number 45 and was due to be seen in the eye clinic; the other Handel, Handel David Thomas from 2 Fish Street, should have been seen in the diabetic clinic.

In circumstances like this, there has been clear negligence by the sister in failing to check that she was taking the right patient to be seen and by the doctor who also did not check. However, apart from causing distress to the patient and a breach of confidentiality of information about the other patient, no harm has been caused to either, so it is not a case that is likely to end up in the courts. However, the potential implications of this type of mistake are terrifying and the tightest control must be kept over patient identification. Unfortunately, one cannot always rely on patients to point out the error since they can become institution-alised and frightened at the prospect of challenging the professionals and stories abound as to what they are prepared to submit to by mistake.

Genito-urinary medicine

Confidentiality

In a genito-urinary department (formerly known as the VD clinic or the 'special clinic'), strict confidentiality must be maintained. This section looks at some of the problems and pitfalls that can arise over confidentiality in this context and also at the statutory provisions.

Practical Dilemma 21.7) **A reasonable request**

Mr Grey had just visited the GUM clinic and samples had been taken. He was told that the results would be available by the Thursday of the following week. He was naturally anxious and, since he lived some 40 miles from the clinic, he phoned up late Thursday morning to find out the results. He gave his name and the nurse asked for his clinic number. She explained that it was on his card. He said that he had lost his card. She therefore told him that she would be unable to give him the result over the phone. He asked if that meant that the results were positive. She said not at all, but because of the principles of confidentiality, she could neither confirm that someone of that name had attended the clinic nor could she give any results over the phone without the clinic number. He became very angry, pointing out the inconvenience that he would suffer if he had to drive the 40 miles there and back, especially if the results were negative. She told him that she could not change the rules. He threatened to complain about her attitude and report her.

There is no doubt that the nurse is correct in not divulging information without being absolutely certain that she is talking to the patient. There are possible ways out of this dilemma. One would be for the nurse to phone a number that had already been given by the patient to the clinic for the notification of the results. The other would be to ensure that all patients are warned of the strict rules of confidentiality from the outset of their care so that they know the rules are firmly adhered to for their own protection, even in circumstances that cause them great inconvenience such as the one above.

A similar difficulty can be seen in Practical Dilemma 21.8.

Requests for information by a spouse

Practical Dilemma 21.8) **Spousely concern**

A man phoned the GUM clinic saying that he was the husband of Mrs Robinson, a patient who had an appointment at the clinic that afternoon. He said that she had lost her appointment card and forgotten the time and, since he was giving her a lift, could they let him know the time of the appointment?

This is the sort of request that few staff in a general outpatients department would hesitate to respond to helpfully. Yet, if confidentiality is to be preserved, it is essential that the person answering the phone does not admit to the fact (if this is indeed the case) that there is a patient of such a name attending the clinic.

Tracing

Obviously, it is essential that, as far as possible, any people who have been in contact with someone who is infected should be traced and advised to have tests. It is important that this be done without revealing the name of the contact. A form is completed to assist the clinic. If original contacts can be persuaded to advise their contacts to have a check, this is preferable to their receiving a call out of the blue.

Venereal disease regulations

These regulations (National Health Service (Venereal Diseases) Regulations 1974 Section 1 No. 29 (as amended by SI 1982 No. 288)) ensure that any information about any sexually transmitted disease is kept confidential. They came into operation on 1 April 1974 and place a duty on every health service body to take all necessary steps to secure that any information capable of identifying an individual obtained by officers of the authority with respect to persons examined or treated for any sexually transmitted disease shall not be disclosed. The exceptions to this rule are disclosures:

(a) for the purpose of communicating that information to a medical practitioner, or to a person employed under the direction of a medical practitioner in connection with the treatment of persons suffering from such disease or the prevention of the spread thereof

(b) for the purpose of such treatment or prevention.

It was suggested in the case of X v. Y and Another (1988)[13] that AIDS came within the scope of these regulations. See Chapter 26 for a consideration of the legal issues in AIDS and infectious diseases.

AIDS testing

The question as to whether the patient's consent is needed for an AIDS test to be carried out and whether it is possible to test secretly without the patient being told the results are discussed in Chapter 26.

Sexual health

The Department of Health initiated a sexual health strategy to reduce sexually transmitted diseases and to reduce unwanted pregnancies. As part of this initiative it published a guide for commissioning and planning.[14]

Day surgery

The NHS Plan saw an increase in day surgery as a means of helping the NHS achieve its targets of treating more patients faster and therefore a key strand of NHS modernisation and predicted that 75 per cent of all elective operations would be carried out as day cases.

This target has not yet been met. In 2001 the Audit Commission considered that day surgery units were not being used to their maximum capacity.[15] An operational guide has been published by the Department of Health[16] to improve efficiency in day surgery units. Funds are available from the NHS Modernisation Programme. Some of the problems identified by the Audit Commission and the British Association of Day Surgery include:

+ inappropriate and inefficient use of units (e.g. treating patients who could be cared for in a treatment room or outpatients)

+ poor management and organisation, especially in relation to the flow of patients

+ clinicians' preference for inpatient surgery

+ mixing of inpatients and day cases on the same list, leading to cancellations due to theatre overruns

+ failure to recognise day surgery as a priority.

All those areas of law that are the concern of inpatient care also apply to those working in day surgery. However, there are additional problems that can arise from the speed of turnover, the fact that patients are seen for a very short time and that significant decisions have to be made urgently. For example, crucial decisions have to be made about whether an operation is to proceed following the necessary tests; should the patient be admitted after surgery or could he/she be allowed to go home, and what information has to be given to the patient before the patient returns home. The pressure of work, the speed of patient throughput and the risk of harm arising means that clear protocols are necessary to ensure that patients receive a satisfactory standard of care and that they and their carers are given essential information pre- and post-surgery. The following is only one of the situations where complaints and litigation can arise. Reference must be made to earlier chapters setting out basic principles of law.

Practical Dilemma 21.9   Day surgery

Barbara was called for day surgery to have an operation for carpal tunnel syndrome. The operation was to be performed under a local anaesthetic. She was told to arrive by 9.00 a.m. even though she would be the last on the list. She waited for two hours before she was seen by a nurse, who then booked her in and told her that she should not have had any breakfast. Barbara queried this, as a general anaesthetic was not planned. The nurse said it was a precaution in case the operation could not be performed under a local anaesthetic. At 2.30 p.m. she was taken down for surgery and told that she must stay in the ward until 6.00 p.m. She asked for and was given a cup of tea at 4.00 p.m. Apart from that, she had no food or drink. No instructions were given to her for post-operative care. She considers that she has been treated poorly. What rights does she have?

This situation is more likely to lead to a complaint than to litigation. There is the possibility of a claim under Article 3 of the Convention on Human Rights (see Chapter 1 and Appendix A) in that she may have been given degrading or inhuman treatment. She is unlikely to benefit from civil litigation for compensation, unless there is long-term harm as a result of the failure to give her post-operative and post-discharge instructions. For example, if she should have been advised not to drive a car after the operation and, as a result of this omission, she was involved in an accident, then there would appear to be a breach of the duty of care owed to her. However, these deplorable circumstances might well be the subject of a complaint and it is hoped that as a result of the complaint there would be significant and substantial review of the procedures in place.

The Healthcare Commission reviewed services for day surgery in 2005 and concluded that there was scope to do much more day surgery within the capacity already available. It recommended that NHS trusts should maintain the momentum in improving the care of patients, and should work closely with clinicians within individual specialties to examine how more patients could be treated on a day surgery basis. It also recommended that trusts should use the recommendations in its local reports to increase the use of day surgery resources.[17]

Conclusions

The provision of A& E services is at the top of the political agenda for the Department of Health as new plans to centralise A&E services to cover wider catchment areas meet with public and professional opposition. The role of the nurse has expanded and continues to expand greatly in this frontline service. The scope of professional practice of the nurse is considered in Chapter 24.

Reflection questions

1 Does the nurse (or doctor) who works in the A&E department have a duty in law to assess the priority to be given to a patient and could she be held liable in the civil courts for failures in making that assessment?

2 Can a patient be lawfully refused treatment in an A&E department and be referred instead to his GP?

3 What remedy does a patient who has waited an excessive amount of time in the A&E department or the outpatients department have?

4 What precautions might be taken to preserve medical confidentiality in the A&E department in relation to:
   (a) the press
   (b) the police
   (c) other staff?

Further exercises

1 Do you consider that the spouse of a patient suffering from a sexually transmitted disease should have a right to be told of the spouse's medical condition? What is the law on this?

2 What remedies does a member of staff have who has been injured by a drunken patient in the A&E department? (See also Chapter 12.)

3 In what way does the duty of staff in A&E departments differ from the duty of those on the wards in relation to the care of the patient's property? (Refer also to Chapter 25.)

4 A patient is admitted into the A&E department with severe bleeding. His clothes have to be cut from him and because they are badly soiled they are sent for incineration. He subsequently complains that there was £300 in the pocket of his jacket. What is the liability of the hospital or of the A&E staff? (Refer to Chapter 25.)

5 A clinical nurse specialist who works in day surgery is asked if she would like to apply for a nurse consultant post in this speciality. What differences would she anticipate in these two roles? (Refer also to Chapter 24.)

References

[1] Royal College of Nursing, A&E: challenging the boundaries, Order No. 00459, RCN, November 1994

[2] Royal College of Nursing and Department of Health, Freedom to Practise: dispelling the myths, RCN and DH 2003

[3] Department of Health press release 2004/0058, Making See and Treat Work for Patients and Staff, 2004

[4] Department of Health, Clinical Exceptions to the four hour Emergency Care Target, DH, 2004

[5] Royal College of Physicians, Reforming Emergency Care, May 2005

[6] Department of Health, Emergency Care Practitioner Report – Right Skill, Right Time, Right Place, DH, 2004

[7] David Ross and Philip Webster, Half of all A&E units marked for closure, *The Times*, 17 May 2007, p. 1

[8] *Deacon* v. *McVicar and Another*, 7 January, available on Lexis (1984) QBD

[9] Department of Health, Handling Major Incidents – an operational doctrine, DH, 2004; www.dh.gov.uk/epcu/opdoctrine.htm

[10] www.dh.gov.uk/emergencycare/collaborative.htm

[11] *Hunter* v. *Mann* (1974) 1 QB 767

[12] Royal College of Nursing, Competencies: an integrated career and competency framework for outpatient nurses, Code 003 042, RCN, 2003

[13] *X* v. *Y and another* [1988] 2 All ER 648

[14] Department of Health, Health Economics of Sexual Health: A guide for Commissioning and Planning, DH, 2003

[15] Audit Commission, Report on Day Surgery, AC, 2001

[16] Department of Health, Day Surgery – operational guide, DH, 2002; available on www.dh.gov.uk/daysurgery/index.htm

[17] Healthcare Commission, Acute hospital portfolio review: Day Surgery, 2005, available on its website.

Chapter 22
Human fertility and genetics

This chapter discusses

+ Artificial insemination
+ Human Fertilisation and Embryology Act 1990
+ *In vitro* fertilisation
+ Embryos
+ Surrogacy
+ Conscientious objection
+ Confidentiality
+ Genetics
+ Gene therapy and genetic diagnosis
+ Gender selection
+ Genetic screening and testing
+ Cloning
+ Future developments

Introduction

Nurses are increasingly likely to be caring for patients in clinics and on the wards who are receiving treatment in connection with problems of fertility. Medical technology has made vast strides in this field and frequently outpaces the law. This chapter provides guidance on the current legislation relating to artificial insemination by donor, embryo implantation, surrogacy and genetic engineering. The legal problems that arise from sterilisation and family planning are considered in Chapter 15 and those relating to organ and tissue removal, donation and storage in Chapter 16. Genetic research using human tissue is considered in Chapter 18. The Human Fertilisation and Embryology Act 1990 introduced statutory controls in this field of medicine.

Artificial insemination

Artificial insemination by husband (AIH)

If a married couple require help in conception such that the husband's semen is artificially transferred to the wife, the law would see the outcome of this as being identical with natural conception. As far as such aspects as inheritance, legal guardianship of the child, etc. are concerned, there is no difference between the artificially and the naturally conceived child. However, the involvement of a third person raises the possibility of other legal issues. For example, it is possible that if a pathology laboratory is involved, there could be a mix-up over the semen and the woman could be given semen from someone other than her husband. With genetic coding, it would now be possible to prove that the child is not the husband's, although, of course, it must be remembered that in order to succeed in a negligence action it must be established that there was a causal link between the negligent act and the harm caused (the woman could have had sex with a third person). Some have opposed AIH on moral grounds, since it is an unnatural form of conception, but the Warnock Committee[1] were of the view that it was an acceptable form of treatment except where a widow used semen that had been stored in a semen bank. They felt that insemination after the husband's death could lead to profound psychological problems for the child and the mother. (See the Diana Blood case on page 521.) The Warnock Committee considered that there was no need or even practical possibility of formal regulation of AIH, but recommended that it should be administered by or under the supervision of a medical practitioner.

No licence is required under the 1990 Act for artificial insemination by the husband. Neither is one required for AIP (artificial insemination of an unmarried woman with her partner's sperm). Neither AIH nor AIP requires the use of donated gametes. GIFT (gamete intrafallopian transfer) does not require a licence if the egg and sperm come from the woman and her partner/husband. The European Court of Human Rights held that the refusal of access to artificial insemination facilities to a life-term prisoner was a disproportionate action by the state and a breach of his Article 8 rights.[2]

Artificial insemination by donor (AID)

Where the donor is not the husband, problems over legitimacy, rights to inheritance and the duties of the husband in relation to the child arise. A report from the Archbishop of Canterbury in 1948 recommended that AID should be made a criminal offence. The Feversham Report set up by the government in 1960 recommended that AID should be discouraged. The opposite has happened. In 1973 a panel under the chairmanship of Sir John Peel recommended the setting up of accreditation centres for AID, but this has not taken place. In an early case[3] (preceding the legislation of 1990), regarding the rights of the father, the father and mother had entered into an agreement that the girl would be artificially inseminated by him and then she would hand over the child on payment of £3,000. She refused to hand the child over and the trial judge gave the father limited rights of access. The Court of Appeal, however, gave him no rights of access.

Artificial insemination by donor is not unlawful, but, in contrast to the child born from AIH, the child born as a result of AID is illegitimate and the husband of the mother has no parental rights and duties in relation to the child, unless he accepts the child as a child of the family. The donor could be held responsible for the maintenance of the child and could apply to the court for access or custody. A consultation paper was published by the government in 1986. As yet, only a few of these recommendations have been implemented in law, one of which is the treating of a child born to a woman as the result of artificial insemination by someone other than her husband as the child of the parties of that marriage. This is enacted by Section 27 of the Family Reform Act 1987. The main condition is that the marriage must be in existence at the time. Proof to the satisfaction of the court that the other party to the marriage did not consent to the insemination will prevent this provision arising. This means that the burden is placed on the husband to show that the insemination was performed without his consent. This provision came into force in April 1988 and applies only to children born subsequently.

In a significant decision, a gay man who had provided sperm for the artificial insemination of a woman on the basis that they would share in the child's upbringing (neither was in a gay relationship at the time) won his application to have joint parental rights over the child. The mother had denied him access to his son, 2 years old, at the time of the court hearing.[4] In another case where a child was conceived to a partner in a lesbian relationship by having sexual intercourse with a man, the man was given parental responsibility subject to a preamble and specified conditions by the Family Division of the High Court.[5]

Anonymity of donors

There were two years of consultation on whether donors should be entitled to keep their anonymity or whether the offspring from donated gametes had a right to know the donors. A summary of the public consultation is available on the Internet.[6] In July 2003 the HFEA called for the removal of laws protecting the anonymity of all future sperm and egg donors and acknowledged the fundamental right of donor offspring to have knowledge of their genetic origins. In a report in *The Times*,[7] Baroness Warnock admitted that she had been wrong to recommend that anonymity should be preserved. Two cases held that Britain was violating Article 8 of the European Convention by depriving children of the right to obtain knowledge of their personal identity. Legislation to give children of sperm, embryo and egg donors the right to find out about their parents was proposed by the government in January 2004[8] and led to new rules[9] to lift anonymity from future donors and allow donor-conceived children to access the identity of their donor when they reach 18 years coming into force on 1 April 2005. These rules do not have retrospective effect. Neither do they create financial or legal obligations on the donor for the child. The HFEA issued guidance on the disclosure of information relating to gamete donation in 2004 following the new disclosure rules.[10] It lists the disclosures to donors which are permissible as long as the disclosure could not lead to the identification of a person whose identity should be protected. The information which could be disclosed includes telling a donor whether a live birth has resulted from the donation and, if so, the number of such births.

Safety of tissue and cells

Concern has been expressed by the Human Fertilisation and Embryology Authority (HFEA) over the purchase of sperm over the Internet. It was announced in January 2004 that the first baby had been born to a lesbian couple following conception by sperm obtained via the Internet. New rules came into force in July 2007[11] relating to standards on quality and safety for the donation, procurement, testing, processing, preservation, storage and distribution of tissues and cells which were set out in an EU directive in 2004.[12] Internet sperm providers must therefore be licensed by the HFEA or have a third party agreement with a licensed centre to ensure standards of quality and safety of the sperm.

Human Fertilisation and Embryology Act 1990

The Act was passed to implement the recommendations of the Warnock Committee.[13] A summary of the provisions of the 1990 Act is set out in the Statute below. It covers three main areas of activity:

1 licensed treatments, i.e. any fertility treatment that involves the use of donated eggs or sperm, or embryos created outside the body (i.e. IVF)

2 storage of eggs, sperm and embryos

3 research on human embryos.

Statute | **Provisions of the Human Fertilisation and Embryology Act 1990**

1 Definition of terms 'embryo' and 'gamete'.

2 Specific activities prohibited:
- Bringing about the creation of an embryo or keeping or using an embryo *except* in pursuance of a licence.
- Placing in a woman a live embryo other than a human embryo or any live gametes other than human gametes.
- A licence cannot authorise:
    (i) keeping or using an embryo after the appearance of the primitive streak, not later than 14 days after the gametes are mixed
    (ii) placing an embryo in any animal
    (iii) keeping or using an embryo in any circumstances in which regulations prohibit its keeping or use
    (iv) replacing a nucleus of a cell of an embryo with a nucleus taken from a cell of any person or embryo or subsequent development of an embryo.
- (i) No person can store gametes, provide treatment services for women (other than AID, AIP or GIFT), or mix gametes with live gametes of an animal, unless in pursuance of a licence.
    (ii) A licence cannot authorise storing or using gametes in any circumstances prohibited by regulations.

3 Human Fertilisation and Embryology Authority established with the function of:
- reviewing information about embryos and advising Secretary of State
- publicising services provided to public by HFEA or in pursuance of licences
- providing advice and information
- other functions specified in regulations
- monitor committees to grant licences
- to give directions.

Statute continued

4 Licences for treatment, storage, research and conditions of holding licence.

5 Code of practice to be issued by HFEA subject to Secretary of State's approval.

6 Definition of 'mother' and 'father'.

7 Register of information to be kept by HFEA with restriction on disclosure.

8 Amendments to Surrogacy Arrangements Act 1985 by providing that no surrogacy arrangement is enforceable by or against any of the persons making it.

9 Changes to Abortion Act 1967 (see Chapter 15).

10 Protection of those with conscientious objection (see page 525).

11 Powers of enforcement given to HFEA including power to enter premises.

12 Offences established.

In vitro fertilisation (IVF)

The Human Fertilisation and Embryology Act 1990 provides a framework for the control of the external fertilisation of an egg, extracted from the ovary, with semen. It covers the disposal of unwanted embryos, their ownership, power to undertake research on these embryos, embryo donation to another woman or genetic engineering to prevent hereditary disorders or to create a superhuman. Fertilisation outside the body coupled with transfer of the embryo into the uterus is, in its most simple form, a means of overcoming a fertility problem in a married couple. However, because of the possibility of egg and semen donation and subsequent transfer to a woman other than the provider of the egg, a complex situation can arise. In addition, it can be coupled with a surrogacy arrangement whereby a couple for whom the woman is unable to carry a child arrange for an embryo created from their egg and semen to be inserted into a host woman who will return the child to the genetic parents after birth. The surrogacy arrangements will be considered later (see pages 523-5). This part will deal with IVF and ET (embryo transfer to the uterus).

The majority of the Warnock Committee recommended a time limit of 14 days on research on an embryo because at about the 15th day after conception the formation of the primitive streak can be identified. This is the first of several identifiable features that develop in and from the embryonic disc during the succeeding days.

Refusal to permit IVF

In a case in 1987,[14] the High Court refused an application for judicial review of decisions by consultants who decided that a woman should be refused IVF treatment, on the grounds of past convictions and her prostitution. Section 13(5) of the 1990 Act makes it a condition of any licence that treatment services are not to be provided unless account has been taken of the welfare of the child who may be born as a result of the treatment (including the need of that child for a father) and of any other child who may be affected by the birth. The Code of Practice issued by HFEA gives further advice on how the licensed centres should assess these welfare issues and its guidance was updated in 2005.[15] In 1994 a 37-year-old woman was refused IVF treatment through the NHS on the grounds of her age.[16] Her application to the High Court to quash the health authority's decision failed on the grounds that, in the light of its limited resources, a health authority policy to set an age limit was not unreasonable. In the draft legislation to replace the 1990 Act a similar clause to 13(5) was included. The Joint Parliamentary Scrutiny Committee recommended that the requirement to consider the need of the child for a father should be put to a free vote in Parliament and possibly be replaced by the phrase 'the need for a second parent', but 'such a condition should not be a barrier to treatment'. The government agreed to remove that phrase from the draft Bill but stated that the general duty to take account of the welfare of the child should be included in primary legislation (see 'Future developments', pages 532–3).

The Court of Appeal overthrew the decision of the High Court in a case where a couple had agreed to have IVF treatment that was unsuccessful on the first attempt. The couple then separated, but the woman did not tell the clinic and then, on the next attempt, became pregnant. Her former partner sought a declaration that he was the child's legal father and wished to establish contact. The High Court ruled that he was the legal father of the 3-year-old girl. However, the woman's appeal succeeded. The Court of Appeal held that the wording of the 1990 Act meant that the partner of a woman receiving treatment with donor sperm will be the father of any resulting child only if the couple are receiving that treatment together, at the time that the sperm or embryo is placed in the womb. The House of Lords dismissed the appeal.[17]

A summary of the provisions of the Human Fertilisation and Embryology Act 1990 on IVF are set out in the Statute on pages 517–18. On 20 July 1994, the Human Fertilisation and Embryology Authority ruled that eggs from aborted foetuses could not be used in fertility treatment, but they could be used in research. The same ruling applies to the eggs of a dead woman, even though she is carrying a donor card. Guidance on the donation of sperm, eggs and embryos was published by the HFEA in January 2006 and implemented on 1 April 2006.[18] The SEED Report covers the adoption of professional standards for donor screening, greater clarity around the number of families that may be created using each donor and new guidance to help centres avoid exceeding this limit, new directions on the reimbursement of donors' expenses and compensation for loss of earnings, guidance on egg sharing and HFEA's policy on authorising imports and exports of gametes and embryos. The SEED Report can be downloaded from the HFEA website.[19] Following the SEED Report, the HFEA set out the principles which apply to the use of donated materials in research and incorporated them into the 7th edition of its Code of Practice which was published in October 2007.

An infertile man who attempted to become a legal father to a sperm-donor baby simply by signing his partner's IVF consent form failed when the Court of Appeal overruled a paternity declaration in his favour by a High Court judge.[20]

Obtaining fertility treatment within the NHS has varied from health authority to health authority, with some couples having to pay as much as £3,000 to obtain each private fertility treatment, while others are able to obtain the treatment on the NHS. In November 2000 the Secretary of State for Health asked the National Institute for Clinical Excellence (as it then was) (NICE, see Chapter 5) to review the various fertility treatments with a view to ending the postcode lottery and to draw up national guidelines for the provision of fertility treatment within the NHS. NICE reported in August 2003 and recommended that women between 23 and 29 should be entitled to free IVF treatment under the NHS. NICE guidelines on IVF were published in February 2004 and recommended that all women between the ages of 23 and 39 should be offered three cycles of IVF. Following this, the Department of Health recommended that initially women under 40 years who had been unable to conceive after two years should have one course of IVF treatment, if appropriate, under the NHS. In its response to the Joint Committee scrutiny of the new Human Tissue and Embryos (draft) Bill, the government stated that legislation was not an option to enforce NICE guidelines covering IVF treatment on primary care trusts and foundation trusts but the DH was funding a three-year programme of work that aims to reduce inequalities in the provision of IVF (see 'Future developments', pages 532-3).

Embryos

The 1990 Act prohibits certain actions in relation to the use of embryos (see Statute on pages 517-18). However, there were doubts as to whether the Act and therefore the HFEA prevented the use of embryos for stem cell research or human cloning. The definition of embryo has been the subject of dispute. Section 1 states that '(a) an embryo means a live human embryo where fertilisation is complete and (b) references to an embryo include an egg in the process of fertilisation'. The House of Lords held that organisms created by cell nuclear replacement (CNR) came within the definition of 'embryo' in Section 1(1) of the 1990 Act and accordingly were subject to regulation by the Human Fertilisation and Embryology Authority.[21] In the High Court[22] it had been held that live human embryos created outside the body by cell nuclear replacement (CNR) were not 'embryos' within Section 1 and accordingly were not subject to regulation under the Act. The Court of Appeal[23] allowed the appeal against this decision and the House of Lords dismissed the appeal against the decision of the Court of Appeal. In the light of the High Court decision (which meant that embryos created by CNR were not subject to the 1990 Act and therefore could be cloned) the Human Reproductive Cloning Act 2001 was passed and came into force on 4 December 2001 to prohibit the placing in a woman of a human embryo which has been created otherwise than by fertilisation. Proceedings can only be brought with the consent of the Director of Public Prosecutions. Regulations to enable research on stem cells to take place within the provisions of the 1990 Act[24] have been enacted (see page 531). These enable a licence to be issued for research for the purposes of increasing the knowledge about the development of embryos, increasing knowledge about serious disease or enabling any such knowledge to be applied in developing treatments for serious disease. The UK Stem Cell Bank has issued a Code of Practice on the use of stem cells but this has no legal force. Proposals to prevent research using hybrid embryos (formed from human and animal cells) which were to be included in new legislation were dropped following pressure from the scientific community (see 'Future developments', pages 532-3).

A new Section 3A was added to the 1990 Act (by the Criminal Justice and Public Order Act 1994) which prohibits the use of female germ cells derived from an embryo or foetus for the provision of treatment services for any woman.

Human Fertilisation and Embryology Authority (HFEA)

The Human Fertilisation and Embryology Authority was established under the provisions of the 1990 Act. It has the power to issue licences for centres to carry out IVF treatment and inspect them. It also issues a Code of Practice for the centres and provides guidance to the government on new areas for litigation and control.[25] The Human Genetics Advisory Commission (HGAC) operated from December 1996 to December 1999, providing the government with independent advice on issues arising from developments in human genetics. It published papers on: insurance and genetic testing (December 1997); cloning (December 1998); and employment and genetic testing (July 1999). It was replaced by the Human Genetics Commission (HGC) in December 1999, which also replaced the Advisory Committee on Genetic Testing and the Advisory Group on Scientific Advances in Genetics. The HGC has the remit of advising on necessary changes to the advisory and regulatory framework, of providing information and guidance to the minister on general issues in human genetics. Other non-statutory bodies advising in this area are: Gene Therapy Advisory Committee; Genetics and Insurance Committee; and the Nuffield Council on Bioethics, an independent body established by the trustees of the Nuffield Foundation in 1991 to consider the ethical issues arising from developments in medicine and biology.

The powers of HFEA to refuse to authorise the implantation of more than three embryos in a particular patient were challenged by the clinic.[26] The court refused the application holding that the court had no authority to intervene to quash the decision of HFEA in circumstances where careful and thorough consideration had been given to the matter and opinion provided that was plainly rational. While the decisions of the authority were open to judicial review, they were only amenable to such scrutiny in circumstances where the authority had either exceeded or abused its powers. HFEA issued a public consultation on the issue of multiple births after IVF in October 2007. At present it only permits a maximum of two embryos to be implanted and it is likely in view of the higher risk to both mother and baby from multiple births that in the future only one embryo for implantation would be permitted. The current limitation on a maximum of two embryos applies to treatment in both the NHS and private sectors.

Consent provisions for retrieval, storage and use of human gametes under the Human Fertilisation and Embryology Act 1990

Diane Blood was refused permission by the Human Fertilisation and Embryology Authority to use the stored sperm from her dead husband on the grounds that the husband had not given written consent for this use as required by the 1990 Act. She brought a case seeking judicial review of the Authority's refusal to license the infertility treatment. The sperm had been taken from her husband as he lay in a coma as a result of meningitis. The Court of Appeal[27] held that, as a result of the restrictions under the 1990 Act, she could not be lawfully treated with the sperm in this country. However, she would be permitted to receive treatment in Belgium according to Article 59 of the EC Treaty. She subsequently became pregnant and gave birth. Following this case, the Minister of Health appointed a committee under the chairmanship of Professor Sheila McLean to review the consent provisions in the Human Fertilisation and Embryology Act 1990. The committee sent out a questionnaire for public consultation and published its report in December 1998. In August 2000, the government published its response to the McLean Report.[28] It accepted all the recommendations of the report and went further, suggesting a retrospective effect. The proposed new Human Tissue and Embryo legislation should incorporate some of these recommendations.

1 The father's name should be allowed to appear on birth certificates where his sperm has been used after his death.

2 The legal position on consent and removal of gametes should remain unchanged: gametes can be taken from an incapacitated person who is likely to recover, if the removal of gametes is in their best interests.

3 The HFEA should have the power to permit the storage of gametes where consent has not been given, so long as the gametes have been lawfully removed. This will also benefit children who are about to undergo treatment that will affect their future fertility. (Legislation was required to implement this.)

4 Families will be able to make these birth certificate changes retrospectively.

5 The best practice is for written consent to be obtained, since this most clearly constitutes effective consent. Where there is doubt over whether an effective consent has been obtained, this should be a matter for the courts.

The government has not recommended that there should be any legislative change over permitting the export of gametes that have been removed lawfully, since the Court of Appeal in the Diane Blood case held that sperm stored with consent can be the subject of export. The legal situation will be reviewed in the debates on the new Human Tissue and Embryo Bill.

Subsequently Diane Blood won her claim to have her late husband legally recognised as the father of her two sons, when the Department of Health dropped its opposition.[29] The judge accepted that her inability to name her deceased husband as the father of her children was contrary to her human rights and he ordered the Department of Health to pay Mrs Blood's £20,000 legal costs. The Human Fertilisation and Embryology (Deceased Fathers) Act 2003, which came into force on 1 December 2003, specifies the circumstances in which a deceased father can be recorded on the birth certificate.

The strict wording of the 1990 Act in relation to consent by both parties to the use of the gametes was applied by the High Court in a case[30] where couples who had agreed that embryos could be created and stored then disagreed over their later disposal. One woman placed six frozen embryos into storage before she had cancer treatment. The judge held that the court had no power to override the unconditional statutory right of either party to withdraw or vary consent to the use of embryos in connection with *in vitro* fertilisation treatment at any time before the fertilised embryo was implanted in the woman. In addition, where consent for treatment had originally been given for treatment together with a named partner, that consent remained neither effective nor valid once the parties ceased to be together. Ms Evans lost her appeal to the Court of Appeal in June 2004.[31] Her application to the ECHR for breach of Articles 2, 8 and 14 failed but a dissenting judgment held that there had been a breach of Article 8 and Article 14 in conjunction with Article 8.[32]

In another case,[33] a woman appealed against the decision of the High Court that sperm of her deceased husband should be allowed to perish or be destroyed. The Court of Appeal held, in applying the provisions relating to consent to the storage and use of gametes under Sections 4(1)(a) and 11 and Schedule 3 of the 1990 Act, that the centre was entitled to rely on a form that gave consent to the perishing of the sperm and embryos in the event of death or mental incapacities. The Court of Appeal held that there was no evidence of undue influence by the centre and, without an effective consent by the husband, the continued storage and later use of his sperm by the centre would be unlawful. The husband had initially agreed that the sperm could be used after his death, but subsequently withdrew this consent at the request of a specialist nursing sister.

Criminal offences and civil wrongs with embryos

The Court had to rule in a case where, at the assisted conception unit of Leeds General Infirmary, eggs were inadvertently fertilised by the wrong man's sperm and as a result mixed race twins were born to white parents Mr and Mrs A. Both couples Mr and Mrs A and Mr and Mrs B were having IVF treatment. The biological father Mr B wished to be declared the legal father of the twins. Dame Elizabeth Butler-Sloss, President of the Family Division, held that Mr B was the twins' legal father. The husband of a mother whose child is born after treatment with another man's sperm is the child's legal father, providing the husband consented to the treatment. Although Mr A had consented to his wife's treatment, he had not consented to the use of another man's sperm. The judge held that the twins' rights to respect for their family life with their mother and Mr A could be met by appropriate family or adoption orders and those orders would be proportionate to the infringements of those rights.[34]

Another mishap occurred in Bristol when frozen sperm from 28 cancer patients whose treatment may have left them sterile was destroyed when a freezer unit broke down. An inquiry was set up.[35] In a criminal case an embryologist was jailed for 18 months for deceiving couples by giving them test tubes containing saline solution instead of embryos.[36] HFEA issued guidelines on the storage of sperm, eggs and embryos in June 2004.

Surrogacy

This might be thought, like IVF, to be a result of the recent developments in medical technology. However, the biblical story of Abraham resorting to the servant who could bear a child for him because Sarah was barren is an early example of one form of surrogacy. The possibility of embryo implantation has, however, increased the number of ways in which surrogacy can take place. The child that is born might have no genetic relationship with the ultimate parents, but be the natural child of the bearing mother or even an embryo from two donors. More likely, however, is the situation where the child is genetically related to the father as a result of artificial insemination, but not to the adopting mother. Prior to the Warnock Report, the only legislation that covered a surrogacy situation was the childcare legislation and rules relating to adoption. Section 50, for example, of the Adoption Act 1958 prohibits any payment in connection with adoption. Such surrogate cases as Baby Cotton[37] revealed the gaps in the law and the uncertainties surrounding basic questions. Is a contract for surrogacy enforceable by either party, neither party or only by the mother? What are the legal implications if the child is handicapped? What controls do the contracting couple have over the standard of life of the mother during the pregnancy, e.g. what if she smokes or drinks heavily? If she changes her mind and has an abortion, are damages then payable?

Case 22.1 — In Re An Adoption (Surrogacy) (1987)

A surrogacy dispute[38]

Mr and Mrs A were unable to have children and, because of their age, had been refused as adoptive parents. They entered into a surrogacy arrangement with Mrs B who wished to help the childless couple. Under the arrangement, it was agreed that Mr and Mrs A would pay £10,000 to Mrs B who would give up her job to have the child. In due course, a child was conceived, but in the event Mrs B accepted only £5,000 and refused the balance. It was clear that the amount did not cover Mrs B's loss of earnings and expenses. After the birth, Mr and Mrs A applied to court for an adoption order. The question arose (a) whether the payment of money had been a payment of reward for adoption within the meaning of the Adoption Act Section 50(1) and (b) if there had been a contravention of the section, whether the court could make a retrospective authorisation in respect of the payment under Section 50(3) of the Act and grant an adoption order.

In Case 22.1 it was held that a payment to the mother in a surrogacy arrangement did not contravene the Act if payments made by those others to the natural mother did not include an element of profit or financial reward. Even if they were made for reward, the court had a discretion under the Act to authorise the payments retrospectively. The court granted the adoption order.

The Surrogacy Arrangements Act 1985 prohibits the making of surrogacy arrangements on a commercial basis. Those companies that had come over from the USA and started to arrange surrogacy contracts were thus forced out of business in the UK. This approach had been recommended by the Warnock Committee, whose recommendations, however, went further and suggested that both profit- and non-profit-making organisations should be made illegal and also that any professional who knowingly assisted in the establishment of a surrogacy pregnancy should be criminally liable. They recommended that all surrogacy arrangements should be held illegal and unenforceable in the courts. Section 36(i) of the Human Fertilisation and Embryology Act 1990 amended the 1985 Act to make a surrogacy arrangement unenforceable. It did not make it illegal.

The 1990 Act Section 30 enables a court to order a child to be treated as a child to the parties of the marriage where another woman has acted as surrogate, provided that certain conditions are met. In a case in 1996,[39] a couple applied under Section 30 for a parental order in respect of a child who was born following a surrogacy arrangement. It was agreed that the unmarried woman would receive £8,280 to cover her expenses and loss of earnings. The High Court judge was satisfied that the requirements of Section 30 were met. In particular, the mother had given consent (although she admitted to tearing her copy in half) and the payments were reasonable and could be granted retrospectively. In this case, there was no man who was to be treated as the father and whose consent was required. In a recent case in 2007 a couple, Mr and Mrs J agreed a surrogacy arrangement whereby Mrs P was fertilised by Mr J's sperm. However, Mrs P refused to hand over the child and brought him up as her own chld. At the time of the hearing the child was 17 months old. The court awarded custody to the couple and ordered Mrs P to hand over the boy to them. The judge found that Mrs P was motivated by a compulsive desire to bear further children and never intended to let Mr J have the child. The Court of Appeal dismissed Mrs P's appeal. A collection order was made by the Court of Appeal empowering High Court staff to travel to Bristol with Mr J to oversee the handover of the child.[40]

In 1997, Professor Margaret Brazier was appointed by the Department of Health to review the existing law relating to surrogacy arrangements. The terms of reference included whether payments for expenses should continue to be allowed; whether there was a case for the regulation of surrogacy arrangements through a recognised body and to advise on whether any changes were necessary to the 1985 Act and Section 30 of the Human Fertilisation and Embryology Act 1990. An extensive consultation exercise was undertaken and subsequently the Brazier Report recommended that the Surrogacy Arrangements Act 1985 and Section 30 of the 1990 Act (see above) should be replaced by new legislation and a code of practice on surrogacy should be drawn up by the Department of Health. The extent to which the Brazier recommendations will be implemented will be seen following the review of the 1990 Act which is taking place at the time of writing. The Joint Parliamentary Scrutiny Committee reviewing the draft Bill recommended that it be amended to bring the regulation of surrogacy within the remit of the HFEA. The government was wary of this recommendation and will consult further on the benefits and disadvantages of further regulation of surrogacy.

Compensation amounts and surrogacy

In a case in 2000,[41] a woman claimed compensation as a result of medical negligence that led to a stillborn child and a subtotal hysterectomy. The defendant health authority accepted liability, but damages were disputed. She claimed in addition to damages for pain, suffering and loss of amenity, compensation for the post-traumatic stress disorder as a result of the stillbirth and hysterectomy, loss of earnings and the cost of surrogacy. The court held that she would be awarded £66,000 for the infertility and the accompanying psychological condition. It refused, however, to compensate her for loss of earnings, since it held that regardless of the stillbirth and hysterectomy, she would not have been able to start her training as a teacher earlier; the court also refused the cost of surrogacy, which the claimant was arranging in the USA. The judge held that under the present UK law surrogacy arrangements were unenforceable and, if commercial, illegal. It would therefore be wrong, and contrary to public policy, that damages should be awarded to enable an unenforceable and unlawful contract to be entered into. The judge did not conclude that it would always be wrong to award damages for the cost of surrogacy, but in the claimant's particular circumstances, she could not succeed.

Conscientious objection

The nurse's personal moral beliefs are taken into account by Section 38 of the Human Fertilisation and Embryology Act 1990, which provides a conscientious objection clause as follows:

1 No person who has a conscientious objection to participating in any activity governed by this Act shall be under any duty, however arising, to do so.

2 In any legal proceedings, the burden of proof of conscientious objection shall rest on the person claiming to rely on it.

3 In any proceedings before a court in Scotland, a statement on oath by any person to the effect that he has a conscientious objection to participating in a particular activity governed by the Act shall be sufficient evidence of that fact for the purpose of discharging the burden of proof imposed by subsection (2) above.

Confidentiality

Section 33 of the 1990 Act placed tight restrictions on the disclosure of information held by the HFEA or a licensing authority. The few exceptions to these restrictions were considered to be inadequate and the Human Fertilisation and Embryology (Disclosure of Information) Act 1992 was passed, amending Section 33 as follows: to enable the patient to give specific and general consent to disclosure; for information to be disclosed by a clinician to his legal adviser in relation to legal proceedings (the 1990 Act had permitted disclosures only in relation to action under the Congenital Disabilities (Civil Liability) Act 1976); and for a couple to obtain information about the legal parentage of a child born to a surrogate mother. A Statutory Instrument[42] restricts the right of access to health records that would disclose information showing that an unidentifiable individual was or might have been born in consequence of treatment services under the Human Fertilisation and Embryology Act 1990. This does not affect the right given by Section 31(3), which enables a person of 18 or over to obtain information from HFEA if that person was born in consequence of treatment services, but an opportunity for proper counselling must be provided before disclosure. The legislation to replace the 1990 Act may allow those over 16 years to obtain non-identifying information from HFEA.

Genetics

Considerable progress has been made in the science of gene identification. The Human Genome Project was an international collaboration by the US government and the Wellcome Trust that started in 1990. It aimed to identify every gene in the human body. At the same time, a private company, Celera Genomics Corp headed by Craig Venter, was pursuing the same object. The project was completed on 26 July 2000 when a dead heat was claimed between the two rival organisations. The mapping of the human genome was declared complete in April 2003, two years ahead of schedule,[43] producing a 'book of life' containing 2.9 billion 'letters' of human DNA. Genes linked with some specific hereditary diseases have now been identified. One of the first genes to be linked with a specific disease was that of cystic fibrosis. Subsequently, there have been claims of genetic links with a wide range of medical conditions and human qualities and characteristics. For example, claims have been made for genetic links for sleeplessness,[44] for heart disease,[45] for dyslexia,[46,47] for hibernation,[48] for diseases of old age,[49] for autism,[50] for early menopause,[51] for asthma[52] and many other disorders and characteristics. These discoveries present many ethical and legal issues: to what extent should parents have the right to modify the genetic inheritance of their children? What controls should there be over individuals purchasing commercial testing kits? Should insurers have the right to compel those seeking insurance to be tested? Baroness Kennedy was appointed by the government to head an inquiry into the implications of the mapping of the human genetic code. A White Paper on genetics was published in June 2003.[53] Its aim was to set out a vision of how patients could benefit in future from advances in genetics in healthcare. It presented a comprehensive plan for preparing the NHS, including the investment of £50 million over the next three years, to realise the benefits of genetics in healthcare. Initiatives included the upgrading of laboratories and increase in the numbers of health professionals involved in genetics including counsellors, consultants and scientists; a new genetics education and development centre and new research programmes in pharmacogenetics, gene therapy and health services research. The Human Genetics Commission and the National Screening Committee studied the ethical, social, scientific, economic and practical considerations of screening and its report[54] Choosing the Future was published in 2004. In November 2007 the HGC began preparation for a citizen's inquiry into the use of DNA, details of which are available on its website.

Genetic testing for pregnant women

Which pregnant women should be offered genetic testing? The Human Genetics Commission[55] has issued guidance for consultation on behalf of the former Advisory Committee on Genetic Testing, whose work it has taken over. The guidance suggests that women should have access to prenatal genetic tests and the expertise she requires appropriate to her risk. There should be resources in primary care and hospitals for referral and subsequent care of the patient. Prenatal genetic testing for rare disorders should be arranged on a supra-regional or national level.

Gene therapy and genetic diagnosis

The Clothier Committee[56] recommended that research should continue for somatic cell gene therapy where treatment is given to an individual patient to alleviate disease (e.g. cystic fibrosis). However, germ-line gene therapy, where future generations are affected, should not as yet be lawful. It recommended the establishment of a supervisory body, the Gene Therapy Advisory Committee (GTAC). In its ninth annual report (which is available online)[57] the GTAC reviewed the use of gene therapy in treating children with X-SCID (leukaemia had developed in two of the children treated with gene therapy) and recommended that recruitment into the trials should only be on a case-by-case basis. The United Kingdom Ethics

Committee Authority recognised GTAC as the UK research ethics committee for all gene trials under the new legislation governing clinical trials (see Chapter 18, page 444). The GTAC issued guidance in 2004 on gene therapy. It must be approved by GTAC, must not interfere with the germ-line and must not put patients at disproportionate risk.[58] In its 13th annual report it stated that it considered 14 applications for gene therapy clinical trials and they were all approved or conditionally approved. Around 1,300 patients had been enrolled on to UK gene therapy trials by December 2006. The report is available on the GTAC website.[59]

The Human Fertilisation and Embryology Authority and the Advisory Committee on Genetic Testing established in 1998 a joint working group to prepare a consultation paper on pre-implantation genetic diagnosis (PGD). This paper was published in November 1999.[60] Pre-implantation refers to the two-stage process in which IVF is used to create embryos that are then tested for a particular genetic disorder or to establish their sex (where the disorder is sex linked). Embryos that do not carry the genetic disorder or are not of the potentially affected sex can then be transferred to the uterus in the hope that a pregnancy of a child without the hereditary condition will develop. Four centres in the UK are licensed to carry out PGD. Testing for CF is the most common reason for pre-implantation diagnosis for a single gene defect. However, there are concerns about the range of conditions for which PGD should be licensed, at the seriousness of the condition to be checked for, whether the late onset of a condition should be taken into account and what the nature of the regulation should be.

PGD has also been used in circumstances where parents wish to have a child who would be compatible with and therefore of life-saving assistance for a sibling who is suffering from a genetic disease. Several cases have been contested.

Case 22.2 — R (Quintavalle) v. HFEA (2002–5)

Tissue typing for the benefit of a sibling[61]

Raj and Shahana Hashmi wished to bear a child who would be free of the genetic blood disorder, beta thalassaemia major, and whose tissue type would match that of their young son Zain, who suffered from the life-threatening disorder. They hoped that stem cells from blood taken from the umbilical cord of a newborn baby with matching tissue would cure their son. They applied to HFEA for a licence for PGD. HFEA decided that tissue typing would only be permitted where PGD was already necessary to avoid the passing on of a serious genetic disorder and that licences would be granted on a case-by-case basis and on certain conditions. HFEA granted a licence permitting PGD and tissue typing as part of the couple's *in vitro* fertilisation treatment. The granting of the licence was challenged by Josephine Quintavalle on behalf of Comment on Reproductive Ethics who succeeded in an application for judicial review of the lawfulness of HFEA actions. HFEA appealed to the Court of Appeal.

The Court of Appeal held that HFEA had the power to grant a licence to permit simultaneous tests to be carried out on an embryo for the purpose not only of identifying genetic defects in the embryo but also of ascertaining whether the tissue type of the embryo would match that of an existing child. The House of Lords dismissed the appeal against the Court of Appeal ruling and held that HFEA's discretion to award a licence for tissue typing of an embryo was not limited to its testing for defects in the embryo.

In a case that contrasts with Case 22.2, the HFEA turned down the application from the Witakers to use IVF techniques to select a baby who would be a perfect tissue match for Charlie, aged 3, who had a rare blood disorder and required a bone marrow transplant.

HFEA refused the application because embryos may be screened only if they might carry a serious genetic risk.[62] The Witakers subsequently obtained treatment in the USA.

These issues were the subject of an extensive consultation by HFEA which published its report in July 2004.[63] It concluded that balancing the likely benefit of pre-implantation tissue typing – to the sick sibling, the new baby and the family as a whole – against a better understanding of the possible physical and psychological risk to the child to be born, pre-implantation tissue typing should be available subject to appropriate safeguards, in cases in which there is a genuine need for potential life-saving tissue and a likelihood of therapeutic benefit for an affected child. The Human Genetics Commission published in January 2006 Making Babies,[64] an overview of reproductive decisions and genetic technologies. One of its many significant recommendations and conclusions was that the anxiety that PGD lies at the slippery slope leading to the possibility of a wide range of potential enhancements, such as intelligence or beauty, is misplaced.

The government has agreed that provision will be included in the revised Bill which replaces the 1990 Act that selecting for saviour siblings should not be limited to 'life-threatening' conditions, but only to 'serious' conditions (see 'Future developments', pages 532–3).

Gender selection

To what extent should parents be able to select the sex of their children? Certainly in some cultures, parental selection could lead to an oversupply of boys and very few girls, but there may be justification for it when hereditary diseases, such as haemophilia, are sex linked. A commercial organisation has been set up to assist couples in obtaining the gender of their choice for their child. Where this does not involve gametes of other persons, it does not come under the provision of the 1990 Act. Some consider, however, that there should be controls in this field. A public consultation paper was issued by the Human Fertilisation and Embryology Authority in January 1993.[65] In November 2003 the HFEA announced its recommendations on sex selection.[66] It found from its survey that public opposition to sex selection for non-medical reasons was clear and consistent. Its recommendations were:

+ Sex selection for non-medical reasons should not be permitted.

+ Centres should be permitted to offer treatment with sperm that has been subjected to flow cytometry (whether alone or in combination with PGD) only to patients with clear medical reasons and subject to licences from the HFEA.

+ Before they consent to treatment, those seeking sex selection should be given clear information and the opportunity to receive counselling about the implications of the procedure.

+ Treatment should not be provided unless a thorough assessment of the welfare of the child has been conducted. This assessment should include any child born as a result of treatment and any other child that may be affected by the birth.

+ Detailed information should be collected relating to all treatments and outcomes where sperm sorting is used. This will allow follow-up studies to assess whether there are any long-term risks and consider the effectiveness of sperm-sorting techniques.

+ Treatment using sperm that has been subjected to gradient methods should not be used for either medical or non-medical purposes.

As a result of the Tissue and Cells Directive, which came into force in July 2007 (see page 517),[67] sperm-sorting services are now subject to regulation.

Genetic screening and testing

Concern at the possibility that insurers and employers would require compulsory genetic screening led to the Nuffield Council on Bioethics reporting on the ethical issues involved in genetic screening. It recommended safeguards in relation to consent, confidentiality and monitoring of genetic screening programmes.[68]

A moratorium has been agreed between the government and the Association of British Insurers on the use of predictive genetic test results (see below).

Commercial screening kits

Do-it-yourself genetic screening test kits are now available and have raised considerable ethical concerns. 'A Code of Practice and Guidance on Human Genetic Testing' was published on 23 September 1997 by the health departments of the United Kingdom.[69] It was put forward by the Advisory Committee on Genetic Testing (ACGT) on the basis of proposals prepared by a subgroup (chaired by Professor Marcus Pembrey). It recommended that a voluntary system of compliance and monitoring should be established rather than a statutory scheme. The Code of Practice and Guidance is intended to be used by those who supply genetic testing services direct to the public. The Code itself covers the following areas: testing laboratories, equipment and reagents; confidentiality and storage of samples and records; proposed tests should be cleared with the ACGT and comply with the Code; tests should not be available to those under 16 years or to those unable to make a competent decision regarding testing; specified information should be provided to the customer; pre- and post-test genetic consultation should be available without additional charge; and, finally, the involvement of medical practitioners. Suggested forms for use by the suppliers are provided as well as addresses of the regional genetic centres and other relevant organisations. If the main users of the testing services are national organisations, and there is little private commerce, then there will be strong commercial reasons for the firms to comply with this guidance and quality standards, otherwise they stand to lose lucrative contracts. The attitudes of the suppliers and the purchasers will also influence the extent to which some of the guidelines become mere tokenism: the supplier is required to provide opportunities for pre- or post-testing genetic consultation (which is widely defined). In practice, this may become a formality (a quick phone call) and, after all, the purchaser might refuse to cooperate.

This voluntary code may work, given suppliers who have goodwill and purchasers who are well informed, without the necessity of statutory controls and criminal sanctions. The Advisory Committee on Genetic Testing requires companies selling the kits to submit them for prior approval, but it has no statutory powers and its guidelines are not enforceable.

Code of Practice on genetic tests from the insurers

The Association of British Insurers published a Code of Practice in 1997. It made further revisions to it in 1999.[70] It is a voluntary code for insurers over genetic tests and gives the following guidance:

1 It should not require a person to take a genetic test in order to obtain insurance cover.
2 If the results of a genetic test are in a person's medical records, they can be taken into account only if they apply to one of seven conditions for which the tests are deemed reliable. (These conditions include breast cancer, Alzheimer's and Huntingdon's chorea.)

3 If the test is later found to be unreliable, the person is entitled to a refund of overpaid premiums and cheaper future payments.

4 A person is obliged to tell an insurance company if he has had a genetic test and disclose the results.

5 Anyone refused insurance cover or who wishes to complain can contact the ABI.[71]

Some evidence is emerging that contrary to the assertion of the ABI, some people are being refused insurance cover on the grounds that they have a genetic disorder.[72,73] It may be that either statutory intervention or some form of state insurance cover is necessary to protect those who are vulnerable. In October 2000, new guidelines were recommended by a genetics and insurance committee established by the Department of Health.[74] The committee recommended that the reliability and relevance of the genetic test for Huntingdon's chorea is sufficient for insurance companies to use the result when assessing applications for life insurance. Insurers will not be able to require prospective clients to take the test, but they will be able to ask clients if they have taken tests for Huntingdon's chorea and to ask for the results to be given. The recommendations have been criticised, for example by the National Consumer Council, on the grounds that they will create a genetic underclass and will dissuade people from taking the tests.[75] In addition, scientists are fearful that potential volunteers for genetic tests will refuse to cooperate in this country. Thus many scientists would have no option but to work outside this country, where potential research subjects would not have to disclose results to insurance companies.[76] The Human Genetics Commission has endorsed a regime of self-regulation for companies supplying genetic tests to the public but their recommendations were criticised by Human Genetics Alert and GeneWatch UK.[77] In April 2003 the Human Genetics Commission issued a report saying that direct sales of such tests raised serious questions and that a 'robust but flexible' regulatory system needed to be established to control them. The HGC did not recommend an outright ban as people have the right to information about themselves, but they did want to ensure proper protection. They recommended that genetic tests should be carried out under the supervision of a doctor within the NHS.[78]

In 2005 the Department of Health and the Association of British Insurers agreed a moratorium on the use of predictive genetic test results which has been extended to 2011. The moratorium applies to life insurance policies up to £500,000 and critical illness, long-term care and income protection up to £300,000.

Genetics and confidentiality

The identification of genes linked to disabilities has raised serious legal and ethical issues as the following practical dilemma illustrates.

Practical Dilemma 22.1   **Concealing information**

Mavis undergoes a genetic test and discovers that she is carrying a gene that is linked with Huntingdon's chorea. Her sister, Rachel, has just got married and Mavis knows her sister intends having children and that both her sister and any children could be at risk of suffering from that disease. Mavis decides that she will keep this information to herself.

In this situation, the ordinary laws of confidentiality (see Chapter 8) apply. There are no specific statutes that require the testers to disclose the results to any members of the family. If Rachel were unaware that there is a family risk of Huntingdon's chorea, she would not have the grounds to have herself tested or to seek a disclosure of the results of the test on Mavis. By the time Rachel has had her children and maybe finds that she is suffering from or is a carrier of the disease, it is too late to take preventive action. (Had she known of the risk, she could have opted for the testing of embryos before implantation – see page 527.)

Cloning

In 1997 Dolly the sheep became the first vertebrate cloned from a cell of an adult animal. Because of the immense significance of this scientific development, the Human Genetics Advisory Commission set up a working group and held a consultation exercise on cloning. It issued a consultation paper in 1998.[79] Following this exercise, HFEA recommended that research should continue into creating cloned tissue that can be transplanted, but that cloning for reproductive purposes should continue to be illegal.[80]

Following the report of the Chief Medical Officer's expert group on therapeutic cloning,[81] the government accepted its recommendations (press announcement, 16 August 2000) and agreed that:

1 The currently permitted grounds for embryo research will include treatment for a range of human diseases and research on human embryonic stem cells should be permitted. (At present research on embryos is restricted to the first 14 days and is permitted for five specific purposes relating to infertility, congenital disease, gene or chromosomal abnormalities, miscarriage or contraception. Additional purposes can be added by Statutory Instrument.)

2 Research involving cell nuclear replacement (so-called 'therapeutic cloning') should be allowed to help understand the biological mechanisms involved in the growth and development of human cells.

3 Specific consent must be given before early embryos can be donated for stem cell research.

On 19 December 2000 the House of Commons passed secondary legislation legalising research on the stem cells of embryos and the House of Lords approved the changes in 2001. A Statutory Instrument was enacted in 2001.[82] This means that it is possible for stem cells to be used in the research for illnesses such a cancer, Parkinson's disease, diabetes, osteoporosis, spinal cord injuries, Alzheimer's, leukaemia and multiple sclerosis. A licence is required from the Human Fertilisation and Embryology Authority and the cloning of human beings for reproductive purposes remains illegal (see page 520).

The United Nations voted in November 2003 not to ban all forms of cloning. This led to a statement by the Department of Health[83] that welcomed the United Nations decision, seeing it as a victory for the UK position. The UK is firmly against reproductive cloning but it believed that therapeutic cloning research offers enormous potential to develop cures for serious diseases such as Alzheimer's, Parkinson's and heart disease and this therapeutic cloning is strictly controlled under licence from the HFEA. In January 2004 a claim was made by Dr Zavos, an American scientist, that he had implanted a cloned embryo in a woman's womb. This led to the president of the Royal Society and other top scientists appealing for a worldwide ban on human reproductive cloning.[84] Under the revised proposals being debated in Parliament in 2008 are the use of inter-species embryos for research, with the power given to the Regulator to permit or refuse licenses in relation to all inter-species embryos.

Future developments

The scientific developments which have taken place since the 1990 Act was drafted have meant that revised legislation is long overdue. A White Paper[85] was published in December 2006 following extended consultation and a draft Human Tissue and Embryos Bill was published in May 2007 and subjected to scrutiny by a committee of both Houses. The government response to the Joint Committee's report was published in October 2007.[86] The Joint Committee rejected the following proposals in the draft Bill:

+ The merger of the Human Fertilisation and Embrylogy Authority and the Human Tissue Authority into the Regulatory Authority for Tissue and Embryos (RATE)
+ The prohibition on the creation and use of inter-species embryos for research
+ The removal of the requirement to take account of the need for the child for a father from the current conditions of every licence to provide IVF treatment services. (The need for a second parent should be considered)
+ A joint committee on bioethics should be established.

In response to these criticisms by the Joint Committee, the government:

+ accepted the recommendation to retain the two separate authorities, but would look at the scope for the two authorities to streamline legislation;
+ welcomed the recommendation that primary care trusts and Foundation Trusts implement NICE guidance on minimum levels of IVF treatment, and accepted that whilst this is not a matter for legislation, the DH was funding a three-year programme of work (being carried out by Infertility Network UK) that aims to reduce inequalities in the provision of IVF;
+ agreed that the use of inter-species embryos for research could be put before Parliament, with the power given to the Regulator to permit or refuse licenses in relation to all inter-species embryos;
+ agreed that a permitted embryo could only be implanted if it was from the genetic material of a woman and a man, and not from two women;
+ agreed that selecting for saviour siblings should not be limited to 'life-threatening' conditions, but only to 'serious' conditions;
+ sex selection should only be for medical reasons in accordance with current HFEA policy;
+ use of an embryo for research involving altering the genetic structure of the embryo could proceed within the 14-day period;
+ where embryos have been created using donor gametes, and a woman no longer wished to consent to the storage of the embryo, the clinic would not have to notify the donor;
+ whether it was in the best interests of a mentally incapacitated person to take gametes for storage should be left to the professional judgement of the clinicians;
+ the need for a father should be removed but the general duty to take account of the welfare of the child should be included in primary legislation;
+ there should be a time limit on the period of storage of gametes or embryos and this should be increased from 5 to 10 years but be subject to review;
+ people intending to marry or cohabit or enter a civil partnership should be entitled to contact the HFEA to see whether they are related as a result of donor insemination, but the consent of both parties is required for this information to be provided;

+ HFEA, which holds a register of all donor treatment since 1990, will be able to run the voluntary contact register which covered donor treatment preceding the 1990 Act;

+ those of 16 years and over can obtain non-identifying information from HFEA, but the age limit of 18 years for those wishing to obtain identifying information is to be retained;

+ putting the fact of donor conception on a birth certificate involves issues of privacy, human rights and data protection and will be kept under review;

+ facilitating counselling for persons seeking donor information from the HFEA is important and will be included in discussions between the government and the HFEA on its annual business plan and priorities;

+ the provision in the draft Bill for not allowing sex selection for non-medical purposes in sperm-sorting kits is to be removed since it relates to a potential development and it will be kept under review;

+ the possibility of bringing surrogacy within the remit of the HFEA will be considered.

As a consequence of these changes to government policy, a new Bill has been drafted and placed before Parliament in 2008. The revised proposals are subject to Parliamentary debate and many further changes may be made before the Bill is enacted. The resulting Act is unlikely to be implemented before 2009.

Conclusions

The long-awaited revisions to the 1990 legislation should be of considerable assistance in this developing area. The decision not to amalgamate the Human Fertilisation and Embryology Authority with the Human Tissue Authority is to be welcomed since both quangos are involved in controlling vast areas of activity and their amalgamation may have led to increased bureaucracy and slowness. It is likely, however, in the light of further scientific developments, especially in the field of genetics and genetic testing, that further legislation, perhaps by statutory instruments, will be necessary even after the 1990 Act is replaced.

Reflection questions

1 Where a child is born as the result of a surrogacy arrangement so that an embryo from a woman and her husband is transplanted into the uterus of another woman, what legal rights do you believe that the woman giving birth to the child should have over the genetic mother? What legal rights does she have at present?

2 To what extent do you think that couples should have the right to obtain treatment for their infertility?

3 Can experimentation on an embryo and its replacement in the uterus to develop as a human being be justified?

Further exercises

1 Look at the daily papers and journals over the next month and collect details on the cases, debates and articles on the topics discussed in this chapter.

2 To what extent do you think the law is an appropriate machinery to determine the choices of parents and professionals in the topics discussed in this chapter?

References

[1] Committee of Inquiry into Human Fertilisation and Embryology chaired by Baroness Warnock 1984, Cmnd 9314, HMSO, London, 1984

[2] *Dickson and Another* v. *United Kingdom*, The Times Law Report, 21 December 2007

[3] *A* v. *C* [1978] 8 Fam Law 170

[4] Frances Gibb, Gay father wins case over baby of lesbian, *The Times*, 7 May 2002

[5] *Re D (Contact and PR: Lesbian mothers and known father) No. 2* [2006] EWHC 2 Fam

[6] www.dh.gov.consultations

[7] Alexandra Frean, Donor children should be able to find fathers, *The Times*, 27 July 2002

[8] Department of Health press release 2004/0023, Anonymity to be Removed from Future Sperm, Egg and Embryo Donors, 2004

[9] The HFEA (Disclosure of Donor Information) Regulations, SI 2004 No. 1511

[10] HFEA Disclosure of information relating to gamete donation, CH(04)07

[11] Human Tissue (Quality and Safety) Regulations, SI 2007 No. 1522; Human Tissue (Quality and Safety for Human Applications) Regulations, SI 2007 No. 1523

[12] 2004/23/EC Tissues and Cells Directive

[13] Committee of Inquiry into Human Fertilisation and Embryology chaired by Baroness Warnock 1984, Cmnd 9314, HMSO, London, 1984

[14] *R* v. *Ethical Committee of St Mary's Hospital ex parte Harriot*, The Times, 27 October 1987; [1988] 1 FLR 512

[15] Human Fertilisation and Embryology Authority, New guidance on Welfare of the Child assessments, CH(05)04, November 2005

[16] *R* v. *Sheffield HA ex parte Seale* (1994) 25 BMLR 1

[17] *Re D (A Child)* [2003] EWCA Civ 182; [2005] UKHL 33

[18] HFEA, Sperm, Egg and Embryo Donation Review (SEED), January 2006

[19] www.hfea.gov.uk/

[20] News item in *The Times*, 20 February 2003

[21] *R (Quintavalle)* v. *Secretary of State for Health*, The Times Law Report, 14 March 2003; [2003] 2 WLR 692 HL

[22] *R (Quintavalle)* v. *Secretary of State for Health*, The Times Law Report, 5 December 2001; [2001] 4 All ER 1013

[23] *R (Quintavalle)* v. *Secretary of State for Health*, The Times Law Report, 25 January 2002; [2002] 2 WLR 550; [2003] UKHL 13

[24] Human Fertilisation and Embryology (Research Purposes) Regulations 2001, SI 2001 No. 188

[25] Human Fertilisation and Embryology Authority Code of Practice, HFEA, London, 1995

[26] *R (on the application of Assisted Reproduction and Gynaecology Centre)* v. *Human Fertilisation and Embryology Authority* [2002] EWCA Civ 20; *The Independent*, 6 February 2002; [2003] 1 FCR 266 CA

[27] *R* v. *Human Fertilisation and Embryology Authority ex p Blood* [1997] 2 WLR 806

[28] Department of Health press announcement, 25 August 2000

[29] Helen Rumbelow, Victory for Mrs Blood changes law of paternity, *The Times*, 1 March 2003

[30] *Evans* v. *Amicus Healthcare Ltd and Others*; *Hadley* v. *Midland Fertility Services Ltd and Others*, The Times Law Report, 2 October 2003; [2003] EWHC 2161; [2007] ECHR 264 (Application No. 6339/05)

31 *Evans* v. *Amicus Healthcare* [2004] EWCA 727

32 *Evans* v. *United Kingdom* [2007] ECHR 264 (Application No. 6339/05)

33 *Mrs U* v. *Centre for Reproductive Medicine* [2002] Lloyd's Law Rep Med 259 CA

34 *Leeds Teaching Hospitals NHS Trust* v. *Mr A, Mrs A, YA and ZA (by their litigation friend the Offcial Solicitor), the Human Fertilisation and Embryology Authority, Mr B and Mrs B* [2003] Lloyd's Rep Med 3 151

35 News item, *The Times*, 20 July 2003

36 Lewis Smith, Despicable conman jailed for IVF fraud, *The Times*, 16 January 2003

37 *Re C (A minor: wardship: Surrogacy)* [1985] FLR 846 (the father was able to obtain a wardship summons in order to obtain custody of the baby)

38 *In re An Adoption (surrogacy)* [1987] 2 All ER 826

39 *Re Q (Parental Order)* [1996] 1 FLR 369

40 Nicola Woodcock, Couple win toddler from mother who broke surrogacy agreement, *The Times*, 27 July 2007

41 *Briody* v. *St Helen's and Knowsley HA* (2000), *The Times*, 1 March 2000; [2001] EWCA Civ 1010

42 Access to Health Records (Control of Access) Regulations, SI 1993 No. 746

43 Department of Health, NHS update, 22 April 2003; www.nhs.uk/nhsupdate/news.asp

44 Nigel Hawkes, Uncontrollable sleepers and hope in gene clue, *The Times*, 6 August 1999

45 A correspondent, Heart gene discovered, *The Times*, 8 November 1999

46 Ian Murray, Genetic link to dyslexia is found, *The Times*, 7 September 1999

47 Mark Henderson, Gene fault clue to tackling dyslexia, *The Times*, 28 August 2003

48 Roger Dobson, Found: the hibernating gene that could send man to the stars, *Sunday Times*, 6 February 2000

49 Nigel Hawkes, Gene discovery may reduce diseases linked to old age, *The Times*, 11 April 2000

50 Mark Henderson, Clue to why men suffer more from autism, *The Times*, 10 September 2003

51 Mark Henderson, Genetic clue to early menopause found, *The Times*, 11 July 2003

52 Mark Henderson, Asthma could be stopped in its tracts, *The Times*, 19 May 2003

53 Department of Health, White Paper, Our Inheritance, Our Future – realising the potential of genetics in the NHS, Cm 5791, The Stationery Office, London, June 2003; www.dh.gov.uk/genetics/whitepaper.htm

54 HGC, Choosing the Future: genetic and reproductive decision making, 2004

55 www.open.gov.uk/dh/genetics.htm

56 Clothier Committee, HMSO, London, January 1992

57 www.dh.gov.uk/genetics/gtac

58 Gene Therapy Advisory Committee 2004, Operational Procedures for the Gene Therapy Advisory Committee in its role as the National Ethics Committee for Gene Therapy Clinical Trials, DH, 2004

59 www.advisorybodies.doh.gov.uk/genetics/gtac

60 Human Fertilisation and Embryology Authority and Advisory Committee on Genetic Testing Consultation document on Pre-implantation Genetic Diagnosis, HFEA and ACGT, London, 1999

61 *R (Quintavalle)* v. *Human Fertilisation and Embryology Authority* [2002] EWHC 3000; [2003] EWCA Civ 667; [2005] UKHL 28

62 Laura Peek, Couple lose fight for designer baby, *The Times*, 2 August 2002

63 HFEA, Report on pre-implantation tissue typing policy review, July 2004

64 HGC, Making Babies: reproductive decisions and genetic technologies, January 2006

65 Human Fertilisation and Embryology Authority, Public Consultation on Sex Selection, HFEA, London, January 1993

[66] Human Fertilisation and Embryology Authority, Sex Selection Report and Summary Document, HFEA, London, November 2003; www.hfea.gov.uk/

[67] 2004/23/EC Tissues and Cells Directive

[68] A citizens' jury on the topic was held in November 1997 at the University of Glamorgan. For further information on the report of the jury's recommendations contact Marcus Longley of the Welsh Institute of Health and Social Care, University of Glamorgan; Tel. 01443 483070

[69] Advisory Committee on Genetic Testing, Code of Practice and Guidance on Human Genetic Testing, Health Departments of the United Kingdom, 23 September 1997

[70] Association of British Insurers, Code of Practice for Genetic Testing, 1999

[71] Association of British Insurers; Tel. 0207 600 3333

[72] News item, Insurers ignore genetics code, *Sunday Times*, 13 December 1998

[73] Robert Winnett, Medical underclass fears insurance blacklisting, *Sunday Times*, 26 March 2000

[74] Department of Health, Committee on Genetics and Insurance Report, DH, October 2000

[75] Mark Henderson, Insurers to check for genetic illness, *The Times*, 13 October 2000

[76] Mark Henderson, Scientists attack gene test ruling, *The Times*, 27 November 2000

[77] Nigel Hawkes, Alarm over unregulated DIY genetic health test, *The Times*, 3 February 2003

[78] Nigel Hawkes, Genetic tests must not go on public sale, government told, *The Times*, 10 April 2003

[79] Human Genetics Advisory Commission (HGAC) and Human Fertilisation and Embryology Authority, Consultation Document on Cloning Issues in Reproduction, Science and Medicine, HGAC, London, 1998

[80] Human Fertilisation and Embryology Authority and Human Genetic Advisory Commission, Cloning Issues in Reproduction, Science and Medicine, HFEA/HGAC, London, December 1998

[81] Chief Medical Officer's Expert Group on Therapeutic Cloning, Stem Cell Research: medical progress with responsibility, DH, August 2000

[82] Human Fertilisation and Embryology (Research Purposes) Regulations 2001, SI 2001 No. 188

[83] Department of Health press release 2003/0429, Statement from the Department of Health

[84] Mark Henderson, Top scientists want 'cowboy cloning' banned, *The Times*, 21 January 2004

[85] White Paper, Review of the Human Fertilisation and Embryology Act: Proposals for revised legislation, Cm 6989, DH, December 2006

[86] Secretary of State for Health, Government response to the report from the Joint Committee, Cm 7209, DH, October 2007

Chapter 23

Community, primary care nursing and palliative care

Introduction

This chapter covers the law relating to nurses who work in the community and in primary care, including community/district nurses, health visitors (known after 2004 as specialist community public health nurses), practice nurses and specialist nurses. Community psychiatric nurses will also find Chapter 20 on mental healthcare of relevance.

The development of community care and the establishment of primary care trusts has meant that the focus for many health professionals has switched from the institution to the community and to primary care and those who have always been community workers, such as the health visitor and the district nurse, are now feeling the increased pressure from the implications of the policy to transfer patients from the institution to the community. Recent developments have seen an increase in specialist posts in the community. Community nurses for the mentally handicapped and community psychiatric nurses are increasing in number and specialist posts for stoma care, incontinence, terminal illness and other specialist areas have been established. Many liaison nurses are now seeking specialist training. There are increased appointments for occupational therapists, physiotherapists and community paediatricians. The organisational changes leading to primary care trusts and care trusts have brought about significant changes for these community nurses and also for practice nurses and these are considered in Chapter 5. Box 23.1 illustrates some of the particular difficulties with which these workers are faced. The configuration of hospitals project aimed at reorganising acute services to enhance the range of secondary care services available to patient's homes and to move towards more integrated patterns of care should clarify and facilitate the role of the community and specialist nurse.[1]

Box 23.1 **Difficulties faced by the nurse in the community**

1 Isolation.
2 Vulnerability.
3 Sole responsibility.
4 Pressure to go beyond job description: definitions of the scope of professional practice.
5 Health and safety hazard and occupier's liability.
6 Variable facilities and resources.

NHS and Community Care Act 1990

The community provisions of this Act came into force on 1 April 1993 and are summarised below. They follow the recommendations of the Griffiths Report and the White Paper 'Caring for People'. The Act required the following:

1 Community care plans. Under Section 46, local authorities in conjunction with health authorities and the voluntary and private sector must prepare plans for the provision of services in the community and revise them annually.

2 Assessment of needs for community care services. Section 47 requires local authorities to carry out an assessment of needs for community services on any individual in its

catchment area who would appear to be in need of any services that it provides or for which it arranges the provision. Where appropriate, the health service body and/or the housing authority may be required to be involved in the assessment. In urgent situations, community care services can be provided temporarily and an assessment should take place as soon as possible.

3   Financial arrangements for nursing and residential accommodation. The local authority had the responsibility for purchasing accommodation for clients from 1 April 1993. Those in residence on 31 March 1993 continued to receive means-tested higher level income support from the Department of Social Security until the preserved rights were abolished in 2001.[2] For those residents who moved in on or after 1 April 1993, the local authority, following an assessment, may purchase a place at a nursing home or residential home and recover the fees from residents, who can claim means-tested income support from the DSS, but only at the ordinary level.

4   Inspection and powers of the Secretary of State. Persons can be authorised by the Secretary of State under Section 48 to inspect premises used for the provision of community care services. Local authorities had inspection units that were replaced by new registration and inspection provisions under the Care Standards Act 2000. The Secretary of State can issue directions as to the exercise of social services functions (Section 50) and has required all local authorities to establish a procedure for considering any representations, including complaints about a failure to discharge local authority social services functions. From April 2004 a new body, the Commission for Social Care Inspection (CSCI), has responsibilities for registering and inspecting accommodation provided in care homes.

5   The Act also made provision for the transfer of health service staff to local authorities (Section 49).

Considerable guidance has been issued by the Department of Health and Social Services Inspectorate on the implementation of these statutory duties. The Audit Commission reported in December 1993[3] that cautious but steady progress has been made with the community care changes. Community health professionals are finding that they are caring for a more acutely ill population as the number of day cases increases and shorter lengths of stay for major surgery become the norm. The 'hospital at home' phenomenon places increasing pressure on community nurses who must ensure that their competence, skill and knowledge develop to meet their new roles. All community health professionals, whether caring for acute, chronically sick, mentally disordered, elderly or disabled patients, are finding that the demands on them are increasing and there are greater pressures on resources. Waiting lists for community services, especially the fitting of equipment and adaptations of buildings for the disabled, are increasing in length. Controversy has developed over the nature of assessment and the extent to which it should identify needs that cannot realistically be met because of a shortage of resources. The practitioner who works in the community should ensure that she plays a full part in the preparation of community care plans and the identification of needs, and in upholding the professional duties to the patient set out in the Code of Professional Conduct.

NHS and social services provision

Considerable problems have arisen in the provision of a seamless service between NHS and social services because NHS care is free at the point of delivery whereas most social services provision is means-tested. Local criteria for the eligibility for NHS continuing care have been

drawn up in each area and those who disagree with the decisions can use the complaints procedures established by the strategic health authority and local authority. From 2010 there
will be a uniform complaints procedure between health and social services (see Chapter 27).

Disputes over eligibility for continuing care have been the concern of the Health Service
Commission. Cases 23.1, 23.2 and 23.3 illustrate concerns about the current system of means
testing for those in residential care.

Case 23.1   *R v. N and E Devon Health Authority ex parte Coughlan (2000)*

NHS or means-tested care?[4]

Pamela Coughlan brought an action against the health authority in 1999 when she was
told that she would have to leave the nursing home she was living in at NHS expense and
move to another home that would be means-tested. She had been grievously injured in a
road traffic accident in 1971. She was tetraplegic, doubly incontinent and partially paralysed
in the respiratory tract. She had been promised by the health authority that she would be
able to stay in Mardon House for life, the costs of her care being met by the NHS.

The Court of Appeal held that nursing care for the chronically sick was not always the sole
responsibility of the NHS, but could, in appropriate circumstances, be provided by a local
authority as a social service and the patient could, depending on her means, be liable to meet
the cost of that care. However, there was no overriding public interest in the health authority breaking its promise to her that she could stay in that home for her life.

There was no appeal against the Court of Appeal's decision. Pamela Coughlan was able to
continue to have NHS funding of her care, but the court had accepted the principle that nursing care did not always have to be funded by the NHS, so in that sense both parties won their
case. However, the principle that nursing and other personal care should be funded by the
NHS was put forward by the majority recommendations in the Royal Commission Report on
the long-term care of the elderly,[5] which is discussed in Chapter 19 together with the National
Framework for continuing care.

A dispute arose in relation to the provision of services to disabled people under the
Chronic Sick and Disabled Persons Act 1970 and the extent to which the local authority could
take into account its financial resources.

Case 23.2   *R v. Gloucester CC and Another ex parte Barry (1997)*

Assessment of disabled persons[6]

A man of 79 with severe disabilities brought an action in Gloucester when the local authority informed him that it was going to withdraw his cleaning and laundry services. He obtained
judicial review of the local authority's decision on the grounds that they had not reassessed
his needs prior to withdrawing the services. The High Court judge refused to grant a declaration that, in carrying out the reassessment, the local authority was not entitled to take into
account the resources available to it. The Court of Appeal allowed his appeal, on the grounds
that the local authority was not entitled to take into account the resources available to it.
The local authority appealed to the House of Lords.

The House of Lords allowed the appeal holding that, for the purposes of Section 2(1) of the 1970 Act, a chronically sick or disabled person's needs were to be assessed in the context of, and by reference to, the provision of certain types of assistance for promoting the welfare of disabled people using eligibility criteria. These criteria had to be set taking into account current acceptable standards of living, the nature and extent of the disability and the relative cost balanced against the relative benefit and the relative need for that benefit. Its impact on its resources had to be evaluated and therefore its financial position was relevant. The authority could not make the decision in a vacuum from which all considerations of costs were expelled. In another significant court decision the Court of Appeal[7] allowed the application for judicial review and held that Sefton Borough Council had behaved unlawfully[8] when it set up a scheme whereby those who were entitled to be provided with accommodation under Section 21 could have their capital taken into account unless it was or fell below £1,500 (this figure was chosen since it would usually leave sufficient for a funeral). Subsequently the Community Care (Residential Accommodation) Act 1998 was passed to put the decision of the Court of Appeal on a statutory basis. Section 1 of the 1998 Act states that in determining whether care and attention are otherwise available to a person, a local authority shall disregard so much of the person's capital as does not exceed the capital limit for the purposes of Section 22 of the National Assistance Act 1948. The regulations on capital disregard must be followed by local authorities in means-testing.[9]

In July 2001 the Department of Health published a consultation document, 'Guidance on Fair Access to Care Services', to ensure greater consistency in the use of eligibility criteria for access to care services.

Case 23.3   *R (on the application of Grogan) v. Bexley NHS Care Trust (2006)*

Continuing care[10]

G applied for judicial review of a decision by an NHS trust that she did not qualify for continuing NHS healthcare. If the NHS provided care, it would be free; if it were the social services, she would be means-tested. The High Court held that an NHS trust should apply a primary health need test to determine whether accommodation should be provided by the NHS or social services. The criteria of the NHS trust for determining whether the patient had continuing care needs were fatally flawed and it failed to give reasons why it considered that the patient's continuing care needs were neither complex nor intense. The Court ordered the trust's decision to be set aside and remitted for fresh consideration.

Following the decision in Case 23.3 (the Grogan case) the DH announced that a national framework for continuing care would be implemented in October 2007. Assessments for continuing NHS care were to be carried out by a multidisciplinary team using the concept of 'a primary health' need as the criteria for the receipt of continuing healthcare.[11]

In 2000 the Audit Commission published its findings on the provision of equipment for older and disabled people.[12] It found that users were not asked basic questions about the sort of help they needed; they had to wait for long periods of time for their equipment; the equipment was not always suitable or of a high quality; and the current organisation of equipment services is a recipe for inequality and inefficiency. Among its many significant recommendations are suggestions for involving users, restructuring of mobility services, the integration of health and social services provision for community equipment under the new powers of the Health Act 1999 and the introduction of policy reviews and dissemination of good practice. Care trusts have now been set up to ensure integration of health and social service provision.

Human rights and care homes

In June 2007 the House of Lords held in a majority decision (in keeping with an earlier decision by the Court of Appeal)[13] that a private care home, which was under contract with a local authority to provide care and accommodation for elderly persons, was not an organisation exercising functions of a public nature.[14] An 84-year-old resident who suffered from Alzheimher's disease was therefore unable to make a claim under Article 8 of the European Convention on Human Rights in respect of her removal from the care home. This decision has led to a campaign for legislation to bring private care homes under the auspices of the Human Rights Act 1998. The campaign to secure legislation placing an obligation upon private care homes to recognise the human rights of residents under the Human Rights Act 1998 was given added momentum following the report of the Parliamentary Joint Committee on Human Rights in August 2007.[15] This report found that more than a fifth of care homes have been found to be failing basic standards of care for privacy and dignity. The report considered that elder abuse is a serious and severe human rights abuse which is perpetrated on vulnerable older people who often depend on their abusers to provide them with care. The Joint Committee criticised the Department of Health and Ministry of Justice for failing to provide proper leadership and guidance on the Human Rights Act to providers of health and residential care. It recommended that care standards regulations should be amended so that all care homes are brought under the Human Rights Act and that eventually the Human Rights Act should be amended to ensure that private care homes came under its remit. It also recognised the importance of the role of staff in protecting human rights and made specific recommendation on the training of staff and suggested that there should be a duty specified in the care standards requiring staff to report abuse, with protection for whistleblowing and confidentiality.

A private member's Bill to extend the meaning of function of a public authority in the Human Rights Act 1998 so that it includes functions performed under a contract or other arrangement with a public authority was introduced into the House of Commons in May 2007.

An allegation that a local authority was in breach of Article 5 of the European Convention on Human Rights succeeded in 2006.[16] The local authority had placed the claimant's husband in a care home, justifying the placement on grounds than any restriction on his liberty was in his best interests and he was not being deprived of his liberty within the meaning of Article 5. The court held that the crucial issue was whether the person was free to leave and concluded that he was not. Since October 2007 the provisions of the Mental Capacity Act 2005 would apply to this situation (see Chapter 20 and the Bournewood gap).

In another successful action alleging a breach of Article 8, the claimant, who was blind, suffered from diabetes and had suffered several strokes, obtained judicial review of a primary care trust's refusal to provide 24-hour nursing care in her own home (her parents ceasing to be able to provide hands-on care). The court held that removing her from her home into residential care would interfere with her right to respect for her family life within Article 8.[17]

In contrast with the previous two cases, the challenge of a wife whose husband was transferred from a nursing home to a hospital because of his health and behavioural problems failed in her claim.[18] The judge held that the without notice application for the transfer by the local authority was justified and there was no breach of Article 8. The injunctions to forbid the wife to interfere with her husband's transfer or his care at the hospital or attempting to see him at the hospital except as agreed and supervised by the local authority were justified.

NHS Plan[19] and community care

The NHS Plan made some radical recommendations to improve joint working of health and social services. These are considered in Chapter 19 on the care of the elderly, but the proposals will affect other client groups. Chapter 7 of the NHS Plan envisaged the establishment of care trusts that will commission and deliver primary and community healthcare as well as social care for older people and other client groups. Social services would be delivered under delegated authority from local councils. Powers to effect this have been enacted in Sections 45-48 of the Health and Social Care Act 2001 (see Chapter 5). Intermediate care is seen as a core element in the services for the elderly and is discussed in Chapter 19. Under Section 47 of the NHS and Community Care Act 1990 the local authority had a duty to carry out a community care assessment. A claimant, an asylum seeker, applied for judicial review of a community care assessment on the basis that it was in breach of its duties under this section. The court upheld the application, concluding that the local authority had been wrong in deciding that community care services would not be provided for the claimant because he did not have an enduring mental illness

Delayed discharges

Problems in bed blocking because accommodation is not found in the community for patients ready for discharge from NHS beds are being met by the Community Care (Delayed Discharges etc.) Act 2003, which makes provision for social services authorities to make payments in cases where the discharge of patients is delayed for reasons relating to the provision of community care services or services for carers. Under the Act the responsible NHS organisation can serve notice on a social services authority (in which the patient is ordinarily resident) that a patient is or is expected to become a qualifying hospital patient at a particular hospital and that it is unlikely to be safe to discharge the patient from hospital unless one or more community care services are made available for him. Before issuing a notice the NHS organisation must consult the patient and a carer (if it is aware of the person's identity). Following the notice the responsible authority must carry out an assessment of the patient's needs with a view to identifying any community care services that need to be made available in order for it to be safe to discharge him and, after consulting the NHS body, decide which of those services, if any, the authority will make available for the patient. The needs of the carer must also be assessed (where the carer has requested such an assessment) in order to identify any services the authority may provide under Section 2 of the Carers and Disabled Children Act 2000 and which need to be made available to the carer in order for it to be safe to discharge the patient and, after consultation with the responsible NHS body, which services the authority decides to be made available to the carer. The NHS body must notify the social services authority of the day it intends to discharge the patient and there must be a period of at least two days between the notice and the day of discharge. Regulations that make provisions for the details of the delayed discharges scheme were published in 2003.[20] The regulations set out the type of care which a patient must be receiving in order to come within the provisions of the Act; set out the details of the notice which the relevant NHS body must give to the local social services authority to inform it that there is a patient who is likely to need community care services on discharge and also set the time limits for notice and the amounts which the local authority must pay. The regulations also provide for resolution of a dispute. Failure by the social services authority to comply with these statutory duties can lead to the authority being liable to make a payment of the amount prescribed in the regulations for each day of the delayed discharge. Disputes over 'ordinary residence' are to be resolved by the Secretary of State or Welsh Assembly by arrangements to be drawn up by them. Regulations are also to be passed to set up a system for dispute resolution. The minister is given power to apply these provisions to patients in care homes; £100 million was allocated in 2005/6 to accompany the delayed discharges legislation. As a consequence of the success of the health and social care partners in reducing delayed transfers of care in acute services, the Department of Health set up a project to look at discharge practice in the non-acute and mental health services and commenced data collection in April 2006.[21] At the time of writing there is no intention to extend reimbursement legislation to these settings. Where a patient refuses to be discharged to a residential care home and no longer requires medical or nursing care in hospital, the patient is not entitled to occupy the bed and the NHS trust is entitled to reclaim possession of its hospital premises from the patient.[22]

Carers

It has been estimated that Great Britain has 5.7 million carers and one in six households contains a carer.[23] The Carers (Recognition and Services) Act 1995 required local authorities to carry out an assessment of the carer's ability to provide and to continue to provide care for the person receiving community care services, but it did not give local authorities the power to offer carers services to support them in their caring role.

In 1999 the government published a Carer's National Strategy Document[24] highlighting the need for legislation to enable local authorities to provide services direct to carers. The Carers and Disabled Children Act 2000 has four main purposes:

1 It gives local authorities the power to supply certain services direct to carers.

2 It enables local authorities to make direct payments to carers, including 16- and 17-year-olds, to persons with parental responsibility for disabled children and to the disabled children. These direct payments can then be used for a provider for those services chosen by the carer.

3 Local authorities can provide short-term break voucher schemes, which will give carers flexibility in the timing and choice of breaks.

4 The local authorities are given power to charge carers for the services they receive. In its assessment, the LA can take into account any assessment made under the 1995 Act. The 2000 Act does not apply if the carer is an employee or a volunteer for a voluntary organisation. The LA must consider the assessment and decide:
   + whether the carer has needs in relation to the care that he provides or intends to provide
   + if so, whether they could be satisfied (wholly or partly) by services which the LA may provide
   + if they could be so satisfied, whether or not to provide services to the carer.

Negligence

Standard of care

> **Practical Dilemma 23.1** Key worker
>
> The Roger Park Community NHS Trust set up a series of location managers and teams of multidisciplinary professionals for clients. Each client was assigned a key worker who would discuss with the team that particular client's difficulties and try to resolve them as far as possible on his own, thus preventing the client from being visited by a whole host of different professionals. This key worker could be any one of a variety of professionals, but as far as possible it was one whose training was most relevant to the client's needs.
>
> Margaret Downs lived on her own and was recovering from a stroke. With the help of the physiotherapist she was making good progress and the community nurse, Angela Hide, was visiting her twice a week to dress a leg ulcer and also to give her a bath. The community nurse was Margaret's key worker. After a few weeks, Angela decided that Margaret would be able to manage to bath herself on her own if she had a bath rail and support. She got in touch with the local authority department that provided home aids and ordered the appropriate devices to be fitted. She told Margaret that once they were installed she would not need any assistance to bath, but that if she got into any difficulties she should let Angela know. A few days later Margaret, who had not been seen by neighbours for a few days, was found dead in the bath. A post mortem showed that she had slipped while trying to get out of the bath, that the hand rail was not in a suitable position and that she had probably died of exposure. The coroner held an inquest and Angela was asked to provide a statement, as was the occupational therapist in the team, since the task of assessment for bath aids was normally that of the occupational therapist.

In Practical Dilemma 23.1 it is possible that the relatives will be present and probably represented by a solicitor or barrister at the inquest. The inquest might well be followed by a civil claim against the NHS trust on the basis of its direct liability for the death of Margaret in failing to lay down an appropriate procedure for caring for patients in the community and also on the basis of its indirect or vicarious liability for Angela's negligence. Was Angela negligent? Obviously, there are very few facts given here on which the answer to such a question could be determined, but at the heart of the negligence action will be the question: did Angela follow the accepted approved practice in making those recommendations about the bath aids? Or if she did not follow the approved practice, was there justification for her not doing so and would that justification be supported by competent professional opinion? The question of whether such a decision was within her competence or whether she should have brought in the occupational therapist, whose training includes that type of assessment, will be crucial. It does not, of course, follow that the mere fact that Angela strayed outside her competence will automatically mean that she failed to follow a reasonable standard of care. In addition, the relatives will also have to establish that there was a causal link between the breach of duty by Angela and the harm caused to Margaret and that that harm was reasonably foreseeable.

The most important feature in any team approach and key worker system is that each should know the limits of their competence and the point at which the patient's safety demands that another person be brought in to advise. In the Wilsher case (considered in detail in Chapter 6), the court has held that there is no concept of team liability. It is a question of individual liability and/or the liability of the NHS trust. (The legal issues arising from the scope of professional practice are considered in Chapter 24.)

To whom is the nurse responsible?

> ### Practical Dilemma 23.2   A clash of duties
>
> Community nurses in the Roger Park Unit had been given instructions that they should not carry drugs in their cars, neither should they personally arrange for drugs on prescriptions to be collected from the chemists. Ruth Green was caring for a terminally ill patient who was being nursed by her husband at home. The GP had left a prescription on his last visit and the husband asked her if she would be kind enough to bring the drugs back from the chemist. He said that he did not have any transport or any neighbours who could help and he did not want to leave his wife on her own. Ruth said that she was not allowed to collect drugs from the chemist for patients. He was clearly distressed and offered to come with her if she could provide the transport, but it would still mean leaving his wife on her own. She agreed to this and took him to the chemist and then home again – a round trip of about seven miles that took 20 minutes. The husband could not understand why he had to go with her, leaving his wife for such a long time and obviously in danger. Ruth herself felt that the rules were not appropriate to that situation and wondered whether there was any law that covered her duties.

Practical Dilemma 23.2, in which there is a clash between what the nurse is told to do and what she feels is her duty to the patient, is not unusual, neither is it confined to the community. Other situations, for example where the nurse is told not to take patients in her car or where she is given instructions about lifting that she cannot carry out because the facilities or staff are not available, place the nurse in a dilemma. Is she to fulfil what she believes to be her duty to the patient or should she obey the NHS trust's or nurse manager's instructions? The clash can be seen as a conflict between the Code of Professional Conduct set down by the NMC and her employer's orders. She has a contractual duty to obey the latter, since it is an implied term of her contract of employment that she obey the reasonable orders of her employer; contrariwise, she has a professional duty to follow the Code of Professional Conduct. If provisions of the Code are included in the contract of employment, then there should in theory be no clash between the two. Instructions by the employer must be reasonable and it can be argued that any instructions that clash with the professional obligations of the registered practitioner cannot be reasonable.

The first task for Ruth Green in a situation like this is for the nurse management to be given the full facts of any potential hardship suffered by the patient as a result of their instructions and procedures. Examples of the difficulties that have and will arise from following these instructions must be provided in detail. It may so happen that, when presented with this evidence, management might well feel that either the whole policy should be revised or that certain exceptions can be made in circumstances where the patient is likely to suffer harm.

Alternatively, it may be possible for other arrangements to be made that will ensure the safety and well-being of the patient. For example, in rural areas, pharmacists sometimes provide a home delivery service for medicines and oxygen. If the management is adamant that the procedures must be followed without any exception, the nurse has a duty to undertake those unless there is likely to be such harm to the patient that it is clearly contrary to her duty of care to the patient. In such a situation, her records would have to be very comprehensive to justify her action. In serious situations, the nurse should raise concerns with senior levels of management in accordance with the Public Interest Disclosure Act, which is discussed in Chapter 4.

In the following case, the fact that a GP relied heavily upon the role of community nurses was the subject of disciplinary action.

Case 23.4   *R v. FHS Appeal Authority ex p Muralidhar* (1999)

Medical treatment: reasonableness of doctor relying on nurses[25]

A GP applied for judicial review of a finding by the chief executive of a family health services authority that he was in breach of his terms of service by relying on district nurses who had visited the patient daily to treat a patient's bedsores. The patient suffered from senile dementia, incontinence and was bedridden. The doctor visited her, prescribed antibiotics for infected bedsores, leaving instructions with staff that he should be contacted if there were any deterioration. He was not contacted, but subsequently the patient was removed to hospital where criticism of her previous nursing care was made. The judge, in granting the application, held that the chief executive had failed to consider whether the doctor had behaved in accordance with his terms of service and had taken irrelevant considerations into account. There was also procedural unfairness in that the chief executive had not alerted the doctor to the importance he attached to these considerations so that the doctor could make relevant representations.

There are clear lessons for nursing staff from this case. If they are concerned about a patient's condition they should ensure that the doctor is called in to examine the patient.

Giving advice

One of the most important tasks of many registered practitioners, and in particular the health visitor (specialist community public health nurse, SCPHN), is giving advice to clients, young and old, on all aspects of their health and ways of keeping healthy. For example, one of the vexed questions these days is the extent to which the SCPHN should encourage a mother to have her child vaccinated and the possibility of the SCPHN herself being held liable for giving advice that turns out to cause harm. The topic of liability for communications was discussed in Chapter 4, where it was stated that exactly the same principles of liability apply in giving advice as apply in using skills. Thus if a health visitor, knowing that a child has a history of convulsions, fails to take this into account in advising the mother to have the child vaccinated and also fails to ensure that the doctor is advised of this fact, the health visitor may well share some responsibility for any harm that befalls the child as a result of undergoing the vaccination. (Vaccinations are considered in Chapter 26.)

Safety of the community professional

Entering other people's homes can be dangerous. Unlike the NHS trust, the occupiers have no obligations under the Health and Safety at Work Act 1974, but they do have obligations under the Occupiers' Liability Act 1957. This is discussed in detail in Chapter 12. The community worker faces problems in relation to both the standard of the structure and the fixtures and fittings. In addition, she might find difficulties caused by the client or the relatives.

Practical Dilemma 23.3   Defective premises

Pam Hughes, a health visitor, had a large caseload in one of the poorer parts of the city. In one council house, conditions were very bad: the wallpaper was peeling off the walls and there were piles of empty milk bottles in the kitchen and a miscellaneous assortment of carpet pieces on the concrete floor. The local authority had been notified of certain defects to the roof and the fittings, but had said that, because of the backlog of maintenance work and staff cuts, it would be several weeks before they could repair the property. The occupiers, Mr and Mrs James and their seven children, could not cope with the situation. Mr James was unemployed and attempted to rectify some of the defects, including putting a new piece of glass in the front door to replace the pane that had been broken when the door was slammed shut. The door had swollen owing to the guttering leaking onto it. Pam Hughes was well used to the family and had been visiting regularly because of her concern over the two youngest children. After one visit, she let herself out – as was her usual custom – and had to pull hard on the front door to open it. As she pulled, the new pane fell out on to her hand, cutting her severely across the wrist. After medical treatment and the advice of a specialist, it appeared that the tendons were severed and she would have very little movement in the four fingers of her right hand. It is certainly questionable whether she will be able to continue her work as a health visitor. Since she is unmarried, and the sole breadwinner, caring for her elderly mother, she is frightened at the prospect of losing her job. She is therefore anxious to recover financial compensation for the injuries.

This particular situation may be unique but it represents the many dangers with which a community worker is faced.

What are the practicalities of obtaining compensation? Is the NHS trust liable? The answer is probably no, unless it can be shown that it was aware of the danger that an employee was in and failed to take reasonable precautions to safeguard her. There is no evidence that this was so in this case. However, the employers may be prepared to ensure that compensation is paid to her on an *ex gratia* basis since she was injured in the course of her employment. Mr and Mrs James are possibly liable. As occupiers, they failed to ensure that the premises were safe for the visitor. Mr James may well have repaired the door negligently. However, unless they are insured, the question is academic, since they are unlikely to be able to pay any compensation.

Since it is a council house, it may be that Pam could establish a case against the council in its capacity as landlord and therefore occupier of the building. However, to succeed it would be important to show that, from the obligations under the lease, the landlord had a duty to carry out repairs and his failure to do so had reasonably foreseeably caused the injury to Pam's arm. However, Mr James's repair work makes a break in this chain of causation. If Pam fails against all three potential defendants, then all she can do is fall back on her own insurance cover. Some household insurance schemes also cover for personal injuries or she may have her own personal accident cover. If not, she is unlikely to obtain any compensation other than the usual statutory sick pay scheme and the DSS injury benefits, which are considerably smaller than the level of compensation awarded in the civil courts.

The lesson is clear: because of the dangers of working in variable conditions, it is probably essential that community workers have some form of insurance cover for personal accidents. Some local authorities, professional associations and trade unions have negotiated group schemes of cover. It is, however, the policy of the NHS not to take out insurance cover. If the professional is working on NHS trust premises all the time, then the authority as occupier has a duty to ensure that she is safe, and if it fails in this duty then it could be held liable under the Occupiers' Liability Act.

Case 23.5 | *R v. Hillingdon Health Authority ex parte Wyatt* (1977)

Aggression in the community[26]

Mrs Wyatt suffered from multiple sclerosis, could do nothing for herself and needed nursing assistance. The health authority had the duty to provide a home nursing service under Section 25 of the NHS Act 1946 (as amended by the 1973 Reorganisation Act). The husband, who was also an invalid, abused the nursing staff when they visited his wife and was aggressive and threatening. He was asked to give an assurance that he would cease to behave so, but he refused. The authority told Mrs Wyatt's solicitors that because of Mr Wyatt's behaviour they could not continue the nursing service.

The Court of Appeal held that the authority was doing all that could be reasonably expected of it and the application to compel the authority to provide the service would be dismissed.

The principle established in the Wyatt case can be applied to other situations, including the dangerous nature of the premises. However, before any service can be justifiably withdrawn, the threat to the safety of the community worker must have reached a serious level and every possible precaution must have been taken. For example, it might be necessary for some nurses to be sent in pairs to clients where they face danger. One question that a community nurse sometimes asks is: Can I refuse to go if I consider that I am in personal danger? If the employer's instruction to go to a particular place is unreasonable with regard to the danger with which the worker is faced and the lack of precautions that the employer has taken for the employee's safety, then the employee can refuse to obey them. What is meant by unreasonable? This is a matter of balancing all the options available, including other precautions that it is reasonable for the employer to take against the risks involved and the needs of the client. Where the danger to the professional is the neighbourhood itself it might, for example, be reasonable for the employer to arrange for an alarm/warning system to be carried by the employee or to ensure that they visit homes in pairs. Where the danger comes from aggressive clients or their relatives, then it might be sufficient if a senior nursing officer accompanies the nurse to ensure her safety. A similar situation of a conflict between patients/carers and the health professionals has arisen in manual handling, where the patient refuses to be lifted by a hoist. This issue is considered in Chapter 12. The HSE has developed a pack for violence management training in healthcare settings which could be applied to work in the community[27] (see Chapter 12).

Practical Dilemma 23.4 | Community dangers

Albert was a man of 32 with learning disabilities who had been living in a community home for about six weeks. He had settled down well and, provided that he took his medication, he coped quite well, taking his share of the household chores. He was due for an injection, but to the surprise of the community nurse, he said that he was not going to take it. She pleaded with him, but to no avail. She said she would return that night, but he again refused the injection. She offered to provide it in tablet form, but he said that he would not take it in any form. The nurse tried to give the injection to him again, but he lost his temper, striking out and severely injuring her.

Several problems emerge from this: one is the issue of consent to treatment in the community, which we shall return to later; the other is the question of the safety of community nurses for the mentally ill and those with learning disabilities.

It is the employer's duty to take reasonable care of the health, safety and welfare of his employee. If it is known that a particular patient is a danger to nursing staff, then the employer has a duty to take reasonable precautions to see that they will be safe. These precautions might mean ensuring that a female nurse never visits the patient on her own. There is quite likely to be a need for refuge to be provided so that, if a client is particularly disturbed, he can leave the community or family house and make use of a respite bed, i.e. providing respite for the family. In the situation above, in deciding whether the NHS trust is liable for the injuries suffered by the community nurse, account would have to be taken of whether it was known that the patient was aggressive and, if so, whether the appropriate precautions had been taken, whether the community nurse followed approved accepted practice in her dealings with the patient or whether she provoked the patient by what she did and was therefore, to some extent, to blame for what happened. (See further discussion on health and safety in Chapter 12.)

Official advice on violence

The Health and Safety Commission has published guidance on the assessment and management of risks of violence and aggression to staff in health services.[28] This includes, in Appendix 3, a home visiting checklist. The three Vs of visiting are 'vet – verify – vigilance'. The checklist for staff is shown in Box 23.2. Another checklist is provided for managers.

Box 23.2 **Checklist for staff who make home visits**

Have you:

+ had all the relevant training about violence to staff?
+ a sound grasp of your unit's safety policy for visitors?
+ a clear idea about the area into which you are going?
+ carefully previewed today's cases? Any 'PVs' (potentially violent clients/patients)?
+ asked to double up, take an escort or use a taxi if unsure?
+ made appointments?
+ left your itinerary and expected departure/arrival times?
+ told colleagues, manager about possible changes of plans?
+ arranged for contact if your return is overdue?

Do you have:

+ forms on which to record and report incidents?
+ a personal alarm or radio? Does it work? Is it handy?
+ a bag/briefcase, wear an outer uniform or car stickers that suggest you have money or drugs with you? Is this wise where you are going today/tonight?
+ out of hours telephone numbers to summon help?

Can you:

+ be certain your attitudes, body language, etc. won't cause trouble?
+ defuse potential problems and manage aggression?

Consent to treatment

Mental capacity

If a person is mentally capable, they are entitled to make their own decisions.[29] A person who has the necessary mental capacity can refuse treatment for a good reason, a bad reason or no reason at all.[30,31] (This is considered further in Chapter 7.) However, it is essential that the capacity of the individual to make decisions is assessed by the health professional since if the person lacks the mental capacity then action has to be taken in their best interests.[32,33] The Mental Capacity Act 2005 applies where a person lacks the requisite mental capacity to make their own decisions (see Chapters 7 and 20).

Mentally disordered

In Chapter 20, which deals with the psychiatric nurse, the problem of giving drugs in the community is discussed. Medication could only be given without consent if it comes within the provisions of the Mental Health Act 1983 as revised by the Mental Health Act 2007 or under the provisions of the Mental Capacity Act 2005 where a person lacks the requisite mental capacity and action is taken in his or her best interests. The Mental Health Act 2007 has introduced a new community treatment order which replaces the provision for aftercare under supervision. It is discussed in Chapter 20.

In Practical Dilemma 23.4, described above, if Albert continues to refuse to take medication considered essential for the treatment of his mental disorder as defined in the Act, he would have to be admitted to a mental hospital as an inpatient in order to be treated compulsorily. The Mental Health Act 2007 has amended the 1983 Act to introduce a community treatment order. Where a person lacks the mental capacity to make their own decisions, the Mental Capacity Act 2005 which came into force fully in October 2007 applies. The principles and basic provisions of the Act are considered in Chapter 7 and the provisions relating to the loss of liberty for those incapable of giving consent, but who are not detained under the Mental Health Act 1983 (known as the Bournewood safeguards), are considered in Chapter 20.

Forcible entry

Another point that often concerns the community nurse and the health visitor is whether they have any rights of entry. As far as the statutory law is concerned, the answer is no. There may be a power of entry at common law where it is feared that an old person is lying in need of help, but it exists only in an emergency to save life.

Practical Dilemma 23.5 **A row of bottles**

Neighbours drew the attention of the community nurse to a row of bottles outside the house of an elderly recluse. They feared for her safety and suggested that they should break into the house to check that all was well. The community nurse was hesitant.

In a case like this, it is preferable from the practical, as well as the theoretical, point of view for the police to be summoned. Their entry would provide legal justification (under the Police and Criminal Evidence Act 1984 S. 17(e)) as well as providing the most realistic means of entry.

Social workers have statutory powers of entry under specific conditions, but health workers do not.

Compulsory removal

Under the Mental Health Act 1983

> **Practical Dilemma 23.6**   **Refusal to leave**
>
> Laura Thomas, a community nurse for the mentally ill, was notified that two sisters who were regarded as recluses had not been seen for several days. Neighbours reported that a number of cats were howling around their home and that the curtains had not been drawn for three days. Laura was also informed that of the two sisters, Annie, the younger one, was considered to be a manic-depressive. Laura went to the house and the door was answered by Agnes. She was abrupt and unwelcoming. When asked about her sister, she said they did not want nosey-parkers and they were quite happy. From the doorway, Laura could see that the house was in a dirty condition and Agnes herself was in a dishevelled state. She feared for the physical and mental well-being of Annie. What could she do?

As a community nurse, Laura has no power to enter the house. However, powers do exist: under Section 115 of the Mental Health Act 1983 as amended by the 2007 Act, an Approved Mental Health Professional (AMHP) (replacing the approved social worker under the 1983 Act) may, at all reasonable times after producing, if asked to do so, some duly authenticated document showing that he is such an Approved Mental Health Professional, enter and inspect any premises (not being a hospital) in the area of that authority in which a mentally disordered patient is living, if he has reasonable cause to believe that the patient is not receiving care. This power enables the AMHP to inspect premises, other than hospitals, where a mentally disordered person is living. It does not, however, give the right to enforce entry, but refusal to permit the inspection could constitute an offence under Section 129 of the Mental Health Act 1983. Premises are not defined, but could include private premises, provided a mentally disordered person is living there and provided there is reasonable cause to believe the patient is not under proper care. Laura would therefore have to arrange for an AMHP to visit the home. If entry were obstructed under Section 115, the AMHP would have to make use of her power to apply to the justice of the peace for a warrant to search and remove patients under Section 135 (see pages 494–5). The AMHP would have to give information on oath that there is reasonable cause to suspect that a person believed to be suffering from mental disorder: (a) has been, or is being, ill treated, neglected, or kept otherwise than under proper control, in any place within the jurisdiction of the justice; or (b) being unable to care for himself, is living alone in any such place. The justice may then issue a warrant authorising any constable to enter, if need be by force, any premises specified in the warrant in which that person is believed to be and if it is thought fit to remove him to a place of safety with a view to the making of an application for his care and treatment. An AMHP must accompany a constable. If it is thought fit, Annie could be removed to a place of safety and kept there for up to 72 hours under Section 135(3). (Amendments have been made to the Mental Health Act 1983 by the Mental Health Act 2007; see Chapter 20.)

Under the National Assistance Act 1948

The provision of the Mental Health Act described in the last paragraph can be used only in the case of a person believed within the meaning of the Act to be suffering from mental disorder. There are occasionally cases where those powers are not appropriate. In the above situation, it may well be that, although Annie suffers from learning disabilities and may well come within the definition of suffering from mental disorder, Agnes might not, but she might equally be in need of help.

Section 47 of the 1948 Act authorises the removal to suitable premises of persons in need of care and control in order to secure the necessary care and attention. Its main provisions are set out in the Statute below.

Statute | **Provisions of Section 47 of the National Assistance Act 1948**

The persons must be (a) suffering from grave chronic disease or being aged, infirm, or physically incapacitated, are living in insanitary conditions, AND (b) are unable to devote to themselves, and are not receiving from other persons, proper care and attention. In order to use this section there must be certification by the community specialist after thorough inquiry and consideration that in the interests of any such person or for preventing injury to the health of, or serious nuisance to other persons, it is necessary to remove any such person. An application is made to Court. Seven days' notice must be given of the application. If granted the person can be kept in a place of safety for a period not exceeding three months. This period can be extended.

Because of the dangers to the health of the person in delaying an application, an emergency application can be made under the provisions of the National Assistance (Amendment) Act 1951 under which the period of detention is three weeks. These provisions provide no power to treat the person compulsorily. The Law Commission has recommended changes to these provisions that are under discussion[34] (see Chapter 19).

Protection of property

If both Annie and Agnes were removed from the house, what happens to their home?

Under Section 48 of the National Assistance Act 1948, the council has a duty to provide temporary protection for the property of persons admitted to hospitals. The section gives the council power to enter the property at all reasonable times and to deal with any movable property in order to prevent or mitigate any loss or damage. The council can recover any reasonable expenses incurred in carrying out this duty from the person who is admitted or any person liable to maintain him.

These provisions cause considerable difficulty for community physicians who may be under considerable pressure from neighbours to make use of these statutory powers, but it is well known that such a removal can be fatal for the person concerned who may fail to thrive in institutional care. The dilemma between the rights of freedom of autonomy and the duty to act in the public interest and to safeguard the person's welfare is evident.

Disclosure of information

This topic is fully discussed in Chapter 8 where an example of the problems faced by community staff is considered (page 184, Practical Dilemma 8.6). The health visitor is more likely to be required to give evidence in court than any other community worker and should refer to Chapter 9 on giving evidence in court. The policy that she should wait to be subpoenaed before giving evidence in cases involving children has changed because of her duty to the child under the Children Act 1989.

Criminal suspicion

Community nurses often work alone and if they are charged with theft it is one professional's word against that of the client or relative. In a case like Practical Dilemma 23.7, Kate could well have been accused of theft by the old lady herself if she was at all absent-minded and had forgotten what she had done. The safest rule is therefore never to accept gifts, even though this might distress the client. If the client is insistent and wishes to make a generous gift, then a health service manager could be called in to give advice, but the client should be represented, since if there were any evidence of undue influence the gift would be voidable. The NMC in its draft Code of Practice under the heading 'Maintain professional boundaries' states that 'You must refuse any gifts, favours or hospitality that might be interpreted as an attempt to gain preferential treatment' replacing the clause in the current Code of Practice: '7.4 You must refuse any gift, favour or hospitality that might be interpreted, now or in the future, as an attempt to obtain preferential consideration.'

> ### Practical Dilemma 23.7　Suspected
>
> Kate Giles was a community nurse who had long been visiting an elderly widow who appeared to have no family apart from two grandchildren, who rarely visited, and few other visitors. One of Kate's tasks was to dress the client's leg. On one occasion, the client was anxious to point out some of her treasures to Kate. They included some very fine pieces of bone china. It was suggested to Kate that she might like to have a tiny cat as a small gift. Kate protested that she was not allowed to receive gifts from clients. Her protests were ignored and the old lady wrapped the gift up in an old paper bag and gave it to Kate. Kate forgot to mention it to her nursing officer the next day and after that it seemed too small a matter to be of any concern. Shortly after this the old lady died. The grandchildren discovered that a piece of Spode was missing. They made some enquiries and Kate stated that she had been given it by the elderly lady, but that they would, of course, be entitled to have it back. Kate was severely reprimanded and the grandchildren said they did not believe her story, since the old lady had never been known to give anything away; they suggested that Kate had, in fact, stolen the china.

Nursing and residential homes

The Registered Homes Act 1984, which required mental nursing homes, nursing homes and residential care homes to be registered – mental nursing homes and nursing homes by the health authority in whose catchment area they were and residential care homes by the local authority – was repealed by the Care Standards Act 2000. The 2000 Act followed a White Paper in 1998 on social services[35] which envisaged a single independent system of regulation and inspection with commissions for care standards. The White Paper also recommended a statutory body known as the General Social Care Council, which would register those involved in social care work together with a national training organisation and thus improve standards in social care. National required standards for residential and nursing homes for older people were published in a consultation document by the Department of Health.[36] A Care Standards Act was passed in 2000 incorporating these recommendations.

Care Standards Act 2000

The main provisions of the Care Standards Act 2000 are given below.

Part 1 establishes a new independent regulatory body for social care and private and voluntary healthcare services in England known as the National Care Standards Commission. (Subsequently replaced by the Commission for Social Care Inspection (CSCI)) In Wales, the National Assembly for Wales set up a department or agency to be the regulatory body in Wales. These regulatory bodies are also responsible for the regulation of nursing agencies.

Part II sets out provisions in relation to registration, right of appeals and provisions for the regulation of establishments and standards and creates offences in respect of the regulations. National minimum standards have been issued for all homes. Local authority homes have to comply with the same standards as those set for independent homes.

Part III provides for the inspection of local authority fostering and adoption by the National Care Standards Commission and the National Assembly for Wales.

Part IV of the Act makes provision for the registration of social care workers by a General Social Care Council for England and a Care Council for Wales. These councils regulate the training of social workers and attempt to raise standards in social care through codes of conduct and practice. The Central Council for Education and Training in Social Work (CCETSW) has been abolished. The use of the title 'social worker' is also protected.

Part V of the Act, in response to the recommendations of the report of inquiry chaired by Sir Ronald Waterhouse,[37] established a Children's Commissioner for Wales (see Chapter 13).

Part VI makes arrangements for the regulation of childminding and day care provision, including checks on the suitability of persons working with children.

Part VII of the Act makes provision for the protection of children and vulnerable adults, including the duty of the Secretary of State to keep a list of persons considered unsuitable to work with children and vulnerable adults. There is a statutory duty on persons providing care for such individuals to refer potential individuals to the list holder.

Subsequent changes

As a consequence of the Health and Social Care (Community Health and Standards) Act 2003, the National Care Standards Commission was abolished and its functions under the Care Standards Act 2000 transferred to the Commission for Health Audit and Inspection (CHAI) (known as the Healthcare Commission) and the Commission for Social Care Inspection (CSCI). Part 2 Chapter 7 of the 2003 Act covers the functions of CHAI and CSCI under the Care Standards Act 2000. Each organisation has a general statutory duty to keep the Secretary of State informed about the provision in England of independent health services (CHAI) or registered social care services (CSCI) and in particular the availability and quality of the services. They are both also required to encourage the improvement in the quality of the services under their aegis. They may give advice to the Secretary of State on any changes that should be made to secure improvement in the quality of those services and must have particular regard to the need to safeguard and promote the rights and welfare of children. Additional functions can be placed on both organisations by regulations drawn up by the Secretary of State. Current government plans envisage that from April 2009 there will be a single regulatory body for all hospitals, NHS and private and residential care replacing the Healthcare Commission, the Mental Health Act Commission and the Commission for Social Care Inspection. This new body will have increased powers of control. Under the Disabled Persons (Independent Living) Bill, provision is made to ensure those with disabilities can make their own decisions about independent living.

Quality in social services

In August 2000, the government published a consultation document on improving quality of social care services in England.[38] It recommended the establishment of a new Social Care Institute for Excellence (SCIE), which will set out guidelines on effective social care practice and also set best practice guidelines 'to create a Lifelong Learning social care workforce culture'. Consultation will also take place on the introduction of a new quality framework for social services departments and on the reform of social work training, including the level and length of training and a formal re-registration scheme for professional staff to be regulated by the General Social Care Council (see above). The JM Consulting Report, published at the same time, recommended significant upgrading of several aspects of qualifying training and proposed a national curriculum for social work training, the development of centres of excellence and a three-year undergraduate qualification. SCIE conducted a survey in 2004 in order to develop a new vision of adult social care. Further details are available on the DH website. The Care Services Improvement Partnership (CSIP) was launched in April 2005 to provide high-quality support to help services improve and to put national policies into practice, involve people who use services and their carers, share positive practice, pass on research findings and encourage organisations to work in partnership across all sectors. Further information about CSIP and its publications can be found on its website.[39]

A claimant, X, succeeded in an application for judicial review of a community care assessment by Lambeth LBC which had refused a rehousing request.[40] X was incontinent and unable to stand or walk unsupported following an accident and lived in a flat. An assessment in 1999 noted that there were concerns about her accommodation and in 2003 an occupational therapist recommended that she be rehoused. However, in 2006 an assessment held that there was no eligible need arising from her accommodation. The judge held that the local authority had failed to take into account the history of her falls and issues relating to manual handling in her two sons, her carers, having to take her upstairs; had failed to follow the relevant guidance; and had failed to give her an opportunity to participate in the assessment process.

Community matrons

The NHS Improvement Plan for 2004 envisaged the use of community matrons to provide case management of people with long-term conditions. Community matrons would be experienced, skilled nurses who would have the following functions:

+ Use data to actively seek out patients who will benefit from the case management approach.
+ Combine high-level assessment of physical, mental and social care needs.

+ Review medication and prescribe medicine via independent and supplementary prescribing arrangements.

+ Provide clinical care and health-promoting interventions.

+ Coordinate inputs from all other agencies, ensuring all needs are met.

+ Teach and educate patients and their carers about warning signs of complications or crises.

+ Provide information so patients and families can make choices about current and future care needs.

+ Are highly visible to patients, and their families and carers and are seen by them as being in charge of their care.

+ Are seen by colleagues across all agencies as having the key role for patients with very high intensity needs.

The result of the employment of community matrons is expected to be the prevention of unnecessary admissions to hospital, a reduction in the length of stay in hospital, improved outcomes for patients, the integration of all elements of care, an improvement in patients' ability to function and their quality of life, helping patients and their families plan for the future, increase choice for patients, enable patients to remain in their home and communities and improve end-of-life care.[41] Best practice guidance was issued by the Department of Health in April 2006 to provide a framework for commissioners and providers of education and training for community matrons and case managers.[42] A confidential web forum has been set up for community matrons to share ideas and good practice.[43]

The specialist community public health nurse

The specialist community public health nurse has been defined by the specialist community public health nursing committee as follows:

> Specialist Community Public Health nursing aims to reduce health inequalities by working with individuals, families, and communities promoting health, preventing ill health and in the protection of health. The emphasis is on partnership working that cuts across disciplinary, professional and organisational boundaries that impact on organised social and political policy to influence the determinants of health and promote the health of whole populations.

Standards were set for specialist community public health nurses by the NMC in 2004 and can be downloaded from the NMC website. Guidance has also been issued for nurses working in public health or as school nurses and occupational health nurses for them to qualify as specialist community public health nurses.[44]

The school nurse

Role of the school nurse

The traditional role of one school nurse per school with a wide job description is dying out to be replaced by a nurse with responsibility for several schools, but having an advisory and teaching role rather than seeing children individually and with no direct involvement in first aid for pupils. She may be employed by the NHS, but works within an educational environment, which could cause tension, as the following Practical Dilemma 23.8 indicates. The Department of Health stated that in March 2006 there were 2,409 school nurses in England and it is the intention of the joint strategy of the Department for Education and Skills (now the DCSF) and the Department of Health to increase these numbers. The aim of the strategy is that there should be at least one full-time qualified nurse working with every cluster of primary schools and their related secondary schools by 2010. 'Looking for a School Nurse'[45] is published by the DfES (now the DCSF) and is aimed at head teachers, setting out the advantages and practical considerations of employing a school nurse.

Extent of duty

Practical Dilemma 23.8   An unexpected attack

The deputy head teacher asked Audrey, the school nurse, if she would cover Form 9A for one lesson, since the school was having difficulty in providing sufficient staff to supervise and teach the children because of the teachers' industrial action and the cut-back on the provision of supply teachers. Audrey said that she was employed by the NHS trust, not the education authority, and that her duty was to act as a school nurse, not a teacher or child-minder. The deputy was adamant she take the class and, protesting, Audrey did so. While she was supervising Form 9A, a child from Year 7, Justin Smith, had an epileptic fit. The form teacher, Kate Jay, sent a child to get the school nurse, but unfortunately Audrey could not be found. Kate had no experience in how to handle an epileptic patient and tried to lift Justin. His tongue slipped into his throat, he choked and went blue. Kate told another child to get the head teacher to call an ambulance. Unfortunately, by the time the ambulance arrived, Justin was dead and could not be resuscitated.

In this tragic situation, many different questions arise. What is the role of the school nurse? Is she on call for the whole time in school hours, waiting for such an emergency to arise? Many would say no, but it does depend, of course, on the individual employment contract and job description. The role she plays as far as teaching is concerned also varies from school to school. In some, she might take on the task of teaching such subjects as personal hygiene, health education, sex education, biology, etc. Where she is undertaking this role, it can hardly be expected that she will be fulfilling an emergency first aid role as well. In such circumstances, Audrey is not to blame for the death of Justin. A more likely action is possible against Kate and the education authority for failing to provide a basic first aid training for staff, especially when it would have been known that Justin was epileptic. Kate's action was the worst possible in the circumstances. An action is also possible against the local education authority for using the school nurse in another capacity so that she was not available. Details of a school nurse practice development resource pack (updated in 2006), a health visitor and school nurse development programme and primary school/primary health links projects operating with the Health Schools Standard are available from the Department of Health website.[46]

Use of car

Like any community worker, a school nurse must ensure that she has the appropriate insurance policy to cover all the uses that she is likely to make of a car for work purposes.

Practical Dilemma 23.9   Car insurance

A child, Mary Pugh, cut her head very badly in the gymnasium. The children had been told to trot around like ponies with their heads up high. Mary trotted straight into the teeth of another child. Blood gushed from the wound. Audrey, the school nurse, realised the importance of getting her to the A&E department for stitches. She put the child in her own car and rushed to the local hospital. In her haste, she came out of a side road too quickly and crashed into a motorcyclist coming along the main road. She got out of the car to see what could be done and, seeing that other people had gathered around, she decided that it was her duty to get Mary to hospital. Subsequently, she was notified that the police were charging her with failing to report an accident and having no adequate insurance cover. Relatives of the motorcyclist were also intending to sue her for causing the accident and failing to provide assistance, since the ambulance had taken 20 minutes to arrive and the cyclist had bled to death.

Any employee who does not usually use their car for work, other than going to and from work, would be well advised to ensure that insurance cover is provided for the exceptional circumstance when a car might be needed. Clinic nurses other than peripatetic nurses, school nurses or outpatient nurses might all find that on very rare occasions they need to use their car for work purposes and then they are not covered. The effect is that, although the insurance company may pay out compensation to the victim, it has the right to claim this money back from the person whose insurance did not cover this use. (If the company refuses to pay out compensation, compensation for physical injuries may be payable by the Motors Insurance Bureau.) If exceptional use of a car is foreseeable, it is wiser for the nurse to ensure that her insurance company is notified of this possibility.

As far as the failure to report the accident is concerned, it is a duty under the Road Traffic Act 1988 as amended to ensure that the police are notified of any accident in which personal injuries are caused. Audrey's failure to ensure that this was done could lead to a successful prosecution. Her failure to stop and help the cyclist is a difficult question. On the one hand, as was pointed out in Chapter 3, there is no obligation to volunteer help. On the other hand, however, in this case Audrey caused the harm and is under a legal obligation to mitigate it as far as possible but she also has a duty to Mary and it is a question of assessing who is in most need. From the facts given here, it would appear that the cyclist was in more danger and Audrey should have checked that there was nothing she could do before she went away.

The clinic nurse

Clinic nurses may spend their time in one clinic assisting at mother and baby clinics, be attached to specialist clinics such as family planning clinics or travel from school to school, assisting the school doctors in provision of medical, eye and other examinations for schoolchildren.

Obtaining consent

> **Practical Dilemma 23.10** Consent to rubella vaccinations
>
> Brenda West provided nursing assistance to the medical team that carried out the school medical examinations. One of their tasks was to offer the Year 8 girls a rubella vaccination. Letters were sent to the parents in advance, advising them of the service and asking for their consent. Unfortunately, Brenda failed to notice that the parents of Rachel Tyne had not signed the consent form and Rachel was given an injection by the school doctor. Shortly afterwards, Rachel came out in an all-over rash. Investigations were made and it appeared that Rachel had recently had a variety of drugs in anticipation of a holiday to Morocco and these had reacted with the rubella vaccination. The parents were threatening to sue since they did not want Rachel to have the vaccination as she had had German measles a few years before. They also felt that the doctor and nurse should have checked with them before they gave the vaccination to ensure that there were no contraindications.

There are two separate issues here: the one is the consent of the parents; the other is the timing of the vaccination. As far as consent is concerned, the basic principles are that parents have the right to consent to treatment for their children. As far as school health is concerned, it could be argued that under the education acts the school can provide the care as long as the parents do not object. This may well cover medical examinations, but is unlikely to cover the giving of injections. Some schools rely on a passive consent: 'We intend to examine and give your child X on . . . If you do not consent, please contact . . .' The validity of such an arrangement has not been tested in court.

However, if the vaccination is to proceed, it is essential that actual consent should be obtained, that any potential contraindications are identified and that the parents advise the school of any recent events in the child's medical history that suggest that a vaccination would be inappropriate at that particular time or, indeed, at any time. Because of the importance of this, it is advisable for the parents to give positive consent to the vaccination and reassure the staff about the non-existence of any contraindications. A child who is Gillick competent (see Chapter 13 and following section) could give a valid consent to treatment which is in her or his best interests.

As far as responsibility between the nurse and the doctor is concerned, much depends on the local policy in relation to who has the duty of ensuring that the parents' consent has been obtained. In some authorities, this would fall on the doctor. However, this does not necessarily mean that the nurse is free of all liability.

Minors

> **Practical Dilemma 23.11** Family planning and the under 16-year-old
>
> Maureen was working as a clinic nurse in the family planning clinic. She recognised one of the patients, Denise Wright, as a friend of her eldest daughter, aged 15. She completed the forms and the girl told her she was 17. Maureen knew that this was a lie. She was uncertain whether to tell the doctor and decided against this. The doctor prescribed the pill and asked Denise the name of her family doctor. Denise said she did not have one. She said she did not want any communication with her family and the doctor said that would not be necessary if she was over 16.

Several issues arise here. One is the question of the nurse's personal knowledge and the extent to which she should inform the doctor of this. The other is the question of the law relating to an under 16-year-old in this context. This latter point is considered in Chapter 13. From the House of Lords' decision in the Gillick case, it can be seen that in exceptional circumstances treatment and advice can be given to a girl under 16 without the parents being involved.

As far as the first issue is concerned, it could be argued that even though the nurse has acquired information about the patient from a different source, if this is relevant to the doctor's care and treatment of the patient, then it should be disclosed, i.e. her duty of care to the patient would require her to tell the doctor that the girl was 15. Similarly, if she knew that the girl suffered from epilepsy, even though the girl had not told the doctor this, the nurse should pass on the information. It could be argued that this principle applies only to information that is relevant to the care of the child. Thus, if she by chance knew that the girl had been charged by the police for shoplifting, this need not be passed on.

The Children Act 1989 requires decisions relating to children to take into account the wishes of the child where the child has the capacity (see Chapter 13).

The practice nurse

The legal situation of the practice nurse can vary, especially as far as employment rights are concerned. Some practice nurses may be employed by a single-handed or group general practitioner; others are employed by primary care trusts. Practice nurses employed by primary care trusts are more likely to be part of a nursing hierarchy and to receive guidance and policies from the employer. Recent years have seen a considerable growth in the educational and management support provided to practice nurses. In many areas, a practice liaison nurse is appointed to provide assistance and professional advice across the PCT area(s).

Scope of professional practice and the practice nurse

Like other nurses, practice nurses are finding that their scope of professional practice is expanding as they are required to undertake a wider range of responsibilities. While practice nurses were not identified in the First Crown Report on nurse prescribing as one of the groups able to prescribe in the community, they were, together with nurses working in walk-in centres, added to the list of nurses who could prescribe in February 2000. The Final Crown Report envisages that many different health professionals will be recognised as dependent or independent prescribers. (This is discussed further in Chapter 28. Legal issues relating to the scope of professional practice are considered in Chapter 24; see especially page 575.)

Cervical screening

The practice nurse may be required to undertake cervical screening. It is essential that they have appropriate approved training. A practice nurse in Birmingham, who had been taught by her GP to undertake cervical screening, was discovered to be using the spatula by the wrong end and her failure to take the correct samples led to non-diagnosis of several women with cervical cancer.

The standard required in cervical screening came before the courts when East Kent Health Authority were alleged to have been liable for the negligent examination of cervical smears.

> **Case 23.6**   *Penney, Palmer and Cannon v. E Kent Health Authority (2000)*
>
> ### Cervical screening[47]
>
> The claimants brought an action on the grounds that their cervical smears were negligently examined and reported as negative between 1989 and 1992. As a consequence, they were deprived of the opportunity of obtaining early treatment that would have prevented the development of endocervical carcinoma. Screening was carried out by qualified biomedical scientists or by qualified cytology screeners. They were not qualified to diagnose; their only function was to report what, using their expertise, they were able to see. If the screener detected an abnormality in the smear or was in doubt whether what he saw was abnormal, he had to pass the smear on to a senior screener known as a checker. The cervical screening programme guidelines required an absolute confidence test. The trial judge decided that this absolute confidence test had not been complied with and found for the claimants.

The judge preferred the views of the claimants' experts as to whether, in the light of what the cytoscreeners saw, it was negligent to fail either to classify the smears as borderline or to refer the smears to the checker and/or to the pathologist.

The Bolam Principle did not apply because the Bolam Test was concerned with acceptable and unacceptable practice, whereas no question of acceptable practice arose in the instant case because the cytoscreeners were wrong in their classification of the smears.

Even if the Bolam Principle were relevant, the defendant's experts' views did not stand up to logical analysis because the cytoscreeners did not have the ability to draw a distinction between benign and precancerous cells and so should have classified the smears as borderline.

The Court of Appeal dismissed the appeal and upheld the finding that the health authority was liable. It held that the Bolam Test was appropriate where the exercise of skill and judgement of the screener was being questioned. In this case, however, the Bolam Test did not apply since the screeners were not expected to exercise judgement.

It was announced in 2000 that the government was to introduce a pilot study of a new form of cervical screening, liquid-based cytology (LBC), together with tests for the virus HPV that causes cervical cancer. The National Institute for Health and Clinical Excellence has suggested that LBC could increase the sensitivity of the slides, reduce the number of badly taken smears and improve the speed and accuracy with which cytoscreeners can read the slides.[48]

Employment situation

The legal position of the practice nurse as an employee differs according to whether she is employed by a practice or single-handed general practitioner or if she is employed by the primary care trust. In the former case, as an employee of someone who employs only a few people, she may not have all the statutory benefits to which the NHS trust employee will be entitled. If she is employed by a single-handed general practitioner, she may find it more difficult to resist pressure for her to go outside her limits of competence and she lacks the back-up of a clear nursing hierarchy and nurse management support. Her professional standards should, however, be the same.

The palliative care nurse

Palliative care nurses may work in the community visiting patients in their own homes or in a hospice or both. Issues relating to resuscitation and DNAR instructions and the distinction between killing and letting die are considered in Chapter 16. In the case of Bodkin Adams, where an Eastbourne doctor was prosecuted for the death of the patient on the grounds that he had prescribed an overdose of morphine, the judge, in directing the jury on the law that applied to the case, said:

> *There has been a good deal of discussion about the circumstances in which a doctor might be justified in giving drugs which would shorten life in cases of severe pain. It is my duty to tell you that the law knows no special defence of this character. But that does not mean that a doctor aiding the sick or dying has to calculate in minutes or hours, or perhaps in days or weeks, the effect on a patient's life of the medicines which he administers.*
>
> *If the first purpose of medicine – the restoration of health – can no longer be achieved, there is still much for the doctor to do, and he is entitled to do all that is proper and necessary to relieve pain and suffering even if the measures he takes may incidentally shorten life . . . It remains a fact, and remains a law, that no doctor has the right to cut off life deliberately . . . [the defence counsel] was saying that the treatment given by the doctor was designed to promote comfort; and if it was the right and proper treatment of the case, the fact that incidentally it shortened life does not give any grounds for convicting him of murder.*[49]

Dr Adams was found not guilty of murder.

However, the level of prescribing must be consistent with the reasonable practice of a competent medical practitioner and any nurse who was concerned about the levels of analgesics given to a patient could check the prescription with another registered medical practitioner or ask a pharmacist for advice in the light of the previous medicinal history of the patient. Further discussion on the law relating to pain management can be found in the author's book.[50] A website has been set up by a clinical nurse specialist in pain management to provide a forum for information giving and discussion on pain management.[51] New guidance[52] was issued in October 2007 by the BMA, the Resuscitation Council (UK) and the RCN on resuscitation which envisaged that a registered nurse could be the responsible clinician making the decision over CPR. It is considered in Chapter 16. A Palliative Care Bill introduced by Baroness Finley into the House of Lords in 2007 received its third reading but failed to progress to the House of Lords. See also the author's book on legal aspects of death.[53]

Conclusions

Following the amalgamation of community health services with primary care services within a primary care trust, the new GP contracts and the establishment of care trusts, covering both social and health services, major changes are being made in the traditional roles of practice nurse, clinic nurse and community nurse. While in the past the majority of practice nurses were employed by a GP practice, now they are increasingly likely to be employed by a primary care trust or care trust and share the same employer with their community nurse colleagues. The potential for improvement and development in community health and primary care services as a result of the Health Act 1999 is now being realised and has major implications for the role of the nurse. In addition, the establishment of care trusts (combining primary healthcare and social service responsibilities) further assists in the integration of health and social care as envisaged in Chapter 7 of the NHS Plan. The emphasis on primary healthcare and the significant role of the PCT in obtaining services from the secondary sector is leading to an increase in treatments being carried out in primary or intermediate care. This refocusing creates both opportunities and challenges for nurses working outside the secondary or tertiary care sector. In particular, there are considerable enhancements in the sphere of professional competence and it is to this area that we turn in the next chapter.

Reflection questions

1 You break an ornament while visiting a patient. The ornament is valued at £5,000. You are personally unable to meet the costs of replacing it. What remedies are available to the owner of the ornament? (See also Chapter 25.)

2 What special concerns does the community professional have in relation to health and safety and what specific precautions should be taken to protect her? (Refer also to Chapter 12.)

3 What difficulties, if any, arise from the fact that the school nurse is employed by the NHS trust and works with education authority staff? Could the school nurse refuse to undertake tasks allocated by the head teacher? What are the likely implications?

4 What differences exist in law between the clinic nurse who spends all her time in a clinic and the nurse who visits patients in their own homes?

5 Consider the expanded-role activities that are sometimes undertaken by the practice nurse or community nurse and outline the legal requirements. (See Chapter 24.)

Further exercises

1 As a community nurse, you visit a patient who appears to you to be incapable of caring for herself. What action would you take? Outline a procedure to cover the situation if the patient shows extreme reluctance to move from her home and there are no relatives to care for her.

2 Obtain details of the procedures for assessment for community care as a result of the 1990 Act. What impact have these had on your practice? How are assessment procedures changed as a result of the NHS Plan?

3 Consider the developments that have taken place with the establishment of primary care trusts and care trusts. How have these affected your professional practice and what improvements have been made in the quality of care provided to the patient?

References

1 Department of Health, Keeping the NHS Local. Guidance Gateway Reference 3487; available on DH website

2 Health and Social Care Act 2001 Sections 50-52; The Preserved Rights (Transfer of Responsibilities to Local Authorities) Regulations 2001, SI 2001 No. 3776; LAC(2002)7

3   The Audit Commission, Taking Care: progress with care in the community, HMSO, London, December 1993

4   R v. *North and East Devon Health Authority ex parte Coughlan* [2000] 3 All ER 850; [2000] 2 WLR 622

5   Royal Commission, Report on the Long-Term Care of the Elderly, with Respect to Old Age, The Stationery Office, London, 1999

6   R v. *Gloucester County Council and Another ex parte Barry* [1997] 2 All ER 1 HL

7   R v. *Sefton Metropolitan Borough Council ex parte Help the Aged* [1997] 3 FCR 573 CA

8   LASSL(97)13 Responsibilities of Local Authority Social Services Departments: implications of recent legal judgments

9   LAC(98)19 Community Care (Residential Accommodation) Act 1998

10 *R (on the application of Grogan)* v. *Bexley NHS Care Trust* [2006] EWHC 44; (2006) 9 CCL 188

11 Department of Health, The National Framework for NHS Continuing Healthcare and NHS-funded Nursing Care, DH, June 2007

12 Audit Commission Report, Fully Equipped: the provision of equipment to older or disabled people by the NHS and social services in England and Wales, AC, March 2000

13 *R (on the application of Johnson)* v. *Havering LBC* [2007] EWCA 26; *The Times*, 2 February 2007

14 *YL* v. *Birmingham City Council and others* [2007] UKHL 22; The Times Law Report 21 June 2007

15 House of Lords and House of Commons Joint Committee on Human Rights of Older People in Healthcare, 18th Session 2006-7, HL 156-I/HC 378-I, August 2007

16 *JE* v. *DE; Sub nom DE, Re,* [2006] EWHC 3459 (Fam)

17 *R (on the application of Gunter)* v. *SouthWestern Staffordshire Primary Care Trust* [2005] EWHC 1894

18 *B Borough Council* v. *S* [2006] EWHC 2584

19 Department of Health, NHS Plan, Cmnd 4818-I, The Stationery Office, London, July 2000

20 Delayed Discharges (England) Regulations 2003, SI 2003 No. 2277

21 Department of Health, Delayed discharges in the non-acute and mental health sectors, DH, 2007

22 *Barnet Primary Care Trust* v. *X* [2006] EWHC 787; (2006) BMLR 17

23 Explanatory notes to the Carers and Disabled Children Act 2000; http://www.legislation.hmso.gov.uk/acts/en/2000en16.htm

24 Carer's National Strategy Document, Caring about Carers, The Stationery Office, London, 8 February 1999

25 R v. *Family Health Services Appeal Authority ex p Muralidhar* [1999] COD 80

26 R v. *Hillingdon Health Authority ex parte Wyatt, The Times,* 20 December 1977 CA

27 Health and Safety Executive, RR495, Violence management training: the development of effective trainers in the delivery of violence management training in healthcare settings, HSE, 2006

28 Health and Safety Commission, Violence and aggression to staff in health services, HSE Books, 1997

29 *Re C (An Adult: refusal of medical treatment)* [1994] 1 All ER 819

30 *Re MB (Adult: medical treatment)* [1997] 2 FLR 426

31 *St George's Healthcare NHS Trust* v. *S* [1998] 3 All ER 673

32 *Re T* [1992] 4 All ER 649

33 *F* v. *Berkshire HA* [1989] 2 All ER 545

34 Law Commission Report No. 231, Mental Incapacity, The Stationery Office, London, 1995

[35] Modernising Social Services, Cm 4169, The Stationery Office, London, DH, 30 November 1998

[36] Department of Health, Fit for the Future? National required standards for residential and nursing homes for older people (consultation document), DH, London, 1999

[37] Lost in care – the report of the tribunal of inquiry (chaired by Sir Ronald Waterhouse) into the abuse of children in care in the former county council areas of Gwynedd and Clwyd since 1974, February 2000, The Stationery Office, London, HC 201

[38] Department of Health, A Quality Strategy for Social Care, DH, August 2000

[39] www.csip.org.uk

[40] *R (On the application of Ireneschild)* v. *Lambeth LBC* [2006] EWHC 2354; (2006) 9 CCL Rep. 686

[41] Department of Health, Community Matrons, DH, May 2007

[42] Department of Health, Best Practice Guidance Framework for commissioners and providers of education and training for community matrons and case managers, DH, April 2006

[43] NHS Networks website from DH website

[44] Nursing and Midwifery Council, Information packs for public health nurses (October 2006); for school and occupational health nurses (December 2006)

[45] DfES, Looking for a School Nurse, DfES, 2006

[46] www.dh.gov.uk/

[47] *Penney, Palmer and Cannon* v. *East Kent Health Authority* [2000] Lloyd's Rep Med 2000 p. 41 CA

[48] Dr Thomas Stuttaford, New screening should cut smear errors, *The Times*, 3 August 2000

[49] *R* v. *Bodkin Adams* [1957] Crim LR 365

[50] B. Dimond, *The Legal Aspects of Pain Management*, Quay Books, Dinton, 2002

[51] www.pain-talk.co.uk; email Glenn Bruce (site manager) info@pain-talk.co.uk

[52] British Medical Association, Resuscitation Council (UK) and the Royal College of Nursing, Decisions Relating to Cardiopulmonary Resuscitation, BMA, October 2007, Paragraph 13, p. 19

[53] B. Dimond, *The Legal Aspects of Death*, Quay Books, Dinton, 2008

Chapter 24
Scope of professional practice, clinical nurse specialist and consultant nurse

Introduction

The government's plans for the new NHS as shown in the White Paper,[1] in the document 'Making a Difference'[2] and in the NHS Plan[3] relied heavily on a widened scope of practice for the nurse. NHS Direct and walk-in clinics are run by nurses and provide an increasingly extensive and popular service. As a consequence of these developments, the role of the nurse is changing radically and these changes have major legal implications. This chapter considers the background to the scope of professional practice and the NMC advice, the role of the consultant nurse and clinical nurse specialist. One development in the scope of professional practice is the change in nurse prescribing and this is considered in Chapter 28.

Scope of professional practice

In June 1992, the UKCC (the predecessor to the NMC) published the 'Scope of Professional Practice'. It marked a major development in the thinking underlying professional practice. Previously, the concept of the extended role highlighted the distinction between the basic training that the practitioner received in order to become a registered professional and post-registration training. Under 'the extended role', professional development was seen as incremental, task oriented and often delegated from other professionals (usually medical). A circular in 1977 (CHC (77)22) gave advice on extended role tasks. This advice has now been superseded by subsequent developments on the scope of professional practice.

In 1986, a working party was set up by the Standing Medical Advisory Committee and the Standing Nursing and Midwifery Committee to review the extended role of the nurse. Its report was circulated under cover of a DHSS letter from the Chief Nursing Officer, dated 26 September 1989, and it paved the way for the publication of the UKCC's 'Scope of Professional Practice'.

The UKCC emphasised that professional practice must be sensitive, relevant and responsive to the needs of individual patients and clients and have the capacity to adjust, where and when appropriate, to changing circumstances (Paragraph 1). It set out principles that should govern adjustment to the scope of professional practice (Paragraph 9). These are laid out in Box 24.1. The 'Scope of Professional Practice' should be seen in the light of the new Code of Professional Conduct drawn up by the NMC.[4] Paragraph 6 of the Code requires practitioners to maintain their professional knowledge and competence. This includes taking part regularly in learning activities that develop competence and performance; acknowledging the limits of professional competence and only undertaking practice and accepting responsibilities for those activities in which the practitioner is competent; where an aspect of practice is beyond one's level of competence or outside one's area of registration, obtaining help and supervision from a competent practitioner, until the practitioner and her employer consider that the requisite knowledge and skill have been acquired. A duty is also recognised by the NMC for the practitioner to facilitate students of nursing and midwifery and others to develop their competence and also the responsibility of delivering care based on current evidence, best practice and, where applicable, validated research when it is available.

> **Box 24.1** **Principles for adjusting the scope of professional practice**
>
> The registered nurse, midwife or health visitor:
>
> 1 must be satisfied that each aspect of practice is directed to meeting the needs and serving the interests of the patient or client
>
> 2 must endeavour always to achieve, maintain and develop knowledge, skill and competence to respond to those needs and interests
>
> 3 must honestly acknowledge any limits of personal knowledge and skill and take steps to remedy any relevant deficits in order effectively and appropriately to meet the needs of patients and clients
>
> 4 must ensure that any enlargement or adjustment of the scope of personal professional practice must be achieved without compromising or fragmenting existing aspects of professional practice and care and that requirements of the Council's Code of Professional Conduct are satisfied throughout the whole area of practice
>
> 5 must recognise and honour the direct or indirect personal accountability borne for all aspects of professional practice
>
> 6 must, in serving the interests of patients and clients and the wider interests of society, avoid any inappropriate delegation to others that compromises those interests.

The post-registration education and practice (PREP), which is the NMC's framework for continuing education, includes a duty on practitioners to have at least five refresher days every three years. Implementation commenced in April 1995. Undoubtedly, there are opportunities for nursing, midwifery and health visiting to develop safely beyond the original boundaries. It enables professional practice to develop naturally into areas that were once seen as delegated medical tasks; it moves development away from new tasks to a more holistic view of professional practice relevant to a nurse, midwife or health visitor (since 2004 known as the specialist community public health nurse, SCPHN).

The National Plan for the NHS,[5] published in July 2000, envisaged that within the reformed NHS there will be radical changes in the ways in which staff work. The new NHS Modernisation Agency (set up by the government to plan and implement the changes) will lead a major drive to ensure that protocol-based care takes hold throughout the NHS. A statement on the future direction of the NHS Modernisation Agency was published by the DH in 2005 which envisaged the original organisation being replaced by a new central organisation smaller than the MA with a focus on innovation and an emphasis on local implementation.

The new approach to the scope of professional practice shatters old demarcations that have held back staff and slowed down care. NHS employers will be required to empower appropriately qualified nurses, midwives and therapists to undertake a wider range of clinical tasks including the right to make and receive referrals, admit and discharge patients, order investigations and diagnostic tests, run clinics and prescribe drugs. The inclusion of the suitably experienced nurse with the consultant and GP in identifying those responsible for making decisions on CPR[6] (see Chapter 16) is a natural development of the scope of professional practice of the registered nurse. It will be the responsibility of the individual nurse to ensure that she has the requisite competence to make such a decision.

The ten key roles identified for the nurse by the Chief Nursing Officer and set out in the NHS Plan are shown in Box 24.2.

Box 24.2   Ten key roles for nurses in the NHS Plan

1 To order diagnostic investigations such as pathology tests and X-rays.
2 To make and receive referrals direct, say, to a therapist or pain consultant.
3 To admit and discharge patients for specified conditions and within agreed protocols.
4 To manage patient caseloads, say for diabetes or rheumatology.
5 To run clinics, say for ophthalmology or dermatology.
6 To prescribe medicines and treatments.
7 To carry out a wide range of resuscitation procedures, including defibrilation.
8 To perform minor surgery and outpatient procedures.
9 To triage patients using the latest IT to the most appropriate health professional.
10 To take a lead in the way local health services are both organised and run.

Delegation and supervision

The scope of professional practice of individual health professionals cannot be expanded unless there is either an increase in those registered professionals or activities are delegated to others such as healthcare assistants or support workers. The Bolam Test (see Chapter 3) applies to the delegation of activities. It is the personal and professional responsibility of each practitioner who delegates activities to ensure that the person to carry out that activity is trained, competent and has the necessary experience to undertake the activity safely. The delegating practitioner must also ensure that the appropriate level of supervision is provided. (Delegation and supervision is considered in Chapter 4.)

At the time of writing the NMC is consulting on a new code. In its new draft Code the NMC states:

+ Delegate effectively

+ You must establish that anyone you delegate to is competent to carry out your instructions

+ You must confirm that the outcome of any delegated task meets required standards

+ You must make sure that everyone you are responsible for is properly supervised

The NMC issued new advice for delegation to non-regulated healthcare staff in 2007[7] which is available on its website. It sets out 10 principles for nurses and midwives to follow when delegating to non-regulated healthcare staff. These principles are as follows:

+ The delegation of nursing or midwifery care must always take place in the best interests of the patient or client and the decision to delegate must always be based on an assessment of the individual patient or client's needs.

+ Where a registrant has authority to delegate tasks to another, they will retain responsibility and accountability for that delegation.

+ A registrant may only delegate an aspect of care to a person whom they deem competent to perform the task and they should assure themselves that the person to whom they have delegated fully understands the nature of the delegated task and what is required of them.

+ Where another, such as an employer, has the authority to delegate an aspect of care, the employer becomes accountable for that delegation. The registrant will, however, continue to carry responsibility to intervene if she feels that the proposed delegation is inappropriate or unsafe.

+ The decision whether or not to delegate an aspect of care and to transfer and/or to rescind delegation is the sole responsibility of the registrant and is based on their professional judgement.

+ The registrant has the right to refuse to delegate if they believe that it would be unsafe to do so or is unable to provide or ensure adequate supervision.

+ It is essential that those delegating care, and those employees undertaking delegated duties, do so within a robust local employment policy framework to protect the public and support safe practice.

+ The decision to delegate is either made by the registrant or the employer and it is the decision maker who is accountable for it.

+ Healthcare can sometimes be unpredictable. It is important that the person to whom aspects of care are being delegated understands their limitations and when not to proceed should the circumstances within which the task has been delegated change.

+ No one should feel pressurised into either delegating or accepting a delegated task. In such circumstances, advice should be sought, in the first instance, from the registrant's professional line manager and then, if necessary, the NMC.

The Nursing and Midwifery Council has also provided guidance on the delegation of tasks by midwives.[8] It states that only a practising midwife (i.e. a registered midwife who has met all the updating requirements for her midwifery practice and has notified her intention to practise to the LSA) is able to provide care and advice during the antenatal, *intra-partum* or post-natal period:

> *It is for the midwife to decide whether the delegation of tasks Is appropriate in the care of a woman or her baby.*
>
> *If the midwife considers that any part of the care programme can be safely delegated to another member of the caring team, she remains accountable for the appropriateness of the delegation. If a task is delegated, the midwife must ensure that the person who does the work is able to do it and must provide adequate supervision and support. Such delegation must not compromise existing care and the midwife must be satisfied that the care meets the needs of the woman.*

Such advice would, of course, apply to all the different specialties covered by NMC registered practitioners.

Nurse consultants

Clinical nurse specialists and consultant nurses are seen as having a major role to play in providing an improved service for patients. The NHS Plan envisaged that there will be 1,000 nurse consultants and therapist consultants will also be appointed. The key features of the consultant nurse as envisaged in the Department of Health's 'Making a Difference',[9] are shown in Box 24.3.

Box 24.3 **Key features of the consultant nurse**

1 Expert practice.
2 Professional leadership and consultancy.
3 Education and development.
4 Practice and service development linked to research and evaluation.

It was envisaged that at least 50 per cent of the time of nurse consultants will be spent on clinical work with career opportunities. NHS trusts were required to agree the posts with regional offices of the DH.

Clinical nurse specialists and specialist nurses

In addition, clinical nurse specialists have taken on a wide range of expanded duties often working within protocols agreed with medical staff. They may also have managerial responsibilities. Other specialist nurses may or may not come within the category of clinical nurse specialists, but are increasingly taking on expanded-role functions. It would be impossible in a book of this type to explore the wide range of specialties covered by nurses, often functioning within a multidisciplinary team, but making many decisions on their own. They include continence care, stoma care, pain management, diabetic and A&E nurse practitioners.

For example, nurses working in breast care in community, general practice and hospital settings are increasingly undertaking expanded roles. In the guidance for breast care nurses from the RCN,[10] a checklist that applies to all expanded-role tasks is provided for extending roles:

Is this new skill/role consistent with nursing practice?

Is it consistent with my current job description?

Does it fit current priorities – nursing and organisational?

What changes will it entail?

Will I need to stop some parts of my current care?

Do I need accreditation?

How will I get it?

Do I need additional skills?

How will I get them?

Do I need a training period before I take on the new responsibility?

Do I have a mentor for this change?

How will I evaluate my performance in the new role?

Have I got clinical supervision?

Clinical nurse specialists and consultant nurses and clinical guidelines

It has been emphasised that when a clinical nurse specialist or consultant nurse takes on an expanded role they must provide the same standard of care which would have been provided by the health professional who would originally have performed that activity. Thus an A&E clinical specialist nurse undertaking activities that would in the past have been performed by junior doctors would be expected to provide the reasonable standard of care of a doctor. Jo Wilson[11] has suggested that guidelines can be very useful in role expansion and assist the expanded role practitioner in delivering a higher standard of care that reflects: additional training and regular updates; additional competency and expertise; skills required for the activity. She lists the considerations that should be taken into account in drafting guidelines:

+ description and limitations to the activity being performed
+ degree of supervision required
+ audit, evaluation and outcome data
+ making the status of the treating nurse known to patient
+ obtaining the patient's consent
+ regular education/training updates.

(Further consideration on the legal significance of guidelines, procedures and protocols can be found in Chapter 3.)

Concerns about developments in scope of professional practice

Practitioners have concerns, however, as a result of the move away from certified tasks and the rapid development in the scope of professional practice, which include the following:

1 How do I know if I am competent?
2 How does my employer know if I am competent?
3 What happens if I undertake an activity that is outside my field of competence?
4 Where do I stand if a doctor/senior manager/other professional ignores my refusal to undertake an activity because I have not sufficient competence or experience to undertake that activity?
5 How can I ensure that I receive the appropriate training for my expanded role?

Some situations will be considered that highlight these dilemmas.

Practical Dilemma 24.1   Scope of professional practice (1)

Mavis, a staff nurse, was asked by the registrar to do the intravenous infusions. The registrar rushed away before she had the chance to explain to him that she had not developed the skills, competence and knowledge to undertake that activity safely. However, she decided that she would carry out his instructions as best she could. Unfortunately, when she was adding a drug to Jimmy Price's intravenous infusion, she failed to set the speed of his drip correctly and as a result Jimmy became very ill. Where do Mavis and the registrar stand in relation to the responsibility for the harm to Jimmy?

As far as Mavis was concerned, she was at fault in failing to mention her lack of competence for that activity to the registrar. No nurse should work outside her range of competence and skill unless a dire emergency arises when the risks in failing to act are greater than the risks in acting. There is no suggestion that this was an emergency. The nurse ignored a fundamental principle of the Code of Professional Conduct (Paragraphs 6.2 and 6.3):

To practise competently, you must possess the knowledge, skills and abilities required for lawful, safe and effective practice without direct supervision. You must acknowledge the limits of your professional competence and only undertake practice and accept responsibilities for those activities in which you are competent.

If an aspect of practice is beyond your level of competence or outside your area of registration, you must obtain help and supervision from a competent practitioner until you and your employer consider that you have acquired the requisite knowledge and skill.

The failure of Mavis to notify the doctor that she was not competent in this area and the resulting mistake that caused harm to the patient could result in a civil action being brought against her employer because of its vicarious liability for the negligent actions of an employee acting in the course of employment (see pages 67–72).

Mavis herself may be subject to fitness to practise proceedings before the NMC Conduct and Competence Committee. Were Jimmy to die, she might also face criminal proceedings. Her employer, of course, would commence its own disciplinary inquiry and proceedings.

What of the registrar? Is he also at fault? If the addition of drugs to intravenous transfusions were seen as a task delegated by a doctor to a nurse practitioner, he would be liable as delegator in failing to ensure that he was delegating to a competent person. However, under the scope of professional practice, such activities are not seen as 'delegated tasks' and the duty is incumbent on the individual nurse practitioner to ensure that, if she herself was not competent, another practitioner, whether medical or nursing, who was competent, performed the activity. The standard of care that the patient is entitled to expect does not depend on which professional is undertaking a particular activity. The reasonable standard of care will be required of any professional carrying out an extended role: if that activity were formerly carried out by a doctor, then a nurse undertaking that activity will be expected to provide the reasonable standard that a doctor would have provided. The Bolam Test, which is discussed in Chapter 3, is used to define the reasonable standard. The managerial responsibilities in ensuring appropriate supervision and allocation of activities are discussed in Chapter 4.

Can a nurse refuse to undertake training in new areas of competency?

It was a principle under the concept of the 'extended role' that nurses could refuse to undertake a new task or activity. However, this approach is probably no longer appropriate in relation to the scope of professional practice. Clause 6.1 of the Code of Professional Conduct requires nurses to 'keep your knowledge and skills up to date throughout your working life'.

It would be entirely inappropriate for a practitioner to refuse to develop her professional practice beyond the level she reached when she became registered. In addition, it is directly contrary to the principles of PREP. She would be contractually entitled to receive from her employer the necessary training to ensure that she was competent in the new range of activities. It is a contractual requirement of the employer to ensure that staff are competent to perform the work they are asked to perform.

There are other contractual considerations. In an interview for a job, for example, a nurse might be told that a contractual requirement for that particular post is that the nurse is competent in a specified area. If the nurse agrees to this condition, then she is contractually bound to develop, with support from the employer, the appropriate skills, knowledge and competence. If she refuses the condition, she will probably not get the post.

Scope of professional practice in primary care

Practical Dilemma 24.2 **Liability and the scope of professional practice (2)**

Practice Nurse Jenny Brown was asked by the GP, her employer, to make a primary visit to a child whose mother had reported him too ill to come to surgery. Jenny Brown visited the child, took his temperature and blood pressure and examined him. She told the mother that she thought he was suffering from the flu that was going round at present, to keep him warm with lots of drinks and, if he worsened or failed to improve within a few days, to let the surgery know. She reported the results of the visit to the GP, who approved of her action. Unfortunately, that same night an emergency call was made by the mother to the out-of-hours service and the boy was rushed to hospital, where he was diagnosed as suffering from meningitis. He eventually died. The mother is now demanding that action be taken against both the nurse and the doctor. What is the responsibility of the nurse and the doctor?

If the nurse had acted outside her competence, been negligent and caused harm as a consequence, then she will be liable. The doctor will be vicariously liable for the actions of a negligent nurse employed by the doctor. In this case, there would be an investigation to establish the tests undertaken by the nurse and the advice that she gave to the mother and whether her actions satisfied the standard of the reasonable medical practitioner. The competence of a nurse in making a primary visit will become of increasing importance with the expansion of nurse prescribing. In any case, even when the doctor is not the employer of the nurse, where there is delegation of a task that is normally performed by a doctor, the doctor will remain liable in civil law for that task unless he has delegated it to a competent, trained person and provides the requisite supervision for the task to be done safely. Here one might question whether it was a suitable case for the practice nurse to undertake. Had she the necessary training and skills to detect whether the patient was suffering from mumps or another condition? Once she had visited the patient, should she not have arranged for the GP to attend or ensured that a closer eye was kept on him? Did she make all the appropriate tests and checks when she visited the boy? If these questions are answered in such a way that the nurse is shown to be at fault, then the GP could well be liable for any harm that has consequentially befallen the boy (there may, in fact, be no harm suffered, since the short delay in diagnosis may have had no effect) and the nurse would also be liable for undertaking a task that she was not competent to perform. In either event, the nurse would be held professionally accountable before the NMC for her actions. Even had there been no negligence on the part of the GP, he, as her employer, would be vicariously liable for the practice nurse's negligence.

Scope of professional practice in theatre nursing

Practical Dilemma 24.3 **Scope of professional practice and theatres**

Myra Jones had worked in theatre for over 20 years and was an extremely experienced nurse. She had asked for training in acting as a first assistant, but the surgeons had stated that this was not a role that should be performed by nurses. One day, she was asked by the registrar to assist in an appendectomy because there was a shortage of junior doctors. She knew that she could do the work competently, but was hesitant. What is the legal situation?

Should she refuse on the grounds that she has not been trained to fulfil this role? What if this request comes at night when there is only a registrar on his own and it is an emergency case? The basic principle is that, whatever duties she is called on to perform, she should undertake no work that she is not competent to undertake.

In an emergency situation, when the harm to the patient of her acting is outweighed by the harm to the patient of her not acting, the balance might be in favour of her acting as assistant (but these occasions are likely to be rare). To refuse to perform certain tasks is not pleasant for the nurse, but it is her duty both in civil law and also as part of the Code of Professional Conduct of her profession. Only in this way can the safety of the patient be ensured. If such situations arise where the nurse is expected to undertake tasks for which she is not trained, this must ultimately be referred to nurse management. If this proves ineffective, then the nurse may need to take advantage of the whistleblower's protection, which is discussed in Chapter 4.

In Practical Dilemma 24.3, it is hoped that the surgeons would ultimately recognise that this is an activity that is suitable for role expansion and ensure that they take part in the necessary training for the nurses selected to develop their practice in this way.

Scope of professional practice in emergency nursing

A joint report by the RCN and the DH[12] has attempted to dispel the myths about what nurses and other health professionals may or are entitled to do in emergency care. The booklet aims to show directors of nursing how they can empower staff to take responsibility for change and to show managers to use it to support staff in developing their roles. It is available from the DH website.[13] Fact sheets cover the myths about the legal and professional framework, clinical governance, the emergency services collaboration, CHD and primary care collaboratives.

Scope of professional practice and X-rays

The ordering of X-rays may constitute an expanded role for the nurse, but she should be aware of the rules relating to this. The Ionising Radiation (Medical Exposure) Regulations 2000[14] were enacted, together with the Ionising Radiations Regulations 1999[15] to comply with European Directive 97/43/Euratom.[16] This directive lays down:

+ basic measures for the health protection of individuals against dangers of ionising radiation in relation to medical exposure
+ duties on those responsible for administering ionising radiation
+ need to protect persons undergoing medical exposure whether as part of their own medical diagnosis or treatment or of occupational health surveillance, health screening, voluntary participation in research or medicolegal procedures.

The regulations do not specify that any specified health professional must be a referrer (i.e. the person ordering the X-ray), but require that the referrer must be entitled in accordance with the employer's procedures to refer individuals for medical exposure to a practitioner. Regulation 6 prohibits any medical exposure from being carried out that has not been justified and authorised and sets out matters to be taken into account for justification.

The referrer has a duty to supply the practitioner with sufficient medical data relevant to the medical exposure requested by the referrer to enable the practitioner to decide whether there is sufficient net benefit as required by Regulation 6(1)(a). Applying these requirements to nurses: this means that nurses may be referrers, i.e. order X-rays, but they must have the training and competence which enables them to provide the medical data to enable the radiographer to decide whether the patient should be exposed to the X-rays.[17] Guidance has been provided by the Department of Health on the regulations and is available on the Internet.[18] The fact sheet provided within the publication 'Freedom to practice: dispelling the myths'[19] points out that nurses requesting radiological examinations can be referrers under the Ionising Regulations provided that they have the competence, conferred by training and experience, to provide the medical data required to enable the practitioner (usually a radiologist) to decide whether there is net benefit to the patient from the exposure. The nurse would require the consent of the employer who would specify the type or range of conditions for which the nurse can be the referrer.

NHS Direct and walk-in clinics

Practical Dilemma 24.4   **Scope of professional practice (3)**

A nurse employed by NHS Direct received a phone call from a woman of 28 who said she was suffering from severe indigestion and asked what was recommended. The nurse failed to clarify whether the woman was pregnant and suggested that she should take some indigestion pills. Subsequently, the woman was admitted in an emergency to hospital with hypertension. The family are now wishing to sue NHS Direct.

In this situation, there would probably be a protocol the nurse should have followed and ascertaining the possibility of pregnancy would have been an essential question to ask. There would appear to be *prima facie* evidence of negligence. Clearly, the safest advice to be given by any nurse answering calls on NHS Direct is for the patient to seek an appointment with his or her general practitioner. However, this might reduce the value of the service.

Similar problems beset the nurse providing the services in walk-in clinics, since the majority are nurse led. It is essential that nurse practitioners have the appropriate training to run such clinics competently and to be aware of the limits of their knowledge and have the confidence to be firm on what they do not know. Minor injuries can probably be dealt with on a one-off basis, such as suturing or bandaging a sprain. However, there may be a need to refer to X-ray, to arrange for further diagnostic tests or to seek specialist advice and the nurse needs to be confident when this is required and when she needs to refer the patient on for medical advice. (See earlier section on X-rays.) In February 2000 practice nurses and nurses who work in walk-in centres were given statutory powers to prescribe from a limited list, as do community nurses and health visitors.[20] Subsequently the new developments in nurse prescribing enable any nurse who has had the appropriate training to prescribe medications within her competence (see Chapter 28). These powers increase the dangers of a nurse working outside her competence. (For further discussion on NHS Direct and walk-in centres, see Chapter 5.)

Modern matrons

The role of matron was reintroduced into the NHS as part of the NHS Plan. It was intended that they should provide strong leadership on wards and be highly visible and accessible to patients; that they should set an example in driving up standards of clinical care and empowering nurses to take on a greater range of clinical tasks to help improve patient care. A report was published in April 2003 on progress in these appointments and the Chief Nursing Officer of the Department of Health set out the plans to extend the role of modern matrons in A&E departments to improve patient experience of NHS emergency care. Each matron in charge of an A&E department was to have a £10,000 budget to help bring these improvements about. A progress report was provided in February 2004 that gave examples of how the monies had been spent.[21] The function of modern matrons in A&E departments includes: clinical leadership; improving patient experience; improving the clinical and patient environment; and managing the ward/departmental environment budget. The intention to appoint 3,000 community matrons was announced in June 2004. In September 2007 the DH announced that it was placing responsibility for the cleanliness of wards and departments upon nurses who would have the right of appealing to the chief management if their recommendations were not accepted. This further emphasises the importance of the role of the matron.

Concerns about the scope of professional practice

Nurses at a conference on the scope of professional practice were asked about their concerns about the development of their professional work. The reservations they had were grouped under the following headings: cultural; training and education; management and resource issues.[22]

Cultural issues

It was clear that to expand the scope of professional practice of the nurse is not simply of concern to the nursing profession alone: it will have an impact on the full multidisciplinary team - patients, carers, managers and many others. Nurses are therefore concerned about potential opposition from some within these groups: open resistance, a reluctance to adjust their own particular ways of practice; being concerned with demarcation lines; undermining a nurse's attempt to undertake further professional activities. In a sense, what is required is almost a complete cultural change within the NHS: a major challenge and one that cannot be accomplished by one single discipline whatever the political pressure for change.

Training and education

The main concern of all participants about the safe development of their professional practice was the need to ensure that the appropriate training was given to them. This was not simply the instruction in a new activity, although this was clearly important. Their concerns were far wider and included the necessity of receiving supervised practice, of competent assessed teachers and having training and experience in a new role rather than just a new task.

Resources

There is a danger that, like care in the community, developing the scope of professional practice might be seen as a cheap alternative to employing more junior doctors. Care in the community has proved to be more expensive than running the large institutions that it replaced. Participants recognised that there were considerable resource issues in the development of the scope of professional practice that, if they were not resolved, could defeat any nurse development.

Professional issues

Obviously, many of the concerns related to the establishment of professional guidelines and agreeing procedures with other members of the multidisciplinary team. One of the basic professional concerns was the need for more guidelines and protocols for determining standards within the expanded role. This is certainly the intention of the government whose NHS Plan published in July 2000 envisaged that NICE will provide more appraisal and protocols to guide staff (see Chapter 5). However, as the discussion in that chapter shows, it cannot be assumed that following a protocol to the letter will always be a defence against any allegation of negligence, since in exceptional circumstances good practice might dictate a different course of action.

Management and insurance

The support given by management to the whole process is seen as vital to the success of the development. This included protecting nurses against legal liability, recognising that they would indemnify the nurse and uphold their actions. One of the crucial concerns of nurse practitioners was that they would not obtain support from management if things went wrong; they were concerned that they would be held personally liable and were also anxious about whether they should take out insurance cover. In Chapter 4, it was explained that an employer is vicariously liable for the negligent actions of an employee who is acting in the course of employment. Where, therefore, a practitioner is undertaking an expanded-role activity, that would normally be seen as in the course of employment. If, therefore, the practitioner is negligent, while she would be professionally accountable both to the NMC and to her employer, she would probably not be held personally liable in the civil courts since her employer would pay compensation on the basis of its vicarious liability. Even when she has not obtained the approval of the employer for this extended activity, it would probably be held vicariously liable as long as she were acting in the interests of the employer's organisation. However, because of uncertainties on this last point, the practitioner would always be well advised to obtain the agreement of the employer to developments in the scope of professional practice. As long as vicarious liability exists, the employee does not require her own personal insurance cover. If, however, she works on her own account or she undertakes Good Samaritan activities that are outside the scope of professional practice, then she needs to ensure that she has professional indemnity insurance. This is often provided by professional associations. (See Chapter 4 where this issue and the NMC consultation paper on indemnity insurance is discussed.)

Clinical supervision

An important part of the support mechanism and professional development of the nurse is clinical supervision. Described by the UKCC in its position paper as 'reflective practice',[23] it provides an opportunity for nurses to discuss in confidence the issues that they have encountered in practice and how they can develop and learn from these experiences. Bond and

Holland have provided guidance on the skills required.[24] Alec Grant raised issues about why clinical supervision is in practice falling short of the theory.[25] The NMC A–Z advice sheet on clinical supervision[26] states that clinical supervision allows registrants to receive professional supervision in the workplace by a skilled supervisor. It enables registrants to:

Identify solutions to problems

Increase understanding of professional issues

Improve standards of patient care

Further develop their skills and knowledge

Enhance their understanding of their own practice

The NMC suggests that clinical supervision should be available to registrants throughout their careers. It considers that it is best developed at a local level in accordance with local needs and therefore does not advocate any particular model of clinical supervision, nor does it provide detailed guidance about its nature and scope. It puts forward the following set of principles which should underpin any system of clinical supervision:

✚ Clinical supervision supports practice, enabling registrants to maintain and improve standards of care.

✚ Clinical supervision is a practice-focused professional relationship, involving a practitioner reflecting on practice guided by a skilled supervisor.

✚ Registrants and managers should develop the process of clinical supervision according to local circumstances. Ground rules should be agreed so that the supervisor and the registrant approach clinical supervision openly, confidently and are aware of what is involved.

✚ Every registrant should have access to clinical supervision and each supervisor should supervise a realistic number of practitioners.

✚ Preparation for supervisors should be flexible and sensitive to local circumstances. The principles and relevance of clinical supervision should be included in pre-registration and post-registration education programmes.

✚ Evaluation of clinical supervision is needed to assess how it influences care and practice standards. Evaluation systems should be determined locally.

Agency nurses

In recent years the shortage in the number of nurses has led to the growth in the use of agencies for the provision of nurse staffing. Many nurses, too, find working for an agency suits their practical needs of combining family and work by giving them greater flexibility and control over their time. Nursing agencies were regulated under the Nurses Agencies Act 1957, but following the implementation of the Care Standards Act 2000, the National Care Standards Commission (NCSC) took over responsibility for their regulation. (In Wales, this is carried out by a department or agency set up by the National Assembly for Wales.) Subsequently, following the Health and Social Care (Community Health and Standards) Act 2003, the NCSC was abolished and its functions taken over by the Commission for Health Audit and Inspection (i.e the Healthcare Commission) and the Commission for Social Care Inspection. (NHS Professionals is discussed in Chapter 10 and the NHS Institute for Innovation and Information in Chapter 11.)

Nurses working for an agency should be clear over the legal implications of their status when they are allocated to an NHS trust. Do they become employees of the trust or are they employees of the agency or are they classified as self-employed practitioners? Their employment status has considerable repercussions for both their legal liability and also for their entitlements to statutory provisions for the employee (see Chapter 10). The RCN has provided a guide for good practice in nursing and care agencies[27] for the assistance of both those who wish to set up a nursing or care agency and those considering a career as a nursing and care agency manager. The guide will require updating in the light of the recent legislation and any rulings by the Healthcare Commission.

Basic principles that apply to the scope of professional practice

1 Always work within the scope of your professional practice.

2 Identify any training or supervised practice needs and take steps to ensure that these are met.

3 Be aware that the law does not accept a principle of team liability: each individual practitioner is personally and professionally accountable for their own actions.

4 Do not obey orders, except in an extreme emergency, unless you are satisfied that they constitute reasonable professional practice.

5 Be prepared to refuse to undertake any activity unless it is within your competence.

6 Do not accept an undertaking that someone else will accept responsibility for what you do. (I'll take responsibility!)

7 Ensure that any development in your professional practice takes place in the context of multidisciplinary discussions, with full management support and an awareness of the need to educate the patient and others to the new situation.

Conclusions

The scope of professional practice of the nurse, midwife and specialist community public health nurse has continued to develop and it is clear that the initial pre-registration training is the foundation upon which an expanded professional role can take place. Registered practitioners are aware of the requirement to work within their competence and ensure that they have the training and supervision to develop their practice in new areas. The most extensive area of expansion has been in the field of prescribing and these developments are considered in Chapter 28. However, other traditional areas of clinical practice such as surgery are opening up to nurses. The repercussions of such developments are significant not just for the individual registered practitioner, but also for the culture and interrelationships of professionals within health and social care. The 'Freedom to practise: dispelling the myths' template has paved the way for further professional development but there is still much further to go. There are very few Acts of Parliament which require certain activities to be carried out by a member of a specified registered health profession.

Reflection questions

1 You have been working as a clinical nurse specialist in the diabetic clinic and have now been asked if you would wish to seek a post of consultant nurse in the same department. What differences would you anticipate there would be between your present post and the post of consultant nurse? What legal implications would there be if you were to obtain the new post?

2 You are aware that your expanded scope of professional practice includes several activities that were originally performed by doctors. In what ways could you assure patients that you are competent to perform these activities?

3 You have been asked to undertake training to be able to act as a clinical supervisor. What are the legal implications of this role?

4 What documentation should be kept in respect of clinical supervision?

Further exercises

1 Study a copy of your NHS trust's policy on the scope of professional practice duties and the principles contained therein. In what ways do you consider that your professional practice could develop? What are the barriers to such development and how could these barriers be overcome?

References

1 Department of Health, The New NHS – modern, dependable, HMSO, London, 1997

2 Department of Health, Making a Difference: the new NHS, DH, July 1999

3 Secretary of State for Health, The NHS Plan, Cm 4818-1, The Stationery Office, London, July 2000

4 Nursing and Midwifery Council, Code of Professional Conduct: standards for performance, conduct and ethics, 2004

5 Secretary of State for Health, The NHS Plan, Cm 4818-1, The Stationery Office, London, July 2000

6 British Medical Association, Resuscitation Council (UK) and the Royal College of Nursing, Decisions Relating to Cardiopulmonary Resuscitation, BMA, October 2007, Paragraph 13, p. 19

7 Nursing and Midwifery Council, New advice for delegation to non-regulated healthcare staff, 2007

8 Nursing and Midwifery Council circular 1/2004, Guidance on Provision of Midwifery Care and Delegation of Midwifery Care to Others, 20 January 2004

9 Department of Health, Making a Difference: the new NHS, DH, July 1999

10 Royal College of Nursing, Developing Roles: nurses working in breast care, Order No. 001957, RCN, May 1999

11 Jo Wilson, Why Clinical Guidelines? A nursing perspective, in John Tingle and Charles Foster (eds) Clinical Guidelines: Law, Policy and Practice, Cavendish Publishing, London, 2002

12 Royal College of Nursing and Department of Health, Freedom to Practise: dispelling the myths, RCN and DH, 2003

[13] Department of Health and Royal College of Nursing, *Freedom to practise: dispelling the myths*, November 2003

[14] The Ionising Radiation (Medical Exposure) Regulations 2000, SI 2000 No. 1059

[15] Ionising Radiations Regulations 1999, SI 1999 No. 3232

[16] European Directive 97/43/Euratom (OJ No. L180, 9.7.97, p. 22)

[17] See B. Dimond, *Legal Aspects of Radiography and Radiology* (Chapter 16), Blackwell Scientific Publications, Oxford, 2002

[18] www.dh.gov.uk/irmer.htm

[19] Department of Health and Royal College of Nursing, *Freedom to practise: dispelling the myths*, November 2003

[20] The National Health Service (Pharmaceutical Services) Amendment Regulations 2000, SI 2000, No. 121

[21] Department of Health press release 2004/0047, Health Minister urges A&E Matrons to Claim their £10,000

[22] B. Dimond, The Scope of Professional Practice, *Healthcare Risk Report*, March 2001, 7(4), pp. 16-17

[23] UKCC, Position Statement on Clinical Supervision, UKCC, London, 1996

[24] M. Bond and S. Holland, *Skills of Clinical Supervision for Nurses*, Open University Press, Milton Keynes, 1998

[25] Alec Grant, Why clinical supervision is not so super in reality, *Nursing Times*, 15 June 2000, 96(24), p. 42

[26] Nursing and Midwifery Council, A-Z advice sheet on clinical supervision, updated March 2006

[27] Royal College of Nursing, Guide to Good Practice in Nursing and Care Agencies, Order No. 000675, RCN, May 1998

Part III
General areas

Chapter 25
Legal aspects of property

Introduction

The nurse may have many concerns about property. She may wonder if she is liable if the patient's property is lost. This becomes of particular concern in those situations where the patient is incompetent to take care of his own possessions. What are the legal requirements? The nurse may also be concerned for her own property. Does the NHS trust as an employer have any duty to make arrangements to care for the nurse's property? What happens if the nurse's car is damaged in the hospital car park? Does it make any difference to the liability of the employer if a patient damages the car?

Principles of liability

> ### Practical Dilemma 25.1   A Christmas casualty
>
> Dora Hardy, a 72-year-old widow, was staying with her son, James, and his family over the Christmas holidays. On the Saturday night, the day before Christmas Eve, she complained of feeling very tired and retired to bed at 7.00 p.m. At 9.00 p.m. James suddenly heard his mother cry out and, rushing upstairs, he found her very pale, gasping for breath and clutching her heart. Ann, his wife, phoned for the ambulance and collected up her mother-in-law's handbag and toilet bag. Dora, still in her nightdress with an overcoat over her shoulders, was taken to Roger Park Hospital within 15 minutes. She was wheeled straight into the admission unit and a staff nurse asked James and Ann to wait in the waiting room. After five minutes, the staff nurse returned to ask them Dora's name, address and age. They waited for over an hour without seeing any sign of anyone and then decided to find out what was happening. James walked into the admission unit and asked the sister on duty if he could see his mother. The sister explained that she had gone up to the medical ward about an hour before. She apologised, but said that, owing to the change of shift, she had not realised that Mrs Hardy had relatives with her and that anyone was waiting. To make up for her oversight, the sister phoned the medical ward and arranged for James and Ann to go straight up. James and Ann, who was still clutching Dora's possessions, were led to the medical ward. There were screens around Dora's bed and Dora seemed to be unconscious. Ann tiptoed to the head of the bed and placed Dora's handbag and toilet bag in the locker. Since it was clear that there was little that they could do, James and Ann left the bedside, calling in to the ward sister's office to make sure that the night nurse had their address and phone number.
>
> Dora remained critically ill for three days, but on the fourth day she seemed to start pulling through. James visited her the day after Boxing Day and for the first time was able to chat with her. He asked if there was anything she needed and she said that she would like some Kleenex and orange squash. The next day, James and Ann took in the Kleenex and squash and £10 in cash to ensure that Dora could buy things from the ward trolley. Ann took the handbag from the locker and opened the purse to put the £10 inside. She noticed that there was already £60 in the purse. However, she added the £10 and replaced the purse in the handbag, which she put in the locker. Over the next few days, a number of relatives visited Dora, but on 3 January James had a phone call to say that she had taken a turn for the worse. James and Ann rushed to the hospital but Dora died later that night.
>
> The next day, James returned to the hospital to collect the death certificate. The ward sister gave him a white plastic bag with 'patient's property' written over it. She handed him a checklist of its contents, which included 'handbag with purse containing 30 pence'. James glanced at the list and pointed out that the purse should have contained about £70. The ward sister stated that she had personally checked through the contents and that was all that there was. James explained that his wife had seen £60 there and had added £10. The ward sister advised him to see the unit manager since there was nothing more that she could do. The unit manager, on interviewing James, ascertained the following:
>
> 1 No warnings had been given at the time that Dora was admitted about the patient's property and hospital rules.
> 2 There was a notice in the ward about the hospital not being liable for patient's property unless it was handed in for safe custody, but this notice was not prominently displayed and James and Ann said that they had not seen it.
>
> Sister Thomas was interviewed and said that she knew that there was a handbag in the locker, but had not looked inside it until after Dora's death when she was drawing up the checklist of contents.

In Practical Dilemma 25.1, the first issue that arises is: Can it be said that the NHS trust is liable for the missing property and is Sister Thomas personally liable? In general, a person does not become liable for another person's property unless he or she can be shown to have assumed some responsibility for it. The person who undertakes to look after the property of another person is known as a *bailee*. The person who owns the property is known as the *bailor*. Thus, if a patient were to give a gold watch to the ward sister, the sister on behalf of the NHS trust acts as bailee of that property entrusted to it by the patient, the bailor. It is the duty of the bailee to carry out the instructions of the bailor and to surrender the property of the bailor when requested to do so or as previously agreed. In most circumstances, the relationship of bailor/bailee is a voluntary one and one person cannot force another into being the bailee of one's property. When the person agrees to act as bailee (and there may be no reward for doing so), a transfer of possession takes place so that the bailee then becomes liable. In contrast with the usual principles of negligence, once the existence of the bailment is established, it is not for the bailor to establish negligence by the bailee, but for the bailee to show that he exercised all reasonable care for the goods and was not negligent. This is a reversal of the usual burdens of proof.

Applying this law to the above situation, it could be argued that at no time did the family or Dora ask the NHS trust or its staff to become bailees of the property and take care of it. There was therefore no liability in law for the missing cash.

However, in the context of hospital care, another duty arises under the law of negligence. If an unconscious patient is brought into the A&E department, the NHS trust and the professionals have a duty to care for the patient and this would include caring for his property if he is unable to look after it. This is known as involuntary bailment. Looking at Dora's situation, were there any occasions when it could be said that the NHS trust became an involuntary bailee of Dora's property and had a duty of care in relation to it? The answer is when she became unconscious and was unable to look after her property herself. However, we have Ann's evidence that the cash was still there after Dora had resumed consciousness, so it could be argued that the NHS trust was no longer a bailee (whether or not it had ever been one). The next point at which an involuntary bailment may have arisen is Dora's death. At this point, the ward staff should assume control and ensure that a list of the property is drawn up and properly witnessed. If this is what Sister Thomas did and the cash was not there at that time, then it could be argued that the NHS trust was not liable for the fact that it is missing.

This is the law in relation to bailment and would mean that in these circumstances the relatives would have difficulty in winning a case against the NHS trust or Sister Thomas.

Administrative failures

However, what is more likely to occur is that there will be a complaint about the administrative procedures in relation to Dora's property, which would be based on failure of the staff to point out to the relatives procedures for dealing with the property or even checking whether they had brought any in for Dora. Complaints of this kind, though they may not lead to a court action, may, however, lead to the NHS trust making an *ex gratia* payment to the patient or relatives. This is not an admission of liability, but an attempt to appease the relatives and make up for administrative shortcomings. Under the complaints scheme that was established in July 2004, any complaint of missing property would be investigated at a local level and an attempt made to resolve it. If the complainant is not satisfied with the outcome, then he/she can apply to the Healthcare Commission for an independent review (see Chapter 27).

> ## Practical Dilemma 25.2   A lost engagement ring
>
> Mavis was admitted for an appendectomy and was expecting to stay in hospital only for a few days. She took very little cash in with her, but did take her engagement ring. When she was using the wash basin in the toilets, she took off her ring, placing it on the side and then forgot to put it back on. She had been back in the ward only a short time when she realised what she had done and rushed back to fetch it, but unfortunately it was gone. She knows that someone must have stolen it. Can she recover compensation from the trust?

There is no legal right for Mavis to obtain compensation from the trust. She did not entrust her property to the trust employees, and at the time that it was lost she was responsible for it. However, she may be able to show that there were administrative failings. For example, it might not have been pointed out to her that she brings her property into the hospital at her own risk. While, therefore, there may be no legal basis for a claim, she may be able to use the complaints procedure to raise concerns and, depending on the results, the trust may make an *ex gratia* payment to her. Contrariwise, if the trust explained the situation about patient's property and a notice (see below) pointing out that the trust did not accept liability was shown to her, she would probably be unable to obtain any compensation.

Exclusion of liability

What is the legal significance of the notice absolving the NHS trust or PCT of all responsibility for the patient's property? Under the Unfair Contract Terms Act 1977 (see Statute on pages 129-30), such an exemption or exclusion notice is effective in relation to the loss or damage of property, provided that it is reasonable to exclude liability for the negligence that has led to such loss or damage. (Liability for negligence that leads to personal injury or death cannot be excluded.) How is reasonableness defined? The requirement of reasonableness is defined in the following Statute.

> ## Statute   Definition of reasonableness in Section 11 of the Unfair Contract Terms Act 1977
>
> [I]t should be fair and reasonable to allow reliance upon it, having regard to all the circumstances obtaining when the liability arose or [but for the Notice] would have arisen (Section 11(3)).
>
> It is for the party claiming that a contract term or notice satisfies the requirement of reasonableness to show that it does (Section 11(5)).

In Practical Dilemma 25.1, where a notice was displayed on the wall, if it could be argued that the NHS trust's employees had been negligent in relation to her property, then the NHS trust might claim to rely on the notice to avoid liability. It would then have to show that it was reasonable for them to rely on it.

Patients should be advised not to bring valuable property into hospital. If they do, then it can be recommended to them that the property should be taken into safekeeping by the nursing staff. If they are unwilling to part with the property, then they can be asked to sign a form whereby they accept responsibility for the care of the property which has the added advantage of impressing upon the patient the dangers of having valuable property in hospital (see Box 25.1).

Box 25.1   Patients' property: form of notice disclaiming liability

I acknowledge that the opportunity has been given to me to hand over my personal property to be placed in safekeeping, that I have been advised to do so and that I have declined the offer of safe-keeping of my personal property.

Signature of patient

Witnessed by

(Member of staff)

Designation

Date

To be filed in patient's case notes folder

Property of the mentally incompetent

What about the property of those who are unconscious or who have learning disabilities or who are mentally ill or the elderly infirm?

Temporary incapacity

Practical Dilemma 25.3   Lost teeth

Arthur Brown was rushed into hospital one night with a cardiac arrest. He survived following a six-hour operation. When he recovered from the operation, he was told that it was touch and go as to whether he would pull through. A few days later, he discovered that his set of teeth was missing. He told the staff nurse who said that a search would be started, but they were not found. What remedies does he have?

In this situation, it is clear that Arthur was incapable of taking care of his personal property on admission and it is likely that his teeth were removed pre-operatively. (There would have to be a check to see if they were removed pre-admission or by the ambulance crew.) If following investigations it appears that the hospital staff did remove them and failed to take reasonable care, the trust would be seen as the bailee of the property and responsible for their loss. It would be advisable for the trust to admit liability and make Arthur a speedy offer of an *ex gratia* payment. Some staff may feel that, in view of the fact that staff saved Arthur's life, it is unreasonable of Arthur to complain. However, if there were a justified complaint, the fact that a patient's life has been saved would not be a successful defence.

Permanent incapacity

In other situations of long-term mental incapacity, there may be tensions between attempting to develop the autonomy of a person and the care of personal property as the following situation indicates.

Practical Dilemma 25.4　　**Pocket money**

Jimmy Jones, an adult of 24 with learning disabilities, lived in a community home with others of a similar condition. He regularly earned himself significant amounts of money from doing odd jobs around the home and thus accumulated over £100. The staff in the home attempted to encourage Jimmy to put this in the bank. However, he could not be persuaded and there were rumours that he slept with it under his pillow at night. One morning, he screamed with distress and it appeared that all his money had been stolen from under his bed. A search revealed nothing and there was no hint as to where it had gone. Is the organisation which ran the home liable for the loss?

From the discussion about Practical Dilemma 25.1 on Dora, it will be apparent that in Practical Dilemma 25.4 there was no transfer of possession from Jimmy to the care home owners or managers, so that the latter is not *prima facie* liable. However, much depends on Jimmy's mental competence and whether sufficient effort was made to persuade him to allow it to be taken for safekeeping. A system of tokens can sometimes be devised to protect patients' property, although care must be taken not to limit their purchasing power and to ensure that the funds are available for them when they want them. In addition, in this case, it could be argued that the care home had a duty of care in relation to the security of the home.

Mental Capacity Act 2005

The Mental Capacity Act 2005 established a new Court of Protection whose jurisdiction covers both personal welfare and property and affairs for those over 16 years. The Court has the power to make orders in respect of those under 16 years if there is reasonable belief that their incapacity will continue beyond 16 years. The Court can make declarations and/or it can appoint a deputy to make decisions on behalf of those lacking mental capacity. In addition a person, over 18 years, when mentally competent can draw up a lasting power of attorney (see below) which gives the power to make decisions to another person over 18 years on both personal welfare and property and affairs. The LPA must be registered with the Office of Public Guardian. The LPA over personal welfare can only take effect when the donor loses the requisite mental capacity. Where small amounts of money are involved the present system whereby appointees can collect DSS moneys on behalf of those incapacitated will continue.

Day-to-day care of money

> **Practical Dilemma 25.5** **Shopping**
>
> At the heart of the philosophy of community care of those with learning disabilities or severe mental health problems is the principle of autonomy. Clients are encouraged to shop and take part in community activities and realise as much of their potential as possible. In these circumstances, moneys might be entrusted to staff to guide clients in making small purchases. On one such shopping expedition, Gary White, the team leader at a community home for those with learning disabilities, took three residents to the shops. Two were able to manage their own purchases, but the third, Leonard, needed some guidance and Gary aided him in purchasing several small items – toiletries, sweets, etc. On their return, Leonard complained to another resident that Gary had spent all his money. This came to the attention of the home manager who asked Gary for an immediate explanation. Gary showed how the money had been spent, but was unable to produce any receipts or supporting evidence. Neither was he able to remember exactly where the money had gone.

In a situation like this, the member of staff is like a trustee for the resident's property and should be able to account for it in detail with supporting receipts. Of course, the receipts do not in themselves show that the money was spent on the patient but, together with evidence from other witnesses, it should be possible to record exactly how the money was spent and that it was spent in the interests of the resident. In a case like this, the home manager would discipline Gary for his failure to follow the correct procedure.

In the community, many residents may have considerable sums to spend and the staff are therefore vulnerable to an accusation that they have spent the money on themselves. One of the requirements under the Care Standards Act and Regulations made under it (see Chapter 23) is that there should be accurate records kept of residents' property. It is essential that staff be trained in good practices of bookkeeping and that there should be, as far as possible, witnesses to give evidence as to how the money has been spent. The ultimate aim is, of course, that the resident should be the watchdog for his own funds, but many residents/ clients may never get beyond the stage of entrusting all such matters to others.

Power of attorney

Patients who have the necessary mental capacity can grant a power of attorney. Under the Powers of Attorney Act 1971 this power was revoked (i.e. withdrawn) if the person granting it became mentally incapable. However, since this is often the very occasion when it would be useful to exercise the power on behalf of the patient, an Enduring Power of Attorney Act 1985 was passed, which came into effect in 1986. This power comes into existence only if the person wishes the power to continue after the time at which he becomes incapable; he must sign to this effect and indicate that he is aware of the significance of the enduring element. From 1 October 2007 it is no longer possible to create an enduring power of attorney (EPA). Instead as the result of the Mental Capacity Act 2005 a lasting power of attorney can be set up. Different forms are completed and registered for an LPA covering personal welfare and one covering property and affairs. Existing EPAs continue to be valid, and if the donor still retains the requisite mental capacity could be replaced by an LPA. Box 25.2 sets out some of the requirements for and the characteristics of a lasting power of attorney.

Box 25.2 **Lasting powers of attorney**

1 Lasting powers of attorney can be set up in respect of personal welfare and property and affairs. The LPA in respect of personal welfare only comes into force when the donor lacks the requisite mental capacity. The LPA in respect of property and affairs can come into effect even though the donor still has the requisite mental capacity.

2 The LPA must be in the exact form prescribed in the Regulations.[1]

3 The LPA may give:
   + a general power - which authorises the attorney to carry out any transactions or make personal welfare decisions on behalf of the donor or
   + a specific power - which authorises the attorney to deal only with those aspects of the donor's affairs that are specified in the power or make specific personal welfare decisions.

4 The donor can revoke or cancel the lasting power at any time while she/he remains mentally capable, but the power cannot be cancelled or revoked once it has been registered, unless the Office of Public Guardian confirms the revocation.

5 When the donor becomes mentally incapable, the attorney must notify the Office of Public Guardian.

6 Once registered, the attorney has the power to act on behalf of the donor - either general or specific.

Court of Protection

In October 2007 a new Court of Protection was established under the Mental Capacity Act 2005. The Court has considerable jurisdiction in relation to both personal welfare and property and affairs of those who lack the requisite mental capacity. It can also determine whether capacity is lacking.

Where there is no enduring or lasting power of attorney in existence and the person is incapable of managing his affairs, an application can be made to the Court of Protection for the appointment of a deputy to manage the affairs. There is a short procedure that can be used where the assets are small. A relative, or perhaps the NHS organisation, could apply for a deputy to be appointed to manage the patient's affairs and to allow money to be spent on the patient. The powers of the Court of Protection are considerable. The applicant will have to pay in to the court a sum of money as a *recognisance*. Notice of the application is given to the patient, who has the opportunity of opposing it. Medical evidence will also be required to show that the patient lacks the requisite mental capacity (as defined in the Mental Capacity Act Sections 2 and 3) to be capable of handling his affairs. This medical evidence can be challenged by the patient. The Court of Protection has the power of making a will in the name of the incompetent person and can arrange for sums to be paid to other persons who would have been dependent on the patient or would have looked to him for help, even though these obligations would not have been legally enforceable. Obviously, there is a power to pay all debts. The powers given to the Court of Protection under Part 7 of the Mental Health Act 1983 have been replaced by those given under the Mental Capacity Act 2005. In Scotland the Adults with Incapacity (Scotland) Act 2000 has been in force since 2001.

Protecting patients from relatives

Practical Dilemma 25.6   Grasping relatives

Mary Bennet was visited regularly by her daughter, Jean, and each week the ward sister noticed that Jean brought the pension book in for her mother to sign. However, it was noticeable that Mary never seemed to have any money for purchases from the ward trolley and if the ward had not supplied her with squash, tissues and soap, she would not have had any of those items. Janice, the ward sister, mentioned it to Jean, who flushed a little and said that she did not have anything to do with her mother's money and by the time she had personally paid for the bus fare to the hospital, she did not have any funds for such purchases and, anyway, the hospital provided that, did they not?

Many nurses would recognise this type of situation and the dilemma that arises for them is this: to what extent is the nurse a protector of the patient, even when she has to protect the patient from his own relatives? In one sense, this type of situation will not continue for very long since certain benefits are reduced and ultimately end after several weeks. However, the same issue can arise in other circumstances, for example, the signing of wills (considered in Chapter 29). In the above situation, there is little that the ward sister can do. In any event, she cannot be sure that the money is not being used to meet Mary's bills at home and the sum is, of course, far too small to consider taking out a Court of Protection order. However, the fact that the relatives are aware of her concern might be of some small influence.[2] The Department for Work and Pensions (DWP) can appoint someone (an appointee) to claim and spend benefits on a person's behalf if that person lacks the requisite mental capacity. The DWP has a responsibility to supervise the situation. Any concerns about misappropriation could be reported to the DWP.

(The law relating to the care of a patient's property on the death of a patient and the making of wills is considered in Chapter 29.)

Returning the patient's property

Practical Dilemma 25.7   Weekend property problems

It was the accepted practice at Roger Park General Hospital for the money on any patients who were admitted in an emergency to be retained by the general office for safekeeping during their stay. On discharge, they were then able to obtain a cheque representing that amount of money from the general office. Most patients, except those with no bank accounts, accepted the system. Problems, however, arose at weekends when no general office staff were on duty or when discharge was sudden and the cheques could not be made available in time. On such occasions, patients complained that the actual cash that was taken from them was not returned and, since not all banks were open on Saturday, they could not change the cheques and some had no cash with which to return home. What is the legal position?

The legal position depends to a certain extent on the circumstances of the money being taken by the NHS trust. If the patient is fully conscious when the money is handed over, he should be told that he will be given a cheque for this amount on discharge. If he refuses to agree to this, then it is open to him to ask relatives to look after his money or to take the risk of keeping that sum on his person. If, however, the money has been taken from the unconscious patient after an emergency admission, then there is no chance of the terms of the bailment being agreed with him. In such circumstances, the hospital holds the money as part of its duty of care to look after the patient. It could be argued that this duty requires the hospital to return to the patient exactly the same coins and notes that were taken from him. Alternatively, it could be said that the hospital carries out its duty of care by giving the patient the equivalent of what was taken in the form of a cheque. Unfortunately, there is no decided case to clarify the position in law. As far as administrative practice is concerned, possibly the best solution is to discuss with the patient as soon as he is conscious and capable of handling his affairs what the patient would prefer and, if the patient is unhappy at receiving a cheque for the entire amount, to consider the possibility of providing part in cash for immediate needs. Where the discharge is contemplated for a weekend, then either the cheque should be prepared in advance or there should be an emergency scheme to provide the patient with a cash advance. Where the patient has no bank account, the hospital should be able to make special arrangements either for the cheque to be cleared at a local branch or for the cash to be made available.

Staff property

> **Practical Dilemma 25.8**   **Lost handbag**
>
> Mavis Jarvis, a staff nurse, was going straight from work to a travel company to pay for her holiday to Greece. She was holidaying with a friend and had £500 in cash to pay for both of them. The money was contained in a wallet inside her handbag. At the hospital, all nursing staff were provided with a locker in a staffroom in their ward or department. The lockers were fitted with a padlock and key. Mavis locked her locker and carried the key around for the whole shift. Several people knew that she was going to the travel agent after work. At the end of the shift, when she went to her locker, she found that it had been broken into: the small padlock had been forced open and the money was missing from the wallet. The police were summoned, but despite intensive questioning and a search the money was never recovered or the thief discovered. Mavis feels that the NHS trust should pay for the missing money since, she argued, the padlock was inadequate and a far tougher system should have been provided for taking care of staff property. Is she right in law?

Unfortunately for Mavis, it is highly unlikely that she would win in a court action against the NHS trust. If we return to the terminology used in Dora's case in Practical Dilemma 25.1, the NHS trust is not the bailee of Mavis's cash; she has not transferred it to its safekeeping. She has, so to speak, brought the property into the hospital at her own risk. If, of course, she had gone to the general office and said, 'Please take care of this for me since I have to go to the travel agent straight after work', and it had done so, the situation would have been very different. In that case, the NHS trust would have become a bailee of her money and would be accountable to her for its return. What about the argument that the locker should have been stronger? The locker should be as strong as is compatible with the value of property that is reasonable to be kept in there. There must be few who would think that attempting to keep £500 is reasonable. Anyone who brings valuable goods to work and keeps them there cannot expect the NHS trust to be held responsible for their loss, unless, of course, it is a requirement of the job that such items are brought to work, or unless the employer has assumed responsibility for the property. The employer can, through the contract of employment, take on a wider responsibility for the property of employees, although this would be unusual. The courts are unlikely to imply a term that the employer has a duty to take care of the property of the employee. There would have to be an explicit undertaking to that effect.

Practical Dilemma 25.9 **Staff car park**

Jean Jones, a staff nurse in the outpatients department, parked her car in the hospital car park, paying the daily fee of £3.00. When she came back, she found that her car had been broken into and the radio/cassette player taken. A pathology laboratory technician whose office overlooked the car park came up to her as she was looking at the damage and said that he had seen the whole incident. He had seen two youths break into the car who were then chased by the car park attendant. When car park charges were introduced, staff had been assured that there would be better protection for their cars. Could Jean Jones hold the security firm or the NHS trust responsible for the damage?

There are two possible causes of action: one against the security firm and the other against the trust. If it were the responsibility of the security firm to protect the cars in the park on a 24-hour basis, then they have failed to fulfil that responsibility. There may be a contractual right against them by the NHS trust, but it depends on the terms of the contract. Although the trust has a right of action in contract, Jean Jones does not have a right of action, unless she can make use of the Contracts (Rights of Third Parties) Act 1999, which enables a person not a party to the contract to sue for benefits under it. In addition, it may be argued that the security firm owed a duty of care in the law of negligence to each employee or user of the car park. This might be difficult to establish. Any liability of the trust depends on Jean's being able to establish that it owed Jean a duty of care in respect of her car and had not excluded any liability by an exemption notice. This would depend on the actual facts. The likelihood is that Jean will be unable to obtain compensation from either the security firm or her employers and will be dependent on any insurance cover she has for theft.

Conclusions

The Mental Capacity Act 2005 in establishing a new Court of Protection, an Office of Public Guardian and the concept of the lasting power of attorney will have a major impact on the property and affairs of those lacking the requisite mental capacity to make decisions. A Code of Practice[3] has been prepared which should assist those responsible for the property of others and help and information on the Mental Capacity Act is available from the Ministry of Justice[4].

Reflection questions

1 Consider the liability of the NHS trust, if any, for the loss of a patient's pyjamas. It appears that they were removed when the patient was given a bath and probably placed with the sheets in the laundry bag. The laundry has denied any knowledge of them.

2 Examine the procedure followed in relation to property when patients are admitted to hospital.

3 You are working at a psychiatric hospital and one of the patients drags a nail along the side of your new car. Is the NHS trust responsible? Would it make any difference if there were a notice by the car park exempting the NHS trust from loss or damage to staff cars parked there?

4 The Court of Protection has been appointed to manage the property of one of the patients on your ward. What powers does it have and who will administer the property?

Further exercises

1 How many disclaimer notices or exclusion notices do you see around the hospital? Consider the extent to which reliance on each notice would be reasonable to exclude liability for damage or loss of property caused by the negligence of the NHS trust or its staff.

2 The relative of a patient in your geriatric wards asks you if you would witness a power of attorney so that the relative can manage the patient's affairs on his behalf. You know that the patient is mentally disordered but is reputed to be quite wealthy. What advice would you give to the relative?

References

[1] The Lasting Powers of Attorney, Enduring Powers of Attorney and Public Guardian Regulations, SI 2007 No. 1253
[2] B. Dimond, *Legal Aspects of Mental Capacity*, Blackwells Scientific Publishing, Oxford, 2007
[3] Code of Practice, Mental Capacity Act 2005, Department for Constitutional Affairs, February 2007, paragraph 7.21
[4] www.justice.gov.uk

Chapter 26
Legal aspects of AIDS and other infectious diseases

This chapter discusses

+ Statutory regulations
+ Characteristics of AIDS
+ AIDS and employment
+ The AIDS patient
+ Consent to screening
+ Government policy on testing
+ Blood donors
+ Haemophiliacs and recipients of blood
+ Confidentiality
+ AIDS Control Act 1987
+ Notifiable diseases
+ Cross-infection control
+ Tuberculosis (TB)
+ Health Protection Agency
+ Vaccination

Introduction

All those general principles of law that have been discussed in relation to health and safety, consent, confidentiality and professional liability apply to the patient suffering from AIDS or who is HIV positive. There are very few specific laws and cases dealing with the AIDS patient. However, because AIDS is at present incurable (although there has been recent progress in medications that delay the onset of AIDS from HIV), because a high proportion of HIV patients eventually suffer from AIDS itself and because of the present hysteria that surrounds it (as can be seen from the way in which different professional groups have argued that the basic principles of law do not apply in relation to such sufferers), it is considered advisable to have a separate chapter on the law relating to AIDS and other infectious diseases, to discuss a few of the dilemmas that arise. The term 'AIDS patient' will be used to cover both the person who has AIDS itself and the person who is HIV positive. The most recent figures from the Health Protection Agency showed that 63,500 adults are now living with HIV in the UK.[1]

This chapter discusses the legal aspects of AIDS and infectious diseases.

Statutory regulations

The government has made regulations (Public Health (Infectious Diseases) Regulations 1985), which came into force on 22 March 1985 and which gave the powers that are set out in the Statute below. In addition, there is the AIDS Control Act 1987, which provides for periodic reports on AIDS to enable the appropriate resources to be allocated and plans to be made. This Act is considered further below.

Statute   **Public Health Act (Infectious Diseases) Regulations 1985**

1 Gives to local authorities the power to apply to a justice of the peace for the removal of an AIDS sufferer to hospital to be detained there.

2 Gives to the justice of the peace the power to make an order for a person believed to be suffering from AIDS to be medically examined. There are also powers in relation to the disposal of the body of an AIDS sufferer.

Apart from these rules and the existing public health laws that would cover AIDS, there has been minimal legislation. Codes of practice have been issued by the DH and by many professional associations, but these do not have the force of law. Although the guidance should usually be followed, failure to do so would not necessarily involve any illegality or give rise to a cause of action in law. Section 23 of the Health and Medicines Act 1988 enables the Secretary of State to make the regulations on HIV testing kits and services which were enacted in 1992.[2]

Characteristics of AIDS

AIDS does, of course, appear to have some characteristics that, taken together, make the disease unique. These are shown in Box 26.1.

Box 26.1   **Characteristics of AIDS**

It is incurable at present.

It is passed through body fluid contact.

It has puny strength once outside body fluids.

A high proportion of those who are HIV positive are thought likely to suffer eventually from AIDS itself.

Screening for HIV positivity is beset with difficulties: there are false negatives and false positives. Early incubation over the first three months does not necessarily show up as HIV positive.

A person who is shown to be HIV negative could become exposed to and acquire the virus immediately after the test.

The combination of these characteristics could possibly justify the judges making the law relating to AIDS an exception to the general principles of law and, until more cases are heard, the situation in law is uncertain.

AIDS and employment

Some of the many questions that arise in employment are as follows:

Can I refuse to nurse an AIDS sufferer?

Can I be compelled to have a test for AIDS?

Can an employee insist that other employees are tested for AIDS?

Can I refuse to work with an employee whom I know is an AIDS sufferer or whom I suspect might be?

Can an employee who suffers from AIDS be fairly dismissed?

Pre-employment medical examination

Can an employer legally insist on a prospective employee being screened for AIDS prior to being taken on as an employee? The simple answer is, yes. An employer's right to choose the most suitable, competent, capable person for the job, while not absolute, is extremely wide. He is constrained by the Sex Discrimination Act 1975, the Race Relations Act 1976 and the Disability Discrimination Act 1995 and other anti-discrimination legislation and cannot choose a particular sex or race or refuse to appoint a disabled person, unless the exceptions to those Acts apply. He is also prevented from compelling an employee to divulge a criminal offence if that conviction is spent for the purposes of the Rehabilitation of Offenders Act 1974. (However, most health service posts are excluded from the provisions of this Act. See Chapter 10.) The requirement that a prospective employee has a medical examination can either be insisted on before the contract of employment commences or it can result in the contract ending after it has commenced, since the medical results are not satisfactory. Many occupational health departments carry out this examination for the NHS trust and considerable hardship can arise if the employee commences the new post, having given in his notice in his previous employment and only after starting work does the medical examination find him unfit and therefore he loses the new job. This could apply to a person suffering from AIDS or who is found to be HIV positive. Many of the codes of practice that exist advise that such tests should not be insisted on. The Disability Discrimination Act 1995 may provide some protection, but the absence of an Act of Parliament that makes it illegal to test for AIDS in such circumstances makes the situation in law uncertain. However, nursing recruits from overseas are required to have tests for AIDS/HIV and other infectious diseases.

Tests for AIDS during employment

Once the employee's contract of employment has commenced, he has certain protection against unreasonable requests by the employer.

Practical Dilemma 26.1   Compulsory testing

Eddie was a staff nurse in the operating theatre. It was well known that he was homosexual. His colleagues were concerned that he might be HIV positive and felt that he should not be allowed to act as a scrub nurse if there were any danger to the patients. They felt that he should be tested. A request was made to the director of nursing services and she asked Eddie to undergo the test. Is this request unreasonable? Can Eddie refuse to comply?

Where the employee's physical or mental capability to do the job is in doubt, the employer can suggest that the employee submits to an independent medical examination, but there is no power to order this. If the employee has refused a medical examination and if subsequently, in consequence, the employee is dismissed on the grounds of the refusal, the employment tribunal will consider whether the employer acted reasonably in all the circumstances. Under the 1985 Regulations, the justice of the peace can make an order for a person believed to be suffering from AIDS to be medically examined by a registered medical practitioner (under the Public Health (Control of Disease) Act 1984 Section 34). This provision is for the purpose of preventing a danger to public health and could be used where a person suspected of being an AIDS sufferer is acting intentionally or recklessly in endangering public health. If the disease were confirmed, the powers of the local authority to apply to a justice of the peace for the removal of the sufferer and detention in hospital could then be used (Public Health Regulations 1985 and Public Health (Control of Disease) Act 1984 Sections 37 and 38). In extreme circumstances, it could be argued that these powers are available where the employer is concerned about a danger to public health. It is extremely unlikely, however, that their use could be justified in the circumstances described in Eddie's case. It could be argued that in Eddie's case the request to be tested for AIDS would be unreasonable for two reasons. If the test proves negative, it is of value only for the day of testing and it does not exclude the possibility that Eddie has recently been exposed to the virus, which has not yet shown up in tests. Frequent tests would have to be carried out to cover this possibility. If the test proves positive, what is the significance of this? It shows that the individual has been exposed to the virus, but there is little indication to show the course of events: it could be many years before Eddie contracts the disease itself (if ever). It does reveal that he is a potential source of infection, but if good hygienic practices are followed, there should be no danger to other employees or patients. It could be argued that, being a theatre nurse, he is a greater danger to patients, but this does not follow if the proper procedures are complied with. In addition, it could be said that, since there is no obvious value to the employer in insisting on such a test, such a request is unreasonable because of the harm it could cause the employee. As long as the disease is incurable and as long as it is impossible to tell which HIV positive patients will contract AIDS or ARC (AIDS-related complex) and when the knowledge of an HIV positive result confers no benefit on the employee and, in fact, brings him considerable harm. It affects his eligibility for a mortgage and life insurance and he may lose his job and be unable to obtain a new one. Tentative conclusions here are that at the present time such a request by an employer would be unreasonable, unless very exceptional circumstances existed. However, if Eddie has been in continuous employment for less than one year and is dismissed because he has refused to take the test, he is ineligible to bring an action for unfair dismissal before an employment tribunal and, provided he has been given the contractual period of notice to which he is entitled, he would probably have no remedy for wrongful dismissal. If he alleges that he is being discriminated against on grounds of disability, then he could bring an action under the Disability Discrimination Act 1995. If he is an NHS employee, he would be entitled to make an internal appeal against dismissal, but his only protection then is the overall policy of the NHS trust and the rules of natural justice. The Department of Health has updated guidance on the management of infected healthcare workers and patient notification.[3] It states that it is no longer necessary to notify every patient who has undergone an exposure-prone procedure by an HIV-infected healthcare worker because of the low risk of transmission and the anxiety caused to patients and the wider public. It recommends that infected healthcare workers should consult with the occupational health department. While they have a duty of confidentiality to the employees, an exception to this duty may arise in the public interest (see Chapter 8). An Expert Advisory Group on AIDS was established as a non-statutory advisory non-departmental public body in 1985 to provide advice to the Chief Medical Officer of the DH on AIDS/HIV.

In the case of *Bliss* v. *SE Thames IRHA* [1985] IRLR 308, the Court of Appeal held that an employee could not be required to submit to a medical examination unless there were reasonable grounds to believe that he might be suffering from physical or mental disability that might cause harm to the patients or adversely affect the quality of the treatment given to them.

Compensation for unfair dismissal

In one case,[4] a tribunal held that a cinema company had acted reasonably in dismissing a projectionist who was reported in the newspaper to have been importuning in a public toilet. The dismissal was not unfair. However, it does not follow that a dismissal on the grounds of homosexual conduct or being infected with AIDS/HIV will always be fair, as the next case shows.

A gay supermarket manager was told to stay away from work after his bosses found out that he was HIV positive. He applied to the employment tribunal alleging sexual and disability discrimination and the employers agreed an out-of-court settlement thought to be in the region of about £250,000.[5]

> ### Practical Dilemma 26.2   The unwitting victim
>
> Unknown to Mary Kemp, her husband was bisexual and was infected with the AIDS virus and eventually she was infected as well. She was not aware of this initially, but after being away from work for an intractable infection, it was discovered that she had AIDS. She was considered fit to return to work for the immediate future. She told her nursing officer of the diagnosis and it was suggested that she should return home and not consider working again. The nursing officer justified her decision on the basis that she was a risk to the staff and the patients and that she was unlikely to perform her job competently anyway.

This situation is likely to be very complex. It is not an established principle that the fact that an employee suffers from AIDS (or is HIV positive) is in itself justification for immediate dismissal. Neither can it be said that the employer's duty to safeguard the health of other employees would automatically require him to dismiss the sufferer or carrier. There may, of course, come a time when that employee is incapable, by reason of his physical or mental condition, of carrying out his duties and a dismissal in those circumstances may well be fair and not an infringement of the Disability Discrimination Act 1995. However, provided a safe system of work is followed and good hygienic practices are implemented, the AIDS sufferer should not be a danger to his fellow employees or the patients and should not be dismissed on those grounds alone. Similarly, a pregnant employee cannot be dismissed just because she is pregnant but, unlike the AIDS sufferer, the pregnant employee has the additional protection of a specific statutory right not to be dismissed solely on the grounds of pregnancy. A similar statutory provision might be required for the protection of AIDS sufferers or HIV positive people.

If there were a clear danger to the health of patients or colleagues from infection, then dismissal, in the event of no suitable alternative work, may be fair. For example, the discovery that a surgeon had died of AIDS led to an extended public debate on the extent to which any health worker should be permitted to continue in work and possibly endanger the lives of his patients. In this particular case, death followed within a few weeks of the knowledge of the illness (the surgeon ceased working as soon as he was aware of the diagnosis) and the health authorities in which the doctor concerned worked made a vigorous effort to contact patients who had been operated on by the surgeon and offer them AIDS tests. Interestingly, and perhaps not surprisingly, the take-up on the offer of tests was very low. The General Medical Council announced that doctors risked being struck off the medical register if they contract AIDS but ignore advice to stop practising. New guidelines were published for doctors that included the advice that doctors should inform the health authorities if they suspected that a colleague had the virus, but was not following advice. The General Medical Council announced that it was unethical for doctors who know or believe themselves to be infected with HIV to put patients at risk by failing to seek appropriate counselling or to act on it when given. It could be added that if a doctor, knowing himself to be HIV positive, infected a patient as a result of his own carelessness, then it could be not only unethical, but also a civil wrong. This is discussed below on the duty of the AIDS patient. The Department of Health has updated its guidance on HIV infected healthcare workers.[6]

The NMC has provided guidance on blood-borne viruses in its A–Z advice sheet.[7] It advises that:

> *Registrants infected with a blood-borne virus should have their viral load monitored regularly and should not return to work unless agreed as fit to resume by a responsible*

medical officer, general practitioner or their occupational health consultant. The agreed viral load varies depending on the infection. Registrants should confirm with their own Occupational Health Department what is acceptable for their particular place of employment. It emphasises the importance of respecting the confidentiality of employees' health status.

The RCN recommends that because the risk of contracting hepatitis B (HBV) from needlestick exposure is much greater than the risk of contracting HIV, all nurses should be vaccinated against hepatitis B.[8]

AIDS and health and safety at work

As explained in Chapter 12, the employer has a duty both under the common law and under the Health and Safety at Work Act 1974 to take care of the health and safety of his employees. Under the common law duty, he is required to ensure that the premises, plant and equipment are safe, that the staff are competent and that a safe system of work is implemented.

Practical Dilemma 26.3 Caring for the AIDS patient

Ruth was a staff nurse in a ward that had been specially adapted for the care of AIDS patients. Unfortunately, because of the financial position of the NHS trust, it was necessary to reduce revenue costs. The recommended practice was that gloves should be worn at all times when dealing with the bodily fluids of the patients. However, the original type of glove that was provided was replaced by a cheaper alternative which tore easily. Since Ruth suffered from eczema, she was very nervous about working in the ward and asked if she could reasonably refuse to work there.

In carrying out its duty in relation to health and safety, an employer must ensure that all reasonable practical precautions are taken to safeguard the employee. A written statement of safety policy is a statutory obligation under the Health and Safety at Work Act 1974. In order to comply with its duties, each employer should ensure that the policy covers potential dangers from the AIDS virus. The employer has a duty to ensure that the equipment and protective clothing that are reasonably necessary to ensure the safety of the employee are provided. If a code of practice requires that, in the circumstances outlined above, gloves should be provided, then it would also be reasonable to provide gloves that met the needs of staff safety. If Ruth can show that the gloves provided are useless in protecting her and others could be purchased that would be effective at reasonable cost, it could be argued that Ruth would be justified in requiring these reasonable precautions to be made for her safety. If she were to be dismissed in such circumstances, it could be argued that the employer was being unreasonable and that it was an unfair dismissal. The employee could not refuse to treat an AIDS patient simply because he had AIDS. There are no statutory grounds for refusing to take part in such care as is provided by the Abortion Act (see Chapter 15).

It is, however, unreasonable of the employer to endanger the safety of the employee when reasonable precautions could be taken but they are not. The employer's duty in this respect would include the laying down of safe codes of practice and ensuring that these were implemented, training of staff in safe systems of work, as well as the provision of reasonable equipment to ensure a safe environment. If, however, an employee failed to follow the safe practices and became infected, any claim for compensation against the employer might be reduced on the grounds of contributory negligence.

The UKCC published guidelines that made it clear that it would regard the refusal by a registered nurse to treat an AIDS patient as professional misconduct. It emphasised that the practitioner has no right to refuse to treat a patient suffering from AIDS or who is HIV positive. The NMC has not yet itself issued any guidance about AIDS/HIV patients or registered practitioners.

If, in the above case, Ruth was provided with gloves that were considered suitable and yet she still refused to work on the AIDS ward, it is highly likely (depending, of course, on the details of the situation) that such conduct would be considered to be unreasonable. It would follow that the employers could use such conduct in refusing to care for the AIDS patient as a statutory reason for a fair dismissal. Ruth might also face disciplinary proceedings from the conduct and competence committee.

The Personal Protective Equipment (PPE) at Work Regulations 1999 require employers to carry out a risk assessment to avoid risks and, where this is not possible, to provide suitable PPE free of charge to employees exposed to these risks. Protection against dismissal in health and safety situations is given by employment legislation (see Chapter 10). Guidance has been issued for clinical healthcare workers on protection against infection with HIV and hepatitis viruses.[9] Advice from the NHS Executive[10] supplements previous guidance on hepatitis B-infected healthcare workers and aims to reduce further the risk of transmission of infection to patients.[11] In February 2004 a doctor who failed to inform his employers that he was carrying hepatitis B and practised surgery and applied for surgical posts without disclosing that fact, contrary to an NHS Directive that banned hepatitis B carriers from 'exposure-prone procedures', lost his appeal against suspension by the GMC.[12] The Department of Health has updated its guidance on HIV-infected healthcare workers.[13]

The AIDS patient

Gradually, a clearer idea is emerging on the rights and duties of the AIDS sufferer. The issues are often concerned with the rights of consent to be tested and also the problems of confidentiality and to whom the information that X is suffering from AIDS be given. There are also some cases directly concerned with the AIDS patient in the criminal law. For example, a threat by an AIDS victim to harm another person can be a criminal offence. In the first successful prosecution for sexually transmitting HIV in England, a man was convicted of inflicting 'biological' grievous bodily harm on two women and sentenced to 4½ years imprisonment.[14] The Court of Appeal set out the basic provisions which apply to this criminal offence in the case of Konzani.[15] A man who had known for three years that he was HIV positive was sentenced to 9 years imprisonment for having unprotected sex with a woman to whom he did not disclose his HIV status.[16]

Other countries have had AIDS-related criminal offences: a man in Missouri, USA, injected his son with HIV to avoid paying child benefit support. The boy has survived. The father stole AIDS-tainted blood from his job as a laboratory technician. He was sentenced to imprisonment and it was recommended that he serve life.[17] A doctor in Louisiana, USA, who injected his nurse lover with the AIDS virus, was given a maximum penalty of 50 years' hard labour.[18]

It would seem that there is no reason why a person who knows that he is suffering from AIDS or is HIV positive and is therefore a potential source of infection should not owe a duty of care to any person whom he can reasonably foresee would be likely to be harmed by his actions. This is the same duty of care that is owed by anyone in the civil law of negligence to take such precautions as are practical to ensure that reasonably foreseeable harm does not occur as the result of their actions or omissions (see Chapter 3).

What is the nature of the duty of care owed by an AIDS sufferer to those who might be contaminated by him? Should he inform those with whom he is in contact that he has AIDS or is HIV positive? Take, for example, a situation where an AIDS sufferer is involved in a road traffic accident; should he tell the ambulance crew and those who are helping him as he lies bleeding in the road to take special precautions? If he fails to do so (and he might well fail to do so for fear that the volunteers might suddenly disappear) and some of the helpers become infected, would he then be liable to them? If the general principles of law are applied, there should be no reason why he is not under the duty to inform them, but the point still needs to be settled in the courts. In a case brought against the Swedish government an HIV patient argued that there had been a breach of his human rights under Article 5(1) of the European Convention on Human Rights when he had been compulsorily isolated for periods amounting to one and a half years over a seven-year period. The European Court on Human Rights held that the authorities had failed to strike a fair balance between the need to ensure that the HIV virus did not spread and the applicant's right to liberty.[19] In contrast the House of Lords held that there was no breach of Article 3 rights when a Ugandan woman was refused asylum even though she was suffering from full-blown AIDS and needed the retroviral drugs available in the UK to stay alive. Article 3 could not be interpreted as requiring contracting states to admit and treat AIDS sufferers from all over the world for the rest of their lives. They came to their unanimous decision despite their considerable sympathy for the woman.[20]

Consent to screening

There has been considerable debate in the press over whether people could be tested for AIDS without their knowledge and consent; for example, in epidemiological research when there is a need to establish the extent of the disease or the existence of HIV positivity in the country for the purposes of planning resources and future policies. Some have argued that if the tests are done on an anonymous basis, and the individuals therefore not informed of the results, then such testing would be lawful. Others have stated that to take blood for such testing without obtaining the patient's consent is a trespass to their person.

One of the difficulties is that while the law requires the consent of an individual for any interference with his person, at present consent is given for blood to be taken and this seems to include consent to all the various tests that are to be carried out on the blood: few doctors or technicians would explain to a patient all the tests that are to be undertaken. For example, in pregnancy it is routine for a Wassermann test (for venereal disease) to be carried out on patients, but very few would be aware of the existence of the test or its purpose. It could be argued that consent to all these various tests is covered by the initial consent to the blood being taken. These tests are undertaken as part of the duty of care for the patient, to enable a proper diagnosis to be carried out and the appropriate treatment given. However, at present it is not clear that testing blood for AIDS or HIV is in the best interests of the patient. The knowledge that a person is HIV positive merely puts an uncertain burden over him with prognosis and timings remaining unknown. Insurance companies, for example, are refusing cover for persons who have received a test, not just for those who are HIV positive.

However, a new scheme whereby insurance cover is not provided for AIDS-related illnesses might take away the need to make any declaration in relation to AIDS tests or to one's sexual preferences.

What are our conclusions? It has been pointed out that there is, under the public health legislation, power for a doctor to be authorised to examine a person suspected of having AIDS. Since this statutory power exists, no further powers that contradict the general principles of consent should be implied, i.e. if Parliament had wished to give wider powers it could have done so under this legislation. In all other cases, the principle that the patient should give consent to the testing should be applied and there should be no secret testing without the patient's knowledge or consent.

As the extent of the disease grows, there may well be specific laws changing this position. For example, there has been a strong plea in favour of anonymous screening for epidemiological reasons and the government has supported the need. The Public Health Laboratory Service commenced a programme of anonymous HIV testing, using blood left over from other tests authorised by the patient. A UKCC Registrar's letter (12/93) dated 6 April 1993 sets guidelines for practitioners involved in such testing.

Government policy on testing

In December 1998 the government launched a campaign to encourage all pregnant women to have an HIV test. The press release stated that only 30 per cent of women who are HIV positive are aware that they are infected. If a pregnant woman is known to be HIV positive, then the risk of passing on HIV to the foetus can be reduced by arranging for delivery to be by Caesarean section. Avoiding breastfeeding also removes the risk of passing on the virus through the milk. However, the law has not been changed and a test for HIV still requires the consent of the woman. The government set a national target to achieve an 80 per cent reduction by December 2002 in the number of children who acquire HIV from their mothers.[21] In their HIV/AIDS Services 2000/2001 allocation and strategy, NHS organisations were instructed that part of the HIV prevention budget was to be used to support antenatal services in recommending an HIV test to all pregnant women. A research project to estimate the cost-effectiveness of a universal, voluntary HIV screening programme has suggested that it is effective and should be implemented in the London area, with other areas being considered for screening.[22] For further information on guidelines for the management of HIV infections in pregnant women see the article by Lyall[23] and guidance from the Department of Health.[24] The Expert Advisory Group on AIDS published guidelines which were updated in 2002. They are available on its website.[25] It points out that all women in England are now offered and recommended an HIV test as part of their antenatal care and it sets out the pre-test discussions which should take place. Named testing should only take place with the consent of the person.

A GP who carried out secret HIV tests on five patients he suspected were indulging in risky sex was given a serious reprimand by the GMC. One of the patients had found out about the test when he applied for a life insurance policy and he notified the GMC. The disciplinary committee of the GMC noted that the GP believed that he was acting in the patients' best interests, but concluded that 'such a benevolent, paternalistic attitude has no place in modern medicine'.[26]

In Case 26.1, an HIV positive mother refused to allow her baby to be tested for HIV.

> ### Case 26.1   *Re C (HIV test)*
>
> **Refusal of HIV test**[27]
>
> The local authority applied for a specific issue order that a baby born to an HIV positive mother be tested for HIV. The mother was sceptical of the conventional treatment for HIV and AIDS, had refused medication during the pregnancy and intended to continue breast-feeding until the child was about 2 years old. The judge found that there was a 20–25 per cent chance that the baby was infected with HIV; the risk had been increased with the breastfeeding. The judge held that the views of the parents were important factors in the decision and any court invited to overrule parental wishes had to move extremely cautiously. He concluded that in the present circumstances the arguments for overruling the wishes of the parents and for testing the baby were overwhelming. The baby had rights of her own, recognised in national and international law, the baby's welfare was paramount and in the baby's interests the test should take place. The parents appealed, but did not attend court on the date their application was due to be heard, having disappeared from their home, tak-ing the child with them. The Court of Appeal refused permission to appeal: the question whether the child should or should not be tested was a matter relating to the welfare of the child, not the rights of the parents, and it was clearly not in the child's best interests for either the parents or the health professionals to remain ignorant of her state of health.

The Royal College of Paediatrics and Child Health published an update report on reducing mother to child transmission of HIV infection in the UK in 2006.[28] It recommends the development of networks for sharing expertise and facilities, the improvement of case management, the evolution in the management of HIV disease (through the use of antiretroviral treatment, Caesarean section and avoidance of breastfeeding) and the long-term follow-up of infants exposed to antiretroviral drugs.

This field is of particular concern to midwives and operating theatre staff who wish to know whether it is possible to insist that all midwifery patients or all surgical patients be screened for AIDS. There is certainly no power to insist on such screening under the laws at present, though there is the power to order an AIDS test on an individual under the public health regulations discussed above. The difficult question is: if there were power to screen prospective surgical or midwifery patients and the tests were carried out and some were found to be positive, what happens then? Can the professional staff refuse to operate or to attend them in their confinements? Can additional precautions for the safety of the staff be taken? If the answer to the latter question is yes, then it gives the staff a false sense of security since, as was pointed out in the section on the characteristics of AIDS, there can be false negatives. It would be better practice for midwifery, operating theatre and other staff to maintain standards of practice that assumed that every patient was HIV positive.

Guidelines on good practice for pupils living with HIV were published by the National Childrens Bureau and the Children and Young People HIV Network[29] which gives guidance to schools on supporting children infected or affected by HIV.

Blood donors

The present practice is for blood donors to be asked to agree that their blood can be tested for AIDS and a leaflet is given to them to sign as to whether they are in any of the high-risk groups and which asks them not to give blood if they are. The donors should not, of course, run any risk of contracting AIDS as a result of giving blood.

Haemophiliacs and recipients of blood

Before the disease of AIDS was recognised in this country as a possible killer, many haemophiliacs were given contaminated blood and have since contracted AIDS. In order to succeed in an action for compensation in respect of the harm caused by being given contaminated blood, they would need to be able to show that those professionals providing the blood should have tested it for AIDS and were in breach of their duty of care in failing to do so and that this failure was contrary to the standard accepted practices of the time. It is unlikely that those who were originally infected could show this and therefore they have been dependent on government *ex gratia* payments and charity to assist them. Any person receiving contaminated blood now, however, which has not been properly tested, would have a *prima facie* case of negligence and might also be able to obtain compensation under the Consumer Protection Act[30] (see Chapter 12). In August 2003 the Secretary of State announced that £100 million was being made available to compensate people who had been infected with hepatitis C from contaminated blood products. The numbers include 2,800 haemophiliacs who were infected through contaminated clotting agents they were given during the 1970s and 1980s. The details of the scheme were announced in January 2004:[31] from April 2004 patients, who were alive on 29 August 2003 and who had been infected with hepatitis C after being given blood by the NHS before September 1999, will receive an initial lump sum of £20,000. This includes those who have contracted hepatitis C through someone infected with the disease. Those with more advanced stages of illness will receive a further £45,000. However, the widows of haemophiliacs who had died from the disease would be excluded from the compensation. An inquiry has been set up under the chairmanship of Lord Archer to look at the supply of contaminated blood and blood products. See Chapter 16. Further information can be obtained from the inquiry website.[32] In January 2004 NICE approved new treatment for those suffering from hepatitis C. It suggested that pegylated interferon should be prescribed on the NHS along with another drug, ribavairin.[33]

Confidentiality

> **Practical Dilemma 26.4** **A justified disclosure?**
>
> Dr Jones, a general practitioner, was treating Ben James for an undiagnosed condition. He thought initially that it could be glandular fever. However, the blood tests revealed that he was suffering from AIDS. Dr Jones was uncertain as to who he could inform about this result. Ben was anxious that no one be told and that the information should be kept from his wife until much later on. Dr Jones wondered if the practice nurse and others working in the health centre who were likely to come into contact with Ben should be notified.

AIDS probably comes under the definition of venereal disease[34] and the Venereal Disease Regulations would therefore apply (sexual health strategies are considered in Chapter 13). AIDS was not a notifiable disease under the Public Health (Control of Disease) Act 1984. It was included in the list of diseases made notifiable under Regulation 3 of the Public Health (Infectious Diseases) Regulations 1988, to which only certain provisions apply. The AIDS Control Act 1987 regulates the reporting of cases and in 1988 this was extended to HIV positive persons. The powers set out in the Statute on page 600 were given to local authorities and justices of the peace to prevent the spread of infection of AIDS (Public Health (Infectious Diseases) Regulations 1985). These were consolidated in the regulations made in 1988.[35] In addition, in Chapter 8, the general exceptions to the principle of confidentiality were discussed and it will be recalled that one of the exceptions was where disclosure was justified on grounds of the public interest. This was one of the most difficult exceptions, since there is no clear judicial or statutory definition over what are the limits and extent of the term 'public interest' in this context. In the story of Ben (Practical Dilemma 26.4), if Dr Jones also treats Ben's wife, it could be argued that he is not fulfilling his duty of care to her if he fails to inform her that she is at risk of contracting AIDS and, even if she is not his patient, he should inform her GP (unless, of course, he can persuade Ben to tell her). This breach in the duty of confidentiality owed to Ben is therefore justifiable on the grounds of the public interest. The same argument could be applied to informing any person in the health centre who is likely to be at risk from infection from Ben. Thus there may be justification in informing the practice nurse, but not the receptionist, since the latter is not likely to acquire the disease from Ben. The fact that the law is uncertain makes for considerable difficulties and ultimately it is up to individual practitioners to decide whether, in the specific circumstances of an individual case, there should be disclosure. The balance between an action for breach of confidentiality and an action for breach of a duty to care for the safety of a fellow employee is a very fine one.

In contrast to the case of X v. Y (see Case 26.2), the Court of Appeal allowed an order of disclosure of the person who had informed the press about an Ashworth patient. Subsequently the House of Lords decided that the journalist did not have to identify his source. (The case is further discussed in Chapter 8, page 171.)

Case 26.2 *X v. Y* (1988)

Order of disclosure and non-disclosure under contempt of court[36]

The High Court held that public interest did not justify a newspaper publishing or using information disclosed by a health authority employee in breach of contract who admitted to a journalist that two identified doctors were being treated for AIDS at an identified hospital. The newspaper was fined £10,000 for contempt of a court order. However, the health authority was not able to obtain disclosure of the name of the informant employee, even though he or she was clearly in breach of the duty of employment, because this was not one of the occasions on which the press were obliged to disclose the source of their information under the contempt of court legislation.

Confidentiality and identifying patients who may be at risk

In one case,[37] the claimant was working as a healthcare worker when he was diagnosed as HIV positive. He informed the health authority and ceased working immediately. The health authority wanted to conduct a 'lookback' exercise that involved contacting various patients of the claimant's who were thought to be potentially at risk of infection. The claimant did not believe that his patients were at sufficient risk to justify that exercise and sought a declaration that the lookback exercise was unlawful on the grounds that it breached clinical confidentiality. He also sought an order restraining the authority from making use of the patient records and from doing anything that might directly or indirectly reveal his identity. An order was in force stating that the parties were only to be identified by initials. A newspaper wished to publish the story and the claimant sought an order to prevent its revealing his identity. The injunction was issued but was subsequently varied on the application of the newspaper so that it could name the health authority, the claimant's specialty and the date of his diagnosis as HIV positive. The Court of Appeal held that it was appropriate for the health authority and claimant to be identified by initials, for the claimant's specialty to be identified, and ordered the claimant to make available to the health authority such patient records as were reasonably required on the understanding that they would not be disclosed without either the permission of the claimant or the court. The updated guidance of the Department of Health on HIV infected healthcare workers emphasises the importance of protecting the rights to confidentiality of any employees and makes it clear that, because of the very low risk of infection, there is no longer a requirement to notify all patients, but whether notification is necessary should be assessed on a case-by-case basis using risk assessment.[38]

AIDS Control Act 1987

This Act requires district health authorities to report to the regional health authorities (or Welsh Office) and for the regional authorities to report to the Secretary of State, giving information set out in the schedule and other such relevant information as the Secretary of State may direct. The schedule includes the following:

1 the number of people known to have AIDS and the timing of the diagnosis

2 the particulars of facilities and services provided by each authority

3 the numbers of people employed by the authority in providing such facilities

4 future provision over the next 12 months.

It also requires details of the action taken to educate members of the public in relation to AIDS and HIV, to provide training for testing for AIDS and for the treatment, counselling and care of persons with AIDS or infected with HIV.

A subsequent statutory instrument has extended the information required to include HIV positive persons.[39] Nurses are likely to be involved in providing information to managers for the necessary returns to be made.

Notifiable diseases

Diseases that are notifiable are shown in Box 26.2.

Box 26.2 **Notifiable diseases**

Category A: cholera, plague, relapsing fever, smallpox, typhus.

Category B: acquired immune deficiency syndrome (AIDS), acute encephalitis, acute poliomyelitis, anthrax, diphtheria, dysentery, leprosy, leptospirosis, malaria, measles, meningitis, meningococcal septicaemia, mumps, ophthalmia neonatorum, paratyphoid fever, rabies, rubella, scarlet fever, tetanus, tuberculosis, typhoid fever, viral haemorrhagic fever, viral hepatitis, whooping cough, yellow fever.

Category A covers those notifiable diseases that come under the duties set by the Public Health (Control of Disease) Act 1984. These diseases must be reported to the local authority. Those diseases under Category B are covered by Regulation 3 of the Public Health (Infectious Diseases) Regulations 1988[40] and the 1984 Act applies to a more limited extent.

Procedure for notification

Under Section 11 of the 1984 Act, a registered medical practitioner has a duty to notify the proper office of the local authority if he becomes aware, or suspects, that a patient whom he is attending within the district of a local authority is suffering from a notifiable disease or from food poisoning. The duty does not apply if he believes, and has reasonable grounds for believing, that some other registered medical practitioner has complied with the duty.

What information must be notified?

Box 26.3 shows the information that must be notified.[41]

Box 26.3　　**Information that must be notified**

1　Name, age and sex of the patient and the address of the premises where the patient is.
2　The disease or, as the case may be, particulars of the poisoning from which the patient is, or is suspected to be, suffering and the date or approximate date of its onset.
3　If the premises is a hospital, the day on which the patient was admitted, the address of the premises from which he came there and whether or not, in the opinion of the person giving the certificate, the disease or poisoning from which the patient is, or is suspected to be, suffering was contracted in hospital.

(NB Section 11(4) imposes a criminal sanction on a person who fails to comply with an obligation imposed on him under the provisions set out above.)

Cross-infection control

A report by the National Audit Office[42] raised major concerns about the level of hospital-acquired infection (HAI). The report suggested that HAI could be the main or a contributory cause in 20,000 or 4 per cent of deaths a year in the UK and that there are at least about 100,000 cases of HAI with an estimated cost to the NHS of £1 billion. The NAO drew conclusions on the strategic management of HAI; surveillance, and the extent and cost of HAI; and the effectiveness of prevention, detection and control measures. Its recommendations include reviewing the following:

1　The value of using an infection control manual should be considered.
2　The 1995 Guidance on Infection Control should be reviewed.
3　Cost-effectiveness of screening patients and staff and isolation of patients together with standards and guidelines should be considered.
4　The policies on provision of education and training.
5　The arrangements for monitoring hospital hygiene and hospital practices.
6　Ensuring advice on handwashing is implemented.

7 Clinical audit arrangements to ensure infection control is covered.

8 Isolation facilities.

9 Guidance on management of HAI outbreaks.

Following this report, the government announced a multi-pronged initiative to tackle hospital-acquired infections. Among the initiatives planned were an antimicrobial strategy, including a clampdown on inappropriate antibiotic use and better infection control measures.[43] In addition, there was to be independent inspection of hospitals by the Audit Commission and Commission for Health Improvement. The government has stated that the Commission for Health Improvement and the Audit Commission would conduct ward inspections and be given the right to seek information on HAI and to publish it.[44] The report on the NHS commissioned by the government from Virgin Group reported that it found grubby wards, litterstrewn entrances and dirty casualty departments throughout the NHS. On 31 July 2000 the Health Minister, Lord Hunt, announced that NHS hospitals were to be given £150,000 each to clean up their wards and disinfect bathrooms as part of a £31 million campaign. The money could be used for extra cleaning staff, materials, equipment and new towels and linen. Patient environment action teams would make unannounced inspections every six months and those hospitals that failed to meet standards would be 'named and shamed'. National standards for cleanliness would form part of performance assessment guidelines for hospitals. In September 2000 eight NHS hospitals were identified by the Department of Health as models for others. They were to assist in drawing up standards for a national action plan for cleanliness to be published in December 2000. The results of the National Audit Office were reinforced by a cross-party report of the House of Commons which suggested that unhygienic hospitals were costing the NHS £1 billion a year by making patients worse. If hospital infection could be cut by just 10 per cent, the NHS could treat 50,000 more patients a year.[45]

In the light of this report the Secretary of State for Health admitted that Methicillin-resistant *Staphylococcus aureus* is endemic in England's hospitals.[46]

Another prong of the government's campaign against cross-infection was to make ward sisters responsible for ward cleaning and reintroduce the role of 'matron'. In a press release in January 2001,[47] the Department of Health announced a further £30 million to raise standards of cleanliness and that ward sisters would have the authority to agree with managers to withhold payments from contracted cleaning companies if standards were not reached. Managers would work closely with ward sisters to ensure that sufficient resources were being spent to provide high-quality cleaning services. As a last resort, ward sisters would be able to request that alternative cleaning arrangements are made. In a press announcement on 4 April 2001[48] the Secretary of State announced that each group of wards in the NHS were to have a matron (male or female) in charge. Four of the ten key functions identified were the following.

1 Making sure the wards are clean.

2 Preventing and controlling hospital-acquired infection.

3 Improving the wards for the patients.

4 Making sure nurses have more power.

The NMC provides advice to registrants on infection control.[49] The RCN has also provided guidance on good practice in infection prevention and control.[50] It covers the general principles of infection prevention and control and provides a 10-step handwashing guide. A progress report on the strategy for infectious diseases was published by the Department of Health in June 2004[51] and the work of the HPA is discussed below.

Practical Dilemma 26.5   Cross-infection nurse

Joan was appointed as the hospital infection control nurse. Immediately on starting her new post, she undertook an audit of existing practices on infection control. She found that basic standards, including handwashing, were extremely lax, particularly among junior doctors. However, her attempts to raise standards appeared to be thwarted. What is the legal situation?

When Joan was appointed, she should have been notified of the organisational support that would be given to her post. This would include such details as to whom she reported, who was her immediate line manager and the strategy of the organisation in setting down and complying with the standards issued by the government. There should be in place a committee for infection control. She would need to prepare a report on her findings, giving her conclusions in a clear, unemotional report with constructive recommendations on the action that could be taken. If there is no follow-up action from her report, then she may have justification in following the procedures set up under the Public Interest Disclosure Act 1998 (see Chapter 4) in order to ensure that action is taken.

Methicillin-resistant *Staphylococcus aureus* (MRSA) and Clostridium difficile

One of the greatest challenges for all those working in healthcare is the control and eradication of Methicillin-resistant *Staphylococcus aureus* (MRSA). At a conference in September 1999, George Duckworth of the Public Health Laboratory Service stated that the proportion of all *S. aureus* bloodstream infections caused by MRSA had increased from less than 3 per cent before 1991 to 37 per cent.[52] This poses a major problem for all hospital and community health professionals. It appears to be accepted that it is a problem that will never be completely eradicated. Robert Munro suggests that poor hygiene standards in hospitals are largely to blame for the increase in MRSA and other infections.[53] The Royal College of Nursing has provided guidance for nurses on MRSA as part of its campaign to wipe out MRSA.[54] MRSA data are available online.[55] In December 2003 the Department of Health announced plans for a crackdown on healthcare-acquired infections, including antibiotic-resistant infections – i.e. superbugs – supporting proposals put forward by the Chief Medical Officer of Health.[56] These include:

+ a designated director of infection control in each NHS trust leading a dedicated infection control team
+ introduction of a new system to cut food poisoning
+ a drive to ensure staff adhere to cross-infection prevention schemes such as frequent handwashing and disinfection
+ reduction in the unnecessary use of catheters and intravenous drips
+ the Healthcare Commission was asked to make infection control a key priority in its assessments of hospital performance
+ £3 million will be spent on research into hospital-acquired infections

✚ a working group including modern matrons, ward housekeepers and allied health professionals to work out ways to improve the prevention and control of healthcare-associated
infection.

In February 2004 the Health Protection Agency announced that the number of persons
dying from MRSA infection had risen more than fifteenfold in the past decade. A total of
1,542 cases of MRSA were announced in England between October and December 2006,
and although this was a slight reduction on previous months, the DH target of halving rates
of MRSA infection before April 2007 was not met. The DH published a strategy for tackling
MRSA in November 2006. It was announced in June 2007 that the Healthcare Commission
was to make unannounced spot checks on NHS trusts to cut rates of hospital-acquired infection.[57] The NHS trusts' performance would be measured against the DH hygiene code, which
sets out 11 compulsory duties to prevent and cope with hospital superbugs. Sanctions for
failure to comply with the code could lead to a trust being placed under special measures.
Further information on the DH strategy to reduce hospital-acquired infections can be found
on the DH website.[58]

Clostridium difficile was described by the Health Protection Agency in 2007 as the most
important cause of hospital-acquired diarrhoea. Further information including the findings
and recommendations from a review of epidemiology by the Directors of Infection Prevention and Control in England[59] can be found on the HPA website[60] and the DH website.[61] In
2007 one of the first acts of the new Secretary of State, Alan Johnson, when appointed
was to give £50 million to tackle MRSA and Clostridium by doubling the size of the DH's
infection improvement team who advise NHS trusts on developing plans to cut infections.
In July 2007 the Healthcare Commission published a national study into healthcare-
associated infection. In order to reduce the risk of infections the report recommended that
trusts should develop a culture of safety, have a good system of corporate and clinical
governance, review performance, manage risk and communicate with patients and the public. A report by the Healthcare Commission in October 2007 into Maidstone and Tunbridge
Wells Trust revealed that up to 90 patients had died between 2004 and 2006 after being
infected with Clostridium difficile. The Minister of Health responded by announcing plans
for a new super-regulator to be established in April 2009, combining the Healthcare
Commission, Mental Health Act Commission and the Commission for Social Care Inspection
with powers to close NHS and private hospitals and residential care homes. The new powers
under the Corporate Manslaughter and Corporate Homicide Act may be used against NHS
trusts which fail to control hospital-acquired infections. It was reported on 17 January 2007
that Lesley Ash, an actress, received a £5 million settlement after she caught MRSA at the
Chelsea and Westminster Hospital. It caused her devastating disabilities and meant that she
would never again be able to play active roles as an actress.

A Risk and Regulatory Advisory Council is being set up to review regulations on health and
safety. Its first project is to look at the government initiatives in relation to MRSA to assess
their effectiveness.[62]

Tuberculosis (TB)

TB was once thought to have been eradicated. However, there is evidence that poor housing
conditions, poverty and malnourishment are leading to an increase in TB levels, often particularly associated with the refugee population. The HPA states that 800 new cases of TB
are reported each year in the UK with most cases occurring in major cities, particularly in

London. The HPA is working with the Department of Health and the NHS towards the elimination of TB and is coordinating a TB programme. Further information on its strategy and local and national surveillance can be obtained from the HPA website.[63]

Health Protection Agency

In April 2003 the Health Protection Agency was created to provide a coordinated approach to health protection and reduce the impact of infectious diseases, poisons, chemicals, biological and radiation hazards. It was set up in the light of the Chief Medical Officer of Health's report, 'Getting Ahead of the Curve',[64] which recognised the need to bring together in one organisation the skills and expertise in a number of organisations to work in a more coordinated way, to reduce the burden and consequences of health protection threats or disease with the aim of providing a more comprehensive and effective response to threats to the public's health. The HPA brings together the following organisations into the one body:

✦ Public Health Laboratory Service (including the Communicable Disease Surveillance Centre and Central Public Health Laboratory)

✦ Centre for Applied Microbiology and Research

✦ National Focus for Chemical Incidents

✦ regional service provider units that support the management of chemical incidents

✦ National Poisons Information Service

✦ NHS public health staff responsible for infectious disease control, emergency planning and other protection support

✦ National Radiological Protection Board (NRPB) (incorporated into the Health Protection Agency in April 2005).

The HPA was established as a special health authority under Section 11 of the National Health Service Act 1977 but under the Health Protection Agency Act 2004 it became a non-departmental public body. Its website[65] prides itself on its independence:

> *People want clear, unambiguous and authoritative information on public health protection issues from an independent source, which they feel they can trust. The Health Protection Agency will give impartial advice to the public, professionals and government alike, which is based on the experience and expertise of the professionals working in the organisation.*

However, with a budget of £175 million a year, it has to be accountable and this is initially to the Department of Health and parliamentary monitoring.

The functions of the HPA, as set out on its website, are as follows:

✦ To provide impartial, authoritative information and advice to professionals and the public, and independent advice to the government on public health protection policies and programmes.

✦ To deliver services and support to the NHS and other organisations to protect people's health from infectious diseases, chemical hazards, poisons and radiation hazards.

✦ To monitor and respond to new threats to public health and provide a rapid response to health protection emergencies, including the deliberate release of poisons, chemicals or microbiological substances.

✚ To improve knowledge about health protection through research, development, education and training.

Further information on its strategy, publications and its local and regional services can be obtained on its website.[66]

Emergency response

The plans of the HPA, to meet a possible terrorist emergency or potential SARS outbreak or other emergency, include the following:

✚ build on the existing major incident plans

✚ develop the infrastructure for surveillance and early recognition of events

✚ continue to produce guidance for health protection for these new hazards

✚ identify specific counter-measures and make sure they are available quickly

✚ provide training and test new plans

✚ coordinate the Health Protection Agency's divisions and expertise in emergency situations.

Vaccination

Compensation for vaccine damage can be obtained in two ways. First, there is a statutory scheme of compensation under the Vaccine Damage Payments Act 1979. Under this scheme, £120,000[67] is now payable to a person who can establish that they have been severely disabled as a result of a vaccination against the specified diseases of diphtheria, tetanus, whooping cough, poliomyelitis, measles, rubella, tuberculosis, smallpox and any other disease specified by the Secretary of State. Subsequent regulations[68] have reduced the severity of the disability, which must be proved to be 60 per cent. Whether the disability has been caused by the vaccination shall be established on a balance of probabilities. The claim must be made before whichever is the later of the date on which the disabled person attains the age of 21 years (or, where he has died, would have attained that age) and the end of a period of six years, beginning on the date of the vaccination against the disease to which the claim relates. Meningococcal Group C has been added to the diseases covered and the person need not be under 18 at the time of vaccination, neither need there be an outbreak of the disease.[69]

This statutory scheme does not prevent a claim being made in the civil courts for negligence in relation to damage caused by vaccine. Clearly, if such a case could succeed, far more than £120,000 would be payable for severely disabled persons. However, civil action faces a further difficulty, as well as having to establish a causal link between the vaccine and the disability. The claimant must also show that the disability occurred as a result of negligence by the professional: for example, the professionals failed to take account of the person's present health condition or previous history and the vaccine was contraindicated for that person. A claim could also be brought against the drug company if there were some defect in the vaccine and this claim could now come under the Consumer Protection Act (considered in Chapter 12), under which it is not necessary to show negligence by a manufacturer, but simply that there was a defect in the product. This would be extremely difficult if the victim was the only one from a particular batch who suffered harm. The civil cases so far have not overcome the problems of proving causation apart from a case in Ireland (see below).

> ### Case 26.3 *Loveday v. Renton and Another* (1988)
>
> **Vaccine damage**[70]
>
> Susan Loveday was vaccinated for whooping cough in 1970 and 1971, following which she suffered permanent brain damage. She claimed compensation from the Wellcome Foundation, which made the vaccine, and from the doctor who administered it.

The judge held that on a balance of probabilities the claimant had failed to show that pertussis vaccine could cause permanent brain damage in young children. The case therefore failed on this point of causation. The judge also said that even if he had found in favour of the claimant on this preliminary point, the claimant would still face insuperable difficulties in establishing negligence on the part of the doctor or nurse who administered the vaccine. Such a claim would have to be based on the ground that the vaccination had been given in spite of the presence of certain contraindications.

In a case in Ireland brought against the Wellcome Foundation,[71] £2.75 million was awarded in respect of brain damage following a vaccination. It was established that a particular batch of vaccine was below standard and should not have been released on to the market. An appeal by a GP against a finding of negligent advice in respect of a polio vaccine succeeded. The Court of Appeal held that the trial judge had wrongly found the GP to be in breach of his duty of care when he advised parents that there was no reason to postpone a polio vaccination because the child had an abscess on his buttocks. Subsequently the child contracted polio. The Court of Appeal held it was not reasonably foreseeable that the GP could have foreseen the results of his failure to explain his advice to the parents. His reasoning was based on possible pain to the child, not the possibility of polio being contracted.[72]

The MMR dispute

Concern about MMR was raised in 1995[73] by Dr Wakefield of the Royal Free Hospital, London, who published claims of a link between the measles vaccination and the inflammatory bowel condition known as Crohn's disease. He subsequently published a second study that showed that some children who had developed the bowel condition also developed autism. The study was too small to demonstrate a causal connection with MMR, but it was suggested by Dr Wakefield that pending further research, MMR should be temporarily abandoned and single doses of the different vaccines should be given. Subsequently, there has been considerable disquiet over whether it was safe for health professionals to recommend MMR and many parents have opted for single dose that is not available on the NHS. There have been government attempts to induce confidence in MMR. For example, on 13 December 2001 a Department of Health press release[74] announced the publication of a report commissioned by the Department of Health and carried out by the Medical Research Council that there was no evidence to link autism with the measles, mumps and rubella vaccine. The apparent increase in prevalence of autism spectrum disorders (ASDs) is likely to have resulted from better diagnosis and clearer definition as well as increased awareness. In January 2004 the Department of Health published an MMR information pack for parents setting out the reasons why MMR is recommended and providing seven information sheets.[75] Further information on supplies and the administration of MMR was issued in May 2005[76] and an assessment of the press coverage of the MMR vaccine was published by the Department of Health two days earlier.[77]

The issue came to the attention of the courts when a dispute arose between two sets of parents over whether the children should be given the MMR: in each case the mother was against the triple vaccine and the father wanted it given. The High Court ruled that it was in the best interest of the children to have the MMR. The Court of Appeal dismissed the appeal on the grounds that the judge had decided the applications by reference to the paramount consideration of the welfare of the two children, in accordance with Section 1 of the Children Act 1989.[78] A practice direction was issued in July 2003 on MMR/MR vaccine litigation, which required such actions to commence in the Royal Courts of Justice and those that have commenced in the county court or district registry must be transferred. The actions had been allocated to the multi-track and came under the Civil Procedure Rules.[79] The independence of Dr Wakefield's research has subsequently been criticised and the safety of MMR reaffirmed. In 2007 an increase in measles was held to be directly linked with the failure in uptake of the MMR vaccine as a result of the controversy. The MMR controversy is explored in a book by Tammy Boyce.[80]

Conclusions

In recent years the focus in infectious diseases has moved away from that of AIDS/HIV infection to that of MRSA/Clostridium difficile. However, the continuing increase in the numbers infected with the HIV virus leaves no room for complacency. The reduction of hospital acquired infections is a priority for the NHS and the Health Protection Agency and criminal proceedings against NHS trust chief executives and chairs may be initiated. Ultimately, however, improvement in the safety of hospitals and the reduction of deaths through hospital acquired infections rests with individual standards of personal hygiene. Provision is made in the Health and Social Care Bill for amending the Public Health (Control of Disease) Act 1984 to provide a more effective and proportionate response to infectious disease.

Reflection questions

1 What is meant by 'reasonably practical precautions to safeguard the safety of other employees'? To what extent do you consider your present practice meets this requirement in relation to the dangers of infection from the AIDS virus? (See also Chapter 12.)

2 Many regard the hepatitis B virus as an even greater danger to health service staff than AIDS. What are the main differences in the law (if any) relating to AIDS and to hepatitis?

3 Look again at the laws relating to the notification of infectious diseases. To what extent do you consider they could impinge on your professional practice?

4 What is meant by the duty of confidentiality in relation to AIDS? Are any exceptions to the duty justified? To what extent do you consider that the duty is carried out and what suggestions would you make for improvements for all staff to observe this duty? (See also Chapter 8.)

Further exercises

1 Obtain a copy of your authority's policy and guidelines on AIDS and discuss the extent to which these are fully implemented.

2 Do you consider that we require an AIDS Discrimination Act? What provisions do you think such an Act would contain?

3 Study the figures of your organisation on the cross-infection of patients following admission. What improvements could be made in cross-infection control?

4 What role do you consider that the individual nurse should play in ensuring that hospitals and other health premises are clean and hygienic?

References

[1] Health Protection Agency, A Complex Picture, HPA, November 2006

[2] HIV Testing Kits and Services Regulations 1992, SI 1992 No. 460

[3] Department of Health, AIDS/HIV Infected Health Care Workers: guidance on the management of infected health care workers and patient notification, DH, London, 1999, updated July 2005

[4] Buck v. Letchworth Palace Ltd, Bulletin of the Institute of Medical Ethics, No. 28, July 1987, p. 5

[5] Paul Wilkinson, Store boss banned over HIV wins cash, The Times, 11 April 2000

[6] Department of Health, AIDS/HIV Infected Health Care Workers: guidance on the management of infected health care workers and patient notification, DH, London, 1999, updated July 2005

[7] Nursing and Midwifery Council A-Z advice sheet, Blood-borne viruses, last updated March 2006

[8] RCN, Managing accidental exposures to blood-borne virus, part of its wipe it out campaign against MRSA, RCN, 2006

[9] UK Health Departments, Guidance of Clinical Health Care Workers: recommendations of the Expert Advisory Group on AIDS, HMSO, London, January 1990

[10] NHS Executive, Hepatitis B Infected Health Care Workers, HSC 2000/020, DH, London, 2000

[11] HSG(93)40, Protecting Health Care Workers and Patients from Hepatitis B; and its addendum EL(96)77

[12] Nursing and Midwifery Council News, 4 February 2004

[13] Department of Health, AIDS/HIV Infected Health Care Workers: guidance on the management of infected health care workers and patient notification, DH, London, 1999, updated July 2005

[14] R v. Dica [2004] EWCA Crim 1103; Michael Horsnell, Lover convicted after infecting women with HIV, The Times, 15 October 2003

[15] R v. Konzani [2005] EWCA Crim 706

[16] Michael Horsnell, HIV chef who recklessly infected his lover is jailed for nine years, The Times, 6 April 2007, p. 26

[17] James Bone, Man injected his son with HIV to avoid payments, The Times, 7 December 1998

[18] News item, The Times, 19 February 1999

[19] Enhorn v. Sweden [2005] ECHR 56529

[20] N v. Secretary of State for the Home Department [2005] UKHL 31

[21] HSC 1999/183

[22] M.J. Postma and Others, Universal HIV Screening of Pregnant Women in England: cost-effectiveness analysis, BMJ, 19 June 1999, 318, pp. 1656-60

[23] E.G. Lyall et al. (2001) Guidelines for the management of HIV infections in pregnant women in prevention of mother to baby transmission, HIV Medicine, 2(4), pp. 314-34

[24] Department of Health, Reducing Mother to Baby Transmission of HIV, HSC 1999/183, DH

[25] www.advisorybodies.doh.gov.uk/eaga/guidelineshivtestdiscuss.htm

[26] News item, HIV test reprimand, *The Times*, 6 January 2000

[27] *Re C (HIV Test)* [1999] 2 FLR 1004

[28] Royal College of Paediatrics and Child Health, Reducing mother to child transmission of HIV in the United Kingdom, July 2006

[29] National Children's Bureau, HIV in schools: good practice to supporting children infected or affected by HIV, 2005

[30] *A and Others* v. *National Blood Authority and Another (sub nom Re Hepatitis C Litigation)*, The Times Law Report, 4 April 2001; [2001] 3 All ER 289

[31] Department of Health press release 2004/0025, Details of Hepatitis C ex gratia payment scheme announced

[32] www.nice.org.uk

[33] www.archbbp.com

[34] See statement by judge in the case of *X* v. *Y and Another* [1988] 2 All ER 648

[35] Public Health (Infectious Diseases) Regulations 1988, SI 1988 No. 1546 as amended by SI 1996 No. 971

[36] *X* v. *Y and Another* [1988] 2 All ER 648

[37] *H (A Healthcare Worker)* v. *Associated Newspapers Ltd; H (A Healthcare Worker* v. *N (A Health Authority)* [2002] Civ 195; [2002] Lloyd's Rep Med 210 CA

[38] Department of Health, AIDS/HIV Infected Health Care Workers: guidance on the management of infected health care workers and patient notification, DH, London, 1999, updated July 2005

[39] Aids (Control) (Contents of Reports) (No. 2) Order 1988, SI 1988 1047

[40] Public Health (Infectious Diseases) Regulations 1988, SI 1988 No. 1546

[41] Public Health (Control of Disease) Act 1984 Section 11

[42] National Audit Office, The Management and Control of Hospital Acquired Infection in Acute NHS Trusts in England, The Stationery Office, London, 2000

[43] http://www.dh.gov.uk/arbstrat.htm

[44] Department of Health press release 12 June 2000; Jill Sherman, Infections caught in hospital to be exposed, *The Times*, 13 June 2000

[45] Helen Rumbelow, Hospitals that make us ill cost the NHS £1 billion a year, *The Times*, 19 January 2001

[46] David Charter, Milburn admits superbug is endemic, *The Times*, 8 January 2001

[47] Department of Health press release, Ward sisters to have greater control over cleaning standards, 17 January 2001

[48] Department of Health press release, Health Secretary to bring back matron to the health service, 4 April 2001

[49] Nursing and Midwifery Council A-Z advice sheet, Infection control, March 2006

[50] Royal College of Nursing, Good practice in infection prevention and control, RCN, 2006

[51] Department of Health, A strategy for Infectious Diseases, June 2004

[52] Esther Leach, Resistance Fighters, *Nursing Times*, 22 September 1999, 95(38), p. 18

[53] Robert Munro, Clean up your act, *Nursing Times*, 22 June 1999, 96(25), pp. 26-7

[54] Royal College of Nursing, Methicillin-Resistant *Staphylococcus Aureus*, Guidance for nursing staff, RCN, 2005

[55] www.dh.gov.uk/cmo/mrsadata/

[56] Department of Health press release 2003/0500, Drive to tackle hospital infections, 5 December 2003; available on www.dh.gov.uk/cmo

[57] David Rose, Hit squads to stamp out hospital superbugs, *The Times*, 4 June 2007, p. 18

58 www.dh.gov.uk/en/Policyandguidance/Healthandsocialcare

59 Directors of Infection Prevention and Control in England, Clostridium difficile: Findings and recommendations from a review of epidemiology and a survey, HPA, July 2006

60 www.hpa.org.uk/infections/topics_az/clostridium_difficile

61 www.dh.gov.uk/en/Policyandguidance/Healthandsocialcare

62 Rosemary Bennett, Risk assessment watchdog set up to halt march of the nanny state, *The Times*, 16 January 2008

63 www.hpa.org.uk/infections/topics_az/tb/

64 Chief Medical Officer of Health, Getting Ahead of the Curve, DH, London, January 2002

65 www.hpa.org.uk/hpa/faqs.htm

66 www.hpa.org.uk

67 The Vaccine Damage Payments Act 1979, Statutory Sum Order, SI 2007 No. 1931

68 Regulatory Reform (Vaccine Damage Payments Act 1979) Order 2002, SI 2002 No. 1592

69 Vaccine Damages Payments (Specific Diseases) Order 2001, SI 2002 No. 1652

70 *Loveday v. Renton and Another, The Times*, 31 March 1988

71 *Best v. Wellcome Foundation, Dr O'Keefe, the Southern Health Board, the Minister for Health of Ireland and the Attorney General* [1994] 5 Med LR 81

72 *Thompson v. Bradford* [2005] EWCA 1439

73 Nigel Hawkes, A lone doctor's fear set parents against experts, *The Times*, 7 February 2002

74 Department of Health, Medical Research Council Autism Review Report, 2001/0615, 13 December 2001

75 Department of Health, MMR Information pack, January 2004, Gateway reference 2004

76 Department of Health, Further Information on Supplies and Administration of MMR, May 2005

77 Department of Health, Measles, mumps and rubella (MMR) vaccine: assessment of press coverage, May 2005

78 *C (A Child: immunisation: parental rights) Re; and Others* [2003] 3 FCR 156 CA

79 www.courtservice.gov.uk/cms/7731.htm

80 Tammy Boyce, *Health, Risk and News: The MMR Vaccine and the Media*, Peter Lang Publ Inc, 2007

Chapter 27
Handling complaints

Introduction

It is highly likely that at some time in her career a nurse will be involved in a complaint, either in relation to her own conduct or in handling a complaint about someone else's. There is no doubt that there is an increase in the number of complaints made about the NHS. To some, this is a very bad sign and indicative of a growing discontent with the health services.

However, others see this as a positive and valuable sign: an opportunity to improve the service and at the same time a sign that patients are more prepared to raise their voices over their concerns. Certainly, the current emphasis on customer and consumer relations is encouraging patients, through consumer satisfaction surveys, to make their views known so that the service can be improved. Feedback from the patient is essential if the quality of care is to be improved. Unfortunately, as the reports of the Health Service Commissioner show only too frequently, whether or not a complaint is initially justified, the way in which the complaint is handled can itself be a cause for complaint. Patients' charters, the Human Rights Act 1998, National Service Frameworks and reports from the Commission for Audit and Inspection and other bodies may also encourage patients to criticise the services they have received in comparison with the standards they were led to expect and their rights as laid down in the European Convention on Human Rights (see Chapter 1 and Appendix A). This section will review the procedures for handling complaints and discuss the legal powers of those statutory bodies that can represent or investigate the grievances of the patient.

Methods of complaining

Figure 27.1 shows the variety of ways of making a complaint about the NHS. Private hospitals have their own system for handling complaints and these tend to be on an individual hospital basis.

Many different motives exist behind a complaint. Some of the reasons why patients complain are shown in Figure 27.2 and the outcomes that they are seeking are shown in Box 27.1. However, it should be appreciated that, for many people, to make a formal complaint

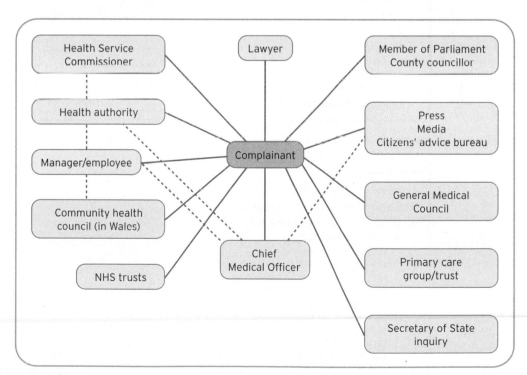

Figure 27.1 Various ways of making a complaint

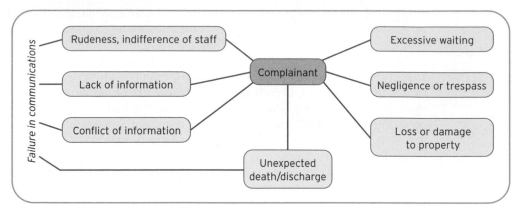

Figure 27.2 Why do people complain?

requires considerable courage and there are many reasons why justifiable grievances are not brought to the attention of management (see Box 27.2). It is very difficult for patients who are suffering from chronic conditions where they are dependent on the continued support of a particular department to make a formal complaint.

Box 27.1 | **What do complainants seek?**

Apology.
Explanation.
Improvement.
Prevention of similar occurrences.
Compensation.
Punishment:
    discipline
    dismissal
    striking off.
Criminal proceedings.

Box 27.2 | **Why do people *not* complain?**

1 No reason to complain.
2 No perceived reason to complain.
3 There is a perceived reason *but*:
  ✦ Positive reasons:
    (i) sympathy with staff
    (ii) immediate apology/explanation offered
    (iii) promise of rectification/improvement
    (iv) immediate interview with consultant/senior manager.
  ✦ Negative reasons:
    (i) apathy/indifference
    (ii) ignorance of how to complain
    (iii) acceptance that errors/inefficiency are inevitable
    (iv) useless to complain – no point
    (v) fear of retribution.

A typical letter of complaint will be considered to illustrate how it should be handled and the role of the nurse.

Handling complaints

Practical Dilemma 27.1 Dear Sir

Dear Sir
I was furious at the way my daughter was treated when we went to the diabetic clinic the other day. We waited two hours to be seen and then we saw a foreign doctor who could barely speak English and who changed her drugs. Since then she has had a diabetic coma and the GP has said that the dose should never have been changed. I think that that doctor should be prevented from practising again.
   Yours sincerely
   Valerie Machin

This type of complaint is typical since, like many, it covers several different complaints, some of which relate to clinical matters and others to non-clinical matters and often a lack of communication underlies the problem. This complaint is not directly concerned with nursing matters, but the nurses in the clinic may well be asked to provide a statement as to what took place in the clinic and whether the parents complained at the time and what was done.

The complaint raises the following issues:

+ waiting time in an outpatient department clinic
+ communication between doctor and patient
+ clinical practice of the doctor
+ patient's current clinical condition.

The normal procedure would be for a letter of this kind to be referred to the hospital complaints manager acting on behalf of the chief executive. Many complainants are not always aware of the procedure and the letter could be sent to anyone. Staff should be aware of a procedure that ensures the letter is received by the complaints manager, who can follow it up to ensure that the correct procedure is followed and an acknowledgement, and later a report, are sent to the complainant by the chief executive.

The designated complaints manager would be responsible for ensuring that every point raised by the complainant is investigated and reported on satisfactorily. The chief executive officer would be expected to sign letters to a complainant personally (see below):

1 The first task would be to refer the last two points listed above urgently to the consultant in charge of the patient to assess: it may be necessary for the consultant to discuss her present condition urgently with the GP to ensure that she is now on the appropriate medication.

2 Once her present clinical condition is satisfactory, the complaints relating to clinical matters would be investigated according to the appropriate procedure, which is considered below.

3 An investigation into the waiting times would be initiated by asking the director of nursing services for a report and also asking for a report from the medical records officer or any administrative officer in charge of that department. There should be a system in place

for recording the times of the patients' arrival and departure and a system for pinpointing unreasonable delays. Some clinics do not operate an appointments system and block booking can often create unacceptable waiting times. Nursing staff will be required to provide information as to the usual way in which the diabetic clinic functioned, whether this could be improved and whether there were any extenuating circumstances on that occasion.

4 The consultant and director of nursing services would also be asked to report on the level of communication of the doctor in question, and whether his English was at an acceptable level. It may be that that aspect of the complaint could be due to some form of racial prejudice, but it should never be assumed that the complaint is without foundation. A full inquiry must always be held.

The usual practice would be for the director of nursing services or his assistant to arrange for any individual nurse who was present at the time of the clinic visit to make a statement on what occurred. It is essential that the nurse receives guidance in preparing such a report and also checks with all the available documentation on the ward or department. (Guidance is given in Chapter 9 on preparing statements.) The nurse should never submit the statement unless she is 100 per cent satisfied with the contents and that she has, where possible, checked its accuracy. The report that is sent to the complainant will be based on what the nurse has said and if there are any inaccuracies in this which are not spotted by other hospital personnel, then the nurse could well be questioned in an investigation by the Healthcare Commission and, possibly, even the Health Service Commissioner and criticism could be made of her (see below).

When the complaints manager has received all the relevant reports, including at this stage the report by the consultant on the clinical complaints, a response will be sent to the complainant. This might be just a letter or it might be an invitation to attend a meeting or both. It is vital that every single point raised by the complainant is answered fully and honestly. This might at this stage mean apologising for some shortcoming that has been revealed in the service.

In serious cases, the NHS trust might decide to set up an inquiry into the complaint. Such inquiries will come under the recommendations set out by the DH in 2001, 'Building a Safer NHS for Patients', and the new statutory complaints regulations (see below).

Hospital Complaints Procedure Act 1985 and the Wilson Report

Under the Hospital Complaints Act 1985 each health authority was required to establish a complaints procedure. Guidance required authorities to establish a procedure in relation to community health services as well. Following a review chaired by Professor Alan Wilson into the handling of hospital complaints, a consultation document was published.[1] The Department of Health accepted the principal recommendations of the Wilson Report and published guidance and directions for its implementation by NHS trusts and health service authorities.[2]

The Wilson Report found the system for dealing with complaints relating to health services to be confusing, bureaucratic, slow and inefficient. The Report reviewed the current situation and set objectives for any effective complaints system. The principles it saw for any effective complaints system are set out in Box 27.3.

The Report recommended that these principles should be incorporated into an NHS complaints system. On 1 April 1996 a new complaints procedure came into effect that implemented the majority of recommendations contained in the Wilson Report.

> ### Box 27.3 Key elements in a complaints procedure
>
> 1 Responsiveness
> 2 Quality enhancement
> 3 Cost-effectiveness
> 4 Accessibility
> 5 Impartiality
> 6 Simplicity
> 7 Speed
> 8 Confidentiality
> 9 Accountability

Complaints within the family health services

Complaints about family health services were brought within the common complaints system in 1996. Disciplinary procedures are kept separate from the complaints system.

New complaints procedure 2004

Research into the complaints system

The Department of Health commissioned an investigation into the effectiveness of the complaints procedure established following the Wilson Report. In its publication, 'NHS Complaints Reform: making things right',[3] the Department of Health noted that criticisms of the existing complaints procedure were that:

+ It is unclear how, and difficult, to pursue complaints and concerns.
+ There is often delay in responding when concerns arise.
+ Too often there is a negative attitude to concerns expressed.
+ Complaints seem not to get a fair hearing.
+ Patients do not get the support they need when they want to complain.
+ The independent review stage does not have the credibility it needs.
+ The process does not provide the redress the patients want.
+ There does not seem to be any systematic processes for using feedback from complaints to drive improvements in services.

The aims of the reforms to the complaints procedure were to establish clear national standards and accountabilities, devolution to clinicians and managers backed up by independent scrutiny, flexibility and ensuring that patients can choose how they wish to pursue their concerns and have the support they need to help them do so.

The Department of Health recommended that there be:

+ Increasing support and information for people who make complaints through local patient advice and liaison services and independent complaints and advice services (see below).
+ Patient feedback and customer care and training for NHS staff, including board members, to improve the way people are dealt with to help resolve complaints quickly.

✦ Subject to legislation, responsibility for independent complaints review placed with the Commission for Healthcare Audit and Inspection (CHAI) (The Healthcare Commission).

New complaints procedure

Under the Department of Health's new complaints procedure there are still three stages: local resolution, independent review, Health Service Commissioner (ombudsman), but there are significant changes to each stage and the support provided to patients.

Local resolution

The vast majority of complaints should be resolved locally and to assist in this process, the patient advice and liaison services (PALS) (see below) will provide assistance to the complainant. In addition, the Department of Health produced a good practice toolkit for local resolution that draws on existing good practice and provides the basis for consistent training and development.[4] A board member should be identified as the person taking overall responsibility for the investigation of and learning from adverse events, complaints and negligence claims.

Independent review

To meet the criticism that there was a lack of independence in determining whether there should be an independent review, the Department of Health decided that the responsibility for the independent review stage should be placed with the Commission for Healthcare Audit and Inspection (CHAI), known as the Healthcare Commission. Under the Health and Social Care (Community Health and Standards) Act, this new body was established in 2004. A Commission for Social Care Inspection (CSCI) was established and this is responsible for the independent stage of complaints about social services and registered homes. CHAI and CSCI are expected to work together on any complaint that crosses health and social services boundaries. Any complainant dissatisfied with the local resolution stage can ask CHAI or CSCI to review the case. CHAI has the options of making recommendations for further action by the NHS organisations complained about, investigating cases in detail and referring particularly complex cases to the ombudsman.

CHAI and CSCI have the following responsibilities:

✦ to strengthen the accountability of those responsible for health and social services
✦ to demonstrate to the public how the additional money being invested in these services is being spent and enable them to judge how performance is improving as a result
✦ to achieve greater rationalisation of inspection arrangements for health and social care.

The Department of Health's plans were set out in a Statement of Purpose.[5] The Department of Health was of the view that giving CHAI and CSCI responsibility for the independent review stage of complaints will provide the necessary independence for the independent stage of complaints procedure, speedier resolution of complaints by allowing certain cases to be referred to the ombudsman more quickly than is possible at present and provide a direct link into quality improvement processes. The Health and Social Care (Community Health and Standards) Act 2003 Part 2 Chapter 9 gives power to the Secretary of State to make regulations on the handling of complaints about healthcare (Section 113), social services (Section 114) and Section 115 sets out topics that could be covered by regulations.

If a complaint is referred to CHAI the following options are available:

+ recommendations from CHAI for further action by the NHS organisation
+ investigation in detail by CHAI
+ referral of case to the ombudsman, where the case is particularly complex.

The Health Service Commissioner (HSC)

The final option for unresolved complaints is recourse to the ombudsman whose jurisdiction was extended in 1996 to cover complaints relating to the exercise of clinical judgement and those about family practitioners. Disciplinary matters were not included in its jurisdiction (see below). If a complainant is not satisfied with the response of the authority to a complaint and the response of the Healthcare Commission, he can apply to the ombudsman for further investigation: the Health Service Commissioner in respect of complaints about the NHS and the Local Authority Commissioner in respect of complaints about local authority services. The HSC has a duty to prepare a report that is submitted to Parliament, under Section 14(4) of the Health Service Commissioners Act 1993. The Select Committee of the House of Commons has the power to investigate further any complaint reported by the HSC, if necessary summoning witnesses to London for questioning. The HSC is completely independent of the NHS and the government and has the jurisdiction to investigate complaints against any part of the NHS, as shown in Box 27.4. It was held in a case heard in 2006 that the Health Service Commissioner had exceeded her statutory powers by going outside the remit of the complaint. The complaint concerned the discontinuation by a trust of a specialist vitamin unit which a father had found benefited his son who had epilepsy and learning and communication difficulties. The Court found that the HSC had not confined herself to the investigation of the complaint but had expanded the ambit of the investigation beyond the scope of the original complaint and had therefore exceeded her statutory powers.[6]

Box 27.4   Jurisdiction of the Health Service Commissioner

Health Service Commissioner's jurisdiction covers:

1 a failure in service
2 a failure to purchase or provide a service one is entitled to receive or
3 maladministration (administrative affairs).

The following are excluded from his investigation:

1 actions where there is already an existing remedy in law (but there is a discretion to hear such matters if the Commissioner is satisfied that it is not reasonable to expect the complainant to resort to this)
2 personnel matters or contractual matters to do with the NHS
3 out-of-time complaints - although there is discretion to extend this
4 complaints that have not yet been referred to the organisation for dealing through the complaints procedure.

The House of Commons Select Committee

A final possibility in the complaints process (and this can be very effective) is for an inquiry to be set up by the Select Committee of the House of Commons, to whom the Health Service Commissioner reports. This committee has the power to investigate a matter further by summoning witnesses to appear before it and if in the report of the HSC it is clear that an authority has ignored its recommendations, the Committee can ask the authority to explain itself – an experience that few witnesses who have appeared before it will ever forget. There is no secrecy. All these cases are fully reported and the proceedings of the Select Committee are themselves published and may also be televised.

There is no doubt that the fact that eventually an authority might have to explain how it dealt with any complaint is an important factor in ensuring that the complaint is properly, speedily and effectively dealt with.

Complaints regulations 2004 and 2006

On 30 July 2004 regulations[7] on a new complaints system came into force. The regulations cover:

+ nature and scope of arrangements for the handling and consideration of complaints
+ handling and consideration of complaints by NHS bodies
+ handling and consideration of complaints by the Healthcare Commission
+ publicity, monitoring and annual reports.

The regulations require each NHS body, CHAI and each primary care trust to make arrangements for the handling of complaints in accordance with the regulations:

> *The arrangements must be accessible and such as to ensure that the complaints are dealt with speedily and efficiently, and that complainants are treated courteously and sympathetically and as far as possible involved in decisions about how their complaints are handled and considered.*

The arrangements must be in writing with a copy given free of charge to any person who requests a copy.

Amendments were made to the regulations in 2006[8] to facilitate the transfer of complaints which relate to social services (see below), extending the persons who can be appointed as complaints managers, changing the time limit for response to a complaint and broadening the remit of the Healthcare Commission in relation to complaints about NHS foundation trusts.

A primary care provider (and this includes pharmacists, opthalmic opticians, dentists, GPs and primary care trusts) must ensure that a complaints procedure is in place. A complex complaint is one that relates to several different NHS bodies or local authority or primary care providers or is already subject to a concurrent investigation. If the NHS trust or primary care trust arranges for the provision of services through an independent provider, they are required to ensure that the independent provider has arrangements in place for the handling of complaints in accordance with the regulations.

Excluded from the complaints regulations are:

+ Complaints made by an NHS body that relate to the exercise of its functions by another NHS body.
+ Complaints by a primary care provider that relate either to the exercise of its functions by an NHS body or to the contract or arrangements under which it provides primary care services.
+ Complaints made by an employee of an NHS body or primary care provider about any matter relating to his contract of employment.
+ Complaints made by an independent provider about any matter relating to arrangements made by an NHS body with that independent provider.

+ Complaints which relates to the provision of primary medical services in accordance with arrangements made by a PCT with a strategic health authority under Section 28C of the NHS Act 1977 or under a transitional agreement.

+ Complaints that are being or have been investigated by the Health Service Commissioner.

+ Complaints arising out of an NHS body's alleged failure to comply with a data subject request under the Data Protection Act 1998 or a request for information under the Freedom of Information Act 2000.

+ A complaint about which the complainant has stated in writing that he intends to take legal proceedings.

+ A complaint about which an NHS body is taking or is proposing to take disciplinary proceedings in relation to the substance of the complaint against a person who is the subject of the complaint.

+ A complaint the subject matter of which has already been investigated under these regulations.

+ A complaint relating to a scheme under the Superannuation Act 1972.

The regulations require a complaints manager to be appointed by each NHS body. This may include a person who is not an employee of the NHS body and a person who is appointed as a complaints manager for more than one NHS body.

A complaint can be made by a patient, or any person who is affected by or likely to be affected by the action, omission or decision of the NHS body which is the subject of the complaint. A complaint may also be made by the representative of a person who has died, is a child or is unable by reason of physical or mental incapacity to make the complaint himself or has asked the representative to act on his behalf.

Time limits for making a complaint are six months of the date on which the matter which is the subject of the complaint occurred or first came to the notice of the complainant, but the complaints manager can investigate complaints outside these time limits if he is of the opinion that, having regard to all the circumstances, the complainant had good reasons for not making the complaint within that period and it is still possible to investigate the complaint effectively and efficiently.

Procedure

+ The complaints manager must send to the complainant a written acknowledgement of the complaint within two working days of the date on which the complaint was made, together with details of the right to assistance from independent advocacy services.

+ Where the complaint was made orally, the acknowledgement must be accompanied by the written record with an invitation to the complainant to sign and return it.

+ The complaints manager must send a copy of the complaint and his acknowledgement to any person identified as the subject of the complaint

Investigation

The complaints manager must investigate the complaint to the extent necessary and in the manner which appears to him most appropriate to resolve it speedily and efficiently. Where the manager thinks it would be appropriate to do so he can, with the agreement of the complainant, make arrangements for conciliation, mediation or other assistance for the purpose of resolving the complaint. The NHS body must ensure that appropriate conciliation or mediation services are available. He must take such steps as are reasonably practicable to keep the complainant informed about the progress of his investigation.

Response

The complaints manager must prepare a written response to the complaint which:

+ summarises the nature and substance of the complaint
+ describes the investigation under regulation 12 and
+ summarises its conclusions.

The letter must be signed by the chief executive of the NHS body except in cases where for good reason the chief executive is not himself able to sign it, in which case it may be signed by a person acting on his behalf.

The letter must be sent to the complainant within 25 (amended from 20 by the 2006 regulations) working days beginning with the date on which the complaint was made unless the complainant agrees to a longer period in which case the response may be sent within that longer period.

+ The letter must notify the complainant of his right to refer the complaint to the Healthcare Commission.
+ Copies of the response must be sent to any person who was the subject of the complaint and any other person to whom the complaint has been sent under the regulations.

Handling and considerations of complaints by CHAI (Healthcare Commission)

Part 111 of the regulations enable a complainant:

+ who is not satisfied with the results of an investigation (except where the complaint relates to an NHS bursary scheme)
+ where the investigation has not been completed within six months of the date on which the complaint was made, or
+ where the complaints manager has decided not to investigate because it was out of time, to request a consideration of the complaint by the Healthcare Commission within six months of the response being made.

The Healthcare Commission is then required to assess the nature and substance of the complaint and decide how it should be handled having regard to the views of the complainant, the views of the body complained about, the views of the independent regulator (where the complaint relates to a foundation trust), any investigation of the complaint and action taken as a result and any other relevant circumstances. The Healthcare Commission must notify the complainant as to whether it has decided to:

+ take no further action
+ make recommendation to the body which is the subject of the complaint as to what action might be taken to resolve it
+ investigate the complaint further, whether by establishing a panel to consider it or otherwise
+ consider the subject matter of the complaint as part of or in conjunction with any other investigation or review

+ refer the complaint to a health regulatory body

+ refer the complaint to the Health Service Commissioner.

Where the Healthcare Commission proposes to investigate the complaint it must, within ten working days of the date on which it sent the notification, send the complainant and any other person to whom the notice was sent its proposed terms of reference for its investigation.

The regulations cover the investigation by the Healthcare Commission, including the use of an independent panel to hear and consider complaints and its powers to request the production of such information and documents as it considers necessary to enable a complaint to be considered properly. Members and employees of an NHS body and any person who is or was a healthcare professional or employee of a health care professional are excluded from being a member of a panel. Detailed procedural rules are laid down for the panels. The report of the Healthcare Commission's investigation must include the specified information and be completed as soon as reasonably practicable. The report must be sent to the complainant with a letter explaining to him his right to take his complaint to the HSC; and also to the NHS body that was the subject of the complaint (and, in the case of a complaint involving a primary care provider, to the PCT), to any relevant strategic health authority and to the independent regulator for complaints about an NHS foundation trust, where he so requests. The independent regulator may make an individual request for a report or make a standing request that identifies a type of complaint for which he wishes to receive a report.

Part IV of the regulations requires each NHS body and the Healthcare Commission to ensure that there is effective publicity for its complaints arrangements. For monitoring purposes, each NHS body must prepare a quarterly report specifying the number of complaints received, the subject matter of the complaints, summarise how they were handled including the outcome and identify any complaints where the recommendations of the Healthcare Commission were not acted upon, giving the reasons. An annual report must be prepared on the handling and consideration of complaints and be sent to specified bodies including the Healthcare Commission, the strategic health authority and PCT, as appropriate.

Criticisms by the Healthcare Commission

In October 2007 the Healthcare Commission published its first audit on how the NHS trusts handled complaints, which is available on its website.[9] It found considerable variation in how complaints were handled across the country. Its report highlighted the issues shown in Box 27.5. The Healthcare Commission announced that it was working on a toolkit for complaints managers which should be available in 2008.

Box 27.5 | **Issues raised by Healthcare Commission on complaints handling**

+ More needs to be done to make the complaints systems open and accessible, especially for those with learning disabilities and from ethnic communities.

+ People who complain should be confident that their care will not suffer.

+ Trusts should use complaints data to inform decision making.

+ Whilst there is no one-size-fits-all approach to investigating complaints, a common approach would improve risk management of complaints and manage the expectations of complainants.

+ There are no nationally available standard tools and resources such as case studies, checklists and training aids for staff.

NHS and social services complaints: a single comprehensive procedure

Regulations relating to social services complaints[10] came into force on 1 September 2006. They impose time limits on making complaints, new timescales for handling stages of the process and provide greater independence at the final review panel stage. They can be downloaded from the Office of Public Sector Information.[11] The NHS complaints regulations have been amended[12] following the White Paper commitment to develop a single comprehensive complaints procedure across health and social care by 2009. The amendments are intended to make the system more responsive and give better links with the arrangements for responding to social care complaints

Commission for Patient and Public Involvement in Health (CPPIH)

In accordance with the strategy set out in the NHS Plan,[13] the Commission for Patient and Public Involvement in Health (CPPIH) was established under Section 20 of the NHS Reform and Health Care Professions Act 2002 in January 2003. Its functions, set out in Section 20(2) of the 2002 Act, included advising the Secretary of State about arrangements for public involvement in and consultation about matters relating to the health service in England and the provision of independent advocacy services. It is to be abolished in 2008 when the Local Government and Public Involvement in Health Act 2007 is enacted (see below).

Independent Complaints Advocacy Service (ICAS)

Under Section 12 of the Health and Social Care Act 2001, the Secretary of State has a responsibility to provide independent advocacy services to assist patients in making complaints against the NHS. The independent complaints advocacy service[14] was available nationally from September 2003. A consultation paper, 'Involving Patients and the Public in Healthcare',[15] was issued by the Department of Health in September 2001 for consultation on proposals for greater public representation to replace the community health councils (CHCs).

ICAS focus on helping individuals to pursue complaints about NHS services. They aim to ensure complainants have access to the support they need to articulate their concerns and navigate the complaints system, maximising the chances of their complaint being resolved more quickly and effectively. ICAS work alongside the trust-based patients' forums and patient advocacy and liaison services. Information about ICAS and the current range of pilot services is available on the Department of Health website.[16] It was announced in January 2006 that following a rigorous exercise, the DH awarded contracts to three organisations to deliver a new and improved Independent Complaints Advocacy Service from 1 April 2006.

These organisations replace CHCs, which were abolished in England in 2003. (But note that CHCs were retained in Wales.)

Patient Advice and Liaison Services (PALS)

A significant proposal in the NHS Plan[17] (see Chapter 17) was the patient advice and liaison services (PALS). The Plan envisaged that by 2002 PALS will be established in every major hospital, with an annual national budget of around £10 million. Their core functions are:

+ To provide on-the-spot help and speed resolution of problems

+ To act as a gateway to independent advice and advocacy services

+ To provide accurate information about the trust's services and other related services

+ As a key source of feedback to the trust, to act as a catalyst for change and improvement

+ To support staff in the development of a responsive, listening culture

Special provision is made in respect of patient and advocacy services for the purposes of the Mental Health Act 1983 and Section 134, which concerns the withholding of correspondence. Under regulations of 2003 correspondence with a patient advice and liaison service is exempt from the provisions of Section 134.[18]

All NHS trusts were required to establish a PALS service by April 2002. A national evaluation of PALS was conducted from January 2005 to January 2007 and a report on the key messages published in October 2006 by the Department of Health and available on its website. Patients can contact their local PALS by phoning the local hospital, clinic, GP surgery or health centre, phoning NHS Direct on 0845 46 47 or searching the office directory on the PALS online webservice which has a direct link to the DH website.

Patients' forums

Under Section 15 of the NHS Reform and Health Care Professions Act, the Secretary of State has a duty to set up in every trust and primary care trust a body to be known as a patients' forum. The members of each patients' forum are appointed by the Commission for Patient and Public Involvement in Health. The statutory functions[19] laid down for them are:

+ monitor and review the range and operation of services provided by or under arrangements made by the trust for which it is established

+ obtain the views of patients and their carers about those matters and report on those views to the trust

+ provide advice and make reports and recommendations about matters relating to the range and operation of those services to the trust

+ make available to patients and their carers advice and information about those services

+ in prescribed circumstances, perform any prescribed function of the trust with respect to the provision of a service affording assistance to patients and their families and carers

+ carry out such other functions as may be prescribed.

The forums are required to cooperate when appropriate. They also have the responsibility for providing independent advocacy services to persons in the trust's area or who have been provided with services by the trust; for giving advice to patients and carers about the making of complaints and representing the views of members of the public about matters affecting their health (Section 16 NHS Reform and Health Care Professions Act 2002).

They are also expected to promote the involvement of members of the public in the area of the trust in consultations about decisions and the formulation of policies that would affect the health of those members of the public.

Regulations give rights to patients' forums to inspect any premises where NHS patients go to receive healthcare. Each patient forum must prepare an annual report and this must include details of the arrangements maintained by the forum in that year for obtaining the views of patients (Section 18 of 2002 Act). Regulations have been enacted on the functions, membership and procedures for patients' forums.[20]

There are now over 400 patient and public involvement forums, one for each NHS trust in England supported by the Commission for Patient and Public Involvement in Health (CPPIH).

Reforms to patient forums

The House of Commons Select Health Committee published a report on Patient and Public Involvement in the NHS in April 2007.[21] As a consequence of its recommendations significant changes were proposed to the existing arrangements for the involvement of the public in healthcare and incorporated in the Local Government and Public Involvement in Health Act 2007. Local involvement networks (LINKS) replace patients' forums and the Commission for Patient and Public Involvement in Health will be abolished. The proposed changes come into force in 2008. LINKS are aimed at genuine involvement of a greater number of people than is currently available, ensuring local communities have a stronger voice in commissioning health and social care and enabling them to influence key decisions about the services they both use and pay for. Section 11 of the Health and Social Care Act 2001 (now Section 242 of the National Health Service Act 2006) places a duty on NHS trusts, primary care trusts and strategic health authorities to make arrangements to involve and consult patients and the public in service planning and operation and in the development of proposals for changes. An action seeking judicial review of a decision to close twin inpatient wards without consultation in breach of Section 11 succeeded; the trust's defence of it being a decision taken in an emergency situation was not accepted.[22]

Complaints and litigation

Under the complaints procedure which was based on the Wilson Report, if the complainant indicated that he or she wished to pursue a legal remedy, the complaints procedure would be halted. The proposals for a new compensation scheme for clinical negligence claims, 'Making Amends' (discussed in Chapter 6), recommended that complaints handling and early investigation of a potential legal action be combined. This recommendation was not included in the NHS redress scheme (see Chapter 6) and the NHS complaints regulations exclude from its procedure a complaint where the complainant has stated in writing that he intends to take legal proceedings.

The nurse and complaints

It is in the interests of all health professionals to ensure that any complaints by patients or relatives relating to the provision of health services are resolved as speedily as possible informally, without requiring the complainant to make use of the formal procedure. Nurses should have the confidence to realise that complaints can be a useful way of monitoring and improving the services to patients, that it takes courage to make a complaint, especially where the patient suffers from a chronic condition, and that improvements can be made if clients are prepared to discuss with the health professionals ways in which the services could be enhanced.

Other quality assurance methods

Individuals who have complaints against the services provided in the NHS do not have any contractual right to bring an action before the court for breach of contract. If harm has been suffered as a result of a failure or omission, they may have a successful claim in the law of negligence (see Chapter 3) or, if a service has not been provided, they may be able to bring a case of breach of statutory duty for failure to provide that service (see Chapter 5). Otherwise, they must rely on the complaints procedure. They could apply for judicial review to the High Court if the principles of natural justice have not been followed, but they would be expected to exhaust appeals procedures within the NHS complaints system first. There are, however, many other mechanisms to ensure the maintenance of high standards of health-care that cannot be directly utilised by the patient. The White Paper on the NHS put forward a strategy for improving quality assurance and its mechanisms which was implemented in the Health Act 1999. These mechanisms include a National Institute for Health and Clinical Excellence (NICE), a Healthcare Commission and a framework for national standards. The establishment of clinical governance whereby chief executives of trusts are held accountable for the clinical performance of their organisations provides more evidence to the patient about the standards of care locally. These innovations are discussed in Chapter 5.

Mental Health Act Commission

Under the 1983 Mental Health Act, there is a statutory duty placed on the Mental Health Act Commission to investigate complaints by detained patients. The jurisdiction could be extended to cover informal patients. The Mental Health Act Commission can also investigate complaints of a clinical nature and, in fact, a high proportion of the complaints that it has investigated are concerned with clinical matters such as medication, medical and nursing care. The MHAC has no power to subpoena witnesses or to take evidence on oath and is itself one of the bodies whose administrative function can be investigated by the HSC.[23] From the biennial reports of the MHAC, it is clear that the number and variety of the complaints that it is investigating are considerable. The Commission pointed out that it has complete discretion over how the complaints are to be investigated – methods range from a word to a ward sister to a full-scale investigation by commissioners. It is also apparent that, while its terms of reference are so far only to cover the detained patient, many of its recommendations are wider and affect the care of the informal patient. For example, its procedure on the consent to treatment of the mentally disordered outside the provisions of Part 4 of the 1983 Act has major implications for the care of the informal patient. In addition, the Code of Practice on the Mental Health Act provides advice about procedures and precautions to take if informal patients are detained in locked wards. The MHAC is a signatory to the Concordat, which is a code of objectives and practices agreed by bodies auditing, inspecting and regulating healthcare in England; 10 objectives were agreed in the Concordat. The Healthcare Commission has a statutory role to coordinate reviews of health and healthcare in the NHS in England. Further information can be obtained on the MHAC website[24] (see also Chapter 20).

Secretary of State inquiries

Statutory powers are given in the NHS legislation for the Secretary of State to set up an inquiry into any case 'where he deems it advisable to do so in connection with any matter arising under this Act'.[25] The powers of such an inquiry are extensive and include the power to summon witnesses and order the production of documents and the taking of evidence on oath. Any person who refuses to give evidence or attend or destroys documents is guilty of a criminal offence.

A public inquiry of this nature is kept for the most serious of complaints with very serious implications.

The Secretary of State can also make an intervention order in relation to an NHS body other than NHS foundation trusts where he considers that the NHS body is not performing one or more of its functions adequately or at all or that there are significant failings in the way the body is being run, and he is satisfied that it is appropriate for him to intervene.[26] The effect of an intervention order is that he can remove all or any members from the board of the NHS body and appoint replacements or suspend any members.[27]

The Secretary of State also has statutory powers known as default powers (re-enacted in Section 68 of the NHS Act 2006), where, if he is satisfied after such inquiry as he thinks fit, that a health authority has failed to carry out its statutory functions or is in breach of the regulations, then he can make an order declaring it to be in default. The effect of this is that the members of the authority in question must vacate their office and the Secretary of State can appoint new persons to undertake the functions. In addition, he has emergency powers to give appropriate directions to ensure that the functions are properly performed. This control enables the Secretary of State to force the health authorities to comply with policies (e.g. keeping within their budgets) set by the government or the DH, which they might otherwise be unwilling to do. The DH also has the power to give directions to NHS trusts. The setting up of inquiries and the role of the Healthcare Commission are considered in a DH document, 'Building a Safer NHS for Patients', which was published in 2001.[28] In October 2007 the government announced that it was to establish a new super-regulator which would have the power to close hospitals within 24 hours. The new regulator will cover all NHS and private hospitals and residential care homes and will combine the existing Healthcare Commission, the Mental Health Act Commission and the Commission for Social Care Inspection.

Conclusions

A new complaints procedure was implemented in 2004 and has been modified to ensure a single comprehensive complaints procedure across health and social care. In addition, the NHS redress scheme, which is discussed in Chapter 6, is coming into force. The extent to which this scheme reduces civil litigation remains to be seen, as does its effect on the handling of complaints (see Chapter 6). Evidence from the Healthcare Commission suggests that the use of independent advocacy services to ensure that patients' complaints are handled speedily and efficiently has not yet improved the handing of complaints and more changes can be anticipated following the establishment of a new super-regulator in April 2009. In November 2003 a one-stop website to access NHS services was launched.[29] The website can be used to access all NHS organisations and will provide information about walk-in clinics, waiting times and local health services. At the time of writing local involvement networks are about to be set up, replacing patients' forums and the Commission for Patient and Public Involvement in Health. It is unclear at present the extent to which these LINKS will facilitate patient and public involvement in healthcare decision making. Further developments in patient and public involvement may follow the review of healthcare services currently being undertaken by Lord Darzi and David Nicholson, 'Our NHS, Our Future', and their interviews with staff, patients and the public.[30]

Reflection questions

1 What do you consider to be the most appropriate system for recording informal complaints?

2 Complaints are one means of obtaining feedback from patients about their stay. Consider other means of a more positive nature to obtain information relating to patient satisfaction and consider the possibility of implementing them.

3 You are a staff nurse on a medical ward. A patient complains to you that he thinks that he is suffering from the side effects of medication. How would you deal with this complaint?

Further exercises

1 Obtain a copy of the complaints procedure of your NHS trust or employer and familiarise yourself with it.

2 Ask the complaints manager in your organisation if you may see the complaints book and, if you can, see how an individual complaint has been followed up. (Remember the duty of confidentiality.)

3 Access the report of the Healthcare Commission on its audit on complaints handling by NHS trusts and consider the extent to which its recommendations could apply in your organisation.

References

1 Being Heard, The Report of a Review Committee chaired by Professor Wilson on NHS complaints procedures, DH, London, 1994

2 NHS Executive, Guidance on the Implementation of the NHS Complaints Procedure, London, DH, March 1996; EL(96)19 Directions to NHS Trusts, Health Authorities and Special Health Authorities for Special Hospitals on Hospital Complaints Procedures; Directions to Health Authorities on Dealing with Complaints about Family Health Services Practitioners; Miscellaneous Directions to Health Authorities for Dealing with Complaints, DH, London, March 1996

3 Department of Health, NHS Complaints Reform: making things right, DH, London, 2003

4 Department of Health, Handling complaints in the NHS – good practice toolkit for local resolution, Gateway reference 2944, 15 April 2005

5 Department of Health, The Commission for Healthcare Audit and Inspection and the Commission for Social Care Inspection – statement of purpose, DH, London, 2003; www.dh.gov.uk/statementofpurpose

6 *R (on the application of Cavanagh, Bhatt and Redmond)* v. *Health Service Commissioner* [2005] EWCA Civ 1578; [2006] 3 All ER 543

7 The National Health Service (Complaints) Regulations 2004, SI 2004 No. 1768

8 The National Health Service (Complaints) Amendment Regulations 2006, SI 2006 No. 2084

9 www.healthcarecommission.org.uk/

10 The Local Authority Social Services Complaints (England) Regulations 2006, SI 2006 No. 1681

11 www.opsi.gov.uk

12 The National Health Service (Complaints) Amendment Regulations 2006, SI 2006 No. 2084

[13] Department of Health, The NHS Plan, Cm 4818-1, DH, London, 1 July 2000 (Chapter 10)

[14] Information on ICAS is available from the DH website: www.dh.gov.uk/complaints/

[15] Department of Health, Involving Patients and the Public in Healthcare, DH, London, September 2001

[16] www.dh.gov.uk/complaints/advocacyservice.htm

[17] Department of Health, The NHS Plan: a plan for investment, a plan for reform, Cm 4818-1, DH, London, 2000; www.nhs.uk/nhsplan/contentspdf.htm

[18] Mental Health (Correspondence of Patients, Patient Advocacy and Liaison Services) Regulations 2003, SI 2003 No. 2042

[19] Section 15(3) NHS Reform and Health Care Professions Act 2002

[20] Patients' Forums (Functions) Regulations 2003, SI 2003 No. 2124; Patients' Forums (Membership and Procedure) Regulations 2003, SI 2003 No. 2123

[21] House of Commons Health Committee, Patient and Public Involvement in the NHS: Third Report of Session 2006-7, HC 278-1, 20 April 2007

[22] *R (On the application of Morris)* v. *Trafford Healthcare NHS Trust* [2006] EWHC 2334

[23] See Health Service Commissioners' Annual Report 1992/93

[24] www.mhac.org.uk/

[25] Section 84 National Health Service Act 1977

[26] Section 66 National Health Service Act 2006 (as re-enacted)

[27] Section 67 National Health Service Act 2006 (as re-enacted)

[28] Department of Health, Building a Safer NHS for Patients, DH, London, 2001

[29] www.nhs.uk

[30] Department of Health, Our NHS, Our Future website: www.ournhs.nhs.uk/

Chapter 28
Legal aspects of medicines

Introduction

Legislation has been passed to give nurses the power to prescribe in the community and further legislation implementing the recommendations of the Final Crown Report was contained in Section 63 of the Health and Social Care Act 2001, which is discussed below.

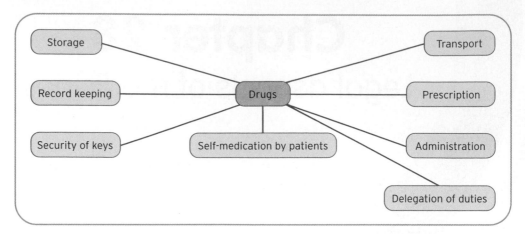

Figure 28.1 Areas that concern the nurse

The main legislation controlling the supply, storage and administration of medicines is the Medicines Act 1968 and the Misuse of Drugs Act 1971 and many subsequent statutory instruments. Of particular importance are the Misuse of Drugs Regulations 2001.[1] The Medicines Act 1968 set up a comprehensive system of medicine controls (as can be seen on pages 645-6). The Medicines Control Agency was absorbed into the Medicines and Healthcare products Regulatory Agency (MHRA) in April 2003 and information on the regulation of medicines can be accessed via the MHRA website[2] (see below). The main provisions of the Misuse of Drugs Act 1971 are seen on page 645 and the 2001 Regulations on pages 647-8. The regulations relating to prescribing prescription-only medicines were consolidated in the Prescription-Only Medicines (Human Use) Order 1997,[3] but there have been subsequent amendments.

Figure 28.1 illustrates the main areas of control of drugs that are the concern of the nurse. The UKCC published guidelines for the administration of medicines, which have been reissued by the NMC and updated in 2004 to bring them in line with the legislative changes to the NMC.[4] While this guidance has no legal force in itself, it establishes principles for safe practice in the management and administration of medicines by registered nurses, midwives and health visitors. The 2004 booklet replaces the standards for administration of medicines that was published in 1992. The new guidelines also cover prescribing by nurses and the use of patient group directions (see below). Local policies may be drawn up that differ from the main guidelines and the advisory paper allows for this, but it sets out principles that should be taken into account in the setting up of these local policies. Any local policy must, of course, comply with the statutory framework.

Shipman Report

In May 2007 the Department of Health and the Royal Pharmaceutical Society of Great Britain published a paper on the safer management of controlled drugs.[5] As a consequence of the Fourth Shipman Inquiry, the Health Act 2006 Sections 17 to 25 introduced new laws in relation to the supervision of management and use of controlled drugs and regulations strengthened the governance and monitoring arrangements for controlled drugs.[6] An Accountable Officer must now be appointed within each trust to have responsibility for the safe use and management of controlled drugs. The guidance builds on the safe and secure handling of medicines (known as the revised Duthie Report, March 2005). In addition, amendments to the Misuse of Drugs Regulations enable all details on prescriptions for controlled drugs, except the signature, to be computer generated and the computerisation of controlled drugs registers for drugs listed in Schedules 2 and 3. The final changes to record-keeping requirements can be obtained from the DH.[7] Powers are given to a constable or other authorised person to enter and inspect premises and stocks and records of controlled drugs.

General principles

Under the Medicines Act, drugs are divided into categories for the purposes of supply to the public. The Part III regulations cover the following:

1 *Pharmacy-only products* (P) i.e. these can be sold or supplied retail only by someone conducting a retail pharmacy business when the product must be sold from a registered pharmacy by or under the supervision of a pharmacist.

2 *General sales list* (GSL) i.e. medicinal products that may be sold other than from a retail pharmacy, as long as provisions relating to Section 53 of the Medicines Act are complied with, i.e. the place of sale must be the premises where the business is carried out; they must be capable of excluding the public; the medicines must have been made up elsewhere and the contents must not have been opened since make-up.

3 *Prescription-only list* (POM) i.e. these medicines are available only on a practitioner's prescription. Schedule 1 of the subsequent regulations lists the prescription-only products and Part II of the schedule lists the prescription-only products that are covered by the Misuse of Drugs Act (see below). Hospitals are exempt from these prescription-only provisions, as are midwives.

The Misuse of Drugs Act and the 2001 Regulations make provision for the classification of controlled drugs and their possession, supply and manufacture. This is considered below.

Statute   **Misuse of Drugs Act 1971**

1 Lists and classifies controlled drugs.

2 Creates criminal offences in relation to the manufacture, supply and possession of controlled drugs.

3 Gives Secretary of State power to make regulations and directions to prevent misuse of controlled drugs.

4 Creates advisory council on misuse of drugs.

5 Gives powers of search, arrest and forfeiture.

Statute   **Medicines Acts 1968 and 1971**

The Acts set up a comprehensive system of medicine controls covering:

1 administrative system

2 licensing system

> *Statute continued*
>
> **3** sale and supply of medicines to the public:
> - pharmacy-only products
> - general sales list
> - prescription-only list
> **4** retail pharmacies
> **5** packing and labelling of medicinal products
> **6** British pharmacopoeia.
>
> NB Exception to Part III Regulations on sale and supply of medicines to the public: Midwives – see Chapter 13.
> Hospitals: 'Prescription medicines may be sold or supplied by a hospital, provided they are in accordance with the written instructions of a doctor, although these instructions need not be contained in a formal prescription.'

Administration of drugs

Box 28.1 shows a checklist that a nurse should go through before a drug is administered to a patient. There is no team liability for negligence, as was seen in the Wilsher case (pages 62–3, Case 4.3). Each professional must ensure that she fulfils her duties according to the approved standard of practice expected of her. If something goes wrong, she is accountable in the criminal courts, the civil courts, before her employer and before the Conduct and Competence Committee of the NMC for her activities and would have to show that she followed the approved accepted practice. Prescription-only medicines can be administered without the direction of a doctor where the situation is an emergency for the purpose of saving a life. For example, a parent or teacher who needed to administer adrenalin when a child has suffered an anaphylactic shock would be covered for such actions.

Box 28.1 **Checklist for the administration of drugs**

A *The correct patient. Consent?*
 Capacity to consent:
   child
   mentally ill or lacking mental capacity.
 Pre-existing disability or contraindications.
 Warnings about side effects; drowsiness, etc.

B *Correct drug*
 Side effects.
 Timing.
 Special precautions.
 Any contraindications.
 Expiry date.

C *Correct dose*
 Type of patient.
 Physique of patient.
 Allergy frequency.

D *Correct site and method of administration*
 Injection: skin, muscular, vein, artery, site on body.

> **Box 28.1 continued**
>
> E   *Correct procedure*
>   Level of competence of nurse.
>   Skill, training.
>   Appropriate delegation.
>   Safe equipment, sound sterile procedure.
>   Correct gauge of needle, form of drug and transport.
> F   *Correct record keeping of dose, time, drug and method*

Controlled drugs

The classification of controlled drugs by the Misuse of Drugs Regulations 2001 is shown in the Statute below. Examples only are given here of the different schedules. The full list can be found in the *British National Formulary*. The nurse should be familiar with the procedure for access to the controlled drugs stock and the record keeping, the way in which any destruction of the drugs is recorded and the changes resulting from the Fourth Shipman Report.

Statute   **Misuse of Drugs Regulations 2001 SI 2001/3988**

Drugs are divided into five schedules, each specifying the requirements governing the import, export, production, supply, possession, prescribing and record keeping.

Schedule 1: e.g. cannabis, lysergide. Possession and supply prohibited except in accordance with Home Office authority.

Schedule 2: e.g. diamorphine, morphine, pethidine, glutethimide, amphetamine – subject to full controlled drug requirements relating to prescriptions, safe custody, the need to keep registers.

Schedule 3: e.g. barbiturates, diethylpropion, mazindol – subject to special prescription requirements but not safe custody requirements (except for diethylpropion) or to the need to keep registers.

Schedule 4 includes 33 benzodiazepines that are subject to minimal control. In particular, controlled drug prescription requirements do *not* apply and they are *not* subject to safe custody.

Schedule 5 preparations that, because of their strength, are exempt from most controlled drug requirements, other than retention of invoices for two years.

Makes provision for:

1   Certain exemptions from the Misuse of Drugs Act 1971 in relation to the production, importation, exportation, possession and supply of controlled drugs.

2   Prescriptions, records and furnishing of information concerning controlled drugs and for the supervision of the destruction of such drugs.

Examples of the Regulations

1   *Persons entitled* to have controlled drugs in their *possession* include under Paragraph 6(7)(f): a person engaged in conveying the drug to a person who may lawfully have that drug in his possession.

> ### Statute continued
>
> **2** *Administration of drugs* in Schedules 2, 3, 4 and 5, Paragraph 7(3): any person other than a doctor or dentist may administer to a patient, in accordance with the direction of a doctor or dentist, any drug specified in Schedules 2, 3 and 4.
>
> #### Production and supply of drugs
>
> *Paragraph 8(2)(e)*
> In the case of Schedule 2 and 5 drugs supplied to her by a person responsible for the dispensing and supply of medicines at the hospital or nursing home, the sister or acting sister for the time being in charge of a ward, theatre or other department in such a hospital or nursing home as aforesaid . . . may, when acting in her capacity as such, supply, or offer to supply any drug specified in Schedule 2 or 5 to any person who may lawfully have that drug in his possession, provided that nothing in the paragraph authorises:
>
> **(a)** . . .
>
> **(b)** a sister or acting sister for the time being in charge of a ward, theatre, or other department to supply any drug otherwise than for the administration to a patient in that ward, theatre or department in accordance with the directions of a doctor or dentist.

Medicines and the operating department practitioner (ODP)

Operating department practitioners are now a registered profession under the aegis of the Health Professions Council. Employers should check with the HPC that any prospective or actual ODP in their employment is on the register. The HPC includes in the standards for proficiency of the ODP the following key concept: 3a.1 Understand how to store, issue, prepare and administer prescribed drugs to patients and monitor the effects of drugs on patients.

They are not identified as one of the registered professions able to become independent prescribers.

Problems in the administration of medicine

Conflict with prescriber

> ### Practical Dilemma 28.1   Challenging the doctor
>
> Staff Nurse Johnson was a children's nurse with some two years' experience. One evening, a child was admitted with suspected meningitis. The house officer on call wrote the child up for antibiotics after having given an injection. Staff Nurse Johnson was surprised at the dosage and queried this with the house officer who was furious to find his treatment questioned by a nurse and confirmed that the nurse should administer that drug at the prescribed dose and at the intervals set out. Since Staff Nurse Johnson had not had many years' experience in paediatrics, she was uncertain what to do since she knew that the child was seriously ill and that a higher dose than usual might be justified in the circumstances. She also knew that it was imperative that there were no delays in administering the drug. She was in charge of the ward.

The nurse is personally accountable for her actions in administering any drug. Only in the most serious emergency where speed is of the essence could she rely on the fact that a doctor ordered her to give the drug and she did not have the opportunity to question the dosage because of the seriousness of the situation. In any case, where the nurse is not satisfied with some aspect of the drug she is instructed to administer, she must ensure the prescription is checked. She would have to do this despite considerable pressure brought by a junior doctor. The difficulties for Staff Nurse Johnson are that, at night, she may have to get someone in to check. She would inform her immediate nurse manager of her concern and would ask the registrar, and, if necessary, the consultant, to confirm that the medication, dosage, frequency and route are correct. If possible, she could obtain the advice of the pharmacist. In extreme circumstances, she is entitled to tell the doctor that she is refusing to administer the drug and the doctor then has the option of administering it himself or of rethinking the position. The nurse, of course, risks disciplinary action for her refusal, but if she has good grounds for her belief that the drug or dosage is inappropriate, she should have the support of her management.

Sources of information

The nurse should also be familiar with the *British National Formulary*. There should be an up-to date copy on the ward and she should have easy access to it. There is some useful information at the beginning, giving guidance on prescribing.

Illegible writing

Nurses often complain that they are unable to read the doctors' writing on the drug charts. If they have any doubt about the drug prescribed, they should not administer it unless they have checked it with the doctor who wrote it, his superior or, in certain circumstances, the pharmacist. If the nurse fails to double-check illegible writing, she could herself become liable as the following case illustrates.

Case 28.1   *Prendergast v. Sam Dee Ltd and Others* (1989)

Illegible writing[8]

One of three items on a prescription was for 21 Amoxil tablets. The pharmacist misread this as Daonil. The patient suffered hypoglycaemia and sustained permanent brain damage. The pharmacist said that he had read the 'A' for a 'D' and the 'x' for an 'n'. There were other indications from which the pharmacist should have realised that his interpretation was for the wrong drug, i.e. the other drugs that were prescribed, the dosage and the fact that the patient paid for his prescription. (Daonil is a drug used by diabetic patients who do not have to pay prescription charges.) Both doctor and pharmacist were held liable for the harm that befell the patient. The doctor was held 25 per cent liable. Damages totalled £137,547.

In a case where a woman was prescribed a top-up epidural following a hysterectomy in a private hospital, the junior doctor mistook a dose of 3 ml of diamorphine for 30 ml. The woman collapsed following its administration and the doctor was unable to use the resuscitation equipment, as he had not had the necessary training. Although the consultant was able to revive her, she died a few days later.[9]

Bad maths

The UKCC advised in 2000 that student nurses should be given more mathematics training following claims that drug calculation errors could be putting patients at risk. Professor Bryn Davis, a UKCC member, stated that the GCSE maths exam, which is a compulsory entry requirement for training, is failing to prepare nurses for complex drug calculations.[10] An example of the fatal effects of miswriting decimals was seen in October 2000 when it was alleged that a baby in a neonatal unit died when a decimal point in a drug prescription was entered in the wrong place.[11] The death had been reported to the coroner.

Management of errors or incidents in the administration of medicines

The NMC in its guidelines for the administration of medicines also gives guidance on the management of errors or incidents in the administration of medicines. It states that the NMC will distinguish between those cases where the error was the result of reckless or incompetent practice or was concealed and those cases that resulted from other causes, such as serious pressure of work, and where there was immediate honest disclosure in the patient's interests, and it urges employers to consider each incident in its particular context and similarly to discriminate between these two categories.[12] In 2004 the Department of Health published a new guide to improve safety in the prescribing, dispensing and administration of medicines.[13] The guide examines the causes and frequency of medication errors, highlights drugs and clinical settings that carry particular risks and identifies models of good practice for health professionals and NHS organisations. The National Patient Safety Agency (NPSA) in its annual report for 2006/7 stated that in partnership with the DH and the Welsh Assembly it had initiated a safe medication practice work programme for 2007/8 which aims to improve the safe use of medicines in the NHS. Patient safety alerts cover five distinct areas of medicines management: anticoagulant medicines management; liquid medicines administered via oral and other enteral routes; injectable medicines; epidural injections and infusions; and paediatric intravenous infusions. In March 2007 the NPSA published 'Safety in doses: improving the use of medicines in the NHS'. It is also looking at preventing medication errors by improving the packaging design. These reports are available on the NPSA website.[14] The NPSA grades patient safety incidents in terms of no harm (including where the incident has been prevented and where it has not been prevented), low harm where the incident required extra observation or minor treatment, moderate harm, severe harm and death.

Shared liability

It may happen that several different practitioners are involved in an incident that causes harm to a patient. The court has to determine the respective responsibility of each person and their employer (if any). Under the Civil Liability (Contribution) Act 1978, a successful claimant can obtain compensation from any one of several defendants and that defendant can then claim from the others reimbursement according to their responsibility for the harm. An example of this is given in Case 28.2. The case does not involve a nurse, but if the situation were in a hospital context rather than in the home, one can imagine a nurse being involved.

> ### Case 28.2 — *Dwyer v. Roderick* (1984)
>
> **Over-prescribing**[15]
>
> It was alleged by Mrs Dwyer that Dr Roderick prescribed a particular drug (Migril) and was negligent in choosing the number and frequency with which the relevant tablets should be taken, so that within a relatively short time she had received a dangerous overdose. The manufacturers had warned that not more than four tablets should be taken for any one attack of migraine and that no more than 12 tablets should be taken in the course of one week. Dr Roderick's prescription was for two tablets to be taken every four hours as necessary. He prescribed a total of 60 tablets. Dr Roderick admitted that this was utterly wrong: 'I have no satisfactory explanation. It was a mental aberration.' When the prescription was taken for dispensing, there were two qualified pharmacists in the shop, neither of whom noticed the error and simply repeated Dr Roderick's instructions on the label. They in turn accepted some liability. Over the next six days, Mrs Dwyer took 36 Migril tablets. As a result of this overdose, she suffered serious personal injuries, i.e. irreversible ergotamine poisoning which resulted in constriction of the blood vessels and gangrene of her toes and lower limbs. As well as suing the chemists and Dr Roderick, Mrs Dwyer sued as second defendant Dr Roderick's partner, Dr Jackson, who saw her three days after the prescription had been given and who failed to discover the fact that his partner had over-prescribed the drug and failed to stop her taking it.

In Case 28.2, the trial judge decided that each defendant was liable: Dr Roderick was 45 per cent liable, Dr Jackson was 15 per cent liable and the pharmacists were 40 per cent liable. The Court of Appeal held by a majority that Dr Jackson was not negligent. It accepted his evidence that it was his usual practice to enquire what medication a patient was on. Liability was thus divided between Dr Roderick and the pharmacists. Mrs Dwyer received £92,000 compensation.

One particularly interesting aspect of this case is that the incident occurred in November 1973, but did not come to court until 1982. Thus the actual evidence of what happened was scanty and undoubtedly made Mrs Dwyer's case against Dr Jackson very difficult. The court commented adversely on the delay and suggested that the time might be ripe for changes designed to enable the court and the judiciary to play a greater part in encouraging the parties and their advisers to speed up the process of litigation. These changes have now taken place (known as the Woolf Reforms) and are discussed in Chapter 6. Cases may still commence only many years after an incident (see Chapter 6 on limitation of time) and therefore nurses must be aware of the importance of record keeping (see Chapter 9). In any such incident, the nurse is likely to have very little personal recall, but will be heavily dependent on the clarity and comprehensiveness of the records.

Fitness to practise case

> ### Case 28.3 — Fitness to practise[16]
>
> A registered general nurse who was employed first as the lead nurse in an ophthalmology department, then on a care of the elderly ward, faced allegations that she put an instruction to 'dilate both eyes' on a patient's notes without medical authorisation, that she administered a drug via the wrong route, and while she was not competent to do so, and made a false entry on a patient's fluid balance chart relating to that drug error. The nurse admitted all the charges except of making the false entry.

In hearing Case 28.3 the Professional Conduct Committee of the NMC found the facts proved and were convinced by the evidence that the nurse had added the letters SC (subcutaneous) at a later date. It found that the proved facts of all the charges amounted to misconduct. It decided that the nurse's name should be removed from the Register.

PRN medication

PRN medication (*pro re nata* – 'as required, whenever necessary') enables a doctor to write the patient up for medication, but leaves to the nurse the discretion as to when, if at all, the drug should be administered, depending on the patient's condition.

The value of this system is that it allows the patient to have a drug when necessary, without calling the doctor for the specific purpose of prescribing the drug for it to be administered immediately. Thus pain relief drugs, sleeping tablets and indigestion drugs can be prescribed in case the patient might need such help. Unfortunately, the doctor does not always ensure that sufficient information is given on the drugs sheet. He or she might, for instance, fail to give the maximum amount that can be given in any 24-hour period. He or she might also fail to specify the dose and the intervals at which it can be given. The hospital pharmacist should check the drugs sheets regularly to ensure that all the relevant information is present and the nurse should not administer these drugs without first checking the limitations. It is also essential that every drug that is administered PRN should be recorded when given, as overdoses could easily occur if a record is not kept. Each hospital should have a policy relating to PRN medication.

Infusion therapy

Since 1968 there have been 23 cases of inadvertent intrathecal injection of the vinca alkaloid drug Vincristine reported around the world (and around half of these have been in England). One of the targets of the National Patient Safety Agency (see Chapter 12) was to reduce the number of patients dying or being paralysed by maladministered spinal injections to zero by the end of 2001. A junior doctor in Nottingham pleaded guilty to manslaughter following the administration of a chemotherapy drug by epidural rather than IV to a patient suffering from leukaemia (see Chapter 2). Guidance on standards for infusion therapy in hospitals and the community has been published by the RCN.[17] These give information on standards on:

+ infection control
+ most appropriate infusion devices and infusion-related equipment
+ infusion-related complications
+ infusion therapies, including chemotherapy, analgesia, transfusion and epidural
+ placement, care and maintenance of vascular access devices.

Updated national guidance on the safe administration of intrathecal chemotherapy was issued by the Department of Health in 2003.[18] The guidance contained in the annexe to the circular was to be fully complied with by NHS trusts by 30 November 2003. A training toolkit and video have been issued to support local induction and training programmes. Under the guidance, the chief executive of a trust is required to identify a designated lead to oversee compliance within the trust; trusts that undertake fewer than ten procedures a year (low-volume trusts) should carry out a risk assessment to decide if they should continue to provide the service; high-level trusts (500+ procedures a year) should carry out a risk assessment to check the capacity and safety of the service; a written local protocol should be drawn up and a register established to identify personnel who have been trained and are authorised to prescribe, dispense, issue, check or administer; automatic inclusion in a hospital's register on the transfer of staff should not occur. There should be annual reviews of competence and a certificate or other written confirmation of competence should be issued. The guidance also includes advice on those eligible to prescribe, documentation, storage, administration of intrathecal chemotherapy after intravenous chemotherapy has been administered, an area should be designated for the administration of intrathecal chemotherapy and it should only be administered in normal working hours. Guidance on waivers is also given.

Instructions by telephone

The following situation is not uncommon.

> ### Practical Dilemma 28.2   Night orders
>
> Ward Sister Dury was the night sister at a small geriatric hospital that was served by GPs. One night she was very worried about the condition of a frail patient whose blood pressure and temperature were raised. She telephoned the duty GP and expressed her anxieties to him. He was of the opinion that she need not be concerned and suggested that the patient should be given paracetamol. She was reluctant to take instructions over the telephone, but decided that, since he would not visit, there was little else she could do for the patient. She gave the dose of paracetamol, but unfortunately the patient's condition deteriorated and she again telephoned the GP, who did not visit until 9.00 a.m. the next day, by which time the patient had died.

What is the position of the ward sister? Should she have taken instructions over the telephone? The NMC guidelines[19] state:

Instruction by telephone to a practitioner to administer a previously unprescribed substance is not acceptable. In exceptional circumstances, where the medication has been previously prescribed and the prescriber is unable to issue a new prescription, but where changes to the dose are considered necessary, the use of information technology (such as fax or email) is the preferred method. This should be followed up by a new prescription confirming the changes within a given time period. The NMC suggests a maximum of 24 hours. In any event, the changes must have been authorised before the new dosage is administered.

It would now be possible for patient group directions to be drawn up so that, following appropriate training, the ward sister could prescribe and administer against an agreed protocol (see below).

Misprescribing of antibiotics

Research carried out by University College London using the NHS General Practice Research Database showed that family doctors are persisting in prescribing antibiotics for conditions against which they do not work. Even patients who were aware that antibiotics were ineffective against viral conditions still pressed GPs for prescriptions for antibiotics.[20]

Self-administration by patients

The involvement of the patient in his own medication is increasingly being adopted as a form of rehabilitation and as a move towards discharge and the assumption by the patient of responsibility for his own health and care. The NMC welcomes this development in its guidance for the administration of medicines,[21] but stresses that the necessary safety, security and storage arrangements must be available and, where necessary, agreed procedures in place. The NMC states that it is also important that if the nurse is delegating the responsibility for the administration of medicines, she must ensure that the patient or carer/care assistant is competent to carry out the task. This will require education, training and assessment of the patient or carer/care assistant and further support if necessary. The retention by the patient of medication in his bedside locker puts additional responsibilities on the nurse, who needs to ensure that there is a clear policy in relation to the safety of the medicines, especially from other patients and visitors and also in relation to the training and supervision of the patient himself and that these policies are implemented. Guidance has been published by the Royal Pharmaceutical Society of Great Britain on the administration and control of medicine in care homes and children's services, which includes advice on the self-administration of medicines.[22]

Covert administration of medicines

It is a basic principle of law that the consent of an adult to treatment including medication is required. However, problems can arise when an adult lacks the mental capacity to give consent. The UKCC published a position statement in 2001[23] on the covert administration of medicines disguised in food or drink. The guidance has been republished by the NMC in the form of a position statement within its A–Z advice sheets.[24] It makes clear that covert administration would not apply to a patient who had the mental capacity to make his or her own decisions even in a life-saving situation and could only be justified where the patient lacked the mental capacity to make his or her own decisions and the administration of medicines in this way was in the best interests of the patient. The NMC states:

> *The covert administration of medicines is only likely to be necessary or appropriate in the case of patients or clients who actively refuse medication but who are judged not to have the capacity to understand the consequences of their refusal.*

It suggests that the following considerations may apply where covert administration of medicines for a patient is being discussed:

+ The best interests of the patient or client must be considered at all times.
+ The medication must be considered essential for the patient's or client's health and well-being or for the safety of others.
+ The decision to administer a medication covertly should not be considered routine and should be a contingency measure. Any decision to do so must be reached after assessing the care needs of the patient or client individually. It should be patient or client specific, in order to avoid the ritualised administration of medicine in this way.

+ There should be broad and open discussion among the multidisciplinary clinical team and the supporters of the patient or client and agreement that this approach is required in the circumstances. Those involved should include carers, relatives, advocates and the multidisciplinary team (especially the pharmacist). Family involvement in the care process should be positively encouraged.

+ The method of administration should be agreed with the pharmacist.

+ The decision and action taken, including the names of all parties concerned, should be documented in the care plan and reviewed at appropriate intervals.

+ Regular attempts should be made to encourage the patient or client to take their medication. This might best be achieved by giving regular information, explanation and encouragement, preferably by the team member who has the best rapport with the individual.

+ There should be a written local policy, taking into account these professional practice guidelines.

Nurse as prescriber

There have been major developments in the scope of professional practice of the nurse, which are considered in Chapter 24. Of these developments, one of the most significant ones is nurse prescribing. This section looks at the developments in prescribing in the community and then considers the recommendations and the implementation of the Crown Reports. (The prescribing powers of the midwife are considered in Chapter 14.)

Community nurse prescribing

Legislation has been passed to give specified practitioners the power to prescribe specified medicines (Medicinal Products (Prescription by Nurses) Act 1992). The legislation followed the recommendations of the report of the advisory group on nurse prescribing (known as the First Crown Report) to the Department of Health in December 1989. Health visitors and community nurses who have had the requisite training can prescribe in the community from a nursing formulary. In February 2000,[25] prescribing powers were given to nurses employed by a doctor on the medical list (i.e. GP) and also to nurses working in walk-in centres, defined in the regulations as 'A centre at which information and treatment for minor conditions is provided to the public under arrangements made by or on behalf of the Secretary of State'.

> **Practical Dilemma 28.3**   **Holding stocks in the community**
>
> Brenda was a community nurse who was eligible to prescribe medicines in the community. Often patients would, when the treatment had ended, offer her dressings and other medicines that they had been prescribed and were left over. She was happy to take them since to dispose of them would be a waste. She thus built up a considerable stock, which she kept in the boot of her car, and would issue to new patients before their prescriptions had been dispensed. She is now concerned to know the legality of what she is doing.

There are considerable dangers in the practice followed by Brenda. In the first place, the medicinal products obtained on prescription for one patient should be used for that patient and not for others. Second, by supplying these medicinal products to others, she could be seen as the supplier under the Consumer Protection Act 1987 (see Chapter 12) and become liable for any defects. In addition, there is the security and safety aspect of keeping such products in the boot of her car. In order to ensure that a safe practice is followed, she should discuss with her manager and the pharmacist the possibility of the pharmacist taking the unwanted goods back into stock.

Prescribing in hospital and primary care

The legal changes permitting nurse prescribing in the community brought into focus the situation in hospitals and family practitioner centres where nurse prescribing was taking place according to protocols or written instructions signed by the delegating doctor. The anomalies raised by this quasi-legal situation led the government to appoint Dr June Crown to review the position on prescribing, supply and administration of medicines and make recommendations.

Group protocols or patient group directions

The Crown Committee first considered the arrangements for and legality of group protocols and reported in March 1998 (see Box 28.2) and recommended legislation to ensure that their legal validity was clarified. The criteria against which any group protocol should be tested are shown in Box 28.3. It recommended that certain products should be excluded from group protocols. These included:

1 new drugs under intensive monitoring and subject to special adverse reaction reporting requirements (the Black Triangle scheme)[26]

2 unlicensed medicines

3 medicines used outside their licensed indications

4 medicines being used in clinical trials.

Box 28.2 **Crown Report on group protocols**

1 The majority of patients should continue to receive medicines on an individual basis. However, there is likely to be a continuing need for supply and administration under group protocols in certain limited situations.

2 Current safe and effective practice using group protocols which are consistent with criteria defined in the report should continue (see Box 28.3).

3 The law should be clarified to ensure that health professionals who supply or administer medicines under group protocols are acting within the law.

4 All group protocols should comply with specified criteria.

5 Current protocols should be reviewed in the light of those criteria.

6 The Department of Health should disseminate the criteria widely.

7 An evaluation study should be undertaken on the use of the group protocols.

8 These recommendations should apply to all sectors of healthcare including the private and charitable sectors.

As a consequence of the Crown Report on group protocols (see Box 28.3), new regulations came into force on 9 August 2000.[27] These provide for patient group directions to be drawn up to make provision for the sale or supply of a prescription-only medicine in hospitals in accordance with the written direction of a doctor or dentist. To be lawful, the patient group direction must cover the particulars that are set out in Part I of Schedule 7 of the Statutory Instrument. These particulars are shown in Box 28.4.

Box 28.3 **Criteria for group protocols**

Group protocol criteria are as follows:

+ should ensure that patient safety is not compromised or put at risk
+ should specify clear arrangements for professional responsibility and accountability
+ should contribute to the effective use of resources
+ should be consistent with the summary of product characteristics, which is part of the marketing authorisation granted for the product
+ content of the protocol should state the clinical need which it is intended to address and the objectives of care which it will provide; the characteristics of staff authorised to take responsibility for the supply or administration of medicines under a group protocol
+ description of treatment available; management and monitoring of group protocols
+ development of group protocols: by whom? approval; employer's final approval; date and signature and monitoring
+ implementation of group protocols.

The classes of individuals by whom supplies may be made are set out in Part III of Schedule 7 and include the following:

1 ambulance paramedics (who are registered or hold a certificate of proficiency)
2 pharmacists
3 registered health visitors
4 registered midwives
5 registered nurses
6 registered ophthalmic opticians
7 state registered chiropodists
8 state registered orthoptists
9 state registered physiotherapists
10 state registered radiographers.

The person who is to supply or administer the medicine must be designated in writing on behalf of the authorising person (see below) for the purpose of the patient group direction. In addition to compliance with the particulars set out in Box 28.4, a patient group direction must be signed on behalf of the authorising person. This is defined as the Common Services Agency, the (special) health authority, the NHS trust or primary care trust. The Department of Health has developed PGDs for certain chemical and biological countermeasures in emergency situations, such as atropine, and these can be downloaded from its website.[28] The Royal

Pharmaceutical Society of Great Britain published in September 2007 a resource pack for pharmacists on patient group directions which would also be of interest to NMC-registered practitioners.

Box 28.4 — Particulars for patient group direction

+ Period during which the direction shall have effect.
+ Description or class of prescription-only medicines to which the direction relates.
+ Whether there are any restrictions on the quantity of medicine which may be supplied on any one occasion and, if so, what restrictions.
+ Clinical situations that prescription-only medicines of that description or class may be used to treat.
+ Clinical criteria under which a person shall be eligible for treatment.
+ Whether any class of person is excluded from treatment under the direction and, if so, what class of person.
+ Whether there are circumstances in which further advice should be sought from a doctor or dentist and, if so, what circumstances.
+ Pharmaceutical form or forms in which prescription-only medicines of that description or class are to be administered.
+ Strength, or maximum strength, at which prescription-only medicines of that description or class are to be administered.
+ Applicable dosage or maximum dosage.
+ Route of administration.
+ Frequency of administration.
+ Any minimum or maximum period of administration applicable to prescription-only medicines of that description or class.
+ Whether there are any relevant warnings to note and, if so, what warnings.
+ Whether there is any follow-up action to be taken in any circumstances and, if so, what action and in what circumstances.
+ Arrangements for referral for medical advice.
+ Details of the records to be kept of the supply or the administration of medicines under the direction.

Final Crown Report 1999

In March 1999 the Final Report was published.[29] Its recommendations are shown in Box 28.5 and they cover the first three terms of reference:

1 to develop a consistent policy framework to guide judgements on the circumstances in which health professionals might undertake new responsibilities with regard to prescribing, supply and administration of medicines
2 to advise on the likely impact of any proposed changes
3 to consider possible implications for legislation, professional training and standards.

Other recommendations are made to professional bodies on the criteria to be followed in making proposals for extensions to prescribing and the arrangements they should make for training; to the General Medical Council and postgraduate deans; and to employers to ensure that staff prescribing medicines have the right training and skills.

> ### Box 28.5 Recommendations of Final Crown Report, March 1999
>
> 1 The legal authority in the UK to prescribe should be extended beyond currently authorised prescribers.
>
> 2 The legal authority to prescribe should be limited to medicines in specific therapeutic areas related to particular competence and expertise of the group.
>
> 3 Two types of prescriber should be recognised: the independent prescriber and the dependent prescriber.
>
> 4 A UK-wide advisory body, provisionally entitled the New Prescribers' Advisory Committee, should be established under Section 4 of the Medicines Act to assess submissions from professional organisations seeking powers for suitably trained members to become independent or dependent prescribers.
>
> 5 Newly authorised groups of prescribers should not normally be allowed to prescribe specified categories of medicines including controlled drugs.
>
> 6 The current arrangements for the administration and self-administration of medicines should continue to apply. Newly authorised prescribers should have the power to administer those parenteral prescription-only medicines that they are authorised to prescribe.
>
> 7 Repeatable prescriptions should be available on the NHS, with limits on the number of repeats and the duration of its validity.
>
> 8 There should be primary legislation that permits ministers, through regulations, to designate new categories of dependent and independent prescribers for the purpose of the Medicines Act, defining what classes of medicines they could prescribe.
>
> 9 The new arrangements should be subject to evaluation.
>
> 10 There should be an evaluation of likely costs and benefits to the NHS in specific areas before general adoption of the recommendations takes place.

Independent and dependent (subsequently known as supplementary) prescribers

Perhaps the most significant recommendation of the Crown Report (1999) is that there should be two types of prescriber:

+ The *independent prescriber* is defined as the person who is responsible for the assessment of patients with undiagnosed conditions and for decisions about the clinical management required including prescribing. This group would include doctors, dentists and certain nurses who are already legally authorised prescribers. Other health professionals may also become newly legally authorised independent prescribers.

+ The *dependent prescriber* (now known as the *supplementary prescriber*) is defined as the person who is responsible for the continuing care of patients who have been clinically assessed by an independent practitioner. The continuing care can include prescribing that will be informed by clinical guidelines and will be consistent with individual treatment plans. Dependent prescribers may also be involved in continuing established treatments by issuing repeat prescriptions, with authority to adjust the dose or dosage form according to patients' needs. There should be provision for regular clinical review by the assessing clinician.

Individual practitioners

The final recommendation of the Crown Report is to individual practitioners:

All legally authorised prescribers should take personal responsibility for maintaining and updating their knowledge and practice related to prescribing, including taking part in clinical audit, and should never prescribe in situations beyond their professional competence.

Situation following the Final Crown Report 1999

Legislation implementing the Final Crown Report recommendations was contained in Section 63 of the Health and Social Care Act 2001, which amends the Medicines Act 1968 and enables the Secretary of State to draw up regulations to lay down the conditions on which prescribing powers can be extended to specified health professionals. On 25 October 2000 the Department of Health issued a consultation paper to extend nurse prescribing. It proposed training about 10,000 nurses to prescribe treatment for a broader range of medical conditions including:

1 minor injuries and ailments such as cuts, burns and hayfever

2 promoting healthier lifestyles such as help with giving up smoking

3 chronic diseases including asthma and diabetes

4 palliative care.

The NHS Act 1977 Regulations were amended to permit an extension of nurse prescribing from September 2001 from an expanded nurse prescribers' formulary. Instead of separate nurse prescribing formularies for different specialties, it was considered preferable to have one nurse prescribers' formulary with individual nurses using their professional judgement to decide the items within it that they were competent to prescribe. Following the consultation, a Statutory Instrument was issued in 2002, which came into force on 1 April 2002.[30] This enabled nurses who met certain conditions and who were to be known as 'extended formulary nurse prescribers', to be able to prescribe certain prescription-only medicines. The extended formulary meant the *Nurse Prescribers' Extended Formulary* supplement in the current edition of the *British National Formulary*. In March 2002 the Department of Health issued guidance for the implementation of extended independent nurse prescribing.[31] This has been followed by similar guidance from the other constituent countries of the UK

Nurse independent prescribing

In May 2006 the *Nurse Prescribers' Extended Formulary* was discontinued[32] and qualified nurse independent prescribers are now able to prescribe any licensed medicine for any medical condition within their competence, including some controlled drugs. Further information is available from the DH website. A nurse independent prescriber means a person (a) who is a registered nurse or registered midwife and (b) against whom is recorded in the professional register an annotation signifying that he is qualified to order drugs, medicines and appliances as a nurse independent prescriber or a nurse independent/supplementary prescriber. Nurse independent prescribers are only able to prescribe or administer a limited range of controlled drugs as set out in Schedule 3A of the Statutory Instrument. Independent prescribing by pharmacists is also facilitated.

The NMC has issued guidance on Criminal Records Bureau checks, and the educational and training requirements for independent prescribing and for specialist community public health nursing programmes.[33]

Additional criteria for eligibility to become an independent nurse prescriber

In its guidance on implementation the Department of Health has advised that in addition to fulfilling the legal criteria, applicants for the prescribing preparation will need:

+ the ability to study at level 3 (degree level)
+ at least three years' post-registration clinical nursing experience (or part-time equivalent): nominees will usually be at E grade or above
+ a medical prescriber willing to contribute and to supervise the nurse's 12-day learning in practice element of preparation
+ the support of the employer and confirmation of certain conditions.

The three key principles to prioritise potential applicants for training as independent nurse prescribers are seen by the DH as being:

+ patient safety
+ maximum benefit to patients in terms of quicker and more efficient access to medicines for patients
+ better use of nurses' skills.

Supplementary prescribing

In April 2002[34] the Department of Health announced its intention of introducing supplementary prescribing by a nurse or pharmacist in 2003. The aim was to enable the pharmacists and nurses to work in partnership with doctors and help treat such conditions as asthma, diabetes, high blood pressure and arthritis. The doctor would draw up a plan with the patient's agreement, laying out the range of medicines that may be prescribed and when to refer back to the doctor. This early announcement was followed by a press release in November 2002,[35] which gave further details of the patient conditions and the medicinal products that would be the subject of supplementary prescribing.

In April 2005 chiropodists and podiatrists, physiotherapists and radiographers were added to the list of those who could become supplementary prescribers and restrictions on their prescribing controlled drugs or unlicensed medicines were removed.[36]

Implications of nurse prescribing for the scope of professional practice

The Crown Report has, in a sense, given its approval to a controlled development of professional competence in areas formerly the sole preserve of medical staff. However, clear checks are to be in place to ensure that these developments take place with well-defined precautions to secure patient safety and also to secure efficient use of resources. While nurses are likely to be the most numerous group to develop prescribing skills, other professionals, such as physiotherapists, radiographers, orthoptists, dietitians, speech therapists and many others, will also find that the new legislation will facilitate professional development or at the minimum validate activities already taking place. The need to obtain a doctor's personal attendance on a patient in order that a specific drug could be prescribed has placed an unnecessary obstacle in the advancement of professional practice for many health professionals and this will now be lifted. (Issues relating to the scope of professional practice and the role of the clinical nurse specialist and the consultant nurse are discussed in Chapter 24.)

Electronic prescriptions

Regulations were enacted in 2001 to allow the use of an electronic signature for the electronic transmission of prescriptions in pilot studies and this is extended to PCTs to facilitate the use of electronic prescriptions.[37] The system allows the patient's prescription to be sent electronically from their GP to a pharmacy. Further information on the current stage of the initiative can be obtained from the Department of Health website.

Safety of medicines

The Committee on Safety of Medicines was one committee set up under Section 4 of the Medicines Act on the advice of the Medicines Commission to the minister. It is regulated under Schedule 1 of the Medicines Act and under Statutory Instrument.[38] It can in turn set up its own subcommittees. Like all other Section 4 committees and the Medicines Commission itself, it must submit an annual report about its work to ministers. The Medicines Control Agency is the licensing authority under the Medicines Act and the European Regulations and has the function of monitoring the safety and quality of medicines. Its website provides access for health professionals, members of the public, academics, the pharmaceutical industry and journalists.[39] It operates a Defective Medicines Report Centre. On 1 April 2003 the Medicines Control Agency was amalgamated with the Medical Devices Agency to form the Medicines and Healthcare products Regulatory Agency (MHRA).

A yellow card adverse drug reaction (ADR) reporting scheme is a voluntary scheme, through which doctors, dentists, coroners and pharmacists notify the Medicines Control Agency (MCA)/Committee on Safety of Medicines (CSM) of suspected adverse drug reactions. The yellow cards for completion can be found at the back of the *BNF/NPF*. The MCA/CSM encourage the reporting of all suspected adverse drug reactions to newly licensed medicines that are under intensive monitoring (identified by a Δ symbol both on the product information for the drug and in the *BNF* and *MIMS*) and all serious suspected adverse drug reactions to all other established drugs. Serious reactions include those that are fatal, life-threatening, disabling, incapacitating or which result in or prolong hospitalisation and/or are medically significant. The yellow card reporting scheme was extended to nurses, midwives and health visitors in 2002. At the same time an electronic reporting system was introduced to enable quicker and easier submission of reports. Patients are able to report adverse medicinal reactions through NHS Direct.

Product liability and drugs

The case brought against the manufacturers of Opren has shown the difficulties and expense of suing a company for harm caused by medication. Initially, a judge decided that a class action could not be brought on behalf of all those who claimed to have suffered side effects, but each person claiming compensation would have to sue individually and contribute his share to the total costs. This has led to a demand for changes in the procedure in respect of such actions involving thousands of litigants, which are currently being considered. Class actions have now been initiated in respect of several drug products.

Under the present laws of negligence it is in any case difficult to show that a firm failed to take all reasonable care in testing and manufacturing its products. The victims of thalidomide did not establish negligence by the Distillers Company in this country, but agreed an *ex gratia* settlement. It is possible that the Consumer Protection Act 1987 Part I, which is applicable to damage suffered after the Act came into force, will make any action for liability by someone harmed by drugs easier on the basis that, provided the patient can prove that he has suffered injury as a result of a defect in a particular drug, it is then up to the manufacturer to show that one of the many defences open to him under the Act was present. (This is further discussed in Chapter 12 and will not be considered further here.)

Misuse of drugs

Nurses may sometimes encounter patients in their work who are addicted to various substances. They should know the law relating to such persons and how it affects their own position. In the past, there was a requirement that doctors should send to the Home Office particulars of drug addicts. However, this requirement was revoked by the Misuse of Drugs (Supply to Addicts) Regulations 1997 in May 1997. Doctors are now expected to report on a standard form cases of drug misuse to their local Drug Misuse Database (DMD). Phone numbers are set out in the *British National Formulary* (*BNF*). The notification to the DMD should be made when a patient first presents with a drug problem or re-presents after a gap of six months or more. All types of problem drug misuse should be reported including opioid, benzodiazepine and CNS stimulant. The data held on the databases is anonymised, so it can not be used to check on multiple prescribing. Under the Misuse of Drugs (Supply to Addicts) Regulations 1997, only medical practitioners who hold a special licence issued by the Home Secretary may prescribe, administer or supply diamorphine, Diconal or cocaine in the treatment of drug addiction. Other practitioners must refer any addict who requires these drugs to a treatment centre.

A National Treatment Agency for substance abuse was established in 2001 as a special health authority to exercise on behalf of the Secretary of State such functions in connection with the treatment of drug misusers and such other functions as he may direct it to perform.[40] Its overall purpose is to improve the availability, capacity and effectiveness of treatment for drug misuse in England. Regulations relating to membership, termination of office and the appointment of committees and the duty to furnish reports and certain other information to the Secretary of State have been passed.[41] Further information is available from its website.[42] Recently the change of status of cannabis from a Class B to Class C drug was implemented despite considerable pressure from organisations such as the British Medical Association and others alleging a link between cannabis usage and psychosis. The Advisory Council on the Misuse of Drugs has concluded that there was no evidence that cannabis caused mental illness.[43] The Home Office launched a £1 million campaign to explain to parents and young people the new law on the possession of cannabis. A private members' Bill, Drugs (Reclassification) Bill, has been introduced to reclassify cannabis. The Department of Health has set up an A-Z guide on all its substance misuse guidance and publications which can be accessed via its website.

Two charity workers were jailed for knowingly permitting or suffering the supply of a Class A drug on the premises.[44] Concerns about breach of confidentiality are considered in Chapter 8. Nurses who remove illegal drugs from patients on admission and who ensure that these drugs are immediately handed into the pharmacy department should be protected from charges of illegal possession of drugs.

Conclusions

Following the implementation of the Crown Reports, prescribing by nurses has developed rapidly and the abolition of the extended formulary was a natural development. The ability of nurses in hospitals and in primary care to issue prescriptions has a major impact on the development of their scope of professional practice. The regulatory impact assessment of the Statutory Instrument abolishing the extended formulary[45] states that 'enabling nurses to prescribe any licensed medicine for any condition subject to clinical competence will not be at the expense of endangering public health'. However, it will be essential to ensure that the additional responsibilities are coupled with adequate resources and training in order to prevent more litigation, complaints and fitness to practise proceedings.

Reflection questions

1 A patient is concerned at the possibility of having suffered side effects from medication. What is the relevant law? (Refer also to the duty of care to inform the patient (Chapter 7).)

2 In your hospital, when a patient is admitted, any drugs that he brings from home are immediately taken from him and destroyed. One patient complains about this practice because it is wasteful and because he paid the prescription price for those drugs. What do you consider should be the correct practice?

3 What are the advantages and disadvantages of administering controlled drugs PRN?

Further exercises

1 Review your practice in the administration of drugs. Are there any ways in which you consider you might not be meeting the legal requirements? Consider any advice and guidance issued by the person in your trust identified as the Accountable Officer for the safe use and management of controlled drugs.

2 Design a policy for handling drugs to be learnt by a first-year student.

3 What safeguards do you consider should be laid down to protect the patient as nurse prescribing extends?

References

1 The Misuse of Drug Regulations 2001, SI 2001 No. 3998
2 www.mhra.gov.uk/
3 Prescription-Only Medicines (Human Use) Order 1997, SI 1997 No. 1830
4 UKCC, Guidance for the Administration of Medicines, October 2000, reissued by the NMC, 2002 and updated 2004
5 Department of Health and Royal Pharmaceutical Society of Great Britain, Safer Management of Controlled Drugs, May 2007
6 The Controlled Drugs (Supervision of Management and Use) Regulations 2006, SI 2006 No. 3148

[7] Department of Health, Safer Management of Controlled Drugs: Changes to Record Keeping Requirements, DH Gateway Ref. 7187, October 2006

[8] *Prendergast* v. *Sam Dee Ltd and Others, The Times*, 14 March 1989

[9] Dominic Kennedy, Hospital blamed in report on overdose drug, *The Times*, 3 July 2000

[10] Rebecca Coombes, Nurses need a dose of maths, *Nursing Times*, 15 June 1999, 96(24), pp. 4-5

[11] Greg Hurst, Baby dies after one decimal point drug dose error, *The Times*, 11 October 2000

[12] UKCC, Guidance for the Administration of Medicines, 2000, p. 9, reprinted by the NMC, 2002 and updated 2004. New NMC Standards for Medicines Management are in press

[13] Chief Pharmaceutical Officer, Department of Health, Building a safer NHS for patients - improving medication safety, DH, London, January 2004

[14] www.npsa.nhs.uk

[15] *Dwyer* v. *Roderick*, 20 June 1984 QBD

[16] Nursing and Midwifery Council, Professional Conduct Annual Report, NMC, London, 2002-3 pp. 17-19

[17] Royal College of Nursing, Standards for Infusion Therapy, RCN, London, October 2003

[18] Department of Health, Updated National Guidance on the Safe Administration of Intrathecal Chemotherapy, HSC 2003/010, DH, London, October 2003

[19] UKCC, Guidance for the Administration of Medicines, 2000, p. 5, reprinted by the NMC, 2002, updated 2004

[20] Nigel Hawkes, Doctors ignore guidelines to prescribe 'ineffective' antibiotics, *The Times*, 26 July 2007, p. 11

[21] UKCC, Guidance for the Administration of Medicines, 2000, p. 8, reprinted by the NMC, 2002, updated 2004

[22] Royal Pharmaceutical Society of Great Britain, The Administration and Control of Medicine in Care Homes and Children's Services, RPSGB, London, June 2003

[23] UKCC, Registrar's letter 26/2001, Position Statement on the Covert Administration of Medicines - disguising medicine in food and drink

[24] Nursing and Midwifery Council A-Z Advice sheet: Medicines Management, last updated March 2006

[25] National Health Service (Pharmaceutical Services) Amendment Regulations 2000, SI 2000 No. 121

[26] The Black Triangle scheme refers to newly introduced drugs, still subject to special monitoring for potential side effects by the Medicine Control Agency (so-called because they are identifed by a black triangle symbol in the *British National Formulary*)

[27] Prescription-Only Medicines (Human Use) Amendment Order 2000, SI 2000 No. 1917

[28] www.dh.gov.uk/Policyandguidance/Emergencyplanning/

[29] Department of Health, Review of Prescribing, Supply and Administration of Medicines Final Report (Crown Report), DH, London, March 1999

[30] Prescription-Only Medicines (Human Use) Amendment Order 2002, SI 2002 No. 549

[31] Department of Health, Extending Independent Nurse Prescribing within the NHS in England: a guide for implementation, DH, London, March 2002

[32] Medicines for Human Use (Prescribing) (Miscellaneous Amendments) Order, SI 2006 No 915

[33] NMC circulars 29/2007; 30/2007 and 31/2007.

[34] Department of Health press release 2002/0189, Groundbreaking new consultation aims to extend prescribing powers for pharmacists and nurses, 16 April 2002

[35] Department of Health press release 2002/0488, Pharmacists to prescribe for the first time; nurses will prescribe for chronic illness, 21 November 2002

[36] The National Health Service (Primary Medical Services) (Miscellaneous Amendments) Regulations, SI 2005 No. 893; The Medicines for Human Use (Prescribing) Order, SI 2005 No. 765

[37] The National Health Service (Primary Medical Services) (Miscellaneous Amendments) Regulations, SI 2005 No. 893

[38] Committee on Safety of Medicines, SI 1970 No. 1257

[39] www.open.gov.uk/mca/mcahome.htm

[40] National Treatment Agency (Establishment and Constitution) Order 2001, SI 2001 No. 713; National Treatment Agency (Amendment) Regulations 2001, SI 2001 No. 4044

[41] National Treatment Agency Regulations 2001, SI 2001 No. 715

[42] www.nta.nhs.uk/home/main.htm

[43] Stewart Tendler, New drug law confuses the public, *The Times*, 16 January 2004

[44] Alan Simpson, What price confidentiality? *Nursing Times*, 2 March 2000, 96(9), p. 35

[45] Medicines for Human Use (Prescribing) (Miscellaneous Amendments) Order, SI 2006 No. 915, Explanatory memorandum and regulatory impact assessment, available on www.opsi.gov.uk/legislation

Chapter 29
Legal aspects of death

Introduction

Nurses inevitably encounter death in their work. It can be a distressing time and uncertainties surrounding legal issues and numerous questions from troubled relatives can add to the nurse's difficulties. It is important that the nurse should have confidence in her knowledge and be well acquainted with the procedures and the law so that she can answer questions or know from where further information is available. Significant recommendations on the certification of and procedures following death have been made by the inquiry set up following the conviction of Dr Shipman and these are considered below. For more detail on the topics in this chapter see the author's work.[1]

Certification and registration of death

Certification of death is a medical task. The complexities in dealing with brain death and organ transplants are considered in Chapter 16, which also discusses the definition of death and the importance of the exact time of death.

Here we consider the nurse's role and the procedures to be followed generally.

Practical Dilemma 29.1   An expanded role?

Night porters at Roger Park Hospital had clear instructions that no body should be taken to the mortuary unless it had been certified dead. This resulted from an unfortunate incident some time before when a body was taken to the mortuary, but was seen to move and therefore quickly returned to the ward. An investigation revealed that the person had been certified dead by a nurse. The nurses were told always to call a doctor to certify death. However, house officers were not happy about being called out just to certify death and considerable pressure was put on the nursing staff. One night, it was clear that one patient was extremely ill. There were no immediate relatives, but a distant relative was notified of the situation. The patient died at 3 a.m. The nurse summoned the doctor, who said that he would not come down, but would see the patient in the mortuary and sign the certificate there in the morning. The nurse was asked by the bed bureau if she had a spare bed, as a GP had just phoned and was sending in an emergency case. The hospital had no spare beds at all, except the one occupied by the dead person. Could the nurse herself identify that death had occurred and arrange for the porters to remove the body?

The law at present requires a doctor to certify a death. The certification cannot be undertaken by nurses. However, a nurse may have had the training to be able to confirm that a patient has died, i.e. to verify a death. In certain parts of the country, the local medical committees have advised nursing homes and residential care homes that the nurse or manager in charge of the home should, where death is expected, confirm that death has taken place and the doctor would sign the certificate at a later time. If the nurse considers that she is unable to confirm that death has taken place, she should not give way to any pressure, however reasonable it might appear. Should the nurse feel unable, she may be able to obtain help from another nurse who is competent or from a doctor who is prepared to come to the ward.

Case 29.1   Fatal diagnosis[2]

The son of Mrs Maureen Jones summoned a GP when he found his mother collapsed in her bedroom. The GP said that she had died and advised the relatives to notify the police. The undertakers were summoned. A policeman called to the scene saw the woman's leg move and applied mouth-to-mouth resuscitation until the paramedics arrived. She then made a full recovery in hospital. She had been in a diabetic coma. A county court judge found the doctor negligent in making a diagnosis of death. Damages were agreed with the Medical Defence Union at £38,500. Following an investigation, the health authority agreed that the doctor could continue in practice, but was given an official reprimand, told to comply more closely with her terms of service and was required to undergo educational assessment and support.

Verification of death is seen as an expanded role activity and the RCN has provided a paper on verification of death by registered nurses.[3] The NMC in its A–Z advice sheet on confirmation of death[4] states that:

A nurse cannot legally certify death. This is one of the few activities required by law to be carried out by a registered medical practitioner; in the case of an expected death, a registered nurse may confirm or verify when death has occurred, providing there is an explicit local policy or protocol in place to allow such an action.

The policy or protocol must only be used in situations where the death is expected.

Nurses undertaking this responsibility should only do so providing they have received appropriate education and training and have been assessed as competent. They must also be aware of their accountability when performing this role.

A central working group is reviewing a national standard and policy for confirmation/ verification of death.

It is advised that local policies should be developed or amended using the information outlined above. Information on updated advice sheets will be published in NMC news. *[Bold as in NMC publication]*

(Issues relating to the scope of professional practice and the expanded role of the nurse are considered in Chapter 24.)

The general office of the hospital or the medical records department discusses with bereaved relatives the administrative details that must be dealt with. Sometimes there is a special office for dealing with the bereaved and during weekdays the relatives can be shown to this place. However, at night and during the weekends and bank holidays the nurse may have to deal with the administrative details. She should know the details relating to the registration of death and the disposal of the body. Box 29.1 sets out the procedure to be followed.

Box 29.1 — **Procedures for dealing with death**

The medical certificate should be taken by the next of kin or, if not available, by any relatives living in the district or present at the death to the registrar for births, marriages and deaths within five days of the death. He will require the following information: the full name of the deceased; the last known address; date of birth; occupation; and whether the deceased was in receipt of a pension. The registrar will give the person registering the death a certificate of disposal form which can be handed to the undertaker. If a cremation is intended, certification by two doctors will be required. If the death has been referred to the coroner, the relatives should be notified that they will not receive the certificate from the hospital. The coroner will issue his own disposal certificate.

The relatives will receive from the registrar, in addition to the certificate of disposal form, a certificate of registration of death. This may be required by the Benefits Agency in order to claim any entitlements. (The death grant is no longer payable but other benefits are available to those who are eligible.) This certificate may also be required to obtain transfer of any bank accounts, etc. and further copies are available from the registrar on payment of a fee.

Disposal of the body

Different arrangements exist according to the local hospital facilities. Some hospital mortuaries also double up as the public mortuary and it is possible for the body to remain there until collected by the undertakers for the funeral. Before the body is taken from the ward, the nurse must ensure that it is properly labelled and that a receipt is signed and that any property on the body, e.g. rings, are carefully noted and signed for. Similar procedures to check identification and property on the body and the giving of receipts must also be followed when the body is handed over by the porters, administrators or even nurses to the undertakers. Unfortunately, mix-up between bodies still occurs and the wrong body is released.

Post mortems

The coroner might require a post mortem to ascertain the cause of death and can direct a legally qualified medical practitioner to carry out the post mortem. A post mortem ordered by a coroner may or may not precede an inquest. If the coroner orders a post mortem, then the person in possession of the body has no choice but to agree. Sometimes, however, medical staff may request the relative's permission to confirm the cause of death or for research purposes. They require the consent of the person in possession of the body (Human Tissue Act 2004). This can be a distressing request to make to relatives and the request should be put to them with sensitivity. Organs should not be retained by hospital doctors without the relatives' consent. (The issue of retention of organs and the provisions of the Human Tissue Act 2004 are considered in Chapter 16.)

Deaths that have to be reported to the coroner

These are shown in Box 29.2.

Box 29.2   **Deaths that have to be reported to the coroner**

1 Where there is reasonable cause to suspect a person has died a violent or unnatural death.
2 Where there is reasonable cause to suspect a person has died a sudden death of which the cause is unknown.
3 The person has died in prison or in such place or under such circumstances as to require an inquest.

Those causes of death which should be reported to the coroner include: abortions; accidents and injuries; alcoholism; anaesthetics and operations; crime or suspected crime; drugs; ill treatment; industrial diseases; infant deaths if in any way obscure; pensioners where death might be connected with a pensionable disability; persons in legal custody; poisoning; septicaemias if originating from an injury; and stillbirths where there may have been a possibility or suspicion that the child may have been born alive.

If it is likely to be a coroner's case, no unofficial post mortem should be undertaken without the coroner's approval. The coroner can order a post mortem examination to be carried out before deciding to hold an inquest.

Inquests

The Coroners Act 1988 covers the appointment of coroners, the holding of inquests, and post mortem examination. A decision by the coroner not to hold an inquest can be the subject of an application to the High Court. For example, in one case where a mother had suffered from a cerebral haemorrhage soon after giving birth in circumstances that suggested that had her blood pressure been properly monitored immediately after the birth her death might have been avoided, the coroner concluded that she had suffered a natural death. The High Court decided that he had erred in deciding not to hold an inquest. The coroner appealed to the Court of Appeal, which dismissed the appeal. The Court of Appeal held that for the purposes of the Coroners Act 1988 Section 8(1)(a) a death by natural causes was an 'unnatural death' where it was wholly unexpected and would not have occurred but for some culpable human failing.[5] A breach of Article 2 rights was claimed when a coroner refused to resume an adjourned hearing (adjourned pending criminal proceedings) into the death of a man who was stabbed and killed in May 2000 even though the death had occurred before the Human Rights Act 1998 came into force in October 2000. The victim's mother claimed that there were failures by the police and local housing authority in failing to avert the death. The Court of Appeal held that the inquest should be resumed and the Commissioner of Police appealed against this decision. The House of Lords found that the coroner's decision was lawful and allowed the appeal.[6] In December 2007 the European Court of Human Rights held that failure by the state to investigate credible allegations about unlawful killings could amount to a breach of Article 2 and the right to life in relation to alleged failings by the Royal Ulster Constabulary.[7]

Practical Dilemma 29.2 | An unexpected death

Bill Arthur was undergoing a stomach operation when the anaesthetist reported that his pulse was becoming very weak. Resuscitative procedures were undertaken, but unfortunately Bill died. The death was reported to the coroner who decided that an inquest should be held.

What is the purpose of the inquest?

The purpose is to ascertain the following:

1 the identity of the deceased

2 how, where and when the deceased came by his death

3 the particulars, for the time being required by the Registration Acts, to be registered concerning the death.

Section 11(6) of the Coroners Act 1988 specifically states that the purpose of the proceedings shall not include the finding of any person guilty of murder, manslaughter or infanticide.

Who should attend?

The coroner has a duty[8] to examine on oath all persons who tender evidence as to the facts of the death and all persons having knowledge of the facts whom he considers it expedient to examine. Under the Coroners' Rules,[9] the coroner has considerable discretion in deciding who should attend. He must notify the date, hour and place of an inquest to:

1 the spouse or a near relative or personal representative of the deceased whose name and address are known to the coroner

2 any other person who:

+ in the opinion of the coroner is within Rule 20(2), i.e. parent, child, spouse (and a partner in a civil partnership); any beneficiary under an insurance policy on the life of the deceased; any person whose act or omission or that of his servant or agent may have caused or contributed to the death of the deceased; any person appointed by a trade union to which the deceased belonged if the death may have been caused by an injury received at work or an industrial disease; an inspector appointed by an enforcing authority or government department to attend; the chief of police; any other person who in the opinion of the coroner is a properly interested person
+ has asked the coroner to notify him of the particulars of the inquest
+ has supplied the coroner with a telephone number or address for the purpose of so notifying him.

Examination of witnesses

Any of the persons listed in the second point under 2 above are entitled to examine the witnesses either in person or through a solicitor or barrister. The coroner has the power to disallow any question that, in his opinion, is not relevant or is otherwise not a proper question.

The procedure is for any witness to be examined by the coroner first and, if the witness is represented at the inquest, by the representative last. No witness is obliged to answer any question tending to incriminate himself. Where it appears to the coroner that a witness has been asked such a question, the coroner must inform the witness that he may refuse to answer.

Any person whose conduct is likely to be called in question shall, if he has not been summoned to give evidence at the inquest, be given reasonable notice of the date, hour and place at which the inquest shall be held. If any such person has not been summoned or notified, then the coroner must adjourn the hearing to enable him to be present. The inquest shall be adjourned by the coroner on notification by the clerk to the magistrates' court that a person has been charged with an offence such as murder, manslaughter, infanticide or causing death by dangerous driving or the offence of aiding and abetting a suicide under Section 2(1) of the Suicide Act 1961. The Director of Public Prosecutions may also ask the coroner to adjourn the hearing. Where the coroner adjourns the hearing, he shall send to the registrar of deaths a certificate stating particulars required for registration.

Nature of the inquest

The coroner's inquest is very different from the hearings in the other courts of law in this country. It is an inquisitorial hearing as opposed to the civil and criminal courts, which are accusatorial or adversarial. This means that in an inquest there are not two opposing parties with the coroner sitting back and hearing them argue out a case, intervening only to ensure fair play. At an inquest, the coroner takes the lead and is in control. It is up to him or her to obtain answers to the questions set out above. He or she calls the witnesses and decides the order in which they are to give evidence and generally controls the court and hearing. There is not always a jury, but where there is a point of public concern then the coroner will usually ensure that a jury is summoned. The decision of the coroner in the inquest into the death of Princess Diana and her companion not to hold a jury was held by the High Court to be wrong.[10]

Returning to Practical Dilemma 29.2, the coroner's officer will have requested statements from relevant people who were present in theatre and who were concerned with Bill's treatment. It is helpful if those making a statement can keep a copy. (Refer to Chapter 9 for the making of statements.) The coroner will probably have requested a post mortem examination to ascertain the cause of death. He will decide which people he requires to summon as witnesses. Clearly, in Bill's case, there will have to be evidence of identity and also of what took place in theatre. The surgeon, anaesthetist and the nurse are all likely to be called to give evidence. If detailed pathology laboratory results are not yet available, there could well be an adjournment until they are ready. Bill's family will obviously wish to be present in order that they can ask for the relevant questions to be put to prepare for a possible case of negligence in the civil courts. The coroner has the power to prevent any question that he does not consider relevant to the inquest.

Preparation for the theatre nurse before attending the inquest

The theatre nurse has, one hopes, kept a copy of the statement that she made for the coroner. The statement should have followed those guidelines discussed in Chapter 9. She should be advised by a senior nursing officer who has had some experience in such matters on the sort of questions she can expect and how to cope. Preferably, she should be advised by the solicitor to the trust. (For further information on this aspect see Chapter 9.) The importance of comprehensive, meaningful record keeping cannot, once again, be overstressed. Prior to the hearing, the solicitor to the trust should take her through her evidence and answer any concerns that she has.

Recommendations of the Shipman Inquiry

Following the conviction of Dr Shipman for murder an inquiry was set up under the chairmanship of Dame Janet Smith DBE. The First Report[11] considered how many patients Shipman killed, the means employed and the period over which the killings took place. The Second Report examined the conduct of the police investigation into Shipman that took place in March 1998 and failed to uncover his crimes.[12] The Third Report[13] considered the present system for death and cremation certification and for the investigation of deaths by coroners, together with the conduct of those who had operated those systems in the aftermath of the deaths of Shipman's victims. The report noted that the present system of death and cremation certification failed to detect that Shipman had killed any of his 215 victims. Even though many of the deaths occurred suddenly and unexpectedly and should under the present procedures have been reported to the coroner, Shipman managed to avoid any coronial investigation in all but two of the cases in which he had killed. He did this by claiming to be in a position to certify the cause of death and by persuading relatives that no autopsy (and therefore no referral to the coroner) was necessary. The present system failed to protect the public. This Third Report made extensive recommendations, which are summarised in Box 29.3. The inquiry took into account feedback to a consultation paper published by the Fundamental Review of Death Certification and the Coroner Services in England, Wales and Northern Ireland chaired by Mr Tom Luce and accepted the recommendations of the coroner's review on changes to scope and conduct of inquests. The Fourth Shipman Report which was published in July 2004[14] considered the regulation of controlled drugs in the community (see Chapter 28).

> **Box 29.3** Summary of the recommendations of the Shipman Inquiry into death and cremation certification and the role of the coroner
>
> + Future of the coronial system
> + Aim and purposes of the new coroner service
> + Need for leadership, training and expertise in the coroner service
> + Structure and organisation of the coroner service
> + Death certification
> + Registration
> + Further investigation
> + Pathology services
> + Statutory duty to report concerns about a death
> + Public education
> + Audit and appeal
> + Transitional arrangements
> + The future

The Fifth Report of this inquiry was published in December 2004.[15] It considered the handling of complaints against GPs, the raising of concerns about GPs, the procedures of the General Medical Council and the revalidation of doctors and made significant recommendations for the more effective regulation of GPs. Many of the detailed changes for GMC procedures recommended in the Fifth Shipman Report could also apply, where appropriate, to the NMC as could the results from a review carried out by the Chief Medical Officer. The Sixth and final Shipman Report considered how many patients Shipman killed during his career as a junior doctor at Pontefract General Infirmary and in his time at Hyde.[16]

The inquiry recommended that a new coronial system should be established that would provide an independent, cohesive system of death investigation and certification, readily accessible and understood by the public. It should seek to establish the cause of every death and to record the formal details accurately for the purposes of registration and the collection of mortality statistics. It should seek to meet the needs and expectations of the bereaved and its procedures should be designed to detect cases of homicide, medical error and neglect. It should provide a thorough and open investigation of all deaths giving rise to public concern. It should ensure that the knowledge gained from death investigation is applied for the prevention of avoidable death and injury in the future. The legal and medical functions of the coroner's office should be carried out respectively by a judicial and medical coroner who should be independent officeholders under the Crown. The Coroner Service should have a corps of trained investigators, who would be the mainstays of the new system. The Coroner Service should be an executive non-departmental public body, independent of the Department for Constitutional Affairs (now the Ministry of Justice) and the Department of Health. A board should govern the service and formulate policy, strategic direction and the promotion of public education of its work. Three members of the board would be the Chief Judicial Coroner, the Chief Medical Coroner and the Chief Coroner's Investigator. There should also be an advisory council.

Recommendations for death certification are that there should be one system for death certification for all deaths, whether death is to be followed by burial or cremation. Two forms will need to be completed: Form 1 would provide an official record of the fact and circumstances of death and be completed by a doctor, accredited nurse or paramedic or a trained and accredited coroner's investigator who confirmed that death had occurred. Form 2 would be completed by the doctor who had treated the deceased person during the last illness or if no doctor had treated the deceased person in the recent past, by the deceased's usual medical practitioner. Form 2 would contain a brief summary of the deceased person's recent medical history and the chain of events leading to death and the doctor could express an opinion as to the cause of death. There would be a statutory duty on doctors to complete the death certificate and the General Medical Council should impose a professional duty for doctors to cooperate with the death certification system.

All deaths would be reported to the Coroner Service, which would have responsibility for certification of death and decide if further investigation were necessary. Where Form 2 stated the doctor's opinion as to the cause of death, the coroner's investigator would consult with the deceased's family and decide if certification could proceed. There should be random and targeted checks to consider whether fuller investigation is required. A new certificate of cause of death should be completed by the coroner's investigator or if an investigation has been undertaken by the medical coroner. There should only be an inquest in a case in which the public interest requires a public investigation for reasons connected with the facts and circumstances of the individual case and decided by the judicial coroner. There would be a mandatory inquest in a few specified circumstances. Where an inquest was not held, a report of further investigations would be prepared by the medical and/or judicial coroner, explaining how and why the deceased died. Any recommendation of the medical or judicial coroner should be submitted to the Chief Coroners, who should take it forward. Statutory powers including powers of entry, search and seizure of documents should be given to the coroners. The family should have the right to appeal against an autopsy being held or to make representations for one to be held. Detailed proposals are made for the investigations by the medical and judicial coroners. The relationship between criminal proceedings relating to a death and investigations by the Health and Safety Executive and the medical and judicial coroners are also spelt out. Deaths which were or might be caused or contributed to by medical error or neglect should be investigated by the Coroner Service, initially by the medical coroner and if after investigation it appears that the death might have been caused or contributed to by medical error or neglect, the case should be referred to the regional coroner's office for investigation by the regional medical coroner and judicial coroner. The recommended statutory duty to report concerns about a death should be placed on any 'qualified' or 'responsible' person. Employers should encourage employees to report any concerns relating to the cause or circumstances of a death and should pass on these reports to the appropriate quarter without delay and without any possibility of the reporter being subject to criticism or reprisal. The public should be educated about the functions of the Coroner Service and should be encouraged to report any concerns about a death. The Report also recommended that there should be a systematic audit of the Coroner Service and rights of appeal.

Following the Third Shipman Report, a position paper was published by the Home Office[17] in March 2004 and constituted the government's response to the Fundamental Review of Death Certification and Coroner Services[18] and the Shipman Inquiry. In February 2006 the Minister of State for Constitutional Affairs announced the implementation of the first set of reforms: those relating to the Coroner Service.[19] Six key reforms were to be introduced:

+ Bereaved people will have a right to contribute to coroners' investigations. They will be able to bring their concerns to coroners even where a death certificate has been issued. A coroners' charter will set out the service bereaved people can expect.

+ A Chief Coroner (accountable to the government) and an advisory Coronial Council would be introduced to provide national leadership, guidance and support. Coroners would continue to be appointed and funded by their local councils and served by coroners' officers drawn from the local police or local authority. The Chief Coroner will have the power to commission audits and inspections and will be responsible for monitoring the coroners' charter for bereaved people. The Chief Coroner will also have power to appoint judges in complex cases. The Coronial Council will include independent lay members and representatives of voluntary groups. It will act as a further check on standards and will advise the Chief Coroner on what service and strategic issues may need further scrutiny.

+ A body of full-time coroners would be created and current boundaries would be reshaped to create a smaller number of coroner jurisdictions. The full-time coroners would be supported by a pool of assistant coroners to act in their absence. All new appointments to the service will be required to have a legal qualification.

+ The investigation and inquest processes would be modernised and coroners would be given new powers to obtain information to help their investigations.

+ In limited and specific cases, such as some suicides and child deaths, coroners will have a new discretion to complete their investigations and decide on the facts without holding inquests, where no public interest is served by doing so.

+ A Chief Medical Adviser will be appointed to support the Chief Coroner to give advice on medical best practice and medical issues related to coroners' investigations.

In addition:

+ At local level funding will be provided to coroners to ensure appropriate local medical advice to support their investigation.

+ Coroners will no longer have the task of determining whether a particular find should be classified as treasure. A new national coroner for treasure will be appointed to take on the work currently undertaken by coroners at local level.

A draft Coroner's Bill, together with a draft charter for the bereaved were published in June 2006 to enable pre-legislative scrutiny to be undertaken by the Select Committee for the Department of Constitutional Affairs. The draft Bill was scrutinised by the DCA Select Committee[20] which made strong criticisms about the fact that many of the proposals contained in the Shipman Report and in the position paper were omitted from the Bill, in particular the changes to the death certification system and a national system for the office of coroner. The Select Committee was also concerned that there was inadequate resourcing of the coronial service. The government responded to these recommendations in November 2006.[21] It did not accept the recommendation that all deaths should be reported to the coroner, since this could lead to unnecessary delays for families in preparing the funeral. It did accept the recommendation that there should be a positive statutory duty for doctors to refer certain categories of death to the coroner and suitable guidance and training to improve doctors' knowledge of death certificate requirements should take place with the GMC and the General Register Office. As a consequence of the Select Committee's recommendations and the government response changes will be required to the draft Bill before its introduction into Parliament. The draft legislative programme for 2007/8 includes the Coroner's Bill but it is unlikely to become law before 2009. The implications for the nurse, if these recommendations are to become law, are significant. Like other health professionals the nurse will have a professional duty to report any concerns that she has about a death. She will also, after the appropriate training, be able to complete the recommended Form 1 and provide an official record of the facts and circumstances of death.

Property of the deceased

When a patient has died, there is an obligation on the staff to ensure that the property is listed and accounted for. Usually, the next of kin will arrange for clothes and small personal items to be taken away. However, any property that looks as though it might be of some value should be handed over to the executor or personal representative only on production of the grant of probate or letters of administration relating to the estate. A form of indemnity may be required to protect the NHS trust. This is the only way in which the NHS trust can defend itself if it is challenged for handing the property over to the wrong person. (See Chapter 25 on property.)

> ### Case 29.2   Property of the deceased[22]
>
> A patient was brought into hospital following a heart attack at a garden centre and was found to be dead on arrival. His widow realised that he was carrying the house keys in his pocket and asked for them so that she could return home. The sister stated that the keys had to be left in the safe until after the post mortem, even though the widow told her that she would not be able to get into her house without them. She returned to the house with her daughter, but was unable to get in and had to hire a locksmith the next day.

Even though the hospital was probably following the set procedure for handling property following an unexpected death which was reported to the coroner, there would appear to be reasonable grounds for permitting the widow to receive the keys, perhaps on receipt of an indemnity. There were no suspicious circumstances relating to the death and the hospital could have safeguarded its position by obtaining the consent of the coroner to the handing over of the keys.

Wills

The best advice to nursing staff in relation to the drawing up or signing of wills for patients is: *do not get involved*. Ideally, if a patient makes it known that he wishes to make his will (the person making a will is known as the *testator*), the unit manager should be advised and the patient's solicitor called. The nurse should not be involved. If there is likely to be any dispute as to the patient's competence to make a will, medical opinion should be obtained to confirm that the patient is mentally competent, since one of the grounds for challenging a will's validity is that the patient lacked the competence to sign it, since he was unaware of the implications of his act. Another ground on which its provisions can be challenged is that the patient was subjected to undue influence at the time of signing it so that its provisions do not represent his real intent. Nursing and medical evidence thus becomes crucial in any such legal dispute. If there is a statement in the medical records that the patient signed his will on such and such a day and that his state of mind was rational, clear and unconfused, while that is not in itself evidence of the truth of what is stated, it should at least contain sufficient information to assist professionals in the recall of events, should they be subjected to cross-examination on the patient's competence or independent state of mind.

> ## Practical Dilemma 29.3   Execution at night
>
> Florence Evans was convinced that she was dying. She fretted that she had not made her will and asked the night sister if she would sign a piece of paper declaring how she would like her property disposed of. The night sister was very reluctant to become involved, although she knew that Florence was, in fact, very ill. Florence showed her the paper on which everything was written and asked her to sign it with the auxiliary as a witness. Just to settle Florence, the night sister agreed and she and the nursing auxiliary together watched Florence sign the piece of paper and then they signed their own names. Florence died that same week.
>
> A few weeks later the sister was told that Florence's daughter was disputing the will which left everything to her two brothers and nothing to her. She said that the formalities were not complied with and that it was not a proper will.

Practical Dilemma 29.3 gives an example of one reason why nursing staff are advised not to become involved with will making. Hospitals should provide advice on what staff should do in this situation. In some hospitals, it would be possible for a sister in this situation to summon the on-call manager to take care of Florence's will. The actual signing and witnessing of the will is known as the *execution* of the will and strict rules are in force in relation to the validity of the process. These have been eased slightly since 1982, but the revised procedures must be strictly followed. Any irregularity in the execution of the will may lead to the will being declared invalid. There are no special forms to be used although these are available. The legal requirements are set out in the following Statute.

> ## Statute   Section 17 Administration of Justice Act 1982 amending Section 9 of the Wills Act 1837
>
> No will shall be valid unless:
>
> + It is in writing and signed by the testator, or by some other person in his presence and by his direction.
> + It appears that the testator intended by his signature to give effect to the will.
> + The signature is made or acknowledged by the testator in the presence of two or more witnesses present at the same time.
> + Each witness either:
>   **(i)** attests and signs the will or
>   **(ii)** acknowledges his signature in the presence of the testator (but not necessarily in the presence of any other witness), but no form of attestation shall be necessary.
>
> Additional requirements:
>
> + the testator must be over 18 (unless in the armed forces or the merchant navy)
> + the testator must have the required mental competence at the time he signs the will.

Any person who signs the will as a witness is prevented from being a beneficiary under the will and this applies to the spouse as well. (In one case where the solicitor allowed the beneficiary's spouse to sign the will, the solicitor was liable for the lost inheritance.) If the testator intends leaving a gift to the NHS trust or its staff, then no one from the NHS trust should be involved in the drawing up or signing of the will, otherwise the gift could be invalidated on the grounds of undue influence.

In Practical Dilemma 29.3, described above, where the sister and the nursing auxiliary witnessed the will, it is unlikely that the will could be declared invalid on the grounds of its actual execution even though it might be challenged on other grounds (the lack of mental competence, undue influence, etc.). However, the possibility of involvement in litigation does illustrate the advantages of nursing staff ensuring that, where possible, the experts are involved.

Conclusions

Significant changes are likely to be made to procedures in the certification of death and in the role of the coroner as a consequence of the recommendations of the Shipman Inquiry. The Coroner's Bill proposed for the draft legislative programme 2007/8 aims at delivering an improved service for bereaved people, introducing national leadership while ensuring that the service remains firmly grounded locally and ensuring more effective investigations and inquests. As a consequence of these reforms, the role of the registered nurse practitioner is likely to be enhanced.

Reflection questions

1 Consider any patient whose death you have witnessed and whose relatives you have had to comfort and assist. Was there any information of which you were ignorant? Could you answer all their questions?

2 In what ways would an inquest differ from a hearing in the criminal or civil courts?

Further exercises

1 Obtain a copy of the local policy and guidelines on dealing with death and familiarise yourself with it.

2 Draft a procedure for preparing a nurse who has been asked to give evidence at an inquest.

3 Obtain a copy of your NHS trust's leaflet for the guidance of patients on the care of property. Does it consider the procedure to be followed at the death of a patient? What precautions would you as a ward sister take to ensure that the property of the deceased was cared for?

References

[1] B. Dimond, *Legal Aspects of Death*, Quay Publications, 2008
[2] Paul Wilkinson, £38,500 for woman given up for dead, *The Times*, 27 September 2000
[3] Royal College of Nursing, Verification of Death by Registered Nurses, Order No. 000594, RCN, May 1996

4 Nursing and Midwifery Council, Confirmation of death A–Z advice sheet, last updated March 2006

5 *R (on the application of Touche)* v. *HM Coroner for Inner North London District* [2001] EWCA Civ 383; [2001] QB 1206 CA

6 *R (on the application of Hurst)* v. *London Northern District Coroner* [2007] UKHL 13; [2007] 2 All ER 1025

7 *Brecknell* v. *United Kingdom*, Application No. 32457/04 (and 4 other applications) The Times Law Report, 7 December 2007

8 Section 11(2) Coroners Act 1988

9 Coroners' Rules 1984, SI 1984 No. 552

10 *R (on the application of Paul and others)* v. *Deputy Coroner of the Queen's Household and Assistant Deputy Coroner for Surrey* [2007] EWHC 408; [2007] 2 All ER 509

11 Shipman Inquiry First Report: Death Disguised, 19 July 2002; www.the-shipman-inquiry.org.uk/reports.asp

12 Shipman Inquiry Second Report: The Police Investigation of March 1998, 14 July 2003; www.the-shipman-inquiry.org.uk/reports.asp

13 Shipman Inquiry Third Report: Death and Cremation Certification, 14 July 2003; www.the-shipman-inquiry.org.uk/reports.asp

14 Shipman Inquiry Fourth Report: The Regulation of Controlled Drugs in the Community, 15 July 2004, Cm 6249, Stationery Office; www.the-shipman-inquiry.org.uk/reports.asp

15 The Shipman Inquiry Fifth Report: Safeguarding Patients: Lessons from the Past – Proposals for the Future, Command Paper Cm 6394, December 2004, Stationery Office; www.the-shipman-inquiry.org.uk/reports.asp

16 The Shipman Inquiry Sixth Report: The Final Report, January 2005, Stationery Office; www.the-shipman-inquiry.org.uk/reports.asp

17 Home Office, Reforming the Coroner and Death Certification Service. A Position Paper, Cm 6159, March 2004, Stationery Office

18 Tom Luce, Chair, Fundamental Review of Death Certification and the Coroner Services in England, Wales and Northern Ireland, Home Office, 2003

19 Department for Constitutional Affairs, Coroners' Service Reform, Briefing Note, February 2006, DCA

20 Department for Constitutional Affairs, Select Committee's Report on the Reform of the Coroners' System and Death Certification, DCA, 2006

21 Government Response to the Report by the Constitutional Affairs Select Committee (Cm 6943, Session 2005–6), November 2006

22 Oliver Wright, Widow forced to break into home, *The Times*, 28 August 2000

Chapter 30
Complementary and alternative therapies

Introduction

A phenomenon in recent years has been the increase in the popularity of complementary and alternative therapies. An information pack for primary care on complementary medicine has been sponsored by the Department of Health.[1] The pack was initiated after a survey found that one in four adults would use alternative therapies at some point in their lives. Other evidence estimates that one-third of the population has tried such remedies or visited such practitioners.[2] The Health Education Authority has published an A–Z guide, which covers 60 therapies.[3] In addition, the House of Lords Select Committee on Science and Technology has reviewed the field of complementary and alternative medicines and made significant recommendations on their control and use within the NHS.[4] Much research needs to be done on the efficacy of these therapies and the Health Authority Council has approved a research project to be undertaken by the National Association of Health Authorities and Trusts (now the NHS Confederation) into the prevalence of complementary therapies and their services for patients, purchasers and providers.[5] A chair in complementary therapy has been provided at Exeter University. The Prince of Wales suggested the setting up of a group to consider the current positions of orthodox, complementary and alternative medicine in the UK and how far it would be appropriate and possible for them to work more closely together. Four working groups looking at research and development, education and training, regulation and delivery mechanisms were established under a steering group chaired by Dr Manon Williams, Assistant Private Secretary to HRH the Prince of Wales. It reported in 1997 and made extensive recommendations.[6] These include encouraging more research and the dissemination of its results; emphasising the common elements in the core curriculum of all healthcare workers, orthodox and complementary and alternative medicine; establishing statutory self-regulatory bodies for those professions that could endanger patient safety; identifing areas of conventional medicine and nursing that are not meeting patients' needs at present. It also recommended the establishment of an Independent Standards Commission for Complementary and Alternative Medicine. In December 2004 the Prince of Wales Foundation for Integrated Health was given £900,000 by the Department of Health to support its work in developing robust systems of regulation for the main complementary healthcare professions. There is every likelihood that more and more pressure will be provided for various complementary therapies to be made available on the NHS. For example, at its conference in 2000, the BMA pressed the government to make acupuncture available on the NHS. Many GP practices are now providing complementary therapy services to their patients. The Department of Health has established working groups that looked at state regulation for herbal medicines and acupuncture (see below). The RCN provided guidance to its members on complementary therapies in 2003, updated in 2007.[7]

This chapter looks at the legal implications of complementary therapy practice for nurses, midwives and health visitors in two respects: one as a practitioner of a complementary therapy alongside the skills for which they are registered with the NMC; the other as a carer of patients who may be receiving complementary therapies as well as care from traditional medicine. For more detailed information on the legal aspects of complementary therapies, see the author's work.[8] Reference should also be made to the many books written by nurses about individual complementary therapies.[9] Further information can be obtained from the website of the Complementary Healthcare Information Service.[10]

Definitions of complementary and alternative therapies

It is perhaps easier to define complementary and alternative therapy negatively in the sense that it is treatment for which health-giving or disease-repelling properties are claimed that are not yet accepted by those who practise orthodox medicine. If this definition is used, it could be argued that chiropractic and osteopathy were once, but are no longer, complementary therapies, but by becoming state-registered professions are now accepted as part of orthodox medicine and there are referrals funded by the NHS. If this definition is used, it would follow that homeopathy has long been part of orthodox medicine; since the Faculty of Homeopathy was established in 1848, five schools of homeopathy have been established and both the schools and the hospitals receive state support. The Cochrane Collaboration defines complementary and alternative medicine as:

A broad domain of healing resources that encompasses all health systems, modalities and practices and their accompanying theories and beliefs, other than those intrinsic to the politically dominant health systems of a particular society or culture in a given historical period.[11]

The term 'complementary and alternative therapy' covers a wide range of practices from the well-established field of homeopathy to claims in respect of dowsing, radionics and astrology. The Health Professions Council, which replaced the Council for the Professions Supplementary to Medicine in 2002, has the capacity to recognise new registered professions. The HPC has published guidelines setting criteria on opening new parts of the Register.[12] Each applicant organisation must: cover a discrete area of activity displaying some homogeneity; apply a defined body of knowledge; practise based on evidence of efficacy; have at least one established professional body which accounts for a significant proportion of that occupational group; operate a voluntary register; have defined routes of entry to the profession; have independently assessed entry qualifications; have standards in relation to conduct, performance and ethics; have fitness to practise procedures to enforce those standards; be committed to continuous professional development. Over 53 organisations have sought statutory registration from the HPC including the Acupuncture Regulatory Working Group, the British Society of Clinical Hypnosis and the Craniosacral Therapy Association of the UK. Once the Council has approved an application, an HPC recommendation and an accompanying report to regulate the profession is submitted to the Secretary of State. If the Secretary of State agrees with the application, an order will be drawn up under Section 60 of the Health Act 1999, submitted for consultation, if necessary amended and then placed before Parliament.

The NMC practitioner as a complementary therapist

The NMC has provided guidance in the use of complementary and alternative therapies in the Code, its guidelines for the administration of medicines and in its A–Z advice sheet.[13] It states that registered practitioners:

> *3.11 . . . must ensure that the use of complementary or alternative therapies is safe and in the interests of patients and clients. This must be discussed with the team as part of the therapeutic process and the patient or client must consent to their use.*

An NMC practitioner who has been trained in a complementary therapy may wish to use it for the benefit of her NHS patients. She may, for example, have acquired skills in aromatherapy, reflexology or acupuncture and believe that these may be more effective in reducing pain or relaxing the patient than medication. What restrictions would there be on her practising her additional skills?

The NMC suggests that employers may wish to have a policy covering the use of complementary and alternative therapies. This should include details about the information that should be given to the employer about qualifications and membership of the relevant associations. Unfortunately, there are considerable variations in the standards of training required and many therapies do not have a single overall professional body that sets standards. West Yorkshire has issued guidance on the information that should be retained by employers about the complementary therapies that staff may wish to practise.[14] The consent of the employer must be obtained as the following situation indicates.

Practical Dilemma 30.1   Aromatherapy without consent

Brenda was an ITU nurse who had undertaken a course in aromatherapy. She knew that it would be relaxing and beneficial to the ventilated patients she was caring for and wished to use aromatherapy oils on them. Her employers were prepared to give consent to her using aromatherapy, but their policy on the use of complementary and alternative therapies required employees to obtain the consent of patients before initiating any treatment. Since most of Brenda's adult patients were unconscious and relatives could not give a valid consent on their behalf, she was thwarted in her plans. What is the law?

It is entirely reasonable for the employer to lay down instructions and protocols for the use of non-orthodox treatments. The requirement of the patient's consent is also consistent with the legal situation. Brenda, therefore, has to accept that until such time, if ever, aromatherapy becomes a recognised part of traditional nursing and medicine and could therefore be used in the best interests of a mentally incompetent patient, she would be unable to use it in ITU, unless she has the patient's consent when mentally capable.

Liability for using complementary therapy at work

If consent is not obtained from the employer but the nurse practises her complementary therapy skills during her work, there could be serious consequences for the nurse. On the one hand, she has disobeyed the reasonable instructions of the employer and she therefore faces disciplinary action, including dismissal. On the other hand, if she causes harm to the patient, she may face personal liability for the harm that she has caused, since the employer might deny that it is vicariously liable for an employee who is disobeying reasonable instructions and who is not therefore acting in the course of employment (see Chapter 4). Even if this argument by the employer did not succeed, since it could be held that the employee is still acting in the employer's interests, the employer might claim from the employee an indemnity for any compensation that it has to pay to the injured patient.

In contrast, if the employee *has* obtained consent from the employer and is working within the guidelines set by the employer, not only would there be no justification for disciplinary action, but if harm were to occur to the patient as the result of negligence by the practitioner, the employer would be vicariously liable for that harm.

Different issues arise if the practitioner wishes to use her complementary therapy skills out of working hours but on the employer's premises, as the following case shows.

Case 30.1   *Watling v. Gloucester County Council* (1995)

Private practice in working hours[15]

An occupational therapist was dismissed when he saw private patients for alternative therapy during working hours. His application for unfair dismissal failed. He had been warned by his employers not to conduct his private business during his working hours and that lunchtimes were for a break, not for private work.

It may be that as the clinical effectiveness of certain therapies is established, then employers will fund study leave for practitioners to develop these new skills as part of the scope of their professional practice (see Chapter 24). At this point, some of these therapies might be seen as part of the reasonable standard of care to be provided to a patient and could then be given to mentally incapacitated adults in their best interests.

Notifying the patients of risks of complementary therapy

There appears to be a common fallacy that complementary and alternative therapies, being natural, can do only good and not harm and there are no risks attached. However, this is not correct as some of the cases reported in the author's work show.[16] Any significant risks, which reasonable professional practice would suggest should be made known to the patient, must be explained to the patient before consent is obtained. Exactly the same principles apply in complementary therapies to the obtaining of consent and the information to be given to a patient as apply in orthodox medicine. These are discussed in Chapter 7. If, for example, a patient were to be given acupuncture and suffered harm, it would be a defence if the defendant could show that there was no negligence on the part of the practitioner, that the patient had given a valid consent and that information about significant risks of substantial harm had been notified by the practitioner to the patient. There are obviously advantages if this information could be conveyed both in writing as well as by word of mouth. The Bolam Test[17] standard would apply as to what information should be given. It may, however, be more difficult to establish this in non-orthodox medicine.

It might be asked if liability for harm in complementary therapies could be excluded by reference to a notice. The Unfair Contract Terms Act 1977 would prevent any exclusion of liability if negligence by the therapist caused personal injury or death (see Chapter 6).

Patients receiving complementary therapies

If it is found that the patient, in addition to being treated by orthodox medicine, is also in receipt of complementary and alternative therapies, then care must be taken to ensure that there are no contraindications between the two treatments and as much information as possible is obtained about the other treatment. The patient may agree to give the name of the complementary therapist who could be contacted for details of their treatment and treatment plan. It may be, for example, that the patient is given conflicting advice: in such a situation, good communication is essential between the orthodox practitioners and the complementary therapist. There are considerable advantages in NMC practitioners obtaining a good understanding of the complementary therapies that their patients are most likely to be using, so that the practitioner can understand the implications for orthodox medicine and know where to obtain further advice and information.[18]

The consent of the client must be obtained, as the following situation indicates.

Practical Dilemma 30.2 Herbal medicine

Daphne asked a patient about the various bottles that she saw on her bedside locker. The patient explained that she was receiving herbal medicine for her arthritis. Daphne asked for details about what she was taking, but the patient said it was nothing to do with Daphne or her stay in hospital because she was being treated for a heart condition. Where does Daphne stand in law?

There are clear dangers here, since it could be that the herbal preparations could react against any medication given for the patient's heart condition or could even exacerbate the condition. Daphne should ensure that the medical staff are aware of the situation and it might be advisable to arrange for the pharmacist to see the patient and try to persuade her to disclose sufficient details about the herbal preparations and the herbalist advising the patient so that any necessary action can be taken to ensure that the patient is safe.

The NMC reported in its news service in January 2004[19] that cancer patients may be risking dangerous side effects by taking herbal remedies or supplements alongside their conventional treatment. A study at the Royal Marsden Hospital in London found that more than half the 300 patients studied took some form of complementary medicine. The NMC reminded practitioners of their Code of Professional Conduct, which requires practitioners to ensure that the use of complementary and alternative therapies is safe and in the interests of patients and clients, and referred them to more detailed guidance in the advice section on its website.[20]

Case 30.2 — *Shakoor (Deceased) v. Situ (2000)*

Standard of care of a complementary therapist[21]

S, who was suffering from a skin condition, consulted a practitioner of traditional Chinese herbal medicine. After taking nine doses of the herbal remedy, S became ill and later died of acute liver failure, which was attributable to a rare and unpredictable reaction to the remedy. His widow brought proceedings against the practitioner, but failed. The High Court held that on the evidence before it the actions of the practitioner had been consistent with the standard of care appropriate to traditional Chinese herbal medicine in accordance with established requirements.

House of Lords Select Committee

In November 2000, the Scientific Committee of the House of Lords[22] reported that there should be regulations of complementary and alternative medicines (CAM) and there should be further research to evaluate their effectiveness. It divided such therapies into three groups:

1 *Professionally organised therapies*, where there is some scientific evidence of their success, although seldom of the highest quality, and there are recognised systems for treatment and training of practitioners. This group includes acupuncture, chiropractic, herbal medicine, homoeopathy and osteopathy.

2 *Complementary medicines* where evidence that they work is generally lacking, but which are used as an adjunct rather than a replacement for conventional therapies, so that lack of evidence may not matter so much. Included in this group are Alexander technique, aromatherapy, nutritional medicine, hypnotherapy and Bach and other flower remedies.

3 *Techniques that offer diagnosis as well as treatment*, but for which scientific evidence is almost completely lacking. This group cannot be supported and includes naturopathy, crystal therapy, kinesiology, radionics, dowsing and iridology.

The Select Committee of the House of Lords considered that some remedies such as acupuncture and aromatherapy should be available on the NHS and NHS patients should have wider access to osteopathy and chiropractic. The implementation of these recommendations has led to the establishment of working groups. Eventually there will be fundamental changes in how complementary and alternative therapies are viewed in relation to orthodox medicine and within the NHS.

Herbal medicines, acupuncture and research

Working groups established by the Department of Health to consider the regulation of herbal medicine practitioners and acupuncturists[23] put forward proposals that herbalists will have to register with a new governing body to be eligible to practise and some herbal treatments will only be available from licensed practitioners.[24] These proposals were put out to consultation and the Department published an analysis of responses to the consultation in February 2005.[25] Its intention was to publish a draft Section 60 (Health Act 1999) Order for consultation on a new Complementary and Alternative Medicine Council for the regulation of herbal medicine and acupuncture in the latter part of 2005. This is still awaited.

State registration is not the only form of regulations and where medicinal products are concerned the MHRA is the enforcement agency. It carried out a public consultation on the regulation of herbal medicines at the same time as the Department of Health[26] and warned in September 2004 of the dangers because of the quality of traditional Chinese medicines. A European Directive on Traditional Herbal Medicinal Products[27] setting out the safety and quality of over-the-counter traditional herbal medicines[28] was implemented in October 2005.[29] Further details of the implications and the transitional regulations can be obtained from the website of the Medicines and Healthcare products Regulations Agency. In February 2007 a Chinese woman was prosecuted for selling customers boar bile, antelope and rare orchids as Chinese cures.[30]

The Department of Health announced a new consolidated, multi-purpose, 'pick and mix' set of model byelaws that can be used for one, several or all types of skin-piercing/skin-colouring that are currently regulated.[31]

A strategy to develop research capacity in complementary and alternative medicine[32] was put forward and the Department of Health invited higher education institutions (HEIs) to register their interest in hosting research into this field.[33] The value of complementary and alternative medicine is increasingly likely to feature as a field of enquiry in general research into specific conditions: thus a study was carried out on the use of complementary and alternative therapies among people undergoing cancer treatment. It reported in January 2006[34] and its report is available on the DH website.[35] CAM were used by slightly less than one-third of the group studied, not to treat the cancer but to manage the day-to-day effects of cancer, its treatment and to counter the side effects of treatment. More would have used CAM had more information and guidance been available. The report concluded that more research was needed on the interface between conventional cancer treatment and CAM and their safety. A report of the working group looking at chronic fatigue syndrome (CFS/ME) considered patients' views on the use of CAM and their value in the management of the illness.[36] A Complementary and Alternative Medicine Council has not yet been set up and the Health Professions Council is reviewing applications for state registration.

Conclusions

The RCN noted in its report on the views of nurses on the future[37] that there had been a burgeoning of interest in complementary therapies in recent years and many nurses had undertaken some form of training in various therapies. However, they were encountering difficulties in integrating them into mainstream services. There was widespread misunderstanding of their use and effectiveness in nursing, too much variation in quality and content of courses available and concerns that attaching these therapies to the old medical model would negate their potential as enhancers of holistic care. The RCN has published guidance on the integration of complementary therapies into clinical practice.[38] Some of the concerns highlighted by the RCN may gradually be resolved by the proposed establishment of a Complementary and Alternative Medicine Council, which, if it goes ahead, may in future include registration provision for other CAM therapists as well as herbalists and acupuncturists. In the meantime several CAMs are applying to the HPC for statutory regulation. The increasing popularity of complementary therapies is accompanied by concerns about their safety and there is still pressure for more research to establish their safety and effectiveness to be carried out and national standards published. In addition, patients are seeking for various therapies to be available within the NHS. Their likely success will depend considerably on the extent to which research can show that there is clear clinical evidence to establish their effectiveness over orthodox medicine alternatives and their endorsement by NICE. In May 2007 it was reported that more than half of the PCTs in England were refusing to pay for homeopathy and other CAMs, on the grounds that their treatments are unproved or disproved.[39]

Reflection questions

1 You have decided that you would like to undertake training in aromatherapy and eventually use it as part of your practice as a clinical nurse specialist in intensive care. What actions would you take to ensure that your plans are compatible with your role as a registered nurse?

2 Identify the ways in which the knowledge that a patient was receiving complementary therapy treatment could affect the care that you give that person.

Further exercises

1 Do you consider that those complementary therapists who so wished should be permitted to have registered status under the Health Professions Council? (Refer also to Chapter 11.) If not, what criteria would you lay down for a profession to receive registered status?

2 Do you consider that patients should be under an obligation to inform their NHS carers if they are receiving complementary therapies?

3 Obtain a copy of the House of Lords Select Committee Report and consider the extent to which it could be implemented within the NHS and the likely consequences of its recommendations.

References

1 Complementary Medicine Information Pack for Primary Care; www.dh.gov.uk

2 Jeremy Laurance, Alternative health: an honest alternative or just magic? *The Times*, 5 February 1996

3 Health Education Authority, A-Z Guide on Complementary Therapies, HEA, London, 1995

[4] House of Lords Select Committee on Science and Technology, 6th Report: complementary and alternafive medicine, Session 1999–2000, 21 November 2000

[5] www.nhsconfed.org

[6] Integrated Healthcare: a way forward for the next five years, Foundation for Integrated Medicine, 1997

[7] Royal College of Nursing, Complementary Therapies in Nursing, Midwifery and Health Visiting Practice, Order No. 002 204, RCN, October 2007

[8] B.C. Dimond, *Legal Aspects of Complementary Therapy Practice*, Churchill Livingstone, Edinburgh, 1998

[9] See, in particular, Denise Rankin-Box (ed.) *The Nurse's Handbook of Complementary Therapies*, Churchill Livingstone, Edinburgh, 1995

[10] www.chisuk.org.uk

[11] www.dh.gov.uk/en/Policyandguidance/Healthandsocialcare

[12] http://www.hpc-uk.org/aboutregistration/new/criteria/

[13] www.nmc-uk.org/; Para 3.11 Code of Professional Conduct: standards for conduct, performance and ethics, NMC, 2004

[14] News item, *Medical Law Monitor*, Jan/Feb 1996, pp. 6–8

[15] *Watling* v. *Gloucester County Council* Employment Tribunal EAT/868/94, 17 March 1995, 23 November 1994, Lexis transcript

[16] B.C. Dimond, *Legal Aspects of Complementary Therapy Practice*, Churchill Livingstone, Edinburgh, 1998

[17] *Bolam* v. *Friern Barnet HMC* [1957] 2 All ER 118

[18] Royal Council for Complementary Medicine, Tel. 0207 833 8897; Institute for Complementary Medicine, Tel. 0207 237 5165; British Medical Association, *Complementary Medicine: New Approaches to Good Practice*, OUP/BMA, Oxford 1993; links to alternative medicine sites: www.medic.org.uk/altmed

[19] *Nursing and Midwifery Council News*, Herbal remedy warning for cancer patients, 21 January 2004

[20] www.nmc-uk.org/nmc

[21] *Shakoor (Deceased)* v. *Situ* [2000] 4 All ER 181

[22] House of Lords Select Committee on Science and Technology, 6th Report: complementary and alternative medicine, Session 1999–2000, 21 November 2000

[23] www.dh.gov.uk/herbalmedicinewg/index.htm and www.dh.gov.uk/acupuncturewg/index.htm

[24] Oliver Wright, Chris Johnston and Rosemary Bennett, Clampdown on alternative medicines, *The Times*, 20 September 2003

[25] Statutory regulation of herbal medicine and acupuncture: Report of the consultation 2005; available on the DH website

[26] www.mhra.gov.uk

[27] European Directive, Traditional Herbal Medicines, 2004/24/EC

[28] www.mhra.gov.uk

[29] Medicines (Traditional Herbal Medicinal Products for Human Use) Regulations 2005, SI 2005 No. 2750

[30] Nicola Woolcock, Woman traded bear bile, antelope and rare orchids as Chinese cures, *The Times*, 15 February 2007, p. 3

[31] DH updated model byelaws for the regulation of acupuncture, tattooing, semi-permanent skin-colouring etc., September 2006

[32] Alison Pighills and Cliff Bailey, Developing Research Capacity in Complementary and Alternative Medicine: a strategy for action, DH, London, April 2002

[33] www.dh.gov.uk/research/rd1/cam.htm

[34] Professor Jessica Corner and others, A study of the use of complementary and alternative therapists among people undergoing cancer treatment: A quantative and qualitative study. Final Report, Department of Health and University of Southampton, January 2006.

[35] www.dh.gov.uk/research/rd3/nhsandd/cam/28_02.htm

[36] www.dh.gov.uk/cmo/cfsmereport/

[37] Royal College of Nursing, Imagining the Future Nursing in the New Millennium, Order No. 000912, RCN, August 1998

[38] Royal College of Nursing, Complementary Therapies in Nursing: Midwifery and health visiting, Order No. 002 204, RCN, 2007; www.rcn.org.uk/direct

[39] Mark Henderson, Hard-up NHS cuts back on homoepathy, *The Times*, 23 May 2007, p. 9

Appendix A
Articles of the European Convention on Human Rights

SCHEDULE 1

OF THE HUMAN RIGHTS ACT 1998

THE ARTICLES

PART I

THE CONVENTION

RIGHTS AND FREEDOMS

Article 2

Right to life

1. Everyone's right to life shall be protected by law. No one shall be deprived of his life intentionally save in the execution of a sentence of a court following his conviction of a crime for which this penalty is provided by law.

2. Deprivation of life shall not be regarded as inflicted in contravention of this Article when it results from the use of force which is no more than absolutely necessary:

(a) in defence of any person from unlawful violence;

(b) in order to effect a lawful arrest or to prevent the escape of a person lawfully detained;

(c) in action lawfully taken for the purpose of quelling a riot or insurrection.

Article 3

Prohibition of torture

No one shall be subjected to torture or to inhuman or degrading treatment or punishment.

Article 4

Prohibition of slavery and forced labour

1. No one shall be held in slavery or servitude.

2. No one shall be required to perform forced or compulsory labour.

3. For the purpose of this Article the term 'forced or compulsory labour' shall not include:

(a) any work required to be done in the ordinary course of detention imposed according to the provisions of Article 5 of this Convention or during conditional release from such detention;

(b) any service of a military character or, in case of conscientious objectors in countries where they are recognised, service exacted instead of compulsory military service;

(c) any service exacted in case of an emergency or calamity threatening the life or well-being of the community;

(d) any work or service which forms part of normal civic obligations.

Article 5

Right to liberty and security

1. Everyone has the right to liberty and security of person. No one shall be deprived of his liberty save in the following cases and in accordance with a procedure prescribed by law:

(a) the lawful detention of a person after conviction by a competent court;

(b) the lawful arrest or detention of a person for non-compliance with the lawful order of a court or in order to secure the fulfilment of any obligation prescribed by law;

(c) the lawful arrest or detention of a person effected for the purpose of bringing him before the competent legal authority on reasonable suspicion of having committed an offence or when it is reasonably considered necessary to prevent his committing an offence or fleeing after having done so;

(d) the detention of a minor by lawful order for the purpose of educational supervision or his lawful detention for the purpose of bringing him before the competent legal authority;

(e) the lawful detention of persons for the prevention of the spreading of infectious diseases, of persons of unsound mind, alcoholics or drug addicts or vagrants;

(f) the lawful arrest or detention of a person to prevent his effecting an unauthorised entry into the country or of a person against whom action is being taken with a view to deportation or extradition.

2. Everyone who is arrested shall be informed promptly, in a language which he understands, of the reasons for his arrest and of any charge against him.

3. Everyone arrested or detained in accordance with the provisions of paragraph 1(c) of this Article shall be brought promptly before a judge or other officer authorised by law to exercise judicial power and shall be entitled to trial within a reasonable time or to release pending trial. Release may be conditioned by guarantees to appear for trial.

4. Everyone who is deprived of his liberty by arrest or detention shall be entitled to take proceedings by which the lawfulness of his detention shall be decided speedily by a court and his release ordered if the detention is not lawful.

5. Everyone who has been the victim of arrest or detention in contravention of the provisions of this Article shall have an enforceable right to compensation.

Article 6

Right to a fair trial

1. In the determination of his civil rights and obligations or of any criminal charge against him, everyone is entitled to a fair and public hearing within a reasonable time by an independent

and impartial tribunal established by law. Judgment shall be pronounced publicly but the press and public may be excluded from all or part of the trial in the interest of morals, public order or national security in a democratic society, where the interests of juveniles or the protection of the private life of the parties so require, or to the extent strictly necessary in the opinion of the court in special circumstances where publicity would prejudice the interests of justice.

2. Everyone charged with a criminal offence shall be presumed innocent until proved guilty according to law.

3. Everyone charged with a criminal offence has the following minimum rights:

(a) to be informed promptly, in a language which he understands and in detail, of the nature and cause of the accusation against him;

(b) to have adequate time and facilities for the preparation of his defence;

(c) to defend himself in person or through legal assistance of his own choosing or, if he has not sufficient means to pay for legal assistance, to be given it free when the interests of justice so require;

(d) to examine or have examined witnesses against him and to obtain the attendance and examination of witnesses on his behalf under the same conditions as witnesses against him;

(e) to have the free assistance of an interpreter if he cannot understand or speak the language used in court.

Article 7

No punishment without law

1. No one shall be held guilty of any criminal offence on account of any act or omission which did not constitute a criminal offence under national or international law at the time when it was committed. Nor shall a heavier penalty be imposed than the one that was applicable at the time the criminal offence was committed.

2. This Article shall not prejudice the trial and punishment of any person for any act or omission which, at the time when it was committed, was criminal according to the general principles of law recognised by civilised nations.

Article 8

Right to respect for private and family life

1. Everyone has the right to respect for his private and family life, his home and his correspondence.

2. There shall be no interference by a public authority with the exercise of this right except such as is in accordance with the law and is necessary in a democratic society in the interests of national security, public safety or the economic well-being of the country, for the prevention of disorder or crime, for the protection of health or morals, or for the protection of the rights and freedoms of others.

Article 9

Freedom of thought, conscience and religion

1. Everyone has the right to freedom of thought, conscience and religion; this right includes freedom to change his religion or belief and freedom, either alone or in community with others and in public or private, to manifest his religion or belief, in worship, teaching, practice and observance.

2. Freedom to manifest one's religion or beliefs shall be subject only to such limitations as are prescribed by law and are necessary in a democratic society in the interests of public safety, for the protection of public order, health or morals, or for the protection of the rights and freedoms of others.

Article 10

Freedom of expression

1. Everyone has the right to freedom of expression. This right shall include freedom to hold opinions and to receive and impart information and ideas without interference by public authority and regardless of frontiers. This Article shall not prevent States from requiring the licensing of broadcasting, television or cinema enterprises.

2. The exercise of these freedoms, since it carries with it duties and responsibilities, may be subject to such formalities, conditions, restrictions or penalties as are prescribed by law and are necessary in a democratic society, in the interests of national security, territorial integrity or public safety, for the prevention of disorder or crime, for the protection of health or morals, for the protection of the reputation or rights of others, for preventing the disclosure of information received in confidence, or for maintaining the authority and impartiality of the judiciary.

Article 11

Freedom of assembly and association

1. Everyone has the right to freedom of peaceful assembly and to freedom of association with others, including the right to form and to join trade unions for the protection of his interests.

2. No restrictions shall be placed on the exercise of these rights other than such as are prescribed by law and are necessary in a democratic society in the interests of national security or public safety, for the prevention of disorder or crime, for the protection of health or morals or for the protection of the rights and freedoms of others. This Article shall not prevent the imposition of lawful restrictions on the exercise of these rights by members of the armed forces, of the police or of the administration of the State.

Article 12

Right to marry

Men and women of marriageable age have the right to marry and to found a family, according to the national laws governing the exercise of this right.

Article 14

Prohibition of discrimination

The enjoyment of the rights and freedoms set forth in this Convention shall be secured without discrimination on any ground such as sex, race, colour, language, religion, political or other opinion, national or social origin, association with a national minority, property, birth or other status.

Article 16

Restrictions on political activity of aliens

Nothing in Articles 10, 11 and 14 shall be regarded as preventing the High Contracting Parties from imposing restrictions on the political activity of aliens.

Article 17

Prohibition of abuse of rights

Nothing in this Convention may be interpreted as implying for any State, group or person any right to engage in any activity or perform any act aimed at the destruction of any of the rights and freedoms set forth herein or at their limitation to a greater extent than is provided for in the Convention.

Article 18

Limitation on use of restrictions on rights

The restrictions permitted under this Convention to the said rights and freedoms shall not be applied for any purpose other than those for which they have been prescribed.

PART II

THE FIRST PROTOCOL

Article 1

Protection of property

Every natural or legal person is entitled to the peaceful enjoyment of his possessions. No one shall be deprived of his possessions except in the public interest and subject to the conditions provided for by law and by the general principles of international law.

The preceding provisions shall not, however, in any way impair the right of a State to enforce such laws as it deems necessary to control the use of property in accordance with the general interest or to secure the payment of taxes or other contributions or penalties.

Article 2

Right to education

No person shall be denied the right to education. In the exercise of any functions which it assumes in relation to education and to teaching, the State shall respect the right of parents to ensure such education and teaching in conformity with their own religious and philosophical convictions.

Article 3

Right to free elections

The High Contracting Parties undertake to hold free elections at reasonable intervals by secret ballot, under conditions which will ensure the free expression of the opinion of the people in the choice of the legislature.

PART III

THE SIXTH PROTOCOL

Article 1

Abolition of the death penalty

The death penalty shall be abolished. No one shall be condemned to such penalty or executed.

Article 2

Death penalty in time of war

A State may make provision in its law for the death penalty in respect of acts committed in time of war or of imminent threat of war; such penalty shall be applied only in the instances laid down in the law and in accordance with its provisions. The State shall communicate to the Secretary General of the Council of Europe the relevant provisions of that law.

Section 10   # SCHEDULE 2

REMEDIAL ORDERS

Orders

1. (1) A remedial order may:
    (a) contain such incidental, supplemental, consequential or transitional provision as the person making it considers appropriate;
    (b) be made so as to have effect from a date earlier than that on which it is made;
    (c) make provision for the delegation of specific functions;
    (d) make different provision for different cases.
   (2) The power conferred by sub-paragraph (1)(a) includes:
    (a) power to amend primary legislation (including primary legislation other than that which contains the incompatible provision); and
    (b) power to amend or revoke subordinate legislation (including subordinate legislation other than that which contains the incompatible provision).
   (3) A remedial order may be made so as to have the same extent as the legislation which it affects.
   (4) No person is to be guilty of an offence solely as a result of the retrospective effect of a remedial order.

Procedure

2. No remedial order may be made unless:
    (a) a draft of the order has been approved by a resolution of each House of Parliament made after the end of the period of 60 days beginning with the day on which the draft was laid; or

(b) it is declared in the order that it appears to the person making it that, because of the urgency of the matter, it is necessary to make the order without a draft being so approved.

Orders laid in draft

3. (1) No draft may be laid under paragraph 2(a) unless:
   (a) the person proposing to make the order has laid before Parliament a document which contains a draft of the proposed order and the required information; and
   (b) the period of 60 days, beginning with the day on which the document required by this sub-paragraph was laid, has ended.
   (2) If representations have been made during that period, the draft laid under paragraph 2(a) must be accompanied by a statement containing:
   (a) a summary of the representations; and
   (b) if, as a result of the representations, the proposed order has been changed, details of the changes.

Appendix B
Congenital Disabilities (Civil Liability) Act 1976 (1976 c 28)

1   Civil liability to child born disabled

(1) If a child is born disabled as the result of such an occurrence before its birth as is mentioned in subsection (2) below, and a person (other than the child's own mother) is under this section answerable to the child in respect of the occurrence, the child's disabilities are to be regarded as damage resulting from the wrongful act of that person and actionable accordingly at the suit of the child.

(2) An occurrence to which this section applies is one which:
   (a) affected either parent of the child in his or her ability to have a normal, healthy child; or
   (b) affected the mother during her pregnancy, or affected her or the child in the course of its birth, so that the child is born with disabilities which would not otherwise have been present.

(3) Subject to the following subsections, a person (here referred to as 'the defendant') is answerable to the child if he was liable in tort to the parent or would, if sued in due time, have been so; and it is no answer that there could not have been such liability because the parent suffered no actionable injury, if there was a breach of legal duty which, accompanied by injury, would have given rise to the liability.

(4) In the case of an occurrence preceding the time of conception, the defendant is not answerable to the child if at that time either or both of the parents knew the risk of their child being born disabled (that is to say, the particular risk created by the occurrence); but should it be the child's father who is the defendant, this subsection does not apply if he knew of the risk and the mother did not.

(5) The defendant is not answerable to the child, for anything he did or omitted to do when responsible in a professional capacity for treating or advising the parent, if he took reasonable care having due regard to then received professional opinion applicable to the particular class of case; but this does not mean that he is answerable only because he departed from received opinion.

(6) Liability to the child under this section may be treated as having been excluded or limited by contract made with the parent affected, to the same extent and subject to the same restrictions as liability in the parent's own case; and a contract term which could have been set up by the defendant in an action by the parent, so as to exclude or limit his liability to him or her, operates in the defendant's favour to the same, but no greater, extent in an action under this section by the child.

(7) If in the child's action under this section it is shown that the parent affected shared the responsibility for the child being born disabled, the damages are to be reduced to such extent as the court thinks just and equitable having regard to the extent of the parent's responsibility.

[1A Extension of Section 1 to cover infertility treatments

    (1) In any case where:

        (a) a child carried by a woman as the result of the placing in her of an embryo or of sperm and eggs or her artificial insemination is born disabled,

        (b) the disability results from an act or omission in the course of the selection, or the keeping or use outside the body, of the embryo carried by her or of the gametes used to bring about the creation of the embryo, and

        (c) a person is under this section answerable to the child in respect of the act or omission,

the child's disabilities are to be regarded as damage resulting from the wrongful act of that person and actionable accordingly at the suit of the child.

    (2) Subject to subsection (3) below and the applied provisions of Section 1 of this Act, a person (here referred to as 'the defendant') is answerable to the child if he was liable in tort to one or both of the parents (here referred to as 'the parent or parents concerned') or would, if sued in due time, have been so; and it is no answer that there could not have been such liability because the parent or parents concerned suffered no actionable injury, if there was a breach of legal duty which, accompanied by injury, would have given rise to the liability.

    (3) The defendant is not under this section answerable to the child if at the time the embryo, or the sperm and eggs, are placed in the woman or the time of her insemination (as the case may be) either or both of the parents knew the risk of their child being born disabled (that is to say, the particular risk created by the act or omission).

    (4) Subsections (5) to (7) of Section 1 of this Act apply for the purposes of this section as they apply for the purposes of that but as if references to the parent or the parent affected were references to the parent or parents concerned.]

2 Liability of woman driving when pregnant

A woman driving a motor vehicle when she knows (or ought reasonably to know) herself to be pregnant is to be regarded as being under the same duty to take care for the safety of her unborn child as the law imposes on her with respect to the safety of other people; and if in consequence of her breach of that duty her child is born with disabilities which would not otherwise have been present, those disabilities are to be regarded as damage resulting from her wrongful act and actionable accordingly at the suit of the child.

3 Disabled birth due to radiation

    (1) Section 1 of this Act does not affect the operation of the Nuclear Installations Act 1965 as to liability for, and compensation in respect of, injury or damage caused by occurrences involving nuclear matter or the emission of ionising radiations.

    (2) For the avoidance of doubt anything which:

        (a) affects a man in his ability to have a normal, healthy child; or

        (b) affects a woman in that ability, or so affects her when she is pregnant that her child is born with disabilities which would not otherwise have been present,

is an injury for the purposes of that Act.

    (3) If a child is born disabled as the result of an injury to either of its parents caused in breach of a duty imposed by any of Sections 7 to 11 of that Act (nuclear site licensees and others to secure that nuclear incidents do not cause injury to persons, etc.), the child's disabilities are to be regarded under the subsequent provisions of that Act (compensation and other matters) as injuries caused on the same occasion, and by the same breach of duty, as was the injury to the parent.

(4) As respects compensation to the child, Section 13(6) of that Act (contributory fault of person injured by radiation) is to be applied as if the reference there to fault were to the fault of the parent.

(5) Compensation is not payable in the child's case if the injury to the parent preceded the time of the child's conception and at that time either or both of the parents knew the risk of their child being born disabled (that is to say, the particular risk created by the injury).

4 Interpretation and other supplementary provisions

(1) References in this Act to a child being born disabled or with disabilities are to its being born with any deformity, disease or abnormality, including predisposition (whether or not susceptible of immediate prognosis) to physical or mental defect in the future.

(2) In this Act:
  (a) 'born' means born alive (the moment of a child's birth being when it first has a life separate from its mother), and 'birth' has a corresponding meaning; and
  (b) 'motor vehicle' means a mechanically propelled vehicle intended or adapted for use on roads

[and references to embryos shall be construed in accordance with Section 1 of the Human Fertilisation and Embryology Act 1990].

(3) Liability to a child under Section 1 [1A] or 2 of this Act is to be regarded:
  (a) as respects all its incidents and any matters arising or to arise out of it; and
  (b) subject to any contrary context or intention, for the purpose of construing references in enactments and documents to personal or bodily injuries and cognate matters,
as liability for personal injuries sustained by the child immediately after its birth.

(4) No damages shall be recoverable under [any] of those sections in respect of any loss of expectation of life, nor shall any such loss be taken into account in the compensation payable in respect of a child under the Nuclear Installations Act 1965 as extended by Section 3, unless (in either case) the child lives for at least 48 hours.

[(4A) In any case where a child carried by a woman as the result of the placing in her of an embryo or of sperm and eggs or her artificial insemination is born disabled, any reference in Section 1 of this Act to a parent includes a reference to a person who would be a parent but for Sections 27 to 29 of the Human Fertilisation and Embryology Act 1990.]

(5) This Act applies in respect of births after (but not before) its passing, and in respect of any such birth it replaces any law in force before its passing, whereby a person could be liable to a child in respect of disabilities with which it might be born; but in Section 1(3) of this Act the expression 'liable in tort' does not include any reference to liability by virtue of this Act, or to liability by virtue of any such law.

(6) References to the Nuclear Installations Act 1965 are to that Act as amended; and for the purposes of Section 28 of that Act (power by Order in Council to extend the Act to territories outside the United Kingdom) Section 3 of this Act is to be treated as if it were a provision of that Act.

5 Crown application

This Act binds the Crown.

6 Citation and extent

(1) This Act may be cited as the Congenital Disabilities (Civil Liability) Act 1976.

(2) This Act extends to Northern Ireland but not to Scotland.

Appendix C
Schedules 2 and 3 of Data Protection Act 1998

SCHEDULE 2

CONDITIONS RELEVANT FOR PURPOSES OF THE FIRST PRINCIPLE:
PROCESSING OF ANY PERSONAL DATA

1. The data subject has given his consent to the processing.

2. The processing is necessary:
   (a) for the performance of a contract to which the data subject is a party, or
   (b) for the taking of steps at the request of the data subject with a view to entering into a contract.

3. The processing is necessary for compliance with any legal obligation to which the data controller is subject, other than an obligation imposed by contract.

4. The processing is necessary in order to protect the vital interests of the data subject

5. The processing is necessary:
   (a) for the administration of justice,
   (b) for the exercise of any functions conferred on any person by or under any enactment,
   (c) for the exercise of any functions of the Crown, a Minister of the Crown or a government department, or
   (d) for the exercise of any other functions of a public nature exercised in the public interest by any person.

6. (1) The processing is necessary for the purposes of legitimate interests pursued by the data controller or by the third party or parties to whom the data are disclosed, except where the processing is unwarranted in any particular case by reason of prejudice to the rights and freedoms or legitimate interests of the data subject.
   (2) The Secretary of State may by order specify particular circumstances in which this condition is, or is not, to be taken to be satisfied.

Section 4(3) SCHEDULE 3

CONDITIONS RELEVANT FOR PURPOSES OF THE
FIRST PRINCIPLE: PROCESSING OF
SENSITIVE PERSONAL DATA

1. The data subject has given his explicit consent to the processing of the personal data.

2. (1) The processing is necessary for the purposes of exercising or performing any right or obligation which is conferred or imposed by law on the data controller in connection with employment.
   (2) The Secretary of State may by order:
   (a) exclude the application of subparagraph (1) in such cases as may be specified, or

    (b) provide that, in such cases as may be specified, the condition in subparagraph (1) is not to be regarded as satisfied unless such further conditions as may be specified in the order are also satisfied.

3. The processing is necessary:
    (a) in order to protect the vital interests of the data subject or another person, in a case where:
        (i) consent cannot be given by or on behalf of the data subject, or
        (ii) the data controller cannot reasonably be expected to obtain the consent of the data subject, or
    (b) in order to protect the vital interests of another person, in a case where consent by or on behalf of the data subject has been unreasonably withheld.

4. The processing:
    (a) is carried out in the course of its legitimate activities by any body or association which:
        (i) is not established or conducted for profit, and
        (ii) exists for political, philosophical, religious or trade union purposes,
    (b) is carried out with appropriate safeguards for the rights and freedoms of data subjects,
    (c) relates only to individuals who either are members of the body or association or have regular contact with it in connection with its purposes, and
    (d) does not involve disclosure of the personal data to a third party without the consent of the data subject.

5. The information contained in the personal data has been made public as a result of steps deliberately taken by the data subject.

6. The processing:
    (a) is necessary for the purpose of, or in connection with, any legal proceedings (including prospective legal proceedings),
    (b) is necessary for the purpose of obtaining legal advice, or
    (c) is otherwise necessary for the purposes of establishing, exercising or defending legal rights.

7. (1) The processing is necessary:
    (a) for the administration of justice,
    (b) for the exercise of any functions conferred on any person by or under an enactment, or
    (c) for the exercise of any functions of the Crown, a Minister of the Crown or a government department.
  (2) The Secretary of State may by order:
    (a) exclude the application of subparagraph (1) in such cases as may be specified, or
    (b) provide that, in such cases as may be specified, the condition in subparagraph (1) is not to be regarded as satisfied unless such further conditions as may be specified in the order are also satisfied.

8. (1) The processing is necessary for medical purposes and is undertaken by:
    (a) a health professional, or
    (b) a person who in the circumstances owes a duty of confidentiality which is equivalent to that which would arise if that person were a health professional.
  (2) In this paragraph 'medical purposes' includes the purposes of preventative medicine, medical diagnosis, medical research, the provision of care and treatment and the management of healthcare services.

9. (1) The processing:
    (a) is of sensitive personal data consisting of information as to racial or ethnic origin,
    (b) is necessary for the purpose of identifying or keeping under review the existence or absence of equality of opportunity or treatment between persons of different

racial or ethnic origins, with a view to enabling such equality to be promoted or maintained, and

(c) is carried out with appropriate safeguards for the rights and freedoms of data subjects.

(2) The Secretary of State may by order specify circumstances in which processing falling within subparagraph (1)(a) and (b) is, or is not, to be taken for the purposes of subparagraph (1)(c) to be carried out with appropriate safeguards for the rights and freedoms of data subjects.

10. The personal data are processed in circumstances specified in an order made by the Secretary of State for the purposes of this paragraph.

Glossary

acceptance an agreement to the terms of an offer which leads to a binding legal obligation, i.e. a **contract**

accusatorial a system of court proceedings where the two sides contest the issue (contrast with **inquisitorial**)

Act of Parliament, **statute**

action legal proceedings

actionable per se a court action where claimant does not have to show loss, **damage** or harm to obtain compensation, e.g. an action for **trespass to the person**

actus reus essential element of a crime that must be proved to secure a conviction, as opposed to the mental state of the accused (*mens rea*)

adversarial approach adopted in an **accusatorial** system

advocate a person who pleads for another: it could be paid and professional, such as a **barrister** or **solicitor**, or it could be a lay advocate either paid or unpaid; a witness is not an advocate

affidavit a statement given under oath

alternative dispute resolution methods to resolve a dispute without going to court such as mediation

approved mental health professional a person recognised under the Mental Health Act 1983 (as amended by the Mental Health Act 2007) as having responsibilities in relation to the admission and detention of persons under the Mental Health Act (replaces the **approved social worker**)

approved social worker a social worker qualified for the purposes of the Mental Health Act

arrestable offence an offence defined in Section 24 of the Police and Criminal Evidence Act 1984 that gives to the citizen the power of arrest in certain circumstances without a warrant

assault a threat of unlawful contact (**trespass to the person**)

balance of probabilities standard of proof in **civil** proceedings

barrister a lawyer qualified to take a case in court

battery an unlawful touching (see **trespass to the person**)

bench magistrates, justices of the peace

Bolam Test test laid down by Judge McNair in the case of *Bolam* v. *Friern HMC* on the standard of care expected of a professional in cases of alleged **negligence**

burden of proof duty of a party to litigation to establish the facts or, in criminal proceedings, the duty of the prosecution to establish both *actus reus* and *mens rea*

cause of action facts that entitle a person to sue

certiorari an **action** taken to challenge an administrative or judicial decision (literally: to make more certain)

citation Each case is reported in an official series of cases according to the following symbols: Re F (i.e. in the matter of F) or F. v. West Berkshire Health Authority 1989 2 All ER 545 which means the year 1989 volume 2 of the All England Law Reports page 545. Each case can be cited by means of this reference system. In the case of Whitehouse v. Jordan (Whitehouse v Jordan [1981] 1 All ER 267), Whitehouse is the claimant, Jordan the defendant and 'v' stands for versus, i.e. against. Other law reports include: AC Appeals Court; EWCA England and Wales Court of Appeal; EWHC England and Wales High Court; EWHL England and Wales House of Lords; QB Queens Bench Division and WLR Weekly Law Reports

civil action proceedings brought in the civil courts

civil wrong an act or omission which can be pursued in the civil courts by the person who has suffered the wrong (see **tort**)

claimant person bringing a **civil action** (originally **plaintiff**)

committal proceedings hearings before the **magistrates** to decide if a person should be sent for **trial** in the Crown Court

common law law derived from the decisions of judges, case law, judge-made law

conditional fee system a system whereby client and lawyer can agree that payment of fees is dependent on the outcome of the court **action**; also known as 'no win, no fee'

conditions terms of a contract (*see* **warranties**)

constructive knowledge knowledge that can be obtained from the circumstances

continuous service length of service an employee must have served to be entitled to receive certain statutory or contractual rights

contract an agreement enforceable in law

contract for services an agreement enforceable in law whereby one party provides services, not being employment, in return for payment or other consideration from the other

contract of service a contract for employment

coroner a person appointed to hold an Inquiry (inquest) into a death that occurred in unexpected or unusual circumstances

counter-offer a response to an offer that suggests different terms and is therefore counted as an offer, not an **acceptance**

criminal wrong an act or omission which can be pursued in the criminal courts

cross-examination questions asked of a witness by the lawyer for the opposing side: leading questions may be asked

damages a sum of money awarded by a court as compensation for a **tort** or breach of contract

declaration a ruling by the court setting out the legal situation

disclosure documents made available to the other party

dissenting judge a judge who disagrees with the decision of the majority of judges

distinguished (of cases) rules of precedent require judges to follow decisions of judges in previous cases, where these are binding on them. However, in some circumstances, it is possible to come to a different decision, because the facts of the earlier case are not comparable to the case now being heard and therefore the earlier decision can be 'distinguished'

examination in chief witness is asked questions in court by the lawyer of the party that has asked the witness to attend. Leading questions may not be asked

ex gratia as a matter of favour, e.g. without admission of **liability**, of payment offered to a claimant

expert witness evidence given by a person whose general opinion, based on training or experience, is relevant to some of the issues in dispute (contrast with **witness of fact**)

frustration (of contracts) ending of a contract by operation of law, because of the existence of an event not contemplated by the parties when they made the contract, e.g. imprisonment, death, blindness

guardian ad litem a person with a social work and childcare background who is appointed to ensure that the court is fully informed of the relevant facts which relate to a child and that the wishes and feelings of the child are clearly established. The appointment is made from a panel set up by the local authority

guilty a finding in a criminal court of responsibility for a criminal offence

hearsay evidence that has been learnt from another person

hierarchy recognised status of courts that results in lower courts following the decisions of higher courts (see **precedent**). Thus decisions of the House of Lords must be followed by all lower courts unless they can be **distinguished**

indictment a written accusation against a person, charging him with a serious crime, triable by jury

informal of a patient who has entered hospital without any statutory requirements

injunction an order of the court restraining a person

inquisitorial a system of justice whereby the truth is revealed by an inquiry into the facts conducted by the judge, e.g. coroner's court

invitation to treat early stages in negotiating a **contract**, e.g. an advertisement or letter expressing interest. An invitation to treat will often precede an **offer** that, when accepted, leads to the formation of an agreement that, if there is consideration and an intention to create legal relations, will be binding

judicial review an application to the High Court for a judicial or administrative decision to be reviewed and an appropriate order made, e.g. **declaration**

justice of the peace (JP) a lay **magistrate**, i.e. not legally qualified, who hears **summary** (minor) **offences** and sometimes indictable (serious) offences in the magistrates' court in a group of three (see **bench**)

liable/liability responsible for the wrongdoing or harm in civil proceedings

litigation civil proceedings

magistrate a person (*see* **justice of the peace** and **stipendiary magistrate**) who hears summary (minor) offences or indictable offences that can be heard in the magistrates' court

mandamus (we command) an order of the court requiring the defendant to take specified action

mens rea mental element in a crime (contrast with **actus reus**)

negligence a civil **action** for compensation, also a failure to follow a reasonable standard of care

next friend a person who brings a court action on behalf of a minor

offer a proposal made by a party that, if accepted, can lead to a **contract**. It often follows an **invitation to treat**

ombudsman a commissioner (e.g. health, local government) appointed by the government to hear complaints

payment into court an offer to settle a dispute at a particular sum, which is paid into court. The claimant's failure to accept the offer means that the claimant is liable to pay costs, if the final award is the same or less than the payment made

pedagogic of the science of teaching

plaintiff term formerly used to describe one who brings an action in the civil courts. Now the term **claimant** is used

plea in mitigation a formal statement to the court aimed at reducing the sentence to be pronounced by the judge

practice direction guidance issued by the head of the court to which they relate on the procedure to be followed

pre-action protocol rules of the Supreme Court that provide guidance on action to be taken before legal proceedings commence

precedent a decision that may have to be followed in a subsequent court hearing (see **hierarchy**)

prima facie at first sight; sufficient evidence brought by one party to require the other party to provide a defence

privilege in relation to evidence, being able to refuse to disclose it to the court

privity relationship that exists between parties as the result of a legal agreement

professional misconduct conduct of a registered health practitioner that could lead to conduct and competence proceedings by the registration body

proof evidence that secures the establishment of a claimant's, prosecution's or defendant's case

prosecution pursuing of criminal offences in court

quantum amount of compensation, or the monetary value of a claim

Queen's Counsel (QC) a senior barrister, also known as a 'silk'

reasonable doubt to secure a conviction in criminal proceedings the prosecution must establish 'beyond reasonable doubt' the guilt of the accused

Re F ruling a professional who acts in the best interests of an incompetent person who is incapable of giving consent does not act unlawfully if he follows the accepted standard of care according to the **Bolam Test**

rescission where a contract is ended by the order of a court or by the cancellation of the contract by one party entitled in law to do so

solicitor a lawyer who is qualified on the register held by the Law Society

specialist community public health nurse replaces the health visiter as a registered practitioner under the Nursing and Midwifery Council

statute law (statutory) law made by Acts of Parliament

stipendiary magistrate a legally qualified magistrate who is paid (i.e. has a stipend)

strict liability liability for a criminal act where the mental element does not have to be proved; in civil proceedings liability without establishing **negligence**

subpoena an order of the court requiring a person to appear as a witness (*subpoena ad testificandum*) or to bring records/documents (*subpoena duces tecum*)

summary judgment a procedure whereby the claimant can obtain judgment without the defendant being permitted to defend the action

summary offence a lesser offence that may only be heard by **magistrates**

tort a civil wrong excluding breach of contract. It includes: **negligence**, **trespass** (**to the person**, goods or land), nuisance, breach of statutory duty and defamation

trespass to the person a wrongful direct interference with another person. Harm does not have to be proved

trial a court hearing before a judge

ultra vires outside the powers given by law (e.g. of a statutory body or company)

vicarious liability liability of an employer for the wrongful acts of an employee committed while in the course of employment

volenti non fit injuria to the willing there is no wrong; voluntary assumption of risk

ward of court a minor placed under the protection of the High Court, which assumes responsibility for him or her and all decisions relating to his or her care must be made in accordance with the directions of the court

warranties terms of a **contract** that are considered to be less important than the terms described as

conditions: breach of a condition entitles the innocent party to see the contract as ended, i.e. repudiated by the other party (breach of warranties entitles the innocent party to claim damages)

Wednesbury principle court will intervene to prevent or remedy abuses of power by public authorities if there is evidence of unreasonableness or perversity. Principle laid down by the Court of Appeal in the case of *Associated Provincial Picture House Ltd* v. *Wednesbury Corporation* [1948] 1 KB 233

without prejudice without detracting from or without disadvantage to. The use of the phrase prevents the other party using the information to the prejudice of the one providing it

witness of fact a person who gives evidence of what they saw, heard, did or failed to do (contrast with **expert witness**)

writ a form of written command, e.g. the document that used to commence civil proceedings. Now a claim form is served

Further reading

Allen, R., Crasnow, R. and Beale, A., *Employment law and human rights*, 2nd edn, Oxford University Press, 2007

Appelbe, G.E. and Wingfield, J. (eds) *Dale and Appelbe's Pharmacy: Law and Ethics*, 8th edn, Pharmaceutical Press, 2005

Archbold, *Criminal Pleadings, Evidence and Practice* (ed. P.J. Richardson) 55th rev. edn, Sweet & Maxwell, 2007

Atkinson, J., *Advance Directives in Mental Health – theory, practice and ethics*, Jessica Kingsley Publications, 2007

Barrett, B. and Howells, R., *Occupational Health and Safety Law: Text and Materials*, Cavendish, 2000

Beale, H.G. (general editor) *Chitty on Contracts*, 3rd cumulative supplement to 29th edn, Sweet & Maxwell, 2006

Beauchamp, T.L. and Childres, J.F., *Principles of Biomedical Ethics*, 5th edn, Oxford University Press, 2001

Benny, R., Sargeant, M. and Jefferson, M., *Employment Law Questions and Answers*, Oxford University Press, 2nd edn, 2006

Blom-Cooper, L., *et al.*, *The Case of Jason Mitchell: Report of the Independent Panel of Inquiry*, Duckworth, 1996

Blom-Cooper, L., Hally, H. and Murphy, E., *The Falling Shadow – One Patient's Mental Health Care 1978–1993* (Report of an Inquiry into the Death of an Occupational Therapist at Edith Morgan Unit, Torbay 1993), Duckworth, 1996

Brazier, M., *Medicine, Patients and the Law*, 4th edn, Penguin, 2007

British Medical Association, *Medical Ethics Today*, BMJ Publishing, 1998

Britton, A., *Health care law and ethics*, W. Green, 2004

Carey, P., *Data Protection – a practical guide to UK and EU law*, 2nd edn, Oxford University Press, 2004

Clements, L., *Community Care and the Law*, 3rd edn, Legal Action Group, 2004

Clerk, J.F., *Clerk and Lindsell on Torts*, 19th edn, Sweet & Maxwell, 2006

Committee of Experts Advisory Group on AIDS, *Guidance for Health Care Workers' Protection against Infection with HIV and Hepatitis*, HMSO, 1994

Connolly, M., *Discrimination Law*, Thomson, Sweet & Maxwell, 2006

Cooper, J. (ed.) *Law, Rights and Disability*, Jessica Kingsley, 2000

Deakin, S., Johnston, A. and Markensinis, B., *Markensinis and Deakin's Tort Law*, 6th edn, Clarendon Press, 2007

Denis, I.H., *The Law of Evidence*, Sweet & Maxwell, 1999

Department of Health, *AIDS/HIV Infected Health Care Workers*, DH, April 1993

Dimond, B.C., *Legal Aspects of Death*, Quay Publications/Mark Allen, 2008

Dimond, B.C., *Legal Aspects of Mental Capacity*, Blackwell Publishing, 2008

Dimond, B.C., *Legal Aspects of Midwifery*, 3rd edn, Books for Midwives Press, 2005

Dimond, B.C., *Legal Aspects of Consent*, Quay Publications/Mark Allen, 2003

Dimond, B.C., *Legal Aspects of Pain Management*, Quay Publications/Mark Allen, 2002

Dimond, B.C., *Legal Aspects of Patient Confidentiality*, Quay Publications/Mark Allen, 2002

Dimond, B.C., *Legal Aspects of Physiotherapy*, Blackwell Science, 1999

Dimond, B.C., *Patients' Rights, Responsibilities and the Nurse*, 2nd edn, Central Health Studies, Quay Publications, 1999

Dimond, B.C., *Legal Aspects of Complementary Therapy Practice*, Churchill Livingstone, 1998

Dimond, B.C., *Legal Aspects of Care in the Community*, Macmillan, 1997

Dimond, B.C., *Legal Aspects of Occupational Therapy*, Blackwell Scientific, 1997

Dimond, B.C., *Mental Health (Patients in the Community) Act 1995: An Introductory Text*, Mark Allen, 1997

Dimond, B.C., *Legal Aspects of Child Health Care*, Mosby, 1996

Dimond, B.C., *Accountability and the Nurse*, Distance Learning Pack, South Bank University, 1992

Dimond, B.C. and Barker, F., *Mental Health Law for Nurses*, Blackwell Science, 1996

Eliot, C., *The English Legal System*, 8th edn, Pearson Education, 2007

Fraser, J. with M. Nolan, *Child Protection: a guide for midwives*, 2nd edn, Books for Midwives, 2004

Glynn, J. and Gomez, D., *Fitness to Practise: Healthcare Regulatory Law, Principles and Process*, Sweet & Maxwell, 2005

Grainger, I. and Fealy, M. with Spencer, M., *Civil Procedure Rules in Action*, 2nd edn, Cavendish, 2000

Harris, D.J., *Cases and Materials on the European Convention on Human Rights*, 2nd rev. edn, Butterworth, 2005

Harris, P., *An Introduction to Law*, 7th edn, Butterworth, 2007

Health and Safety Commission, *Management of Health and Safety at Work Regulations: Approved Code of Practice*, HMSO, 1999

Health and Safety Commission, *Guidelines on Manual Handling in the Health Services*, HMSO, 1992

Health and Safety Commission, *Manual Handling Regulations: Approved Code of Practice*, HMSO, 1992

Hendrick, J., *Law and Ethics in Nursing and Healthcare*, 2nd edn, Nelson Thornes Publishers, 2006

Herring, J., *Medical Law and Ethics*, Oxford University Press, 2006

Heywood-Jones, I. (ed.) *The UKCC Code of Conduct: A Critical Guide*, Nursing Times Books, 1999

Hockton, A., *The Law on Consent to Treatment*, Sweet & Maxwell, 2002

Hoggett, B., *Mental Health Law*, 5th edn, Sweet & Maxwell, 2005

Holland, J. and Burnett, S., *Employment Law*, Oxford University Press, 2006

Howarth, D.R. and O'Sullivan J.A., *Hepple, Howarth and Matthews, Tort: Cases and Materials*, 5th edn, Butterworth, 2000

Howells, G. and Weatherill, S., *Consumer Protection Law*, 2nd edn, Dartmouth, 2005

Humphreys, N., *Trade Union Law and Collective Employment Rights*, 2nd edn, Jordans, 2005

Hunt, G. and Wainwright, P. (eds) *Expanding the Role of the Nurse*, Blackwell Scientific, 1994

Hurwitz, B., *Clinical Guidelines and the Law*, Oxford Radcliffe Medical Press, 1998

Hurwitz, B. and Paquita, Z., *Everyday ethics in primary care*, BMJ, 2006

Ingman, T., *The English Legal Process*, 11th edn, Blackstone Press, 2006

Jay, R., *Data Protection Law and Practice*, 3rd rev. edn, Sweet & Maxwell, 2007

Jones, M.A., *Textbook on Torts*, 9th edn, Oxford University Press, 2007

Jones, M.A., *Medical Negligence*, 3rd edn, Sweet & Maxwell, 2003

Jones, M.A. and Morris, A.E., *Blackstone's Statutes on Medical Law*, 4th edn, Oxford University Press, 2005

Jones, R., *Mental Health Act Manual*, 10th edn, Sweet & Maxwell, 2006

Keenan, D., *Smith and Keenan's English Law*, 14th edn, Harlow, Longman, 2004

Kennedy, I. and Grubb, A., *Medical Law*, 3rd edn, Butterworth, 2000

Kennedy, T., *Learning European Law*, Sweet & Maxwell, 1998

Kidner, R., *Blackstone's Statutes on Employment Law*, 13th edn, Oxford University Press, 2003

Kloss, D., *Occupational Health Law*, 4th edn, Blackwell Scientific, 2005

Leach, P., *Taking a Case to the European Court of Human Rights*, 2nd edn, Blackstone Press, 2005

Lee, R.G. and Morgan, D. *Human Fertilisation and Embryology*, Blackstone Press, 2001

Lewis, T., *Employment Law*, 6th edn, Legal Action Group, 2005

Lockton, D., *Employment Law 2007-8*, 5th edn, Routledge-Cavendish, 2007

Mandelstam, M., *Community Care Practice and the Law*, 3rd edn, Jessica Kingsley, 2005

Mandelstam, M., *An A-Z of Community Care Law*, Jessica Kingsley, 1998

Mason, D. and Edwards, P., *Litigation: A Risk Management Guide for Midwives*, Royal College of Midwives, 1993

Mason, J.K., McCall-Smith, R.A. and Laurie, G.T., *Law and Medical Ethics*, 6th edn, Butterworth, 2002

McHale, J. and Fox, M., *Health Care Law*, 2nd edn, Sweet & Maxwell, 2007

McHale, J. and Tingle, J., *Law and Nursing*, 2nd edn, Elsevier Health Sciences, 2007

McLean, S., *Impairment and Disability: Law and ethics at the beginning and end of life*, Routledge-Cavendish, 2007

Metzer, A. and Weinberg, J., *Criminal Litigation*, Legal Action Group, 1999

Miers, D. and Page, A., *Legislation*, 2nd edn, Sweet & Maxwell, 1990

Miles, A., Hampton, J. and Hurwitz, B., *NICE, CHI and the NHS reforms - enabling excellence or imposing contro?* Aesculapius, 2000

Montague, A., *Legal Problems in Emergency Medicine*, Oxford University Press, 1996

Montgomery, J., *Health Care Law*, 2nd edn, Oxford University Press, 2003

Murphy, J., *Street on Torts*, 12th edn, London: Butterworth, 2006

Nairns, J., *Discrimination Law: text, cases and materials*, Oxford University Press, 2006

National Association of Theatre Nurses, *Principles of Safe Practice in the Perioperative Environment*, NATN, 1998

National Association of Theatre Nurses, *Safeguards for Invasive Procedures*, NATN, 1998

National Association of Theatre Nurses, *The Role of the Nurse as First Assistant in the Operating Department*, NATN, 1993

Painter, R.W. and Holmes, A.E.M., *Cases and Materials on Employment Law*, 6th edn, Oxford University Press, 2006

Pitt, G., *Employment Law*, 6th edn, Sweet & Maxwell, 2007

Pyne, R.H., *Professional Discipline in Nursing, Midwifery and Health Visiting*, 3rd edn, Blackwell Scientific, 1998

Rogers, W.V.H., *Winfield and Jolowicz on Tort*, 17th edn, Thomson, Sweet & Maxwell, 2006

Rose, W. (ed.) *Blackstone's Civil Practice 2008*, Oxford University Press, 2007

Rowson, R., Working *Ethics - how to be fair in a culturally complex world*, Jessica Kingsley, 2006

Rowson, R., *An Introduction to Ethics for Nurses*, Scutari Press, 1990

Royal College of Midwives, *Examples of Effective Midwifery Management*, RCM, 1993

Royal College of Midwives, *The Midwife: Her Legal Status and Accountability*, RCM, 1993

Royal College of Nursing, *Focus on Restraint*, 2nd edn, RCN, 1992

Rubenstein, M., *Discrimination - guide to relevant case law*, 15th edn, Eclipse Group, 2002

Rumbold, G., *Ethics in Nursing Practice*, 3rd edn, Baillière Tindall, 1999

Salvage, J., *Nurses at Risk: Guide to Health and Safety at Work*, 2nd edn, Heinemann, 1998

Sellars, C., *Risk Assessment with People with Learning Disabilities*, Blackwell, 2002

Selwyn, N., *Selwyn's Law of Employment*, 14th edn, Butterworth, 2006

Sime, S., *Practical Approach to Civil Procedure*, 9th edn, Blackstone Press, 2006

Skegg, P.D.G., *Law, Ethics and Medicine*, 2nd edn, Oxford University Press, 1998

Slapper, G. and Kelly, D., *The English Legal System*, 8th edn, Routledge-Cavendish, 2006

Social Security Inspectorate, Department of Health, *No Longer Afraid: Safeguard of Older People in Domestic Settings*, HMSO, 1993

Stauch, M., *Text and Materials on Medical Law*, 3rd edn, Cavendish, 2005

Steiner, J., *Textbook on EC Law*, 9th edn, Oxford University Press, 2006

Stone, J. and Matthews, J., *Complementary Medicine and the Law*, Oxford University Press, 1996

Storch, J., *Towards a Moral Horizon: Nursing Ethics for Leadership and Practice*, Pearson Education, 2004

Taylor, S. and Emir, A., *Employment Law: An introduction*, Oxford University Press, 2006

Tingle, J. and Cribb, A., *Nursing law and ethics*, 3rd edn, Blackwell Publishers, 2007

Tingle, J. and Foster, C., *Clinical Guidelines: Law, Policy and Practice*, Cavendish, 2002

Tolley's Health and Safety at Work Handbook, 19th edn, Tolley, 2007

Tschudin, V., *Ethics in Nursing: the caring relationship*, 3rd edn, Butterworth-Heinemann, 2002

Vincent, C. (ed.) *Clinical Risk Management*, BMJ Publishing, 1995

Wheeler, J., *The English Legal System*, 2nd edn, Pearson Education, 2006

White, R., Carr, P. and Lowe, N., *A Guide to the Children Act 1989*, 3rd edn, Butterworth, 2002

Wilkinson, R. and Caulfield, H., *The Human Rights Act: A Practical Guide for Nurses*, Whurr Publishers, 2000

Young, A.P., *Law and Professional Conduct in Nursing*, 2nd edn, Scutari Press, 1994

Young, A.P., *Legal Problems in Nursing Practice*, Harper & Row, 1989

Zander, M., *Police and Criminal Evidence Act*, 1st supplement to 5th edn, Sweet & Maxwell, 2005

Websites

Action for Advocacy	**www.actionforadvocacy.org**
Action on Elder Abuse	**www.elderabuse.org.uk**
Age Concern	**www.ageconcern.org.uk**
Alert	**www.donoharm.org.uk**
Alzheimer's Research	**www.Alzheimers-research.org.uk**
Alzheimer's Society	**www.alzheimers.org.uk**
ASA Advice	**www.advice.org.uk**
Association of Contentious Trust and Probate Solicitors	**www.actaps.com**
Audit Commission	**www.audit-commission.gov.uk**
Carers UK	**www.carersonline.org.uk**
	www.carersuk.org
Care Services Improvement Partnership	**www.csip.org.uk**
Central Office for Research Ethics Committees	**www.corec.org.uk**
Citizen Advocacy Information and Training	**www.citizenadvocacy.org.uk**
Citizens' Advice Bureau	**www.citizensadvice.org.uk**
Civil Procedure Rules	**www.open.gov.uk/lcd/civil/procrules_fin/crules.htm**
	www.justice.gov.uk/civil/procrules_fin/index
Clinical Negligence Scheme for Trusts	**www.nhsla.com/Claims/Schemes/CNST/**
Commission for Patient and Public Involvement in Health	**www.cppih.org/**
Commission for Racial Equality	**www.cre.gov.uk/**
Commission for Social Care and Inspection	**www.csci.gov.uk**
Community Legal Service Direct	**www.clsdirect.org.uk**
Complementary Healthcare Information Service	**www.chisuk.org.uk**
Contact the Elderly	**www.contact-the-elderly.org**
Convention on the International Protection of Adults	**www.hcch.net/index_en.php?**
Council for Healthcare Regulatory Excellence	**www.chre.org.uk**

Counsel and Care	**www.counselandcare.org.uk**
Court Funds Office	**www.hmcourts-service.gov.uk/infoabout/cfo/index.htm**
Court of Protection	via the Office of Public Guardian or HM Courts Services
Dementia Care Trust	**www.dct.org.uk**
Department for Business, Enterprise and Regulatory Reform (DBERR)	**www.berr.gov.uk**
Department for Children, Schools and Families (DCSF)	**www.dfes.gov.uk**
Department for Education and Skills (now DCSF)	**www.dfes.gov.uk**
Department for Work and Pensions	**www.dwp.gov.uk/**
Department of Health	**www.dh.gov.uk**
Department of Trade and Industry (now DBERR)	**www.dti.gov.uk/**
Disability Law Service	**www.dls.org.uk/**
Domestic Violence	**www.domesticviolence.gov.uk**
Down's Syndrome Association	**www.downs-syndrome.org.uk**
	www.dsa-uk.com
Equality and Human Rights Commission	**www.equalityhumanrights.com.**
Family Carer Support Service	**www.familycarers.org.uk**
Family Mediation Helpline	**www.familymediationhelpline.co.uk**
Foundation for People with Learning Disabilities	**www.learningdisabilities.org.uk**
General Medical Council	**www.gmc-uk.org**
Headway (brain Injury) Association	**www.headway.org.uk**
Health and Safety Commission	**www.hsc.gov.uk**
Health and Safety Executive	**www.hse.gov.uk**
Help the Aged	**www.helptheagedorg.uk**
Help the Hospices	**www.hospiceinformation.info**
Healthcare Commission	**www.healthcarecommission.org.uk/**
Health Professions Council	**www.hc-uk.org**
HM Courts Service	**www.hmcourts-service.gov.uk**
Home Farm Trust	**www.hft.org.uk**
Human Fertilisation and Embryology Authority	**www.hfea.gov.uk/**
Human Genetics Commission	**www.hgc.gov.uk**
Human Rights	**www.humanrights.gov.uk**
Independent Mental Capacity Advocate	**www.dh.gov.uk.imca**
Information Commissioner's Office	**www.ico.gov.uk**
Law Centres Federation	**www.lawcentres.org.uk**

Law Society	**www.lawsociety.org.uk/choosingandusing/ findingasolicitor.law**
Legal cases (England and Wales)	**www.bailli.org/ew/cases**
Legislation	**www.opsi.gov.uk/legislation** or **www.legislation.hmso.gov.uk**
Linacre Centre for Healthcare Ethics	**www.linacre.org**
Making Decisions Alliance	**www.makingdecisions.org.uk**
Manic Depression Fellowship	**www.mdf.org.uk**
MedicAlert Foundation	**www.medicalert.org.uk**
Medicines and Healthcare products Regulatory Agency	**www.mhra.gov.uk**
MENCAP	**www.mencap.org.uk**
Mental Health Act Commission	**www.mhac.org.uk/**
Mental Health Foundation	**www.mentalhealth.org.uk**
Mental Health Lawyers Association	**www.mhla.co.uk**
Mental Health Matters	**www.mentalhealthmatters.com/**
Mind	**www.mind.org.uk**
Ministry of Justice	**www.justice.gov.uk**
Motor Neurone Disease Association	**www.mndassociation.org.uk**
National Audit Office	**www.nao.gov.uk**
National Autistic Society	**www.nas.org.uk** **www.autism.org.uk**
National Care Association	**www.nca.gb.com**
National Family Carer Network	**www.familycarers.org.uk**
National Health Service Litigation Authority	**www.nhsla.com**
National Mediation Helpline	**www.nationalmediationhelpline.com**
National Patient Safety Agency	**www.npsa.gov.uk**
National Perinatal Epidemiology Unit	**www.npeu.ox.ac.uk/**
National Treatment Agency	**www.nta.nhs.uk/**
NHS Direct	**www.nhsdirect.nhs.uk**
NHS Professionals	**www.nhsprofessionals.nhs.uk**
NHS website	**www.nhs.uk**
NICE	**www.nice.org.uk**
Nursing and Midwifery Council	**www.nmc-uk.org/**
Office of Public Guardian	**www.guardianship.gov.uk**
Office of Public Sector Information	**www.opsi.gov.uk**
Official Solicitor	**www.officialsolicitor.gov.uk**
Open Government	**www.open.gov.uk**
Pain website	**www.pain-talk.co.uk**
Patient Concern	**www.patientconcern.org.uk**
Patients' Association	**www.patients-association.org.uk**

People First	**www.peoplefirst.org.uk**
Prevention of Professional Abuse Network	**www.popan.org.uk**
Princess Royal Trust for Carers	**www.carers.org/**
Relatives and Residents Association	**www.releres.org/**
RESCARE (The National Society for mentally disabled people in residential care)	**www.rescare.org.uk**
Respond	**www.respond.org.uk**
Rethink (formerly the National Schizophrenia Fellowship)	**www.rethink.org**
Royal College of Nursing	**www.rcn.org.uk**
Royal College of Psychiatrists	**www.rcpsych.ac.uk**
SANE	**www.sane.org.uk**
Scope	**www.scope.org.uk**
Sense	**www.sense.org.uk**
Shipman Inquiry	**www.the-shipman-inquiry.org.uk/reports.asp**
Skipton Fund	**www.skiptonfund.org/Eng**
Solicitors for the Elderly	**www.solicitorsfortheelderly.com**
Speakability	**www.speakability.org.uk**
Speaking Up	**www.speakingup.org/**
Stroke Association	**www.stroke.org.uk**
Together: Working for Wellbeing	**www.together-uk.org**
Turning Point	**www.turning-point.co.uk**
UK Homecare Association	**www.ukhca.co.uk**
UK Parliament	**www.parliament.uk**
United Response	**www.unitedresponse.org.uk**
Values into Action	**www.viauk.org**
Veterans Agency	**www.veteransagency.org.uk**
VOICE UK	**www.voiceuk.clara.net**
Voluntary Euthanasia Society	**www.ves.org.uk**
Welsh Assembly Government	**www.wales.gov.uk**
World Medical Association	**www.wma.net/e/policy/b3.htm**

Index